𝔚𝔦𝔱𝔱𝔯𝔶,

𝔚𝔦𝔱𝔯𝔶,

𝔙𝔦𝔱𝔯𝔶

The Family Tree – 2007

THE COAT OF ARMS OF THE CITY OF VITRY-SUR-ORNE IN FRANCE,
THE SOURCE OF THE NAME OF THE AUTHOR'S FAMILY

Eugene J. Wittry

HERITAGE BOOKS
2008

HERITAGE BOOKS

AN IMPRINT OF HERITAGE BOOKS, INC.

Books, CDs, and more—Worldwide

For our listing of thousands of titles see our website
at
www.HeritageBooks.com

Published 2008 by
HERITAGE BOOKS, INC.
Publishing Division
100 Railroad Ave. #104
Westminster, Maryland 21157

Other books by the author:

Tripping Over Europe: Expert Advice on Making Travel Easy
Wittry, Witry, Vitry: A Family History
Wittry, Witry, Vitry: The Family Tree, 2001

International Standard Book Numbers
Paperbound: 978-0-7884-4567-5
Clothbound: 978-0-7884-7695-2

This book is dedicated to my parents, Albert A. Wittry and Margaret E. (Kneipper) Wittry. They gave outstanding example to their sons by the way they conducted their lives, and they engendered a pride of heritage that deserves to be passed on to future generations. I hope that we who received our name from them can pass on the same pride of heritage by the way we live.

Contents

Preface

It has been six years since I wrote the book that lists the members of our family, *Wittry, Witry, Vitry: The Family Tree - 2001*. It is time to provide interested members of the family with an updated tree, since the amount of information has grown about thirty percent since the publication of that book. I was ready to send the book to the publisher late in 2006. But then I learned that the National Archives of Luxembourg had released genealogical records from the years 1895 through 1923. I decided it would be best to include the information from those records before publishing the book. That work has taken me a little over a year to complete.

Certainly I must repeat the credits from the first book. Thanks are due to my aunt, Lena Florence, who maintained the Jacob Wittry family tree for many years. Thanks to my mother who took responsibility for the tree upon Lena's death. Thanks also to Barbara Theis, Lena's daughter, who took over the task for many years after my mother's death. Thanks to the many people who have provided me with copies of the tree of their immediate families. Thanks to those who send me updates on their families. Thanks to those who send me interesting peripheral information. Thanks to those who put me in contact with other members of the family. There is no way that I am going to list all of these people, for fear of offending someone whose name I forgot to include. Oh yes, thanks to our granddaughter Shanna (Wittry) Malone, who has volunteered to take over the maintenance of the family tree when I am no longer able to do so.

If you find any errors in this book, and errors are here, please send me corrections. If you find missing information, please send it to me. If there are any new births, marriages or deaths in your family, please tell me. The only way that the family tree can grow and improve in accuracy is through your interest and cooperation. Send me information at any time. Please also send me the names and addresses of family members at any time.

My snail mail address is:

Eugene J Wittry
623 W Timothy Dr
Peoria IL 61614-2049
U S A

My email address is:

ewittry@comcast.net

I promise that if you send me new information about your branch of the family, I will send you an updated list of your branch by return mail.

Note too that I publish a ten-page newsletter about the family four times a year. This has been going on since the first book was published, primarily to provide you with corrections and additions as they become available. The newsletter still performs that function, but it also includes stories, photos and other items of interest that will never be included in the family tree. If you are interested in the newsletter, please contact me.

1

How to Use the Book

Structure

This book is intended to be as simple to use as current software and the creativity of the author can make possible. Both are limited.

This first chapter describes how the book is organized and how to use it to find information about the family members who interest you. There are three chapters and two appendices in the book. The second chapter tells how to look up families in Appendix B, the index to all of the marriages in the family database. The third chapter tells how to interpret the information about each family. This family information is contained in Appendix A.

Some information in my files is missing from Appendix A. I have over 3000 copies of original documents from Luxembourg, Germany, France and Belgium. These documents have been transcribed and translated from the original 17th to 20th century, hand-written Latin, German and French, and are recorded in the database. They are not included in this book so that its size and price can be reasonable. All of these documents helped me to record the family history as accurately as possible. This doesn't mean that I didn't make mistakes. It also doesn't mean that I found all of the relevant documents. For example, a document recording a marriage is likely to tell where each of the couple was born. However, it will not tell where they plan to live. It is difficult, but not impossible, to trace a family back in time. It is a matter of luck if one can manage to trace a family forward in time.

Relationship to the first book

Don't throw my first book *Wittry, Witry, Vitry: A Family History* away. This book does not replace it, but supplements it. In essence, this book replaces only two chapters in the first book that have become obsolete. It does, however, replace my second book *Wittry, Witry, Vitry: The Family Tree – 2001*.

Other families

The first book contained information about two other families in Appendices B and C. One is a family from Kentucky, named Wittry. The other is a family from Louisiana, named Vitry. Both believe that their roots are from Alsace-Lorraine in France. To date we have been unsuccessful in finding a relationship between our families, or in demonstrating that the sharing of the same name is only coincidental. I have not included these families in this book, but continue to maintain communication with them in the hope that a common ancestor might come to light.

Expansion of the family tree

In the five years since the first book was published, the number of people in the family tree has more than doubled by the time that *Wittry, Witry, Vitry: The Family Tree - 2001* was published six years ago. It has grown by another 30% since then. Part of this is due to people sending me information about their branches of the family. Part is due to the fact that Luxembourg released another 15 years of records, thus extending my sources of information from 1880 through 1894. A second release included records from the years 1895 through 1923. Part is due to the kindness of Rob Deltgen, a distant relative and an accomplished genealogist in Luxembourg. He is summarizing records for public use, and

2

forwards to me any that he thinks might be of interest. Those of you who cannot find all of your immediate family information in the first book should have better luck here. If you don't, it is because nobody has provided the information to me.

My research into the family tree for the first book ended where the available records ended. There are no known records of the family in Luxembourg before the early part of the 17th century. That was the time when pastors of parishes first began to record baptisms, marriages, and interments.

At the time I finished my original historical research there were no available records after the date of 1880. This was due to national laws that generally prohibit general access to records less than a hundred years old. The purpose is to avoid fraudulent use of the information.

As I neared the end of my research I discovered that I had been far more interested in the dead than in the living. Certainly the book was not for the dead, so, I began to search out the living. I obtained addresses from known relatives. I searched the Internet for addresses of people who bore any reasonable variant of the family name, and wrote to them. A surprising number of people answered my letters and provided information.

Then, I began to publish a newsletter four times a year. This generated more incentive for people to give me information about their families. People like to see their name in print. Besides, if a person is sending me payment for a copy of the newsletter, it is a simple matter to enclose a bit of new information in the envelope.

Finally, I began to add to the family tree the parents of people who married into the family. The software that generates the tree in Appendix A is capable of adding that parenthetical information to spouses.

For all of these reasons, as well as the passage of time, the content of the family tree has grown significantly. People began to tell me that they found it difficult to find the information they wanted. And when they found it, it was often out of date. That clearly demonstrated that it is time to offer the family an updated book.

Expansion of the index to marriages

In the first book each marriage of a male Wittry/Witry has a sequence number. The printed family tree contains these marriages in the order of that sequence number. Because the original book was already large - 505 pages - I only provided an index based on an alphabetized list of the women who had married these men. Many people are interested in the family even though the name Wittry/Witry doesn't appear in their ancestry for a number of generations. An example might illustrate. A man from Germany attended a reunion of the family in Luxembourg in April, 2001. He brought his two sons. It was the great-great-grandmother of the boys who carried the name Witry.

All of this goes to say that many people find it difficult to locate themselves or their parents in the family tree. For this reason Appendix B of this book contains a complete index to all marriages, both by the name of the wife and by the name of the husband.

Finding a person

The way to find a person in Appendix A is to first find an associated marriage in the index in Appendix B. If the person is not married, you will need to know the names of the person's parents or other ancestors. Find the appropriate marriage in Appendix B. Note the sequence number of that marriage. Then look in Appendix A for the marriage with that sequence number. It is just that easy. Good hunting.

Other information in the first book

The first book, *Wittry, Witry, Vitry: A Family History,* contains a lot of background information that is missing from this book. If you want to know more than you can find in Appendix A of this book, you might want to refer to that book. It tells of the origin of the family name. It tells about famous people and places that bore a variant of the family name. It describes the history and culture of the early centuries of our forefathers. It describes how people lived in the old country, why some of them emigrated, and where they went. It also contains brief stories of different family groups, things

4

that could only be learned by careful analysis of the details in Appendix A or even by reading the original documents from past centuries.

Future books?

It is highly unlikely that I will ever write a replacement of the first book *Wittry, Witry, Vitry: A Family History.* My research found a few records from the 1600's and none from earlier times. From everything that I have been able to learn, there are no older records to discover. The only records that are likely to expand my knowledge of the original families in Luxembourg will be newly released records from Luxembourg. By past practice, no new records should become available until about 2016. Then it would take me two years to study those records, extract family information from them, compile a new family tree book to replace this one, and then have it published. This would take us to 2018. At that time I will be 86 years old. Only God knows if I will be alive, or what my health will be if I am.

2

How to Use the Index

Structure

The index to marriages is in Appendix B, and is formatted into four columns. The first column contains the names of partners (male and female) in a family marriage. The married couple are listed twice in the list, once with the man's name first, and once with the woman's name first. The second column contains the year (sometimes known and sometimes estimated) of the marriage. The third column contains the sequence number of the marriage. The fourth column contains sequence number(s) that help you locate the parents of the partner in that marriage who is descended from Peter Witry (seq. 001,) our first known ancestor. The sequence numbers show where the marriage appears in the full family tree in Appendix A. Note that the marriage might not be shown in Appendix A as a separate topic. If it is not, then look for the topic headed by the sequence number in the fourth column

As an example, consider marriage 323.01 - Firmin Rob and Marie Machus. There is no topic heading in Appendix A for that marriage, because it is the second marriage of Firmin Rob. The marriage number in column 4 is 002. That sequence number is the marriage of the parents of Firmen Rob, and it is the bold sequence number at the top of the paragraph in Appendix A that contains Rob Firmin's parents. In that paragraph you will find that the sequence number of Firmin Rob's first marriage is 323. Go to the paragraph with the topic heading 323, and you will find both marriages.

Now consider another case, that of marriage 015.21, Barbara-Marie Wagner and Edward Farrall. The sequence number in column 4 is 015.19.50. The parents of Marie Wagner are sequence number 015.20, but, since theirs is a second marriage, it is found in Appendix A in the paragraph with the heading 015.19.50, the sequence number of the first marriage of Barbara-Marie Wagner's mother. The purpose of this indirect reference is to aid you in finding parents of a person by simply looking in the paragraph headed by the sequence number in column 4.

Why is there a need for indirect references? There are two reasons. The bold-faced heading above the "paragraph" for each family grouping is that of a couple with children. If you look up in Appendix B a couple who have no children, there is no corresponding paragraph in Appendix A headed with the sequence number of their marriage. The record of their marriage appears in the paragraph headed by the sequence number of the marriage of the parents of the one who descended from the original Peter Witry. Another reason could be that the first named parent in the paragraph was married more than once. All of the marriages are listed under the sequence number of the earliest marriage.

Finding a marriage

Hopefully you know the names of both parties in any marriage that is of interest to you. If so, look up either the name of the husband or the wife in the first column. The names are listed in alphabetical order, by last name, and then by given names. The last name for a woman is her maiden name. If you don't know the wife's maiden name, then look up the name of the husband.

If you find that there are several couples with similar names, look at both names and at the date of marriage in column 2 to find the couple you seek. Then note the sequence number of the marriage, shown in the third column. Usually, but not always, it is just that simple.

Complications

Nothing is ever as simple as it seems. There can be complications, especially as you look for a marriage from the early days.

The spelling of the names varies. The first two columns contain the names as they appear in the family tree in Appendix A. The name is written as the person wrote it, if the person could write. This was not a common skill in the early days. If the person could not write, or if I didn't find a document with his or her signature, I recorded the name as written on an official document. If I had no documents, I recorded the name as it was provided by someone else in the family. So, a man's given name might be John, Johann, Johannes, or Jean, depending on the source of the information. Last names can vary too, since there were no rules for spelling in the old days. For example, Haas, Huss and Hassen are variations of the same name, as are Hoffman and Hoffmann; and Wittry, Witry, and Vitry.

Sometimes I don't have a spouse's family name or given name, or either name. Sometimes a person was known by a second name. An example of both is our oldest known ancestor, Peter. He probably didn't have a family name, since his son Peter was known by the name of the estate, Thies, where he lived and worked. Presumably the original Peter had a wife, since he had a son, but there is no record of his wife's name. The first records in the table all begin with <Unnamed>. Note the one that reads <Unnamed> and Witry, Peter. Toward the end of the list you will find the corresponding record of Witry, Peter & <Unnamed>

Interpreting the sequence number

The sequence number in the third column tells you where to find the desired marriage in Appendix A. All of the marriages in Appendix A are organized by sequence number. The original sequence number has been retained from the first book on the family. For all marriages that didn't have an original sequence number, I have developed a new number. To keep these numbers sequential in listings of the family tree, I have added suffixes as necessary. For example, there are several marriages between sequence numbers 261 and 262. I gave them the numbers 261.01 and 261.02. Then later I recorded two new marriages that appear between 262.02 and 262.03. So, I gave them the numbers 262.02.01 and 262.02.02. This might become awkward in time, but it allows a given marriage to always be known by the same sequence number in newsletters and in possible future books.

Multiple descent

Some people are descended from two different lines of the family tree. This is the case for my grandparents, John Wittry and Barbara (née Wittry) Wittry. Their marriage is sequence number 182.

So how do you deal with this multiple ancestry? First of all, note that in such cases the fourth column contains two sequence numbers for the parents of the couple listed in the first column. Look up the marriage of John Wittry and Barbara Wittry. You will see two sequence numbers in column 4. One (167) is sequence number of the marriage of John's parents. The other (271) is the sequence number of Barbara's parents.

Try it

Yes, that is all complicated and confusing. But it works, and it is the best way I know to enable you to find families that you are interested in. So look up some families that you know well. You will find it to be easy. You will soon forget these instructions and will be able to navigate through the family tree at will. Have fun!

3

Family Tree of Peter Witry

Structure

The tree begins with Peter Witry, born about 1575, whose wife's name is not known. It will probably never be known, since I have not found any records that far in the past from the area where he lived. Peter's marriage is identified as sequence 001. Succeeding marriages are shown in numerical order by sequence number. The sequence number scheme was designed to keep the families in order, oldest child to youngest child in each generation of each branch of the family tree.

The marriages are shown with just the children and the children's marriages, if any. This technique makes the book bulkier than its predecessor, but it also makes it easier for you to gain a perspective on each individual family. In the previous book, the grandchildren of a couple could be scattered throughout the whole book. I hope you find the new format more convenient. Certainly it will be easier for you to organize replacement pages when I publish updates to families.

The marriages and their children are listed in sequence number order. The first person listed in the marriage is the parent who is a direct descendent from Peter Witry (seq. 001.) The second person in the list is the spouse. The spouse is followed by the children from oldest to youngest.

The marriage of Peter's oldest son is sequence 002. The marriage of the oldest child of the second Peter is sequence 003. The sequence of marriages progresses from the oldest married child to the oldest married child of the next generation. Thus, all of the families of descendants of the oldest child of the first Peter will appear before the record of the second child of Peter. If a person married more than a single time, the second marriage will appear in the same family list, but will be placed after all of the descendants of the first marriage.

This is an accurate description of the organization of the marriages in the book. However, it might be confusing. If you browse the book a bit, it will become clear. It would be best if you begin browsing a family that is very familiar to you.

Contents

The items of data for each person are coded in an abbreviated fashion to save space and to limit the size of the book. The abbreviations are as follows:
- generation number of the person beginning with 1 for Peter Witry (there are 14 generations in the family) followed by the family name in capital letters, followed by given names

a: - any alias or other name(s) by which the person was known

b: - date and location of birth

c: - number of children of this marriage

d: - date, location and cause of death

h: - name or number of the house where the person lived

i: - any interesting fact, including the date, if known

r: - the letters b-birth, d-death, m-marriage, x-other, to indicate that a copy of the original birth, death, etc. record was translated, and a copy of the translation is in the database (Note that if you want a copy of the original document and its translation, it is available for the asking.)

f: - name of the father of the spouse of the descendent

m: - name of the mother of the spouse of the descendent

t: - any title by which the person was known

v: - village or town where the person lived
w: - date and location of the marriage (wedding)

The people in the tree

Not all members of the family are in the tree. It will never be complete, and it would not fit in a book if it were complete. To know who is in the tree, it is necessary to trace the history of my research into the family and the rules I developed over time for inclusion and exclusion.

When I started looking up documents for births, marriages and deaths in the family, my first rule was to find as many of my own direct ancestors as possible. Therefore, I traced each of the paternal and maternal ancestors of my father as far back as I could find records. I also included all of the children of these couples.

When I began to look for the grandchildren of these people, I realized that I was in danger of making the job bigger than I could accomplish, and of making the tree bigger than most members of the family would be interested in. So I developed another rule. I would try to find the children of any married Witry man., I would try to find the marriages of these children, and I would try to find the children of these marriages - the grandchildren of the original couple. Another way of saying it is that I tried to find any marriage where one of the parties was a Witry, and any birth or death where at least one of the parents was named Witry.

Finally, I developed a last rule - that I would record the names of the parents of any person who married a Witry. This would hopefully give anyone a head start when trying to trace his or her own non-Witry ancestors.

If any reader of this book wants to know more about ancestors who are not named Witry, I recommend accessing the website deltgen.com to study the largest single-source tree that I know of. Rob Deltgen, the genealogist who developed the tree is a cousin of ours and is in this book. Thanks, Rob.

Tracing your ancestry

To trace your ancestry, first find your marriage or the marriage of your parents in the index in Appendix B, and note the sequence number in column 3. Look for the marriage with that sequence number in this chapter. If the first parent in the marriage married again, that subsequent marriage will be listed in the same family listing, but will follow the last child of the previous marriage.

To search downwards, note the sequence number of the marriage of a child in the family of interest to you. If this marriage produced children, the sequence number in front of the wife's name tells you where to look in this chapter for the family of that marriage. In this way, you can discover all of the descendants in the marriage that you looked up in the table in Appendix B.

To search upwards, go back to Appendix B and look up the names of the parents in the family of interest to you (the same names you originally looked up.) The right hand column in the table contains the sequence number of the paragraph that contains the records of the parents of the person listed in the marriage you started with. That person is a direct descendent of Peter Witry (seq. 001.) If there are two sequence numbers in the right hand column, it means that the second parent in that family is also descended from Peter Witry.

Let's take my family for an example. Start with me. Why not? My wife's name is Nancy Link. In Appendix B you will see that our marriage is sequence number 193. In Appendix A the record of our marriage says that I am generation 10. Our oldest son is listed immediately below our names and his marriage has the sequence number 194.

Now let's look for my ancestors. Look for my wife's and my name in the table in Appendix B. You will see the sequence number 192 in the right-hand column. That is the sequence number of my parents. Returning to Appendix A, look for marriage 192 to find my parents and my siblings.

Now let's look for my grandparents. Look up my parents' names in Appendix B. You will find the sequence number 182 in the right-hand column. Back to Appendix A. The marriage with sequence number 182 lists my grandparents. Go back to Appendix B one more time to look up their names. Note that there are two sequence numbers in the right hand column. The first is for my grandfather, who is descended from Peter Witry (seq. 001,) and the other is for my grandmother, who is also descended from Peter, but by a different line of descent.

If you have the patience to perform such a search, and don't make any mistakes, you will be able to trace all of the generations between you and Peter Witry. If you don't have the patience, or if you get stuck, write to me. I will be happy to send you a list of your ancestors. This method of looking up ancestors is a bit tedious, but it is less tedious than the one in the old book.

Multiple marriages

In tracing your ancestry, you could run into a complication if an ancestor was married more than once. Which marriage is the one you descended from? The right-hand column on the table on page 2 lists the sequence number of the first marriage. Return to that marriage in this chapter and read through the marriages and children within that family to locate the specific marriage you descended from. To help you identify multiple marriages, a number like [2] is shown in front of to the name of the person who has multiple marriages.

This same convention is used to identify people who have married other people within the family. An example is my grandparents, John Wittry and Barbara Wittry (seq. 182.)

The future

Well, that is it. There is no more text after this point. The remainder of the book is the appendices with the family tree and the table of marriages. Like a new car, the book immediately became a bit obsolete as soon as I sent it to the publisher. I will be telling you of changes by means of the quarterly newsletter. My hope is that by using this book you might learn more about your family, you might meet new cousins, and you might send me new information. Enjoy!

APPENDIX A

Family Tree

001

1 WITRY, Peter b: Abt. 1575 in Budange, France a: Robert h:
  Robert v: Budange, France c: 2
+ seq: 001 b: Abt. 1575 w: Abt. 1600 in Budange, France v:
  Budange, France c: 2
2 WITRY, Peter b: Abt. 1605 in Budange, France d: 02 Aug 1695
  in Schrondweiler, Lux a: Thies v: Schrondweiler, Lux c: 11
+ seq: 002 THIES, Anna b: Abt. 1615 d: 03 Nov 1694 in
  Schrondweiler, Lux w: Abt. 1635 in Fameck, France v:
  Schrondweiler, Lux r: d c: 11
2 MARCHAL, Nicolas b: Abt. 1610 in Budange, France d: 06
  Jan 1671 in Budange, France v: Budange, France r: d c: 4
+ seq: 324 PAULUS, Elisabeth b: Abt. 1610 d: 27 Jun 1688 in
  Budange, France w: Abt. 1640 in Budange, France v:
  Budange, France r: d c: 4

002

2 WITRY, Peter b: Abt. 1605 in Budange, France d: 02 Aug 1695
  in Schrondweiler, Lux a: Thies v: Schrondweiler, Lux c: 11
+ seq: 002 THIES, Anna b: Abt. 1615 d: 03 Nov 1694 in
  Schrondweiler, Lux w: Abt. 1635 in Fameck, France v:
  Schrondweiler, Lux r: d c: 11
3 WITRY, Adam b: Abt. 1636 in Budange, France a: Thies a:
  Ludwig v: Beidweiler, Lux o: Builder r: x c: 10

+ seq: 003 KUHNEN, Marie-Magdalena (Elisabeth) b: Abt. 1665 in Betzdorf, Lux d: 15 Jan 1742 in Beidweiler, Lux w: 23 Jan 1685 in Nommern, Lux a: Ludwig a: Connen a: Baydes v: Beidweiler, Lux r: mx r: d c: 10

3 WITRY, Nicolas b: 13 Jun 1638 in Schrondweiler, Lux r: b

3 WITRY, Susanne b: 05 Jul 1639 in Schrondweiler, Lux r: b

3 THIES, Margaretha b: 18 Sep 1643 in Schrondweiler, Lux d: 09 Jan 1742 in Blaschette, Lux a: Witry v: Blaschette, Lux r: bd c: 6

+ seq: 017.05 REUTER, Louis b: Abt. 1660 in Blaschette, Lux d: 06 Oct 1728 in Blaschette, Lux w: 11 Jan 1688 in Nommern, Lux v: Blaschette, Lux r: m t: Parish elder r: d c: 6

3 THIES, Johann b: 07 Mar 1646 in Schrondweiler, Lux a: Rob a: Witry h: Rob v: Glabach, Lux r: b c: 6

+ seq: 018 Margaretha b: Abt. 1650 w: Abt. 1675 v: Glabach, Lux c: 6

3 THIES, Johann b: 09 May 1649 in Schrondweiler, Lux a: Witry h: Thies v: Schrondweiler, Lux r: b c: 2

+ seq: 019 REULAND, Susanne b: Abt. 1650 in Blaschette, Lux d: 02 Jul 1707 in Schrondweiler, Lux w: Abt. 1675 a: Thies h: Thies v: Schrondweiler, Lux r: d c: 2

3 WITRY, Nicolas b: 07 Jan 1652 in Schrondweiler, Lux d: Aft. 1729 a: Thies h: Thies v: Schrondweiler, Lux t: Mayor r: b c: 8

+ seq: 020 REUTER, Elisabeth b: Abt. 1660 in Blaschette, Lux d: Aft. 1716 w: 11 Jan 1688 in Nommern, Lux v: Schrondweiler, Lux r: m c: 8

3 WITRY, Peter b: 09 Apr 1654 in Schrondweiler, Lux d: 17 Feb 1708 in Schrondweiler, Lux a: Weidert h: Weidert v: Schrondweiler, Lux o: Overseer r: bd c: 7

+ seq: 311 GLASENER, Anna-Elisabeth b: Abt. 1660 in Schrondweiler, Lux w: 11 Nov 1685 in Nommern, Lux a: Weidert h: Weidert v: Schrondweiler, Lux r: m c: 7

3 WITRY, Franzisca b: 02 Jan 1656 in Schrondweiler, Lux a: Thies v: Schrondweiler, Lux r: b c: 6

+ seq: 321.08 GOEDERT, Mathias b: Abt. 1655 in Schrondweiler, Lux w: 02 Feb 1681 in Nommern, Lux v: Schrondweiler, Lux r: m c: 6

3 [1] ROB, Firmin b: Abt. 1660 in Budange, France d: 22 Jun 1756 in Useldange, Lux a: Thies a: Machus a: Witry a: Kob(?) a: Koob(?) a: Maclus a: Mockels h: Machus v: Useldange,

Lux r: d a: Mockels c: 11

+ seq: 322 MATHIEU, Catherine b: Abt. 1675 in Useldange, Lux
d: 14 Aug 1712 in Useldange, Lux w: 14 Nov 1700 in
Nommern, Lux a: Machus h: Machlus v: Useldange, Lux r: m
r: d f: Nicolas Mathieu c: 5

* 2nd Wife of [1] ROB, Firmin:

+ seq: 323 MACHUS, Marie b: Abt. 1690 d: 02 Aug 1742 in
Useldange, Lux w: Abt. 1712 a: Mockels a: Macklus v:
Useldange, Lux c: 6

3 [2] WITRY, Johanna b: Abt. 1664 in Schrondweiler, Lux d: 02
Feb 1734 in Marnach, Lux a: Thies a: Schmitt v: Marnach, Lux
r: d c: 9

+ seq: 323.01 SCHMITT, Theodor b: Abt. 1664 in Marnach, Lux
d: 1704 in Marnach, Lux w: 19 Feb 1691 in Nommern, Lux v:
Marnach, Lux r: m t: Parish elder r: d c: 7

* 2nd Husband of [2] WITRY, Johanna:

+ seq: 323.04 SCHMITT, Johann-Wilhelm b: Abt. 1677 in
Oberwampach, Lux d: 14 Dec 1754 in Marnach, Lux w: 07
Jan 1705 in Munschausen, Lux v: Marnach, Lux r: m r: d c: 2

003

3 WITRY, Adam b: Abt. 1636 in Budange, France a: Thies a:
Ludwig v: Beidweiler, Lux o: Builder r: x c: 10

+ seq: 003 KUHNEN, Marie-Magdalena (Elisabeth) b: Abt. 1665
in Betzdorf, Lux d: 15 Jan 1742 in Beidweiler, Lux w: 23 Jan
1685 in Nommern, Lux a: Ludwig a: Connen a: Baydes v:
Beidweiler, Lux r: mx r: d c: 10

4 WITRY, Johann-Frederic b: 28 Mar 1687 in Betzdorf, Lux v:
Beidweiler, Lux r: b

4 WITRY, Marie b: 28 Mar 1687 in Betzdorf, Lux

4 WITRY, Johann b: 12 Oct 1688 in Betzdorf, Lux v: Bivange,
Lux r: b

+ seq: 004 EYNERS, Anna b: Abt. 1715 in Reckange, Lux w: 11
Jan 1735 in Bettange, Lux a: Zyners v: Bivange, Lux r: m

4 WITRY, Anna-Catherine b: 05 May 1698 in Hoesdorf, Lux r: b

4 WITRY, Mathias b: 25 Jun 1702 in Betzdorf, Lux v:
Ettelbruck, Lux r: b c: 1

+ seq: 005 Anna b: Abt. 1695 w: Abt. 1720 v: Ettelbruck, Lux
c: 1

4 WITRY, Johann-Peter b: 08 May 1704 in Beidweiler, Lux d: 21
Jul 1774 in Beidweiler, Lux a: Ludwigs a: Hansen v:

Beidweiler, Lux r: b c: 12
+ seq: 006 HANSEN, Angela b: 13 Apr 1716 in Beidweiler, Lux
   d: 21 Apr 1769 in Beidweiler, Lux w: 07 Jan 1731 in
   Rodenbourg, Lux a: Schirm v: Beidweiler, Lux r: mx r: b f:
   Nicolas Hansen m: Elisabeth c: 12
4 WITRY, Mathias b: 06 Jul 1706 in Beidweiler, Lux d: 03 Jun
   1776 in Beidweiler, Lux v: Beidweiler, Lux r: bd
4 WITRY, Johann-Bernard b: 02 Oct 1708 in Beidweiler, Lux a:
   Ludwig a: Claudon h: Claudon v: Warken, Lux i: 1734 Family
   tree chart t: Mass server r: bx c: 12
+ seq: 011 CLAUDON, Susanne b: 25 Aug 1719 in Warken, Lux
   d: 26 Jul 1775 in Warken, Lux w: 02 Feb 1734 in Ettelbruck,
   Lux v: Warken, Lux i: 1734 Family tree chart r: mx r: bd f:
   Mauritius Claudon m: Maria Behm c: 12
4 WITRY, Margaretha b: 23 Oct 1712 in Betzdorf, Lux r: b
+ seq: 017.02 DRAILLY, Lambert b: 1715 in Bois-et-Borsu,
   Belgium d: 1787 in Haltinne, Belgium w: 21 Jul 1737 in Bois
   et Borsu, Belgium r: m f: Remy-Joseph de Railly m: Marie-
   Jacqueline Quinet
4 WITRY, Anna b: 11 Jan 1717 in Beidweiler, Lux d: 24 Dec
   1789 in Waldbillig, Lux a: Ludwigs v: Beidweiler, Lux r: bd
   c: 3
+ seq: 017.03 ADAMY, Peter b: Abt. 1712 in Meysembourg,
   Lux d: 07 Jan 1790 in Waldbillig, Lux w: 28 Nov 1746 in
   Rodenbourg, Lux v: Beidweiler, Lux i: Served as mayor in
   Waldbillig r: m r: d c: 3

005
4 WITRY, Mathias b: 25 Jun 1702 in Betzdorf, Lux v:
   Ettelbruck, Lux r: b c: 1
+ seq: 005 Anna b: Abt. 1695 w: Abt. 1720 v: Ettelbruck, Lux
   c: 1
5 WITRY, Anna-Margaretha b: 24 Sep 1724 in Ettelbruck, Lux

006
4 WITRY, Johann-Peter b: 08 May 1704 in Beidweiler, Lux d: 21
   Jul 1774 in Beidweiler, Lux a: Ludwigs a: Hansen v:
   Beidweiler, Lux o: Merchant r: b c: 12
+ seq: 006 HANSEN, Angela b: 13 Apr 1716 in Beidweiler, Lux
   d: 21 Apr 1769 in Beidweiler, Lux w: 07 Jan 1731 in
   Rodenbourg, Lux a: Schirm v: Beidweiler, Lux r: b r: mx f:

Nicolas Hansen m: Elisabeth c: 12

5 WITRY, Elisabeth b: 31 Aug 1732 in Beidweiler, Lux a:
Ludwigs h: Ludwigs v: Beidweiler, Lux r: b

5 WITRY, Johann-Michel b: 21 Jan 1735 in Beidweiler, Lux d:
26 Mar 1812 in Beidweiler, Lux a: Hansen h: Hansen v:
Beidweiler, Lux o: Clerk of the court in Junglinster o: Farmer
r: bd c: 6

+ seq: 007 MOUCHANT, Anna-Marie b: Abt. 1745 in Livange,
Lux w: 04 May 1767 in Rodenbourg, Lux a: Meschamps v:
Beidweiler, Lux r: m c: 6

5 WITRY, Johann-Nicolas b: 02 Oct 1737 in Beidweiler, Lux d:
24 Jan 1804 a: Hansen h: Hansen v: Beidweiler, Lux o:
Farmer r: bd

5 WITRY, Marie-Catherine b: 12 Aug 1740 in Beidweiler, Lux
d: 12 Feb 1742 a: Hansen h: Hansen v: Beidweiler, Lux r: b

5 WITRY, Elisabeth b: 30 Jan 1743 in Beidweiler, Lux d: 06 Sep
1806 in Beidweiler, Lux v: Beidweiler, Lux o: Farmer r: bd

5 WITRY, Susanne b: 11 Oct 1745 in Beidweiler, Lux r: b

5 WITRY, Anna b: 01 Jun 1747 in Beidweiler, Lux d: 09 Dec
1792 in Heffingen, Lux a: Ludwigs h: Maisch v: Heffingen,
Lux o: Farmer r: bd c: 9

+ seq: 009.40 KIRSCH, Valentin b: Abt. 1745 d: 09 Jul 1802 in
Heffingen, Lux w: Abt. 1770 a: Maisch a: Meiesch h: Maisch
v: Heffingen, Lux o: Farmer r: d c: 9

5 WITRY, Peter b: 28 Aug 1749 in Beidweiler, Lux d: 05 Jan
1767 in Beidweiler, Lux a: Ludwigs h: Ludwigs v: Beidweiler,
Lux o: Farmer r: b

5 WITRY, Peter b: 17 Dec 1751 in Beidweiler, Lux a: Ludwigs
h: Ludwigs v: Beidweiler, Lux r: b c: 1

+ seq: 010 PINK, Susanne b: Abt. 1775 w: Abt. 1800 v:
Beidweiler, Lux c: 1

5 WITRY, Angela b: 23 Aug 1753 in Beidweiler, Lux d: 11 Feb
1775 in Beidweiler, Lux v: Beidweiler, Lux r: bd

5 WITRY, Catherine b: 08 Mar 1756 in Beidweiler, Lux d: 09
Jan 1804 in Beidweiler, Lux a: Ludwigs h: Ludwigs v:
Beidweiler, Lux r: bd

5 WITRY, Anna b: 23 Jun 1760 in Beidweiler, Lux d: 26 Aug
1811 in Petange, Lux h: No. 17 Klein St. v: Petange, Lux r: bd
c: 9

+ seq: 010.01 KLEIN, Peter b: Abt. 1765 in Petange, Lux w: 24
Oct 1785 in Mersch, Lux h: No. 17 Klein St. v: Petange, Lux

o: Day laborer o: Farmer r: m f: Martin Klein m: Elisabeth Goedert c: 9

007

5 WITRY, Johann-Michel b: 21 Jan 1735 in Beidweiler, Lux d: 26 Mar 1812 in Beidweiler, Lux a: Hansen h: Hansen v: Beidweiler, Lux o: Clerk of the court in Junglinster o: Farmer r: bd c: 6

+ seq: 007 MOUCHANT, Anna-Marie b: Abt. 1745 in Livange, Lux w: 04 May 1767 in Rodenbourg, Lux a: Meschamps v: Beidweiler, Lux r: m c: 6

6 WITRY, Johann-Nicolas b: 09 Jul 1768 in Beidweiler, Lux v: Beidweiler, Lux r: b c: 1

+ seq: 008 b: Abt. 1780 w: Abt. 1805 v: Beidweiler, Lux c: 1

6 WITRY, Johann-Mathias b: 20 Feb 1771 in Beidweiler, Lux d: 07 May 1843 in Reckange, Lux a: Hansen a: Hans h: Hansen/Meisch v: Reckange, Lux v: Beidweiler, Lux o: Farmer r: bd c: 6

+ seq: 009 WESTER, Susanne b: 10 Apr 1769 in Reckange, Lux d: 10 Nov 1844 in Beidweiler, Lux w: 30 Mar 1799 in Betzdorf, Lux h: Hansen v: Beidweiler, Lux o: No profession r: bd r: m f: Peter Wester m: Barbara Adamy c: 6

6 WITRY, Michel b: 12 Feb 1773 in Beidweiler, Lux r: b

6 WITRY, Magdalena b: 28 Nov 1774 in Beidweiler, Lux r: b

6 WITRY, Angela (Angelica) b: 28 Nov 1776 in Beidweiler, Lux d: 15 Mar 1844 in Niederanven, Lux v: Niederanven, Lux r: bd

+ seq: 009.37 SCHNEIDER, Johann b: Abt. 1771 in Niederanven, Lux d: 08 Jan 1797 in Beidweiler, Lux w: 20 Sep 1792 in Rodenbourg, Lux v: Niederanven, Lux o: Farmer r: m f: Jacob Schneider m: Magdalena Thinnes

6 [1] WITRY, Anna-Margaretha b: 13 Mar 1779 in Beidweiler, Lux v: Wallendorf, Lux o: Farmer r: b

+ seq: 009.38 MALDING, Johann-Baptist b: Abt. 1770 w: 28 Dec 1799 in Leudelange, Lux

* 2nd Husband of [1] WITRY, Anna-Margaretha:

+ seq: 009.39 HOFFMANN, Gerard b: Abt. 1780 in Wallendorf, Lux w: 13 Apr 1806 in Wallendorf, Lux v: Wallendorf, Lux o: Laborer r: m f: Wilhelm Hoffmann m: Susanne Betzen

008

6 WITRY, Johann-Nicolas b: 09 Jul 1768 in Beidweiler, Lux v:

Beidweiler, Lux r: b c: 1

+ seq: 008 b: Abt. 1780 w: Abt. 1805 v: Beidweiler, Lux c: 1

7 WITRY, Michel b: 29 Mar 1812 in Beidweiler, Lux

009

6 WITRY, Johann-Mathias b: 20 Feb 1771 in Beidweiler, Lux d:
07 May 1843 in Reckange, Lux a: Hansen a: Hans h:
Hansen/Meisch v: Reckange, Lux v: Beidweiler, Lux o:
Farmer r: bd c: 6

+ seq: 009 WESTER, Susanne b: 10 Apr 1769 in Reckange, Lux
d: 10 Nov 1844 in Beidweiler, Lux w: 30 Mar 1799 in
Betzdorf, Lux h: Hansen v: Beidweiler, Lux o: No profession
r: bd r: m f: Peter Wester m: Barbara Adamy c: 6

7 WITRY, Johanna b: 22 May 1799 in Beidweiler, Lux d: 07
Aug 1845 in Beidweiler, Lux h: Hames v: Beidweiler, Lux o:
No profession r: d c: 5

+ seq: 009.01 SIMON, Johann b: 31 Jan 1802 in Garnich, Lux
w: 03 Jun 1828 in Rodenbourg, Lux a: Kammes a: Hames h:
Hames v: Beidweiler, Lux o: Soldier o: Farmer r: m f:
Johann Simon m: Elisabeth Ketter c: 5

7 WITRY, Peter b: 17 Jan 1803 in Beidweiler, Lux d: 31 Jan
1803 in Beidweiler, Lux h: Hansen v: Beidweiler, Lux o: No
profession r: bd

7 WITRY, Margaretha b: 20 Feb 1804 in Beidweiler, Lux d: 01
Feb 1879 in Munsbach, Lux h: Weber v: Olingen, Lux o: No
profession r: bd c: 6

+ seq: 009.04 OLINGER, Johann b: 18 Jun 1801 in Munsbach,
Lux d: 20 Apr 1853 in Munsbach, Lux w: 01 Dec 1830 in
Schuttrange, Lux h: Weber v: Olingen, Lux o: Painter o:
Farmer r: m f: Johann Olinger m: Marie Jung c: 6

7 WITRY, Catherine b: 20 Feb 1804 in Beidweiler, Lux d: 05
May 1889 in Weyer, Lux h: Hoimes v: Weyer, Lux o: No
profession r: bd c: 6

+ seq: 009.15 STRONCK, Johann-Peter b: 29 Oct 1798 in
Weyer, Lux d: 19 Mar 1859 in Weyer, Lux w: 20 May 1829 in
Fischbach, Lux h: Hoimes v: Weyer, Lux o: Laborer o:
Farmer r: bd r: m f: Peter Stronck m: Marie Bernard c: 6

7 WITRY, Susanne b: 27 Jan 1807 in Beidweiler, Lux d: 11 Feb
1891 in Reisdorf, Lux v: Reisdorf, Lux o: No profession r: bd
c: 5

+ seq: 009.26 Reiland, Nicolas b: 13 Mar 1805 in Reisdorf, Lux

d: Bef. 1891 w: 13 Jan 1835 in Reisdorf, Lux v: Reisdorf, Lux
o: Cobbler o: Farmer r: m f: Peter Reiland m: Anna Chilartz
c: 5

7 [1] WITRY, Anne-Marie b: 01 Jan 1810 in Beidweiler, Lux d:
in Abweiler, Lux v: Verlorenhart, Lux i: Paulis o: No
profession r: b c: 4

+ seq: 009.35 PIERRE, Johann-Mathias b: Abt. 1805 w: 1839 v:
Verlorenhart, Lux i: Paulis o: Gardener

* 2nd Husband of [1] WITRY, Anne-Marie:

+ seq: 009.36 PLETSCHET, Peter b: 03 Mar 1805 in Grosbous,
Lux d: in Boulaide, Lux w: 03 Sep 1839 in Rodenbourg, Lux
v: Verlorenhart, Lux o: Miller r: m f: Johann Pletschet m:
Catherine Wester c: 4

009.01

7 WITRY, Johanna b: 22 May 1799 in Beidweiler, Lux d: 07
Aug 1845 in Beidweiler, Lux h: Hames v: Beidweiler, Lux o:
No profession r: d c: 5

+ seq: 009.01 SIMON, Johann b: 31 Jan 1802 in Garnich, Lux
w: 03 Jun 1828 in Rodenbourg, Lux a: Kammes a: Hames h:
Hames v: Beidweiler, Lux o: Soldier o: Farmer r: m f:
Johann Simon m: Elisabeth Ketter c: 5

8 SIMON, Susanne b: 17 Aug 1829 in Beidweiler, Lux r: b

8 SIMON, Mathias b: 13 Jan 1831 in Beidweiler, Lux r: b

8 SIMON, Nicolas b: 17 Dec 1832 in Beidweiler, Lux v:
Macheren, France r: b

8 SIMON, Angela b: 27 Mar 1836 in Beidweiler, Lux v:
Herborn, Lux r: b c: 4

+ seq: 009.02 HANSEN w: Abt. 1860 v: Herborn, Lux c: 4

8 SIMON, Jean

+ seq: 009.03 REICHLING w: Abt. 1860

009.02

8 SIMON, Angela b: 27 Mar 1836 in Beidweiler, Lux v:
Herborn, Lux r: b c: 4

+ seq: 009.02 HANSEN w: Abt. 1860 v: Herborn, Lux c: 4

9 HANSEN, Nicolas

9 HANSEN, Susanne

9 HANSEN, Jean

9 HANSEN, Michel

7 WITRY, Margaretha b: 20 Feb 1804 in Beidweiler, Lux d: 01 Feb 1879 in Munsbach, Lux h: Weber v: Olingen, Lux o: No profession r: bd c: 6

+ seq: 009.04 OLINGER, Johann b: 18 Jun 1801 in Munsbach, Lux d: 20 Apr 1853 in Munsbach, Lux w: 01 Dec 1830 in Schuttrange, Lux h: Weber v: Olingen, Lux o: Painter o: Farmer r: m f: Johann Olinger m: Marie Jung c: 6

8 OLINGER, Johann b: 30 Jan 1832 in Munsbach, Lux r: b c: 4

+ seq: 009.05 w: Abt. 1850 c: 4

8 OLINGER, Mathias b: 02 Sep 1834 in Munsbach, Lux v: Munsbach, Lux o: Farmer r: b

8 OLINGER, Peter b: 24 May 1837 in Munsbach, Lux d: 22 Feb 1842 in Munsbach, Lux v: Munsbach, Lux r: b

8 OLINGER, Johann b: 04 Oct 1839 in Munsbach, Lux d: 15 Dec 1839 in Munsbach, Lux v: Munsbach, Lux r: b

8 OLINGER, Barbara b: 07 Dec 1840 in Munsbach, Lux r: b c: 4

+ seq: 009.09 HELLERS b: in Manternach, Lux w: Abt. 1860 c: 4

8 OLINGER, Marie b: 14 Nov 1843 in Munsbach, Lux r: b c: 4

+ seq: 009.14 WEISS b: in Munsbach, Lux w: Abt. 1870 c: 4

8 OLINGER, Johann b: 30 Jan 1832 in Munsbach, Lux r: b c: 4

+ seq: 009.05 w: Abt. 1850 c: 4

9 OLINGER, Johann

+ seq: 009.06 PIRRY b: in Colmar. Lux w: Abt. 1880

9 OLINGER, Mathias o: Engineer

+ seq: 009.07 SWOBODA, Olga b: in Russia w: Abt. 1880

9 OLINGER, Margareta

+ seq: 009.08 HELLERS b: in Obersyren, Lux w: Abt. 1880

9 OLINGER, Peter

8 OLINGER, Barbara b: 07 Dec 1840 in Munsbach, Lux r: b c: 4

+ seq: 009.09 HELLERS b: in Manternach, Lux w: Abt. 1860 c: 4

9 HELLERS, Catherine

+ seq: 009.10 WILMES b: in Ingeldorf, Lux w: Abt. 1890

9 HELLERS, Jean

+ seq: 009.11 KURTH b: in Schuttrange, Lux w: Abt. 1890

9 HELLERS, Mathias
+ seq: 009.12 SCHILTZ b: in Manternach, Lux w: Abt. 1890
9 HELLERS, Jacob
+ seq: 009.13 STEID b: in Herborn, Lux w: Abt. 1890

009.14

8 OLINGER, Marie b: 14 Nov 1843 in Munsbach, Lux r: b c: 4
+ seq: 009.14 WEISS b: in Munsbach, Lux w: Abt. 1870 c: 4
9 WEISS, Jean
9 WEISS, Victor
9 WEISS, Marguerite
9 WEISS, Joseph

009.15

7 WITRY, Catherine b: 20 Feb 1804 in Beidweiler, Lux d: 05
  May 1889 in Weyer, Lux h: Hoimes v: Weyer, Lux o: No
  profession r: bd c: 6
+ seq: 009.15 STRONCK, Johann-Peter b: 29 Oct 1798 in
  Weyer, Lux d: 19 Mar 1859 in Weyer, Lux w: 20 May 1829 in
  Fischbach, Lux h: Hoimes v: Weyer, Lux o: Laborer o:
  Farmer r: bd r: m f: Peter Stronck m: Marie Bernard c: 6
8 STRONCK, Marie b: 02 Apr 1830 in Weyer, Lux h: Hoimes v:
  Weyer, Lux r: b c: 8
+ seq: 009.16 BERTRANG, Peter w: Abt. 1860 h: Hoimes v:
  Weyer, Lux f: Johann Bertrang m: Catharina Flammang c: 8
8 STRONCK, Nicolas b: 01 Jan 1834 in Weyer, Lux h: Hoimes
  v: Weyer, Lux r: b c: 1
+ seq: 009.21 KOEMPTGEN, Susanna w: Abt. 1860 c: 1
8 STRONCK, Anna b: 01 Nov 1837 in Weyer, Lux h: Hoimes v:
  Weyer, Lux o: Nun r: b
8 STRONCK, Michel b: 02 Mar 1840 in Weyer, Lux h: Hoimes
  v: Weyer, Lux o: Doctor r: b
+ seq: 009.23 JACQUEMIN, Julie w: Abt. 1870
8 STRONCK, Helene b: 17 Sep 1843 in Weyer, Lux d: 01 Nov
  1843 in Weyer, Lux h: Hoimes v: Weyer, Lux r: bd
8 STRONCK, Johann b: 11 Aug 1847 in Weyer, Lux h: Hoimes
  v: Weyer, Lux r: b c: 2
+ seq: 009.24 REDING, Catherine b: in Lintgen, Lux w: Abt.
  1870 c: 2

009.16

8 STRONCK, Marie b: 02 Apr 1830 in Weyer, Lux h: Hoimes v:
Weyer, Lux r: b c: 8
+ seq: 009.16 BERTRANG, Peter w: Abt. 1860 h: Hoimes v:
Weyer, Lux f: Johann Bertrang m: Catharina Flammang c: 8
9 BERTRANG, Hubert c: 3
+ seq: 009.17 PETTINGER, Marianna w: Abt. 1890 c: 3
9 BERTRANG, Gustave
9 BERTRANG, Jean-Michel
9 BERTRANG, Nicolas v: Godbrange, Lux c: 1
+ seq: 009.18 MULLER, Leonie w: Abt. 1890 v: Godbrange,
Lux c: 1
9 BERTRANG, Barbe
9 BERTRANG, Mathias v: Junglinster, Lux c: 5
+ seq: 009.19 WILTGEN, Marie w: Abt. 1890 v: Junglinster,
Lux c: 5
9 BERTRANG, Anna v: Mersch, Lux c: 5
+ seq: 009.20 SCHWARTZ, Joseph w: Abt. 1890 v: Mersch,
Lux c: 5
9 BERTRANG, Edouard

009.17

9 BERTRANG, Hubert c: 3
+ seq: 009.17 PETTINGER, Marianna w: Abt. 1890 c: 3
10BERTRANG, Valerie
10BERTRANG, Camile
10BERTRANG, Florentine

009.18

9 BERTRANG, Nicolas v: Godbrange, Lux c: 1
+ seq: 009.18 MULLER, Leonie w: Abt. 1890 v: Godbrange,
Lux c: 1
10BERTRANG, Maria

009.19

9 BERTRANG, Mathias v: Junglinster, Lux c: 5
+ seq: 009.19 WILTGEN, Marie w: Abt. 1890 v: Junglinster,
Lux c: 5
10BERTRANG, Francoise
10BERTRANG, Prosper
10BERTRANG, Jean-Pierre

10BERTRANG, Johanna
10BERTRANG, Leonie

009.20
9 BERTRANG, Anna v: Mersch, Lux c: 5
+ seq: 009.20 SCHWARTZ, Joseph w: Abt. 1890 v: Mersch,
   Lux c: 5
10SCHWARTZ, Edouard
10SCHWARTZ, Maria
10SCHWARTZ, Henriette
10SCHWARTZ, Alice
10SCHWARTZ, Henry

009.21
8 STRONCK, Nicolas b: 01 Jan 1834 in Weyer, Lux h: Hoimes
   v: Weyer, Lux r: b c: 1
+ seq: 009.21 KOEMPTGEN, Susanna w: Abt. 1860 c: 1
9 STRONCK, Peter c: 3
+ seq: 009.22 WEISS, Helena w: Abt. 1890 c: 3

009.22
9 STRONCK, Peter c: 3
+ seq: 009.22 WEISS, Helena w: Abt. 1890 c: 3
10STRONCK, Edouard
10STRONCK, Anna
10STRONCK, Virginie

009.24
8 STRONCK, Johann b: 11 Aug 1847 in Weyer, Lux h: Hoimes
   v: Weyer, Lux r: b c: 2
+ seq: 009.24 REDING, Catherine b: in Lintgen, Lux w: Abt.
   1870 c: 2
9 STRONCK, Johanna
+ seq: 009.25 WOLTER, Nicolas w: Abt. 1900
9 STRONCK, Juliette

009.26
7 WITRY, Susanne b: 27 Jan 1807 in Beidweiler, Lux d: 11 Feb
   1891 in Reisdorf, Lux v: Reisdorf, Lux o: No profession r: bd
   c: 5

+ seq: 009.26 Reiland, Nicolas b: 13 Mar 1805 in Reisdorf, Lux
   d: Bef. 1891 w: 13 Jan 1835 in Reisdorf, Lux v: Reisdorf, Lux
   o: Cobbler o: Farmer r: m f: Peter Reiland m: Anna Chilartz
   c: 5
8 Reiland, Anna
8 Reiland, Susanne v: Reisdorf, Lux c: 2
+ seq: 009.27 TERRENS w: Abt. 1880 v: Reisdorf, Lux c: 2
8 Reiland, Nicolas b: 1841 v: Reisdorf, Lux o: Miller c: 6
+ seq: 009.29 DOSTERT, Marie w: Abt. 1870 v: Reisdorf, Lux
   c: 6
8 Reiland, Catherine c: 5
+ seq: 009.32 MEHLEN w: Abt. 1860 c: 5
8 Reiland, Marie v: Manternach, Lux c: 3
+ seq: 009.33 FELL w: Abt. 1860 v: Manternach, Lux c: 3

009.27

8 Reiland, Susanne v: Reisdorf, Lux c: 2
+ seq: 009.27 TERRENS w: Abt. 1880 v: Reisdorf, Lux c: 2
9 TERRENS, Nicolas
9 TERRENS, Susanne
+ seq: 009.28 SCHOOMARS, N. b: in Bohmuhle, Lux w: Abt.
   1910

009.29

8 Reiland, Nicolas b: 1841 v: Reisdorf, Lux o: Miller c: 6
+ seq: 009.29 DOSTERT, Marie w: Abt. 1870 v: Reisdorf, Lux
   c: 6
9 Reiland, Michel
+ seq: 009.30 POERTERS, Susanne w: Abt. 2000
9 Reiland, Marguerite
+ seq: 009.31 DUHR b: in Ahn, Lux w: Abt. 2000
9 Reiland, Catherine o: Nun
9 Reiland, Josephine o: Nun
9 Reiland, Lucie
9 Reiland, Mathias o: Religious

009.32

8 Reiland, Catherine c: 5
+ seq: 009.32 MEHLEN w: Abt. 1860 c: 5
9 MEHLEN, Susanne
9 MEHLEN, Catherine

9 MEHLEN, Mathias
9 MEHLEN, Lucie
9 MEHLEN, Nicolas

009.33

8 Reiland, Marie v: Manternach, Lux c: 3
+ seq: 009.33 FELL w: Abt. 1860 v: Manternach, Lux c: 3
9 FELL, Mathias
+ seq: 009.34 KLEIN, M. w: Abt. 1890
9 FELL, Catherine
9 FELL, Lucie

009.35

7 [1] WITRY, Anne-Marie b: 01 Jan 1810 in Beidweiler, Lux d:
in Abweiler, Lux v: Verlorenhart, Lux i: Paulis o: No
profession r: b c: 4
+ seq: 009.35 PIERRE, Johann-Mathias b: Abt. 1805 w: 1839 v:
Verlorenhart, Lux i: Paulis o: Gardener
* 2nd Husband of [1] WITRY, Anne-Marie:
+ seq: 009.36 PLETSCHET, Peter b: 03 Mar 1805 in Grosbous,
Lux d: in Boulaide, Lux w: 03 Sep 1839 in Rodenbourg, Lux
v: Verlorenhart, Lux o: Miller r: m f: Johann Pletschet m:
Catherine Wester c: 4
8 WITRY, Peter b: 08 Mar 1839 in Eich, Lux d: 15 Feb 1840 in
Verlorenhart, Lux r: bd
8 WITRY, Mathias b: 19 Aug 1840 in Oberfeulen, Lux d: 10 Oct
1840 in Oberfeulen, Lux
8 WITRY, Jean b: 29 Apr 1842 in Oberfeulen, Lux d: in
Abweiler, Lux
8 WITRY, Marie b: 24 Mar 1844 in Oberfeulen, Lux d: in
Abweiler, Lux

009.40

5 WITRY, Anna b: 01 Jun 1747 in Beidweiler, Lux d: 09 Dec
1792 in Heffingen, Lux a: Ludwigs h: Maisch v: Heffingen,
Lux o: Farmer r: bd c: 9
+ seq: 009.40 KIRSCH, Valentin b: Abt. 1745 d: 09 Jul 1802 in
Heffingen, Lux w: Abt. 1770 a: Maisch a: Meiesch h: Maisch
v: Heffingen, Lux o: Farmer r: d c: 9
6 KIRSCH, Anna-Catherine b: 13 Jan 1771 in Heffingen, Lux a:
Maisch r: b

+ seq: 009.41 WEIDERT, Peter b: Abt. 1770 in Mensdorf, Lux
  w: 08 Jan 1794 in Betzdorf, Lux r: m
6 KIRSCH, Barbara b: 01 Nov 1772 in Heffingen, Lux d: 11 Sep
  1802 in Heffingen, Lux a: Maisch v: Heffingen, Lux r: bd
+ seq: 009.42 STIREN, Nicolas b: Abt. 1770 in Consdorf, Lux
  w: 07 Oct 1796 in Betzdorf, Lux v: Heffingen, Lux r: m
6 KIRSCH, Theodor b: 27 Jun 1775 in Heffingen, Lux a: Maisch
  r: b
6 KIRSCH, Nicolas b: 07 Aug 1777 in Heffingen, Lux d: 27 Mar
  1778 in Heffingen, Lux a: Maisch v: Bergem, Lux o: Plowman
  r: bd
6 KIRSCH, Anna-Marie b: 23 Jan 1779 in Heffingen, Lux a:
  Maisch r: b
6 KIRSCH, Marie-Catherine b: 09 May 1781 in Heffingen, Lux
  d: 07 Dec 1781 in Heffingen, Lux a: Maisch v: Heffingen, Lux
  r: bd
6 KIRSCH, Elisabeth b: 07 Jul 1783 in Heffingen, Lux a: Maisch
  r: b
6 KIRSCH, Margaretha b: 14 Jan 1786 in Heffingen, Lux a:
  Maisch v: Heffingen, Lux r: b
+ seq: 009.43 BRAUN, Nicolas b: Abt. 1785 in Heffingen, Lux
  w: 17 Jan 1810 in Betzdorf, Lux v: Heffingen, Lux r: m
6 KIRSCH, Georg b: 08 Jun 1791 in Heffingen, Lux d: 10 Jun
  1793 in Heffingen, Lux a: Maisch v: Heffingen, Lux r: bd

010

5 WITRY, Peter b: 17 Dec 1751 in Beidweiler, Lux a: Ludwigs
  h: Ludwigs v: Beidweiler, Lux r: b c: 1
+ seq: 010 PINK, Susanne b: Abt. 1775 w: Abt. 1800 v:
  Beidweiler, Lux c: 1
6 WITRY, Susanne b: 09 Sep 1805

010.01

5 WITRY, Anna b: 23 Jun 1760 in Beidweiler, Lux d: 26 Aug
  1811 in Petange, Lux h: No. 17 Klein St. v: Petange, Lux r: bd
  c: 9
+ seq: 010.01 KLEIN, Peter b: Abt. 1765 in Petange, Lux w: 24
  Oct 1785 in Mersch, Lux h: No. 17 Klein St. v: Petange, Lux
  o: Day laborer o: Farmer r: m f: Martin Klein m: Elisabeth
  Goedert c: 9
6 KLEIN, Anna-Marie b: 21 Oct 1787 in Petange, Lux d: 21 Apr

1793 in Petange, Lux v: Petange, Lux r: bd
6 KLEIN, Elisabeth b: 06 Feb 1789 in Petange, Lux d: 01 Oct
  1790 in Petange, Lux v: Petange, Lux r: bd
6 KLEIN, Catherine b: 15 Jul 1791 in Petange, Lux d: 11 Apr
  1793 in Petange, Lux v: Petange, Lux r: bd
6 KLEIN, Frederic b: 12 Jan 1793 in Petange, Lux d: 07 Apr
  1793 in Petange, Lux v: Petange, Lux r: bd
6 KLEIN, Jacob b: 27 Apr 1794 in Petange, Lux r: b
6 KLEIN, Mathias b: 07 Mar 1796 in Petange, Lux d: 08 Jul 1796
  in Petange, Lux v: Petange, Lux r: bd
6 KLEIN, Michel b: 19 Apr 1801 in Petange, Lux r: b
6 KLEIN, Elisabeth b: 18 Jul 1802 in Petange, Lux r: b
6 KLEIN, Peter b: 19 Apr 1805 in Petange, Lux r: b

011
4 WITRY, Johann-Bernard t: Mass server b: 02 Oct 1708 in
  Beidweiler, Lux a: Ludwig a: Claudon h: Claudon v: Warken,
  Lux i: Family tree chart o: Farmer r: bx c: 12
+ seq: 011 CLAUDON, Susanne b: 25 Aug 1719 in Warken, Lux
  d: 26 Jul 1775 in Warken, Lux w: 02 Feb 1734 in Ettelbruck,
  Lux v: Warken, Lux i: Family tree chart r: bd r: mx f:
  Mauritius Claudon m: Maria Behm c: 12
5 WITRY, Philipp-Frederic b: 19 Feb 1737 in Warken, Lux r: b
5 WITRY, Jean-Mathias t: Peasant b: 08 Mar 1739 in Warken,
  Lux d: 16 Dec 1803 in Warken, Lux v: Warken, Lux i: Sold
  Warken mill with Domini and Susanne o: Miller o: Carpenter
  o: Farmer o: Machinist, Lathe operator r: bd c: 11
+ seq: 012 KNEIP, Anna-Catherine b: Abt. 1740 in Eschdorf, Lux
  d: 25 Feb 1809 in Warken, Lux w: 12 Oct 1766 in Ettelbruck,
  Lux v: Warken, Lux r: m f: Nicolas Kneip m: Anna-Elisabeth
  c: 11
5 WITRY, Johann-Nicolas b: 18 Oct 1741 in Warken, Lux r: b
5 WITRY, Johann b: 20 Feb 1743 in Warken, Lux r: b
5 WITRY, Catherine b: 05 Jan 1746 in Warken, Lux d: 09 Feb
  1803 in Dippach, Lux v: Bettange, Lux r: bd
+ seq: 015.98 KIPGEN, Jacob b: Abt. 1740 w: Abt. 1770 v:
  Bettange, Lux
5 WITRY, Susanne b: 05 Jan 1746 in Warken, Lux d: 24 Jul
  1821 in Luxembourg, Lux h: 23 Possenthal v: Luxembourg,
  Lux o: Baker r: bd
+ seq: 015.99 SCHEUR, Nicolas b: Abt. 1740 w: 12 Sep 1766 in

Ettelbruck, Lux h: 23 Possenthal v: Luxembourg, Lux o: Baker

5 WITRY, Marie-Elisabeth b: 09 Jan 1749 in Warken, Lux r: b

5 WITRY, Marie-Catherine b: 29 Apr 1751 in Warken, Lux d: 03 Jan 1823 in Luxembourg, Lux v: Luxembourg, Lux o: No profession r: bd

+ seq: 015.99.01 MORIS, Charles b: Abt. 1745 w: Abt. 1775 v: Luxembourg, Lux o: Brewer

5 WITRY, Johann-Michel b: 05 Sep 1753 in Warken, Lux d: 11 Feb 1832 in Warken, Lux v: Warken, Lux o: Day laborer o: Linen weaver r: bd c: 2

+ seq: 016 THIEL, Marie b: 04 Jan 1767 in Schrondweiler, Lux d: 15 May 1845 in Warken, Lux w: 27 Oct 1794 in Nommern, Lux a: Goeders v: Warken, Lux o: Day laborer r: bd r: m f: Nicolas Thiel m: Elisabeth Roob c: 2

5 WITRY, Marie-Regina b: 17 Feb 1756 in Warken, Lux d: 29 Apr 1804 in Ettelbruck, Lux v: Ettelbruck, Lux o: Day laborer r: bd c: 10

+ seq: 017.01 UNDEN, Heinrich b: Abt. 1742 in Ettelbruck, Lux d: in Warken, Lux w: 09 Dec 1779 in Ettelbruck, Lux a: Onden v: Ettelbruck, Lux o: Tavern keeper o: Banker o: Day laborer, Merchant r: m c: 10

5 WITRY, Anna-Barbara b: 31 Oct 1758 in Warken, Lux r: b

5 WITRY, Marie-Elisabeth b: 03 Apr 1760 in Warken, Lux d: 05 Jun 1831 in Warken, Lux v: Warken, Lux o: Farmer r: bd

012

5 WITRY, Jean-Mathias t: Peasant b: 08 Mar 1739 in Warken, Lux d: 16 Dec 1803 in Warken, Lux v: Warken, Lux i: Sold Warken mill with Domini and Susanne o: Miller o: Carpenter o: Farmer o: Machinist, Lathe operator r: bd c: 11

+ seq: 012 KNEIP, Anna-Catherine b: Abt. 1740 in Eschdorf, Lux d: 25 Feb 1809 in Warken, Lux w: 12 Oct 1766 in Ettelbruck, Lux v: Warken, Lux r: m f: Nicolas Kneip m: Anna-Elisabeth c: 11

6 WITRY, Susanne b: Abt. 1767 in Warken, Lux v: Warken, Lux c: 2

+ seq: 012.01 DRAUDEN, Martin t: Peasant b: Abt. 1760 in Berg, Lux w: 30 Jan 1786 in Ettelbruck, Lux v: Warken, Lux o: Miller o: Farmer r: m f: Johann-Peter Drauden m: Marie Schemper c: 2

6 WITRY, Dominic b: 11 Sep 1769 in Warken, Lux d: 31 May

1847 in Warken, Lux h: Grols v: Warken, Lux i: Owned
Warken mill once more o: Farmer o: Miller r: bd c: 13
+ seq: 013 WAGNER, Christina b: Abt. 1785 in Bissen, Lux w:
19 Feb 1809 in Ettelbruck, Lux h: Grols v: Warken, Lux o:
Farmer o: Miller r: mx c: 13
6 WITRY, Marie-Catherine b: 15 May 1772 in Warken, Lux r: b
+ seq: 015.01 MONS, Karl b: Abt. 1770 w: 04 Mar 1796 in
Schieren, Lux
6 WITRY, Regina b: 14 Mar 1775 in Warken, Lux d: 15 Jan
1850 in Ettelbruck, Lux h: Gaessel v: Ettelbruck, Lux o: Day
laborer r: bd
+ seq: 015.02 KAUFFMANN, Nicolas b: 28 Jan 1788 in
Ettelbruck, Lux d: 26 Dec 1858 in Ettelbruck, Lux w: 20 Aug
1817 in Ettelbruck, Lux h: Gaessel v: Ettelbruck, Lux o: Day
laborer r: d r: m f: Johann-Nicolas Kauffmann m: Catherine
Adamy
6 WITRY, Marie-Anna-Christina b: 29 Nov 1777 in Warken, Lux
d: 18 Sep 1791 in Warken, Lux v: Warken, Lux r: bd
6 WITRY, Johann-Michel b: 06 Mar 1780 in Warken, Lux r: b
6 WITRY, Margaretha b: 19 Nov 1782 in Warken, Lux r: b
6 WITRY, Elisabeth b: Abt. 1783 in Warken, Lux d: 20 Jan 1784
in Warken, Lux v: Warken, Lux r: d
6 WITRY, Johann b: 29 Oct 1784 in Warken, Lux r: b
6 WITRY, Marie b: 08 Oct 1786 in Warken, Lux d: 15 Nov 1854
in Ettelbruck, Lux h: Gross Street v: Ettelbruck, Lux o: Farmer
r: bd c: 8
+ seq: 015.03 SPANIER, Dominique b: 24 Dec 1790 in
Ettelbruck, Lux d: 09 Nov 1854 in Ettelbruck, Lux w: 24 Sep
1811 in Ettelbruck, Lux h: Gross Street v: Ettelbruck, Lux o:
Day laborer o: Farmer r: d r: m f: Georg Spanier m: Catherine
Wolk c: 8
6 WITRY, Marie-Barbara b: 28 Dec 1790 in Warken, Lux d: 17
Oct 1869 in Warken, Lux v: Warken, Lux o: No profession r:
bd c: 7
+ seq: 015.97 BISSENER, Michel b: 09 Oct 1780 in Oberfeulen,
Lux d: 07 May 1845 in Warken, Lux w: 09 Aug 1815 in
Ettelbruck, Lux v: Warken, Lux o: Farmer r: d r: m f:
Theodor Bissener m: Magdalena Polter c: 7

012.01
6 WITRY, Susanne b: Abt. 1767 in Warken, Lux v: Warken, Lux

c: 2

+ seq: 012.01 DRAUDEN, Martin t: Peasant b: Abt. 1760 in
Berg, Lux w: 30 Jan 1786 in Ettelbruck, Lux v: Warken, Lux
o: Miller o: Farmer r: m f: Johann-Peter Drauden m: Marie
Schemper c: 2

7 DRAUDEN, Marie-Salome b: 25 Feb 1787 in Warken, Lux d:
08 Jul 1790 in Warken, Lux v: Warken, Lux r: bd

7 DRAUDEN, Johann b: 19 Jan 1789 in Warken, Lux r: b

013

6 WITRY, Dominic b: 11 Sep 1769 in Warken, Lux d: 31 May
1847 in Warken, Lux h: Grols v: Warken, Lux i: Owned
Warken mill once more o: Farmer o: Miller r: bd c: 13

+ seq: 013 WAGNER, Christina b: Abt. 1785 in Bissen, Lux w:
19 Feb 1809 in Ettelbruck, Lux h: Grols v: Warken, Lux o:
Farmer o: Miller r: mx c: 13

7 WITRY, Michel b: 09 Jan 1810 in Warken, Lux d: 10 Mar
1896 in Warken, Lux v: Warken, Lux o: Land owner o: Farmer
o: Miller r: bd c: 5

+ seq: 014 MULLER, Marie-Catherine b: 23 Sep 1814 in
Michelau, Lux d: 1881 in Warken, Lux w: 19 Dec 1841 in
Ettelbruck, Lux v: Warken, Lux i: Prenuptial agreement o:
Farmer r: mx f: Mathias Muller m: Marie-Elisabeth Maillette
c: 5

7 WITRY, Margaretha b: 31 Aug 1811 in Warken, Lux d: 18
Nov 1892 in Ettelbruck, Lux v: Warken, Lux i: In 1848 she
purchased a piece of land in Warken, and gave it to her brother,
Michel Witry o: Farmer r: bd c: 2

+ seq: 014.01 DE WAHA, Nicolas b: 15 Apr 1806 in
Grummelscheid, Lux d: 1880 w: 22 Jun 1836 in Winseler, Lux
v: Warken, Lux i: Before the French Revolution the family
owned the castle of Grummelscheid o: Farmer r: b r: mx f:
Jean-Baptist De Waha m: Margaretha Lutgen c: 2

7 WITRY, Martin b: 26 Jun 1813 in Warken, Lux d: 05 Jan 1820
in Warken, Lux v: Warken, Lux r: bd

7 WITRY, Mathias b: 07 Mar 1815 in Warken, Lux d: 12 Aug
1815 in Warken, Lux v: Warken, Lux r: bd

7 WITRY, Anna-Catherine b: 09 Oct 1816 in Warken, Lux d: 08
May 1817 in Warken, Lux v: Warken, Lux r: bd

7 WITRY, Michel b: 08 Apr 1818 in Warken, Lux d: 27 Jan 1820
in Warken, Lux v: Warken, Lux r: bd

7 WITRY, Johann b: 11 May 1820 in Warken, Lux d: 21 Dec 1898 in Warken, Lux v: Warken, Lux o: Estate owner o: Day laborer o: Miller r: bd

+ seq: 015 PROBST, Margaretha b: 25 Aug 1823 in Warken, Lux d: 25 Jul 1899 in Warken, Lux w: 26 Jan 1848 in Ettelbruck, Lux v: Warken, Lux o: Property owner o: Farmer r: bd r: m f: Mathias Probst m: Marie Mai

7 WITRY, Barbara b: 08 May 1822 in Warken, Lux d: 02 May 1825 in Warken, Lux v: Warken, Lux r: bd

7 WITRY, Michel b: 28 Nov 1823 in Warken, Lux d: 09 Jun 1841 in Warken, Lux v: Warken, Lux r: bd

7 WITRY, Nicolas b: 23 Oct 1825 in Warken, Lux d: 01 Mar 1827 in Warken, Lux v: Warken, Lux r: bd

7 WITRY, Marie b: 01 Mar 1828 in Warken, Lux d: 06 Mar 1828 in Warken, Lux v: Warken, Lux r: bd

7 WITRY, Johann-Peter b: 30 Dec 1829 in Warken, Lux d: 06 Jul 1831 in Warken, Lux v: Warken, Lux r: bd

7 WITRY, Margaretha (Anna-Marie) b: 05 Oct 1831 in Warken, Lux d: 12 Dec 1831 in Warken, Lux v: Warken, Lux r: bd

014

7 WITRY, Michel b: 09 Jan 1810 in Warken, Lux d: 10 Mar 1896 in Warken, Lux v: Warken, Lux o: Land owner o: Farmer o: Miller r: bd c: 5

+ seq: 014 MULLER, Marie-Catherine b: 23 Sep 1814 in Michelau, Lux d: 1881 in Warken, Lux w: 19 Dec 1841 in Ettelbruck, Lux v: Warken, Lux o: Farmer r: m f: Mathias Muller m: Marie-Elisabeth Maillette c: 5

8 WITRY, Christina b: 17 Sep 1842 in Warken, Lux r: b

8 WITRY, Jean-Pierre b: 27 Jan 1844 in Warken, Lux v: Warken, Lux o: Farmer r: b

8 WITRY, Johann b: 17 May 1846 in Warken, Lux d: 10 Mar 1907 in Warken, Lux v: Warken, Lux o: Farmer r: bd

8 WITRY, Margaretha b: 12 Nov 1851 in Warken, Lux d: 15 Jul 1860 in Warken, Lux v: Warken, Lux o: No profession r: bd

8 WITRY, Nicolas b: 12 Feb 1854 in Warken, Lux d: 12 Oct 1908 in Warken, Lux v: Warken, Lux i: Emigrated to Nebraska o: Farmer o: Locksmith r: bd

014.01

7 WITRY, Margaretha b: 31 Aug 1811 in Warken, Lux d: 18

Nov 1892 in Ettelbruck, Lux v: Warken, Lux i: In 1848 she
purchased a piece of land in Warken, and gave it to her brother,
Michel Witry o: Farmer r: bd c: 2

+ seq: 014.01 DE WAHA, Nicolas b: 15 Apr 1806 in
Grummelscheid, Lux d: 1880 w: 22 Jun 1836 in Winseler, Lux
v: Warken, Lux i: Before the French Revolution the family
owned the castle of Grummelscheid o: Farmer r: b r: mx f:
Jean-Baptist De Waha m: Margaretha Lutgen c: 2

8 DE WAHA, Maria b: 03 May 1837 in Grummelscheid, Lux o:
Farmer c: 3

+ seq: 014.50 KAELL, Jean b: 16 Dec 1825 in Weiler la Tour,
Lux w: 28 Mar 1854 in Ettelbruck, Lux o: Farmer r: m f:
Francois Kaell m: Anna Salfy c: 3

8 DE WAHA, Melanie b: 06 Jan 1843 in Winseler, Lux r: b

014.50

8 DE WAHA, Maria b: 03 May 1837 in Grummelscheid, Lux o:
Farmer c: 3

+ seq: 014.50 KAELL, Jean b: 16 Dec 1825 in Weiler la Tour,
Lux w: 28 Mar 1854 in Ettelbruck, Lux o: Farmer r: m f:
Francois Kaell m: Anna Salfy c: 3

9 KAELL, Anne b: 1855

9 KAELL, Marguerite b: 1858

9 [1] KAELL, Charles (Joseph) b: 26 Mar 1861 in Warken, Lux
d: 01 Jun 1939 in Warken, Lux v: Warken, Lux o: Farmer o:
Innkeeper c: 3

+ seq: 014.55 JACOBY, Catherine b: 10 Mar 1875 in Vichten,
Lux d: 06 Aug 1906 in Warken, Lux w: 28 Jan 1902 in
Ettelbruck, Lux o: No profession f: Philippe Jacoby m:
Catherine Welter

* 2nd Wife of [1] KAELL, Charles (Joseph):

+ seq: 014.60 STROESSER, Anne b: 24 Dec 1873 in
Niederwampach, Lux d: 16 Feb 1944 in Warken, Lux w: 1908
r: m c: 3

014.55

9 [1] KAELL, Charles (Joseph) b: 26 Mar 1861 in Warken, Lux
d: 01 Jun 1939 in Warken, Lux v: Warken, Lux o: Farmer o:
Innkeeper c: 3

+ seq: 014.55 JACOBY, Catherine b: 10 Mar 1875 in Vichten,
Lux d: 06 Aug 1906 in Warken, Lux w: 28 Jan 1902 in

Ettelbruck, Lux o: No profession f: Philippe Jacoby m:
Catherine Welter
* 2nd Wife of [1] KAELL, Charles (Joseph):
+ seq: 014.60 STROESSER, Anne b: 24 Dec 1873 in
   Niederwampach, Lux d: 16 Feb 1944 in Warken, Lux w: 1908
   r: m c: 3
10KAELL, Francois b: 19 Nov 1908 in Warken, Lux d: 27 Sep
   1986 in Ettelbruck, Lux v: Warken, Lux o: Farmer o:
   Innkeeper o: Salesman c: 3
+ seq: 014.65 SIEBENALER, Marguerite b: 23 Jan 1923 in
   Filsdorf, Lux d: 25 Dec 2006 in Vianden, Lux w: 07 Feb 1945
   v: Warken, Lux f: Nicolas Siebenaler m: Catherine Willem c:
   3
10KAELL, Pauline b: 10 Feb 1910 in Warken, Lux d: 12 Apr
   1998 in Ettelbruck, Lux v: Warken, Lux
+ seq: 014.65.90 EISEN, Joseph b: 15 Dec 1906 in Bastendorf,
   Lux d: 03 Nov 1971 in Ettelbruck, Lux w: 22 Feb 1955 in
   Ettelbruck, Lux v: Warken, Lux o: Clerk f: Philippe Eisen m:
   Anne Dumong
10KAELL, Marguerite b: 04 Apr 1911 in Warken, Lux d: 01 Feb
   1998 in Ettelbruck, Lux v: Grosbous, Lux c: 3
+ seq: 014.70 LIES, Alphonse b: 10 Mar 1911 in Ettelbruck, Lux
   d: 09 May 1983 in Ettelbruck, Lux w: 31 Jan 1940 in
   Ettelbruck, Lux f: Michael Lies m: Marie Dennemeyer c: 3

014.65

10KAELL, Francois b: 19 Nov 1908 in Warken, Lux d: 27 Sep
   1986 in Ettelbruck, Lux v: Warken, Lux o: Farmer o:
   Innkeeper o: Salesman c: 3
+ seq: 014.65 SIEBENALER, Marguerite b: 23 Jan 1923 in
   Filsdorf, Lux d: 25 Dec 2006 in Vianden, Lux w: 07 Feb 1945
   v: Warken, Lux f: Nicolas Siebenaler m: Catherine Willem c:
   3
11KAELL, Joseph b: 16 Nov 1945 in Warken, Lux v: Schieren,
   Lux o: Teacher c: 4
+ seq: 014.65.20 ODUBER, Marlene b: 16 Oct 1947 in Aruba,
   Antilles w: 18 Aug 1971 in Aruba, Antilles v: Schieren, Lux
   o: Teacher f: Emanuel Oduber m: Teresita Baiz c: 4
11KAELL, Emile b: 17 May 1950 in Ettelbruck, Lux v: Warken,
   Lux o: Clerk c: 3
+ seq: 014.65.60 COLLE, Michele b: 08 Feb 1952 in

Schifeflange, Lux w: 01 Sep 1972 in Ettelbruck, Lux v:
Warken, Lux o: Decorator f: Raymond Colle m: Lucie
Wagner c: 3
11 KAELL, Marianne b: 31 Oct 1955 in Ettelbruck, Lux v:
Warken, Lux c: 2
+ seq: 014.65.80 KERGER, Paul b: 29 Jan 1950 in Ettelbruck,
Lux w: 20 Dec 1974 in Ettelbruck, Lux v: Warken, Lux o:
Teacher f: Jean-Pierre Kerger m: Margot Geisen c: 2

014.65.20

11 KAELL, Joseph b: 16 Nov 1945 in Warken, Lux v: Schieren,
Lux o: Teacher c: 4
+ seq: 014.65.20 ODUBER, Marlene b: 16 Oct 1947 in Aruba,
Antilles w: 18 Aug 1971 in Aruba, Antilles v: Schieren, Lux
o: Teacher f: Emanuel Oduber m: Teresita Baiz c: 4
12 KAELL, Francis-Aaron b: 30 Jun 1972 in Ettelbruck, Lux v:
Bissen, Lux o: Cadastral engineer o: Pianist c: 2
+ seq: 014.65.40 VAN GRYSPERRE, Isabel b: 10 Jun 1976 in
Izegem, Belgium w: 29 Dec 2000 in Izegem, Belgium v:
Bissen, Lux o: Violonist f: Freddy van Grysperre m: Yvette
Strynk c: 2
12 KAELL, Jonathan-Emanuel b: 17 May 1975 in Ettelbruck, Lux
v: Schieren, Lux o: Musician (Conductor)
12 KAELL, Dennis-Philippe b: 04 Aug 1979 in Ettelbruck, Lux v:
Luxembourg, Lux o: Luxair Airline pilot
12 KAELL, Jennifer-Margaret-Therese b: 05 Jun 1982 in
Ettelbruck, Lux v: Schieren, Lux o: Translator Chinese-
English-German

014.65.40

12 KAELL, Francis-Aaron b: 30 Jun 1972 in Ettelbruck, Lux v:
Bissen, Lux o: Cadastral engineer o: Pianist c: 2
+ seq: 014.65.40 VAN GRYSPERRE, Isabel b: 10 Jun 1976 in
Izegem, Belgium w: 29 Dec 2000 in Izegem, Belgium v:
Bissen, Lux o: Violonist f: Freddy van Grysperre m: Yvette
Strynk c: 2
13 KAELL, Oceana-Amethys b: 26 Jun 2002 in Luxembourg, Lux
v: Bissen, Lux
13 KAELL, Olympia-Maeva b: 05 Aug 2005 in Luxembourg, Lux
v: Bissen, Lux

014.65.60

11 KAELL, Emile b: 17 May 1950 in Ettelbruck, Lux v: Warken, Lux o: Clerk c: 3

+ seq: 014.65.60 COLLE, Michele b: 08 Feb 1952 in Schifeflange, Lux w: 01 Sep 1972 in Ettelbruck, Lux v: Warken, Lux o: Decorator f: Raymond Colle m: Lucie Wagner c: 3

12 KAELL, Sandrine b: 12 Dec 1979 in Ettelbruck, Lux v: Wahl, Lux o: Teacher

12 KAELL, Danielle b: 21 Dec 1983 in Ettelbruck, Lux v: Warken, Lux o: Teacher

12 KAELL, Pascale b: 01 Oct 1987 in Ettelbruck, Lux v: Warken, Lux

014.65.80

11 KAELL, Marianne b: 31 Oct 1955 in Ettelbruck, Lux v: Warken, Lux c: 2

+ seq: 014.65.80 KERGER, Paul b: 29 Jan 1950 in Ettelbruck, Lux w: 20 Dec 1974 in Ettelbruck, Lux v: Warken, Lux o: Teacher f: Jean-Pierre Kerger m: Margot Geisen c: 2

12 KERGER, Malou b: 18 Mar 1976 in Ettelbruck, Lux v: Oberfeulen, Lux o: Teacher c: 3

+ seq: 014.65.85 BESENIUS, Jeff b: 26 Sep 1974 in Ettelbruck, Lux w: 21 Dec 2001 in Feulen, Lux v: Oberfeulen, Lux o: Technical engineer f: Eloi Besenius m: Mady Mathias c: 3

12 KERGER, Claude b: 21 Aug 1978 in Ettelbruck, Lux v: Warken, Lux o: Teacher

+ seq: 014.65.88 HEIN, Nadia b: 23 Nov 1977 in Ettelbruck, Lux w: 10 Sep 2005 in Eschdorf, Lux o: Teacher f: Claude Hein m: Josee Hermes

014.65.85

12 KERGER, Malou b: 18 Mar 1976 in Ettelbruck, Lux v: Oberfeulen, Lux o: Teacher c: 3

+ seq: 014.65.85 BESENIUS, Jeff b: 26 Sep 1974 in Ettelbruck, Lux w: 21 Dec 2001 in Feulen, Lux v: Oberfeulen, Lux o: Technical engineer f: Eloi Besenius m: Mady Mathias c: 3

13 BESENIUS, Pol b: 12 Aug 2002 in Ettelbruck, Lux v: Oberfeulen, Lux

13 BESENIUS, Charel b: 11 Nov 2004 in Ettelbruck, Lux v: Oberfeulen, Lux

13BESENIUS, Marie b: 28 Sep 2006 in Ettelbruck, Lux

014.70

10KAELL, Marguerite b: 04 Apr 1911 in Warken, Lux d: 01 Feb 1998 in Ettelbruck, Lux v: Grosbous, Lux c: 3
+   seq: 014.70 LIES, Alphonse b: 10 Mar 1911 in Ettelbruck, Lux d: 09 May 1983 in Ettelbruck, Lux w: 31 Jan 1940 in Ettelbruck, Lux f: Michael Lies m: Marie Dennemeyer c: 3
11LIES, Anne-Marie b: 29 Nov 1940 in Ettelbruck, Lux d: 06 Oct 2006 v: Warken, Lux c: 2
+   seq: 014.75 RASQUIN, Jean-Pierre b: 25 Apr 1936 d: 29 Jan 1995 w: 1964 in Grosbous, Lux v: Esch-sur-Alzette, Lux o: Optician f: Rasquin m: Conzemius c: 2
11LIES, Eugenie-Pauline b: 22 Dec 1943 in Ettelbruck, Lux v: Crauthem, Lux c: 2
+   seq: 014.80 HUBERTY, Camille b: 04 Feb 1942 in Burden, Lux w: 15 Apr 1964 in Grosbous, Lux v: Crauthem, Lux o: Clerk of the court of justice f: Guillaume Huberty m: Christine Weber c: 2
11LIES, Alphonse-Emile b: 19 Apr 1950 in Ettelbruck, Lux d: 11 Oct 1981 in Ettelbruck, Lux o: Bank clerk

014.75

11LIES, Anne-Marie b: 29 Nov 1940 in Ettelbruck, Lux d: 06 Oct 2006 v: Warken, Lux c: 2
+   seq: 014.75 RASQUIN, Jean-Pierre b: 25 Apr 1936 d: 29 Jan 1995 w: 1964 in Grosbous, Lux v: Esch-sur-Alzette, Lux o: Optician f: Rasquin m: Conzemius c: 2
12RASQUIN, Mireille b: 29 Jun 1965 in Esch-sur-Alzette, Lux v: Beckerich, Lux o: Optician c: 3
+   seq: 014.77 BERTRANG, Marco b: 19 Apr 1958 in Esch-sur-Alzette, Lux w: Abt. 1990 v: Beckerich, Lux c: 3
12RASQUIN, Carmen b: 02 Jul 1966 in Esch-sur-Alzette, Lux v: Esch-sur-Alzette, Lux i: 2 children o: Kinetical therapeutist
+   seq: 014.78 IONICA, Dumitrel w: Abt. 1980 i: 2 children

014.77

12RASQUIN, Mireille b: 29 Jun 1965 in Esch-sur-Alzette, Lux v: Beckerich, Lux o: Optician c: 3
+   seq: 014.77 BERTRANG, Marco b: 19 Apr 1958 in Esch-sur-Alzette, Lux w: Abt. 1990 v: Beckerich, Lux c: 3

13 BERTRANG, Mike b: 07 Nov 1991 in Esch-sur-Alzette, Lux v: Beckerich, Lux

13 BERTRANG, Sam b: 31 Aug 1992 in Esch-sur-Alzette, Lux v: Beckerich, Lux

13 BERTRANG, Carrie b: 12 Jun 1998 in Esch-sur-Alzette, Lux v: Beckerich, Lux

014.80

11 LIES, Eugenie-Pauline b: 22 Dec 1943 in Ettelbruck, Lux v: Crauthem, Lux c: 2

+ seq: 014.80 HUBERTY, Camille b: 04 Feb 1942 in Burden, Lux w: 15 Apr 1964 in Grosbous, Lux v: Crauthem, Lux o: Clerk of the court of justice f: Guillaume Huberty m: Christine Weber c: 2

12 HUBERTY, Pascale b: 08 May 1967 in Luxembourg, Lux v: Gasperich, Lux o: Clerk of the court of justice c: 1

+ seq: 014.85 KAISER, Frank b: 09 Feb 1965 in Differdange, Lux v: Gasperich, Lux o: Publicist f: Kaiser m: Angela Vettor c: 1

12 HUBERTY, Patrick b: 02 Nov 1973 in Luxembourg, Lux v: Steinfort, Lux o: Barrister

+ seq: 014.90 STRAUS, Annik v: Steinfort, Lux o: Teacher f: Jean-Paul Straus m: Yvette Schreiner

014.85

12 HUBERTY, Pascale b: 08 May 1967 in Luxembourg, Lux v: Gasperich, Lux o: Clerk of the court of justice c: 1

+ seq: 014.85 KAISER, Frank b: 09 Feb 1965 in Differdange, Lux v: Gasperich, Lux o: Publicist f: Kaiser m: Angela Vettor c: 1

13 KAISER, Lou b: 16 Jun 1999 in Luxembourg, Lux

015.03

6 WITRY, Marie b: 08 Oct 1786 in Warken, Lux d: 15 Nov 1854 in Ettelbruck, Lux h: Gross Street v: Ettelbruck, Lux o: Farmer r: bd c: 8

+ seq: 015.03 SPANIER, Dominique b: 24 Dec 1790 in Ettelbruck, Lux d: 09 Nov 1854 in Ettelbruck, Lux w: 24 Sep 1811 in Ettelbruck, Lux h: Gross Street v: Ettelbruck, Lux o: Day laborer o: Farmer r: d r: m f: Georg Spanier m: Catherine Wolk c: 8

7 SPANIER, Marie-Catherine b: 27 Apr 1812 in Ettelbruck, Lux
  d: in Ettelbrook, Lux v: Ettelbruck, Lux r: b c: 7
+ seq: 015.04 SCHROEDER, John b: 23 Jan 1803 in Arlon,
  Belgium d: Aug 1864 in Ettelbrook, Lux w: 1838 v:
  Ettelbruck, Lux c: 7
7 SPANIER, Barbara b: 11 Jun 1814 in Ettelbruck, Lux d: 26
  Mar 1821 in Ettelbruck, Lux v: Ettelbruck, Lux r: bd
7 SPANIER, Regina b: 25 Oct 1816 in Ettelbruck, Lux r: b
7 SPANIER, Marie b: 17 Feb 1818 in Ettelbruck, Lux r: b
+ seq: 015.93 SOANNY, George w: Abt. 1840
7 [1] SPANIER, Nicolas b: 19 Sep 1820 in Ettelbruck, Lux v:
  Ettelbruck, Lux o: Farmer r: b
+ seq: 015.94 CLEES, Susanna d: 03 Oct 1858 in Ettelbruck, Lux
  w: Abt. 1840 o: Farmer
* 2nd Wife of [1] SPANIER, Nicolas:
+ seq: 015.95 MASSELTER, Clara b: 12 May 1827 in Eisenach,
  Germany w: 11 Aug 1860 in Ettelbruck, Lux o: Farmer r: m
  f: Michel Masselter m: Anna Wolsfelt
7 SPANIER, Jean b: 26 Nov 1822 in Ettelbruck, Lux d: 08 Apr
  1825 in Ettelbruck, Lux v: Ettelbruck, Lux r: bd
7 SPANIER, Susanne b: 23 Feb 1825 in Ettelbruck, Lux r: b
+ seq: 015.96 KLEIN, H. w: Abt. 1850
7 SPANIER, Anna-Margaretha b: 12 Jan 1827 in Ettelbruck, Lux
  d: 12 Jan 1827 in Ettelbruck, Lux v: Ettelbruck, Lux r: bd

015.04
7 SPANIER, Marie-Catherine b: 27 Apr 1812 in Ettelbruck, Lux
  d: in Ettelbrook, Lux v: Ettelbruck, Lux r: b c: 7
+ seq: 015.04 SCHROEDER, John b: 23 Jan 1803 in Arlon,
  Belgium d: Aug 1864 in Ettelbrook, Lux w: 1838 v:
  Ettelbruck, Lux c: 7
8 SCHROEDER, Nicolas b: 1838 in Ettelbrook, Lux
8 SCHROEDER, Catherine b: 1840 in Ettelbrook, Lux
8 SCHROEDER, Michel b: 04 Nov 1842 in Ettelbruck, Lux d:
  1904 v: Ettelbruck, Lux c: 7
+ seq: 015.05 WAGENER, Josephine b: 18 Apr 1840 in
  Ettelbruck, Lux d: in Ettelbrook, Lux w: 20 Jun 1868 v:
  Ettelbruck, Lux f: Jean Wagener m: Susanne Kaufmann c: 7
8 SCHROEDER, Susanne b: 1846 in Ettelbrook, Lux
8 SCHROEDER, Franz b: 1848 in Ettelbruck, Lux d: in
  Ettelbrook, Lux v: Ettelbruck, Lux c: 2

+ seq: 015.85 STAUDT, Catherine (Ann) b: 1844 in Ettelbrook, Lux d: 1900 w: 1873 c: 2
8 SCHROEDER, Johann b: 1852 in Ettelbrook, Lux
8 SCHROEDER, Josephine b: Dec 1853 in Ettelbrook, Lux d: Jul 1932 in Chicago, IL i: Emigrated to U. S. with husband and nephew c: 7
+ seq: 015.91 HOFFMAN, Peter b: Jun 1851 in Luxembourg, Lux w: 1871 i: Emigrated to U. S. with wife and nephew c: 7

015.05
8 SCHROEDER, Michel b: 04 Nov 1842 in Ettelbruck, Lux d: 1904 v: Ettelbruck, Lux c: 7
+ seq: 015.05 WAGENER, Josephine b: 18 Apr 1840 in Ettelbruck, Lux d: in Ettelbrook, Lux w: 20 Jun 1868 v: Ettelbruck, Lux f: Jean Wagener m: Susanne Kaufmann c: 7
9 SCHROEDER, Anna b: Abt. 1865 in Ettelbrook, Lux d: Bef. 1880
9 SCHROEDER, Johann b: 1869 in Ettelbrook, Lux
9 SCHROEDER, Nicolas b: 1871 in Ettelbrook, Lux
9 SCHROEDER, Marie-Anna b: 1873 in Ettelbrook, Lux
9 SCHROEDER, Johann-Peter b: 09 Jan 1875 in Ettelbrook, Lux d: 01 Sep 1959 in Escanaba, MI i: Emigrated to U. S. with aunt, Josephine, and uncle, Peter i: Became a U. S. citizen c: 11
+ seq: 015.06 DAHM, Matilda (Tillie) b: 12 Jun 1885 in Essen, Germany d: 14 Apr 1967 in Escanaba, MI w: 22 Nov 1902 in Escanaba, MI f: Michael Dahm m: Louise Kozitzsky c: 11
9 SCHROEDER, Anna b: 1880 in Ettelbrook, Lux
9 SCHROEDER, Michel b: 1882 in Ettelbruck, Lux d: 1934 in Ettelbruck, Lux v: Ettelbruck, Lux

015.06
9 SCHROEDER, Johann-Peter b: 09 Jan 1875 in Ettelbrook, Lux d: 01 Sep 1959 in Escanaba, MI i: Emigrated to U. S. with aunt, Josephine, and uncle, Peter i: Became a U. S. citizen c: 11
+ seq: 015.06 DAHM, Matilda (Tillie) b: 12 Jun 1885 in Essen, Germany d: 14 Apr 1967 in Escanaba, MI w: 22 Nov 1902 in Escanaba, MI f: Michael Dahm m: Louise Kozitzsky c: 11
10[1] SCHROEDER, Ernest b: 16 Dec 1904 in Escanaba, MI d: 17 Aug 1982 in Milwaukee, WI v: Milwaukee, WI c: 6
+ seq: 015.07 MEYER, Esther b: 02 Nov 1907 in Waterloo, WI d: 05 May 1950 in Chicago, IL w: 11 Oct 1924 in Milwaukee,

WI f: August Meyer m: Marie Wolff c: 2
* 2nd Wife of [1] SCHROEDER, Ernest:
+ seq: 015.34 NAPRUSZEWSKI, Alyce-Clara b: 02 Nov 1917 in
   Milwaukee, WI w: 11 Jul 1942 in Escanaba, MI v: Milwaukee,
   WI c: 4
10 SCHROEDER, Bernard b: 27 Dec 1905 in Escanaba, MI d: 28
   Dec 1905 in Escanaba, MI v: Escanaba, MI
10 SCHROEDER, James b: 26 Mar 1906 in Escanaba, MI d: 12
   Aug 1970 in Milwaukee, WI v: Milwaukee, WI c: 1
+ seq: 015.44 BRZYCKI, Alice b: 20 Jul 1917 in Milwaukee, WI
   d: 08 Mar 1997 in Shoshone, IN w: 29 Aug 1935 in Escanaba,
   MI v: Milwaukee, WI c: 1
10 [2] SCHROEDER, Paul J. b: 25 Nov 1908 in Escanaba, MI d:
   14 Nov 1979 in Escanaba, MI v: Escanaba, MI c: 7
+ seq: 015.59.30 w: Abt. 1930
* 2nd Wife of [2] SCHROEDER, Paul J.:
+ seq: 015.59.40 LARSEN, Marie w: 1934 c: 3
* 3rd Wife of [2] SCHROEDER, Paul J.:
+ seq: 015.59.50 Loretta w: Abt. 1935 c: 1
* 4th Wife of [2] SCHROEDER, Paul J.:
+ seq: 015.59.60 CLINE, Frances-Marie b: 06 Apr 1915 in
   Escanaba, MI d: Nov 1935 w: 04 Mar 1935
* 5th Wife of [2] SCHROEDER, Paul J.:
+ seq: 015.60 FRENCH, Merle b: 1921 d: 1966 Cause of death:
   Heart attack w: Abt. 1950 c: 3
10 SCHROEDER, Josephine b: 11 Dec 1910 in Escanaba, MI d:
   15 Apr 1993 in Escanaba, MI v: Escanaba, MI c: 1
+ seq: 015.70 WILSON, Hjalmer (Hack) b: 07 Jan 1910 d: 11
   Nov 1977 in Escanaba, MI w: 21 Aug 1933 v: Escanaba, MI
   c: 1
10 SCHROEDER, Edward b: 02 Dec 1912 in Escanaba, MI d: 15
   Dec 1995 in Escanaba, MI v: Escanaba, MI c: 2
+ seq: 015.78 LARSON, Dorothy w: 06 Jun 1939 c: 2
10 SCHROEDER, Ruth b: 07 Oct 1913 in Escanaba, MI d: 23 Jul
   1915 in Escanaba, MI v: Escanaba, MI
10 SCHROEDER, Florence b: 07 Oct 1913 in Escanaba, MI d: 24
   Jul 1915 in Escanaba, MI v: Escanaba, MI
10 SCHROEDER, Edna b: 08 Dec 1915 in Escanaba, MI d: 14
   Sep 1973 in Escanaba, MI v: Escanaba, MI i: A swinger in the
   1930's i: Rumored to be a hooker in 1940's
+ seq: 015.81 PEARSON, William w: Abt. 1935 v: Escanaba,

MI

10 SCHROEDER, Walter b: 17 Oct 1920 in Escanaba, MI d: 23 Jul 1921 in Escanaba, MI v: Escanaba, MI

10[3] SCHROEDER, John b: 20 Sep 1922 in Escanaba, MI d: 25 Apr 1994 in Gladstone, MI v: Escanaba, MI i: Mechanic i: Raced boats c: 2

+ seq: 015.83 COLE, Doris-Margaret b: 19 Dec 1924 in Gladstone, MI d: 28 Jul 1976 in Gladstone, MI w: 06 Jul 1946 in Escanaba, MI c: 2

* 2nd Wife of [3] SCHROEDER, John:

+ seq: 015.84.50 Virginia w: Abt. 1950

015.07

10[1] SCHROEDER, Ernest b: 16 Dec 1904 in Escanaba, MI d: 17 Aug 1982 in Milwaukee, WI v: Milwaukee, WI c: 6

+ seq: 015.07 MEYER, Esther b: 02 Nov 1907 in Waterloo, WI d: 05 May 1950 in Chicago, IL w: 11 Oct 1924 in Milwaukee, WI f: August Meyer m: Marie Wolff c: 2

11 SCHROEDER, Barbara-Marie b: 31 Mar 1925 in Milwaukee, WI d: 23 Oct 1960 in Elgin, IL Cause of death: Cancer c: 4

+ seq: 015.08 LOSER, George-Andrew b: 29 Sep 1923 in Chicago, IL d: 27 Feb 1992 in McHenry, IL w: Abt. 1942 i: Lost one foot and half of the other to diabetes c: 4

11 SCHROEDER, Robert-Bernard b: 11 Dec 1926 in Milwaukee, WI i: Served in U. S. Army during WWII c: 4

+ seq: 015.29 CESARINI, Gloria-Fern b: 14 Oct 1927 in Chicago, IL d: 03 May 2000 in Dunedin, FL w: 26 Jul 1945 in Chicago, IL f: Giorgio Cesarini m: Leonora Lepore c: 4

* 2nd Wife of [1] SCHROEDER, Ernest:

+ seq: 015.34 NAPRUSZEWSKI, Alyce-Clara b: 02 Nov 1917 in Milwaukee, WI w: 11 Jul 1942 in Escanaba, MI v: Milwaukee, WI c: 4

11 SCHROEDER, Judy-Ellen b: 13 Dec 1943 in Milwaukee, WI v: Milwaukee, WI c: 2

+ seq: 015.35 PRZYBYL, Philip-Eugene b: 06 Jul 1938 in Ripon, WI w: 20 Aug 1966 in Milwaukee, WI v: Milwaukee, WI c: 2

11[2] SCHROEDER, Thomas-Ernest b: 24 Apr 1944 in Milwaukee, WI v: Milwaukee, WI c: 4

+ seq: 015.36.50 PALASZ, Patricia-Ann w: 06 Jun 1956 in Milwaukee, WI

* 2nd Wife of [2] SCHROEDER, Thomas-Ernest:

+ seq: 015.37 KOLP, Sharon-Raye-Marie b: 20 Jun 1949 w: Abt.
   1965 in Milwaukee, WI v: Milwaukee, WI c: 4
11[3] SCHROEDER, Sandra-Elaine b: 29 Apr 1945 in Milwaukee,
   WI v: Milwaukee, WI c: 2
+ seq: 015.40 BROTHERHOOD, Roy b: 07 Mar 1948 in
   Milwaukee, WI w: 27 Jan 1968 in Milwaukee, WI v:
   Milwaukee, WI c: 2
* 2nd Husband of [3] SCHROEDER, Sandra-Elaine:
+ seq: 015.42 STELMASZEWSKI, Robert-Eugene b: 08 Mar
   1940 in Milwaukee, WI w: 07 Jul 1990 in Milwaukee, WI
11 SCHROEDER, Kathleen-Elizabeth b: 08 Jun 1946 in
   Milwaukee, WI
+ seq: 015.43 CORRIVEAU, Dennis-Eric b: 12 May 1947 in
   Milwaukee, WI w: 12 Jul 1969 in Milwaukee, WI i: One of
   two surviving triplets i: Changed name from Dennis to Eric

015.08
11 SCHROEDER, Barbara-Marie b: 31 Mar 1925 in Milwaukee,
   WI d: 23 Oct 1960 in Elgin, IL Cause of death: Cancer c: 4
+ seq: 015.08 LOSER, George-Andrew b: 29 Sep 1923 in
   Chicago, IL d: 27 Feb 1992 in McHenry, IL w: Abt. 1942 i:
   Lost one foot and half of the other to diabetes c: 4
12 LOSER, George-Noel b: 28 Dec 1944 in Chicago, IL v:
   Woodstock, IL c: 2
+ seq: 015.09 STEADMAN, Loraine-Marie b: 04 Oct 1946 in
   Woodstock, IL w: 31 Jul 1965 in McHenry, IL v: Woodstock,
   IL c: 2
12[1] LOSER, Katherine-Marie b: 06 Nov 1946 in Chicago, IL v:
   Woodstock, IL c: 3
+ seq: 015.12 HEBER, Paul-John b: 25 Feb 1947 in McHenry, IL
   w: 03 Jul 1965 in McHenry, IL v: Woodstock, IL c: 3
* 2nd Husband of [1] LOSER, Katherine-Marie:
+ seq: 015.16 MCKENNA, Kenneth b: 27 Feb 1944 w: 09 Sep
   1972 in Woodstock, IL
* 3rd Husband of [1] LOSER, Katherine-Marie:
+ seq: 015.17 ETTNER, Thomas w: Nov 1976
* 4th Husband of [1] LOSER, Katherine-Marie:
+ seq: 015.18 OFFLING, Frank w: Jan 1980
* 5th Husband of [1] LOSER, Katherine-Marie:
+ seq: 015.19 SMELL, Jack w: Jun 1986
12[2] LOSER, Cinthia-Ann b: 31 Oct 1950 in Chicago, IL v:

Woodstock, IL c: 3
+ seq: 015.19.50 ARMSTRONG, Robert w: Abt. 1965
* 2nd Husband of [2] LOSER, Cinthia-Ann:
+ seq: 015.20 WAGNER, Rick w: Abt. 1965 v: Woodstock, IL
   c: 3
* 3rd Husband of [2] LOSER, Cinthia-Ann:
+ seq: 015.26 THOMFOHRDA, Woody w: May 1991 in
   Woodstock, IL
12 LOSER, Steven-Mark b: 03 Aug 1955 in Chicago, IL v:
   Woodstock, IL c: 4
+ seq: 015.27 BRYAN, Kathy b: 18 Oct 1955 w: 16 Feb 1974 in
   Woodstock, IL v: Woodstock, IL c: 4

015.09

12 LOSER, George-Noel b: 28 Dec 1944 in Chicago, IL v:
   Woodstock, IL c: 2
+ seq: 015.09 STEADMAN, Loraine-Marie b: 04 Oct 1946 in
   Woodstock, IL w: 31 Jul 1965 in McHenry, IL v: Woodstock,
   IL c: 2
13 LOSER, Michelle-Ann (Schelly) b: 26 Apr 1967 in Woodstock,
   IL v: Barrington, IL c: 3
+ seq: 015.10 TUEBER, Christopher-Andrew b: 27 May 1966 in
   Woodstock, IL w: 24 Oct 1987 in McHenry, IL v: Barrington,
   IL c: 3
13 LOSER, Stacy-Ann b: 27 Dec 1972 in Woodstock, IL
+ seq: 015.11 HENDERSON, Russell w: 27 Dec 1997 in
   McHenry, IL

015.10

13 LOSER, Michelle-Ann (Schelly) b: 26 Apr 1967 in Woodstock,
   IL v: Barrington, IL c: 3
+ seq: 015.10 TUEBER, Christopher-Andrew b: 27 May 1966 in
   Woodstock, IL w: 24 Oct 1987 in McHenry, IL v: Barrington,
   IL c: 3
14 TUEBER, Sarah-Marie b: 06 Jun 1989 in Barrington, IL
14 TUEBER, Keely-Shaye b: 09 May 1992 in Barrington, IL
14 TUEBER, Zakary-Thomas b: 30 Sep 1994 in Barrington, IL

015.12

12 [2] LOSER, Katherine-Marie b: 06 Nov 1946 in Chicago, IL v:
   Woodstock, IL c: 3

+ seq: 015.12 HEBER, Paul-John b: 25 Feb 1947 in McHenry, IL
  w: 03 Jul 1965 in McHenry, IL v: Woodstock, IL c: 3
13 HEBER, Paul-Joseph b: 1966 in Woodstock, IL d: 20 Jan 1972
  in McHenry, IL Cause of death: Drowning i: Fell through the
  ice on a lake
13 [1] HEBER, Robert-Wayne b: 03 May 1967 in Woodstock, IL
  v: Texas c: 2
+ seq: 015.13 w: Abt. 1980
* 2nd Wife of [1] HEBER, Robert-Wayne:
+ seq: 015.14 Laurie b: 05 Nov 1966 w: 15 Nov 1990 v: Texas
  c: 2
13 HEBER, David-John b: 14 Oct 1970 in Woodstock, IL
+ seq: 015.15 WINIARSKI, Wendy R. w: 02 Dec 1995 in
  McHenry, IL
* 2nd Husband of [2] LOSER, Katherine-Marie:
+ seq: 015.16 MCKENNA, Kenneth b: 27 Feb 1944 w: 09 Sep
  1972 in Woodstock, IL
* 3rd Husband of [2] LOSER, Katherine-Marie:
+ seq: 015.17 ETTNER, Thomas w: Nov 1976
* 4th Husband of [2] LOSER, Katherine-Marie:
+ seq: 015.18 OFFLING, Frank w: Jan 1980
* 5th Husband of [2] LOSER, Katherine-Marie:
+ seq: 015.19 SMELL, Jack w: Jun 1986

015.13
13 [1] HEBER, Robert-Wayne b: 03 May 1967 in Woodstock, IL
  v: Texas c: 2
+ seq: 015.13 w: Abt. 1980
* 2nd Wife of [1] HEBER, Robert-Wayne:
+ seq: 015.14 Laurie b: 05 Nov 1966 w: 15 Nov 1990 v: Texas
  c: 2
14 HEBER, Brianna-Marie b: 09 Dec 1991 in Dallas, TX
14 HEBER, Riley-Elyse b: 26 Apr 1996 in Misawa, Japan

015.19.50
12 [1] LOSER, Cinthia-Ann b: 31 Oct 1950 in Chicago, IL v:
  Woodstock, IL c: 3
+ seq: 015.19.50 ARMSTRONG, Robert w: Abt. 1965
* 2nd Husband of [1] LOSER, Cinthia-Ann:
+ seq: 015.20 WAGNER, Rick w: Abt. 1965 v: Woodstock, IL
  c: 3

13[2] WAGNER, Barbara-Marie b: 25 Mar 1968 in Woodstock, IL
  c: 2
+ seq: 015.21 FARRALL, Edward b: in Florida w: 1984 c: 1
* 2nd Husband of [2] WAGNER, Barbara-Marie:
+ seq: 015.22 PARKER, Jeffery b: 07 Mar 1963 w: 1987 in
  Florida c: 1
13 WAGNER, Dianne-Theresa b: 28 Jul 1970 in Woodstock, IL
+ seq: 015.23 ANGE, Michael w: Abt. 1995 in Florida
13 WAGNER, Debra (Debbie) b: 28 Jul 1970 in Woodstock, IL c:
  1
+ seq: 015.24 w: Abt. 1995 c: 1
* 3rd Husband of [1] LOSER, Cinthia-Ann:
+ seq: 015.26 THOMFOHRDA, Woody w: May 1991 in
  Woodstock, IL

015.21
13[1] WAGNER, Barbara-Marie b: 25 Mar 1968 in Woodstock, IL
  c: 2
+ seq: 015.21 FARRALL, Edward b: in Florida w: 1984 c: 1
14 FARRALL, Heather b: 11 Jan 1985 in Woodstock, IL
* 2nd Husband of [1] WAGNER, Barbara-Marie:
+ seq: 015.22 PARKER, Jeffery b: 07 Mar 1963 w: 1987 in
  Florida c: 1
14 PARKER, Jeffery b: 09 Jun 1988 in Florida

015.24
13 WAGNER, Debra (Debbie) b: 28 Jul 1970 in Woodstock, IL c:
  1
+ seq: 015.24 w: Abt. 1995 c: 1
14? b: 1997

015.27
12 LOSER, Steven-Mark b: 03 Aug 1955 in Chicago, IL v:
  Woodstock, IL c: 4
+ seq: 015.27 BRYAN, Kathy b: 18 Oct 1955 w: 16 Feb 1974 in
  Woodstock, IL v: Woodstock, IL c: 4
13 LOSER, Brandy b: 16 Sep 1974 in Woodstock, IL
+ seq: 015.28 LUND, Mike w: 30 Sep 1995 in Woodstock, IL
13 LOSER, Christopher b: 17 Oct 1978 in Woodstock, IL
13 LOSER, Nicholas b: 03 Nov 1984 in Woodstock, IL
13 LOSER, Brittany b: 25 Jan 1987 in Woodstock, IL

015.29

11 SCHROEDER, Robert-Bernard b: 11 Dec 1926 in Milwaukee, WI i: Served in U. S. Army during WWII c: 4

+ seq: 015.29 CESARINI, Gloria-Fern b: 14 Oct 1927 in Chicago, IL d: 03 May 2000 in Dunedin, FL w: 26 Jul 1945 in Chicago, IL f: Giorgio Cesarini m: Leonora Lepore c: 4

12 SCHROEDER, Kenneth-Mark b: 01 Dec 1947 in Chicago, IL c: 3

+ seq: 015.30 MARSCH, Susan-Marie b: 09 Aug 1949 in Milwaukee, WI w: 05 May 1973 in Racine, WI c: 3

12 SCHROEDER, Duane-Matthew b: 28 Jun 1949 in Chicago, IL v: Des Plaines, IL c: 2

+ seq: 015.31 REEDY, Nancy-Lee b: 21 Oct 1955 in Evanston, IL w: 21 Aug 1981 in Skokie, IL v: Des Plaines, IL c: 2

12 SCHROEDER, Bruce-Steven-Mark b: 02 Oct 1950 in Chicago, IL c: 3

+ seq: 015.32 RICE, Helen-Ann b: 16 Dec 1950 in Beloit, WI w: 04 May 1974 in Beloit, WI f: Charles Rice m: Leona Houghton c: 3

12 SCHROEDER, Curtis-Lee-Joseph b: 15 Jun 1956 in Highwood, IL

+ seq: 015.33 COOPER, Kim-Therese b: 08 Aug 1960 in Park Ridge, IL w: 10 Jun 1983 in Northbrook, IL

015.30

12 SCHROEDER, Kenneth-Mark b: 01 Dec 1947 in Chicago, IL c: 3

+ seq: 015.30 MARSCH, Susan-Marie b: 09 Aug 1949 in Milwaukee, WI w: 05 May 1973 in Racine, WI c: 3

13 SCHROEDER, Brian-James b: 29 Jan 1977 in Indianapolis, IN

13 SCHROEDER, Shanon-Marie b: 02 Mar 1979 in Indianapolis, IN

13 SCHROEDER, Anthony-Douglas b: 21 Dec 1983 in Columbus, OH

015.31

12 SCHROEDER, Duane-Matthew b: 28 Jun 1949 in Chicago, IL v: Des Plaines, IL c: 2

+ seq: 015.31 REEDY, Nancy-Lee b: 21 Oct 1955 in Evanston, IL w: 21 Aug 1981 in Skokie, IL v: Des Plaines, IL c: 2

13 SCHROEDER, Kathleen-Mercedes b: 10 Sep 1985 in Des

Plaines, IL

13 SCHROEDER, Kelly-Sheffield b: 24 Sep 1990 in Des Plaines, IL

015.32

12 SCHROEDER, Bruce-Steven-Mark b: 02 Oct 1950 in Chicago, IL c: 3

+ seq: 015.32 RICE, Helen-Ann b: 16 Dec 1950 in Beloit, WI w: 04 May 1974 in Beloit, WI f: Charles Rice m: Leona Houghton c: 3

13 SCHROEDER, Nicholas-John b: 23 Feb 1979 in Highland Park, IL

13 SCHROEDER, Joseph-Bliven b: 22 Dec 1981 in Libertyville, IL

13 SCHROEDER, Natalie-Ann b: 09 Jul 1988 in Park Ridge, IL

015.35

11 SCHROEDER, Judy-Ellen b: 13 Dec 1943 in Milwaukee, WI v: Milwaukee, WI c: 2

+ seq: 015.35 PRZYBYL, Philip-Eugene b: 06 Jul 1938 in Ripon, WI w: 20 Aug 1966 in Milwaukee, WI v: Milwaukee, WI c: 2

12 PRZYBYL, Steven-Philip b: 20 Mar 1968 in Elmhurst, IL c: 1

+ seq: 015.36 GRAZIANO, Teresa b: 23 Aug 1967 in Charlottesville, VA w: 24 Sep 1994 in Madison, WI c: 1

12 PRZYBYL, Scott-Kevin b: 19 Jan 1970 in Milwaukee, WI

015.36

12 PRZYBYL, Steven-Philip b: 20 Mar 1968 in Elmhurst, IL c: 1

+ seq: 015.36 GRAZIANO, Teresa b: 23 Aug 1967 in Charlottesville, VA w: 24 Sep 1994 in Madison, WI c: 1

13 PRZYBYL, Grace-Elizabeth b: 16 Mar 1999 in Madison, WI

015.36.50

11 [1] SCHROEDER, Thomas-Ernest b: 24 Apr 1944 in Milwaukee, WI v: Milwaukee, WI c: 4

+ seq: 015.36.50 PALASZ, Patricia-Ann w: 06 Jun 1956 in Milwaukee, WI

* 2nd Wife of [1] SCHROEDER, Thomas-Ernest:

+ seq: 015.37 KOLP, Sharon-Raye-Marie b: 20 Jun 1949 w: Abt. 1965 in Milwaukee, WI v: Milwaukee, WI c: 4

12SCHROEDER, Leslie-Ann b: 25 Mar 1966 in Milwaukee, WI
+ seq: 015.38 ZEIMET, Michael-Louis b: 04 May 1965 in
   Milwaukee, WI w: 20 Mar 1999 in West Allis, WI
12SCHROEDER, Christopher-Thomas b: 28 Jul 1969 in
   Milwaukee, WI
12SCHROEDER, Lori-Lynn b: 09 Mar 1972 in Milwaukee, WI
12SCHROEDER, Sarah-Rebecca b: 01 May 1977 in Milwaukee,
   WI

015.40

11[1] SCHROEDER, Sandra-Elaine b: 29 Apr 1945 in Milwaukee,
   WI v: Milwaukee, WI c: 2
+ seq: 015.40 BROTHERHOOD, Roy b: 07 Mar 1948 in
   Milwaukee, WI w: 27 Jan 1968 in Milwaukee, WI v:
   Milwaukee, WI c: 2
12BROTHERHOOD, Jason-Richard b: 19 Jul 1970 in Milwaukee,
   WI
12BROTHERHOOD, Tina-Faye b: 22 Jun 1973 in Milwaukee, WI
   c: 2
+ seq: 015.41 w: Abt. 1990 c: 2
* 2nd Husband of [1] SCHROEDER, Sandra-Elaine:
+ seq: 015.42 STELMASZEWSKI, Robert-Eugene b: 08 Mar
   1940 in Milwaukee, WI w: 07 Jul 1990 in Milwaukee, WI

015.41

12BROTHERHOOD, Tina-Faye b: 22 Jun 1973 in Milwaukee, WI
   c: 2
+ seq: 015.41 w: Abt. 1990 c: 2
13BROTHERHOOD, Nicolas-Alexander b: 18 Feb 1992 in
   Milwaukee, WI
13VANN, Nadia-Michelle b: 30 Dec 1992 in Milwaukee, WI

015.44

10SCHROEDER, James b: 26 Mar 1906 in Escanaba, MI d: 12
   Aug 1970 in Milwaukee, WI v: Milwaukee, WI c: 1
+ seq: 015.44 BRZYCKI, Alice b: 20 Jul 1917 in Milwaukee, WI
   d: 08 Mar 1997 in Shoshone, IN w: 29 Aug 1935 in Escanaba,
   MI v: Milwaukee, WI c: 1
11[1] SCHROEDER, Gloria-Patricia b: 07 May 1937 in
   Milwaukee, WI v: Milwaukee, WI c: 9
+ seq: 015.45 RASMUSSEN, Robert w: 1952 in Milwaukee, WI

v: Milwaukee, WI c: 6
* 2nd Husband of [1] SCHROEDER, Gloria-Patricia:
+ seq: 015.55 BAST, Seno w: 1961 v: Milwaukee, WI c: 2
* 3rd Husband of [1] SCHROEDER, Gloria-Patricia:
+ seq: 015.58 WILDE, Donald w: 1965 c: 1

015.45

11[1] SCHROEDER, Gloria-Patricia b: 07 May 1937 in
   Milwaukee, WI v: Milwaukee, WI c: 9
+ seq: 015.45 RASMUSSEN, Robert w: 1952 in Milwaukee, WI
   v: Milwaukee, WI c: 6
12 RASMUSSEN, Patricia b: 29 Sep 1952 in Milwaukee, WI c: 4
+ seq: 015.46 DAVIS, Larry w: 1970 c: 4
12 RASMUSSEN, Pamela b: 29 Sep 1952 in Milwaukee, WI c: 3
+ seq: 015.48 SKOGLIE, Lawrence b: 01 Oct 1952 w: 1971 c: 3
12 RASMUSSEN, Terry b: 06 Nov 1953 in Milwaukee, WI c: 2
+ seq: 015.50 HAYNES, Kenny w: Abt. 1975 c: 2
12 RASMUSSEN, Theresa b: 03 Oct 1956 in Milwaukee, WI c: 3
+ seq: 015.52 NELSON, Curtis w: 1976 c: 3
12 RASMUSSEN, Debbra b: 24 Sep 1958 in Milwaukee, WI c: 3
+ seq: 015.53 SLADE, William w: 1977 c: 3
12 RASMUSSEN, Dawn b: 09 Aug 1960 in Milwaukee, WI c: 2
+ seq: 015.54 WATTS, Steve w: Abt. 1985 c: 2
* 2nd Husband of [1] SCHROEDER, Gloria-Patricia:
+ seq: 015.55 BAST, Seno w: 1961 v: Milwaukee, WI c: 2
12 BAST, Cindy b: 25 Jul 1962 in Milwaukee, WI c: 2
+ seq: 015.56 MOSS, David w: Abt. 1985 c: 2
12 BAST, James b: 06 Jan 1964 in Milwaukee, WI c: 3
+ seq: 015.57 WILDE, Pamela w: Abt. 1984 c: 3
* 3rd Husband of [1] SCHROEDER, Gloria-Patricia:
+ seq: 015.58 WILDE, Donald w: 1965 c: 1
12 WILDE, Donald b: 10 May 1966 in Grass Valley, CA c: 1
+ seq: 015.59 Debbie w: Abt. 1985 c: 1

015.46

12 RASMUSSEN, Patricia b: 29 Sep 1952 in Milwaukee, WI c: 4
+ seq: 015.46 DAVIS, Larry w: 1970 c: 4
13 DAVIS, Shannon b: 15 Mar 1971 c: 2
+ seq: 015.47 Craig w: 1990 c: 2
13 DAVIS, Jason b: 20 Apr 1975
13 DAVIS, Melisha b: 09 Aug 1979

13DAVIS, Joshua b: 12 May 1983

015.47
13DAVIS, Shannon b: 15 Mar 1971 c: 2
+ seq: 015.47 Craig w: 1990 c: 2
14CRISHAN b: 19 Oct 1990
14CRAIGSHAN b: 23 Apr 1995

015.48
12RASMUSSEN, Pamela b: 29 Sep 1952 in Milwaukee, WI c: 3
+ seq: 015.48 SKOGLIE, Lawrence b: 01 Oct 1952 w: 1971 c: 3
13SKOGLIE, Shadwell b: 15 Jul 1972
13SKOGLIE, Chadwick b: 15 Jul 1972
13SKOGLIE, Tammy b: 15 Dec 1973 c: 1
+ seq: 015.49 MORGAN, Phillip w: Abt. 1995 c: 1

015.49
13SKOGLIE, Tammy b: 15 Dec 1973 c: 1
+ seq: 015.49 MORGAN, Phillip w: Abt. 1995 c: 1
14MORGAN, Jacob b: 13 Dec 1996

015.50
12RASMUSSEN, Terry b: 06 Nov 1953 in Milwaukee, WI c: 2
+ seq: 015.50 HAYNES, Kenny w: Abt. 1975 c: 2
13HAYNES, Kenny b: 08 May 1976 c: 2
+ seq: 015.51 Jillan w: Abt. 1995 c: 2
13HAYNES, Chastity b: 27 Jul 1978

015.51
13HAYNES, Kenny b: 08 May 1976 c: 2
+ seq: 015.51 Jillan w: Abt. 1995 c: 2
14HAYNES, Savana b: 08 Dec 1997
14HAYNES, Gavin b: 1999

015.52
12RASMUSSEN, Theresa b: 03 Oct 1956 in Milwaukee, WI c: 3
+ seq: 015.52 NELSON, Curtis w: 1976 c: 3
13NELSON, Curtis b: 01 Sep 1976
13NELSON, Nicole b: 29 Jun 1980
13NELSON, Kayla b: 30 Apr 1985

015.53

12RASMUSSEN, Debbra b: 24 Sep 1958 in Milwaukee, WI c: 3
+ seq: 015.53 SLADE, William w: 1977 c: 3
13SLADE, Corrine b: 14 Jul 1978
13SLADE, William b: 27 Jul 1979
13SLADE, Jesse b: 15 Feb 1981

015.54

12RASMUSSEN, Dawn b: 09 Aug 1960 in Milwaukee, WI c: 2
+ seq: 015.54 WATTS, Steve w: Abt. 1985 c: 2
13WATTS, Clint b: 15 Feb 1987
13WATTS, Daren b: 23 Mar 1990

015.56

12BAST, Cindy b: 25 Jul 1962 in Milwaukee, WI c: 2
+ seq: 015.56 MOSS, David w: Abt. 1985 c: 2
13MOSS, Hope b: 30 Apr 1988
13MOSS, Chelse b: 17 Dec 1991

015.57

12BAST, James b: 06 Jan 1964 in Milwaukee, WI c: 3
+ seq: 015.57 WILDE, Pamela w: Abt. 1984 c: 3
13BAST, James b: 26 Feb 1986
13BAST, Angela b: 12 Aug 1987
13BAST, Cody b: 16 Apr 1991

015.59

12WILDE, Donald b: 10 May 1966 in Grass Valley, CA c: 1
+ seq: 015.59 Debbie w: Abt. 1985 c: 1
13WILDE, Donald b: 22 Dec 1990

015.59.30

10[1] SCHROEDER, Paul J. b: 25 Nov 1908 in Escanaba, MI d:
    14 Nov 1979 in Escanaba, MI v: Escanaba, MI c: 7
+ seq: 015.59.30 w: Abt. 1930
* 2nd Wife of [1] SCHROEDER, Paul J.:
+ seq: 015.59.40 LARSEN, Marie w: 1934 c: 3
11SCHROEDER, Paula b: in Escanaba, MI c: 3
+ seq: 015.59.45 w: Abt. 1965 c: 3
11SCHROEDER, Babe
11SCHROEDER, Margy

* 3rd Wife of [1] SCHROEDER, Paul J.:
+ seq: 015.59.50 Loretta w: Abt. 1935 c: 1
11 SCHROEDER, Romayne b: in Escanaba, MI v: Escanaba, MI
    c: 1
+ seq: 015.59.55 PALMER, Paul w: Abt. 1965 v: Escanaba, MI
    c: 1
* 4th Wife of [1] SCHROEDER, Paul J.:
+ seq: 015.59.60 CLINE, Frances-Marie b: 06 Apr 1915 in
    Escanaba, MI d: Nov 1935 w: 04 Mar 1935
* 5th Wife of [1] SCHROEDER, Paul J.:
+ seq: 015.60 FRENCH, Merle b: 1921 d: 1966 Cause of death:
    Heart attack w: Abt. 1950 c: 3
11 SCHROEDER, Penny b: 05 Nov 1953 in Escanaba, MI v:
    Escanaba, MI c: 3
+ seq: 015.61 MALLORY w: Abt. 1969 v: Escanaba, MI c: 3
11 SCHROEDER, Robin b: 07 Oct 1955 in Escanaba, MI v:
    Escanaba, MI c: 3
+ seq: 015.62 CASTOR, Eric b: 23 Apr 1955 in Michigan w:
    Abt. 1974 v: Escanaba, MI c: 3
11 SCHROEDER, John-Paul b: 07 Feb 1960 in Escanaba, MI c: 2
+ seq: 015.63 Julia w: Abt. 1985 c: 2

015.59.45

11 SCHROEDER, Paula b: in Escanaba, MI c: 3
+ seq: 015.59.45 w: Abt. 1965 c: 3
12 Daniel
12 Laura
12 Lynn

015.59.55

11 SCHROEDER, Romayne b: in Escanaba, MI v: Escanaba, MI
    c: 1
+ seq: 015.59.55 PALMER, Paul w: Abt. 1965 v: Escanaba, MI
    c: 1
12 PALMER, Trace b: 1970 in Escanaba, MI

015.61

11 SCHROEDER, Penny b: 05 Nov 1953 in Escanaba, MI v:
    Escanaba, MI c: 3
+ seq: 015.61 MALLORY w: Abt. 1969 v: Escanaba, MI c: 3
12 MALLORY, Robin b: 27 Jul 1971 in Escanaba, MI

12MALLORY, Thomas b: 1974 in Escanaba, MI
12MALLORY, Mathew b: 1977 in Escanaba, MI

015.62
11SCHROEDER, Robin b: 07 Oct 1955 in Escanaba, MI v:
Escanaba, MI c: 3
+ seq: 015.62 CASTOR, Eric b: 23 Apr 1955 in Michigan w:
Abt. 1974 v: Escanaba, MI c: 3
12CASTOR, Amber-Lynn b: 28 Jan 1976 in Escanaba, MI
12CASTOR, Amanda-Lynn b: 14 Dec 1976 in Escanaba, MI
12CASTOR, Clayton-John b: 12 Jun 1979 in Escanaba, MI

015.63
11SCHROEDER, John-Paul b: 07 Feb 1960 in Escanaba, MI c: 2
+ seq: 015.63 Julia w: Abt. 1985 c: 2
12SCHROEDER, Brian-John b: 24 Apr
12SCHROEDER, Adam-Gary b: 27 Sep

015.70
10SCHROEDER, Josephine b: 11 Dec 1910 in Escanaba, MI d:
15 Apr 1993 in Escanaba, MI v: Escanaba, MI c: 1
+ seq: 015.70 WILSON, Hjalmer (Hack) b: 07 Jan 1910 d: 11
Nov 1977 in Escanaba, MI w: 21 Aug 1933 v: Escanaba, MI
c: 1
11[1] WILSON, Darlene b: 1933 in Escanaba, MI d: 26 Jun 1999
v: Escanaba, MI c: 6
+ seq: 015.71 JOHNSON, Craig w: Abt. 1950 v: Escanaba, MI
c: 3
* 2nd Husband of [1] WILSON, Darlene:
+ seq: 015.74 REYNOLDS, Alan w: Abt. 1950 c: 1
* 3rd Husband of [1] WILSON, Darlene:
+ seq: 015.75 LEMARAND, Robert w: Mar 1952 in Escanaba,
MI i: Stock car racer c: 2

015.71
11[2] WILSON, Darlene b: 1933 in Escanaba, MI d: 26 Jun 1999
v: Escanaba, MI c: 6
+ seq: 015.71 JOHNSON, Craig w: Abt. 1950 v: Escanaba, MI
c: 3
12[1] JOHNSON, Rick b: 18 Feb 1957 in Escanaba, MI c: 4
+ seq: 015.72 REDEFORD, Carmen w: Abt. 1975 c: 2

* 2nd Wife of [1] JOHNSON, Rick:
+ seq: 015.73 Laura w: Abt. 1980 c: 2
12JOHNSON, Lee-Ann b: 01 Sep 1961 in Escanaba, MI
12JOHNSON, Donald b: 20 Sep 1958 in Escanaba, MI
* 2nd Husband of [2] WILSON, Darlene:
+ seq: 015.74 REYNOLDS, Alan w: Abt. 1950 c: 1
12REYNOLDS, Lee-Ann b: 01 Sep 1961 in Escanaba, MI
* 3rd Husband of [2] WILSON, Darlene:
+ seq: 015.75 LEMARAND, Robert w: Mar 1952 in Escanaba,
   MI i: Stock car racer c: 2
12LEMARAND, Connie b: 19 Apr 1952 in Escanaba, MI c: 2
+ seq: 015.76 HOULE, Ray w: Abt. 1972 c: 2
12LEMARAND, Cinthia b: 23 Feb 1954 in Escanaba, MI c: 2
+ seq: 015.77 CARLSON, Robert w: Abt. 1977 c: 2

015.72
12[1] JOHNSON, Rick b: 18 Feb 1957 in Escanaba, MI c: 4
+ seq: 015.72 REDEFORD, Carmen w: Abt. 1975 c: 2
13JOHNSON, Heather b: 05 Dec 1976 in Escanaba, MI
13JOHNSON, Jennifer b: 02 Apr 1978 in Escanaba, MI
* 2nd Wife of [1] JOHNSON, Rick:
+ seq: 015.73 Laura w: Abt. 1980 c: 2
13JOHNSON, Ashley b: 02 Jan 1983 in Black River Falls, WI
13JOHNSON, Devon b: 06 Nov 1987 in Black River Falls, WI

015.76
12LEMARAND, Connie b: 19 Apr 1952 in Escanaba, MI c: 2
+ seq: 015.76 HOULE, Ray w: Abt. 1972 c: 2
13HOULE, Cristine b: 17 Jul 1974
13HOULE, Brian b: 02 Dec 1977

015.77
12LEMARAND, Cinthia b: 23 Feb 1954 in Escanaba, MI c: 2
+ seq: 015.77 CARLSON, Robert w: Abt. 1977 c: 2
13CARLSON, Aoysa b: 11 Sep 1979 in Minneapolis, MN
13CARLSON, Erica b: 11 Sep 1979 in Minneapolis, MN

015.78
10SCHROEDER, Edward b: 02 Dec 1912 in Escanaba, MI d: 15
   Dec 1995 in Escanaba, MI v: Escanaba, MI c: 2
+ seq: 015.78 LARSON, Dorothy w: 06 Jun 1939 c: 2

11 SCHROEDER, Clinton c: 1
+ seq: 015.79 Catherine w: Abt. 1970 c: 1
11 SCHROEDER, Mary-Dell b: 02 Oct 1942 c: 2
+ seq: 015.80 Bob w: Abt. 1970 c: 2

015.79
11 SCHROEDER, Clinton c: 1
+ seq: 015.79 Catherine w: Abt. 1970 c: 1
12 SCHROEDER, Lisa

015.80
11 SCHROEDER, Mary-Dell b: 02 Oct 1942 c: 2
+ seq: 015.80 Bob w: Abt. 1970 c: 2
12 Anthony
12 ?

015.83
10 [1] SCHROEDER, John b: 20 Sep 1922 in Escanaba, MI d: 25
    Apr 1994 in Gladstone, MI v: Escanaba, MI i: Mechanic i:
    Raced boats c: 2
+ seq: 015.83 COLE, Doris-Margaret b: 19 Dec 1924 in
    Gladstone, MI d: 28 Jul 1976 in Gladstone, MI w: 06 Jul 1946
    in Escanaba, MI c: 2
11 SCHROEDER, Colleen-Margaret b: 13 Feb 1949 in Milwaukee,
    WI
11 SCHROEDER, Randy-John b: 10 Dec 1953 in Escanaba, MI v:
    Gladstone, MI c: 1
+ seq: 015.84 Kathy w: Abt. 1980 v: Gladstone, MI c: 1
* 2nd Wife of [1] SCHROEDER, John:
+ seq: 015.84.50 Virginia w: Abt. 1950

015.84
11 SCHROEDER, Randy-John b: 10 Dec 1953 in Escanaba, MI v:
    Gladstone, MI c: 1
+ seq: 015.84 Kathy w: Abt. 1980 v: Gladstone, MI c: 1
12 SCHROEDER, Tarra b: 1980 in Gladstone, MI

015.85
8 SCHROEDER, Franz b: 1848 in Ettelbruck, Lux d: in
    Ettelbrook, Lux v: Ettelbruck, Lux c: 2
+ seq: 015.85 STAUDT, Catherine (Ann) b: 1844 in Ettelbrook,

Lux d: 1900 w: 1873 c: 2
9 SCHROEDER, Franz b: 1877 d: 1878
9 SCHROEDER, Michel b: 25 Dec 1879 in Ettelbruck, Lux d:
   1934 v: Ettelbruck, Lux o: Plumber o: Police officer c: 2
+ seq: 015.86 HIPP, Margaret Jacoby b: 1883 in Ettelbruck, Lux
   d: 1959 in Ettelbruck, Lux w: 12 Jul 1907 in Ettelbruck, Lux v:
   Ettelbruck, Lux o: Laundress r: m m: Catharina Hipp c: 2

015.86
9 SCHROEDER, Michel b: 25 Dec 1879 in Ettelbruck, Lux d:
   1934 v: Ettelbruck, Lux o: Plumber o: Police officer c: 2
+ seq: 015.86 HIPP, Margaret Jacoby b: 1883 in Ettelbruck, Lux
   d: 1959 in Ettelbruck, Lux w: 12 Jul 1907 in Ettelbruck, Lux v:
   Ettelbruck, Lux o: Laundress r: m m: Catharina Hipp c: 2
10SCHROEDER, Francois b: 11 Feb 1909 in Ettelbruck, Lux d:
   1996 in Ettelbruck, Lux v: Ettelbruck, Lux r: b c: 1
+ seq: 015.87 LANHERS, Margit w: Abt. 1930 c: 1
10SCHROEDER, Pierre b: 10 Jan 1911 in Ettelbrook, Lux d:
   1954 r: b

015.87
10SCHROEDER, Francois b: 11 Feb 1909 in Ettelbruck, Lux d:
   1996 in Ettelbruck, Lux v: Ettelbruck, Lux r: b c: 1
+ seq: 015.87 LANHERS, Margit w: Abt. 1930 c: 1
11SCHROEDER, Marcel b: 1933 in Ettelbruck, Lux d: 1994 in
   Ettelbruck, Lux v: Ettelbruck, Lux c: 2
+ seq: 015.88 BIERI, Margrit b: 1932 in Ettelbruck, Lux w: Abt.
   1955 v: Ettelbruck, Lux c: 2

015.88
11SCHROEDER, Marcel b: 1933 in Ettelbruck, Lux d: 1994 in
   Ettelbruck, Lux v: Ettelbruck, Lux c: 2
+ seq: 015.88 BIERI, Margrit b: 1932 in Ettelbruck, Lux w: Abt.
   1955 v: Ettelbruck, Lux c: 2
12SCHROEDER, Margot b: 1958 in Ettelbrook, Lux c: 3
+ seq: 015.89 PIXIUS, Jacques b: 1955 in Luxembourg, Lux w:
   1981 c: 3
12SCHROEDER, Pia b: 1962 in Ettelbrook, Lux c: 3
+ seq: 015.90 CORRING, Antoine w: 1988 c: 3

015.89

12SCHROEDER, Margot b: 1958 in Ettelbrook, Lux c: 3
 + seq: 015.89 PIXIUS, Jacques b: 1955 in Luxembourg, Lux w:
    1981 c: 3
13PIXIUS, Patrick b: 1983 in Wolferdange, Lux
13PIXIUS, Paul b: 1985 in Wolferdange, Lux
13PIXIUS, Pierre b: 1989 in Wolferdange, Lux

015.90

12SCHROEDER, Pia b: 1962 in Ettelbrook, Lux c: 3
 + seq: 015.90 CORRING, Antoine w: 1988 c: 3
13CORRING, Kim b: 1989
13CORRING, Anne b: 1991
13CORRING, Luc b: 1994

015.91

8 SCHROEDER, Josephine b: Dec 1853 in Ettelbrook, Lux d: Jul
    1932 in Chicago, IL i: Emigrated to U. S. with husband and
    nephew c: 7
 + seq: 015.91 HOFFMAN, Peter b: Jun 1851 in Luxembourg,
    Lux w: 1871 i: Emigrated to U. S. with wife and nephew c: 7
9 HOFFMAN, ? i: Died in infancy
9 HOFFMAN, ? i: Died in infancy
9 HOFFMAN, ? i: Died in infancy
9 HOFFMAN, ? i: Died in infancy
9 HOFFMAN, John b: Dec 1880 in Michigan d: Feb 1964
9 HOFFMAN, Katherine b: Dec 1883 in Michigan d: Nov 1961
 + seq: 015.92 DRURNLELLER, Frank d: Nov 1951 w: Abt.
    1910
9 HOFFMAN, Annie b: Oct 1890 in Michigan

015.97

6 WITRY, Marie-Barbara b: 28 Dec 1790 in Warken, Lux d: 17
    Oct 1869 in Warken, Lux v: Warken, Lux o: No profession r:
    bd c: 7
 + seq: 015.97 BISSENER, Michel b: 09 Oct 1780 in Oberfeulen,
    Lux d: 07 May 1845 in Warken, Lux w: 09 Aug 1815 in
    Ettelbruck, Lux v: Warken, Lux o: Farmer r: d r: m f:
    Theodor Bissener m: Magdalena Polter c: 7
7 BISSENER, Christina b: 31 Aug 1816 in Warken, Lux v:
    Warken, Lux o: Day laborer r: b

+ seq: 015.97.50 FABRICIUS, Johann b: 22 Sep 1809 in Schieren, Lux w: 29 Aug 1855 in Ettelbruck, Lux o: Farmer r: m f: Frantz Fabricius m: Maria Strirn

7 BISSENER, Anna-Marie b: 10 Feb 1818 in Warken, Lux r: b
7 BISSENER, Nicolas b: 21 Nov 1819 in Warken, Lux r: b
7 BISSENER, Marie b: 26 Mar 1822 in Warken, Lux r: b
7 BISSENER, Peter b: 11 Jun 1824 in Warken, Lux d: 20 Jun 1824 in Warken, Lux v: Warken, Lux r: bd
7 BISSENER, Johann b: 07 Aug 1826 in Warken, Lux v: Warken, Lux o: Day laborer o: Carpenter r: b
7 BISSENER, Michel b: 17 Apr 1829 in Warken, Lux r: b

016

5 WITRY, Johann-Michel b: 05 Sep 1753 in Warken, Lux d: 11 Feb 1832 in Warken, Lux v: Warken, Lux o: Day laborer o: Linen weaver r: bd c: 2
+ seq: 016 THIEL, Marie b: 04 Jan 1767 in Schrondweiler, Lux d: 15 May 1845 in Warken, Lux w: 27 Oct 1794 in Nommern, Lux a: Goeders v: Warken, Lux o: Day laborer r: bd r: m f: Nicolas Thiel m: Elisabeth Roob c: 2
6 WITRY, Johann-Adam b: 04 Nov 1795 in Nommern, Lux d: 15 Jan 1866 in Warken, Lux a: Michel h: Witry v: Warken, Lux o: Lathe operator o: Carpenter r: bd c: 5
+ seq: 017 WAGNER, Susanne b: 17 Sep 1798 in Schieren, Lux d: 10 Jun 1871 in Warken, Lux w: 14 Jan 1829 in Ettelbruck, Lux h: Witry v: Warken, Lux o: No profession r: bd r: m f: Johann Wagner m: Barbara Lanners c: 5
6 WITRY, Johann b: 26 Oct 1799 in Nommern, Lux d: 19 Jan 1861 in Warken, Lux v: Warken, Lux o: Carpenter r: bd

017

6 WITRY, Johann-Adam b: 04 Nov 1795 in Nommern, Lux d: 15 Jan 1866 in Warken, Lux a: Michel h: Witry v: Warken, Lux o: Lathe operator o: Carpenter r: bd c: 5
+ seq: 017 WAGNER, Susanne b: 17 Sep 1798 in Schieren, Lux d: 10 Jun 1871 in Warken, Lux w: 14 Jan 1829 in Ettelbruck, Lux h: Witry v: Warken, Lux o: No profession r: bd r: m f: Johann Wagner m: Barbara Lanners c: 5
7 WITRY, Johann b: 06 May 1831 in Warken, Lux d: 13 Apr 1863 in Warken, Lux v: Warken, Lux o: Carpenter r: bd
7 WITRY, Christina b: 03 Apr 1833 in Warken, Lux d: 08 Mar

1837 in Warken, Lux v: Warken, Lux r: bd

7 WITRY, Nicolas b: 30 Apr 1835 in Warken, Lux d: 16 May 1838 in Warken, Lux v: Warken, Lux r: bd

7 WITRY, Anna b: 05 Feb 1839 in Warken, Lux d: 04 Jan 1905 in Ettelbruck, Lux v: Warken, Lux i: Spent his last days in a sanitarium in Ettelbruck o: No profession r: b

7 WITRY, Nicolas b: 05 Oct 1841 in Warken, Lux d: 22 Jan 1901 in Ettelbruck, Lux v: Warken, Lux o: Lathe operator o: Day laborer o: Carpenter r: bd

017.01

5 WITRY, Marie-Regina b: 17 Feb 1756 in Warken, Lux d: 29 Apr 1804 in Ettelbruck, Lux v: Ettelbruck, Lux o: Day laborer r: bd c: 10

+ seq: 017.01 UNDEN, Heinrich b: Abt. 1742 in Ettelbruck, Lux d: in Warken, Lux w: 09 Dec 1779 in Ettelbruck, Lux a: Onden v: Ettelbruck, Lux o: Tavern keeper o: Banker o: Day laborer, Merchant r: m c: 10

6 UNDEN, Elisabeth b: 13 Sep 1780 in Ettelbruck, Lux r: b

6 UNDEN, Peter b: 13 Sep 1780 in Ettelbruck, Lux d: 30 Nov 1780 in Ettelbruck, Lux v: Ettelbruck, Lux r: d

6 UNDEN, Philipp b: 23 Nov 1781 in Ettelbruck, Lux d: 12 Jan 1786 in Ettelbruck, Lux v: Ettelbruck, Lux r: bd

6 UNDEN, Anna-Marie b: 29 Nov 1783 in Ettelbruck, Lux r: bd

6 UNDEN, Susanne b: 17 Jan 1785 in Ettelbruck, Lux d: 29 Jan 1786 in Ettelbruck, Lux r: bd

6 UNDEN, Catherine b: 04 Feb 1787 in Ettelbruck, Lux r: b

6 UNDEN, Susanne b: 10 Feb 1790 in Ettelbruck, Lux r: b

6 UNDEN, Peter b: 10 Oct 1792 in Ettelbruck, Lux d: 03 Nov 1792 in Ettelbruck, Lux r: bd

6 UNDEN, Anna-Marie b: 06 Aug 1794 in Ettelbruck, Lux d: 07 Mar 1844 in Ettelbruck, Lux v: Warken, Lux o: No profession r: bd

6 UNDEN, Peter b: 06 Apr 1802 in Ettelbruck, Lux r: b

017.03

4 WITRY, Anna b: 11 Jan 1717 in Beidweiler, Lux d: 24 Dec 1789 in Waldbillig, Lux a: Ludwigs v: Beidweiler, Lux r: bd c: 3

+ seq: 017.03 ADAMY, Peter b: Abt. 1712 in Meysembourg, Lux d: 07 Jan 1790 in Waldbillig, Lux w: 28 Nov 1746 in

Rodenbourg, Lux v: Beidweiler, Lux i: Served as mayor in
Waldbillig r: d r: m c: 3

5 ADAMY, Marie-Barbara b: 18 Sep 1748 in Beidweiler, Lux r:
b

5 ADAMY, Peter b: 16 Feb 1756 in Beidweiler, Lux r: b

5 ADAMY, Mathias (Peter) b: 18 Nov 1759 in Beidweiler, Lux
d: 25 Jul 1800 in Waldbillig, Lux h: A Ludes v: Waldbillig,
Lux r: b c: 5

+ seq: 017.03.01 SCHOLER, Anne-Marie b: 06 Dec 1767 in
Waldbillig, Lux d: 18 Feb 1858 in Waldbillig, Lux w: 14 Feb
1787 in Waldbillig, Lux h: A Ludes v: Waldbillig, Lux r: m f:
Nicolas Scholer m: Susanne Becker c: 5

017.03.01

5 ADAMY, Mathias (Peter) b: 18 Nov 1759 in Beidweiler, Lux
d: 25 Jul 1800 in Waldbillig, Lux h: A Ludes v: Waldbillig,
Lux r: b c: 5

+ seq: 017.03.01 SCHOLER, Anne-Marie b: 06 Dec 1767 in
Waldbillig, Lux d: 18 Feb 1858 in Waldbillig, Lux w: 14 Feb
1787 in Waldbillig, Lux h: A Ludes v: Waldbillig, Lux r: m f:
Nicolas Scholer m: Susanne Becker c: 5

6 ADAMY, Susanne b: 18 May 1788 in Waldbillig, Lux

+ seq: 017.03.02 MICHELS, Mathias w: Abt. 1810

6 ADAMY, Marie-Marguerite b: 16 Jul 1791 in Waldbillig, Lux
d: 17 Feb 1856 in Waldbillig, Lux v: Waldbillig, Lux

+ seq: 017.03.03 LAICHES, Mathias b: 11 Feb 1791 in Biver,
Lux d: 13 Sep 1864 in Waldbillig, Lux w: 09 Feb 1818 in
Waldbillig, Lux v: Waldbillig, Lux

6 ADAMY, Pierre-Nicolas b: 24 Feb 1793 in Waldbillig, Lux d:
08 Aug 1871 in Waldbillig, Lux v: Waldbillig, Lux c: 3

+ seq: 017.03.04 KEYSER, Anne-Marie b: 05 Dec 1799 in
Waldbillig, Lux d: 22 Aug 1880 in Waldbillig, Lux w: 19 Jan
1830 in Waldbillig, Lux v: Waldbillig, Lux f: Jacques Keyser
m: Anne Kasel c: 3

6 ADAMY, Nicolas b: 19 Aug 1795 in Waldbillig, Lux d: 12
Mar 1872 in Waldbillig, Lux v: Waldbillig, Lux c: 1

+ seq: 017.03.14 MAJERUS, Anne-Marie b: 28 Aug 1794 in
Waldbillig, Lux d: 12 Dec 1871 in Waldbillig, Lux w: 02 Feb
1836 in Waldbillig, Lux v: Waldbillig, Lux f: Nicolas Majerus
m: Madeleine Zens c: 1

6 ADAMY, Anne b: 20 Oct 1798 in Waldbillig, Lux d: 02 Feb

1882 in Waldbillig, Lux h: An Gaspers v: Waldbillig, Lux c: 2
+ seq: 017.03.15 BROOS, Martin b: 28 Oct 1804 in Waldbillig,
   Lux d: 10 Apr 1879 in Waldbillig, Lux w: 10 Dec 1823 in
   Waldbillig, Lux h: An Gaspers v: Waldbillig, Lux f: Michel
   Broos m: Catherine Krier c: 2

017.03.04

6 ADAMY, Pierre-Nicolas b: 24 Feb 1793 in Waldbillig, Lux d:
   08 Aug 1871 in Waldbillig, Lux v: Waldbillig, Lux c: 3
+ seq: 017.03.04 KEYSER, Anne-Marie b: 05 Dec 1799 in
   Waldbillig, Lux d: 22 Aug 1880 in Waldbillig, Lux w: 19 Jan
   1830 in Waldbillig, Lux v: Waldbillig, Lux f: Jacques Keyser
   m: Anne Kasel c: 3
7 ADAMY, Marguerite b: 23 Apr 1832 in Waldbillig, Lux v:
   Waldbillig, Lux c: 4
+ seq: 017.03.05 JUNG, Mathias b: 17 Jun 1832 in Scheidleck,
   Lux d: 24 Aug 1898 in Waldbillig, Lux w: 27 Aug 1857 in
   Waldbillig, Lux v: Waldbillig, Lux f: Jacques Jung m:
   Marguerite Husse c: 4
7 ADAMY, Susanne b: 23 May 1836 in Waldbillig, Lux d: 02
   Mar 1919 in Christnach, Lux v: Christnach, Lux c: 1
+ seq: 017.03.13 SCHAAFF, Henri b: 29 Jan 1834 in Christnach,
   Lux d: 20 Aug 1922 in Christnach, Lux w: 25 Oct 1865 in
   Waldbillig, Lux v: Christnach, Lux o: Day laborer f: Jean
   Schaff m: Marie Lax c: 1
7 ADAMY, Anne b: 17 Nov 1838 in Waldbillig, Lux

017.03.05

7 ADAMY, Marguerite b: 23 Apr 1832 in Waldbillig, Lux v:
   Waldbillig, Lux c: 4
+ seq: 017.03.05 JUNG, Mathias b: 17 Jun 1832 in Scheidleck,
   Lux d: 24 Aug 1898 in Waldbillig, Lux w: 27 Aug 1857 in
   Waldbillig, Lux v: Waldbillig, Lux f: Jacques Jung m:
   Marguerite Husse c: 4
8 JUNG, Pierre b: 23 Jun 1858 in Waldbillig, Lux d: 18 Mar
   1943 in Waldbillig, Lux v: Waldbillig, Lux c: 6
+ seq: 017.03.06 FLAMMANG, Marguerite b: 14 May 1862 in
   Consdorf, Lux d: 19 Aug 1926 in Waldbillig, Lux w: 09 Nov
   1888 in Waldbillig, Lux v: Waldbillig, Lux f: Jean Fla m:
   Catherine Ernzen c: 6
8 JUNG, Susanne b: 14 Apr 1862 in Waldbillig, Lux

+ seq: 017.03.11 FABER, Charles b: 16 Jun 1853 in Strassem,
    Lux w: 10 Nov 1888 in Waldbillig, Lux
8 JUNG, Anne b: 02 May 1866 in Waldbillig, Lux
+ seq: 017.03.12 JUNG, Mathias b: 02 Mar 1871 in
    Rollingergrund, Lux w: 02 Jul 1895 in Waldbillig, Lux
8 JUNG, Catherine b: 15 Nov 1869 in Waldbillig, Lux d: 15 Nov
    1869 in Waldbillig, Lux v: Waldbillig, Lux

017.03.06

8 JUNG, Pierre b: 23 Jun 1858 in Waldbillig, Lux d: 18 Mar
    1943 in Waldbillig, Lux v: Waldbillig, Lux c: 6
+ seq: 017.03.06 FLAMMANG, Marguerite b: 14 May 1862 in
    Consdorf, Lux d: 19 Aug 1926 in Waldbillig, Lux w: 09 Nov
    1888 in Waldbillig, Lux v: Waldbillig, Lux f: Jean Fla m:
    Catherine Ernzen c: 6
9 JUNG, Jean b: 22 Jan 1890 in Waldbillig, Lux
9 JUNG, Catherine b: 04 May 1891 in Waldbillig, Lux
+ seq: 017.03.07 GILLESSEN, Pierre b: 31 Mar 1887 in
    Heinerscheid, Lux w: 02 Mar 1919 in Waldbillig, Lux o:
    Railroad worker
9 JUNG, Charles b: 08 Mar 1893 in Waldbillig, Lux v:
    Waldbillig, Lux c: 3
+ seq: 017.03.08 KARELS, Marie b: 14 Oct 1896 in
    Schrondweiler, Lux w: 05 Sep 1922 in Waldbillig, Lux f:
    Francois Karels m: Anne Heintz c: 3
9 JUNG, Elise b: 21 Oct 1894 in Waldbillig, Lux
9 JUNG, Elise-Hilde b: 03 Mar 1897 in Waldbillig, Lux
9 JUNG, Catherine-Irma b: 15 Dec 1902 in Waldbillig, Lux
+ seq: 017.03.10 GREISCH, Theodore b: Abt. 1898 in
    Christnach, Lux w: 1930

017.03.08

9 JUNG, Charles b: 08 Mar 1893 in Waldbillig, Lux v:
    Waldbillig, Lux c: 3
+ seq: 017.03.08 KARELS, Marie b: 14 Oct 1896 in
    Schrondweiler, Lux w: 05 Sep 1922 in Waldbillig, Lux f:
    Francois Karels m: Anne Heintz c: 3
10JUNG, Jean-Pierre-Joseph b: 18 Jan 1924 in Waldbillig, Lux v:
    Waldbillig, Lux
+ seq: 017.03.09 PRIM, Berthie b: Abt. 1927 in Christnach, Lux
    w: 1952

10 JUNG, Roger b: 15 Jul 1925 in Waldbillig, Lux d: 30 Dec 1925 in Waldbillig, Lux v: Waldbillig, Lux

10 JUNG, Irma b: 01 Jun 1927 in Waldbillig, Lux d: 06 Nov 1946 in Waldbillig, Lux v: Waldbillig, Lux

017.03.13

7 ADAMY, Susanne b: 23 May 1836 in Waldbillig, Lux d: 02 Mar 1919 in Christnach, Lux v: Christnach, Lux c: 1

+ seq: 017.03.13 SCHAAFF, Henri b: 29 Jan 1834 in Christnach, Lux d: 20 Aug 1922 in Christnach, Lux w: 25 Oct 1865 in Waldbillig, Lux v: Christnach, Lux o: Day laborer f: Jean Schaff m: Marie Lax c: 1

8 SCHAAFF, Jean b: 07 Nov 1876 in Christnach, Lux d: 08 Feb 1961 in Christnach, Lux v: Christnach, Lux c: 6

+ seq: 017.03.13.30 BAUM, Catherine-Elisabeth b: 28 Jul 1875 in Christnach, Lux d: 06 Feb 1958 in Christnach, Lux w: 21 Apr 1902 in Waldbillig, Lux v: Christnach, Lux f: Pierre Baum m: Catherine Koch c: 6

017.03.13.30

8 SCHAAFF, Jean b: 07 Nov 1876 in Christnach, Lux d: 08 Feb 1961 in Christnach, Lux v: Christnach, Lux c: 6

+ seq: 017.03.13.30 BAUM, Catherine-Elisabeth b: 28 Jul 1875 in Christnach, Lux d: 06 Feb 1958 in Christnach, Lux w: 21 Apr 1902 in Waldbillig, Lux v: Christnach, Lux f: Pierre Baum m: Catherine Koch c: 6

9 SCHAAF, Catherine b: 20 Jan 1903 in Christnach, Lux

9 SCHAAF, Susanne-Julie b: 07 Jul 1905 in Christnach, Lux d: 09 Mar 1908 in Christnach, Lux

9 SCHAAF, Barbe b: 11 Nov 1907 in Christnach, Lux o: Seanstress

9 SCHAAF, Claire b: 01 Oct 1909 in Christnach, Lux

9 SCHAAF, Albert-Mathieu b: 22 May 1912 in Christnach, Lux

9 SCHAAF, Jean-Pierre b: 24 Jan 1916 in Christnach, Lux d: Bef. 2004 v: Solgne, France v: Christnach, Lux o: Transportation entrepreneur c: 5

+ seq: 017.03.13.50 FEHRENTZ, Elise b: 05 May 1920 in Bosenbach, Germany d: 15 Oct 2004 in Ettelbruck, Lux w: 07 Mar 1943 in Solgne, France v: Solgne, France v: Christnach, Lux f: Albert Fehrentz m: Elisabeth Sattler c: 5

017.03.13.50

9 SCHAAF, Jean-Pierre b: 24 Jan 1916 in Christnach, Lux d: Bef. 2004 v: Solgne, France v: Christnach, Lux o: Transportation entrepreneur c: 5

+ seq: 017.03.13.50 FEHRENTZ, Elise b: 05 May 1920 in Bosenbach, Germany d: 15 Oct 2004 in Ettelbruck, Lux w: 07 Mar 1943 in Solgne, France v: Solgne, France v: Christnach, Lux f: Albert Fehrentz m: Elisabeth Sattler c: 5

10 SCHAAF, Irmgard b: 03 Aug 1943 in Solgne, France

10 SCHAAF, Raymond-Michel-Jean-Erneste b: 20 Oct 1946 in Christnach, Lux

10 SCHAAF, Robert-Pierre b: 01 Oct 1948 in Christnach, Lux

10 SCHAAF, Margot-Claire b: 22 Sep 1954 in Christnach, Lux

10 SCHAAF, Elaine b: 23 Feb 1963 in Luxembourg, Lux o: Medical secretary

+ seq: 017.03.13.70 KAEPPELI, Paul b: 14 Jan 1957 in Diekirch, Lux w: 21 Feb 1986 in Diekirch, Lux o: Master tinsmith-installer

017.03.14

6 ADAMY, Nicolas b: 19 Aug 1795 in Waldbillig, Lux d: 12 Mar 1872 in Waldbillig, Lux v: Waldbillig, Lux c: 1

+ seq: 017.03.14 MAJERUS, Anne-Marie b: 28 Aug 1794 in Waldbillig, Lux d: 12 Dec 1871 in Waldbillig, Lux w: 02 Feb 1836 in Waldbillig, Lux v: Waldbillig, Lux f: Nicolas Majerus m: Madeleine Zens c: 1

7 ADAMY, Mathias b: 20 Nov 1836 in Waldbillig, Lux d: 27 Mar 1843 in Waldbillig, Lux v: Waldbillig, Lux

017.03.15

6 ADAMY, Anne b: 20 Oct 1798 in Waldbillig, Lux d: 02 Feb 1882 in Waldbillig, Lux h: An Gaspers v: Waldbillig, Lux c: 2

+ seq: 017.03.15 BROOS, Martin b: 28 Oct 1804 in Waldbillig, Lux d: 10 Apr 1879 in Waldbillig, Lux w: 10 Dec 1823 in Waldbillig, Lux h: An Gaspers v: Waldbillig, Lux f: Michel Broos m: Catherine Krier c: 2

7 BROOS, Mathias b: 18 Jan 1832 in Waldbillig, Lux d: 16 Jun 1922 in Waldbillig, Lux v: Waldbillig, Lux

+ seq: 017.03.16 KONSBRUCK, Anne-Marie b: 10 May 1831 in Waldbillig, Lux d: 22 Dec 1892 in Waldbillig, Lux w: 27 Jan 1863 in Waldbillig, Lux v: Waldbillig, Lux

7 BROOS, Theodor b: 12 Jan 1825 in Waldbillig, Lux d: 29 Oct 1878 in Waldbillig, Lux v: Waldbillig, Lux c: 2

+ seq: 017.03.17 GIRST, Anne-Marie b: 03 Sep 1824 in Waldbillig, Lux d: 06 Feb 1876 in Waldbillig, Lux w: 13 Feb 1849 in Waldbillig, Lux v: Waldbillig, Lux f: Pierre Girst m: Anne Henckes c: 2

017.03.17

7 BROOS, Theodor b: 12 Jan 1825 in Waldbillig, Lux d: 29 Oct 1878 in Waldbillig, Lux v: Waldbillig, Lux c: 2

+ seq: 017.03.17 GIRST, Anne-Marie b: 03 Sep 1824 in Waldbillig, Lux d: 06 Feb 1876 in Waldbillig, Lux w: 13 Feb 1849 in Waldbillig, Lux v: Waldbillig, Lux f: Pierre Girst m: Anne Henckes c: 2

8 BROOS, Marie b: 12 Mar 1854 in Waldbillig, Lux d: 28 Nov 1937 in Waldbillig, Lux v: Waldbillig, Lux

+ seq: 017.03.18 MEDERNACH, Balthasar b: 11 Aug 1856 in Hemsthal, Lux d: 22 Sep 1912 in Waldbillig, Lux w: 09 Nov 1880 in Waldbillig, Lux v: Waldbillig, Lux

8 BROOS, Marie-Anne b: 19 Mar 1858 in Waldbillig, Lux v: Waldbillig, Lux c: 1

+ seq: 017.03.19 NEU, Mathias b: Abt. 1858 w: Bef. 1886 v: Waldbillig, Lux c: 1

017.03.19

8 BROOS, Marie-Anne b: 19 Mar 1858 in Waldbillig, Lux v: Waldbillig, Lux c: 1

+ seq: 017.03.19 NEU, Mathias b: Abt. 1858 w: Bef. 1886 v: Waldbillig, Lux c: 1

9 NEU, Pierre b: 24 Mar 1886 in Waldbillig, Lux

017.05

3 THIES, Margaretha b: 18 Sep 1643 in Schrondweiler, Lux d: 09 Jan 1742 in Blaschette, Lux a: Witry v: Blaschette, Lux r: bd c: 6

+ seq: 017.05 REUTER, Louis t: Parish elder b: Abt. 1660 in Blaschette, Lux d: 06 Oct 1728 in Blaschette, Lux w: 11 Jan 1688 in Nommern, Lux v: Blaschette, Lux r: d r: m c: 6

4 REUTER, Susanne b: 27 Mar 1689 in Blaschette, Lux r: b

4 REUTER, Johann-Bernard b: 29 Oct 1690 in Blaschette, Lux v: Blaschette, Lux r: b c: 6

+ seq: 017.06 MEYERS, Marie b: Abt. 1690 in Breidweiler, Lux
   w: Abt. 1715 v: Blaschette, Lux c: 6
4 REUTER, Catherine b: 26 Feb 1692 in Blaschette, Lux r: b
4 REUTER, Elisabeth b: 24 Mar 1693 in Blaschette, Lux r: b
4 REUTER, Margaretha b: 19 Jan 1696 in Blaschette, Lux v:
   Altlinster, Lux r: b
+ seq: 017.07 PRINTZ, Heinrich b: Abt. 1695 in Altlinster, Lux
   w: 16 Jan 1720 in Blaschette, Lux v: Altlinster, Lux r: m f:
   Bernard Printz
4 REUTER, Nicolas b: 02 Sep 1698 in Blaschette, Lux a:
   Stechgen v: Blaschette, Lux r: b
+ seq: 017.08 Marie b: Abt. 1695 in Blaschette, Lux w: Abt.
   1717 v: Blaschette, Lux

017.06
4 REUTER, Johann-Bernard b: 29 Oct 1690 in Blaschette, Lux v:
   Blaschette, Lux r: b c: 6
+ seq: 017.06 MEYERS, Marie b: Abt. 1690 in Breidweiler, Lux
   w: Abt. 1715 v: Blaschette, Lux c: 6
5 REUTER, Michel b: 14 Oct 1716 in Blaschette, Lux r: b
5 REUTER, Marie-Catherine b: 19 Oct 1718 in Blaschette, Lux r:
   b
5 REUTER, Elisabeth b: 06 Oct 1721 in Blaschette, Lux r: b
5 REUTER, Johann b: 05 Mar 1724 in Blaschette, Lux r: b
5 REUTER, Marie b: 24 Feb 1728 in Blaschette, Lux r: b
5 REUTER, Anna b: 29 Jun 1731 in Blaschette, Lux r: b

018
3 THIES, Johann b: 07 Mar 1646 in Schrondweiler, Lux a: Rob
   a: Witry h: Rob v: Glabach, Lux r: b c: 6
+ seq: 018 Margaretha b: Abt. 1650 w: Abt. 1675 v: Glabach,
   Lux c: 6
4 THIES, Elisabeth b: 16 Nov 1678 in Glabach, Lux a: Rob v:
   Eschweiler, Lux v: Beidweiler, Lux r: b
4 THIES, Philipp b: 09 Aug 1681 in Glabach, Lux a: Rob r: b
4 THIES, Marie b: 04 Feb 1685 in Glabach, Lux a: Rob v:
   Glabach, Lux r: b c: 10
+ seq: 018.01 MATHIEU, Johann b: Abt. 1690 in Rollingen, Lux
   w: 09 Feb 1716 in Nommern, Lux a: Thies v: Glabach, Lux r:
   m c: 10
4 THIES, Gertrud b: 25 Nov 1687 in Glabach, Lux a: Rob r: b

+ seq: 018.04 BETTENDORF, Peter b: Abt. 1685 in
  Goebelsmuhle, Lux w: 17 Nov 1710 in Nommern, Lux o:
  Builder r: m
4 THIES, Catherine b: 16 Jun 1690 in Glabach, Lux a: Rob v:
  Mertzig, Lux r: b
+ seq: 018.05 SCHROEDER, Johann b: Abt. 1690 in Mertzig,
  Lux w: 20 Jan 1716 in Nommern, Lux v: Mertzig, Lux r: m
4 THIES, Margaretha b: 20 May 1693 in Glabach, Lux a: Rob r:
  b

018.01

4 THIES, Marie b: 04 Feb 1685 in Glabach, Lux a: Rob v:
  Glabach, Lux r: b c: 10
+ seq: 018.01 MATHIEU, Johann b: Abt. 1690 in Rollingen, Lux
  w: 09 Feb 1716 in Nommern, Lux a: Thies v: Glabach, Lux r:
  m c: 10
5 MATHIEU, Louis b: 23 Dec 1716 in Glabach, Lux r: b
5 MATHIEU, Susanne b: 23 Apr 1718 in Glabach, Lux d: 16 Jun
  1784 in Glabach, Lux a: Thies v: Glabach, Lux r: bd
+ seq: 018.02 HUSS, Michel b: Abt. 1730 in Eschweiler, Lux d:
  18 Jun 1779 in Glabach, Lux w: 04 Sep 1759 in Nommern, Lux
  v: Glabach, Lux o: Farmer r: d r: m
5 MATHIEU, Johann b: 26 Mar 1720 in Glabach, Lux r: b
5 MATHIEU, Christian b: 22 Mar 1722 in Glabach, Lux r: b
5 MATHIEU, Theodor b: 02 Apr 1726 in Glabach, Lux d: 14 Apr
  1754 in Glabach, Lux v: Glabach, Lux r: bd
5 MATHIEU, Mathias b: 27 Feb 1728 in Glabach, Lux r: b
5 MATHIEU, Philipp b: 03 Apr 1730 in Glabach, Lux r: b
5 MATHIEU, Catherine b: 04 Feb 1732 in Glabach, Lux r: b
5 MATHIEU, Catherine b: 15 Jul 1736 in Glabach, Lux v:
  Heffingen, Lux r: b
+ seq: 018.03 WEBER, Conrad b: Abt. 1730 in Heffingen, Lux
  w: 03 Dec 1758 in Nommern, Lux v: Heffingen, Lux r: m
5 MATHIEU, Elisabeth b: 30 Jun 1739 in Glabach, Lux r: b

019

3 THIES, Johann b: 09 May 1649 in Schrondweiler, Lux a: Witry
  h: Thies v: Schrondweiler, Lux r: b c: 2
+ seq: 019 REULAND, Susanne b: Abt. 1650 in Blaschette, Lux
  d: 02 Jul 1707 in Schrondweiler, Lux w: Abt. 1675 a: Thies h:
  Thies v: Schrondweiler, Lux r: d c: 2

4 THIES, Peter b: 07 Aug 1680 in Schrondweiler, Lux a: Witry
r: b

4 THIES, Hubert b: 01 May 1684 in Schrondweiler, Lux a: Witry
r: b

020

3 WITRY, Nicolas t: Mayor b: 07 Jan 1652 in Schrondweiler,
Lux d: Aft. 1729 a: Thies h: Thies v: Schrondweiler, Lux o:
Farmer r: b c: 8

+ seq: 020 REUTER, Elisabeth b: Abt. 1660 in Blaschette, Lux
d: Aft. 1716 w: 11 Jan 1688 in Nommern, Lux v:
Schrondweiler, Lux r: m c: 8

4 WITRY, Marie b: 15 Oct 1688 in Schrondweiler, Lux d: 16
Mar 1777 in Schrondweiler, Lux a: Thies h: Thies v:
Schrondweiler, Lux r: bd c: 8

+ seq: 020.01 RADERMACHER, Anton b: Abt. 1685 in
Niederanven, Lux d: 16 Dec 1780 in Schrondweiler, Lux w:
Abt. 1705 a: Thies h: Thies v: Schrondweiler, Lux c: 8

4 WITRY, Johann-Baptist b: 15 Mar 1692 in Schrondweiler, Lux
d: Aft. 1745 a: Thies h: Thies v: Bergem, Lux r: b c: 10

+ seq: 021 DONDELINGER, Magdalena b: Abt. 1695 in
Schiffelange, Lux d: Aft. 1758 w: Abt. 1715 in Bergem, Lux
h: Thies v: Bergem, Lux r: x f: Theodor Dondelinger m:
Marie Steichen c: 10

4 WITRY, Elisabeth b: 07 Jan 1694 in Schrondweiler, Lux a:
Thies r: b

4 WITRY, Elisabeth b: 23 Apr 1695 in Schrondweiler, Lux a:
Thies r: b

4 WITRY, Michel b: 08 Feb 1698 in Schrondweiler, Lux a: Thies
r: b

4 WITRY, Catherine b: 25 Jun 1699 in Schrondweiler, Lux a:
Thies v: Berg, Lux r: b

4 [1] WITRY, Marie-Franzisca-Xaveria (Severa) b: 26 Feb 1702
in Schrondweiler, Lux a: Thies h: Peffer v: Niederglabach, Lux
r: b c: 8

+ seq: 119.05 PEFFER, Adam b: Abt. 1697 in Niederglabach,
Lux d: 16 Aug 1754 in Niederglabach, Lux w: 1722 h: Peffer
v: Niederglabach, Lux o: Farmer r: d f: Jean Peffer m:
Marguerite Mehlen c: 8

* 2nd Husband of [1] WITRY, Marie-Franzisca-Xaveria (Severa):

+ seq: 119.10 HAMES, Corneille b: 1700 in Senningen, Lux d:

12 Jan 1789 in Niederglabach, Lux w: 19 Nov 1754 in
Nommern, Lux v: Niederglabach, Lux r: d r: m
4 [2] WITRY, Nicolas b: 11 Jun 1708 in Schrondweiler, Lux d:
Aft. 1780 v: Beidweiler, Lux v: Bergem, Lux o: Laborer o:
Farmer r: b c: 11
+ seq: 120 PIERE, Anna b: 02 Apr 1724 in Rumelange, Lux d:
Abt. 1763 in Schiffelange, Lux w: Abt. 1744 in Bergem, Lux
a: Fischbach v: Bergem, Lux r: b r: x f: Jacques (Jacob) Piere
m: Margaretha (Anna-Marie) Weinand c: 10
* 2nd Wife of [2] WITRY, Nicolas:
+ seq: 309 HYMBERT, Marie b: Abt. 1740 in Kayl, Lux w: 27
Jan 1765 in Schiffelange, Lux v: Bergem, Lux r: x c: 1

020.01

4 WITRY, Marie b: 15 Oct 1688 in Schrondweiler, Lux d: 16
Mar 1777 in Schrondweiler, Lux a: Thies h: Thies v:
Schrondweiler, Lux r: bd c: 8
+ seq: 020.01 RADERMACHER, Anton b: Abt. 1685 in
Niederanven, Lux d: 16 Dec 1780 in Schrondweiler, Lux w:
Abt. 1705 a: Thies h: Thies v: Schrondweiler, Lux c: 8
5 RADERMACHER, Heinrich b: Abt. 1707 in Schrondweiler,
Lux d: 06 Dec 1780 in Schrondweiler, Lux a: Meyer h: Meyer
v: Nommern, Lux r: d
+ seq: 020.02 BOURTZ, Marie b: Abt. 1710 in Schrondweiler,
Lux w: Abt. 1735 in Nommern, Lux h: Meyer v: Nommern,
Lux
5 RADERMACHER, Peter-Heinrich b: 10 Feb 1709 in
Schrondweiler, Lux a: Thies v: Schrondweiler, Lux r: b
+ seq: 020.03 BREYDEN, Angela b: Abt. 1710 w: Abt. 1736 v:
Schrondweiler, Lux
5 RADERMACHER, Johann b: 27 Sep 1711 in Schrondweiler,
Lux d: 25 Nov 1780 in Schrondweiler, Lux a: Meyer h: Meyer
v: Schrondweiler, Lux r: b
+ seq: 020.04 SCHONS, Susanne b: Abt. 1715 in Schrondweiler,
Lux w: Abt. 1738 h: Meyer v: Schrondweiler, Lux
5 RADERMACHER, Marie-Catherine b: Abt. 1713 in
Schrondweiler, Lux d: 05 Feb 1764 in Schrondweiler, Lux v:
Schrondweiler, Lux r: d c: 8
+ seq: 020.05 RIES, Johann b: Abt. 1710 in Eichelbour, Lux d:
27 Jan 1764 in Schrondweiler, Lux w: Abt. 1735 in Nommern,
Lux v: Schrondweiler, Lux o: Steward r: d c: 8

5 RADERMACHER, Anna-Marie (Catherine) b: 19 Oct 1720 in Schrondweiler, Lux d: 08 Mar 1788 in Niedermertzig, Lux h: Koob v: Niedermertzig, Lux o: Farmer r: bd c: 7

+ seq: 020.06 WEILAND, Johann-Peter b: 05 Jun 1717 in Niedermertzig, Lux d: 04 Sep 1788 in Niedermertzig, Lux w: 04 Feb 1742 in Feulen, Lux a: Koob h: Koob v: Niedermertzig, Lux o: Farmer r: bd r: m f: Johann Koob m: Catherine c: 7

5 RADERMACHER, Catherine b: 12 Sep 1723 in Schrondweiler, Lux d: 19 Nov 1786 in Schrondweiler, Lux v: Schrondweiler, Lux r: b

+ seq: 020.07 CLEMENTEN, Johann b: Abt. 1720 in Medernach, Lux w: Abt. 1745 in Nommern, Lux v: Schrondweiler, Lux

5 RADERMACHER, Philipp b: 01 Nov 1726 in Schrondweiler, Lux d: 23 Jan 1807 in Schrondweiler, Lux v: Schrondweiler, Lux r: b

5 RADERMACHER, Nicolas b: 31 Jan 1733 in Schrondweiler, Lux d: 04 Jan 1807 in Schrondweiler, Lux v: Schrondweiler, Lux

020.05

5 RADERMACHER, Marie-Catherine b: Abt. 1713 in Schrondweiler, Lux d: 05 Feb 1764 in Schrondweiler, Lux v: Schrondweiler, Lux r: d c: 8

+ seq: 020.05 RIES, Johann b: Abt. 1710 in Eichelbour, Lux d: 27 Jan 1764 in Schrondweiler, Lux w: Abt. 1735 in Nommern, Lux v: Schrondweiler, Lux o: Steward r: d c: 8

6 RIES, Marie-Catherine b: 12 Nov 1738

6 RIES, Anna-Marie b: 30 Jul 1740

6 RIES, Heinrich b: 13 Apr 1743 d: 17 Apr 1798 in Schrondweiler, Lux

+ seq: 020.05.01 KRIPPES, Catherine b: Abt. 1735 w: 22 Sep 1760 in Echtenach, Lux

6 RIES, Catherine b: 27 Feb 1746 in Schrondweiler, Lux

6 RIES, Philipp b: 28 Jul 1748 in Eichelbour, Lux

6 RIES, Valentin b: 16 Feb 1751

+ seq: 020.05.02 HECHT, Susanne b: Abt. 1755 w: 24 Nov 1778 in Diekirch, Lux

6 RIES, Mathias b: 12 Feb 1754 d: 06 Jun 1846

+ seq: 020.05.03 KIPGEN, Catherine b: Abt. 1755 w: 06 Nov 1788 in Glabach, Lux

6 RIES, Nikolaus b: 20 Aug 1757 d: 17 Jan 1839 in Oberglabach, Lux

020.06

5 RADERMACHER, Anna-Marie (Catherine) b: 19 Oct 1720 in Schrondweiler, Lux d: 08 Mar 1788 in Niedermertzig, Lux h: Koob v: Niedermertzig, Lux o: Farmer r: bd c: 7
+ seq: 020.06 WEILAND, Johann-Peter b: 05 Jun 1717 in Niedermertzig, Lux d: 04 Sep 1788 in Niedermertzig, Lux w: 04 Feb 1742 in Feulen, Lux a: Koob h: Koob v: Niedermertzig, Lux o: Farmer r: bd r: m f: Johann Koob m: Catherine c: 7
6 WEILAND, Marie-Catherine b: 06 Apr 1745 in Niedermertzig, Lux r: b
6 WEILAND, Susanne b: 20 Oct 1747 in Niedermertzig, Lux d: 27 Feb 1754 in Niedermertzig, Lux v: Niedermertzig, Lux r: bd
6 WEILAND, Catherine b: 15 Jan 1750 in Niedermertzig, Lux d: 28 Jan 1750 in Niedermertzig, Lux v: Niedermertzig, Lux r: bd
6 WEILAND, Elisabeth b: 05 Feb 1752 in Niedermertzig, Lux r: b
6 WEILAND, Anna-Marie b: 24 Oct 1754 in Niedermertzig, Lux r: b
6 WEILAND, Marie-Catherine b: 29 Jul 1758 in Niedermertzig, Lux d: 03 Jun 1765 in Niedermertzig, Lux v: Niedermertzig, Lux r: bd
6 WEILAND, Margaretha b: 06 Sep 1760 in Niedermertzig, Lux d: 01 Mar 1765 in Niedermertzig, Lux v: Niedermertzig, Lux r: bd

021

4 WITRY, Johann-Baptist b: 15 Mar 1692 in Schrondweiler, Lux d: Aft. 1745 a: Thies h: Thies v: Bergem, Lux r: b c: 10
+ seq: 021 DONDELINGER, Magdalena b: Abt. 1695 in Schiffelange, Lux d: Aft. 1758 w: Abt. 1715 in Bergem, Lux h: Thies v: Bergem, Lux r: x f: Theodor Dondelinger m: Marie Steichen c: 10
5 WITRY, Theodor b: 28 Aug 1716 in Bergem, Lux a: Peters h: Peters v: Reuland, Lux o: Day laborer o: Farmer r: b
5 [1] WITRY, Heinrich (Henri-Jean) b: 18 May 1719 in Bergem, Lux d: 20 Nov 1795 in Seymerich, Belgium Cause of death: Apoplexy v: Seymerich, Belgium o: Farmer r: b c: 8

+ seq: 021.01 MORIAME, Anne-Marie b: 14 Mar 1723 in
Seymerich, Belgium d: 15 Sep 1757 in Seymerich, Belgium w:
27 Sep 1745 in Seymerich, Belgium v: Seymerich, Belgium r:
bd r: m f: Nicolas Moriame m: Marie-Catherine Bernard c: 3
* 2nd Wife of [1] WITRY, Heinrich (Henri-Jean):
+ seq: 021.24 FISCHER, Margaretha w: 16 Aug 1761 in Arlon,
Belgium v: Seymerich, Belgium r: m f: Mathias Fischer m:
Margaretha Caspar c: 5
5 WITRY, Johann-Baptiste b: 21 Jan 1721 in Bergem, Lux r: b
5 WITRY, Michel b: 22 Sep 1722 in Bergem, Lux r: b
5 WITRY, Marie b: 25 Apr 1724 in Bergem, Lux v: Leudelange,
Lux r: b
+ seq: 021.30 DONLINGER, Theodor w: 01 Feb 1743 in
Leudelange, Lux v: Leudelange, Lux
5 WITRY, Willebrord t: Parish elder b: 04 Mar 1726 in Bergem,
Lux d: 27 Apr 1801 in Schloewenhoff, Lux a: Schloewenhoff
v: Schloewenhoff, Lux o: Farmer r: bdx c: 6
+ seq: 022 HANSEN, Anna b: 06 Dec 1737 in Leudelange, Lux
d: 13 Feb 1804 in Leudelange, Lux w: 29 Apr 1754 in
Leudelange, Lux a: Sadler v: Schloewenhoff, Lux o: Farmer r:
bd r: m f: Ludwig Hansen m: Susanne c: 6
5 WITRY, Margaretha b: 26 Dec 1727 in Bergem, Lux r: b
5 WITRY, Marie-Catherine b: 06 Apr 1730 in Bergem, Lux d: 08
Jun 1796 in Heffingen, Lux h: Mausch v: Heffingen, Lux r: bd
+ seq: 036.03 KIRSCH, Nicolas t: Village trustee b: Abt. 1725 in
Heffingen, Lux d: 22 May 1786 in Heffingen, Lux w: 25 Jan
1749 in Heffingen, Lux a: Maisch v: Heffingen, Lux o: Farmer
r: d r: m f: Johann Kirsch m: Margaretha
5 WITRY, Anna-Catherine b: 04 Dec 1731 in Bergem, Lux h:
Villa Jean Henry r: b
5 WITRY, Theodor b: 24 Feb 1734 in Bergem, Lux d: 25 Dec
1819 in Reuland, Lux a: Petry h: Petry v: Reuland, Lux r: bd
c: 11
+ seq: 037 PETRY, Anna-Marie b: Abt. 1735 in Reuland, Lux d:
31 Dec 1807 in Reuland, Lux w: 21 Feb 1759 in Heffingen, Lux
a: Boudeler h: Peters v: Reuland, Lux o: Farmer r: d r: m f:
Peter Petry c: 11

021.01
5 [1] WITRY, Heinrich (Henri-Jean) b: 18 May 1719 in Bergem,
Lux d: 20 Nov 1795 in Seymerich, Belgium Cause of death:

Apoplexy v: Seymerich, Belgium o: Farmer r: b c: 8
+ seq: 021.01 MORIAME, Anne-Marie b: 14 Mar 1723 in
    Seymerich, Belgium d: 15 Sep 1757 in Seymerich, Belgium w:
    27 Sep 1745 in Seymerich, Belgium v: Seymerich, Belgium r:
    bd r: m f: Nicolas Moriame m: Marie-Catherine Bernard c: 3
6 WITRY, Jean-Nicolas b: 02 Dec 1746 in Arlon, Belgium d: 08
    Apr 1808 in Seimerich, Belgium v: Colpach Bas, Lux v:
    Seymerich, Belgium o: Administrator of the properties of
    Georgi of Horkheim o: Farmer r: bd c: 9
+ seq: 021.02 BROSIUS, Barbara b: in Schwarzenhoff, Lux w:
    26 Sep 1773 in Arlon, Belgium v: Colpach Bas, Lux v:
    Seymerich, Belgium r: m f: Jacob Brosius m: Barbara Gerardy
    c: 9
6 WITRY, Jean-Louis b: 06 Dec 1749 in Seymerich, Belgium r:
    bd
6 WITRY, Anne-Marie b: 29 Oct 1756 in Seymerich, Belgium d:
    07 Mar 1801 in Seymerich, Belgium v: Arlon, Belgium r: bd c:
    3
+ seq: 021.23 COLLART, Mathias w: 20 May 1784 in Arlon,
    Belgium v: Arlon, Belgium o: Day laborer o: Farmer r: m c: 3
* 2nd Wife of [1] WITRY, Heinrich (Henri-Jean):
+ seq: 021.24 FISCHER, Margaretha w: 16 Aug 1761 in Arlon,
    Belgium v: Seymerich, Belgium r: m f: Mathias Fischer m:
    Margaretha Caspar c: 5
6 WITRY, Henri b: 20 May 1763 in Seymerich, Belgium v:
    Arlon, Belgium i: Serf in Guirsch, Belgium i: Emigrated to
    Stockholm, Sweden o: Farmer r: b
+ seq: 021.25 GUILLAUME, Maria-Josepha b: 30 Oct 1772 in
    Arlon, Belgium w: 07 Oct 1788 in Beckerich, Lux v: Arlon,
    Belgium r: b r: m f: Paul Guillaume m: Catharina Theis
6 WITRY, Peter b: 01 Oct 1764 in Seymerich, Belgium d: 29
    Dec 1833 v: Stockem, Belgium o: Farmer o: Day laborer r: b
    c: 12
+ seq: 021.26 REINERT, Anne-Elisabeth b: 16 Jun 1762 in
    Petersmuhle, Belgium w: 07 Oct 1793 in Arlon, Belgium v:
    Stockem, Belgium r: b r: m f: Peter Reinert m: Catharina
    Schmit c: 12
6 WITRY, Anna b: 04 Jul 1766 in Seymerich, Belgium d: 19 Jan
    1831 in Seymerich, Belgium r: bd
+ seq: 021.27 WILWERTZ, Christophe b: Abt. 1761 in Pisport,
    Belgium d: 12 Jan 1806 in Arlon, Belgium w: 03 Feb 1790 in

Arlon, Belgium o: Carpenter o: Day laborer r: d r: m f: Henry
Wilwertz m: Maria-Johannata Pauli

6 WITRY, Maria-Theresa b: 11 Mar 1768 in Seymerich, Belgium
 d: 06 Jan 1838 in Consthum, Belgium v: Consthum, Belgium r:
 bd

+ seq: 021.28 FREILING, Peter d: Bef. 1838 w: 03 May 1793 in
 Arlon, Belgium v: Consthum, Belgium r: m f: Michael Freiling
 m: Maria Schmit

6 WITRY, Anna-Margaretha b: 15 Nov 1770 in Seymerich,
 Belgium d: 11 Jul 1830 in Seymerich, Belgium v: Stockem,
 Belgium r: bd c: 1

+ seq: 021.29 SIMON, Andre w: 08 Jun 1797 v: Stockem,
 Belgium o: Day laborer r: m f: Nicolas Simon m: Magdalena
 Jieres c: 1

021.02

6 WITRY, Jean-Nicolas b: 02 Dec 1746 in Arlon, Belgium d: 08
 Apr 1808 in Seimerich, Belgium v: Colpach Bas, Lux v:
 Seymerich, Belgium o: Administrator of the properties of
 Georgi of Horkheim o: Farmer r: bd c: 9

+ seq: 021.02 BROSIUS, Barbara b: in Schwarzenhoff, Lux w:
 26 Sep 1773 in Arlon, Belgium v: Colpach Bas, Lux v:
 Seymerich, Belgium r: m f: Jacob Brosius m: Barbara Gerardy
 c: 9

7 [1] WITRY, Marie-Barbara b: 05 Jul 1774 in Seymerich,
 Belgium d: 04 Jan 1832 in Seymerich, Belgium v: Seymerich,
 Belgium o: Farmer r: bd c: 6

+ seq: 021.03 ZIMMER, Johann-Viria (Jean) w: Abt. 1800 v:
 Mondercange, Lux c: 2

* 2nd Husband of [1] WITRY, Marie-Barbara:

+ seq: 021.05 KUNTZIGER, Jacques b: Abt. 1771 in Noerdange,
 Lux d: 29 Dec 1831 in Seymerich, Belgium w: 13 Mar 1808 in
 Arlon, Belgium v: Seymerich, Belgium o: Farmer r: d r: m f:
 Henry Kuntziger m: Marguerithe Kispach c: 4

7 WITRY, Jean-Etienne b: 03 Oct 1775 in Seymerich, Belgium
 d: 16 Dec 1851 in Seymerich, Belgium v: Seymerich, Belgium
 v: Paris, France i: St. Donatus parish r: bd c: 1

+ seq: 021.10 GODEFROY, Marie-Catherine-Josepha b: Abt.
 1792 w: Abt. 1810 o: Housekeeper c: 1

7 WITRY, Marie-Catherine b: 25 Dec 1776 in Seymerich,
 Belgium v: Rouver, Germany o: Farmer r: b

+ seq: 021.11 CHRISTNACH, Antoine b: Abt. 1774 in Arlon, Belgium w: 17 Jun 1810 in Arlon, Belgium v: Rouver, Germany o: Churchwarden r: m f: Nicolas Christnach m: Elisabeth Thill

7 WITRY, Johann-Nicolas b: 08 Nov 1779 in Colpach Bas, Lux d: 13 Apr 1808 in Arlon, Belgium o: Farmer r: bd

7 WITRY, Johann-Baptiste b: 03 Apr 1781 in Colpach Bas, Lux r: b

7 WITRY, Marie-Francoise b: 28 Jun 1782 in Colpach Bas, Lux d: in Seymerich, Belgium v: Seymerich, Belgium r: b

7 WITRY, Johann-Nicolas-Francis b: 07 Feb 1784 in Colpach Bas, Lux r: b

7 WITRY, Margaretha-Juliana (Marie-Julienne) b: 19 Jun 1786 in Colpach Bas, Lux d: 28 Aug 1859 in Arlon, Belgium v: Arlon, Belgium o: No profession r: bd

+ seq: 021.12 MENAGE, Pierre b: in Arlon, Belgium w: Abt. 1810 v: Arlon, Belgium o: Butcher

7 WITRY, Michel b: 07 Apr 1788 in Colpach-Bas, Lux d: 17 Jan 1870 in Seymerich, Belgium v: Seymerich, Belgium i: Two other children died young i: Godmother was Maria-Christina of Horkheim i: Military retiree i: St. Donatus parish o: Day laborer o: Farmer r: bd c: 10

+ seq: 021.13 JUNGERS, Marie-Anne b: in Arlon, Belgium d: 02 Jan 1887 in Seymerich, Belgium w: 22 Apr 1830 in Arlon, Belgium v: Seymerich, Belgium o: No profession r: d r: m f: Jean-Baptiste Jungers m: Margaretha Kries c: 10

021.03

7 [1] WITRY, Marie-Barbara b: 05 Jul 1774 in Seymerich, Belgium d: 04 Jan 1832 in Seymerich, Belgium v: Seymerich, Belgium o: Farmer r: bd c: 6

+ seq: 021.03 ZIMMER, Johann-Viria (Jean) w: Abt. 1800 v: Mondercange, Lux c: 2

8 ZIMMER, Jean

8 ZIMMER, Johann-Nicolas b: 08 Nov 1801 in Seymerich, Belgium i: Several children o: Rural guard o: Day laborer r: b

+ seq: 021.04 w: Abt. 1830 in Frassem, Belgium

* 2nd Husband of [1] WITRY, Marie-Barbara:

+ seq: 021.05 KUNTZIGER, Jacques b: Abt. 1771 in Noerdange, Lux d: 29 Dec 1831 in Seymerich, Belgium w: 13 Mar 1808 in Arlon, Belgium v: Seymerich, Belgium o: Farmer r: d r: m f:

Henry Kuntziger m: Marguerithe Kispach c: 4
8 KUNTZIGER, Barbe v: Arlon, Belgium
+ seq: 021.06 WAVER, Joseph w: Abt. 1840 in Arlon, Belgium
v: Arlon, Belgium o: Cap merchant
8 KUNTZIGER, Francoise v: Arlon, Belgium
+ seq: 021.07 MOERIS, Michel w: Abt. 1840 v: Arlon, Belgium
o: Professor at Royal Athenium of Arlon
8 KUNTZIGER, Jacques b: Abt. 1808 v: Seymerich, Belgium i:
Several children o: Farmer
+ seq: 021.08 w: Abt. 1835
8 KUNTZIGER, Andre b: Abt. 1813 v: Seymerich, Belgium i:
Several children o: Farmer
+ seq: 021.09 w: Abt. 1840

021.10
7 WITRY, Jean-Etienne b: 03 Oct 1775 in Seymerich, Belgium
d: 16 Dec 1851 in Seymerich, Belgium v: Seymerich, Belgium
v: Paris, France i: St. Donatus parish r: bd c: 1
+ seq: 021.10 GODEFROY, Marie-Catherine-Josepha b: Abt.
1792 w: Abt. 1810 o: Housekeeper c: 1
8 WITRY, Daughter b: in Paris, France d: in Paris, France v:
Paris, France

021.13
7 WITRY, Michel b: 07 Apr 1788 in Colpach-Bas, Lux d: 17 Jan
1870 in Seymerich, Belgium v: Seymerich, Belgium i: Two
other children died young i: Godmother was Maria-Christina of
Horkheim i: Military retiree i: St. Donatus parish o: Day
laborer o: Farmer r: bd c: 10
+ seq: 021.13 JUNGERS, Marie-Anne b: in Arlon, Belgium d:
02 Jan 1887 in Seymerich, Belgium w: 22 Apr 1830 in Arlon,
Belgium v: Seymerich, Belgium o: No profession r: d r: m f:
Jean-Baptiste Jungers m: Margaretha Kries c: 10
8 WITRY, Suzanne b: 14 Feb 1831 in Seymerich, Belgium d:
1921 in Seymerich, Belgium v: Seymerich, Belgium r: b
8 WITRY, Andre-Michel b: 28 Mar 1832 in Seymerich, Belgium
d: 12 Dec 1832 in Seymerich, Belgium v: Seymerich, Belgium
r: bd
8 WITRY, Andre-Francois b: 13 May 1833 in Seymerich,
Belgium d: 1896 in Seymerich, Belgium v: Seymerich,
Belgium o: Farmer r: b

8 WITRY, Catherine b: 22 Jan 1835 in Seymerich, Belgium d: 1901 in Messancy, Belgium r: b

8 WITRY, Marie-Marguerite-Juliana b: 16 Apr 1836 in Seymerich, Belgium d: 1906 in Seymerich, Belgium v: Seymerich, Belgium r: b

8 WITRY, Jacques b: 14 Nov 1837 in Seymerich, Belgium d: 14 Nov 1837 in Seymerich, Belgium r: bd

8 WITRY, Marie-Catherine b: 15 Nov 1838 in Seymerich, Belgium d: 22 Aug 1859 in Seymerich, Belgium v: Seymerich, Belgium o: No profession r: bd

8 WITRY, Francois-Michel b: 10 Apr 1841 in Seymerich, Belgium d: 1933 v: Seymerich, Belgium v: Frassem, Belgium r: b

+ seq: 021.14 KULTGEN, Catherine b: in Frassem, Belgium d: 1933 in Seymerich, Belgium w: Abt. 1870 v: Frassem, Belgium

8 WITRY, Andre b: 24 Jan 1845 in Seymerich, Belgium d: 15 Nov 1907 in Seymerich, Belgium r: b c: 3

+ seq: 021.15 SCHROBILTGEN, Appoline b: 15 Nov 1867 in Messancy, Belgium d: Jul 1935 in Seymerich, Belgium w: 02 Dec 1893 c: 3

8 WITRY, Jacques b: 21 Oct 1846 in Seymerich, Belgium d: 31 Jan 1926 in Arlon, Belgium i: Senior cure of Messancy, Belgium i: Chevalier of the Order of Leopold i: Dean of Vielsalm, Belgium i: Cure of Ourthe, Belgium i: Ordained a priest o: Priest r: b

021.15

8 WITRY, Andre b: 24 Jan 1845 in Seymerich, Belgium d: 15 Nov 1907 in Seymerich, Belgium r: b c: 3

+ seq: 021.15 SCHROBILTGEN, Appoline b: 15 Nov 1867 in Messancy, Belgium d: Jul 1935 in Seymerich, Belgium w: 02 Dec 1893 c: 3

9 WITRY, Andre-Joseph b: 12 Nov 1897 d: 01 Jun 1937 v: Seymerich, Belgium c: 4

+ seq: 021.16 THOMAS, Josephine b: 18 Sep 1896 in Harlange, Lux d: 13 Nov 1954 w: May 1923 v: Seymerich, Belgium c: 4

9 WITRY, Julienne-Marie-Marguerite

+ seq: 021.21 GANGLER, Lucien b: in Tintange, Belgium w: Abt. 1925

9 WITRY, Marie-Catherine
+ seq: 021.22 HAAS, Rene-Jean-Baptiste b: in Metzert, Belgium
   w: Abt. 1925

021.16

9 WITRY, Andre-Joseph b: 12 Nov 1897 d: 01 Jun 1937 v:
   Seymerich, Belgium c: 4
+ seq: 021.16 THOMAS, Josephine b: 18 Sep 1896 in Harlange,
   Lux d: 13 Nov 1954 w: May 1923 v: Seymerich, Belgium c:
   4
10 WITRY, Maria b: 13 Apr 1924
10 WITRY, Appoline (Pauline) b: 18 May 1927 d: 20 Jun 2000 in
   Seymerich, Belgium v: Seymerich, Belgium c: 1
+ seq: 021.17 AREND, Jean b: 31 Dec 1921 d: 06 Feb 1992 w:
   31 May 1964 c: 1
10 WITRY, Jacqueline b: 28 Jan 1931
10 WITRY, Leon b: 18 Feb 1936 in Seymerich, Belgium d: 21
   Mar 1999 in Mont-Godinne, Belgium v: Arlon, Belgium c: 4
+ seq: 021.18 LIMPACH, Monique b: 30 Jun 1934 w: 06 May
   1961 v: Arlon, Belgium c: 4

021.17

10 WITRY, Appoline (Pauline) b: 18 May 1927 d: 20 Jun 2000 in
   Seymerich, Belgium v: Seymerich, Belgium c: 1
+ seq: 021.17 AREND, Jean b: 31 Dec 1921 d: 06 Feb 1992 w:
   31 May 1964 c: 1
11 AREND, Jacqueline b: 09 Jul 1965

021.18

10 WITRY, Leon b: 18 Feb 1936 in Seymerich, Belgium d: 21
   Mar 1999 in Mont-Godinne, Belgium v: Arlon, Belgium c: 4
+ seq: 021.18 LIMPACH, Monique b: 30 Jun 1934 w: 06 May
   1961 v: Arlon, Belgium c: 4
11 WITRY, Marie-Josee b: 15 Sep 1962 in Arlon, Belgium
11 WITRY, Astrid b: 02 Feb 1964 in Arlon, Belgium c: 1
+ seq: 021.19 ROISIN, Francois b: 19 Jan 1960 w: 03 Jul 1989
   c: 1
11 WITRY, Michel b: 31 Jul 1966 in Arlon, Belgium v: Namur,
   Belgium c: 3
+ seq: 021.20 MEUNIER, Martine b: 19 Jun 1968 w: Abt. 1990
   v: Namur, Belgium c: 3

11 WITRY, Jacques b: 06 Aug 1970 o: Priest

021.19
11 WITRY, Astrid b: 02 Feb 1964 in Arlon, Belgium c: 1
+ seq: 021.19 ROISIN, Francois b: 19 Jan 1960 w: 03 Jul 1989
   c: 1
12 ROISIN, Alice b: 12 Feb 1992 in Namur, Belgium

021.20
11 WITRY, Michel b: 31 Jul 1966 in Arlon, Belgium v: Namur,
   Belgium c: 3
+ seq: 021.20 MEUNIER, Martine b: 19 Jun 1968 w: Abt. 1990
   v: Namur, Belgium c: 3
12 WITRY, Julie b: 14 Aug 1994 in Namur, Belgium
12 WITRY, Jean b: 02 Sep 1997 in Namur, Belgium
12 WITRY, Antoine b: 29 Sep 2000 in Namur, Belgium

021.23
6 WITRY, Anne-Marie b: 29 Oct 1756 in Seymerich, Belgium d:
   07 Mar 1801 in Seymerich, Belgium v: Arlon, Belgium r: bd c:
   3
+ seq: 021.23 COLLART, Mathias w: 20 May 1784 in Arlon,
   Belgium v: Arlon, Belgium o: Day laborer o: Farmer r: m c:
   3
7 COLLART, Anna-Maria b: 14 Feb 1785 in Seymerich, Belgium
   r: b
7 COLLART, Johann-Nicolas b: 06 Jun 1793 in Bivercy, Belgium
   r: b
7 COLLART, Anna b: 25 Sep 1797 in Arlon, Belgium r: b

021.26
6 WITRY, Peter b: 01 Oct 1764 in Seymerich, Belgium d: 29
   Dec 1833 v: Stockem, Belgium o: Farmer o: Day laborer r: b
   c: 12
+ seq: 021.26 REINERT, Anne-Elisabeth b: 16 Jun 1762 in
   Petersmuhle, Belgium w: 07 Oct 1793 in Arlon, Belgium v:
   Stockem, Belgium r: b r: m f: Peter Reinert m: Catharina
   Schmit c: 12
7 WITRY, Elisabetha b: 13 Aug 1792 d: 07 Dec 1793 in
   Altenhoven, Belgium r: d
7 WITRY, Michael b: 13 Aug 1792

7 WITRY, Johann b: 03 May 1794 in Seymerich, Belgium r: b
7 WITRY, Marie b: 1795 in Strassem, Lux d: 17 Feb 1832 in
   Nothomb, Belgium o: Day laborer r: d
+ seq: 021.26.10 PILIER, Pierre w: Abt. 1820
7 WITRY, Heinrich b: 03 Feb 1796 in Seymerich, Belgium r: b
7 WITRY, Nicolas b: 03 Mar 1797 in Seymerich, Belgium v:
   Tontelange, Belgium o: Guardian of Tonetlange o: Day laborer
   r: b c: 3
+ seq: 021.26.20 WEILAND, Marguerite b: 09 Mar 1789 in Etta,
   Belgium d: 10 Mar 1862 in Attert, Belgium w: 23 Dec 1823 in
   Oberpallen, Lux v: Tontelange, Belgium o: Day laborer r: d r:
   m f: Nicolas Weiland m: Magdalena Barnich c: 3
7 WITRY, Peter b: 03 Mar 1797 in Seymerich, Belgium r: b
7 WITRY, Jonann b: 19 Dec 1798 in Seymerich, Belgium r: b
7 WITRY, Elisabetha b: 11 Aug 1800 in Seymerich, Belgium r: b
7 WITRY, Johann-Nicolas b: 23 Aug 1802 in Seymerich,
   Belgium o: Day laborer r: b
+ seq: 021.26.40 BARNICH, Catherine b: 03 May 1786 in
   Bonnert, Belgium w: 20 Jan 1835 in Attert, Belgium o: Day
   laborer r: m f: Pierre Barnich m: Catherine Raden
7 WITRY, Michael b: 23 Aug 1802 in Seymerich, Belgium v:
   Beckerich, Lux o: Day laborer r: b c: 3
+ seq: 021.26.50 LUCAS, Christina b: 24 Jul 1798 in Beckerich,
   Lux w: 10 Jan 1828 in Koerich, Lux a: Lux v: Beckerich, Lux
   r: m f: Johann Lux m: Catharina Lux c: 3
7 WITRY, Margaretha b: 24 Nov 1805 in Seymerich, Belgium r:
   b

021.26.20
7 WITRY, Nicolas b: 03 Mar 1797 in Seymerich, Belgium v:
   Tontelange, Belgium o: Guardian of Tonetlange o: Day laborer
   r: b c: 3
+ seq: 021.26.20 WEILAND, Marguerite b: 09 Mar 1789 in Etta,
   Belgium d: 10 Mar 1862 in Attert, Belgium w: 23 Dec 1823 in
   Oberpallen, Lux v: Tontelange, Belgium o: Day laborer r: d r:
   m f: Nicolas Weiland m: Magdalena Barnich c: 3
8 WITRY, Jean b: 19 Feb 1825 in Tontelange, Belgium v: Attert,
   Belgium o: Day laborer o: Shepherd r: b c: 3
+ seq: 021.26.30 THOMAS, Jeanne b: 22 Apr 1825 in
   Schockville, Belgium w: 18 Feb 1857 in Attert, Belgium v:
   Attert, Belgium o: Day laborer r: m f: Henry Thomas m:

Catherine Scholler c: 3
8 WITRY, Jean b: 1827 in Tontelange, Belgium
8 WITRY, Jean-Nicolas b: 29 May 1830 in Tontelange, Belgium
v: Attert, Belgium o: Day laborer o: Shepherd r: b c: 7
+ seq: 021.26.40 GOERENS, Susanne b: 25 Sep 1838 in Koerich,
Lux w: 23 Apr 1865 in Attert, Belgium v: Attert, Belgium o:
Day laborer r: m f: Jacques Goerens m: Anne-Marguerite
Useldinger c: 7

021.26.30
8 WITRY, Jean b: 19 Feb 1825 in Tontelange, Belgium v: Attert,
Belgium o: Day laborer o: Shepherd r: b c: 3
+ seq: 021.26.30 THOMAS, Jeanne b: 22 Apr 1825 in
Schockville, Belgium w: 18 Feb 1857 in Attert, Belgium v:
Attert, Belgium o: Day laborer r: m f: Henry Thomas m:
Catherine Scholler c: 3
9 WITRY, Jean b: 04 Dec 1857 in Attert, Belgium r: b
9 WITRY, Nicolas b: 28 Oct 1839 in Attert, Belgium r: b
9 WITRY, Andre b: 01 Dec 1864 in Schadeck, Belgium d: 14
Dec 1864 in Schadeck, Belgium r: bd

021.26.32
8 WITRY, Jean-Nicolas b: 29 May 1830 in Tontelange, Belgium
v: Attert, Belgium o: Day laborer o: Shepherd r: b c: 7
+ seq: 021.26.32 GOERENS, Susanne b: 25 Sep 1838 in Koerich,
Lux w: 23 Apr 1865 in Attert, Belgium v: Attert, Belgium o:
Day laborer r: m f: Jacques Goerens m: Anne-Marguerite
Useldinger c: 7
9 WITRY, Catherine b: 27 Jan 1866 in Attert, Belgium r: b
9 WITRY, Madeleine b: 17 May 1867 in Attert, Belgium d: 12
Feb 1869 in Attert, Belgium r: bd
9 WITRY, Elisabeth b: 03 Mar 1869 in Attert, Belgium r: b
9 WITRY, Susanne b: 26 Jan 1871 in Attert, Belgium r: b
9 WITRY, Mathias b: 01 Aug 1873 in Attert, Belgium r: b
9 WITRY, Catherine b: 02 Oct 1876 in Attert, Belgium r: b
9 WITRY, Johann-Baptiste b: 04 Dec 1882 in Attert, Belgium o:
Day laborer
+ seq: 021.26.34 BOURGEOIS, Marie-Julie w: 25 Dec 1906 in
Bertrange, Lux o: No profession r: m f: Louis Bourgeois

021.26.50

7 WITRY, Michael b: 23 Aug 1802 in Seymerich, Belgium v: Beckerich, Lux o: Day laborer r: b c: 3

+ seq: 021.26.50 LUCAS, Christina b: 24 Jul 1798 in Beckerich, Lux w: 10 Jan 1828 in Koerich, Lux a: Lux v: Beckerich, Lux r: m f: Johann Lux m: Catharina Lux c: 3

8 WITRY, Susanne b: 20 Sep 1828 in Koerich, Lux d: Bef. 1905 o: No profession r: b c: 1

+ seq: 021.26.60 THOMAS, Wilhelm b: 26 Jun 1825 in Beckerich, Lux d: Bef. 1905 w: 14 Jul 1852 in Koerich, Lux o: Day laborer r: m f: Heinrich Thomas m: Anne-Marie Brucker c: 1

8 WITRY, Anne b: 30 Jan 1831 in Koerich, Lux d: 09 Aug 1844 in Koerich, Lux v: Koerich, Lux o: No profession r: b

8 WITRY, Catherine b: 07 Apr 1834 in Koerich, Lux d: 04 Jun 1893 in Koerich, Lux v: Steinfort, Lux o: No profession r: bd c: 4

+ seq: 021.26.70 BEIDELER, Peter b: 30 Dec 1820 in Dippach, Lux d: 03 Jan 1894 in Koerich, Lux w: 13 Oct 1858 in Koerich, Lux v: Steinfort, Lux o: Pig herder o: Day laborer r: m f: Martin Beideler m: Marguerite Thomas c: 4

021.26.60

8 WITRY, Susanne b: 20 Sep 1828 in Koerich, Lux d: Bef. 1905 o: No profession r: b c: 1

+ seq: 021.26.60 THOMAS, Wilhelm b: 26 Jun 1825 in Beckerich, Lux d: Bef. 1905 w: 14 Jul 1852 in Koerich, Lux o: Day laborer r: m f: Heinrich Thomas m: Anne-Marie Brucker c: 1

9 THOMAS, Heinrich b: 04 Feb 1864 in Koerich, Lux d: 10 Mar 1905 in Schweich, Lux v: Schweich, Lux o: Shepherd r: d

+ seq: 021.26.65 SCHUH, Elisabeth b: 31 May 1856 in Mertert, Lux w: 16 Oct 1886 in Strassem, Lux v: Schweich, Lux o: Maid servant r: m f: Mathias Schuh m: Catherine Herweis

021.26.70

8 WITRY, Catherine b: 07 Apr 1834 in Koerich, Lux d: 04 Jun 1893 in Koerich, Lux v: Steinfort, Lux o: No profession r: bd c: 4

+ seq: 021.26.70 BEIDELER, Peter b: 30 Dec 1820 in Dippach, Lux d: 03 Jan 1894 in Koerich, Lux w: 13 Oct 1858 in

Koerich, Lux v: Steinfort, Lux o: Pig herder o: Day laborer r: m f: Martin Beideler m: Marguerite Thomas c: 4

9 BEIDELER, Jean b: 20 Jun 1860 in Koerich, Lux d: 01 Jul 1860 in Koerich, Lux v: Koerich, Lux o: No profession r: d

9 BEIDELER, Nicolas b: 15 Feb 1869 in Koerich, Lux r: b

9 BEIDELER, Antoine b: 15 Dec 1870 in Koerich, Lux o: Laborer r: b

9 BEIDELER, Antoine b: 05 Nov 1873 in Koerich, Lux r: b

021.29

6 WITRY, Anna-Margaretha b: 15 Nov 1770 in Seymerich, Belgium d: 11 Jul 1830 in Seymerich, Belgium v: Stockem, Belgium r: bd c: 1

+ seq: 021.29 SIMON, Andre w: 08 Jun 1797 v: Stockem, Belgium o: Day laborer r: m f: Nicolas Simon m: Magdalena Jieres c: 1

7 SIMON, Peter b: 04 Nov 1788 in Stockem, Belgium r: b

022

5 WITRY, Willebrord t: Parish elder b: 04 Mar 1726 in Bergem, Lux d: 27 Apr 1801 in Schloewenhoff, Lux a: Schloewenhoff v: Schloewenhoff, Lux o: Farmer r: bdx c: 6

+ seq: 022 HANSEN, Anna b: 06 Dec 1737 in Leudelange, Lux d: 13 Feb 1804 in Leudelange, Lux w: 29 Apr 1754 in Leudelange, Lux a: Sadler v: Schloewenhoff, Lux o: Farmer r: bd r: m f: Ludwig Hansen m: Susanne c: 6

6 WITRY, Jacob b: 26 Mar 1755 in Schloewenhoff, Lux d: 21 Nov 1836 in Redange, Lux h: Number 5 v: Redange, Lux o: Deputy justice of the peace o: Carpenter o: Assistant miller r: bd

+ seq: 022.01 WEYLAND, Elisabeth b: 01 May 1755 in Niedermertzig, Lux d: 16 Mar 1833 in Redange, Lux w: 25 Apr 1792 in Attert, Belgium r: d f: Francois Weyland m: Catherine Schwebach

6 WITRY, Susanne b: 21 Aug 1756 in Schloewenhoff, Lux d: 12 Apr 1828 in Arlon, Belgium v: Merl, Lux o: Farmer r: bd c: 1

+ seq: 022.02 REDING, Nicolas b: 01 Jan 1752 in Arlon, Belgium d: 26 Mar 1813 in Arlon, Belgium w: 20 Mar 1782 in Dudelange, Lux v: Arlon, Belgium v: Merl, Lux o: Day laborer o: Farmer r: bd r: m f: Nicolas Reding m: Marie Meyers c: 1

6 WITRY, Anna-Catherine b: 20 Mar 1758 in Schloewenhoff,

Lux d: 24 Feb 1825 in Lorentzweiler, Lux v: Blaschette, Lux
o: No profession r: bd c: 9

+ seq: 022.03 WAGNER, Heinrich t: Parish elder b: 26 Apr 1750
in Blaschette, Lux d: 08 Sep 1820 in Blaschette, Lux w: 09 Dec
1788 in Lorentzweiler, Lux h: Ras v: Blaschette, Lux o:
Laborer o: Farmer r: bd r: m f: Peter Wagner m: Marie
Bigeler c: 9

6 [1] WITRY, Johann b: 30 May 1759 in Schloewenhoff, Lux d:
12 Feb 1837 in Junglinster, Lux a: Weisger h: Weisger v:
Junglinster, Lux o: Plowman o: Landlord o: Farmer o: Laborer
r: bd c: 8

+ seq: 023 NILLES, Marie-Catherine b: Abt. 1765 in Junglinster,
Lux d: 07 Jan 1806 in Junglinster, Lux w: 22 Feb 1788 in
Junglinster, Lux h: Weisger v: Junglinster, Lux r: m f: Peter
Nilles m: Marie Brummer c: 6

* 2nd Wife of [1] WITRY, Johann:

+ seq: 032 COPONS, Barbara-Josefine-Charlotte b: 24 Jun 1774
in Altlinster, Lux d: 28 Apr 1849 in Bourglinster, Lux w: 30
Apr 1806 in Junglinster, Lux a: \De Copons\ v: Junglinster, Lux
o: Pensioneer o: Property owner r: d r: m f: Franz-Carl Copons
m: Margaretha Frisch c: 2

6 WITRY, Anna-Margaretha b: 23 May 1761 in Schloewenhoff,
Lux d: 17 Jul 1838 in Schloewenhoff, Lux h: Uselding v:
Schloewenhoff, Lux o: No profession r: bd c: 6

+ seq: 032.03 USELDING, Anton b: Abt. 1770 in Niederpallen,
Lux w: 18 Feb 1794 in Leudelange, Lux h: Uselding v:
Schloewenhoff, Lux o: Laborer o: Farmer o: Plowman r: m f:
Johann Uselding m: Susanne Reding c: 6

6 WITRY, Nicolas t: Mayor b: 16 Sep 1763 in Schloewenhoff,
Lux d: 04 Jul 1836 in Lorentzweiler, Lux v: Lorentzweiler, Lux
i: Revalidated marriage o: Plowman o: Property owner o: Day
laborer o: Innkeeper r: bd c: 6

+ seq: 033 WEIS, Angela b: 03 Sep 1776 in Gonderange, Lux d:
20 Mar 1831 in Lorentzweiler, Lux w: 24 Jan 1797 in
Junglinster, Lux v: Lorentzweiler, Lux i: Revalidated marriage
r: mx f: Michel Weis m: Susanne Decker c: 6

022.02

6 WITRY, Susanne b: 21 Aug 1756 in Schloewenhoff, Lux d: 12
Apr 1828 in Arlon, Belgium v: Merl, Lux o: Farmer r: bd c: 1

+ seq: 022.02 REDING, Nicolas b: 01 Jan 1752 in Arlon,

Belgium d: 26 Mar 1813 in Arlon, Belgium w: 20 Mar 1782 in Dudelange, Lux v: Arlon, Belgium v: Merl, Lux o: Day laborer o: Farmer r: bd r: m f: Nicolas Reding m: Marie Meyers c: 1

7 REDING, Anna-Margarita b: 07 Oct 1788 in Noerdange, Lux r: b

022.03

6 WITRY, Anna-Catherine b: 20 Mar 1758 in Schloewenhoff, Lux d: 24 Feb 1825 in Lorentzweiler, Lux v: Blaschette, Lux o: No profession r: bd c: 9

+ seq: 022.03 WAGNER, Heinrich t: Parish elder b: 26 Apr 1750 in Blaschette, Lux d: 08 Sep 1820 in Blaschette, Lux w: 09 Dec 1788 in Lorentzweiler, Lux h: Ras v: Blaschette, Lux o: Laborer o: Farmer r: bd r: m f: Peter Wagner m: Marie Bigeler c: 9

7 WAGNER, Willebrord b: 03 Nov 1789 in Blaschette, Lux h: Ras v: Blaschette, Lux o: Farmer r: b

7 WAGNER, Anna-Margaretha b: 01 Mar 1792 in Blaschette, Lux r: b

7 WAGNER, Marie-Catherine b: 21 Mar 1793 in Blaschette, Lux r: b

7 WAGNER, Anna b: 06 May 1794 in Blaschette, Lux r: b

7 WAGNER, Nicolas b: 30 Jan 1796 in Blaschette, Lux r: b

7 WAGNER, Anton b: 12 Mar 1798 in Blaschette, Lux r: b

7 WAGNER, Nicolas b: 27 Jul 1799 in Blaschette, Lux r: b

7 WAGNER, Andreas b: 18 Aug 1801 in Blaschette, Lux r: b

7 WAGNER, Catherine b: 11 Dec 1806 in Blaschette, Lux d: 18 Mar 1807 in Blaschette, Lux r: bd

023

6 [1] WITRY, Johann b: 30 May 1759 in Schloewenhoff, Lux d: 12 Feb 1837 in Junglinster, Lux a: Weisger h: Weisger v: Junglinster, Lux o: Plowman o: Landlord o: Farmer o: Laborer r: bd c: 8

+ seq: 023 NILLES, Marie-Catherine b: Abt. 1765 in Junglinster, Lux d: 07 Jan 1806 in Junglinster, Lux w: 22 Feb 1788 in Junglinster, Lux h: Weisger v: Junglinster, Lux r: m f: Peter Nilles m: Marie Brummer c: 6

7 WITRY, Marie b: 28 Aug 1789 in Junglinster, Lux d: 19 Mar 1877 in Junglinster, Lux v: Senningen, Lux o: Farmer o:

Laborer r: bd c: 10
+ seq: 023.01 GROOS, Nicolas b: 04 Apr 1785 in Junglinster, Lux
  d: 26 Apr 1867 in Junglinster, Lux w: 20 Dec 1815 in
  Junglinster, Lux v: Senningen, Lux o: Craftsman o: Plowman
  o: Farmer r: d r: m f: Francois Gros m: Elisabeth Coner c: 10
7 WITRY, Nicolas b: 17 Jul 1791 in Junglinster, Lux d: 25 Apr
  1792 in Junglinster, Lux v: Junglinster, Lux o: Notary o:
  Plowman r: bd
7 WITRY, Jacob b: 21 Apr 1793 in Junglinster, Lux d: 10 Jun
  1793 in Junglinster, Lux v: Junglinster, Lux o: Notary r: bd
7 WITRY, Anna b: 21 Jun 1794 in Junglinster, Lux d: 22 Apr
  1885 in Zittig, Lux h: Webers v: Bech, Lux o: Farmer r: bd c:
  12
+ seq: 023.02 MULLER, Theodor b: 26 Feb 1790 in Zittig, Lux
  d: 28 May 1861 in Zittig, Lux w: 14 Jan 1818 in Bech, Lux a:
  Miller h: Webers v: Zittig, Lux o: Farmer r: d r: m f:
  Heinrich Muller m: Elisabeth Kobsbruck c: 12
7 WITRY, Heinrich b: 09 Nov 1796 in Junglinster, Lux d: 17
  Mar 1860 in Junglinster, Lux v: Junglinster, Lux o: Mayor o:
  Farmer r: bd c: 5
+ seq: 026 NEPPER, Marie b: 05 May 1792 in Strassem, Lux d:
  Aft. 1862 w: 21 Jan 1817 in Junglinster, Lux v: Junglinster,
  Lux o: Farmer r: m f: Peter Nepper m: Margaretha Schroeder
  c: 5
7 WITRY, Marie-Margaretha b: 18 Sep 1798 in Junglinster, Lux
  d: 17 Oct 1824 in Godbrange, Lux h: Braun v: Godbrange, Lux
  r: bd c: 1
+ seq: 031.02 HILBERT, Nicolas b: 05 Mar 1798 in Godbrange,
  Lux d: 08 Jun 1872 in Godbrange, Lux w: 04 Dec 1823 in
  Junglinster, Lux h: Braun v: Godbrange, Lux o: Farmer r: m
  f: Johann Hilbert m: Catherine Blanz c: 1
* 2nd Wife of [1] WITRY, Johann:
+ seq: 032 COPONS, Barbara-Josefine-Charlotte b: 24 Jun 1774
  in Altlinster, Lux d: 28 Apr 1849 in Bourglinster, Lux w: 30
  Apr 1806 in Junglinster, Lux a: \De Copons\ v: Junglinster, Lux
  o: Pensioneer o: Property owner r: d r: m f: Franz-Carl Copons
  m: Margaretha Frisch c: 2
7 WITRY, Marie-Therese b: 25 Sep 1807 in Junglinster, Lux d:
  06 May 1847 in Junglinster, Lux v: Junglinster, Lux o: No
  profession r: bd
+ seq: 032.01 FINSTERWALD, Nicolas b: 20 Jul 1810 in

Junglinster, Lux w: 17 May 1836 in Junglinster, Lux v:
Junglinster, Lux o: Innkeeper o: Master carpenter r: b r: m f:
Hubert Finsterwald m: Marie-Catherine Finsterwald
7 WITRY, Marie-Catherine b: 28 Aug 1813 in Junglinster, Lux
  d: 28 Sep 1888 in Cottonville, IA v: St. Donatus, IA i:
  Emigrated to the U. S. o: No profession r: bd c: 4
+ seq: 032.02 HEBELER, Nicolas b: 03 Aug 1811 in Junglinster,
  Lux w: 10 May 1837 in Junglinster, Lux v: St. Donatus, IA i:
  Emigrated to the U. S. o: Farmer r: m f: Johann Hebeler m:
  Susanne Reckinger c: 4

023.01
7 WITRY, Marie b: 28 Aug 1789 in Junglinster, Lux d: 19 Mar
  1877 in Junglinster, Lux v: Senningen, Lux o: Farmer o:
  Laborer r: bd c: 10
+ seq: 023.01 GROOS, Nicolas b: 04 Apr 1785 in Junglinster,
  Lux d: 26 Apr 1867 in Junglinster, Lux w: 20 Dec 1815 in
  Junglinster, Lux v: Senningen, Lux o: Craftsman o: Plowman
  o: Farmer r: d r: m f: Francois Gros m: Elisabeth Coner c: 10
8 WITRY, Nicolas b: 22 Sep 1814 in Junglinster, Lux d: 31 Dec
  1814 in Junglinster, Lux v: Junglinster, Lux r: bd
8 GROOS, Barbara (Barbe) b: 18 Sep 1816 in Junglinster, Lux r:
  b
+ seq: 023.01.01 PHILIPPS, Jean-Pierre w: 06 Feb 1839 in
  Graulinster, Lux
8 GROOS, Maria-Margaretha b: 29 Jan 1818 in Junglinster, Lux
  d: 03 Feb 1847 in Junglinster, Lux v: Junglinster, Lux o: No
  profession r: bd
+ seq: 023.01.50 [1] HUSS, Heinrich b: 01 Apr 1811 in Brouch,
  Lux w: 07 Mar 1843 in Junglinster, Lux v: Brouch, Lux o:
  Farmer o: Plowman r: m f: Frantz Huss m: Anna-Marie
  Wagner
8 GROOS, Elisabetha b: 24 Nov 1819 in Junglinster, Lux v:
  Junglinster, Lux o: No profession r: b
+ seq: 023.01.70 DUSCHING, Nicolas b: 17 Jun 1807 in
  Junglinster, Lux w: 09 Jun 1845 in Junglinster, Lux v:
  Junglinster, Lux o: Day laborer r: m f: Johann Dusching m:
  Margareta Diderich
8 GROOS, Theodor b: 20 May 1821 in Junglinster, Lux o:
  Farmer r: b
8 GROOS, Anne b: 03 Jul 1825 in Junglinster, Lux o: No

profession r: b

+ seq: 023.01.75 [1] HUSS, Heinrich b: 01 Apr 1811 in Brouch,
   Lux w: 07 Mar 1840 in Junglinster, Lux v: Brouch, Lux o:
   Farmer o: Plowman r: m f: Frantz Huss m: Anna-Marie
   Wagner

8 GROOS, Catherine b: 08 Jan 1827 in Junglinster, Lux d: 08 Jan
   1827 in Junglinster, Lux r: bd

8 GROOS, Anne b: 08 Jun 1828 in Junglinster, Lux o: No
   profession r: b

+ seq: 023.01.80 PHILIPS, Jean b: 31 Jan 1821 in Graulinster,
   Lux w: 13 Feb 1850 in Junglinster, Lux o: Day laborer r: m f:
   Nicolas Philips m: Catherine Mollitor

8 GROOS, Johan b: 21 Oct 1830 in Junglinster, Lux d: 25 Apr
   1831 in Junglinster, Lux r: bd

8 GROOS, Catharina b: 17 May 1832 in Junglinster, Lux d: 20
   Nov 1858 in Junglinster, Lux o: No profession r: bd

+ seq: 023.01.85 LUDWIG, Nicolas b: 04 Sep 1822 in
   Junglinster, Lux w: 05 Feb 1851 in Junglinster, Lux o: Farmer
   r: m f: Peter Ludwig m: Catherine Lenz

023.02

7 WITRY, Anna b: 21 Jun 1794 in Junglinster, Lux d: 22 Apr
   1885 in Zittig, Lux h: Webers v: Bech, Lux o: Farmer r: bd c:
   12

+ seq: 023.02 MULLER, Theodor b: 26 Feb 1790 in Zittig, Lux
   d: 28 May 1861 in Zittig, Lux w: 14 Jan 1818 in Bech, Lux a:
   Miller h: Webers v: Zittig, Lux o: Farmer r: d r: m f:
   Heinrich Muller m: Elisabeth Kobsbruck c: 12

8 MULLER, Elisabeth b: 17 Oct 1818 in Zittig, Lux r: b

8 MULLER, Johann b: 14 Sep 1820 in Zittig, Lux r: bd

8 MULLER, Bernard b: 05 Sep 1821 in Zittig, Lux r: b

8 MULLER, Catherine b: 09 May 1824 in Zittig, Lux r: b

8 MULLER, Johann b: 19 Jan 1826 in Zittig, Lux r: b

8 MULLER, Anna Maria b: 15 Mar 1828 in Zittig, Lux d: 15 Sep
   1846 in Zittig, Lux o: No profession r: bd

8 MULLER, Tresia b: 17 Apr 1830 in Zittig, Lux r: b

8 MULLER, Anna b: 17 Aug 1832 in Zittig, Lux r: b

8 [1] MULLER, Catherine b: 07 Jan 1835 in Zittig, Lux o: No
   profession r: b

+ seq: 023.50 METZ, Evrard b: 17 Nov 1830 d: 06 Apr 1867 in
   Vianden, Lux w: 16 Jan 1861 in Vianden, Lux r: m f:

Reinhard Eltz m: Anna-Marie Alff
* 2nd Husband of [1] MULLER, Catherine:
+ seq: 023.70 ELTZ, Johann-Baptiste b: 24 Dec 1830 in Vianden,
  Lux w: 01 Jul 1868 in Vianden, Lux o: Municipal tax collector
  r: m f: Reinhart Eltz m: Anna-Maria Alff
8 MULLER, Johann b: 19 Jan 1836 in Zittig, Lux
8 MULLER, Elisabeth b: 06 Apr 1837 in Zittig, Lux v:
  Beidweiler, Lux o: Innkeeper r: b c: 5
+ seq: 024 WITRY, Nicolas b: 21 Jun 1831 in Beidweiler, Lux
  d: 16 Dec 1868 in Beidweiler, Lux w: 23 Feb 1859 in
  Rodenbourg, Lux v: Beidweiler, Lux i: Both are descendents
  of the family tree o: Farmer r: bd r: m f: Johann Witry m:
  Barbara Meyers c: 5
8 MULLER, Elisabeth b: 30 Apr 1840 in Zittig, Lux r: b

024

8 MULLER, Elisabeth b: 06 Apr 1837 in Zittig, Lux v:
  Beidweiler, Lux o: Innkeeper r: b c: 5
+ seq: 024 WITRY, Nicolas b: 21 Jun 1831 in Beidweiler, Lux d:
  16 Dec 1868 in Beidweiler, Lux w: 23 Feb 1859 in Rodenbourg,
  Lux v: Beidweiler, Lux i: Both are descendents of the family
  tree o: Farmer r: bd r: m f: Johann Witry m: Barbara Meyers
  c: 5
9 WITRY, Anna b: 27 Nov 1859 in Beidweiler, Lux h: Koims v:
  Beidweiler, Lux o: Farmer r: b c: 4
+ seq: 024.01 STEYER, Heinrich b: 26 Aug 1856 in Scheidgen,
  Lux w: 08 Jan 1879 in Rodenbourg, Lux a: Stiren a: Koims h:
  Koims v: Beidweiler, Lux o: Farmer r: m f: Nicolas Steyer m:
  Anna Molitor c: 4
9 WITRY, Peter b: 09 Jan 1861 in Beidweiler, Lux v: Paris,
  France o: Cartwright r: b
+ seq: 025 PERQUIN, Eugenie-Victorine b: 07 Jan 1869 in Paris,
  France w: 15 Jun 1889 in Paris, France v: Paris, France o:
  Seamstress r: m f: Jean Perquin m: Eugenie-Aglentarie Karbe
9 WITRY, Barbara b: 24 Aug 1863 in Beidweiler, Lux r: b
9 WITRY, Franz b: 28 Jun 1866 in Beidweiler, Lux r: b
9 WITRY, Johann-Peter b: 29 Feb 1868 in Beidweiler, Lux v:
  Germany o: Waiter in a cafe r: b

24.01

9 WITRY, Anna b: 27 Nov 1859 in Beidweiler, Lux h: Koims v:

Beidweiler, Lux o: Farmer r: b c: 4

+ seq: 024.01 STEYER, Heinrich b: 26 Aug 1856 in Scheidgen,
Lux w: 08 Jan 1879 in Rodenbourg, Lux a: Stiren a: Koims h:
Koims v: Beidweiler, Lux o: Farmer r: m f: Nicolas Steyer m:
Anna Molitor c: 4

10STEYER, Barbara b: 06 Sep 1879 in Beidweiler, Lux r: b

10STEYER, Magdalena (Catharina) b: 14 May 1881 in
Beidweiler, Lux o: No profession

+ seq: 024.20 FOEHR, Mathias b: 28 Apr 1876 in Ernster, Lux
w: 09 Dec 1909 in Rodenbourg, Lux o: Farmer r: m f: Mathias
Foehr m: Maria-Anna Weber

10STEYER, Maria b: 15 Nov 1883 in Beidweiler, Lux o: No
profession

+ seq: 024.50 KONSBRUCK, Pierre b: 22 Jan 1864 in
Beidweiler, Lux w: 22 Apr 1902 in Mondercange, Lux o:
Landowner r: m f: Franz Konsbruck m: Maria Kinnen

10STEYER, Nicolas Aloyse (Aloys) b: 15 May 1899 in
Beidweiler, Lux d: 12 Sep 1910 in Beidweiler, Lux o: No
profession r: bd

026

7 WITRY, Heinrich b: 09 Nov 1796 in Junglinster, Lux d: 17
Mar 1860 in Junglinster, Lux v: Junglinster, Lux o: Mayor o:
Farmer r: bd c: 5

+ seq: 026 NEPPER, Marie b: 05 May 1792 in Strassem, Lux d:
Aft. 1862 w: 21 Jan 1817 in Junglinster, Lux v: Junglinster,
Lux o: Farmer r: m f: Peter Nepper m: Margaretha Schroeder
c: 5

8 WITRY, Josefine b: 15 Jan 1818 in Junglinster, Lux d: 02 Mar
1896 in Junglinster, Lux v: Junglinster, Lux o: Farmer r: bd c:
1

+ seq: 026.01 RIES, Johann b: 12 Jul 1815 in Rodenbourg, Lux d:
25 Jan 1888 in Junglinster, Lux w: 27 Dec 1838 in Junglinster,
Lux v: Junglinster, Lux o: Farmer r: d r: m f: Adam Ries m:
Marie Engel c: 1

8 WITRY, Marie b: 04 May 1819 in Junglinster, Lux d: 11 Mar
1863 in Beaufort, Lux v: Beaufort, Lux o: No profession r: bd
c: 1

+ seq: 026.02 RECKINGER, Nicolas b: 22 Jul 1811 in
Angelsberg, Lux d: Aft. 1862 w: 17 Apr 1844 in Junglinster,
Lux v: Beaufort, Lux o: Merchant o: Trader r: m f: Nicolas

Reckinger m: Margaretha Hames c: 1

8 WITRY, Michel H. b: 24 Dec 1820 in Junglinster, Lux d: 1867 in Wisconsin v: La Crosse, WI v: Junglinster, Lux i: Emigrated to Iowa o: Farmer r: b c: 5

+ seq: 027 CONSBRUCK, Susanne b: 24 Apr 1838 in Junglinster, Lux d: 1873 in Garnett, KS w: 18 Mar 1858 in Junglinster, Lux v: Dubuque, IA v: Junglinster, Lux v: La Crosse, WI o: Ran a boarding house r: b r: m f: Nicolas Consbruck m: Catherine Fenning c: 5

8 WITRY, Johann-Michel b: 02 Mar 1823 in Junglinster, Lux d: 27 Dec 1917 in Luxembourg, Lux v: Junglinster, Lux o: Property owner o: Farmer r: bd c: 4

+ seq: 031 MULLER, Elisabeth (Luise) b: 01 May 1840 in Zittig, Lux d: Aft. 1917 w: 07 May 1862 v: Junglinster, Lux o: Farmer r: m c: 4

8 WITRY, Therese b: 23 Jan 1831 in Junglinster, Lux d: 14 Jul 1920 in Dubuque, IA v: Dubuque IA v: Nommern, Lux i: Emigrated to St. Catherine, IA i: moved to Dubuque, IA o: No profession r: b c: 1

+ seq: 031.01.80 STOLTZ, Valentin b: 21 May 1827 in Lorentzweiler, Lux d: 1895 in Duuque, IA w: 18 Mar 1857 in Junglinster, Lux h: Bofferding v: Dubuque,IA v: Nommern, Lux i: Emigrated to St. Catherine, IA i: moved to Dubuque, IA o: Gentleman r: b r: m f: Johann Stoltz m: Marie Siren c: 1

026.01

8 WITRY, Josefine b: 15 Jan 1818 in Junglinster, Lux d: 02 Mar 1896 in Junglinster, Lux v: Junglinster, Lux o: Farmer r: bd c: 1

+ seq: 026.01 RIES, Johann b: 12 Jul 1815 in Rodenbourg, Lux d: 25 Jan 1888 in Junglinster, Lux w: 27 Dec 1838 in Junglinster, Lux v: Junglinster, Lux o: Farmer r: d r: m f: Adam Ries m: Marie Engel c: 1

9 RIES, Heinrich b: 18 Dec 1839 in Junglinster, Lux v: Junglinster, Lux o: Farmer r: b

026.02

8 WITRY, Marie b: 04 May 1819 in Junglinster, Lux d: 11 Mar 1863 in Beaufort, Lux v: Beaufort, Lux o: No profession r: bd c: 1

+ seq: 026.02 RECKINGER, Nicolas b: 22 Jul 1811 in

Angelsberg, Lux d: Aft. 1862 w: 17 Apr 1844 in Junglinster,
Lux v: Beaufort, Lux o: Merchant o: Trader r: m f: Nicolas
Reckinger m: Margaretha Hames c: 1
9 RECKINGER, Therese b: Abt. 1852 v: Beaufort, Lux o:
Storekeeper

027

8 WITRY, Michel H. b: 24 Dec 1820 in Junglinster, Lux d: 1867
in Wisconsin v: La Crosse, WI v: Junglinster, Lux i: Emigrated
to Iowa o: Farmer r: b c: 5
+ seq: 027 CONSBRUCK, Susanne b: 24 Apr 1838 in
Junglinster, Lux d: 1873 in Garnett, KS w: 18 Mar 1858 in
Junglinster, Lux v: Dubuque, IA v: Junglinster, Lux v: La
Crosse, WI o: Ran a boarding house r: b r: m f: Nicolas
Consbruck m: Catherine Fenning c: 5
9 [1] WITRY, Theresa W. b: 23 Jan 1858 d: 18 Apr 1934 v:
Dubuque, IA o: Grocer c: 2
+ seq: 027.01 JUNGLES, Nicolas w: 23 Oct 1876 in Dubuque,
IA v: Dubuque,IA o: Storekeeper c: 1
* 2nd Husband of [1] WITRY, Theresa W.:
+ seq: 027.03 BADE d: Abt. 1926 w: 1892 v: Dubuque, IA o:
Grocer c: 1
9 WITRY, Mary b: 20 Sep 1859 d: 13 Mar 1926
+ seq: 027.04 HAGER w: Abt. 1880
9 WITRY, Katherine (Kate) b: 23 Apr 1861 v: Chicago, IL
+ seq: 027.05 CULBERTSON, J. M. w: Abt. 1885 v: Chicago,
IL
9 WITTRY, Gustave b: 20 Apr 1863 in La Crosse, WI d: 11 Apr
1947 v: Greeley, KS o: Farmer c: 4
+ seq: 028 OSWALD, Elizabeth (Lucy) b: 06 Jul 1870 in
Anderson County, KS d: 23 Dec 1923 w: 09 Apr 1890 in
Garnett, KS f: John Oswald m: Catherine Weber c: 4
9 WITRY, Lucy b: 18 Oct 1866 d: 15 Jul 1911
+ seq: 030.14 HODGE, Richard w: Abt. 1890

027.01

9 [1] WITRY, Theresa W. b: 23 Jan 1858 d: 18 Apr 1934 v:
Dubuque, IA o: Grocer c: 2
+ seq: 027.01 JUNGLES, Nicolas w: 23 Oct 1876 in Dubuque,
IA v: Dubuque,IA o: Storekeeper c: 1
10JUNGLES, Norma v: Mason City, IA

+ seq: 027.02 MUTSCHELER, C. E. w: Abt. 1915 v: Mason City, IA
* 2nd Husband of [1] WITRY, Theresa W.:
+ seq: 027.03 BADE d: Abt. 1926 w: 1892 v: Dubuque, IA o: Grocer c: 1
10BADE, Walter W. v: Dubuque, IA

028

9 WITTRY, Gustave b: 20 Apr 1863 in La Crosse, WI d: 11 Apr 1947 v: Greeley, KS o: Farmer c: 4
+ seq: 028 OSWALD, Elizabeth (Lucy) b: 06 Jul 1870 in Anderson County, KS d: 23 Dec 1923 w: 09 Apr 1890 in Garnett, KS f: John Oswald m: Catherine Weber c: 4
10WITTRY, John b: 07 Dec 1890 d: 07 Dec 1890
10WITTRY, Eleanor (Lenora) b: 19 Feb 1893 d: 06 Feb 1920 in Berger Cause of death: influenza c: 3
+ seq: 028.01 BERGERHAUS, Leo b: 24 Aug 1891 d: 02 Feb 1920 w: 16 Feb 1915 c: 3
10WITTRY, Arthur O. b: 25 Aug 1895 d: 20 May 1957 v: Greeley, KS o: Farmer c: 5
+ seq: 029 LITSCH, Frances b: 06 Nov 1896 d: 19 Nov 1981 w: 24 Sep 1919 in Garnett, KS v: Greeley, KS c: 5
10WITTRY, Hubert (Hubie) b: 25 Aug 1898 d: 07 Feb 1920

028.01

10WITTRY, Eleanor (Lenora) b: 19 Feb 1893 d: 06 Feb 1920 in Berger Cause of death: influenza c: 3
+ seq: 028.01 BERGERHAUS, Leo b: 24 Aug 1891 d: 02 Feb 1920 w: 16 Feb 1915 c: 3
11BERGERHAUS, Ellen b: 19 Dec 1915 v: Kansas City, MO
11BERGERHAUS, Coletta E. b: 11 Oct 1917 in Greeley, KS d: 21 Aug 2005 in Overland Park, KS v: Kansas City, MO o: Executive secretary at General Motors
11BERGERHAUS, Maurice W. b: 15 Oct 1919 d: 29 Dec 1970 v: Denver, CO c: 2
+ seq: 028.02 YOUNG, Merna-Belle b: 29 Mar 1923 d: 17 Jun 1973 w: 09 Jun 1943 c: 2

028.02

11BERGERHAUS, Maurice W. b: 15 Oct 1919 d: 29 Dec 1970 v: Denver, CO c: 2

+ seq: 028.02 YOUNG, Merna-Belle b: 29 Mar 1923 d: 17 Jun
   1973 w: 09 Jun 1943 c: 2
12 BERGERHAUS, Dennis b: 13 May 1944 v: Denver, CO
12 BERGERHAUS, Carol J. b: 04 May 1948 v: Bennett, CO c: 3
+ seq: 028.03 DISHONG, John b: 31 Jul 1945 w: 18 Feb 1967
   v: Bennett, CO o: Fireman in Aurora, CO c: 3

028.03

12 BERGERHAUS, Carol J. b: 04 May 1948 v: Bennett, CO c: 3
+ seq: 028.03 DISHONG, John b: 31 Jul 1945 w: 18 Feb 1967
   v: Bennett, CO o: Fireman in Aurora, CO c: 3
13 DISHONG, Bridgette b: 21 Jun 1968 c: 3
+ seq: 028.04 CUMLEY, Earl R. b: 02 May 1968 w: 05 Apr
   1991 c: 3
13 DISHONG, Wade b: 07 Apr 1970
13 DISHONG, Tammy b: 05 May 1972

028.04

13 DISHONG, Bridgette b: 21 Jun 1968 c: 3
+ seq: 028.04 CUMLEY, Earl R. b: 02 May 1968 w: 05 Apr
   1991 c: 3
14 CUMLEY, Chris b: 14 Oct 1985
14 CUMLEY, Tyler b: 21 Dec 1991
14 CUMLEY, Casey b: 28 Mar 1993

029

10 WITTRY, Arthur O. b: 25 Aug 1895 d: 20 May 1957 v:
   Greeley, KS o: Farmer c: 5
+ seq: 029 LITSCH, Frances b: 06 Nov 1896 d: 19 Nov 1981 w:
   24 Sep 1919 in Garnett, KS v: Greeley, KS c: 5
11 WITTRY, Richard H. b: 22 Apr 1924 in Greeley, KS v:
   Greeley, KS o: Farmer
+ seq: 029.01 BURRITT, Jo-Anne b: 24 Mar 1938 w: 30 Jul
   1977 in Garnett, KS
11 WITTRY, Gustave E. (Gus) b: 25 Nov 1929 in Greeley, KS v:
   Greeley, KS o: Farmer c: 7
+ seq: 030 SETTER, Ruth-Margaret b: 09 Apr 1936 w: 23 Aug
   1955 in Garnett, KS v: Greeley, KS f: Edward-William Setter
   m: Rose R. Heiman c: 7
11 WITTRY, Gladys b: 11 Jun 1920 in Greeley, KS v: Topeka, KS
+ seq: 030.07 NICHOLS, Roy b: 03 Mar 1923 d: 19 Oct 1982

w: 31 May 1947 v: Topeka, KS

11[1] WITTRY, Helen b: 21 Jan 1922 in Greeley, KS v: Topeka, KS c: 2

+ seq: 030.08 KELLEY, Charles A. b: 25 May 1920 w: 15 Oct 1942 in Anderson County, KS c: 1

* 2nd Husband of [1] WITTRY, Helen:

+ seq: 030.10 MCKNIGHT, Forrest b: 19 Jun 1916 d: 13 May 1979 w: Abt. 1956 v: Topeka, KS o: State highway c: 1

11[2] WITTRY, Betty-Jo b: 28 Jul 1932 in Greeley, KS v: Auburn, KS c: 1

+ seq: 030.11 BROWNBACK, Bill b: Mar 1930 w: Abt. 1951 in Topeka, KS v: Parker, KS c: 1

* 2nd Husband of [2] WITTRY, Betty-Jo:

+ seq: 030.13 DUTTON, Kirk b: 19 Jul 1917 w: 15 Oct 1971 in Topeka, KS v: Auburn, KS o: Dentist

030

11 WITTRY, Gustave E. (Gus) b: 25 Nov 1929 in Greeley, KS v: Greeley, KS o: Farmer c: 7

+ seq: 030 SETTER, Ruth-Margaret b: 09 Apr 1936 w: 23 Aug 1955 in Garnett, KS v: Greeley, KS f: Edward-William Setter m: Rose R. Heiman c: 7

12 WITTRY, Alan-Edward b: 21 May 1956 in Houston, TX v: Houston, TX o: Petroleum engineer c: 3

+ seq: 030.01 FRANK, Dorothy b: 09 Apr 1957 w: 21 May 1977 c: 3

12 WITTRY, Thomas-John (Tom) b: 07 Jun 1957 in Garnett, KS v: Greeley, KS o: Construction c: 2

+ seq: 030.02 CRONISTER, Terri b: 03 Dec 1956 in Joplin, MO w: 20 Apr 1992 in Olathe, KS c: 2

12 WITTRY, Patricia-Frances (Patty) b: 17 Mar 1959 v: Lawrence, KS o: Teacher

+ seq: 030.03 PEREZ, Maximo Martinez b: 20 Feb 1958 w: 21 Jun 1983 o: Computer

12 WITTRY, Christopher-Anthony (Chris) b: 24 Sep 1960 v: Louisburg, KS o: Welder c: 2

+ seq: 030.04 KATZER, Jo-Ann b: 31 Jul 1964 in Garnett, KS w: 04 Oct 1985 in Garnett, KS o: Teacher f: Harold-Edward (Bud) Katzer m: Judith-Ann Miner c: 2

12 WITTRY, Carl-Joseph b: 06 May 1962 v: Greeley, KS o: Construction foreman c: 2

+ seq: 030.05 HUETTENMUELLER, Karen-Ann b: 25 Jun 1963
  w: 13 Jun 1986 in Greeley, KS v: Greeley, KS f: Robert
  Huettenmueller m: Elizabeth (Betty) Miner c: 2
12 WITTRY, Ruth b: 15 Dec 1963 in Greeley, KS d: 16 Dec 1963
  in Greeley, KS
12 WITTRY, Janet-Susan b: 16 Dec 1965 v: Olathe, KS o: Bank
  auditor c: 1
+ seq: 030.06 WRIGHT, James b: 21 Oct 1956 w: 11 Aug 1990
  v: Olathe, KS o: Electrician c: 1

030.01
12 WITTRY, Alan-Edward b: 21 May 1956 in Houston, TX v:
  Houston, TX o: Petroleum engineer c: 3
+ seq: 030.01 FRANK, Dorothy b: 09 Apr 1957 w: 21 May 1977
  c: 3
13 WITTRY, Jared b: 01 Nov 1979 o: Plant design with Santa Rita
  Design
13 WITTRY, Nathan b: 27 Apr 1983 o: Student of Aerospace
  Engineering in U. of Texas
13 WITTRY, Eric b: 08 Aug 1987

030.02
12 WITTRY, Thomas-John (Tom) b: 07 Jun 1957 in Garnett, KS
  v: Greeley, KS o: Construction c: 2
+ seq: 030.02 CRONISTER, Terri b: 03 Dec 1956 in Joplin, MO
  w: 20 Apr 1992 in Olathe, KS c: 2
13 WITTRY, Tara-Ann b: 28 Nov 1983 in Joplin, MO o: Nursing
  student at Kansas U.
13 WITTRY, Katie b: 18 Apr 1987 in Garnett, KS

030.04
12 WITTRY, Christopher-Anthony (Chris) b: 24 Sep 1960 v:
  Louisburg, KS o: Welder c: 2
+ seq: 030.04 KATZER, Jo-Ann b: 31 Jul 1964 in Garnett, KS
  w: 04 Oct 1985 in Garnett, KS o: Teacher f: Harold-Edward
  (Bud) Katzer m: Judith-Ann Miner c: 2
13 WITTRY, Jacob-Joseph b: 27 Dec 1992
13 WITTRY, Rachel b: 13 Nov 1995

030.05
12 WITTRY, Carl-Joseph b: 06 May 1962 v: Greeley, KS o:

Construction foreman c: 2

+ seq: 030.05 HUETTENMUELLER, Karen-Ann b: 25 Jun 1963
   w: 13 Jun 1986 in Greeley, KS v: Greeley, KS f: Robert
   Huettenmueller m: Elizabeth (Betty) Miner c: 2

13 WITTRY, Chelsea-Jo b: 10 Mar 1989

13 WITTRY, Ryan-James b: 04 May 1993

030.06

12 WITTRY, Janet-Susan b: 16 Dec 1965 v: Olathe, KS o: Bank
   auditor c: 1

+ seq: 030.06 WRIGHT, James b: 21 Oct 1956 w: 11 Aug 1990
   v: Olathe, KS o: Electrician c: 1

13 WRIGHT, Marie-Susan b: 08 Aug 1996

030.08

11 [1] WITTRY, Helen b: 21 Jan 1922 in Greeley, KS v: Topeka,
   KS c: 2

+ seq: 030.08 KELLEY, Charles A. b: 25 May 1920 w: 15 Oct
   1942 in Anderson County, KS c: 1

12 KELLEY, Sharlys b: 17 Nov 1944 in Garnett, KS v: Topeka,
   KS

+ seq: 030.09 VIERGEVER, James b: Feb 1942 w: Abt. 1970 v:
   Overland Park, KS o: Veterinarian

* 2nd Husband of [1] WITTRY, Helen:

+ seq: 030.10 MCKNIGHT, Forrest b: 19 Jun 1916 d: 13 May
   1979 w: Abt. 1956 v: Topeka, KS o: State highway c: 1

12 MCKNIGHT, Douglas b: 04 Aug 1959 v: Topeka, KS o:
   Dental hygienist

030.11

11 [1] WITTRY, Betty-Jo b: 28 Jul 1932 in Greeley, KS v:
   Auburn, KS c: 1

+ seq: 030.11 BROWNBACK, Bill b: Mar 1930 w: Abt. 1951 in
   Topeka, KS v: Parker, KS c: 1

12 BROWNBACK, Cynthia-Kay b: 03 Oct 1952 v: Auburn, KS
   c: 2

+ seq: 030.12 JOHNSON, Jerry b: 26 Apr 1952 d: 15 Jun 1988
   w: Abt. 1970 c: 2

* 2nd Husband of [1] WITTRY, Betty-Jo:

+ seq: 030.13 DUTTON, Kirk b: 19 Jul 1917 w: 15 Oct 1971 in
   Topeka, KS v: Auburn, KS o: Dentist

030.12

12 BROWNBACK, Cynthia-Kay b: 03 Oct 1952 v: Auburn, KS
c: 2
+   seq: 030.12 JOHNSON, Jerry b: 26 Apr 1952 d: 15 Jun 1988
w: Abt. 1970 c: 2
13 JOHNSON, Amber-Lee b: 26 Aug 1975 v: Topeka, KS o:
Student at Washburn
13 JOHNSON, Dallas A. b: 14 Jun 1979 v: Lawrence, KS o:
Student at Kansas U.

031

8 WITRY, Johann-Michel b: 02 Mar 1823 in Junglinster, Lux d:
27 Dec 1917 in Luxembourg, Lux v: Junglinster, Lux o:
Property owner o: Farmer r: bd c: 4
+ seq: 031 MULLER, Elisabeth (Luise) b: 01 May 1840 in Zittig,
Lux d: Aft. 1917 w: 07 May 1862 v: Junglinster, Lux o:
Farmer r: m c: 4
9 WITRY, Michel-Valentin b: 21 May 1863 in Junglinster, Lux
d: 29 May 1872 in Junglinster, Lux v: Junglinster, Lux o: No
profession r: bd
9 WITRY, Marie-Therese b: 03 Oct 1864 in Junglinster, Lux d:
23 Jul 1943 in Tres Arroyos, Argentina Cause of death: of
chronic myocarditis v: Tres Arroyos, Argentina o: No
profession r: b c: 6
+ seq: 031.00.05 MULLER, Ludwig-Michel (Luis) b: 08 Nov
1864 in Nancy, France d: 02 Nov 1938 in Tres Arroyos,
Argentina Cause of death: of caridac arrest w: 27 Jan 1886 in
Junglinster, Lux v: Tres Arroyos, Argentina i: Arrived in
Argentina on 9-Nov-1886 o: Farmer r: m f: Mathias Muller m:
Maria Muller c: 6
9 WITRY, Anna b: 25 Apr 1868 in Junglinster, Lux d: 12 Sep
1898 in Junglinster, Lux v: Luxembourg, Lux o: No profession
r: b
+ seq: 031.01.60 [1] BOFFERDING, Nicolas b: 12 Apr 1863 in
Junglinster, Lux w: Abt. 1890 v: Luxembourg, Lux o: Prison
warden f: Johann Bofferding m: Susanna Altmann
9 WITRY, Elisabeth b: 16 May 1873 in Junglinster, Lux o: No
profession
+ seq: 031.01.70 [1] BOFFERDING, Nicolas b: 12 Apr 1863 in
Junglinster, Lux w: 27 Nov 1900 in Junglinster, Lux v:
Luxembourg, Lux o: Prison warden f: Johann Bofferding m:

Susanna Altmann

031.00.05

9 WITRY, Marie-Therese b: 03 Oct 1864 in Junglinster, Lux d:
  23 Jul 1943 in Tres Arroyos, Argentina Cause of death: of
  chronic myocarditis v: Tres Arroyos, Argentina o: No
  profession r: b c: 6

+ seq: 031.00.05 MULLER, Ludwig-Michel (Luis) b: 08 Nov
  1864 in Nancy, France d: 02 Nov 1938 in Tres Arroyos,
  Argentina Cause of death: of caridac arrest w: 27 Jan 1886 in
  Junglinster, Lux v: Tres Arroyos, Argentina i: Arrived in
  Argentina on 9-Nov-1886 o: Farmer r: m f: Mathias Muller
  m: Maria Muller c: 6

10 MULLER, Ludwig-Michel b: 07 Dec 1886 in Junglinster, Lux
  r: b

10 MULLER, Juan-Mauricio b: 25 May 1892 in Colonia Jerua,
  Depto de Concordia, Argentina c: 10

+ seq: 031.00.10 w: Abt. 1920 c: 10

10 MULLER, Rosa-Anna (Irene) b: 26 Aug 1894 in Colonia Jerua,
  Depto de Concordia, Argentina d: 24 Jul 1969 in Tres Arroyos,
  Argentina

10 MULLER, Maria-Teresa-Otillia (Matilde) b: 03 Aug 1896 in
  Colonia Jerua, Depto de Concordia, Argentina d: 22 Aug 1990
  in Tres Arroyos, Argentina

10 MULLER, Maria b: 26 Feb 1900 in Entre Rios, Argentina c: 3

+ seq: 031.00.40 CANUETO, Manuel w: Abt. 1925 c: 3

10 MULLER, Felix b: 07 Jul 1901 in Talita, Depto de Uruguay,
  Argentina d: 28 Jan 1991 in Tres Arroyos, Argentina v: Tres
  Arroyos, Argentina o: Small business owner c: 3

+ seq: 031.00.60 ALONSO, Maria b: 16 Jun 1903 in Tres
  Arroyos, Argentina d: 23 Jul 1997 in Tres Arroyos, Argentina
  w: 29 Dec 1924 in Tres Arroyos, Argentina v: Tres Arroyos,
  Argentina f: Domingo Alonso m: Carolina Rodriguez c: 3

031.00.10

10 MULLER, Juan-Mauricio b: 25 May 1892 in Colonia Jerua,
  Depto de Concordia, Argentina c: 10

+ seq: 031.00.10 w: Abt. 1920 c: 10

11 MULLER, Juan

11 MULLER, Roberto

11 MULLER, Felipe

11 MULLER, Carlos-Alberto b: Abt. 1932 d: 18 Mar 2005 in
   Bahia Blanca, Argentina c: 3
+ seq: 031.00.15 GOICOCHEA, Gladis w: Abt. 1955 c: 3
11 MULLER, Rosita
11 MULLER, Vilma
+ seq: 031.00.35 ZUBILLAGA w: Abt. 1960
11 MULLER, Elisa
11 MULLER, Miguel
11 MULLER, Mario
11 MULLER, Luis

030.00.15
11 MULLER, Carlos-Alberto b: Abt. 1932 d: 18 Mar 2005 in
   Bahia Blanca, Argentina c: 3
+ seq: 031.00.15 GOICOCHEA, Gladis w: Abt. 1955 c: 3
12 MULLER, Monica
+ seq: 031.00.20 LEMUS, Nestor w: Abt. 1985
12 MULLER, Isabel
+ seq: 031.00.25 DI MARCO, Gustavo w: Abt. 1985
12 MULLER, Paola
+ seq: 031.00.30 SEPULVEDA, Alejandro w: Abt. 1985

031.00.40
10 MULLER, Maria b: 26 Feb 1900 in Entre Rios, Argentina c: 3
+ seq: 031.00.40 CANUETO, Manuel w: Abt. 1925 c: 3
11 CANUETO, Blanca
+ seq: 031.00.45 LANCE, Alfredo w: Abt. 1950
11 CANUETO, Mita c: 3
+ seq: 031.00.50 VASSOLO, Ricardo w: Abt. 1975 c: 3
11 CANUETO, Hilda
+ seq: 031.00.55 DUCA, Esteban w: Abt. 1950

031.00.50
11 CANUETO, Mita c: 3
+ seq: 031.00.50 VASSOLO, Ricardo w: Abt. 1975 c: 3
12 VASSOLO, Guillermo
12 VASSOLO, Hugo
12 VASSOLO, Josefina

031.00.60
10 MULLER, Felix b: 07 Jul 1901 in Talita, Depto de Uruguay,

Argentina d: 28 Jan 1991 in Tres Arroyos, Argentina v: Tres
Arroyos, Argentina o: Small business owner c: 3
+ seq: 031.00.60 ALONSO, Maria b: 16 Jun 1903 in Tres
   Arroyos, Argentina d: 23 Jul 1997 in Tres Arroyos, Argentina
   w: 29 Dec 1924 in Tres Arroyos, Argentina v: Tres Arroyos,
   Argentina f: Domingo Alonso m: Carolina Rodriguez c: 3
11 MULLER, Felix-Raul b: 26 Oct 1925 in Tres Arroyos,
   Argentina o: Small business owner c: 2
+ seq: 031.00.65 ANSO, Blanca-Ovidia b: 24 Mar 1928 in Tres
   Arroyos, Argentina w: Abt. 1945 c: 2
11 MULLER, Hugo-Alberto b: 22 Jul 1929 in Tres Arroyos,
   Argentina d: 01 Feb 2006 in Claromeco, Argentina o: Attorney
   c: 2
+ seq: 031.00.80 ZAPPETTINI, Lydia-Hesther b: 01 Apr 1933 in
   La Plata, Argentina w: 16 Aug 1960 in La Plata, Argentina c: 2
11 MULLER, Alfredo-Oscar b: Dec 1931 in Tres Arroyos,
   Argentina v: Tres Arroyos, Argentina o: Lawyer c: 4
+ seq: 031.00.90 ZUBIRI, Ana-Maria b: Dec 1939 in Coronel
   Dorrego, Argentina w: 21 Nov 1964 in Tres Arroyos,
   Argentina v: Tres Arroyos, Argentina f: Emilio Zubiri m:
   Rolindes Carrera c: 4

030.00.65
11 MULLER, Felix-Raul b: 26 Oct 1925 in Tres Arroyos,
   Argentina o: Small business owner c: 2
+ seq: 030.00.65 ANSO, Blanca-Ovidia b: 24 Mar 1928 in Tres
   Arroyos, Argentina w: Abt. 1945 c: 2
12 MULLER, Blanca-Susana b: 11 Oct 1952 in Tres Arroyos,
   Argentina c: 4
+ seq: 031.00.70 PRADO, Ruben-Oscar b: 24 Mar 1949 w: 27
   Jul 1973 in Tres Arroyos, Argentina o: Certified Public
   Accountant c: 4
12 MULLER, Alberto-Raul b: 22 Nov 1955 in Tres Arroyos,
   Argentina d: 06 Feb 2003 in Tres Arroyos, Argentina o:
   Attorney c: 1
+ seq: 031.00.75 RE, Andrea-Viviana b: 23 Mar 1966 in Tres
   Arroyos, Argentina w: 04 Sep 1999 in Tres Arroyos, Argentina
   c: 1

031.00.70
12 MULLER, Blanca-Susana b: 11 Oct 1952 in Tres Arroyos,

Argentina c: 4
+ seq: 031.00.70 PRADO, Ruben-Oscar b: 24 Mar 1949 w: 27
Jul 1973 in Tres Arroyos, Argentina o: Certified Public
Accountant c: 4
13 PRADO, Mariano-Gaston b: 27 May 1974 in Rio Plata,
Argentina o: Teacher c: 2
+ seq: 031.00.72 BARILE, Carla b: 28 Jul 1977 in Tres Arroyos,
Argentina w: 16 Aug 1998 in Tres Arroyos, Argentina c: 2
13 PRADO, Juan-Manuel b: 15 Feb 1978 in La Plata, Argentina
13 PRADO, Maria-Constanza b: 22 Dec 1982 in Tres Arroyos,
Argentina
13 PRADO, Maria-Eloisa b: 22 Dec 1982 in Tres Arroyos,
Argentina

031.00.72

13 PRADO, Mariano-Gaston b: 27 May 1974 in Rio Plata,
Argentina o: Teacher c: 2
+ seq: 031.00.72 BARILE, Carla b: 28 Jul 1977 in Tres Arroyos,
Argentina w: 16 Aug 1998 in Tres Arroyos, Argentina c: 2
14 PRADO, Milagros b: 12 Jul 1999 in Tres Arroyos, Argentina
14 PRADO, Maria-Lucero b: 01 Apr 2005 in Tres Arroyos,
Argentina

031.00.75

12 MULLER, Alberto-Raul b: 22 Nov 1955 in Tres Arroyos,
Argentina d: 06 Feb 2003 in Tres Arroyos, Argentina o:
Attorney c: 1
+ seq: 031.00.75 RE, Andrea-Viviana b: 23 Mar 1966 in Tres
Arroyos, Argentina w: 04 Sep 1999 in Tres Arroyos, Argentina
c: 1
13 MULLER, Felipe-Alberto b: 27 Jun 2001 in Tres Arroyos,
Argentina

031.00.80

11 MULLER, Hugo-Alberto b: 22 Jul 1929 in Tres Arroyos,
Argentina d: 01 Feb 2006 in Claromeco, Argentina o: Attorney
c: 2
+ seq: 031.00.80 ZAPPETTINI, Lydia-Hesther b: 01 Apr 1933 in
La Plata, Argentina w: 16 Aug 1960 in La Plata, Argentina c: 2
12 MULLER, Guillermo-Hugo b: 28 Jun 1961 in La Plata,
Argentina v: Barcelona, Spain o: Architect c: 1

+ seq: 031.00.85 AVELAR, Margareth b: 01 May 1963 in Belo
  Horizonte, Brazil w: Abt. 1990 in Barcelona, Spain v:
  Barcelona, Spain o: Dentist c: 1
12 MULLER, Maria-Andrea b: 03 Nov 1962 in La Plata, Argentina

031.00.85
12 MULLER, Guillermo-Hugo b: 28 Jun 1961 in La Plata,
   Argentina v: Barcelona, Spain o: Architect c: 1
+ seq: 031.00.85 AVELAR, Margareth b: 01 May 1963 in Belo
  Horizonte, Brazil w: Abt. 1990 in Barcelona, Spain v:
  Barcelona, Spain o: Dentist c: 1
13 MULLER, Sofia b: 16 Mar 2003 in Barcelona, Spain

031.00.90
11 MULLER, Alfredo-Oscar b: Dec 1931 in Tres Arroyos,
   Argentina v: Tres Arroyos, Argentina o: Lawyer c: 4
+ seq: 031.00.90 ZUBIRI, Ana-Maria b: Dec 1939 in Coronel
  Dorrego, Argentina w: 21 Nov 1964 in Tres Arroyos,
  Argentina v: Tres Arroyos, Argentina f: Emilio Zubiri m:
  Rolindes Carrera c: 4
12 MULLER, Maria-Ines b: 1966 in Tres Arroyos, Argentina v:
   Hoboken, NJ o: Attorney o: Financial analyst c: 3
+ seq: 031.00.95 KAPLUN, Luis-Alberto b: 1960 in Salta,
  Argentina w: 1993 in New York, NY v: Hoboken, NJ c: 3
12 MULLER, Maria-Eugenia b: 1967 in Tres Arroyos, Argentina
12 MULLER, Ana-Josefina b: 1969 in Tres Arroyos, Argentina v:
   Tres Arroyos, Argentina c: 2
+ seq: 031.01.30 OLSEN, Pablo-Humberto b: 1962 in Tres
  Arroyos, Argentina w: 30 Apr 1992 in Tres Arroyos, Argentina
  v: Tres Arroyos, Argentina o: Landlord f: Ejnar Olsen m:
  Clara Groenemberg c: 2
12 MULLER, Carolina b: 1973 in Tres Arroyos, Argentina

031.00.95
12 MULLER, Maria-Ines b: 1966 in Tres Arroyos, Argentina v:
   Hoboken, NJ o: Attorney o: Financial analyst c: 3
+ seq: 031.00.95 KAPLUN, Luis-Alberto b: 1960 in Salta,
  Argentina w: 1993 in New York, NY v: Hoboken, NJ c: 3
13 KAPLUN-MULLER, Emma b: 17 Feb 2004 in New York, NY
   v: Hoboken, NJ
13 KAPLUN-MULLER, Nicolas b: 04 Mar 2006 in New York, NY

v: Hoboken, NJ

13 KAPLUN-MULLER, Benjamin b: 04 Mar 2006 in New York, NY v: Hoboken, NJ

031.01.30

12 MULLER, Ana-Josefina b: 1969 in Tres Arroyos, Argentina v: Tres Arroyos, Argentina c: 2

+ seq: 031.01.30 OLSEN, Pablo-Humberto b: 1962 in Tres Arroyos, Argentina w: 30 Apr 1992 in Tres Arroyos, Argentina v: Tres Arroyos, Argentina o: Landlord f: Ejnar Olsen m: Clara Groenemberg c: 2

13 OLSEN-MULLER, Ingo-Pablo b: 03 Aug 1994 in Tres Arroyos, Argentina

13 OLSEN-MULLER, Irene b: 22 Nov 1996 in Tres Arroyos, Argentina

031.01.80

8 WITRY, Therese b: 23 Jan 1831 in Junglinster, Lux d: 14 Jul 1920 in Dubuque, IA v: Dubuque IA v: Nommern, Lux i: Emigrated to St. Catherine, IA i: moved to Dubuque, IA o: No profession r: b c: 1

+ seq: 031.01.80 STOLTZ, Valentin b: 21 May 1827 in Lorentzweiler, Lux d: 1895 in Duuque, IA w: 18 Mar 1857 in Junglinster, Lux h: Bofferding v: Dubuque,IA v: Nommern, Lux i: Emigrated to St. Catherine, IA i: moved to Dubuque, IA o: Gentleman r: b r: m f: Johann Stoltz m: Marie Siren c: 1

9 STOLTZ, John v: Dubuque, IA

031.02

7 WITRY, Marie-Margaretha b: 18 Sep 1798 in Junglinster, Lux d: 17 Oct 1824 in Godbrange, Lux h: Braun v: Godbrange, Lux r: bd c: 1

+ seq: 031.02 HILBERT, Nicolas b: 05 Mar 1798 in Godbrange, Lux d: 08 Jun 1872 in Godbrange, Lux w: 04 Dec 1823 in Junglinster, Lux h: Braun v: Godbrange, Lux o: Farmer r: m f: Johann Hilbert m: Catherine Blanz c: 1

8 HILBERT, Johann b: 08 Sep 1824 in Godbrange, Lux o: Farmer r: b

+ seq: 031.50 NEPPER, Anna-Maria b: 20 Mar 1833 in Nagem, Lux w: 10 Apr 1861 in Junglinster, Lux o: No profession r: m f: Peter Nepper m: Marie-Johanna Wantz

032.02

7 WITRY, Marie-Catherine b: 28 Aug 1813 in Junglinster, Lux
   d: 28 Sep 1888 in Cottonville, IA v: St. Donatus, IA i:
   Emigrated to the U. S. o: No profession r: bd c: 4
+ seq: 032.02 HEBELER, Nicolas b: 03 Aug 1811 in Junglinster,
   Lux w: 10 May 1837 in Junglinster, Lux v: St. Donatus, IA i:
   Emigrated to the U. S. o: Farmer r: m f: Johann Hebeler m:
   Susanne Reckinger c: 4
8 HEBELER, Theresia b: 02 Feb 1838 in Junglinster, Lux r: b
8 HEBELER, Josephine b: 04 Mar 1840 in Junglinster, Lux r: b
8 HEBELER, Peter b: 25 Feb 1845 in Junglinster, Lux r: b
8 HEBELER, Nicolas b: 02 Oct 1847 in Junglinster, Lux r: b

032.03

6 WITRY, Anna-Margaretha b: 23 May 1761 in Schloewenhoff,
   Lux d: 17 Jul 1838 in Schloewenhoff, Lux h: Uselding v:
   Schloewenhoff, Lux o: No profession r: bd c: 6
+ seq: 032.03 USELDING, Anton b: Abt. 1770 in Niederpallen,
   Lux w: 18 Feb 1794 in Leudelange, Lux h: Uselding v:
   Schloewenhoff, Lux o: Laborer o: Farmer o: Plowman r: m f:
   Johann Uselding m: Susanne Reding c: 6
7 USELDING, Anna b: 28 Jan 1795 in Schloewenhoff, Lux d: 25
   Mar 1796 in Schloewenhoff, Lux v: Schloewenhoff, Lux r: bd
7 USELDING, Willebrord b: 09 Feb 1797 in Schloewenhoff, Lux
   r: b
7 USELDING, Johann-Baptist b: 28 Dec 1799 in Schloewenhoff,
   Lux r: b
7 USELDING, Johann b: 06 Jan 1800 in Schloewenhoff, Lux r: b
7 USELDING, Susanne b: Mar 1802 in Schloewenhoff, Lux r: b
7 USELDING, Michel b: 19 Jan 1804 in Schloewenhoff, Lux r: b

033

6 WITRY, Nicolas t: Mayor b: 16 Sep 1763 in Schloewenhoff,
   Lux d: 04 Jul 1836 in Lorentzweiler, Lux v: Lorentzweiler, Lux
   i: Revalidated marriage o: Plowman o: Property owner o: Day
   laborer o: Innkeeper r: bd c: 6
+ seq: 033 WEIS, Angela b: 03 Sep 1776 in Gonderange, Lux d:
   20 Mar 1831 in Lorentzweiler, Lux w: 24 Jan 1797 in
   Junglinster, Lux v: Lorentzweiler, Lux i: Revalidated marriage
   r: mx f: Michel Weis m: Susanne Decker c: 6
7 WITRY, Michel t: Knight of the Order of the Crown of Oak b:

18 Dec 1797 in Lorentzweiler, Lux d: 01 May 1874 in Echternach, Lux h: Hovelock v: Liege, Belgium i: Secretery of canton of Echternach o: Retiree o: Property owner o: Royal notary r: bd c: 3

+ seq: 034 THIRY, Barbara-Franzisca-Josefine b: 20 Aug 1808 in Echternach, Lux w: 01 Sep 1830 in Echternach, Lux h: Hovelock v: Liege, Belgium v: Echternach, Lux o: Retiree o: No profession r: b r: m f: Georg-Andres Thiry m: Susanne Muller c: 3

7 WITRY, Marie b: 08 Mar 1802 in Lorentzweiler, Lux d: 18 Dec 1870 in Dippach, Lux v: Sprinkange, Lux o: No profession r: bd c: 7

+ seq: 035.01 KLEIN, Nicolas b: 12 Nov 1786 in Sprinkange, Lux d: 02 Jan 1865 in Dippach, Lux w: 21 Nov 1821 in Dippach, Lux v: Sprinkange, Lux o: Pig herder o: Farmer r: m f: Nicolas (Johannes) Klein m: Magdalena (Marie-Madelaine) Majerus c: 7

7 WITRY, Elisabeth b: 04 Jul 1804 in Lorentzweiler, Lux v: Schandel, Lux o: No profession r: b

+ seq: 035.02 FRANZ, Heinrich b: 25 Jul 1801 in Schandel, Lux w: 27 Sep 1826 in Useldange, Lux v: Schandel, Lux o: Farmer r: m f: Frederic Franz m: Catherine Schandeler

7 WITRY, Anna-Catherine b: 27 Dec 1806 in Lorentzweiler, Lux d: 30 Dec 1806 in Lorentzweiler, Lux v: Lorentzweiler, Lux r: d

7 WITRY, Heinrich t: Mayor b: 09 May 1808 in Lorentzweiler, Lux v: Lintgen, Lux o: Farmer o: Property owner r: b c: 5

+ seq: 036 HEUARDT, Petronille-Claudine b: 07 Jul 1814 in Lintgen, Lux w: 11 Feb 1839 in Lintgen, Lux v: Lintgen, Lux o: Property owner r: b r: m f: Ambrose Heuardt m: Marie-Petronille Biver c: 5

7 WITRY, Catherine b: 30 Jun 1811 in Lorentzweiler, Lux d: 30 Jan 1888 in Redange, Lux v: Redange, Lux o: Farmer r: bd c: 5

+ seq: 036.02 SCHLEICH, Denis b: 20 Mar 1802 in Redange, Lux d: 17 Jun 1863 in Redange, Lux w: 27 Oct 1830 in Redange, Lux v: Redange, Lux o: Farmer r: d r: m f: Peter Schleich m: Marie Nicolay c: 5

034

7 WITRY, Michel t: Knight of the Order of the Crown of Oak b:

18 Dec 1797 in Lorentzweiler, Lux d: 01 May 1874 in Echternach, Lux h: Hovelock v: Liege, Belgium i: Secretery of canton of Echternach o: Retiree o: Property owner o: Royal notary r: bd c: 3

+ seq: 034 THIRY, Barbara-Franzisca-Josefine b: 20 Aug 1808 in Echternach, Lux w: 01 Sep 1830 in Echternach, Lux h: Hovelock v: Liege, Belgium v: Echternach, Lux o: Retiree o: No profession r: b r: m f: Georg-Andres Thiry m: Susanne Muller c: 3

8 WITRY, Nicolas-Leopold b: 21 Aug 1831 in Echternach, Lux d: 27 Jan 1909 in Echternach, Lux v: Echternach, Lux o: Pensioner o: No profession r: bd

8 WITRY, George-Alphonse b: 23 Nov 1833 in Echternach, Lux d: 21 Nov 1874 in Echternach, Lux h: Hovelock v: Echternach, Lux o: Retiree r: bd

8 WITRY, Emil-Nicolas b: 14 Sep 1836 in Echternach, Lux d: 22 Sep 1870 in Echternach, Lux h: Hovelock v: Liege, Belgium v: Lintgen, Lux o: Industrialist r: bd c: 1

+ seq: 035 WITRY, Catherine-Petronille-Eudoxie b: 02 Mar 1844 in Lintgen, Lux d: 18 Aug 1897 in Luxembourg, Lux w: 28 Jul 1867 in Lintgen, Lux v: Liege, Belgium v: Lintgen, Lux o: Singer r: bd r: m f: Heinrich Witry m: Petronille-Claudine Heuardt c: 1

035

8 WITRY, Emil-Nicolas b: 14 Sep 1836 in Echternach, Lux d: 22 Sep 1870 in Echternach, Lux h: Hovelock v: Liege, Belgium v: Lintgen, Lux o: Industrialist r: bd c: 1

+ seq: 035 WITRY, Catherine-Petronille-Eudoxie b: 02 Mar 1844 in Lintgen, Lux d: 18 Aug 1897 in Luxembourg, Lux w: 28 Jul 1867 in Lintgen, Lux v: Liege, Belgium v: Lintgen, Lux o: Singer r: bd r: m f: Heinrich Witry m: Petronille-Claudine Heuardt c: 1

9 WITRY, Josefine-Henrietta-Fanny (Fanny) b: 03 Jul 1868 in Lintgen, Lux h: 43 Konigung Gasse v: Carroll, IA i: Emigrated to the U. S. - Carroll, IA o: No profession r: bx

+ seq: 035.00.50 LETELLIER, Gustav-August-Moritz (Maurice) b: 28 May 1862 in Luxembourg, Lux d: 04 Jan 1899 in Luxembourg, Lux w: 21 May 1889 in Lintgen, Lux h: 43 Konigung Gasse v: Luxembourg, Lux o: Lawyer o: Director of the Wilhelm Luxembourg Railroad Company r: d r: m f:

Remy-Augustin Letellier m: Anna-Malvina Neyke

035.01

7 WITRY, Marie b: 08 Mar 1802 in Lorentzweiler, Lux d: 18
   Dec 1870 in Dippach, Lux v: Sprinkange, Lux o: No profession
   r: bd c: 7

+ seq: 035.01 KLEIN, Nicolas b: 12 Nov 1786 in Sprinkange,
   Lux d: 02 Jan 1865 in Dippach, Lux w: 21 Nov 1821 in
   Dippach, Lux v: Sprinkange, Lux o: Pig herder o: Farmer r:
   m f: Nicolas (Johannes) Klein m: Magdalena (Marie-
   Madelaine) Majerus c: 7

8 KLEIN, Marie-Madelaine b: 07 Feb 1823 in Sprinkange, Lux r:
   b

+ seq: 035.01.50 MARX, Jean Baptiste b: 05 Sep 1822 in
   Schouweiler, Lux w: 21 Sep 1853 in Dippach, Lux o: Farmer
   r: m f: Jean Baptiste Marx m: Marie Burns

8 KLEIN, Nicolas b: 13 Oct 1824 in Sprinkange, Lux d: 23 Feb
   1890 in Sprinkange, Lux o: Property owner o: Lay judge r: bd

8 KLEIN, Catherine b: 13 Jun 1826 in Sprinkange, Lux r: b

8 KLEIN, Anne-Margarethe b: 24 Apr 1830 in Sprinkange, Lux
   r: b

8 KLEIN, Boy b: 08 May 1833 in Sprinkange, Lux d: 08 May
   1833 in Sprinkange, Lux r: b

8 KLEIN, Marie-Madelaine b: 19 Jul 1836 in Sprinkange, Lux d:
   01 Apr 1837 in Sprinkange, Lux r: bd

8 KLEIN, Marie-Madelaine b: 23 Jun 1838 in Sprinkange, Lux d:
   08 Dec 1852 in Sprinkange, Lux r: bd

036

7 WITRY, Heinrich t: Mayor b: 09 May 1808 in Lorentzweiler,
   Lux v: Lintgen, Lux o: Farmer o: Property owner r: b c: 5

+ seq: 036 HEUARDT, Petronille-Claudine b: 07 Jul 1814 in
   Lintgen, Lux w: 11 Feb 1839 in Lintgen, Lux v: Lintgen, Lux
   o: Property owner r: b r: m f: Ambrose Heuardt m: Marie-
   Petronille Biver c: 5

8 WITRY, Michel-August b: 29 Nov 1839 in Lintgen, Lux v:
   Lintgen, Lux o: Credit secretary o: Notary r: b

8 WITRY, Eugen-Paul b: 30 Jun 1841 in Lintgen, Lux v:
   Lintgen, Lux o: Civil engineer r: b

8 [1] WITRY, Catherine-Petronille-Eudoxie b: 02 Mar 1844 in
   Lintgen, Lux d: 18 Aug 1897 in Luxembourg, Lux v: Liege,

Belgium v: Lintgen, Lux o: Singer r: bd c: 1
+ seq: 035 WITRY, Emil-Nicolas b: 14 Sep 1836 in Echternach,
  Lux d: 22 Sep 1870 in Echternach, Lux w: 28 Jul 1867 in
  Lintgen, Lux h: Hovelock v: Liege, Belgium v: Lintgen, Lux o:
  Industrialist r: bd r: m f: Michel Witry m: Barbara-Franzisca-
  Josefine Thiry c: 1
* 2nd Husband of [1] WITRY, Catherine-Petronille-Eudoxie:
+ seq: 036.01 LAVALLAYE, Nicolas-Maria-Edouard b: 28 Jul
  1838 in Liege, Belgium w: 27 Jul 1880 in Lintgen, Lux v:
  Liege, Belgium o: Lawyer o: Judge of the Civil Court r: m f:
  Philipp-Franz-Evrard Lavalle m: Marie-Elisabeth Lambert
8 WITRY, Mathilde-Victoire b: 17 Apr 1846 in Lintgen, Lux d:
  19 Apr 1847 in Lintgen, Lux v: Lintgen, Lux r: bd
8 WITRY, Johann-Peter-Viktor b: 25 Jul 1849 in Lintgen, Lux v:
  Lintgen, Lux r: b

036.02
7 WITRY, Catherine b: 30 Jun 1811 in Lorentzweiler, Lux d: 30
  Jan 1888 in Redange, Lux v: Redange, Lux o: Farmer r: bd c:
  5
+ seq: 036.02 SCHLEICH, Denis b: 20 Mar 1802 in Redange,
  Lux d: 17 Jun 1863 in Redange, Lux w: 27 Oct 1830 in
  Redange, Lux v: Redange, Lux o: Farmer r: d r: m f: Peter
  Schleich m: Marie Nicolay c: 5
8 SCHLEICH, Maria b: 19 Sep 1831 in Redange, Lux r: b
8 SCHLEICH, Heinrich b: 04 Jul 1836 in Redange, Lux d: 02
  May 1881 in Redange, Lux h: Schatgen v: Redange, Lux o:
  Farmer r: bd
8 SCHLEICH, Michel b: 07 Jan 1840 in Redange, Lux v:
  Redange, Lux o: Farmer r: b
8 SCHLEICH, Catherine b: 26 Jul 1844 in Redange, Lux r: b
8 SCHLEICH, Petronille-Leonie b: 10 Apr 1847 in Redange, Lux
  r: b

037
5 WITRY, Theodor b: 24 Feb 1734 in Bergem, Lux d: 25 Dec
  1819 in Reuland, Lux a: Petry h: Petry v: Reuland, Lux r: bd
  c: 11
+ seq: 037 PETRY, Anna-Marie b: Abt. 1735 in Reuland, Lux d:
  31 Dec 1807 in Reuland, Lux w: 21 Feb 1759 in Heffingen,
  Lux a: Boudeler h: Peters v: Reuland, Lux o: Farmer r: d r:

m f: Peter Petry c: 11

6 WITRY, Barbara b: 18 Feb 1760 in Reuland, Lux d: 21 Mar
1827 in Reuland, Lux a: Peters h: Peters v: Reuland, Lux o:
Farmer r: b c: 11

+ seq: 037.01 FRANCK, Nicolas b: 29 Oct 1750 in Leudelange,
Lux d: 13 Mar 1816 in Reuland, Lux w: 30 Jan 1781 in
Heffingen, Lux a: Peters h: Peters v: Reuland, Lux o: Farmer
r: bd r: m f: Wilhelm Franck m: Anna-Magdalena Reuter c:
11

6 WITRY, Anna-Catherine b: 21 Sep 1762 in Reuland, Lux d: 28
Jan 1829 in Biwer, Lux h: Weydig v: Biwer, Lux r: bd c: 1

+ seq: 037.03 SPOETLER, Johann b: Abt. 1765 in Biwer, Lux
w: 25 Apr 1791 in Biwer, Lux h: Weydig v: Biwer, Lux o:
Linen weaver r: m f: Spoetler m: Catherine Nicolai c: 1

6 WITRY, Elisabeth (Elise) b: 26 Jun 1764 in Reuland, Lux r: b

6 WITRY, Michel b: 07 Mar 1767 in Reuland, Lux r: b

6 WITRY, Peter b: 27 May 1768 in Reuland, Lux d: 19 Feb 1843
in Schieren, Lux a: Peters h: Peters v: Schieren, Lux o: Day
laborer o: Farmer r: bd c: 8

+ seq: 038 THERENS, Catherine b: Abt. 1778 in Schieren, Lux
d: 23 Jan 1853 in Schieren, Lux w: 22 Mar 1798 in Heffingen,
Lux h: Peters v: Schieren, Lux o: Day laborer o: Farmer r: m
f: Heinrich Therens m: Marie Dondelinger c: 8

6 WITRY, Marie-Catherine b: Abt. 1770 in Reuland, Lux

+ seq: 050.02 WEBER, Jacob b: Abt. 1765 in Beaufort, Lux w:
18 Jan 1790 in Beaufort, Lux r: m f: Peter Weber m:
Appolonia Werion

6 WITRY, Jean-Baptiste b: 15 Jul 1772 in Reuland, Lux d: 21
May 1848 in Schieren, Lux h: Schieren v: Reuland, Lux o: Day
laborer o: Farmer r: bdx c: 14

+ seq: 051 SCHROEDER, Anna-Marie b: 08 Feb 1780 in
Schieren, Lux d: 03 Dec 1859 in Schieren, Lux w: 30 Dec
1798 in Diekirch, Lux v: Schieren, Lux o: Farmer r: dx r: m
c: 14

6 WITRY, Nicolas b: 11 Aug 1775 in Reuland, Lux d: 18 Mar
1808 in Bromberg, Lux Cause of death: Nervous fever v:
Reuland, Lux i: Fought against Austria at Marizell in 1805 i:
Fought in Poland o: Grenadier in 2nd batallion of Grand Army
r: b

6 WITRY, Anna-Marie b: 07 Mar 1777 in Reuland, Lux d: 11
Mar 1837 in Roodt, Lux a: Peters a: Schneider h: Schneider v:

Roodt, Lux o: No profession r: bd c: 5

+ seq: 119.02 GEORGE, Johann b: 10 Jan 1772 in Roodt, Lux d:
14 Apr 1837 in Roodt, Lux w: 30 Dec 1801 in Betzdorf, Lux
a: Schneider h: Schneider v: Roodt, Lux o: Plowman o: Day
laborer o: Farmer r: d r: m f: Jacob George m: Anna-
Margaretha Wagner c: 5

6 WITRY, Stillborn Girl b: 22 Mar 1780 in Reuland, Lux d: 22
Mar 1780 in Reuland, Lux h: Peters v: Reuland, Lux r: d

6 WITRY, Margaretha b: 03 Dec 1781 in Reuland, Lux d: 05 Jan
1783 in Reuland, Lux h: Peters v: Reuland, Lux r: bd

037.01

6 WITRY, Barbara b: 18 Feb 1760 in Reuland, Lux d: 21 Mar
1827 in Reuland, Lux a: Peters h: Peters v: Reuland, Lux o:
Farmer r: b c: 11

+ seq: 037.01 FRANCK, Nicolas b: 29 Oct 1750 in Leudelange,
Lux d: 13 Mar 1816 in Reuland, Lux w: 30 Jan 1781 in
Heffingen, Lux a: Peters h: Peters v: Reuland, Lux o: Farmer
r: bd r: m f: Wilhelm Franck m: Anna-Magdalena Reuter c:
11

7 FRANCK, Johann b: 15 Jan 1782 in Reuland, Lux r: b

+ seq: 037.02 WEIS, Catherine b: Abt. 1790 in Manternach, Lux
w: 13 Feb 1811 in Manternach, Lux r: m

7 FRANCK, Theodor b: 10 Nov 1783 in Reuland, Lux r: b

7 FRANCK, Marie-Catherine b: 15 Dec 1785 in Reuland, Lux r:
b

7 FRANCK, Peter b: 06 Jun 1788 in Reuland, Lux r: b

7 FRANCK, Marie-Catherine b: 22 Nov 1790 in Reuland, Lux r:
b

7 FRANCK, Nicolas b: 27 Feb 1793 in Reuland, Lux r: b

7 FRANCK, Anna-Marie b: 03 Sep 1795 in Reuland, Lux r: b

7 FRANCK, Anna-Margaretha b: 17 Mar 1798 in Reuland, Lux
r: b

7 FRANCK, Margaretha b: 18 Aug 1799 in Reuland, Lux r: b

7 FRANCK, Margaretha b: 26 Jan 1800 in Reuland, Lux r: b

7 FRANCK, Marie b: 25 Jan 1802 in Reuland, Lux d: 21 Sep
1811 in Reuland, Lux r: bd

037.03

6 WITRY, Anna-Catherine b: 21 Sep 1762 in Reuland, Lux d: 28
Jan 1829 in Biwer, Lux h: Weydig v: Biwer, Lux r: bd c: 1

+ seq: 037.03 SPOETLER, Johann b: Abt. 1765 in Biwer, Lux
  w: 25 Apr 1791 in Biwer, Lux h: Weydig v: Biwer, Lux o:
  Linen weaver r: m f: Spoetler m: Catherine Nicolai c: 1
7 SPOETLER, Anna-Marie b: 19 Mar 1792 in Biwer, Lux r: b

038

6 WITRY, Peter b: 27 May 1768 in Reuland, Lux d: 19 Feb 1843
  in Schieren, Lux a: Peters h: Peters v: Schieren, Lux o: Day
  laborer o: Farmer r: bd c: 8
+ seq: 038 THERENS, Catherine b: Abt. 1778 in Schieren, Lux
  d: 23 Jan 1853 in Schieren, Lux w: 22 Mar 1798 in Heffingen,
  Lux h: Peters v: Schieren, Lux o: Day laborer o: Farmer r: m
  f: Heinrich Therens m: Marie Dondelinger c: 8
7 WITRY, Theodor b: 29 Dec 1798 in Schieren, Lux d: 04 Aug
  1875 in Schieren, Lux v: Schieren, Lux o: Property owner o:
  Craftsman o: Day laborer r: bd c: 3
+ seq: 039 KRIER, Margaretha b: 19 May 1805 in Schieren, Lux
  d: 18 Jan 1880 in Schieren, Lux w: 07 Feb 1836 in Ettelbruck,
  Lux v: Schieren, Lux o: Craftsman o: Day laborer r: bd r: m
  f: Lorens Krier m: Elisabeth Welter c: 3
7 WITRY, Barbara b: 14 Oct 1800 in Schieren, Lux d: 25 May
  1830 in Schieren, Lux h: Peters v: Schieren, Lux o: Day
  laborer r: bd
7 WITRY, Johann b: 22 Jun 1803 in Schieren, Lux d: 21 Jan
  1861 in Schieren, Lux v: Schieren, Lux o: Day laborer r: bd c:
  2
+ seq: 045 HIRTZIG, Marie b: 10 Jul 1812 in Niedermertzig,
  Lux d: 08 Mar 1869 in Schieren, Lux w: 07 Jan 1848 in
  Ettelbruck, Lux v: Schieren, Lux o: Day laborer r: d r: m f:
  Jacob Hirtzig m: Catherine Schmitt c: 2
7 WITRY, Marie-Elisabeth b: 10 Aug 1806 in Schieren, Lux d:
  31 Oct 1860 in Schieren, Lux h: Witry v: Schieren, Lux o: No
  profession r: bd c: 1
+ seq: 047 b: Abt. 1805 w: Abt. 1830 c: 1
7 WITRY, Therese b: 08 Jan 1809 in Schieren, Lux d: 14 Apr
  1889 in Schieren, Lux h: Bonels v: Schieren, Lux r: bd
7 WITRY, Wilhelm b: 14 Sep 1811 in Schieren, Lux d: 18 Sep
  1831 in Hosingen, Lux h: Closen v: Hosingen, Lux o: Servant
  r: bd
7 WITRY, Peter b: 09 May 1815 in Schieren, Lux r: b
7 WITRY, Johann b: 29 Sep 1819 in Schieren, Lux d: 11 Feb

1897 in Ettelbruck, Lux v: Ancy-sur-Moselle, France v: Steinsel, Lux i: Spent his last days in the central hospice of Ettelbruck o: Quarryman o: Day laborer o: Forger r: bd c: 5

+ seq: 049 MOISS, Anna-Marie b: 29 May 1824 in Steinsel, Lux d: 25 Feb 1871 in Ancy-sur-Moselle, France w: 07 Oct 1847 in Steinsel, Lux v: Ancy-sur-Moselle, France v: Steinsel, Lux o: No profession r: b r: m f: Johann Moiss m: Anna Haffe c: 5

039

7 WITRY, Theodor b: 29 Dec 1798 in Schieren, Lux d: 04 Aug 1875 in Schieren, Lux v: Schieren, Lux o: Property owner o: Craftsman o: Day laborer r: bd c: 3

+ seq: 039 KRIER, Margaretha b: 19 May 1805 in Schieren, Lux d: 18 Jan 1880 in Schieren, Lux w: 07 Feb 1836 in Ettelbruck, Lux v: Schieren, Lux o: Craftsman o: Day laborer r: bd r: m f: Lorens Krier m: Elisabeth Welter c: 3

8 WITRY, Peter b: 05 Nov 1836 in Schieren, Lux d: 08 Jan 1911 in Schieren, Lux v: Schieren, Lux o: Property owner o: Day laborer o: Farmer r: bd

8 [1] WITRY, Heinrich b: 19 Jul 1840 in Schieren, Lux d: 23 Jul 1917 in Schieren, Lux v: Schieren, Lux o: Property owner o: Day laborer o: Farmer r: bd c: 5

+ seq: 040 HENNES, Susanne b: 20 Dec 1834 in Schieren, Lux d: 21 Jul 1870 in Schieren, Lux w: 26 Feb 1867 in Schieren, Lux v: Schieren, Lux o: No profession r: b r: m f: Georg Hennes m: Catherine Kugeler c: 2

* 2nd Wife of [1] WITRY, Heinrich:

+ seq: 041 FREDERES, Susanne b: 15 Jul 1844 in Michelau, Lux d: 26 Nov 1881 in Schieren, Lux w: 27 May 1877 in Schieren, Lux v: Schieren, Lux o: No profession r: d r: m f: Nicolas Frederes m: Margaretha Majerus c: 4

8 WITRY, Anna b: 06 Nov 1842 in Schieren, Lux h: Geis Mill v: Berg, Lux o: No profession r: b c: 3

+ seq: 044.02 REULAND, Johann b: 17 Nov 1832 in Berg, Lux d: 28 Feb 1896 in Geismuhle, Lux w: 04 Feb 1866 in Berg, Lux h: Geis Mill v: Geismuhle, Lux v: Berg, Lux o: Day laborer o: Craftsman r: d r: m f: Conrad Reuland m: Catherine Wagner c: 3

040

8 [1] WITRY, Heinrich b: 19 Jul 1840 in Schieren, Lux d: 23 Jul

1917 in Schieren, Lux v: Schieren, Lux o: Property owner o:
Day laborer o: Farmer r: bd c: 5
+ seq: 040 HENNES, Susanne b: 20 Dec 1834 in Schieren, Lux
  d: 21 Jul 1870 in Schieren, Lux w: 26 Feb 1867 in Schieren,
  Lux v: Schieren, Lux o: No profession r: b r: m f: Georg
  Hennes m: Catherine Kugeler c: 2
9 WITRY, Elisabeth (Elise) b: 24 Apr 1868 in Schieren, Lux d:
  24 Dec 1885 in Schieren, Lux r: bd
9 WITRY, Catherine b: 21 Mar 1870 in Schieren, Lux d: 22 Sep
  1870 in Schieren, Lux v: Schieren, Lux o: No profession r: bd
* 2nd Wife of [1] WITRY, Heinrich:
+ seq: 041 FREDERES, Susanne b: 15 Jul 1844 in Michelau, Lux
  d: 26 Nov 1881 in Schieren, Lux w: 27 May 1877 in Schieren,
  Lux v: Schieren, Lux o: No profession r: d r: m f: Nicolas
  Frederes m: Margaretha Majerus c: 4
9 WITRY, Pierre-Frederis b: 01 Jun 1878 in Schieren, Lux d: 03
  Dec 1936 in Nitro, WV v: Nitro, WV i: Emigrated to the U.S.
  i: Arrived on the Southwark from Antwerp i: Possibly visited
  Luxembourg and returned to the U.S. on the Finland from
  Antwerp o: Grocer (owned store) r: b c: 3
+ seq: 042 FRIOB, Anna b: 13 Sep 1884 in Dalheim, Lux d: 21
  Nov 1960 in Nitro, WV w: Abt. 1920 v: Nitro, WV i: Visited
  Luxembourg i: Arrived on the Lapland from Antwerp c: 3
9 WITRY, Heinrich b: 10 Nov 1879 in Schieren, Lux r: b
9 WITRY, Elisabeth (Elise) b: 10 Nov 1879 in Schieren, Lux d:
  1962 v: Schieren, Lux o: Midwife c: 3
+ seq: 044.01 CLOOS, Mathias b: Abt. 1875 in Schieren, Lux d:
  1914 w: 10 Feb 1903 in Schieren, Lux v: Schieren, Lux o:
  Farmer r: m f: Heinrich Cloos m: Margaretha May c: 3

042
9 WITRY, Pierre-Frederis b: 01 Jun 1878 in Schieren, Lux d: 03
  Dec 1936 in Nitro, WV v: Nitro, WV i: Emigrated to the U.S.
  i: Arrived on the Southwark from Antwerp i: Possibly visited
  Luxembourg and returned to the U.S. on the Finland from
  Antwerp o: Grocer (owned store) r: b c: 3
+ seq: 042 FRIOB, Anna b: 13 Sep 1884 in Dalheim, Lux d: 21
  Nov 1960 in Nitro, WV w: Abt. 1920 v: Nitro, WV i: Visited
  Luxembourg i: Arrived on the Lapland from Antwerp c: 3
10 WITRY, John-Phillip b: 18 Sep 1923 in Nitro, WV v:
  Waynesboro, VA c: 3

+ seq: 043 ESKEW, Dorothy-Louise b: 01 Jun 1924 in Putnam
County, WV w: 05 Jun 1943 v: Waynesboro, VA f: Eskew
m: Flora E. Truett c: 3
10WITRY, Henry-John (Harry)
10WITRY, Suzanne-Virginia (Sue) b: 1919 i: Visited
Luxembourg with mother

043
10WITRY, John-Phillip b: 18 Sep 1923 in Nitro, WV v:
Waynesboro, VA c: 3
+ seq: 043 ESKEW, Dorothy-Louise b: 01 Jun 1924 in Putnam
County, WV w: 05 Jun 1943 v: Waynesboro, VA f: Eskew
m: Flora E. Truett c: 3
11WITRY, Anne-Truett b: 26 Jun 1953 in Charlottesville, VA c:
1
+ seq: 043.01 GOLLADAY, David b: Abt. 1950 w: Abt. 1973
c: 1
11WITRY, Cynthia-Louise b: 26 Jul 1956 in Waynesboro, VA c:
2
+ seq: 043.02 JENKINS, Thomas b: Abt. 1950 w: Abt. 1978 c:
2
11WITRY, John-Phillip (Phil) b: 20 Dec 1957 in Waynesboro, VA
v: Charlottesville, VA c: 2
+ seq: 044 WOODSON, Sue b: Abt. 1955 w: Abt. 1980 v:
Charlottesville, VA c: 2

043.01
11WITRY, Anne-Truett b: 26 Jun 1953 in Charlottesville, VA c:
1
+ seq: 043.01 GOLLADAY, David b: Abt. 1950 w: Abt. 1973
c: 1
12GOLLADAY, James-David b: 02 Jul 1975

043.02
11WITRY, Cynthia-Louise b: 26 Jul 1956 in Waynesboro, VA c:
2
+ seq: 043.02 JENKINS, Thomas b: Abt. 1950 w: Abt. 1978 c:
2
12JENKINS, Christopher-Wilson b: 19 Sep 1980
12JENKINS, Bryan-Phillip b: 01 Jun 1984

044

11 WITRY, John-Phillip (Phil) b: 20 Dec 1957 in Waynesboro, VA
v: Charlottesville, VA c: 2
+ seq: 044 WOODSON, Sue b: Abt. 1955 w: Abt. 1980 v:
Charlottesville, VA c: 2
12 WITRY, John-Phillip b: 01 Sep 1984 v: Charlottesville, VA
12 WITRY, Sidney-Andrew b: 28 Oct 1986

044.01

9 WITRY, Elisabeth (Elise) b: 10 Nov 1879 in Schieren, Lux d:
1962 v: Schieren, Lux o: Midwife c: 3
+ seq: 044.01 CLOOS, Mathias b: Abt. 1875 in Schieren, Lux d:
1914 w: 10 Feb 1903 in Schieren, Lux v: Schieren, Lux o:
Farmer r: m f: Heinrich Cloos m: Margaretha May c: 3
10 CLOOS, Gredchen
10 CLOOS, Mariechen
10 CLOOS, Johann

044.02

8 WITRY, Anna b: 06 Nov 1842 in Schieren, Lux h: Geis Mill
v: Berg, Lux o: No profession r: b c: 3
+ seq: 044.02 REULAND, Johann b: 17 Nov 1832 in Berg, Lux
d: 28 Feb 1896 in Geismuhle, Lux w: 04 Feb 1866 in Berg, Lux
h: Geis Mill v: Geismuhle, Lux v: Berg, Lux o: Day laborer
o: Craftsman r: d r: m f: Conrad Reuland m: Catherine
Wagner c: 3
9 REULAND, Catherine b: 06 Jan 1867 in Berg, Lux r: b
9 REULAND, Anna-Maria b: 27 Dec 1868 in Berg, Lux r: b
+ seq: 044.50 NILLES, Jean b: 25 Dec 1870 in Biwer, Lux w: 11
May 1897 in Berg, Lux o: Sand caster r: m f: Peter Nilles m:
Anna Besch
9 REULAND, Margaretha b: 12 Jul 1871 in Berg, Lux r: b

045

7 WITRY, Johann b: 22 Jun 1803 in Schieren, Lux d: 21 Jan
1861 in Schieren, Lux v: Schieren, Lux o: Day laborer r: bd c:
2
+ seq: 045 HIRTZIG, Marie b: 10 Jul 1812 in Niedermertzig, Lux
d: 08 Mar 1869 in Schieren, Lux w: 07 Jan 1848 in Ettelbruck,
Lux v: Schieren, Lux o: Day laborer r: d r: m f: Jacob Hirtzig
m: Catherine Schmitt c: 2

8 WITRY, Nicolas b: 22 Feb 1849 in Schieren, Lux d: 19 Nov 1908 in Schieren, Lux h: Witry v: Schieren, Lux o: Teamster o: Day laborer r: bd c: 7

+ seq: 046 LEONARD, Margaretha b: 08 Jun 1849 in Schieren, Lux w: 25 May 1875 in Ettelbruck, Lux h: Witry v: Schieren, Lux o: No profession r: b r: m f: Theodor Leonard m: Catherine Zoller c: 7

8 WITRY, Stillborn Boy b: 11 Jan 1852 in Schieren, Lux d: 11 Jan 1852 in Schieren, Lux v: Schieren, Lux r: bd

046

8 WITRY, Nicolas b: 22 Feb 1849 in Schieren, Lux d: 19 Nov 1908 in Schieren, Lux h: Witry v: Schieren, Lux o: Teamster o: Day laborer r: bd c: 7

+ seq: 046 LEONARD, Margaretha b: 08 Jun 1849 in Schieren, Lux w: 25 May 1875 in Ettelbruck, Lux h: Witry v: Schieren, Lux o: No profession r: b r: m f: Theodor Leonard m: Catherine Zoller c: 7

9 WITRY, Jean b: 03 Sep 1876 in Schieren, Lux h: 45 Vincenz h: Brill v: Esch-sur-Alzette, Lux o: Teamster r: b c: 6

+ seq: 046.20 BLEY, Anna b: 11 Nov 1875 in Schieren, Lux w: 02 Feb 1898 in Schieren, Lux h: Vincenz v: Esch-sur-Alzette, Lux o: No profession r: m f: Mathieu Bley m: Susanne Karpes c: 6

9 WITRY, Theodor b: 07 Sep 1878 in Schieren, Lux d: 26 Oct 1881 in Schieren, Lux v: Schieren, Lux o: No profession r: bd

9 WITRY, Charles (Karl) b: 28 Oct 1881 in Schieren, Lux v: Esch-sur-Alzette o: Conductor o: Teamster r: b

9 [1] WITRY, Nicolas b: 26 May 1884 in Schieren, Lux v: Esch-sur-Alzette o: Master tailor o: Mechanic o: Locksmith o: Blacksmith r: b c: 2

+ seq: 046.50 STIRN, Anna b: 28 Feb 1888 in Schieren, Lux w: 27 Apr 1910 in Schieren, Lux o: Seamstress r: m m: Marie-Catherine Stirn c: 2

* 2nd Wife of [1] WITRY, Nicolas:

+ seq: 046.60 REUTER, Marie Barbe b: 15 Nov 1890 in Diekirch, Lux w: 01 Nov 1920 in Diekirch, Lux f: Nicolas Reuter m: Rosalie Merten

9 WITRY, Philippe b: 10 Jan 1887 in Schieren, Lux o: Conductor

+ seq: 046.65 LACARE, Catherine (Ketty) b: 05 Jul 1891 in Esch-sur-Alzette w: 29 Oct 1919 in Esch-sur-Alzette o: No profession r: m f: Egid Lacare m: Catharina Kanen

9 WITRY, Michel b: 22 Mar 1889 in Schieren, Lux r: b

9 WITRY, Elise b: 16 Sep 1891 in Schieren, Lux o: No
profession r: b c: 2

+ seq: 046.70 BLEY, Peter b: 05 Mar 1882 in Schieren, Lux w:
02 Feb 1913 in Schieren, Lux o: Trader o: Grocer r: m f:
Mathias Bley m: Susanna Karpes c: 2

046.20

9 WITRY, Jean b: 03 Sep 1876 in Schieren, Lux h: 45 Vincenz h:
Brill v: Esch-sur-Alzette, Lux o: Teamster r: b c: 6

+ seq: 046.20 BLEY, Anna b: 11 Nov 1875 in Schieren, Lux w:
02 Feb 1898 in Schieren, Lux h: Vincenz v: Esch-sur-Alzette,
Lux o: No profession r: m f: Mathieu Bley m: Susanne Karpes
c: 6

10 WITRY, Nicolas b: 1898 in Schieren, Lux d: 11 Apr 1898 in
Schieren, Lux r: d

10 WITRY, Mathias-Alphons b: 21 May 1899 in Ectingen, Lux o:
Cartwright

+ seq: 046.30 MERGEN, Catherine b: 04 Apr 1907 in Ettelbruck,
Lux r: b r: m f: Johann Mergen m: Louise Lanners

10 WITRY, Marie b: 13 Jun 1903 in Esch-sur-Alzette d: 01 Feb
1907 in Esch-sur-Alzette, Lux h: 45 Vicenz Strasse r: bd

10 WITRY, Catherine b: 25 Jan 1905 in Esch-sur-Alzette r: b

10 WITRY, Johann-Peter b: 10 Feb 1907 in Esch-sur-Alzette r: b

10 WITRY, Anne b: 18 Feb 1910 in Esch-sur-Alzette d: 02 Apr
1911 in Esch-sur-Alzette, Lux h: Weiser Strasse r: bd

046.50

9 [1] WITRY, Nicolas b: 26 May 1884 in Schieren, Lux v: Esch-
sur-Alzette o: Master tailor o: Mechanic o: Locksmith o:
Blacksmith r: b c: 2

+ seq: 046.50 STIRN, Anna b: 28 Feb 1888 in Schieren, Lux w:
27 Apr 1910 in Schieren, Lux o: Seamstress r: m m: Marie-
Catherine Stirn c: 2

10 WITRY, Johann b: 14 Mar 1911 in Esch-sur-Alzette r: b

10 WITRY, Charles b: 25 Oct 1912 in Esch-sur-Alzette d: 02 Aug
1969 in Luxembourg, Lux r: b

* 2nd Wife of [1] WITRY, Nicolas:

+ seq: 046.60 REUTER, Marie Barbe b: 15 Nov 1890 in
Diekirch, Lux w: 01 Nov 1920 in Diekirch, Lux f: Nicolas

Reuter   m: Rosalie Merten

046.70

9 WITRY, Elise b: 16 Sep 1891 in Schieren, Lux o: No
profession r: b c: 2

+ seq: 046.70 BLEY, Peter b: 05 Mar 1882 in Schieren, Lux w:
02 Feb 1913 in Schieren, Lux o: Trader o: Grocer r: m f:
Mathias Bley m: Susanna Karpes c: 2

10BLEY, Mathias b: 13 Dec 1913 in Schieren, Lux r: b

10BLEY, Marie b: 02 Apr 1915 in Schieren, Lux r: b

047

7 WITRY, Marie-Elisabeth b: 10 Aug 1806 in Schieren, Lux d:
31 Oct 1860 in Schieren, Lux h: Witry v: Schieren, Lux o: No
profession r: bd c: 1

+ seq: 047 b: Abt. 1805 w: Abt. 1830 c: 1

8 WITRY, Peter b: 11 Apr 1831 in Schieren, Lux v: Paris, France
o: Cobbler r: b c: 1

+ seq: 048 WAGNER, Susanne b: Abt. 1825 in Diekirch, Lux w:
Abt. 1855 v: Paris, France o: No profession c: 1

048

8 WITRY, Peter b: 11 Apr 1831 in Schieren, Lux v: Paris, France
o: Cobbler r: b c: 1

+ seq: 048 WAGNER, Susanne b: Abt. 1825 in Diekirch, Lux w:
Abt. 1855 v: Paris, France o: No profession c: 1

9 WITRY, Remy b: Aug 1857 in Paris, France d: 04 Mar 1859 in
Diekirch, Lux v: Paris, France r: d

049

7 WITRY, Johann b: 29 Sep 1819 in Schieren, Lux d: 11 Feb
1897 in Ettelbruck, Lux v: Ancy-sur-Moselle, France v:
Steinsel, Lux i: Spent his last days in the central hospice of
Ettelbruck o: Quarryman o: Day laborer o: Forger r: bd c: 5

+ seq: 049 MOISS, Anna-Marie b: 29 May 1824 in Steinsel, Lux
d: 25 Feb 1871 in Ancy-sur-Moselle, France w: 07 Oct 1847 in
Steinsel, Lux v: Ancy-sur-Moselle, France v: Steinsel, Lux o:
No profession r: b r: m f: Johann Moiss m: Anna Haffe c: 5

8 WITRY, Anna-Marie b: 19 Aug 1848 in Steinsel, Lux h:
Schoug/Witry v: Schieren, Lux o: No profession r: b c: 6

+ seq: 049.01 SCHOUG, Johann-Baptist b: 13 Jun 1852 in

Ettelbruck, Lux w: 20 Apr 1875 in Schieren, Lux a: Peters h:
Peters h: Schoug/Witry v: Schieren, Lux o: Factory worker o:
Day laborer o: Locksmith r: m f: Michel Schoug m: Marie
Weis c: 6

8 WITRY, Johann b: 27 Oct 1850 in Steinsel, Lux d: 1895 v:
Ancy-sur-Moselle, France o: Tinsmith o: Factory worker o:
Forger r: b c: 5

+ seq: 050 COURTIOL, Jeanne b: 08 Jun 1853 in Ancy-sur-
Moselle, France w: 02 Jun 1873 in Ancy-sur-Moselle, France v:
Ancy-sur-Moselle, France o: No profession r: b r: m f: Peter
Courtiol m: Catherine Goernier c: 5

8 WITRY, Johann b: 08 Feb 1859 in Ancy-sur-Moselle, France
v: Bettembourg, Lux o: Master cobbler r: b c: 2

+ seq: 050.00.50 FEDERSPIEL, Elisabeth b: Abt. 1856 w: Abt.
1885 v: Bettembourg, Lux o: No profession c: 2

8 WITRY, Melanie b: 23 Sep 1861 in Ancy-sur-Moselle, France
r: b

8 WITRY, Michel (Andrew) (Andreas) b: 18 Oct 1864 in Ancy-
sur-Moselle, France d: 17 Feb 1913 in Ettelbruck, Lux a:
Adrien Witry h: Gessel v: Ettelbruck, Lux v: Schieren, Lux o:
Day laborer o: Traveling salesman o: Storeclerk r: bd c: 5

+ seq: 050.01 KOETZ, Catherine b: 27 Jun 1871 in Ettelbruck,
Lux w: 05 Jan 1894 in Ettelbruck, Lux h: Gessel v: Ettelbruck,
Lux o: Luggage merchant o: Laborer r: m f: Peter Koetz m:
Margaretha Funck c: 5

049.01

8 WITRY, Anna-Marie b: 19 Aug 1848 in Steinsel, Lux h:
Schoug/Witry v: Schieren, Lux o: No profession r: b c: 6

+ seq: 049.01 SCHOUG, Johann-Baptist b: 13 Jun 1852 in
Ettelbruck, Lux w: 20 Apr 1875 in Schieren, Lux a: Peters h:
Peters h: Schoug/Witry v: Schieren, Lux o: Factory worker o:
Day laborer o: Locksmith r: m f: Michel Schoug m: Marie
Weis c: 6

9 SCHOUG, Johann b: 13 Mar 1876 in Schieren, Lux d: 09 Nov
1876 in Schieren, Lux h: Peters v: Schieren, Lux r: bd

9 SCHOUG, Magdalena b: 10 Feb 1878 in Schieren, Lux r: b

9 SCHOUG, Melanie b: 07 Jan 1880 in Schieren, Lux r: b

9 SCHOUG, Michael b: 21 Jun 1882 in Schieren, Lux r: b

9 SCHOUG, Joseph b: 20 Mar 1885 in Schieren, Lux r: b

9 SCHOUG, Marie b: 20 Feb 1890 in Schieren, Lux r: b

050

8 WITRY, Johann b: 27 Oct 1850 in Steinsel, Lux d: 1895 v:
Ancy-sur-Moselle, France o: Tinsmith o: Factory worker o:
Forger r: b c: 5
+ seq: 050 COURTIOL, Jeanne b: 08 Jun 1853 in Ancy-sur-
Moselle, France w: 02 Jun 1873 in Ancy-sur-Moselle, France
v: Ancy-sur-Moselle, France o: No profession r: b r: m f:
Peter Courtiol m: Catherine Goernier c: 5
9 WITRY, Marie-Anna b: 02 Oct 1873 in Ancy-sur-Moselle,
France d: 31 Aug 1874 in Ancy-sur-Moselle, France v: Ancy-
sur-Moselle, France r: bd
9 WITRY, Leonie b: 22 Mar 1875 in Ancy-sur-Moselle, France
d: 1936 in Blenod les Pont a Mousson r: b
9 WITRY, Edmond b: 14 Aug 1877 in Ancy-sur-Moselle, France
r: b
9 WITRY, Emile b: 08 Sep 1880 in Ancy-sur-Moselle, France r:
b
9 WITRY, Josefine b: 20 Mar 1883 in Ancy-sur-Moselle, France
r: b

050.00.50

8 WITRY, Johann b: 08 Feb 1859 in Ancy-sur-Moselle, France
v: Bettembourg, Lux o: Master cobbler r: b c: 2
+ seq: 050.00.50 FEDERSPIEL, Elisabeth b: Abt. 1856 w: Abt.
1885 v: Bettembourg, Lux o: No profession c: 2
9 WITRY, Catherine b: 07 May 1888 in Bettembourg, Lux o:
Milliner r: b
+ seq: 050.00.60 EIFFES, Jean b: 03 Sep 1889 in Dudelange, Lux
w: 25 Jun 1913 in Dudelange, Lux o: Professor of music f:
Francois Eiffes m: Catherine Flammang
9 WITRY, Johann-Nicolas b: 19 Aug 1890 in Bettembourg, Lux
o: Cobbler r: b c: 2
+ seq: 050.00.70 GIVENES, Albertine-Anna b: 21 May 1891 in
Kayl, Lux w: 09 May 1914 in Bettembourg, Lux o: No
profession r: m f: Johann Winknes m: Susanna Gros c: 2

050.00.70

9 WITRY, Johann-Nicolas b: 19 Aug 1890 in Bettembourg, Lux
o: Cobbler r: b c: 1
+ seq: 050.00.70 GIVENES, Albertine-Anna b: 21 May 1891 in
Kayl, Lux w: 09 May 1914 in Bettembourg, Lux o: No

profession r: m f: Johann Winknes m: Susanna Gros c: 1
10WITRY, Johanna-Maria-Esthel b: 02 May 1916 in
Bettembourg, Lux r: b

050.01

8 WITRY, Michel (Andrew) (Andreas) b: 18 Oct 1864 in Ancy-
sur-Moselle, France d: 17 Feb 1913 in Ettelbruck, Lux a:
Adrien Witry h: Gessel v: Ettelbruck, Lux v: Schieren, Lux o:
Day laborer o: Traveling salesman o: Storeclerk r: bd c: 5
+   seq: 050.01 KOETZ, Catherine b: 27 Jun 1871 in Ettelbruck,
Lux w: 05 Jan 1894 in Ettelbruck, Lux h: Gessel v:
Ettelbruck, Lux o: Luggage merchant o: Laborer r: m f: Peter
Koetz m: Margaretha Funck c: 5
9 WITRY, Margaretha b: 27 Sep 1894 in Ettelbruck, Lux i:
Immigrated to Chicago, IL r: b c: 3
+   seq: 050.01.50 LOSCH, John b: Jun 1896 in Chicago, IL w:
Abt. 1920 in Chicago, IL i: Veteran of WWI f: Stephan Losch
m: Luisa Reding c: 3
9 WITRY, Jean-Pierre b: 27 Nov 1895 in Ettelbruck, Lux r: b
9 WITRY, Jean-Baptiste b: 22 Jul 1898 in Ettelbruck, Lux r: b
9 WITRY, Maria b: 23 May 1900 in Ettelbruck, Lux r: b
9 WITRY, Charles b: 01 Oct 1902 in Ettelbruck, Lux r: b

050.01.50

9 WITRY, Margaretha b: 27 Sep 1894 in Ettelbruck, Lux i:
Immigrated to Chicago, IL r: b c: 3
+   seq: 050.01.50 LOSCH, John b: Jun 1896 in Chicago, IL w:
Abt. 1920 in Chicago, IL i: Veteran of WWI f: Stephan Losch
m: Luisa Reding c: 3
10LOSCH, John b: Abt. 1922
10LOSCH, James b: Abt. 1923
10LOSCH, LaVerne b: 1929

051

6 WITRY, Jean-Baptiste b: 15 Jul 1772 in Reuland, Lux d: 21
May 1848 in Schieren, Lux h: Schieren v: Reuland, Lux o: Day
laborer o: Farmer r: bdx c: 14
+ seq: 051 SCHROEDER, Anna-Marie b: 08 Feb 1780 in
Schieren, Lux d: 03 Dec 1859 in Schieren, Lux w: 30 Dec 1798
in Diekirch, Lux v: Schieren, Lux o: Farmer r: dx r: m c: 14
7 WITRY, Nicolas b: 05 Oct 1799 in Schieren, Lux d: 14 Jun

1827 in Schieren, Lux v: Schieren, Lux r: bd

7 WITRY, Peter b: 18 Mar 1802 in Schieren, Lux d: 25 Mar 1881 in Schieren, Lux h: Schroeder v: Schieren, Lux o: Farmer r: bd c: 9

+ seq: 052 HOFFMANN, Marie-Anna b: 04 Jan 1812 in Stegen, Lux d: 31 May 1866 in Schieren, Lux w: 08 Dec 1835 in Ettelbruck, Lux v: Schieren, Lux o: Farmer r: bd r: m f: Mathias Hoffmann m: Anna-Marie Reuland c: 9

7 WITRY, Johann-Peter b: 25 Mar 1805 in Schieren, Lux d: 12 Jan 1808 in Schieren, Lux v: Schieren, Lux r: bd

7 WITRY, Johann b: 29 Aug 1807 in Schieren, Lux d: 03 Sep 1807 in Schieren, Lux v: Schieren, Lux r: bd

7 WITRY, Jeanette (Anna) b: 25 May 1809 in Berg, Lux d: 19 Apr 1880 in Berg, Lux h: Geis Mill v: Grossmuhle, Lux v: Berg, Lux o: No profession r: bd c: 4

+ seq: 091.01 BADEN, Corneil b: 12 Sep 1806 in Berg, Lux d: 03 Feb 1874 in Berg, Lux w: 21 Jun 1837 in Berg, Lux h: Geis Mill v: Berg, Lux i: Blacksmith o: Day laborer o: Forger r: bd r: m f: Heinrich Baden m: Anna-Marie Schmarm c: 4

7 WITRY, Margaretha b: 31 Oct 1811 in Schieren, Lux d: 23 Nov 1811 in Schieren, Lux v: Schieren, Lux r: bd

7 WITRY, Johann b: 30 Nov 1812 in Schieren, Lux d: 12 Jan 1813 in Schieren, Lux v: Schieren, Lux r: bd

7 WITRY, Marie b: Abt. 1814 in Schieren, Lux d: 15 Dec 1817 in Schieren, Lux v: Schieren, Lux

7 WITRY, Nicolas b: 08 Feb 1817 in Schieren, Lux d: 16 Jan 1873 in Berg, Lux h: Schwartz v: Berg, Lux o: Day laborer o: Farmer r: bd c: 7

+ seq: 092 SCHWARTZ, Catherine b: 27 Jan 1828 in Schieren, Lux d: 04 Oct 1878 in Berg, Lux w: 30 Mar 1853 in Berg, Lux h: Schwartz v: Berg, Lux o: No profession r: d r: m f: Dominique Schwartz m: Catherine Braun c: 7

7 WITRY, Jean b: 02 Dec 1819 in Schieren, Lux d: 09 Mar 1873 in Gilsdorf, Lux v: Gilsdorf, Lux o: Day laborer o: Farmer r: bd c: 4

+ seq: 094 HIRTZ, Anna-Marie b: 25 Mar 1820 in Gilsdorf, Lux d: 23 Aug 1873 in Gilsdorf, Lux w: 29 Feb 1848 in Bettendorf, Lux v: Gilsdorf, Lux o: Farmer r: d r: m f: Adam Hirtz m: Barbara Regener c: 4

7 WITRY, Heinrich b: 24 Feb 1822 in Schieren, Lux d: 22 Feb 1896 in Mersch, Lux v: Boevange, Lux v: Schieren, Lux v:

Athis, France o: Soldier o: Rural guard o: Day laborer o: Farmer r: bdx c: 8

+ seq: 107 HOLZMACHER, Catherine b: 04 Mar 1834 in Boevange, Lux d: 06 Mar 1878 in Boevange, Lux w: 16 Feb 1859 in Schieren, Lux v: Schieren, Lux o: Farmer o: Day laborer r: bdx r: mx f: Nicolas Holzmacher m: Elisabeth Weber c: 8

7 WITRY, Martin b: 02 May 1824 in Schieren, Lux d: 18 May 1824 in Schieren, Lux v: Schieren, Lux r: bd

7 WITRY, Peter b: 27 Feb 1826 in Schieren, Lux d: 14 Apr 1827 in Schieren, Lux v: Schieren, Lux r: bd

7 WITRY, Peter b: 20 Mar 1829 in Schieren, Lux d: 23 May 1829 in Schieren, Lux v: Schieren, Lux r: bd

052

7 WITRY, Peter b: 18 Mar 1802 in Schieren, Lux d: 25 Mar 1881 in Schieren, Lux h: Schroeder v: Schieren, Lux o: Farmer r: bd c: 9

+ seq: 052 HOFFMANN, Marie-Anna b: 04 Jan 1812 in Stegen, Lux d: 31 May 1866 in Schieren, Lux w: 08 Dec 1835 in Ettelbruck, Lux v: Schieren, Lux o: Farmer r: bd r: m f: Mathias Hoffmann m: Anna-Marie Reuland c: 9

8 WITRY, Johann b: 05 Sep 1836 in Schieren, Lux d: 30 Oct 1918 in Schieren, Lux h: Schneider v: Schieren, Lux o: Teamster o: Day laborer o: Farmer o: Contractor r: bd c: 13

+ seq: 053 BIEVER, Margaretha b: 11 Jan 1841 in Hunerhoff, Lux d: 05 Dec 1887 in Schieren, Lux w: 23 Feb 1863 in Schieren, Lux h: Schneider v: Schieren, Lux o: No profession o: Day laborer r: m f: Johann Biever m: Magdalena Weis c: 13

8 WITRY, Frederic b: 01 Jun 1838 in Schieren, Lux d: 19 Sep 1838 in Schieren, Lux h: Schroeder v: Schieren, Lux r: bd

8 [1] WITRY, Anna b: 16 Aug 1839 in Schieren, Lux d: 19 Sep 1919 in Schieren, Lux v: Schieren, Lux o: Day laborer r: bd c: 5

+ seq: 086.23 HANSEN, Peter b: 25 Dec 1830 in Cruchten, Lux d: 22 Oct 1873 in Schieren, Lux w: 22 Dec 1862 in Schieren, Lux a: Henson v: Schieren, Lux o: Farm hand r: d r: m f: Peter-Franz Hansen m: Marie Karmes c: 5

* 2nd Husband of [1] WITRY, Anna:

+ seq: 086.50 KORIER, Nicolas b: 03 Aug 1841 in Schieren, Lux w: 15 Aug 1866 in Schieren, Lux o: Day laborer r: m f: August

Korier

8 WITRY, Heinrich b: 07 Jul 1841 in Schieren, Lux v: Schieren, Lux o: Border guard r: b
8 WITRY, Margaretha b: 15 Apr 1843 in Schieren, Lux r: b
8 WITRY, Marie b: 08 Aug 1845 in Schieren, Lux r: b
8 WITRY, Johann b: 08 Oct 1847 in Schieren, Lux r: b
8 WITRY, Peter (Pierre) b: 23 Nov 1849 in Schieren, Lux d: 1901 in Bourgogne, France v: Bourgogne, France o: Farmer r: b c: 3
+ seq: 087 KOENTGE, Catherine b: 1861 d: 1936 w: Abt. 1885 v: Bourgogne, France o: Farmer c: 3
8 WITRY, Elisabeth b: 17 Nov 1854 in Schieren, Lux r: b

053

8 WITRY, Johann b: 05 Sep 1836 in Schieren, Lux d: 30 Oct 1918 in Schieren, Lux h: Schneider v: Schieren, Lux o: Teamster o: Day laborer o: Farmer o: Contractor r: bd c: 13
+ seq: 053 BIEVER, Margaretha b: 11 Jan 1841 in Hunerhoff, Lux d: 05 Dec 1887 in Schieren, Lux w: 23 Feb 1863 in Schieren, Lux h: Schneider v: Schieren, Lux o: No profession o: Day laborer r: m f: Johann Biever m: Magdalena Weis c: 13
9 WITRY, John b: 10 Jun 1864 in Schieren, Lux d: 03 Jul 1931 in Chicago, IL v: Chicago, IL v: Schieren, Lux i: Emigrated to the U.S. i: Installed an early refrigeration unit in the Chicago Stock Yards r: bx c: 6
+ seq: 054 MELSEN, Anna b: 29 Sep 1864 in Schieren, Lux d: 02 Mar 1947 in Chicago, IL w: Abt. 1890 v: Chicago, IL v: Schieren, Lux o: No profession r: b f: Nicolas Melsen m: Anna Stirn c: 6
9 WITRY, Johann-Peter b: 27 Aug 1865 in Schieren, Lux v: Dubuque, IA o: Farmer r: b c: 5
+ seq: 074 FRISCH, Susanne b: 27 Oct 1865 in Fennberg, Lux d: 01 Jul 1921 in Gilsdorf, Lux w: 06 Jun 1894 in Bettendorf. Lux v: Dubuque, IA o: Maid r: d r: m m: Anna Frisch c: 5
9 WITRY, Marie b: 22 Dec 1866 in Schieren, Lux r: b
9 WITRY, Catherine b: 25 Aug 1868 in Schieren, Lux d: 02 Dec 1868 in Schieren, Lux v: Schieren, Lux r: bd
9 WITRY, Anna b: 21 Nov 1869 in Schieren, Lux d: 29 May 1919 in Luxembourg, Lux v: Schieren, Lux o: No profession r: bd c: 3
+ seq: 074.00.95 KUGENER, Anton b: 03 Aug 1867 in

Niedermertzig, Lux d: 13 Sep 1914 in Schieren, Lux w: 08 Jan 1895 in Schieren, Lux o: Cobbler r: m f: Paul Kugener m: Catharina Olsem c: 3

9 WITRY, Stillborn Girl b: 21 Nov 1869 in Schieren, Lux d: 21 Nov 1869 in Schieren, Lux v: Schieren, Lux r: d

9 WITRY, Peter b: 08 Nov 1870 in Schieren, Lux d: 09 Nov 1870 in Schieren, Lux v: Schieren, Lux r: bd

9 WITRY, Johann-Peter b: 08 Nov 1870 in Schieren, Lux d: 12 Nov 1870 in Schieren, Lux v: Schieren, Lux r: bdx

9 WITRY, Helene (Madeline) b: 24 May 1872 in Schieren, Lux d: 06 Jul 1950 v: Milwaukee, WI v: Schieren, Lux i: Emigrated to Milwaukee, WI o: No profession r: bx c: 2

+ seq: 074.01 MELSEN, Johann-Peter (JP) b: 1868 d: 11 Apr 1931 w: Abt. 1900 v: Schieren, Lux o: House painter o: Sexton r: x c: 2

9 WITRY, Nicholas b: 30 May 1874 in Schieren, Lux d: 03 Dec 1947 v: Chicago, IL i: Emigrated to the U.S. r: bx c: 8

+ seq: 075 Margaret T. b: 30 Apr 1876 d: 15 Jun 1970 w: Abt. 1899 v: Chicago, IL c: 8

9 WITRY, Peter b: 27 Feb 1876 in Schieren, Lux d: 02 Oct 1968 in Dudelange, Lux v: Dudelange, Lux o: Oiler o: Chief roller in a steel mill, ARBED o: Foreman r: b c: 6

+ seq: 079 SCHUSTER, Magdalena (Helena) b: 02 Aug 1877 in Schieren, Lux d: 05 Feb 1959 in Dudelange, Lux w: 02 Aug 1898 in Esch-sur-Alzette v: Dudelange, Lux o: No profession r: m f: Peter Schuster m: Susanna Simon c: 6

9 WITRY, Charles b: 27 May 1878 in Schieren, Lux d: 25 Jan 1943 in Cruchten, Lux h: Fischer h: Schule h: Siebfried v: Schrondweiler, Lux v: Cruchten, Lux o: Servant o: Farmhand o: Cruchten-Larochette railroad r: b c: 3

+ seq: 084 SAUBER, Lucie b: 27 Feb 1877 in Bech, Lux d: 14 Mar 1956 in Cruchten, Lux w: 04 Jan 1904 in Beck, Lux v: Schrondweiler, Lux v: Cruchten, Lux o: No profession r: m f: Gregoir Sauber m: Maria Federspiel c: 3

9 WITRY, Marie b: 25 Apr 1881 in Schieren, Lux d: 14 Mar 1951 v: Chicago, IL i: Emigrated to Chicago, IL i: Arrived on the Friesland from Antwerp r: b c: 3

+ seq: 086.01 CLEMES, John-Peter b: 27 Apr 1879 d: 07 Nov 1937 w: Abt. 1902 v: Chicago, IL i: Emigrated Chicago, IL c: 3

054

9 WITRY, John b: 10 Jun 1864 in Schieren, Lux d: 03 Jul 1931
in Chicago, IL v: Chicago, IL v: Schieren, Lux i: Emigrated to
the U.S. i: Installed an early refrigeration unit in the Chicago
Stock Yards r: bx c: 6
+ seq: 054 MELSEN, Anna b: 29 Sep 1864 in Schieren, Lux d:
02 Mar 1947 in Chicago, IL w: Abt. 1890 v: Chicago, IL v:
Schieren, Lux o: No profession r: b f: Nicolas Melsen m:
Anna Stirn c: 6
10 WITRY, John-Peter b: 31 Mar 1891 in Chicago, IL d: 30 Jun
1960 in Chicago, IL v: Chicago, IL c: 2
+ seq: 055 FREITAG, Frieda b: 07 Aug 1895 d: 31 Jan 1974 in
Chicago, IL w: Abt. 1920 v: Chicago, IL c: 2
10 WITRY, Nicholas b: 02 Feb 1894 d: 06 Oct 1899
10 WITRY, Louis-John b: 25 Nov 1895 d: 16 Nov 1967 v:
Chicago, IL i: Served in Luxembourg in US army c: 2
+ seq: 060 INGERSKI, Vic b: 25 Jun 1898 d: 07 Jul 1987 w:
Abt. 1925 c: 2
10 WITRY, George-Nicholas b: 06 Jun 1898 d: 31 Oct 1962 c: 2
+ seq: 063 MCGRATH, Alice b: 18 Jan 1901 d: 22 Mar 1990 w:
Abt. 1930 c: 2
10 WITRY, Edward-Adam b: 25 Jul 1901 d: 10 Aug 1978 in
Florida v: Chicago, IL c: 3
+ seq: 068 BETCHER, Rose A. b: 18 Mar 1904 d: 05 Aug 2002
w: Abt. 1927 v: Chicago, IL c: 3
10 WITRY, Joseph-John b: 16 Nov 1905 d: 05 Jun 1967 v:
Chicago, IL o: Consul General of Luxembourg o: Lawyer c: 4
+ seq: 071 BURKE, Catherine b: 19 Feb 1910 d: 16 Nov 1971 in
Illinois w: Abt. 1932 v: Chicago, IL c: 4

055

10 WITRY, John-Peter b: 31 Mar 1891 in Chicago, IL d: 30 Jun
1960 in Chicago, IL v: Chicago, IL c: 2
+ seq: 055 FREITAG, Frieda b: 07 Aug 1895 d: 31 Jan 1974 in
Chicago, IL w: Abt. 1920 v: Chicago, IL c: 2
11 WITRY, Bernard-John b: 25 May 1925 in Chicago, IL d: 13
Mar 1999 in Chicago, IL v: Chicago, IL i: 42nd Rainbow
Division in WWII o: Director of Superior Graphite Co. o:
Auditor for Price Waterhouse c: 5
+ seq: 056 KENNEDY, Mary b: 08 Dec 1926 w: Abt. 1950 v:
Chicago, IL c: 5

11 WITRY, Leonard b: 18 Nov 1930 d: 09 Jan 1931 in Chicago, IL

056

11 WITRY, Bernard-John b: 25 May 1925 in Chicago, IL d: 13 Mar 1999 in Chicago, IL v: Chicago, IL i: 42nd Rainbow Division in WWII o: Director of Superior Graphite Co. o: Auditor for Price Waterhouse c: 5
+ seq: 056 KENNEDY, Mary b: 08 Dec 1926 w: Abt. 1950 v: Chicago, IL c: 5
12 WITRY, Mary-Ellen b: 09 Dec 1952 in Chicago, IL v: Chicago, IL c: 2
+ seq: 056.01 LESTER, John-Jay b: 21 Jun 1950 w: Abt. 1974 v: Chicago, IL c: 2
12 WITRY, Bernard-John b: 30 Mar 1956 in Chicago, IL v: Tinley Park, IL c: 4
+ seq: 057 DONNERSBERGER, Catherine A. b: 21 Sep 1961 w: Abt. 1985 v: Tinley Park, IL c: 4
12 WITRY, Lawrence-Joseph b: 05 Sep 1957 in Chicago, IL v: Chicago, IL c: 2
+ seq: 058 TOMASZEK, Margaret V. (Peg) b: 04 Mar 1953 w: Abt. 1981 v: Chicago, IL c: 2
12 WITRY, Kathleen-Frances b: 23 Feb 1959 in Chicago, IL v: Chesapeake, VA c: 3
+ seq: 058.01 SHEAHAN, Michael P. b: 09 Mar 1959 w: Abt. 1985 v: Chesapeale, VA c: 3
12 WITRY, Paul-Gerard b: 19 Sep 1964 in Chicago, IL v: Chicago, IL c: 2
+ seq: 059 MITCHELL, Mary-Kate b: Abt. 1965 w: Abt. 1990 v: Chicago, IL c: 2

056.01

12 WITRY, Mary-Ellen b: 09 Dec 1952 in Chicago, IL v: Chicago, IL c: 2
+ seq: 056.01 LESTER, John-Jay b: 21 Jun 1950 w: Abt. 1974 v: Chicago, IL c: 2
13 LESTER, Caroline-Marie b: 14 Aug 1976 in Chicago, IL
13 LESTER, Michael b: 20 May 1980 in Chicago, IL

057

12 WITRY, Bernard-John b: 30 Mar 1956 in Chicago, IL v: Tinley

Park, IL c: 4
+ seq: 057 DONNERSBERGER, Catherine A. b: 21 Sep 1961
   w: Abt. 1985 v: Tinley Park, IL c: 4
13 WITRY, Brendan-John b: 24 Jul 1990 in Tinley Park, IL
13 WITRY, Sean-Thornton b: 12 Jul 1991 in Tinley Park, IL
13 WITRY, Connor-Ryan b: 25 Jun 1993 in Tinley Park, IL
13 WITRY, Ryan-Patrick b: 21 Jun 1997 in Tinley Park, IL

058
12 WITRY, Lawrence-Joseph b: 05 Sep 1957 in Chicago, IL v:
   Chicago, IL c: 2
+ seq: 058 TOMASZEK, Margaret V. (Peg) b: 04 Mar 1953 w:
   Abt. 1981 v: Chicago, IL c: 2
13 WITRY, Christopher-Lawrence b: 20 Jul 1984 in Chicago, IL
13 WITRY, Daniel-Joseph b: 19 May 1987 in Chicago, IL

058.01
12 WITRY, Kathleen-Frances b: 23 Feb 1959 in Chicago, IL v:
   Chesapeake, VA c: 3
+ seq: 058.01 SHEAHAN, Michael P. b: 09 Mar 1959 w: Abt.
   1985 v: Chesapeale, VA c: 3
13 SHEAHAN, Kelly-Patricia b: 06 Jul 1989 in Chicago, IL
13 SHEAHAN, Michael-Thomas b: 20 Oct 1991 in Chicago, IL
13 SHEAHAN, Erin-Elizabeth b: 10 May 1995 in Chicago, IL

059
12 WITRY, Paul-Gerard b: 19 Sep 1964 in Chicago, IL v:
   Chicago, IL c: 2
+ seq: 059 MITCHELL, Mary-Kate b: Abt. 1965 w: Abt. 1990
   v: Chicago, IL c: 2
13 WITRY, Paul-Raymond b: 03 Jan 1997 in Chicago, IL
13 WITRY, William-Bernard b: 21 Dec 2000

060
10 WITRY, Louis-John b: 25 Nov 1895 d: 16 Nov 1967 v:
   Chicago, IL i: Served in Luxembourg in US army c: 2
+ seq: 060 INGERSKI, Vic b: 25 Jun 1898 d: 07 Jul 1987 w:
   Abt. 1925 c: 2
11 WITRY, Jean b: 22 Sep 1927 v: Oak Lawn, IL c: 4
+ seq: 060.01 BURKE, Phillip b: 17 Oct 1927 w: Abt. 1950 v:
   Oak Lawn, IL c: 4

11 WITRY, Louis-Allan (Al) b: 03 Jul 1929 in Chicago, IL v:
  Orland Park, IL o: Attorney at Law c: 5
 + seq: 061 SWEENEY, Catherine E b: 25 Oct 1932 in Evergreen
    Park, IL d: 31 May 1995 in Orland Park, IL w: 08 Oct 1955 in
    Chicago, IL v: Orland Park, IL c: 5

060.01

11 WITRY, Jean b: 22 Sep 1927 v: Oak Lawn, IL c: 4
 + seq: 060.01 BURKE, Phillip b: 17 Oct 1927 w: Abt. 1950 v:
    Oak Lawn, IL c: 4
12 BURKE, John-Phillip b: 30 Jul 1953 v: Winnetka, IL c: 2
 + seq: 060.02 GROBLE, Maryann b: 27 Feb 1953 w: Abt. 1980
    v: Winnetka, IL c: 2
12 BURKE, Thomas-Francis b: 25 Dec 1956 v: Hinsdale, IL c: 2
 + seq: 060.03 KLEIN, Karen b: 09 Apr 1957 w: Abt. 1980 v:
    Hinsdale, IL c: 2
12 BURKE, Robert-Michael b: 29 Dec 1958 v: LaGrange, IL c: 2
 + seq: 060.04 DETTLOFF, Susan b: 17 Dec 1963 w: Abt. 1985
    v: LaGrange, IL c: 2
12 BURKE, Joseph-Richard b: 09 Aug 1962 v: Lockport, IL c: 1
 + seq: 060.05 DALTON, Mary-Carol b: 30 Dec 1963 w: Abt.
    1988 v: Lockport, IL c: 1

060.02

12 BURKE, John-Phillip b: 30 Jul 1953 v: Winnetka, IL c: 2
 + seq: 060.02 GROBLE, Maryann b: 27 Feb 1953 w: Abt. 1980
    v: Winnetka, IL c: 2
13 BURKE, Elizabeth-Ann b: 27 Nov 1989
13 BURKE, Katherine-Jean b: 24 Aug 1993

060.03

12 BURKE, Thomas-Francis b: 25 Dec 1956 v: Hinsdale, IL c: 2
 + seq: 060.03 KLEIN, Karen b: 09 Apr 1957 w: Abt. 1980 v:
    Hinsdale, IL c: 2
13 BURKE, Alexander b: 18 May 1992
13 BURKE, William-Henry b: 08 Oct 1995

060.04

12 BURKE, Robert-Michael b: 29 Dec 1958 v: LaGrange, IL c: 2
 + seq: 060.04 DETTLOFF, Susan b: 17 Dec 1963 w: Abt. 1985
    v: LaGrange, IL c: 2

13BURKE, Lauren-Ann b: 14 Sep 1991
13BURKE, Robert-Phillip b: 23 Feb 1994

060.05

12BURKE, Joseph-Richard b: 09 Aug 1962 v: Lockport, IL c: 1
+ seq: 060.05 DALTON, Mary-Carol b: 30 Dec 1963 w: Abt.
  1988 v: Lockport, IL c: 1
13BURKE, Patrick-Joseph b: 04 May 1992

061

11WITRY, Louis-Allan (Al) b: 03 Jul 1929 in Chicago, IL v:
  Orland Park, IL o: Attorney at Law c: 5
+ seq: 061 SWEENEY, Catherine E b: 25 Oct 1932 in Evergreen
  Park, IL d: 31 May 1995 in Orland Park, IL w: 08 Oct 1955 in
  Chicago, IL v: Orland Park, IL c: 5
12WITRY, Beth-Ann b: 02 Jul 1956 in Orland Park, IL v: Peoria,
  IL c: 3
+ seq: 061.01 SPARROW, Robert (Bob) b: 06 May 1954 w:
  Abt. 1983 v: Peoria, IL c: 3
12WITRY, Patricia-Louise b: 04 Oct 1957 in Orland Park, IL v:
  Calgary, Canada c: 1
+ seq: 061.02 URBAN, Robert b: 05 Jan 1964 w: Abt. 1990 v:
  Calgary, Canada c: 1
12WITRY, Alene-Marie b: 12 May 1959 in Orland Park, IL v:
  Medina, MN c: 3
+ seq: 061.03 CORKEN, Matthew b: 22 Jul 1959 w: Abt. 1985
  v: Medina, MN c: 3
12WITRY, David-Allen b: 13 Jul 1961 in Orland Park, IL v: Park
  Ridge, IL c: 3
+ seq: 062 SCHULTZ, Karen b: 18 Feb 1962 w: Abt. 1985 v:
  Park Ridge, IL c: 3
12WITRY, Nancy-Jean b: 04 Oct 1965 in Orland Park, IL v: New
  Lenox, IL
+ seq: 062.01 LEGO, Thomas b: 28 Aug 1964 w: Abt. 1990 v:
  New Lenox, IL

061.01

12WITRY, Beth-Ann b: 02 Jul 1956 in Orland Park, IL v: Peoria,
  IL c: 3
+ seq: 061.01 SPARROW, Robert (Bob) b: 06 May 1954 w:
  Abt. 1983 v: Peoria, IL c: 3

13 SPARROW, Christopher T. b: 11 May 1985
13 SPARROW, Mark b: 22 Mar 1987
13 SPARROW, Lindsey b: 21 Jun 1990

061.02
12 WITRY, Patricia-Louise b: 04 Oct 1957 in Orland Park, IL v:
   Calgary, Canada c: 1
+ seq: 061.02 URBAN, Robert b: 05 Jan 1964 w: Abt. 1990 v:
   Calgary, Canada c: 1
13 URBAN, Kenzie b: 20 Jun 1993

061.03
12 WITRY, Alene-Marie b: 12 May 1959 in Orland Park, IL v:
   Medina, MN c: 3
+ seq: 061.03 CORKEN, Matthew b: 22 Jul 1959 w: Abt. 1985
   v: Medina, MN c: 3
13 CORKEN, Catie b: 23 Feb 1989
13 CORKEN, Emily b: 19 Jun 1991
13 CORKEN, Amanda b: 17 Jun 1994

062
12 WITRY, David-Allen b: 13 Jul 1961 in Orland Park, IL v: Park
   Ridge, IL c: 3
+ seq: 062 SCHULTZ, Karen b: 18 Feb 1962 w: Abt. 1985 v:
   Park Ridge, IL c: 3
13 WITRY, Maris b: 19 Feb 1991
13 WITRY, Olivia b: 15 Aug 1992 i: Soccer player
13 WITRY, Nolan b: 28 Aug 1994

063
10 WITRY, George-Nicholas b: 06 Jun 1898 d: 31 Oct 1962 c: 2
+ seq: 063 MCGRATH, Alice b: 18 Jan 1901 d: 22 Mar 1990 w:
   Abt. 1930 c: 2
11 WITRY, George-Kerwin (Bud) b: 30 Oct 1932 d: 28 Jul 2007
   in Chicago, IL Cause of death: complications from surgery v:
   Oak Lawn, IL i: U. S. Navy o: Chicago fireman o: Union
   electrician c: 6
+ seq: 064 HODGES, Edna-Mae b: 30 Dec 1933 w: 28 Jun 1958
   in Chicago, IL v: Oak Lawn, IL f: Frank J. Hodges m: Edna E.
   Porte c: 6
11 WITRY, John-Daniel (Jack) b: 15 May 1935 v: Sacramento,

CA o: VP and controller of Tony Ingoglia Salami and Cheese
Co. o: High school administrator o: Basketball coach o:
Teacher c: 2
+ seq: 067 DONATO, Ramona M. (Mona) b: 13 Jul 1942 w: 14
Aug 1965 in Sacramento, CA v: Sacramento, CA i: Co-
composer of "Oowee, Oowee" o: Musician o: Registered nurse
f: Alfred Donato m: La Tona Walker c: 2

064

11 WITRY, George-Kerwin (Bud) b: 30 Oct 1932 d: 28 Jul 2007
in Chicago, IL Cause of death: complications from surgery v:
Oak Lawn, IL i: U. S. Navy o: Chicago fireman o: Union
electrician c: 6
+ seq: 064 HODGES, Edna-Mae b: 30 Dec 1933 w: 28 Jun 1958
in Chicago, IL v: Oak Lawn, IL f: Frank J. Hodges m: Edna E.
Porte c: 6
12 WITRY, George-John (Bud) b: 07 Jul 1959 v: Chicago, IL o:
Electrical wizard o: Fireman c: 3
+ seq: 065 SCHAAL, Bobbette (Mae) b: 07 May 1964 w: Abt.
1984 v: Chicago, IL f: Carol A. Reeher m: Michael Schaal c: 3
12 WITRY, Joseph-Francis b: 14 Sep 1960 v: Tinley Park, IL o:
Electrical foreman c: 2
+ seq: 066 BAUSKE, Bonnie M. b: 07 Mar 1967 w: Abt. 1985 v:
Tinley Park, IL c: 2
12 WITRY, Mary-Alice b: 09 Dec 1961 v: Chicago, IL c: 2
+ seq: 066.01 PATRICK, Michael b: 05 Mar 1959 w: Abt. 1985
v: Chicago, IL o: Telephone company foreman c: 2
12 WITRY, Timothy-Gerard b: 10 Jan 1963 v: Chicago, IL o:
Electrical foreman
+ seq: 066.01.50 GALEN, Janelle w: 03 Jun 2006
12 WITRY, Mary-Elizabeth (Mary Beth) b: 20 May 1964 v:
Lemont, IL o: Bookkeeper o: Beautician c: 2
+ seq: 066.02 GILIANO, Michael P. b: Abt. 1960 w: Abt. 1990
v: Lemont, IL o: Auto parts sales c: 2
12 WITRY, Mary-Carol b: 16 Dec 1967 v: Oak Lawn, IL

065

12 WITRY, George-John (Bud) b: 07 Jul 1959 v: Chicago, IL o:
Electrical wizard o: Fireman c: 3
+ seq: 065 SCHAAL, Bobbette (Mae) b: 07 May 1964 w: Abt.
1984 v: Chicago, IL f: Carol A. Reeher m: Michael Schaal c:

13 WITRY, Leah-Marie b: 14 Jun 1985
13 WITRY, Ashley-Marie b: 09 Apr 1987
13 WITRY, Mallory-Marie b: 20 Sep 1993

066

12 WITRY, Joseph-Francis b: 14 Sep 1960 v: Tinley Park, IL o: Electrical foreman c: 2
+ seq: 066 BAUSKE, Bonnie M. b: 07 Mar 1967 w: Abt. 1985 v: Tinley Park, IL c: 2
13 WITRY, Amanda-Lee b: 22 Jan 1987
13 WITRY, Amber-Lynn b: 03 Mar 1989

066.01

12 WITRY, Mary-Alice b: 09 Dec 1961 v: Chicago, IL c: 2
+ seq: 066.01 PATRICK, Michael b: 05 Mar 1959 w: Abt. 1985 v: Chicago, IL o: Telephone company foreman c: 2
13 PATRICK, Michael b: 16 Oct 1987
13 PATRICK, Daniel-Joseph (Danny) b: 23 Jun 1990

066.02

12 WITRY, Mary-Elizabeth (Mary Beth) b: 20 May 1964 v: Lemont, IL o: Bookkeeper o: Beautician c: 2
+ seq: 066.02 GILIANO, Michael P. b: Abt. 1960 w: Abt. 1990 v: Lemont, IL o: Auto parts sales c: 2
13 GILIANO, Mitchell-Paul b: 08 Jan 1994
13 GILIANO, Regina-Mae b: 16 May 1996

067

11 WITRY, John-Daniel (Jack) b: 15 May 1935 v: Sacramento, CA o: VP and controller of Tony Ingoglia Salami and Cheese Co. o: High school administrator o: Basketball coach o: Teacher c: 2
+ seq: 067 DONATO, Ramona M. (Mona) b: 13 Jul 1942 w: 14 Aug 1965 in Sacramento, CA v: Sacramento, CA i: Co-composer of "Oowee, Oowee" o: Musician o: Registered nurse f: Alfred Donato m: La Tona Walker c: 2
12 WITRY, Kathleen M. (Kathy) b: 19 Jul 1966 v: Sacramento, CA o: Analyst for the California state retirement system
+ HALSTEAD, James-Steven b: 02 Oct 1954 in Hartford, CT w: 13 Jan 2007 in Sacramento, CA v: Sacramento, CA o: Sales

manager for Wrigley Gum f: Aubrey Halstead m: Philomena
Torchia
12 WITRY, John-Nicholas (Nick) b: 14 Sep 1968 v: Sacramento,
CA o: Senior vice president of Wachovia Securities c: 3
+ seq: 067.01 ALLEN, Michele w: 05 May 2000 in Sacramento,
CA v: Sacramento, CA c: 3

067.01

12 WITRY, John-Nicholas (Nick) b: 14 Sep 1968 v: Sacramento,
CA o: Senior vice president of Wachovia Securities c: 3
+ seq: 067.01 ALLEN, Michele w: 05 May 2000 in Sacramento,
CA v: Sacramento, CA c: 3
13 WITRY, Madisyn b: 06 Oct 1993 in Sacramento, CA
13 WITRY, Lily-Kate b: 03 Apr 2002 in Sacramento, CA
13 WITRY, John-Howard (Jack) b: 17 May 2007 in Sacramento,
CA

068

10 WITRY, Edward-Adam b: 25 Jul 1901 d: 10 Aug 1978 in
Florida v: Chicago, IL c: 3
+ seq: 068 BETCHER, Rose A. b: 18 Mar 1904 d: 05 Aug 2002
w: Abt. 1927 v: Chicago, IL c: 3
11 WITRY, Gerald-Edward b: 01 Apr 1929 v: Hickory Hills, IL
c: 4
+ seq: 069 DOZIER, Joan M. b: 18 Jan 1934 w: Abt. 1955 v:
Hickory Hills, IL c: 4
11 WITRY, Dorinne b: 07 May 1934 v: Spring Valley, CA c: 2
+ seq: 070.02 SANDERS, Norbert b: 04 Dec 1930 w: Abt. 1957
v: Spring Valley, CA c: 2
11 WITRY, Loretta b: 24 Mar 1939 v: Chicago, IL c: 3
+ seq: 070.05 COSGROVE, Frank b: 08 Oct 1935 d: 05 Feb
1987 w: Abt. 1960 v: Chicago, IL c: 3

069

11 WITRY, Gerald-Edward b: 01 Apr 1929 v: Hickory Hills, IL
c: 4
+ seq: 069 DOZIER, Joan M. b: 18 Jan 1934 w: Abt. 1955 v:
Hickory Hills, IL c: 4
12 WITRY, Brenda b: 15 Mar 1957 v: Worth, IL
12 WITRY, Laura b: 08 Jul 1958 v: Orland Park, IL c: 3
+ seq: 069.01 BAILEY, Luke b: 01 Nov 1958 w: Abt. 1983 v:

Orland Park, IL c: 3

12 WITRY, Matthew b: 19 Apr 1960 v: Chicago, IL c: 2

+ seq: 070 WOLFF, Mary-Patricia (Mary Pat) b: 19 Jan 1964 w: 1987 in Chicago, IL v: Chicago, IL c: 2

12 WITRY, Julie b: 12 Nov 1964 v: Tinley Park, IL c: 2

+ seq: 070.01 MERKLE, James b: 12 Jul 1964 w: Abt. 1990 v: Tinley Park, IL c: 2

069.01

12 WITRY, Laura b: 08 Jul 1958 v: Orland Park, IL c: 3

+ seq: 069.01 BAILEY, Luke b: 01 Nov 1958 w: Abt. 1983 v: Orland Park, IL c: 3

13 BAILEY, Kenneth b: 29 Apr 1985

13 BAILEY, Erin b: 21 Mar 1989

13 BAILEY, Brianne b: 17 Mar 1992

070

12 WITRY, Matthew b: 19 Apr 1960 v: Chicago, IL c: 2

+ seq: 070 WOLFF, Mary-Patricia (Mary Pat) b: 19 Jan 1964 w: 1987 in Chicago, IL v: Chicago, IL c: 2

13 WITRY, Caitlin b: 19 Mar 1991

13 WITRY, Nicholas b: 27 Nov 1992

070.01

12 WITRY, Julie b: 12 Nov 1964 v: Tinley Park, IL c: 2

+ seq: 070.01 MERKLE, James b: 12 Jul 1964 w: Abt. 1990 v: Tinley Park, IL c: 2

13 MERKLE, Jordan b: 15 Nov 1991

13 MERKLE, Jenna b: 12 Jan 1994

070.02

11 WITRY, Dorinne b: 07 May 1934 v: Spring Valley, CA c: 2

+ seq: 070.02 SANDERS, Norbert b: 04 Dec 1930 w: Abt. 1957 v: Spring Valley, CA c: 2

12 SANDERS, Jeffrey b: 28 Apr 1959 v: San Diego, CA c: 1

+ seq: 070.03 DAVIDSON, Marlene b: 08 Oct 1962 w: Abt. 1985 v: San Diego, CA c: 1

12 SANDERS, Marc b: 11 Jul 1961 v: San Diego, CA

+ seq: 070.04 CALVIN, Cyrise b: Abt. 1965 w: Abt. 1990 v: San Diego, CA

070.03

12SANDERS, Jeffrey b: 28 Apr 1959 v: San Diego, CA c: 1
+ seq: 070.03 DAVIDSON, Marlene b: 08 Oct 1962 w: Abt.
   1985 v: San Diego, CA c: 1
13SANDERS, Janey b: 01 Jun 1992

070.05

11WITRY, Loretta b: 24 Mar 1939 v: Chicago, IL c: 3
+ seq: 070.05 COSGROVE, Frank b: 08 Oct 1935 d: 05 Feb
   1987 w: Abt. 1960 v: Chicago, IL c: 3
12COSGROVE, Steven b: 23 Dec 1961 v: Oak Lawn, IL c: 2
+ seq: 070.06 CRILLY, Joan b: 13 Feb 1961 w: Abt. 1990 v:
   Oak Lawn, IL c: 2
12COSGROVE, Timothy b: 08 Jan 1964 v: Hometown, IL
+ seq: 070.07 WINTER, Pamela b: 06 Nov 1967 w: Abt. 1990
   v: Hometown, IL
12COSGROVE, Jill b: 22 Dec 1965 v: Orland Hills, IL c: 1
+ seq: 070.08 BARTKOWSKI, Mark b: 27 Sep 1965 w: Abt.
   1990 v: Orland Hills, IL c: 1

070.06

12COSGROVE, Steven b: 23 Dec 1961 v: Oak Lawn, IL c: 2
+ seq: 070.06 CRILLY, Joan b: 13 Feb 1961 w: Abt. 1990 v:
   Oak Lawn, IL c: 2
13COSGROVE, Brittany b: 22 Jul 1993
13COSGROVE, Megan b: 02 Jun 1995

070.08

12COSGROVE, Jill b: 22 Dec 1965 v: Orland Hills, IL c: 1
+ seq: 070.08 BARTKOWSKI, Mark b: 27 Sep 1965 w: Abt.
   1990 v: Orland Hills, IL c: 1
13BARTKOWIAK, Allison b: 11 Jan 1991

071

10WITRY, Joseph-John b: 16 Nov 1905 d: 05 Jun 1967 v:
   Chicago, IL o: Consul General of Luxembourg o: Lawyer c: 4
+ seq: 071 BURKE, Catherine b: 19 Feb 1910 d: 16 Nov 1971 in
   Illinois w: Abt. 1932 v: Chicago, IL c: 4
11WITRY, Patricia-Ann b: 04 Aug 1934 v: Arlington Heights, IL
   c: 4
+ seq: 071.01 CARBERY, John b: 11 Jun 1933 w: Abt. 1956 v:

Arlington Heights, IL c: 4

11 WITRY, Joan-Marie b: 20 Oct 1937 in Evanston, IL v:
Poulsbo, WA

+ seq: 071.06 GORNER, Denis b: 29 Dec 1931 in London,
England w: 28 Dec 1968 in Comarillo, CA v: Poulsbo, WA

11 WITRY, Joseph-John (Joe) b: 18 Oct 1941 d: 12 Sep 1998 in
Woodstock, IL v: Bay St. Louis, MS c: 2

+ seq: 072 ARMSTRONG, Sharon L. b: 21 Dec 1942 w: Abt.
1970 v: Wellington, FL c: 2

11 WITRY, Richard-James t: Counsel General of Luxembourg b:
08 Apr 1950 v: Skokie, IL o: Lawyer c: 1

+ seq: 073 LEWIS, Patricia b: 06 Nov 1952 w: Abt. 1980 v:
Skokie, IL c: 1

071.01

11 WITRY, Patricia-Ann b: 04 Aug 1934 v: Arlington Heights, IL
c: 4

+ seq: 071.01 CARBERY, John b: 11 Jun 1933 w: Abt. 1956 v:
Arlington Heights, IL c: 4

12 CARBERY, John-W. b: 07 Apr 1958 v: Arlington Heights, IL
c: 3

+ seq: 071.02 AMAITIS, Laurie b: 11 Mar 1958 w: Abt. 1980
v: Arlington Heights, IL c: 3

12 CARBERY, James-Richard b: 16 Jun 1959 v: Hoffman Estates,
IL c: 1

+ seq: 071.03 MEZMALIS, Parsla b: 13 Sep 1961 w: Abt. 1985
v: Hoffman Estates, IL c: 1

12 CARBERY, Mary-Janet b: 02 Sep 1960 v: Chesterfield, MO c:
2

+ seq: 071.04 MODERHACK, Lawrence b: 01 Feb 1955 w: Abt.
1985 v: Chesterfield, MO c: 2

12 CARBERY, Thomas-Joseph b: 27 Aug 1962 v: Elk Grove
Village, IL c: 1

+ seq: 071.05 PADOCK, Marcia b: Abt. 1965 w: Abt. 1990 v:
Elk Grove Village, IL c: 1

071.02

12 CARBERY, John-W. b: 07 Apr 1958 v: Arlington Heights, IL
c: 3

+ seq: 071.02 AMAITIS, Laurie b: 11 Mar 1958 w: Abt. 1980
v: Arlington Heights, IL c: 3

13CARBERY, Christie-Marie b: 23 Feb 1984
13CARBERY, Matthew-John b: 21 Dec 1987
13CARBERY, Jackie-Lynn b: 05 Jul 1990

071.03

12CARBERY, James-Richard b: 16 Jun 1959 v: Hoffman Estates, IL c: 1
+ seq: 071.03 MEZMALIS, Parsla b: 13 Sep 1961 w: Abt. 1985 v: Hoffman Estates, IL c: 1
13CARBERY, Janis b: 19 Sep 1986

071.04

12CARBERY, Mary-Janet b: 02 Sep 1960 v: Chesterfield, MO c: 2
+ seq: 071.04 MODERHACK, Lawrence b: 01 Feb 1955 w: Abt. 1985 v: Chesterfield, MO c: 2
13MODERHACK, Brian-Donald b: 09 Mar 1988
13MODERHACK, Bradley

071.05

12CARBERY, Thomas-Joseph b: 27 Aug 1962 v: Elk Grove Village, IL c: 1
+ seq: 071.05 PADOCK, Marcia b: Abt. 1965 w: Abt. 1990 v: Elk Grove Village, IL c: 1
13CARBERY, Natalie-Patricia b: 20 Jan 1994

072

11WITRY, Joseph-John (Joe) b: 18 Oct 1941 d: 12 Sep 1998 in Woodstock, IL v: Bay St. Louis, MS c: 2
+ seq: 072 ARMSTRONG, Sharon L. b: 21 Dec 1942 w: Abt. 1970 v: Wellington, FL c: 2
12WITRY, Joseph-Dale b: 07 Mar 1973 v: Wellington, FL
12WITRY, Catherine-Ashley (Katie) b: 27 Apr 1976 v: Louisiana o: Social worker o: Realtor
+ seq: 072.50 RICHE, Todd w: 26 May 2007 in New Orleans, LA

073

11WITRY, Richard-James t: Counsel General of Luxembourg b: 08 Apr 1950 v: Skokie, IL o: Lawyer c: 1
+ seq: 073 LEWIS, Patricia b: 06 Nov 1952 w: Abt. 1980 v:

Skokie, IL c: 1
12 WITRY, Daniel-Joseph b: 24 Sep 1985

074

9 WITRY, Johann-Peter b: 27 Aug 1865 in Schieren, Lux v:
  Dubuque, IA o: Farmer r: b c: 5
+ seq: 074 FRISCH, Susanne b: 27 Oct 1865 in Fennberg, Lux
   d: 01 Jul 1921 in Gilsdorf, Lux w: 06 Jun 1894 in Bettendorf.
   Lux v: Dubuque, IA o: Maid r: d r: m m: Anna Frisch c: 5
10 WITRY, Pierre b: 08 Mar 1895 in Gilsdorf, Lux d: 10 Jul 1975
   in Gilsdorf, Lux h: Streidesch v: Gilsdorf, Lux o: Farmer r: b
   c: 3
+ seq: 074.00.50 WAMBACH, Barbara b: 20 Apr 1896 in
   Beforterheide, Lux w: 06 Jul 1918 in Bettendorf, Lux h:
   Streidesch v: Gilsdorf, Lux o: No profession r: m f: Mathias
   Wambach m: Susanna Kramp c: 3
10 WITRY, Jean b: 24 Jul 1898 in Gilsdorf, Lux d: 27 Sep 1898 in
   Gilsdorf, Lux r: bd
10 WITRY, Jean b: 24 Sep 1900 in Gilsdorf, Lux d: 13 Apr 1958
   in Diekirch, Lux o: Chauffeur r: b
+ seq: 074.00.90 BROCHMANN, Louise b: 25 Apr 1904 in
   Welscheid, Lux w: 10 Feb 1928 in Bourscheid, Lux o: No
   profession r: m f: Reinhard Brochmann m: Catharina Schiltz
10 WITRY, Jean-Pierre b: 28 Jan 1904 in Gilsdorf, Lux d: 22 Mar
   1904 in Gilsdorf, Lux r: bd
10 WITRY, Anton b: 02 Dec 1906 in Gilsdorf, Lux r: b

074.00.50

10 WITRY, Pierre b: 08 Mar 1895 in Gilsdorf, Lux d: 10 Jul 1975
   in Gilsdorf, Lux h: Streidesch v: Gilsdorf, Lux o: Farmer r: b
   c: 3
+ seq: 074.00.50 WAMBACH, Barbara b: 20 Apr 1896 in
   Beforterheide, Lux w: 06 Jul 1918 in Bettendorf, Lux h:
   Streidesch v: Gilsdorf, Lux o: No profession r: m f: Mathias
   Wambach m: Susanna Kramp c: 3
11 WITRY, Suzanne b: 03 Jun 1919 in Gilsdorf, Lux d: 01 Aug
   2003 in Gilsdorf, Lux o: No profession r: bd
+ seq: 074.00.60 REDING, Johann-Peter b: 27 Dec 1902 in
   Clairefontaine, Lux w: 18 Jul 1930 in Bettendorf, Lux o:
   Farmer r: m f: Nikolaus Reding m: Josephine Benck
11 WITRY, Jean b: 22 Apr 1922 in Gilsdorf, Lux d: 04 Jan 1990

in Gilsdorf, Lux i: 5 children r: bd
+ seq: 074.00.70 w: 1952
11WITRY, Madeleine b: Abt. 1924 c: 1
+ seq: 074.00.80 w: Abt. 1950 c: 1

074.00.80
11WITRY, Madeleine b: Abt. 1924 c: 1
+ seq: 074.00.80 w: Abt. 1950 c: 1
12Mom c: 1
+ seq: 074.00.85 KLENSCH w: Abt. 1970 c: 1

074.00.85
12Mom c: 1
+ seq: 074.00.85 KLENSCH w: Abt. 1970 c: 1
13KLENSCH, John

074.00.95
9 WITRY, Anna b: 21 Nov 1869 in Schieren, Lux d: 29 May
   1919 in Luxembourg, Lux v: Schieren, Lux o: No profession r:
   bd c: 3
+ seq: 074.00.95 KUGENER, Anton b: 03 Aug 1867 in
   Niedermertzig, Lux d: 13 Sep 1914 in Schieren, Lux w: 08 Jan
   1895 in Schieren, Lux o: Cobbler r: m f: Paul Kugener m:
   Catharina Olsem c: 3
10KUGENER, Johann b: 21 Sep 1895 in Schieren, Lux o:
   Cobbler
+ seq: 074.00.99 KAYSER, Marie b: 10 Jan 1900 in Oberglabach,
   Lux w: 02 Jun 1922 in Schieren, Lux o: No profession r: m f:
   Mathias Kayser m: Susanna Weber
10KUGENER, Johann Peter b: 1898 v: Schieren, Lux o: Usher
10KUGENER, Susanna b: 04 Sep 1900 in Schieren, Lux o: No
   profession
+ seq: 074.00.97 FRANTZEN, Joseph b: 09 Jun 1900 in Mersch,
   Lux o: Railroad official r: m f: Johann Frantzen m: Maria
   Colesch

074.01
9 WITRY, Helene (Madeline) b: 24 May 1872 in Schieren, Lux
   d: 06 Jul 1950 v: Milwaukee, WI v: Schieren, Lux i: Emigrated
   to Milwaukee, WI o: No profession r: bx c: 2
+ seq: 074.01 MELSEN, Johann-Peter (JP) b: 1868 d: 11 Apr

1931 w: Abt. 1900 v: Schieren, Lux o: House painter o: Sexton r: x c: 2

10MELSEN, Leo-Johannn b: 09 Dec 1912 in Schieren, Lux d: 08 Jul 1950 r: b
+ seq: 074.02 FRIDERES, Elise b: Abt. 1915 w: Abt. 1940

10MELSEN, Susanna-Magdalena b: 26 Jul 1915 in Schieren, Lux r: b c: 2
+ seq: 074.03 SHER, Mathias b: Abt. 1910 w: Abt. 1940 c: 2

074.03

10MELSEN, Anna b: Abt. 1914 c: 2
+ seq: 074.03 SHER, Mathias b: Abt. 1910 w: Abt. 1940 c: 2
11SHER, Jean-Pierre
11SHER, Leon b: Abt. 1945 c: 1
+ seq: 074.04 Monique b: Abt. 1945 w: Abt. 1970 c: 1

074.04

11SHER, Leon b: Abt. 1945 c: 1
+ seq: 074.04 Monique b: Abt. 1945 w: Abt. 1970 c: 1
12SHER, Claude

075

9 WITRY, Nicholas b: 30 May 1874 in Schieren, Lux d: 03 Dec 1947 v: Chicago, IL i: Emigrated to the U.S. r: bx c: 8
+ seq: 075 Margaret T. b: 30 Apr 1876 d: 15 Jun 1970 w: Abt. 1899 v: Chicago, IL c: 8

10WITRY, John b: 17 Oct 1900 d: 02 Feb 1977 in Chicago, IL v: Chicago, IL c: 1
+ seq: 075.01 Kathleen M. (Kitty) b: 08 Nov 1906 d: 11 Apr 1995 w: Abt. 1930 v: Chicago, IL c: 1

10WITRY, Peter J. b: 25 Jan 1902 d: 01 Dec 1989 v: St. Petersburg, FL c: 2
+ seq: 075.02 MORGE, Marion b: 25 Dec 1913 in Illinois d: 07 Nov 2000 in Lake Geneva, IL w: Abt. 1930 v: Lake Geneva, IL c: 2

10WITRY, Anna b: 27 Oct 1903 d: 16 May 1992 c: 1
+ seq: 075.03 BRUIN, James b: Abt. 1900 w: Abt. 1925 c: 1

10WITRY, Mary-Agnes b: Abt. 1905 d: 1993 c: 3
+ seq: 075.05 BEHEN, Francis-Edward (Frank) b: 1903 d: 1981 w: Abt. 1930 c: 3

10WITRY, Albert b: 16 Jan 1908 v: Mountain Home, AR

+   seq: 075.05.50 June b: 1910 d: 10 Dec 1990 in Mountain
    Home, AR w: Abt. 1930
10 WITRY, Helen b: 10 Apr 1910 d: 18 Feb 1991
+   seq: 075.06 REICHENBERGER, John b: Abt. 1905 w: Abt.
    1935
10 WITRY, Henry b: 08 Aug 1912 d: 27 Apr 1985 in Illinois
+   seq: 075.07 HYLACZEK, Estelle b: 14 Jul 1909 d: 27 Aug
    1983 in Illinois w: Abt. 1940
10 WITRY, William-Louis (Pops) b: 01 Sep 1914 d: 05 Sep 1999
    v: Chicago, IL c: 3
+   seq: 076 MARTIN, Marie-Therese b: 15 Jun 1920 w: Abt.
    1940 v: Chicago, IL c: 3

075.01

10 WITRY, John b: 17 Oct 1900 d: 02 Feb 1977 in Chicago, IL v:
    Chicago, IL c: 1
+   seq: 075.01 Kathleen M. (Kitty) b: 08 Nov 1906 d: 11 Apr
    1995 w: Abt. 1930 v: Chicago, IL c: 1
11 WITRY, June b: Abt. 1935

075.02

10 WITRY, Peter J. b: 25 Jan 1902 d: 01 Dec 1989 v: St.
    Petersburg, FL c: 2
+   seq: 075.02 MORGE, Marion b: 25 Dec 1913 in Illinois d: 07
    Nov 2000 in Lake Geneva, IL w: Abt. 1930 v: Lake Geneva,
    IL c: 2
11 WITRY, Marilyn b: Abt. 1933 c: 1
+   seq: 075.02.01 HANNA, Thomas w: Abt. 1960 c: 1
11 WITRY, PeterJ. b: Abt. 1935 d: 27 Mar 1967 in Illinois Cause
    of death: Auto crash

075.02.01

11 WITRY, Marilyn b: Abt. 1933 c: 1
+   seq: 075.02.01 HANNA, Thomas w: Abt. 1960 c: 1
12 HANNA, Mari v: Mount Holly, NJ o: Teacher of computers o:
    Head of Technology Dept. c: 2
+   seq: 075.02.02 PISCITELLI, Michael w: Abt. 1990 v: Mount
    Holly, NJ o: Airline pilot - Captain at Southwest Airlines c: 2

075.02.02

12 HANNA, Mari v: Mount Holly, NJ o: Teacher of computers o:

Head of Technology Dept. c: 2
+ seq: 075.02.02 PISCITELLI, Michael w: Abt. 1990 v: Mount
 Holly, NJ o: Airline pilot - Captain at Southwest Airlines c: 2
13 PISCITELLI, Christina b: Jan 1991
13 PISCITELLI, Stephanie b: 1993

075.03
10 WITRY, Anna b: 27 Oct 1903 d: 16 May 1992 c: 1
+ seq: 075.03 BRUIN, James b: Abt. 1900 w: Abt. 1925 c: 1
11 BRUIN, Nancy b: Abt. 1930
+ seq: 075.04 RICHTER b: Abt. 1925 w: Abt. 1955

075.05
10 WITRY, Mary-Agnes b: Abt. 1905 d: 1993 c: 3
+ seq: 075.05 BEHEN, Francis-Edward (Frank) b: 1903 d: 1981
 w: Abt. 1930 c: 3
11 BEHEN, Mary-Jane b: 1925 d: 2007 c: 1
+ seq: 075.05.10 HOLT, Raymond-Agner b: 1918 d: 2006 w:
 Abt. 1945 c: 1
11 BEHEN, Francis-Edward b: 1926 d: 1992
+ seq: 075.05.30 WINBECH, Matilda (Thilda) w: Abt. 1950
11 BEHEN, Edward-Nicholas b: 1948 c: 5
+ seq: 075.05.40 WALTERS, Katerine-Ann b: 1950 w: Abt.
 1970 c: 5

075.05.10
11 BEHEN, Mary-Jane b: 1925 d: 2007 c: 1
+ seq: 075.05.10 HOLT, Raymond-Agner b: 1918 d: 2006 w:
 Abt. 1945 c: 1
12 [1] HOLT, Diane b: 1948 c: 1
+ seq: 075.05.25 RABER, Conrad w: Abt. 1970 c: 1
* 2nd Husband of [1] HOLT, Diane:
+ seq: 075.05.27 HIGH, Thomas w: Abt. 1980

075.05.25
12 [1] HOLT, Diane b: 1948 c: 1
+ seq: 075.05.25 RABER, Conrad w: Abt. 1970 c: 1
13 RABER, Brea
* 2nd Husband of [1] HOLT, Diane:
+ seq: 075.05.27 HIGH, Thomas w: Abt. 1980

075.05.40

11BEHEN, Edward-Nicholas b: 1948 c: 5
+ seq: 075.05.40 WALTERS, Katerine-Ann b: 1950 w: Abt. 1970 c: 5
12BEHEN, Jennifer-Ann b: 1974
12BEHEN, Edward-Nicholas b: 1977
12BEHEN, Francis-Edward b: 1983
12BEHEN, Raymond-Michael b: 1985
12BEHEN, Bridgette b: 1986

076

10WITRY, William-Louis (Pops) b: 01 Sep 1914 d: 05 Sep 1999 v: Chicago, IL c: 3
+ seq: 076 MARTIN, Marie-Therese b: 15 Jun 1920 w: Abt. 1940 v: Chicago, IL c: 3
11WITRY, William-James b: 30 Nov 1942 v: Oak Forest, IL c: 4
+ seq: 077 GARFIELD, Elaine b: 01 Dec 1949 w: Abt. 1960 v: Oak Forest, IL c: 4
11WITRY, Suzanne b: 12 Oct 1948
+ seq: 077.03 GORHAM, John P. b: 25 Mar 1947 w: Abt. 1970
11WITRY, Robert-Edward b: 08 Sep 1951 v: Palos Heights, IL c: 1
+ seq: 078 NORTHSTRUM, Mary A. b: 11 Mar 1954 w: Abt. 1980 v: Palos Heights, IL c: 1

077

11WITRY, William-James b: 30 Nov 1942 v: Oak Forest, IL c: 4
+ seq: 077 GARFIELD, Elaine b: 01 Dec 1949 w: Abt. 1960 v: Oak Forest, IL c: 4
12WITRY, Christopher b: 14 May 1966 c: 1
+ seq: 077.01 YOUNG, Kim b: 20 Aug 1966 w: Abt. 1990 c: 1
12WITRY, Lisa b: 19 Dec 1967
+ seq: 077.02 WINTER, Robert b: 25 Mar 1967 w: Abt. 1990
12WITRY, Traci b: 26 Aug 1969 o: Attorney
12WITRY, Nicole K. (Nicky) b: 26 Jul 1973 v: Champaign, IL

077.01

12WITRY, Christopher b: 14 May 1966 c: 1
+ seq: 077.01 YOUNG, Kim b: 20 Aug 1966 w: Abt. 1990 c: 1
13WITRY, Katie b: 22 Jul 1994

078

11 WITRY, Robert-Edward b: 08 Sep 1951 v: Palos Heights, IL
 c: 1
+ seq: 078 NORTHSTRUM, Mary A. b: 11 Mar 1954 w: Abt.
 1980 v: Palos Heights, IL c: 1
12 WITRY, Eric-Daniel b: 23 Apr 1989

079

9 WITRY, Peter b: 27 Feb 1876 in Schieren, Lux d: 02 Oct 1968
 in Dudelange, Lux v: Dudelange, Lux o: Oiler o: Chief roller
 in a steel mill, ARBED o: Foreman r: b c: 6
+ seq: 079 SCHUSTER, Magdalena (Helena) b: 02 Aug 1877 in
 Schieren, Lux d: 05 Feb 1959 in Dudelange, Lux w: 02 Aug
 1898 in Esch-sur-Alzette v: Dudelange, Lux o: No profession
 r: m f: Peter Schuster m: Susanna Simon c: 6
10 WITRY, Suzanne b: 30 Jul 1899 in Dudelange, Lux v:
 Dudelange, Lux i: Died young r: b
10 WITRY, Johann-Peter b: 18 Mar 1901 in Dudelange, Lux d: 12
 Jun 1920 in Dudelange, Lux v: Dudelange, Lux r: bd
10 WITRY, Josephine b: 15 Oct 1903 in Dudelange, Lux d: 22
 Sep 1976 r: b c: 2
+ seq: 079.01 HIRSCHLER, Mathias b: 19 Dec 1901 d: 21 Dec
 1972 w: Abt. 1925 c: 2
10 WITRY, Anna-Susanna b: 27 Dec 1906 in Dudelange, Lux d:
 23 Dec 1912 in Dudelange, Lux v: Dudelange, Lux r: bd
10 WITRY, Nicolas b: 30 Mar 1911 in Dudelange, Lux d: 26 Nov
 1977 in Dudelange, Lux v: Dudelange, Lux o: Maintenance
 foreman in ARBED steel mill r: b c: 1
+ seq: 080 ROOS, Catherine b: 26 Jun 1913 in Lellig, Lux d: 10
 Nov 1985 in Dudelange, Lux w: Abt. 1934 v: Dudelange, Lux
 c: 1
10 WITRY, Joseph-Nicolas b: 29 Jan 1913 in Dudelange, Lux d:
 06 Jan 1995 in Dudelange, Lux v: Dudelange, Lux o: Retiree
 o: Steel mill ARBED c: 2
+ seq: 083 MICHAUX, Marguerite b: 18 Apr 1920 in Dudelange,
 Lux w: 14 Nov 1942 in Dudelange, Lux v: Dudelange, Lux c:
 2

079.01

10 WITRY, Josephine b: 15 Oct 1903 in Dudelange, Lux d: 22
 Sep 1976 c: 2

+ seq: 079.01 HIRSCHLER, Mathias b: 19 Dec 1901 d: 21 Dec 1972 w: Abt. 1925 c: 2

11 HIRSCHLER, Alice b: 28 Jun 1928 in Dudelange, Lux d: 20 Jan 1977 in Nancy, France c: 3

+ seq: 079.02 KOSCH, Roger b: 14 Feb 1926 in Mamer, Lux w: 19 Jun 1949 v: Dudelange, Lux c: 3

11 HIRSCHLER, Robert b: 1925 d: 1944 in Russia

079.02

11 HIRSCHLER, Alice b: 28 Jun 1928 in Dudelange, Lux d: 20 Jan 1977 in Nancy, France c: 3

+ seq: 079.02 KOSCH, Roger b: 14 Feb 1926 in Mamer, Lux w: 19 Jun 1949 v: Dudelange, Lux c: 3

12 KOSCH, Carlo b: 20 Feb 1951 in Luxembourg, Lux o: Teacher c: 2

+ seq: 079.03 BASTIAN, Lotty b: 10 Sep 1948 in Luxembourg, Lux w: 20 Dec 1973 c: 2

12 KOSCH, Marco b: 05 Jan 1957 in Dudelange, Lux v: Dudelange, Lux o: Employee of C.F.L. railroad c: 2

+ seq: 079.04 GIAMPRINI, Diana b: 14 Sep 1963 in Esch-sur-Alzette, Lux w: 16 Sep 1989 in Kayle, Lux v: Dudelange, Lux c: 2

12 KOSCH, Roby b: 26 Feb 1966 in Dudelange, Lux v: Dudelange, Lux o: Master butcher c: 1

+ seq: 079.05 THORNTON, Josette b: 03 Jan 1964 in Weimerskirch, Lux w: 05 Nov 1994 in Luxembourg, Lux v: Dudelange, Lux c: 1

079.03

12 KOSCH, Carlo b: 20 Feb 1951 in Luxembourg, Lux o: Teacher c: 2

+ seq: 079.03 BASTIAN, Lotty b: 10 Sep 1948 in Luxembourg, Lux w: 20 Dec 1973 c: 2

13 KOSCH, Christian b: 20 Jan 1977 in Luxembourg, Lux

13 KOSCH, Corinne b: 04 Aug 1979 in Luxembourg, Lux

079.04

12 KOSCH, Marco b: 05 Jan 1957 in Dudelange, Lux v: Dudelange, Lux o: Employee of C.F.L. railroad c: 2

+ seq: 079.04 GIAMPRINI, Diana b: 14 Sep 1963 in Esch-sur-Alzette, Lux w: 16 Sep 1989 in Kayle, Lux v: Dudelange, Lux

c: 2
13 KOSCH, Sammy b: 22 Jun 1990 in Esch-sur-Alzette, Lux
13 KOSCH, Stevie b: 01 Sep 1993 in Esch-sur-Alzette, Lux

079.05
12 KOSCH, Roby b: 26 Feb 1966 in Dudelange, Lux v:
   Dudelange, Lux o: Master butcher c: 1
+ seq: 079.05 THORNTON, Josette b: 03 Jan 1964 in
   Weimerskirch, Lux w: 05 Nov 1994 in Luxembourg, Lux v:
   Dudelange, Lux c: 1
13 KOSCH, Bob b: 22 Jul 1993 in Luxembourg, Lux

080
10 WITRY, Nicolas b: 13 Mar 1911 in Dudelange, Lux d: 27 Nov
   1978 in Dudelange, Lux v: Dudelange, Lux o: Maintenance
   foreman in ARBED steel mill c: 1
+ seq: 080 ROOS, Catherine b: 26 Jun 1913 in Lellig, Lux d: 10
   Nov 1985 in Dudelange, Lux w: Abt. 1934 v: Dudelange, Lux
   c: 1
11 WITRY, Francois (Franco) b: 01 Jun 1936 in Dudelange, Lux
   v: Dudelange, Lux i: Named in a patent with ARBED for a
   lance to refine liquid metals i: Retired o: Technical engineer in
   steel mill ARBED c: 3
+ seq: 081 SCHALBAR, Nelly b: 14 Mar 1936 in Bettembourg,
   Lux w: 03 Oct 1959 in Bettembourg, Lux v: Dudelange, Lux
   c: 3

081
11 WITRY, Francois (Franco) b: 01 Jun 1936 in Dudelange, Lux
   v: Dudelange, Lux i: Named in a patent with ARBED for a
   lance to refine liquid metals i: Retired o: Technical engineer in
   steel mill ARBED c: 3
+ seq: 081 SCHALBAR, Nelly b: 14 Mar 1936 in Bettembourg,
   Lux w: 03 Oct 1959 in Bettembourg, Lux v: Dudelange, Lux
   c: 3
12 WITRY, Manon b: 18 Nov 1960 in Bettembourg, Lux v:
   Dudelange, Lux o: Nurse c: 3
+ seq: 081.01 BASSANI, Romain b: 14 Feb 1959 in Dudelange,
   Lux w: 05 Dec 1981 v: Dudelange, Lux c: 3
12 WITRY, Alain b: 21 Feb 1963 in Bettembourg, Lux v: Bergem,
   Lux o: Technical manager in Singapore o: Construction

engineer in steel mill ARBED c: 2

+ seq: 082 ROBERT, Claudine b: 27 Nov 1963 in Merl, Lux w:
   09 Apr 1988 in Merl, Lux v: Bergem, Lux c: 2

12 WITRY, Luc b: 16 Jul 1971 in Luxembourg, Lux v: Elvange,
   Lux o: Finance Ministry of Luxembourg c: 2

+ seq: 082.02 SCHollar, Claudine b: 15 Jan 1970 in Esch-sur-
   Alzette, Lux w: 20 Jul 1996 in Dudelange, Lux v: Elvange,
   Lux o: Teacher c: 2

081.01

12 WITRY, Manon b: 18 Nov 1960 in Bettembourg, Lux v:
   Dudelange, Lux o: Nurse c: 3

+ seq: 081.01 BASSANI, Romain b: 14 Feb 1959 in Dudelange,
   Lux w: 05 Dec 1981 v: Dudelange, Lux c: 3

13 BASSANI, Stephanie b: 08 Aug 1985 in Esch-sur-Alzette, Lux
13 BASSANI, Sam b: 24 Sep 1987 in Esch-sur-Alzette, Lux
13 BASSANI, Maite b: 15 Mar 1992 in Esch-sur-Alzette, Lux

082

12 WITRY, Alain b: 21 Feb 1963 in Bettembourg, Lux v: Bergem,
   Lux o: Technical manager in Singapore o: Construction
   engineer in steel mill ARBED c: 2

+ seq: 082 ROBERT, Claudine b: 27 Nov 1963 in Merl, Lux w:
   09 Apr 1988 in Merl, Lux v: Bergem, Lux c: 2

13 WITRY, Daniel b: 02 Jan 1992 in Luxembourg, Lux
13 WITRY, Philip b: 27 Jun 1994 in Luxembourg, Lux

082.02

12 WITRY, Luc b: 16 Jul 1971 in Luxembourg, Lux v: Elvange,
   Lux o: Finance Ministry of Luxembourg c: 2

+ seq: 082.02 SCHollar, Claudine b: 15 Jan 1970 in Esch-sur-
   Alzette, Lux w: 20 Jul 1996 in Dudelange, Lux v: Elvange,
   Lux o: Teacher c: 2

13 WITRY, Charel b: 02 Dec 2000 in Esch-sur-Alzette, Lux
13 WITRY, Mia b: 21 Oct 2004 in Esch-sur-Alzette, Lux

083

10 WITRY, Joseph b: 29 Jan 1913 in Dudelange, Lux d: 06 Jan
   1995 in Dudelange, Lux v: Dudelange, Lux o: Retiree o: Steel
   mill ARBED c: 2

+ seq: 083 MICHAUX, Marguerite b: 18 Apr 1920 in Dudelange,

Lux w: 14 Nov 1942 in Dudelange, Lux v: Dudelange, Lux c: 2

11 WITRY, Monique b: 23 Oct 1943 in Dudelange, Lux v: Bettembourg, Lux c: 1

+ seq: 083.01 STROTZ, Fernand b: 18 Sep 1944 in Bettembourg, Lux d: 08 Feb 1990 in Luxembourg, Lux w: 28 Apr 1967 v: Bettembourg, Lux c: 1

11 WITRY, Marcel b: 15 Dec 1944 in Dudelange, Lux d: 05 Feb 1968 in Dudelange, Lux Cause of death: Traffic accident v: Dudelange, Lux

083.01

11 WITRY, Monique b: 23 Oct 1943 in Dudelange, Lux v: Bettembourg, Lux c: 1

+ seq: 083.01 STROTZ, Fernand b: 18 Sep 1944 in Bettembourg, Lux d: 08 Feb 1990 in Luxembourg, Lux w: 28 Apr 1967 v: Bettembourg, Lux c: 1

12 STROTZ, Nadine b: 05 Jun 1968 in Dudelange, Lux v: Filsdorf, Lux c: 2

+ seq: 083.02 RAUSCH, Claude b: 10 Sep 1965 in Bettembourg, Lux w: 17 Jul 1993 in Bettembourg, Lux v: Filsdorf, Lux o: Mailman c: 2

083.02

12 STROTZ, Nadine b: 05 Jun 1968 in Dudelange, Lux v: Filsdorf, Lux c: 2

+ seq: 083.02 RAUSCH, Claude b: 10 Sep 1965 in Bettembourg, Lux w: 17 Jul 1993 in Bettembourg, Lux v: Filsdorf, Lux o: Mailman c: 2

13 RAUSCH, Ben b: 22 Sep 1996 in Dudelange, Lux

13 RAUSCH, Lena b: 28 Jun 2001

084

9 WITRY, Charles b: 27 May 1878 in Schieren, Lux d: 25 Jan 1943 in Cruchten, Lux h: Fischer h: Schule h: Siebfried v: Schrondweiler, Lux v: Cruchten, Lux o: Servant o: Farmhand o: Cruchten-Larochette railroad r: b c: 3

+ seq: 084 SAUBER, Lucie b: 27 Feb 1877 in Bech, Lux d: 14 Mar 1956 in Cruchten, Lux w: 04 Jan 1904 in Beck, Lux v: Schrondweiler, Lux v: Cruchten, Lux o: No profession r: m f: Gregoir Sauber m: Maria Federspiel c: 3

10WITRY, Maria (Marichen) b: 11 Nov 1904 in Schrondweiler,
Lux d: 23 Jan 1923 in Petange, Lux v: Petange, Lux o: Maid
servant r: bd
10WITRY, Anna b: 26 Sep 1906 in Schrondweiler, Lux d: 25 Feb
1978 in Cruchten, Lux v: Cruchten, Lux r: b c: 1
+ seq: 084.01 SEIL, Andre b: 26 Sep 1949 in Cruchten, Lux d: 30
Aug 1950 in Cruchten, Lux Cause of death: Industrial accident
on railroad w: 11 Jun 1948 v: Cruchten, Lux o: Railroad
employee c: 1
10WITRY, Jean-Pierre b: 20 Jun 1909 in Schrondweiler, Lux d:
25 Sep 1994 in Ettelbruck, Lux v: Cruchten, Lux i: Retired o:
Worked at Paul Wurth metalworks r: b c: 2
+ seq: 085 STOOS, Louise b: 01 Aug 1914 in Cruchten, Lux d:
11 Aug 2005 w: 16 Apr 1940 in Nommern, Lux v: Cruchten,
Lux f: Pierre-Nicolas Stoos m: Anna-Margaretha Zenners c: 2

084.01
10WITRY, Anna b: 26 Sep 1906 in Schrondweiler, Lux d: 25 Feb
1978 in Cruchten, Lux v: Cruchten, Lux c: 1
+ seq: 084.01 SEIL, Andre b: 26 Sep 1949 in Cruchten, Lux d:
30 Aug 1950 in Cruchten, Lux Cause of death: Industrial
accident on railroad w: 11 Jun 1948 v: Cruchten, Lux o:
Railroad employee c: 1
11SEIL, Rene b: 30 Dec 1949 in Ettelbruck, Lux d: 28 Apr 1991
in Arlon, Belgium v: Cruchten, Lux o: Bank clerk at
International Bank of Luxembourg c: 1
+ seq: 084.02 NIESEN, Sylvie b: 16 Jun 1946 in Luxembourg,
Lux w: 05 Sep 1970 v: Cruchten, Lux o: Bank clerk at
International Bank of Luxembourg c: 1

084.02
11SEIL, Rene b: 30 Dec 1949 in Ettelbruck, Lux d: 28 Apr 1991
in Arlon, Belgium v: Cruchten, Lux o: Bank clerk at
International Bank of Luxembourg c: 1
+ seq: 084.02 NIESEN, Sylvie b: 16 Jun 1946 in Luxembourg,
Lux w: 05 Sep 1970 v: Cruchten, Lux o: Bank clerk at
International Bank of Luxembourg c: 1
12SEIL, Guy b: 29 Apr 1977 o: Apprentice electrician c: 1
+ seq: 084.50 MATTIOLI, Diane w: Abt. 2000 c: 1

084.50

12 SEIL, Guy b: 29 Apr 1977 o: Apprentice electrician c: 1
+ seq: 084.50 MATTIOLI, Diane w: Abt. 2000 c: 1
13 SEIL, Larissa b: 10 Jun 2005

085

10 WITRY, Jean-Pierre b: 20 Jan 1909 in Schrondweiler, Lux d:
25 Sep 1994 in Ettelbruck, Lux v: Cruchten, Lux i: Retired o:
Worked at Paul Wurth metalworks c: 2
+ seq: 085 STOOS, Louise b: 01 Aug 1914 in Cruchten, Lux d:
11 Aug 2005 w: 16 Apr 1940 in Nommern, Lux v: Cruchten,
Lux f: Pierre-Nicolas Stoos m: Anna-Margaretha Zenners c: 2
11 WITRY, Lucianne b: 02 Sep 1941 in Cruchten, Lux v:
Heisdorf, Lux o: Office employee for Goodyear c: 1
+ seq: 085.01 PETTINGER, Nic b: 31 May 1937 w: 03 Sep
1963 v: Heisdorf, Lux o: Office employee for Neuberg c: 1
11 WITRY, Charles b: 15 Sep 1947 in Luxembourg, Lux v:
Lintgen, Lux o: Linotypist at Luxemburger Wort c: 1
+ seq: 086 LEISEN, Nicole b: 14 Mar 1947 in Ettelbruck, Lux
w: 06 Jun 1970 v: Lintgen, Lux o: Office employee for social
services c: 1

085.01

11 WITRY, Lucianne b: 02 Sep 1941 in Cruchten, Lux v:
Heisdorf, Lux o: Office employee for Goodyear c: 1
+ seq: 085.01 PETTINGER, Nic b: 31 May 1937 w: 03 Sep
1963 v: Heisdorf, Lux o: Office employee for Neuberg c: 1
12 PETTINGER, Daniele b: 10 Nov 1966 in Ettelbruck, Lux v:
Heisdorf, Lux o: Nurse c: 2
+ seq: 085.02 RUGO, Robert b: 16 Jul 1963 in Luxembourg, Lux
w: 20 Nov 1992 v: Heisdorf, Lux o: Auto mechanic c: 2

085.02

12 PETTINGER, Daniele b: 10 Nov 1966 in Ettelbruck, Lux v:
Heisdorf, Lux o: Nurse c: 2
+ seq: 085.02 RUGO, Robert b: 16 Jul 1963 in Luxembourg, Lux
w: 20 Nov 1992 v: Heisdorf, Lux o: Auto mechanic c: 2
13 RUGO, Tommy b: 16 Jan 1995 in Luxembourg, Lux
13 RUGO, Liz b: 19 Dec 1997 in Luxembourg, Lux

086

11 WITRY, Charles b: 15 Sep 1947 in Luxembourg, Lux v:
Lintgen, Lux o: Linotypist at Luxemburger Wort c: 1
+ seq: 086 LEISEN, Nicole b: 14 Mar 1947 in Ettelbruck, Lux
w: 06 Jun 1970 v: Lintgen, Lux o: Office employee for social
services c: 1
12 WITRY, Annick b: 17 Dec 1975 in Luxembourg, Lux v:
Nospelt, Lux o: Deputy secretary in commune administration of
Lintgen c: 1
+ seq: 086.00.01 HALSDORF, Jos b: in Germany w: 11 May
2002 v: Nospelt, Lux c: 1

086.00.01

12 WITRY, Annick b: 17 Dec 1975 in Luxembourg, Lux v:
Nospelt, Lux o: Deputy secretary in commune administration of
Lintgen c: 2
+ seq: 086.00.01 HALSDORF, Jos b: in Germany w: 11 May
2002 v: Nospelt, Lux c: 2
13 HALSDORF, Louis b: 01 Feb 2005 in Nospelt, Lux
13 HALSDORF, Claire b: 11 Dec 2006 in Nospelt, Lux

086.01

9 WITRY, Marie b: 25 Apr 1881 in Schieren, Lux d: 14 Mar
1951 v: Chicago, IL i: Emigrated to Chicago, IL i: Arrived on
the Friesland from Antwerp r: b c: 3
+ seq: 086.01 CLEMES, John-Peter b: 27 Apr 1879 d: 07 Nov
1937 w: Abt. 1902 v: Chicago, IL i: Emigrated Chicago, IL c:
3
10 CLEMES, Lena (Helen) b: 11 Jul 1902 c: 3
+ seq: 086.02 CARTWRIGHT, Eli b: Abt. 1900 w: Abt. 1935 c:
3
10 CLEMES, John-Peter b: 30 Nov 1903 d: 21 Jan 1973 c: 3
+ seq: 086.05 WIERSCHEM, Marie b: 08 Sep 1908 d: 30 Mar
1983 w: Abt. 1926 c: 3
10 CLEMES, William b: 26 Sep 1906 c: 1
+ seq: 086.21 MORROSCO, Antoinette b: Abt. 1910 w: Abt.
1935 c: 1

086.02

10 CLEMES, Lena (Helen) b: 11 Jul 1902 c: 3
+ seq: 086.02 CARTWRIGHT, Eli b: Abt. 1900 w: Abt. 1935 c:

11 CARTWRIGHT, Mary-Jane b: Abt. 1940
11 CARTWRIGHT, Elizabeth b: Abt. 1940
+ seq: 086.03 SODERHOLM b: Abt. 1935 w: Abt. 1965
11 CARTWRIGHT, Girl b: Abt. 1940
+ seq: 086.04 CLANCY b: Abt. 1935 w: Abt. 1965

086.05

10 CLEMES, John-Peter b: 30 Nov 1903 d: 21 Jan 1973 c: 3
+ seq: 086.05 WIERSCHEM, Marie b: 08 Sep 1908 d: 30 Mar
1983 w: Abt. 1926 c: 3
11 CLEMES, Annabelle b: 24 Dec 1928 v: Palos Heights, IL c: 4
+ seq: 086.06 STOLARSKI, Leonard b: 15 Aug 1929 w: Abt.
1950 v: Palos Heights, IL c: 4
11 CLEMES, Genevieve-Leona b: 04 Jan 1931 v: Burbank, IL c:
5
+ seq: 086.10 HANDZIK, Thomas b: 18 Sep 1928 d: 04 Aug
1995 w: Abt. 1952 v: Burbank, IL c: 5
11 CLEMES, John-Joseph b: 10 Sep 1935 v: Tinley Park, IL c: 5
+ seq: 086.16 NEFFLE, Winifred b: 11 Mar 1936 w: Abt. 1955
v: Tinley Park, IL c: 5

086.06

11 CLEMES, Annabelle b: 24 Dec 1928 v: Palos Heights, IL c: 4
+ seq: 086.06 STOLARSKI, Leonard b: 15 Aug 1929 w: Abt.
1950 v: Palos Heights, IL c: 4
12 STOLARSKI, Judith-Ann b: 27 Aug 1951 v: New Lenox, IL c:
2
+ seq: 086.07 MACK, Charles b: 13 Jun 1951 w: Abt. 1975 v:
New Lenox, IL c: 2
12 STOLARSKI, Leonard-Paul b: 29 Jun 1953 v: New Lenox, IL
c: 2
+ seq: 086.08 KLEINFELDT, Janet b: 10 Feb 1958 w: Abt. 1978
v: New Lenox, IL c: 2
12 STOLARSKI, Richard-George b: 05 Jul 1954 v: Palos Heights,
IL
12 STOLARSKI, Paul-Edward b: 18 Oct 1966 v: Grand Haven,
MI c: 1
+ seq: 086.09 Holly b: Abt. 1970 w: Abt. 1995 v: Grand Haven,
MI c: 1

086.07

12STOLARSKI, Judith-Ann b: 27 Aug 1951 v: New Lenox, IL c: 2

+ seq: 086.07 MACK, Charles b: 13 Jun 1951 w: Abt. 1975 v: New Lenox, IL c: 2

13MACK, Erin b: 19 Nov 1980

13MACK, Emily b: May 1990

086.08

12STOLARSKI, Leonard-Paul b: 29 Jun 1953 v: New Lenox, IL c: 2

+ seq: 086.08 KLEINFELDT, Janet b: 10 Feb 1958 w: Abt. 1978 v: New Lenox, IL c: 2

13STOLARSKI, Christopher b: 14 Feb 1980

13STOLARSKI, Meghan b: 09 May 1984

086.09

12STOLARSKI, Paul-Edward b: 18 Oct 1966 v: Grand Haven, MI c: 1

+ seq: 086.09 Holly b: Abt. 1970 w: Abt. 1995 v: Grand Haven, MI c: 1

13STOLARSKI, Kevin

086.10

11CLEMES, Genevieve-Leona b: 04 Jan 1931 v: Burbank, IL c: 5

+ seq: 086.10 HANDZIK, Thomas b: 18 Sep 1928 d: 04 Aug 1995 w: Abt. 1952 v: Burbank, IL c: 5

12HANDZIK, Joyce b: 05 Sep 1954 v: Joliet, IL c: 4

+ seq: 086.11 NAHORSKI, Jan b: 25 Nov 1952 w: Abt. 1975 v: Joliet, IL c: 4

12HANDZIK, Thomas b: 05 Oct 1955 v: Lockport, IL c: 1

+ seq: 086.12 BENNEY, Jodi b: 19 Jan 1956 w: Abt. 1980 v: Lockport, IL c: 1

12HANDZIK, Leslie b: 22 Jun 1957 v: Darien, IL c: 3

+ seq: 086.13 BERTRAM, David b: 10 Jun 1956 w: Abt. 1978 v: Darien, IL c: 3

12HANDZIK, Karla b: 19 Jul 1959 v: New Lenox, IL

+ seq: 086.14 KRAEMER, Garry b: 28 Apr 1955 w: Abt. 1980 v: New Lenox, IL

12HANDZIK, Joseph b: 24 Apr 1961 v: Frankfort, IL c: 3

+ seq: 086.15 CARR, Kathleen b: 22 May 1960 w: Abt. 1985 v: Frankfort, IL c: 3

086.11

12 HANDZIK, Joyce b: 05 Sep 1954 v: Joliet, IL c: 4
+ seq: 086.11 NAHORSKI, Jan b: 25 Nov 1952 w: Abt. 1975 v: Joliet, IL c: 4
13 NAHORSKI, Jennifer b: 08 Feb 1976
13 NAHORSKI, Jacob b: 22 May 1978
13 NAHORSKI, Jessica b: 16 Mar 1983
13 NAHORSKI, Joanna b: 13 Apr 1987

086.12

12 HANDZIK, Thomas b: 05 Oct 1955 v: Lockport, IL c: 1
+ seq: 086.12 BENNEY, Jodi b: 19 Jan 1956 w: Abt. 1980 v: Lockport, IL c: 1
13 HANDZIK, Amy-Alise b: 13 Mar

086.13

12 HANDZIK, Leslie b: 22 Jun 1957 v: Darien, IL c: 3
+ seq: 086.13 BERTRAM, David b: 10 Jun 1956 w: Abt. 1978 v: Darien, IL c: 3
13 BERTRAM, Scot b: 06 Jun 1980
13 BERTRAM, Eric b: 15 Apr 1982
13 BERTRAM, Ryan b: 30 Dec 1983

086.15

12 HANDZIK, Joseph b: 24 Apr 1961 v: Frankfort, IL c: 3
+ seq: 086.15 CARR, Kathleen b: 22 May 1960 w: Abt. 1985 v: Frankfort, IL c: 3
13 HANDZIK, Joseph
13 HANDZIK, Steven
13 HANDZIK, Joshua

086.16

11 CLEMES, John-Joseph b: 10 Sep 1935 v: Tinley Park, IL c: 5
+ seq: 086.16 NEFFLE, Winifred b: 11 Mar 1936 w: Abt. 1955 v: Tinley Park, IL c: 5
12 CLEMES, Patricia-Ann b: 27 Jul 1956 v: Manhatten, IL c: 2
+ seq: 086.17 COOK, James b: Abt. 1950 w: Abt. 1980 v: Manhatten, IL c: 2

12CLEMES, Cynthia-Sue b: 10 Oct 1957
12CLEMES, Jacqueline-Marie b: 25 Dec 1959 v: Oak Forest, IL
  c: 2
 + seq: 086.18 MULLIGAN, Michael b: 23 Feb 1959 w: Abt.
  1978 v: Oak Forest, IL c: 2
12CLEMES, Janis-Scheryl b: 02 Aug 1963 v: Oak Forest, IL
 + seq: 086.19 DEVUONO, Sam b: 01 Apr 1956 w: Abt. 1990 v:
  Oak Forest, IL
12CLEMES, Kimberly-Therese b: 31 Jul 1965 v: Lockport, IL c:
  2
 + seq: 086.20 HAMBA, James b: 25 Jan 1959 w: Abt. 1985 v:
  Lockport, IL c: 2

086.17
12CLEMES, Patricia-Ann b: 27 Jul 1956 v: Manhatten, IL c: 2
 + seq: 086.17 COOK, James b: Abt. 1950 w: Abt. 1980 v:
  Manhatten, IL c: 2
13COOK, Joshua b: 25 Mar 1985
13COOK, Matthew b: 25 Mar 1985

086.18
12CLEMES, Jacqueline-Marie b: 25 Dec 1959 v: Oak Forest, IL
  c: 2
 + seq: 086.18 MULLIGAN, Michael b: 23 Feb 1959 w: Abt.
  1978 v: Oak Forest, IL c: 2
13MULLIGAN, Amber-Lynn b: 23 Jul 1980
13MULLIGAN, Patrick-Michael b: 23 Jan 1984

086.20
12CLEMES, Kimberly-Therese b: 31 Jul 1965 v: Lockport, IL c:
  2
 + seq: 086.20 HAMBA, James b: 25 Jan 1959 w: Abt. 1985 v:
  Lockport, IL c: 2
13HAMBA, Samantha-Lynn b: 06 Aug 1989
13HAMBA, Alex-James b: 03 Jun 1992

086.21
10CLEMES, William b: 26 Sep 1906 c: 1
 + seq: 086.21 MORROSCO, Antoinette b: Abt. 1910 w: Abt.
  1935 c: 1
11CLEMES, Gail b: Abt. 1940

+ seq: 086.22 MENGEL b: Abt. 1935 w: Abt. 1965

086.23

8 [1] WITRY, Anna b: 16 Aug 1839 in Schieren, Lux d: 19 Sep
1919 in Schieren, Lux v: Schieren, Lux o: Day laborer r: bd c:
5

+ seq: 086.23 HANSEN, Peter b: 25 Dec 1830 in Cruchten, Lux
d: 22 Oct 1873 in Schieren, Lux w: 22 Dec 1862 in Schieren,
Lux a: Henson v: Schieren, Lux o: Farm hand r: d r: m f:
Peter-Franz Hansen m: Marie Karmes c: 5

9 HANSEN, Marie b: Abt. 1863 in Grentzingen, Lux d: 31 May
1866 in Schieren, Lux v: Schieren, Lux r: d

9 HANSEN, Johann b: Abt. 1866 in Grentzingen, Lux d: 24 Jun
1866 in Schieren, Lux v: Schieren, Lux r: d

9 HANSEN, Nicolas b: 03 Jul 1867 in Schieren, Lux r: b

9 HANSEN, Johann b: 02 Aug 1871 in Schieren, Lux o: Railroad
worker r: b

9 HANSEN, Johann b: 11 Jun 1874 in Schieren, Lux d: 20 May
1876 in Schieren, Lux r: bd

* 2nd Husband of [1] WITRY, Anna:

+ seq: 086.50 KORIER, Nicolas b: 03 Aug 1841 in Schieren, Lux
w: 15 Aug 1866 in Schieren, Lux o: Day laborer r: m f: August
Korier

087

8 WITRY, Peter (Pierre) b: 23 Nov 1849 in Schieren, Lux d:
1901 in Bourgogne, France v: Bourgogne, France o: Farmer r:
b c: 3

+ seq: 087 KOENTGE, Catherine b: 1861 d: 1936 w: Abt. 1885
v: Bourgogne, France o: Farmer c: 3

9 WITRY, Henri b: 1890 in Bourgogne, France d: 1966 in
Bourgogne, France v: Bourgogne, France o: Farmer c: 3

+ seq: 088 JUPPIN, Germaine b: 1906 d: 1986 w: Abt. 1930 v:
Bourgogne, France o: Farmer c: 3

9 WITRY, Suzanne b: 1892 d: 1968 o: Farmer

9 WITRY, Pierre o: Farmer

+ seq: 091 GROUD, Henriette w: Abt. 1915 o: Farmer

088

9 WITRY, Henri b: 1890 in Bourgogne, France d: 1966 in

Bourgogne, France v: Bourgogne, France o: Farmer c: 3
+ seq: 088 JUPPIN, Germaine b: 1906 d: 1986 w: Abt. 1930 v:
  Bourgogne, France o: Farmer c: 3
10 WITRY, Therese b: in Bourgogne, France i: Died at 4 months
10 WITRY, Elisabeth b: 1931 in Bourgogne, France v:
  Bourgogne, France o: Farmer c: 3
+ seq: 088.01 GUERLET, Gilbert b: Abt. 1925 w: Abt. 1953 v:
  Bourgogne, France o: Farmer c: 3
10 WITRY, Michel b: 1934 in Bourgogne, France d: 1987 in
  Bourgogne, France v: Bourgogne, France o: Farmer c: 1
+ seq: 089 LHOTELAIN, Monique b: 1938 w: Abt. 1958 v:
  Bourgogne, France o: Farmer c: 1

088.01

10 WITRY, Elisabeth b: 1931 in Bourgogne, France v:
  Bourgogne, France o: Farmer c: 3
+ seq: 088.01 GUERLET, Gilbert b: Abt. 1925 w: Abt. 1953 v:
  Bourgogne, France o: Farmer c: 3
11 GUERLET, Marie-Catherine b: 1955 in Bourgogne, France o:
  Teacher c: 2
+ seq: 088.02 PARMENTIER, Thierry b: Abt. 1955 w: Abt.
  1985 o: Farmer c: 2
11 GUERLET, Francine b: 1956 in Bourgogne, France o: Teacher
  c: 1
+ seq: 088.03 CHARLIER, Michel w: Abt. 1980 o: Teacher c: 1
11 GUERLET, Sylvette b: 1958 in Bourgogne, France o: Teacher
  c: 1
+ seq: 088.04 RAMIRES DE LA ROSA, Hector b: Abt. 1955 d:
  Abt. 1995 w: Abt. 1978 c: 1

088.02

11 GUERLET, Marie-Catherine b: 1955 in Bourgogne, France o:
  Teacher c: 2
+ seq: 088.02 PARMENTIER, Thierry b: Abt. 1955 w: Abt.
  1985 o: Farmer c: 2
12 PARMENTIER, Alexandre b: 1992 i: Twin
12 PARMENTIER, Christophe b: 1992 i: Twin

088.03

11 GUERLET, Francine b: 1956 in Bourgogne, France o: Teacher
  c: 1

+ seq: 088.03 CHARLIER, Michel w: Abt. 1980 o: Teacher c: 1
12 GUERLET, Anne b: 1991

088.04

11 GUERLET, Sylvette b: 1958 in Bourgogne, France o: Teacher
  c: 1
+ seq: 088.04 RAMIRES DE LA ROSA, Hector b: Abt. 1955 d:
  Abt. 1995 w: Abt. 1978 c: 1
12 RAMIRES DE LA ROSA, Flavy b: 1979

089

10 WITRY, Michel b: 1934 in Bourgogne, France d: 1987 in
  Bourgogne, France v: Bourgogne, France o: Farmer c: 1
+ seq: 089 LHOTELAIN, Monique b: 1938 w: Abt. 1958 v:
  Bourgogne, France o: Farmer c: 1
11 WITRY, Eric b: 06 Jun 1960 in Bourgogne, France v:
  Bourgogne, France o: Commercial representative c: 3
+ seq: 090 CARAMELLE, Anne b: 08 Apr 1963 w: 31 Mar
  1990 in Cormontreuil, France v: Bourgogne, France o: Realtor
  c: 3

090

11 WITRY, Eric b: 06 Jun 1960 in Bourgogne, France v:
  Bourgogne, France o: Commercial representative c: 3
+ seq: 090 CARAMELLE, Anne b: 08 Apr 1963 w: 31 Mar
  1990 in Cormontreuil, France v: Bourgogne, France o: Realtor
  c: 3
12 WITRY, Aurelie b: 06 Jun 1987 in Bourgogne, France
12 WITRY, Julien b: 10 Jul 1990 in Bourgogne, France i: Twin
12 WITRY, Nicolas b: 10 Jul 1990 in Bourgogne, France i: Twin

091.01

7 WITRY, Jeanette (Anna) b: 25 May 1809 in Berg, Lux d: 19
  Apr 1880 in Berg, Lux h: Geis Mill v: Grossmuhle, Lux v:
  Berg, Lux o: No profession r: bd c: 4
+ seq: 091.01 BADEN, Corneil b: 12 Sep 1806 in Berg, Lux d:
  03 Feb 1874 in Berg, Lux w: 21 Jun 1837 in Berg, Lux h: Geis
  Mill v: Berg, Lux i: Blacksmith o: Day laborer o: Forger r:
  bd r: m f: Heinrich Baden m: Anna-Marie Schmarm c: 4
8 BADEN, Jean b: 28 Mar 1838 in Berg, Lux r: b
8 BADEN, Anna-Maria (Marie) b: 03 Jun 1840 in Berg, Lux o:

No profession r: b

+ seq: 091.30 REISCH, Johann b: 23 Sep 1829 in Ettelbruck, Lux
   w: 05 Jun 1867 in Berg, Lux o: Cobbler r: m f: Nicolas Reisch
   m: Marie Wolff

8 BADEN, Theresia b: 14 Apr 1843 in Berg, Lux o: No
   profession r: b

+ seq: 091.50 SCHWARTZ, Johann b: 12 Dec 1839 in Berg, Lux
   w: 27 Sep 1864 in Berg, Lux o: Day laborer o: Stone mason r:
   m f: Dominique Schwartz m: Katharina Braun

8 BADEN, Peter b: 09 Feb 1850 in Berg, Lux d: 15 Jul 1850 in
   Berg, Lux r: bd

092

7 WITRY, Nicolas b: 08 Feb 1817 in Schieren, Lux d: 16 Jan
   1873 in Berg, Lux h: Schwartz v: Berg, Lux o: Day laborer o:
   Farmer r: bd c: 7

+ seq: 092 SCHWARTZ, Catherine b: 27 Jan 1828 in Schieren,
   Lux d: 04 Oct 1878 in Berg, Lux w: 30 Mar 1853 in Berg, Lux
   h: Schwartz v: Berg, Lux o: No profession r: d r: m f:
   Dominique Schwartz m: Catherine Braun c: 7

8 WITRY, Catherine b: 04 Feb 1854 in Berg, Lux d: 05 Feb 1854
   in Berg, Lux h: Schwartz v: Berg, Lux r: bd

8 WITRY, Catherine b: 14 Nov 1855 in Berg, Lux h: Geis Mill
   v: Berg, Lux o: No profession r: b c: 7

+ seq: 092.01 BETTENDORF, Heinrich b: 16 Nov 1853 in
   Scheidgen, Lux d: 03 Dec 1901 in Bettembourg, Lux w: 31
   Dec 1878 in Berg, Lux h: Geis Mill v: Berg, Lux o: Stone
   mason o: Mason r: m f: Nicolas Bettendorf m: Margaretha
   Rillung c: 7

8 WITRY, Stillborn Girl b: 24 Oct 1857 in Berg, Lux d: 24 Oct
   1857 in Berg, Lux h: Schwzrtz v: Berg, Lux r: bd

8 WITRY, Anna b: 04 Nov 1858 in Berg, Lux d: 20 Sep 1943 in
   Los Angeles, CA r: b

+ seq: 092.02 GOOLSBY w: Abt. 1880

8 WITRY, Johann b: 20 May 1861 in Berg, Lux v: Milwaukee,
   WI i: Emigrated to U. S. o: Locksmith r: bx c: 2

+ seq: 093 SAND, Anna b: Abt. 1865 in Dubuque, IA w: 20 Nov
   1889 in Dubuque, IA v: Milwaukee, WI r: dx r: m c: 2

8 WITRY, Stillborn Girl b: 08 Mar 1864 in Berg, Lux d: 08 Mar
   1864 in Berg, Lux h: Schwartz v: Berg, Lux r: bd

8 WITRY, Margaretha b: 16 Nov 1866 in Berg, Lux r: b

092.01

8 WITRY, Catherine b: 14 Nov 1855 in Berg, Lux h: Geis Mill
  v: Berg, Lux o: No profession r: b c: 7

+ seq: 092.01 BETTENDORF, Heinrich b: 16 Nov 1853 in
  Scheidgen, Lux d: 03 Dec 1901 in Bettembourg, Lux w: 31
  Dec 1878 in Berg, Lux h: Geis Mill v: Berg, Lux o: Stone
  mason o: Mason r: m f: Nicolas Bettendorf m: Margaretha
  Rillung c: 7

9 BETTENDORF, Catherine b: 20 Oct 1879 in Berg, Lux d: 18
  Mar 1888 in Berg, Lux r: bd

9 BETTENDORF, Nicolas b: 21 Sep 1881 in Berg, Lux r: b

9 BETTENDORF, Marguerite b: 21 Aug 1884 in Berg, Lux r: b

+ seq: 092.01.30 SCHNEIDER, Nicolas o: Butcher r: m f:
  Johann-Peter Schneider m: Marie Garth

9 BETTENDORF, Elisabeth b: 21 May 1887 in Berg, Lux o: No
  profession r: b

+ seq: 092.01.50 FRIEDEN, Peter-Joseph b: 10 Nov 1884 in
  Greiveldange, Lux w: 08 Jul 1910 in Berg, Lux o: Master
  tailor r: m f: Peter Frieden m: Marie Linden

9 BETTENDORF, Susanne b: 21 Jun 1890 in Berg, Lux o: No
  profession

+ seq: 092.01.70 POECKER, Jean b: 29 Jul 1881 in Ermsdorf,
  Lux w: 29 Oct 1913 in Berg, Lux o: Pig farmer r: m f: Johann
  Poecker m: Maria Konnen

9 BETTENDORF, Franziska b: 28 Dec 1895 in Berg, Lux r: b

9 BETTENDORF, Margaretha-Josephine b: 25 Sep 1900 in Berg,
  Lux d: 08 Apr 1982 in Berg, Lux r: b

093

8 WITRY, Johann b: 20 May 1861 in Berg, Lux v: Milwaukee,
  WI i: Emigrated to U. S. o: Locksmith r: bx c: 2

+ seq: 093 SAND, Anna b: Abt. 1865 in Dubuque, IA w: 20 Nov
  1889 in Dubuque, IA v: Milwaukee, WI r: dx r: m c: 2

9 WITRY, Eugenia b: Abt. 1891 in Milwaukee, WI v:
  Milwuakee, WI

+ seq: 093.01 SCHAEDLE, Allen b: Abt. 1885 w: 15 Jan 1913
  in Milwaukee, WI v: Milwaukee, WI o: Print machine installer

9 WITRY, Henrietta b: 1894 in Milwaukee, WI d: 11 Sep 1909 in
  Milwaukee, WI v: Milwaukee, WI r: d

094

7 WITRY, Jean b: 02 Dec 1819 in Schieren, Lux d: 09 Mar 1873 in Gilsdorf, Lux v: Gilsdorf, Lux o: Day laborer o: Farmer r: bd c: 4

+ seq: 094 HIRTZ, Anna-Marie b: 25 Mar 1820 in Gilsdorf, Lux d: 23 Aug 1873 in Gilsdorf, Lux w: 29 Feb 1848 in Bettendorf, Lux v: Gilsdorf, Lux o: Farmer r: d r: m f: Adam Hirtz m: Barbara Regener c: 4

8 WITRY, Heinrich b: 29 Sep 1849 in Gilsdorf, Lux d: 18 Sep 1850 in Gilsdorf, Lux v: Gilsdorf, Lux o: No profession r: bd

8 WITRY, Heinrich b: 23 Sep 1851 in Gilsdorf, Lux d: 08 Mar 1900 in Gilsdorf, Lux v: Gilsdorf, Lux o: Stone mason o: Day laborer o: Farmer r: bd c: 5

+ seq: 095 LUTGEN, Margaretha b: 13 Nov 1845 in Bourscheid, Lux d: 14 Mar 1904 in Gilsdorf, Lux w: 18 Mar 1874 in Bettendorf, Lux v: Gilsdorf, Lux o: No profession r: d r: m f: Mathias Lutgen m: Margaretha Clarens c: 5

8 WITRY, Nicolas b: 26 Jun 1859 in Gilsdorf, Lux d: 1882 in Gilbertsville, IA Cause of death: Accidental drowning v: Waterloo, IA i: Emigrated to Waterloo, IA r: b

8 WITRY, Peter b: 15 Jun 1864 in Gilsdorf, Lux d: 25 Jun 1942 in Blackhawk County, IA Cause of death: Old age v: Blackhawk County, IA i: Emigrated to Gilbertville, IA o: Farmer r: b c: 3

+ seq: 096 BLITSCH, Lizzie b: 18 Sep 1872 in Blackhawk County, IA d: 16 Jul 1968 in Blackhawk County, IA w: 24 Jan 1893 in Eagle Center, IA v: Blackhawk County, IA f: John Blitsch m: Elizabeth Brausch c: 3

095

8 WITRY, Heinrich b: 23 Sep 1851 in Gilsdorf, Lux d: 08 Mar 1900 in Gilsdorf, Lux v: Gilsdorf, Lux o: Stone mason o: Day laborer o: Farmer r: bd c: 5

+ seq: 095 LUTGEN, Margaretha b: 13 Nov 1845 in Bourscheid, Lux d: 14 Mar 1904 in Gilsdorf, Lux w: 18 Mar 1874 in Bettendorf, Lux v: Gilsdorf, Lux o: No profession r: d r: m f: Mathias Lutgen m: Margaretha Clarens c: 5

9 [1] WITRY, Mathias b: 04 Jan 1875 in Gilsdorf, Lux d: 14 Aug 1910 in Gilsdorf, Lux v: Gilsdorf, Lux o: Blacksmith o: Forger r: b c: 4

+ seq: 095.01 HUSS, Virginie b: 15 Dec 1884 in Medernach, Lux d: 01 Sep 1909 in Gilsdorf, Lux w: 05 Oct 1904 in Bettendorf,

Lux o: No profession r: d r: m f: Franz Huss m: Margaretha
Schmit c: 4

* 2nd Wife of [1] WITRY, Mathias:
+ seq: 095.05 KARIGER, Anne-Marie b: 18 Apr 1879 in
  Godbrange, Lux w: 18 Apr 1910 in Junglinster, Lux o: No
  profession r: m f: Peter Kariger m: Elisabeth Schreiner
9 WITRY, Susanne b: 13 Oct 1876 in Gilsdorf, Lux v: Beaufort,
  Lux o: No profession r: b c: 6
+ seq: 095.06 ERPELDING, Jean b: 15 Oct 1872 in Beaufort, Lux
  d: 26 Jan 1914 in Beaufort, Lux w: 11 Apr 1902 in Beaufort,
  Lux v: Beaufort, Lux o: Day laborer o: Farmer o: Stone mason
  r: d r: m f: Nicolas Erpelding m: Maria Pech c: 6
9 WITRY, Johann-Mathias b: 19 Sep 1878 in Gilsdorf, Lux d: 06
  Sep 1881 in Gilsdorf, Lux v: Gilsdorf, Lux o: No profession r:
  bd
9 WITRY, Peter-Johann b: 05 May 1882 in Gilsdorf, Lux d: 06
  May 1882 in Gilsdorf, Lux r: bd
9 WITRY, Peter (Pierre) b: 29 Mar 1884 in Gilsdorf, Lux d: 15
  Mar 1948 in Diekirch, Lux v: Diekirch, Lux o: Stonecutter o:
  Woodcutter o: Sculptor c: 4
+ seq: 095.12 BREYER, Elisabeth (Elise) b: 10 Aug 1885 in
  Freilingerhoehe, Germany w: 30 Jan 1914 in Diekirch, Lux v:
  Diekirch, Lux o: No profession r: m f: Johann Breyer m: Anna
  Flammann c: 4

095.01

9 [1] WITRY, Mathias b: 04 Jan 1875 in Gilsdorf, Lux d: 14 Aug
  1910 in Gilsdorf, Lux v: Gilsdorf, Lux o: Blacksmith o: Forger
  r: b c: 4
+ seq: 095.01 HUSS, Virginie b: 15 Dec 1884 in Medernach, Lux
  d: 01 Sep 1909 in Gilsdorf, Lux w: 05 Oct 1904 in Bettendorf,
  Lux o: No profession r: d r: m f: Franz Huss m: Margaretha
  Schmit c: 4
10 WITRY, Peter b: 21 Jul 1905 in Gilsdorf, Lux d: 08 Sep 1905
   in Gilsdorf, Lux r: bd
10 WITRY, Peter b: 19 Oct 1906 in Gilsdorf, Lux r: b
10 WITRY, Suzanne b: 13 Jan 1908 in Gilsdorf, Lux d: 22 Oct
   1975 in Rueil-Malmaison, France v: Paris, France o: Merchant
   r: b c: 2
+ seq: 095.02 HEBERT, Georges-Maurice b: 02 Nov 1909 in
  Paris, France d: 27 Apr 1974 in Paris, France w: 07 Nov 1931

in Paris, France v: Paris, France c: 2
10 WITRY, Jean b: 18 Aug 1909 in Gilsdorf, Lux d: 19 Aug 1909
 in Gilsdorf, Lux r: bd
 * 2nd Wife of [1] WITRY, Mathias:
 + seq: 095.05 KARIGER, Anne-Marie b: 18 Apr 1879 in
 Godbrange, Lux w: 18 Apr 1910 in Junglinster, Lux o: No
 profession r: m f: Peter Kariger m: Elisabeth Schreiner

095.02

10 WITRY, Suzanne b: 13 Jan 1908 in Gilsdorf, Lux d: 22 Oct
 1975 in Rueil-Malmaison, France v: Paris, France o: Merchant
 r: b c: 2
 + seq: 095.02 HEBERT, Georges-Maurice b: 02 Nov 1909 in
 Paris, France d: 27 Apr 1974 in Paris, France w: 07 Nov 1931
 in Paris, France v: Paris, France c: 2
11 HEBERT, Christiane b: 06 Aug 1942 in Paris, France v:
 Boulogne-Billancourt, France o: Secretary c: 2
 + seq: 095.03 GRELON, Christian b: 25 Aug 1939 in
 Chantonnay, France w: 26 Sep 1964 in Paris, France c: 2
11 HEBERT, Georges (Remi) b: 24 Jul 1943 in Paris, France v: La
 Frette-sur-Seine, France o: Bank employee c: 1
 + seq: 095.04 DUCROCQ, Arlette b: 27 Oct 1942 in Meulan,
 France w: 16 Dec 1967 in Boulogne-Billancourt, France v: La
 Frette-sur-Seine, France c: 1

095.03

11 HEBERT, Christiane b: 06 Aug 1942 in Paris, France v:
 Boulogne-Billancourt, France o: Secretary c: 2
 + seq: 095.03 GRELON, Christian b: 25 Aug 1939 in
 Chantonnay, France w: 26 Sep 1964 in Paris, France c: 2
12 GRELON, Jean-Christophe b: 06 Jul 1966 in Boulogne-
 Billancourt, France c: 1
 + seq: 095.03.50 LILAZ-POLLETAZ, Nadege w: Abt. 2000 c: 1
12 GRELON, Carine b: 02 May 1968 in Boulogne-Billancourt,
 France

095.03.50

12 GRELON, Jean-Christophe b: 06 Jul 1966 in Boulogne-
 Billancourt, France c: 1
 + seq: 095.03.50 LILAZ-POLLETAZ, Nadege w: Abt. 2000 c: 1
13 GRELON-POLLETAZ, Jean-Baptiste b: 16 Mar 2006 in Saint

Maur, France

095.04

11 HEBERT, Georges (Remi) b: 24 Jul 1943 in Paris, France v: La
Frette-sur-Seine, France o: Bank employee c: 1
+ seq: 095.04 DUCROCQ, Arlette b: 27 Oct 1942 in Meulan,
France w: 16 Dec 1967 in Boulogne-Billancourt, France v: La
Frette-sur-Seine, France c: 1
12 HEBERT, Mathias b: 06 Nov 1977 in Paris, France o: Student
c: 1
+ seq: 095.04.50 FOURMOND, Fanny w: Abt. 2000 c: 1

095.04.50

12 HEBERT, Mathias b: 06 Nov 1977 in Paris, France o: Student
c: 1
+ seq: 095.04.50 FOURMOND, Fanny w: Abt. 2000 c: 1
13 HEBERT-FOURMOND, Edel b: 18 Nov 2005 in Paris, France

095.06

9 WITRY, Susanne b: 13 Oct 1876 in Gilsdorf, Lux v: Beaufort,
Lux o: No profession r: b c: 6
+ seq: 095.06 ERPELDING, Jean b: 15 Oct 1872 in Beaufort,
Lux d: 26 Jan 1914 in Beaufort, Lux w: 11 Apr 1902 in
Beaufort, Lux v: Beaufort, Lux o: Day laborer o: Farmer o:
Stone mason r: d r: m f: Nicolas Erpelding m: Maria Pech c:
6
10 ERPELDING, Mathias b: 23 Dec 1902 in Beaufort, Lux d: Abt.
1976 in Dillingen, Lux r: b c: 1
+ seq: 095.07 w: Abt. 1925 c: 1
10 ERPELDING, Pierre b: 29 Mar 1904 in Beaufort, Lux v:
Beaufort, Lux r: b
+ seq: 095.09 w: Abt. 1930 i: 1 daughter and 2 sons
10 ERPELDING, Virginie b: 14 Feb 1906 in Beaufort, Lux r: b c:
1
+ seq: 095.10 ALTMANN w: Abt. 1930 c: 1
10 ERPELDING, Paul-Nicolas b: 18 Apr 1909 in Beaufort, Lux d:
28 Aug 1909 in Beaufort, Lux r: bd
10 ERPELDING, Martin b: 01 Jun 1910 in Beaufort, Lux d: 07
May 1911 in Beaufort, Lux r: bd
10 ERPELDING, Anna b: 14 Mar 1913 in Beaufort, Lux d: 27
Nov 1913 in Beaufort, Lux r: bd

095.07

10ERPELDING, Mathias b: 23 Dec 1902 in Beaufort, Lux d: Abt.
  1976 in Dillingen, Lux r: b c: 1
+ seq: 095.07 w: Abt. 1925 c: 1
11ERPELDING, Nicolas b: Abt. 1927 d: Abt. 1978
+ seq: 095.08 w: Abt. 1950 i: 2 or 3 children

095.10

10ERPELDING, Virginie b: 14 Feb 1906 in Beaufort, Lux r: b c:
  1
+ seq: 095.10 ALTMANN w: Abt. 1930 c: 1
11ALTMANN, Rene b: Abt. 1935
+ seq: 095.11 w: Abt. 1960 i: 1 son and one daughter

095.12

9 WITRY, Peter (Pierre) b: 29 Mar 1884 in Gilsdorf, Lux d: 15
  Mar 1948 in Diekirch, Lux v: Diekirch, Lux o: Stonecutter o:
  Woodcutter o: Sculptor c: 4
+ seq: 095.12 BREYER, Elisabeth (Elise) b: 10 Aug 1885 in
  Freilingerhoehe, Germany w: 30 Jan 1914 in Diekirch, Lux v:
  Diekirch, Lux o: No profession r: m f: Johann Breyer m: Anna
  Flammann c: 4
10WITRY, Henri b: 01 Feb 1915 in Diekirch, Lux d: 1970 in
  Ettelbruck, Lux r: b c: 1
+ seq: 095.13 ELSEN, Helene b: Abt. 1920 in Gilsdorf, Lux w:
  Abt. 1950 c: 1
10WITRY, Jean (Johnny) b: 08 Mar 1916 in Diekirch, Lux d: 10
  Dec 2005 v: Diekirch, Lux o: Marble cutter r: b c: 2
+ seq: 095.14 WALDBILLIG, Germaine w: Abt. 1950 c: 2
10WITRY, Francis b: 21 Nov 1919 in Diekirch, Lux d: 24 Dec
  1987 in Diekirch, Lux v: Diekirch, Lux i: General secretary of
  the government of Diekirch o: Municipal employee r: b c: 3
+ seq: 095.16 POECKER, Anne-Marguerite (Anny) b: 17 Nov
  1927 in Ermsdorf, Lux w: 23 Dec 1955 in Diekirch, Lux v:
  Diekirch, Lux o: No profession r: m f: Pierre Poecker m:
  Barbe-Suzanne Eischen c: 3
10WITRY, Rene-Joseph-Pierre b: 09 Jun 1922 in Diekirch, Lux
  d: 1944 in Russia i: Conscripted into the German army r: b

095.13

10WITRY, Henri b: 01 Feb 1915 in Diekirch, Lux d: 1970 in

Ettelbruck, Lux r: b c: 1

+ seq: 095.13 ELSEN, Helene b: Abt. 1920 in Gilsdorf, Lux w: Abt. 1950 c: 1

11 WITRY, Jean (Johny) b: Abt. 1955 o: Clerk of the court in Diekirch, Lux

095.14

10 WITRY, Jean (Johnny) b: 08 Mar 1916 in Diekirch, Lux d: 10 Dec 2005 v: Diekirch, Lux o: Marble cutter r: b c: 2

+ seq: 095.14 WALDBILLIG, Germaine w: Abt. 1950 c: 2

11 WITRY, Francis b: Abt. 1955 i: 2 sons o: Marble cutter

+ seq: 095.15 w: Abt. 1980 i: no children

11 WITRY, Patrice b: Abt. 1959

095.16

10 WITRY, Francis b: 21 Nov 1919 in Diekirch, Lux d: 24 Dec 1987 in Diekirch, Lux v: Diekirch, Lux i: General secretary of the government of Diekirch o: Municipal employee r: b c: 3

+ seq: 095.16 POECKER, Anne-Marguerite (Anny) b: 17 Nov 1927 in Ermsdorf, Lux w: 23 Dec 1955 in Diekirch, Lux v: Diekirch, Lux o: No profession r: m f: Pierre Poecker m: Barbe-Suzanne Eischen c: 3

11 WITRY, Robert (Roby) b: 12 Nov 1956 in Diekirch, Lux

11 [1] WITRY, Sanny b: 14 Jan 1959 in Diekirch, Lux v: Steinfort, Lux o: Clerk of the court in Luxembourg City c: 2

+ seq: 095.17 TESCHER, Paul b: 02 Mar 1955 in Luxembourg, Lux w: 1980 c: 1

* 2nd Husband of [1] WITRY, Sanny:

+ seq: 095.18 BRAUN, Alex w: 04 Dec 1992 v: Steinfort, Lux c: 1

11 WITRY, Remy b: 15 Apr 1963 in Diekirch, Lux v: Hesperange, Lux o: Bus driver

095.17

11 [1] WITRY, Sanny b: 14 Jan 1959 in Diekirch, Lux v: Steinfort, Lux o: Clerk of the court in Luxembourg City c: 2

+ seq: 095.17 TESCHER, Paul b: 02 Mar 1955 in Luxembourg, Lux w: 1980 c: 1

12 TESCHER, Daniel b: 1982

* 2nd Husband of [1] WITRY, Sanny:

+ seq: 095.18 BRAUN, Alex w: 04 Dec 1992 v: Steinfort, Lux

c: 1

12BRAUN, Nora b: 07 Mar 1996 in Luxembourg, Lux

096

8 WITRY, Peter b: 15 Jun 1864 in Gilsdorf, Lux d: 25 Jun 1942
in Blackhawk County, IA Cause of death: Old age v: Blackhawk
County, IA i: Emigrated to Gilbertville, IA o: Farmer r: b c: 3
+ seq: 096 BLITSCH, Lizzie b: 18 Sep 1872 in Blackhawk
County, IA d: 16 Jul 1968 in Blackhawk County, IA w: 24 Jan
1893 in Eagle Center, IA v: Blackhawk County, IA f: John
Blitsch m: Elizabeth Brausch c: 3
9 WITRY, Clara-Elizabeth b: 24 Nov 1893 in Blackhawk County,
IA d: 17 Feb 1982 in Waterloo, IA v: Hudson, IA c: 3
+ seq: 096.01 CAVANAUGH, Charles J. b: 22 Jun 1891 in
Sheldon, IA d: 28 Mar 1972 in Buckingham, IA Cause of
death: Head injury from a fall w: 06 May 1920 in Blackhawk
County, IA v: Hudson, IA i: Served in military during WW I
o: Farmer f: Joseph Cavanaugh m: Mary Longeran c: 3
9 [1] WITRY, Walter-John b: 21 Oct 1896 in Blackhawk County,
IA d: 01 Feb 1973 in Blackhawk County, IA Cause of death:
Heart failure v: Waterloo, IA o: Worked for John Deere o:
Farmer c: 1
+ seq: 097 SIMONS, Grace b: 19 Jul 1893 in Urbana, IL d: 21
Sep 1956 in Waterloo, IA Cause of death: Lung cancer w: 11
Feb 1929 in Waterloo, IA v: Waterloo, IA o: Office worker f:
William-James Simons m: Ellen-Catherine Haley c: 1
* 2nd Wife of [1] WITRY, Walter-John:
+ seq: 101 DIEFENBAUGH, Mabel-Alvina b: 1895 d: 1971 in
Waterloo, IA w: 20 Dec 1958 in California v: Waterloo, IA v:
California o: Operated a nursing home in California f: Joseph
Diefenbaugh m: Alvina
9 WITRY, Harold C. (Breeze) b: 03 Sep 1902 in Waterloo, IA d:
23 Aug 1973 in Waterloo, IA v: Hudson, IA c: 5
+ seq: 102 CONRY, Lucille K. b: 08 Jul 1904 in Waterloo, IA d:
Jan 1979 in Waterloo, IA w: 14 Sep 1935 in Hudson, IA v:
Hudson, IA c: 5

096.01

9 WITRY, Clara-Elizabeth b: 24 Nov 1893 in Blackhawk County,
IA d: 17 Feb 1982 in Waterloo, IA v: Hudson, IA c: 3
+ seq: 096.01 CAVANAUGH, Charles J. b: 22 Jun 1891 in

Sheldon, IA d: 28 Mar 1972 in Buckingham, IA Cause of
death: Head injury from a fall w: 06 May 1920 in Blackhawk
County, IA v: Hudson, IA i: Served in military during WW I
o: Farmer f: Joseph Cavanaugh m: Mary Longeran c: 3

10CAVANAUGH, Harry-Charles b: 13 May 1922 in Blackhawk
County, IA d: 16 Oct 1949 in Waterloo, IA Cause of death:
Brain cancer v: Hudson, IA

10CAVANAUGH, Erwin-Francis b: 02 Sep 1923 in Blackhawk
County, IA d: 13 Aug 1950 in Waterloo, IA Cause of death:
Auto accident v: Hudson, IA i: Served in U. S. Army c: 2

+ seq: 096.02 BUCHANAN, Margaret (Peg) b: Abt. 1920 d: 28
Oct 1971 in Davenport, IA w: 02 Oct 1944 in Newport News,
VA v: Blackhawk County, IA f: Elza Buchanan c: 2

10CAVANAUGH, Norma-Louise b: 20 Dec 1927 in Blackhawk
County, IA v: Hudson, IA c: 4

+ seq: 096.06 STEIMEL, William-Paul b: 22 Apr 1927 in
Blackhawk County, IA d: 17 Apr 2006 in Waterloo, IA w: 19
Apr 1949 in Blackhawk County, IA v: Hudson, IA o: Raised
Angus cattle o: Farmer f: William J. Steimel m: Esther
Mathern c: 4

096.02

10CAVANAUGH, Erwin-Francis b: 02 Sep 1923 in Blackhawk
County, IA d: 13 Aug 1950 in Waterloo, IA Cause of death:
Auto accident v: Hudson, IA i: Served in U. S. Army c: 2

+ seq: 096.02 BUCHANAN, Margaret (Peg) b: Abt. 1920 d: 28
Oct 1971 in Davenport, IA w: 02 Oct 1944 in Newport News,
VA v: Blackhawk County, IA f: Elza Buchanan c: 2

11[1] CAVANAUGH, Michael-Erwin b: 02 Jun 1945 v: Cedar
Falls, IA i: Served in U. S. Navy o: Truck driver

+ seq: 096.03 STEEGE, Kathie b: Abt. 1945 w: 14 Sep 1965 in
Plainfield, IA

* 2nd Wife of [1] CAVANAUGH, Michael-Erwin:

+ seq: 096.04 HUFFMAN, Gloria-Jean w: 08 Sep 1984 v: Cedar
Falls, IA o: Dispatcher for trucking company

11CAVANAUGH, Sarah-Sue b: 21 Aug 1948 in Waterloo, IA v:
Cedar Falls, IA v: Denver, IA o: Office worker c: 2

+ seq: 096.05 BECKEL, Richard b: Abt. 1945 w: 07 Nov 1971
in Denver, IA v: Denver, IA o: Farmer f: Tom Beckel c: 2

096.05

11CAVANAUGH, Sarah-Sue b: 21 Aug 1948 in Waterloo, IA v: Cedar Falls, IA v: Denver, IA o: Office worker c: 2

+ seq: 096.05 BECKEL, Richard b: Abt. 1945 w: 07 Nov 1971 in Denver, IA v: Denver, IA o: Farmer f: Tom Beckel c: 2

12BECKEL, Trisha b: 02 Sep 1975 in Waterloo, IA

12BECKEL, Tom b: 05 Feb 1980 in Waterloo, IA

096.06

10CAVANAUGH, Norma-Louise b: 20 Dec 1927 in Blackhawk County, IA v: Hudson, IA c: 4

+ seq: 096.06 STEIMEL, William-Paul b: 22 Apr 1927 in Blackhawk County, IA d: 17 Apr 2006 in Waterloo, IA w: 19 Apr 1949 in Blackhawk County, IA v: Hudson, IA o: Raised Angus cattle o: Farmer f: William J. Steimel m: Esther Mathern c: 4

11STEIMEL, Julia-Ann b: 06 Jun 1951 in Waterloo, IA v: Waterloo, IA o: Office worker for the American Cancer Society c: 2

+ seq: 096.07 BARTH, Donald E. (Don) b: 14 Sep 1949 w: 24 Nov 1973 in Blackhawk County, IA v: Waterloo, IA i: Served in U. S. Army o: Mailman f: Harold Barth m: Helen c: 2

11STEIMEL, Mary-Ellen b: 30 Nov 1953 in Waterloo, IA v: Cedar Falls, IA o: Medical assistant in Cedar Falls, IA o: Office worker c: 3

+ seq: 096.08 YUSKO, Mark A. b: 30 Dec in Streator, IL w: 10 May 1980 in Cedar Falls, IA v: Cedar Falls, IA o: Draftsman at John Deere Co. f: Steven Yusko m: Mary c: 3

11STEIMEL, Paula-Sue b: 11 Apr 1957 in Hudson, IA i: Member of Sweet Adelines chorus o: Business manager of Cedar Valley Hospital in Waterloo, IA

11STEIMEL, Kathleen-Renee b: 12 Apr 1960 in Waterloo, IA v: Chicago, IL i: Volunteer in the Coast Guard Auxiliary i: Member of Mellodiers chorus o: Administrative office of Catholic Order of Cervites in Chicago, IL

096.07

11STEIMEL, Julia-Ann b: 06 Jun 1951 in Waterloo, IA v: Waterloo, IA o: Office worker for the American Cancer Society c: 2

+ seq: 096.07 BARTH, Donald E. (Don) b: 14 Sep 1949 w: 24

Nov 1973 in Blackhawk County, IA v: Waterloo, IA i: Served
in U. S. Army o: Mailman f: Harold Barth m: Helen c: 2

12 BARTH, Laura-Ann b: 14 Oct 1974 in Waterloo, IA v:
Waterloo, IA o: Office worker for GMAC Mortgage Co. in
Waterloo, IA c: 2

+ seq: 096.07.50 HOODJER, Jason b: in Waterloo, IA w: 17 Jun
2000 v: Janesville, IA c: 2

12 BARTH, Brian-Donald (Mark) b: 30 Nov 1976 in Waterloo, IA

096.07.50

12 BARTH, Laura-Ann b: 14 Oct 1974 in Waterloo, IA v:
Waterloo, IA o: Office worker for GMAC Mortgage Co. in
Waterloo, IA c: 2

+ seq: 096.07.50 HOODJER, Jason b: in Waterloo, IA w: 17 Jun
2000 v: Janesville, IA c: 2

13 HOODJER, Jared b: 02 Feb 2004 in Waterloo, IA v: Janesville,
IA

13 HOODJER, Tyler-Jeffrey b: 15 Jun 2006 in Waterloo, IA v:
Janesville, IA

096.08

11 STEIMEL, Mary-Ellen b: 30 Nov 1953 in Waterloo, IA v:
Cedar Falls, IA o: Medical assistant in Cedar Falls, IA o: Office
worker c: 3

+ seq: 096.08 YUSKO, Mark A. b: 30 Dec in Streator, IL w: 10
May 1980 in Cedar Falls, IA v: Cedar Falls, IA o: Draftsman
at John Deere Co. f: Steven Yusko m: Mary c: 3

12 YUSKO, Lisa-Marie b: 20 Oct 1984 in Cedar Falls, IA o:
Student at the University of Northern Iowa

12 YUSKO, Elizabeth-Marie b: 22 Oct 1985 in Cedar Falls, IA o:
Student at the University of Northern Iowa

12 YUSKO, Matthew-Alan b: 19 Dec 1986 in Cedar Falls, IA o:
Student at the University of Northern Iowa

097

9 [1] WITRY, Walter-John b: 21 Oct 1896 in Blackhawk County,
IA d: 01 Feb 1973 in Blackhawk County, IA Cause of death:
Heart failure v: Waterloo, IA o: Worked for John Deere o:
Farmer c: 1

+ seq: 097 SIMONS, Grace b: 19 Jul 1893 in Urbana, IL d: 21
Sep 1956 in Waterloo, IA Cause of death: Lung cancer w: 11

Feb 1929 in Waterloo, IA v: Waterloo, IA o: Office worker f: William-James Simons m: Ellen-Catherine Haley c: 1

10 WITRY, Harlan-Earl b: 17 Dec 1929 in Waterloo, IA v: Waterloo, IA o: Farmer o: Tractor mechanic for John Deere c: 3

+ seq: 098 O'CONNOR, Charlotte-Alma b: 25 Nov 1933 in Washburn, IA w: 26 Sep 1953 in La Porte City, IA v: Waterloo, IA o: Legal secretary f: Paul-John O'Connor m: Ines-Fae Bagenstos c: 3

* 2nd Wife of [1] WITRY, Walter-John:

+ seq: 101 DIEFENBAUGH, Mabel-Alvina b: 1895 d: 1971 in Waterloo, IA w: 20 Dec 1958 in California v: Waterloo, IA v: California o: Operated a nursing home in California f: Joseph Diefenbaugh m: Alvina

098

10 WITRY, Harlan-Earl b: 17 Dec 1929 in Waterloo, IA v: Waterloo, IA o: Farmer o: Tractor mechanic for John Deere c: 3

+ seq: 098 O'CONNOR, Charlotte-Alma b: 25 Nov 1933 in Washburn, IA w: 26 Sep 1953 in La Porte City, IA v: Waterloo, IA o: Legal secretary f: Paul-John O'Connor m: Ines-Fae Bagenstos c: 3

11 [1] WITRY, Craig-Joseph b: 18 Jul 1957 in Waterloo, IA v: Hudson, IA v: Waterloo, IA o: City building inspector o: Manager of Astro Buildings c: 2

+ seq: 099 HARWOOD, Faye w: 1979 v: Waterloo, IA

* 2nd Wife of [1] WITRY, Craig-Joseph:

+ seq: 100 HARKEN, Sheree D. b: 20 Sep 1955 in Aplington, IA w: 30 Jan 1993 in Cedar Falls, IA v: Hudson, IA v: Waterloo, IA o: Works for insurance company o: Sold pharmaceuticals f: Wallace Oelmann m: Jeanette Kalkwarf c: 2

11 WITRY, Sharon-Ines b: 27 Aug 1958 in Waterloo, IA v: Waterloo, IA v: Hudson, IA o: Secretary at the University of Northern Iowa c: 2

+ seq: 100.01 CORY, Jeffrey-Lynn (Jeff) b: 06 Dec 1957 in Hudson, IA w: 03 Oct 1980 in Waterloo, IA v: Hudson, IA o: Utilities technologist for Northern Natural Gas Co. in Waterloo, IA o: Machinist f: Max Cory m: Louann Richards c: 2

11 WITRY, Karen-Grace b: 27 Aug 1958 in Waterloo, IA v: Cedar Falls, IA o: Registered nurse in the emergency room of Sartori

Hospital in Cedar Falls, IA c: 2
+   seq: 100.02 ARENDS, Ronald-Dale b: 07 Mar 1950 in
    Wellsburg, IA w: 08 Aug 1986 in Blackhawk County, IA v:
    Cedar Falls, IA o: Civil engineer f: Arnold Arends m: Helen
    Geerdes c: 2

099

11[1] WITRY, Craig-Joseph b: 18 Jul 1957 in Waterloo, IA v:
    Hudson, IA v: Waterloo, IA o: City building inspector o:
    Manager of Astro Buildings c: 2
+   seq: 099 HARWOOD, Faye w: 1979 v: Waterloo, IA
*   2nd Wife of [1] WITRY, Craig-Joseph:
+   seq: 100 HARKEN, Sheree D. b: 20 Sep 1955 in Aplington, IA
    w: 30 Jan 1993 in Cedar Falls, IA v: Hudson, IA v: Waterloo,
    IA o: Works for insurance company o: Sold pharmaceuticals
    f: Wallace Oelmann m: Jeanette Kalkwarf c: 2
12 HARKEN, Bradley-Jay (Brad) b: 05 Oct 1980 in Hampton, IA
    v: Des Moines, IA i: Marketing degree from the University of
    Northern Iowa o: Manager of ToysRUs in Clive, IA
12 HARKEN, Kristi-Kay b: 29 Mar 1984 in Hampton, IA v:
    Wellsburg, IA o: Credit Business Enterprise Group in Waterloo,
    IA

100.01

11 WITRY, Sharon-Ines b: 27 Aug 1958 in Waterloo, IA v:
    Waterloo, IA v: Hudson, IA o: Secretary at the University of
    Northern Iowa c: 2
+   seq: 100.01 CORY, Jeffrey-Lynn (Jeff) b: 06 Dec 1957 in
    Hudson, IA w: 03 Oct 1980 in Waterloo, IA v: Hudson, IA o:
    Utilities technologist for Northern Natural Gas Co. in Waterloo,
    IA o: Machinist f: Max Cory m: Louann Richards c: 2
12 CORY, Shawna-Lynn b: 21 Sep 1983 in Waterloo, IA v:
    Waterloo, IA o: Legal assistant
+   seq: 100.01.50 WALTON, Todd w: 29 Oct 2005 in Hudson, IA
    v: Waterloo, IA o: Assembler f: Ken Walton m: Peggy
    McMenomy Walton
12 CORY, Blake-Jeffrey b: 25 Sep 1986 in Waterloo, IA v: Cedar
    Falls, IA o: Student at Hawkeye Community College

100.02

11 WITRY, Karen-Grace b: 27 Aug 1958 in Waterloo, IA v: Cedar

Falls, IA o: Registered nurse in the emergency room of Sartori Hospital in Cedar Falls, IA c: 2

+ seq: 100.02 ARENDS, Ronald-Dale b: 07 Mar 1950 in Wellsburg, IA w: 08 Aug 1986 in Blackhawk County, IA v: Cedar Falls, IA o: Civil engineer f: Arnold Arends m: Helen Geerdes c: 2

12 ARENDS, Daniel-Mark (Dan) b: 22 Mar 1987 in Cedar Falls, IA v: Cedar Falls, IA v: Ames, IA o: student at Iowa State University

12 ARENDS, Amanda-Sue b: 14 Mar 1990 in Cedar Falls, IA v: Cedar Falls, IA o: Student in high school

102

9 WITRY, Harold C. (Breeze) b: 03 Sep 1902 in Waterloo, IA d: 23 Aug 1973 in Waterloo, IA v: Hudson, IA c: 5

+ seq: 102 CONRY, Lucille K. b: 08 Jul 1904 in Waterloo, IA d: Jan 1979 in Waterloo, IA w: 14 Sep 1935 in Hudson, IA v: Hudson, IA c: 5

10 WITRY, William-Peter (Bill) b: 13 Sep 1937 in Waterloo, IA d: 28 Jun 2006 in Marshalltown, IA v: Waterloo, IA v: Santa Monica, CA i: Served in U. S. Marine Corps o: Worked for John Deere o: Country club attendant c: 2

+ seq: 103 ENGH, Eli b: 1943 in Oslo, Norway w: 1962 in Santa Monica, CA v: Norway o: Travel agent f: Arne Engh c: 2

10 WITRY, Robert-Daniel (Bob) b: 13 Sep 1937 in Waterloo, IA v: La Place, LA v: Hudson, IA v: Waterloo, IA i: Served in U. S. Marine Corps o: Salesman c: 2

+ seq: 104 HOMOLAR, Darlene-Dorothy b: 30 Dec 1935 in Alberon, IA w: 17 Dec 1959 in Cedar Falls, IA v: Laplace, LA o: Registered nurse f: Alvin Holomar m: Gladys c: 2

10[1] WITRY, Ardith-Elaine b: 22 Apr 1941 in Waterloo, IA v: West Des Moines, IA v: Hudson, IA v: Marshalltown/IA v: Louisiana o: Clerical worker c: 3

+ seq: 104.01 WARNELL, Gary b: Abt. 1941 w: 1959 c: 3

* 2nd Husband of [1] WITRY, Ardith-Elaine:

+ seq: 104.06 THEOPHILLUS, Morgan b: 25 Feb 1939 in South Dakota w: Abt. 1970 v: West Des Moines, IA o: Production manager f: Daniel Theopillus m: Merial Roberts

10 WITRY, Bernard-Michael (Bernie) b: 27 Jul 1943 in Waterloo, IA v: Tipton, IA i: Served in U. S. Army o: Teacher c: 2

+ seq: 105 HALL, Mary B. b: 26 Feb 1943 in Charles City, IA d:

18 May 2005 in Iowa City, IA Cause of death: Cancer w: 03
Sep 1966 in Waterloo, IA v: Tipton, IA o: Investment Officer
o: Stock broker f: Robert J. Hall m: Agnes Lynch c: 2
10 WITRY, Thomas-Harold (Tom) b: 24 Mar 1947 in Waterloo, IA
v: Dubuque, IA i: Served in U. S. Army o: Teacher c: 2
+ seq: 106 FRIDAY, Carol-Ann b: 28 Sep 1949 in Sac City, IA
w: 12 Jun 1971 in Odebolt, IA v: Dubuque, IA o: Director of
Religious Education f: Lawrence Friday m: Carolyn Spindler
c: 2

103

10 WITRY, William-Peter (Bill) b: 13 Sep 1937 in Waterloo, IA
d: 28 Jun 2006 in Marshalltown, IA v: Waterloo, IA v: Santa
Monica, CA i: Served in U. S. Marine Corps o: Worked for
John Deere o: Country club attendant c: 2
+ seq: 103 ENGH, Eli b: 1943 in Oslo, Norway w: 1962 in Santa
Monica, CA v: Norway o: Travel agent f: Arne Engh c: 2
11 ELVSVEEN, Kristin b: 18 Jul 1963 in Santa Monica, CA v:
Oslo, Norway o: Teacher c: 1
+ seq: 103.00.50 w: Abt. 1990 c: 1
11 ELVSVEEN, Robert (Bobby) b: 12 Nov 1964 in Santa Monica,
CA v: Trondheim, Norway o: Mason c: 2
+ seq: 103.01 TONE w: Abt. 1990 c: 2

103.00.50

11 ELVSVEEN, Kristin b: 18 Jul 1963 in Santa Monica, CA v:
Oslo, Norway o: Teacher c: 1
+ seq: 103.00.50 w: Abt. 1990 c: 1
12 ELVSVEEN, Aurora b: Abt. 1991 in Oslo, Norway

103.01

11 ELVSVEEN, Robert (Bobby) b: 12 Nov 1964 in Santa Monica,
CA v: Trondheim, Norway o: Mason c: 2
+ seq: 103.01 TONE w: Abt. 1990 c: 2
12 ELVSVEEN, Preban b: Abt. 1991 in Trondheim, Norway
12 ELVSVEEN, Aslak b: 18 Mar 1996 in Trondheim, Norway

104

10 WITRY, Robert-Daniel (Bob) b: 13 Sep 1937 in Waterloo, IA
v: La Place, LA v: Hudson, IA v: Waterloo, IA i: Served in U.
S. Marine Corps o: Salesman c: 2

+ seq: 104 HOMOLAR, Darlene-Dorothy b: 30 Dec 1935 in
Alberon, IA w: 17 Dec 1959 in Cedar Falls, IA v: Laplace, LA
o: Registered nurse f: Alvin Holomar m: Gladys c: 2
11 WITRY, Timothy-Conry b: 16 Oct 1974 in Blackhawk County,
IA v: Seattle, WA o: Aero-space engineer at Boeing
+ seq: 104.00.30 JANTZ, Jessica w: 19 Nov 2005 in Baton
Rouge, LA v: Seattle, WA o: Teacher f: Paul Jantz m: Lillie
11 WITRY, Susan-Marie b: 12 May 1976 in Blackhawk County,
IA v: La Place, LA o: Student at Northeast Louisiana U. c: 2
+ seq: 104.00.60 FOREWOOD, Brant w: 08 Nov 2003 in
Monroe, LA c: 2

104.00.60
11 WITRY, Susan-Marie b: 12 May 1976 in Blackhawk County,
IA v: La Place, LA o: Student at Northeast Louisiana U. c: 2
+ seq: 104.00.60 FOREWOOD, Brant w: 08 Nov 2003 in
Monroe, LA c: 2
12 FORWOOD, Jonathan b: 28 Apr 2005 in Monroe, LA
12 FORWOOD, Ellie-Marie b: 29 May 2006 in LaPlatte, LA

104.01
10[2] WITRY, Ardith-Elaine b: 22 Apr 1941 in Waterloo, IA v:
West Des Moines, IA v: Hudson, IA v: Marshalltown/IA v:
Louisiana o: Clerical worker c: 3
+ seq: 104.01 WARNELL, Gary b: Abt. 1941 w: 1959 c: 3
11 WARNELL, Jeffrey-Glen b: 03 Feb 1960 in Waterloo, IA v:
Marshalltown/IA v: Iowa o: Clerk c: 2
+ seq: 104.02 HARRELL, Sue b: Abt. 1965 w: Abt. 1995 v:
Louisiana, IA o: Cosmetologist c: 2
11[1] WARNELL, Jami-Marie b: 14 Oct 1961 in Marshalltown,
IA v: Louisiana, IA o: Clerk c: 1
+ seq: 104.03 HEBERT, Keith b: Abt. 1960 w: Abt. 1980 c: 1
* 2nd Husband of [1] WARNELL, Jami-Marie:
+ seq: 104.04 SMALDT, Alan b: Abt. 1960 w: Abt. 1990 v:
Louisiana, IA
11 WARNELL, Chris-Anthony b: 08 Jul 1964 in Marshalltown, IA
v: Marshall County/LA v: Iowa c: 3
+ seq: 104.05 HILLARD, Carolyn b: Abt. 1965 w: Abt. 1990 v:
Marshalltown, IA o: Office worker c: 3
* 2nd Husband of [2] WITRY, Ardith-Elaine:
+ seq: 104.06 THEOPHILLUS, Morgan b: 25 Feb 1939 in South

Dakota w: Abt. 1970 v: West Des Moines, IA o: Production
manager f: Daniel Theopillus m: Merial Roberts

104.02

11 WARNELL, Jeffrey-Glen b: 03 Feb 1960 in Waterloo, IA v:
Marshalltown/IA v: Iowa o: Clerk c: 2
+ seq: 104.02 HARRELL, Sue b: Abt. 1965 w: Abt. 1995 v:
Louisiana, IA o: Cosmetologist c: 2
12 WARNELL, Elizabeth-Ann b: 04 Mar 1996 in Marshalltown,
IA
12 WARNELL, Allison

104.03

11 [1] WARNELL, Jami-Marie b: 14 Oct 1961 in Marshalltown,
IA v: Louisiana, IA o: Clerk c: 1
+ seq: 104.03 HEBERT, Keith b: Abt. 1960 w: Abt. 1980 c: 1
12 HEBERT, Bryan-Keith b: 03 Feb 1982 in Baton Rouge, LA
* 2nd Husband of [1] WARNELL, Jami-Marie:
+ seq: 104.04 SMALDT, Alan b: Abt. 1960 w: Abt. 1990 v:
Louisiana, IA

104.05

11 WARNELL, Chris-Anthony b: 08 Jul 1964 in Marshalltown, IA
v: Marshall County/LA v: Iowa c: 3
+ seq: 104.05 HILLARD, Carolyn b: Abt. 1965 w: Abt. 1990 v:
Marshalltown, IA o: Office worker c: 3
12 WARNELL, Shaun-Clay b: 07 Sep 1991 in Marshalltown, IA
12 WARNELL, Andrew
12 WARNELL, Anthony

105

10 WITRY, Bernard-Michael (Bernie) b: 27 Jul 1943 in Waterloo,
IA v: Tipton, IA i: Served in U. S. Army o: Teacher c: 2
+ seq: 105 HALL, Mary B. b: 26 Feb 1943 in Charles City, IA d:
18 May 2005 in Iowa City, IA Cause of death: Cancer w: 03
Sep 1966 in Waterloo, IA v: Tipton, IA o: Investment Officer
o: Stock broker f: Robert J. Hall m: Agnes Lynch c: 2
11 WITRY, Theresa-Ann b: 28 Aug 1968 in Ft. Hood, TX v:
Bondurant, IA o: Social worker c: 2
+ seq: 105.01 GLASER, Neil-Edwin b: 10 Jul 1969 in Algona,

IA w: 16 Oct 1993 in Tipton, IA v: Polk City, IA o: Security
dispatcher f: Donald Glaser m: Annabelle Teitz c: 2

11 WITRY, Amy-Lynn b: 30 Apr 1971 in Lake City, IA v: Los
Angeles, CA o: Office adminstrative assistant

105.01

11 WITRY, Theresa-Ann b: 28 Aug 1968 in Ft. Hood, TX v:
Bondurant, IA o: Social worker c: 2

+ seq: 105.01 GLASER, Neil-Edwin b: 10 Jul 1969 in Algona,
IA w: 16 Oct 1993 in Tipton, IA v: Polk City, IA o: Security
dispatcher f: Donald Glaser m: Annabelle Teitz c: 2

12 GLASER, Shannon-Elizabeth b: 22 Jun 1995 in Des Moines, IA
12 GLASER, Sean

106

10 WITRY, Thomas-Harold (Tom) b: 24 Mar 1947 in Waterloo, IA
v: Dubuque, IA i: Served in U. S. Army o: Teacher c: 2

+ seq: 106 FRIDAY, Carol-Ann b: 28 Sep 1949 in Sac City, IA
w: 12 Jun 1971 in Odebolt, IA v: Dubuque, IA o: Director of
Religious Education f: Lawrence Friday m: Carolyn Spindler
c: 2

11 WITRY, Michael-Thomas b: 29 Jul 1981 in Iowa City, IA o:
Student at U. of Idaho Law School

11 WITRY, Matthew-John b: 02 Apr 1983 in Dubuque, IA o:
Student at U. of Iowa School of Pharmacy

107

7 WITRY, Heinrich b: 24 Feb 1822 in Schieren, Lux d: 22 Feb
1896 in Mersch, Lux v: Boevange, Lux v: Schieren, Lux v:
Athis, France o: Soldier o: Rural guard o: Day laborer o:
Farmer r: bdx c: 8

+ seq: 107 HOLZMACHER, Catherine b: 04 Mar 1834 in
Boevange, Lux d: 06 Mar 1878 in Boevange, Lux w: 16 Feb
1859 in Schieren, Lux v: Schieren, Lux o: Farmer o: Day
laborer r: bdx r: mx f: Nicolas Holzmacher m: Elisabeth
Weber c: 8

8 WITRY, Anna b: 12 Mar 1860 in Boevange, Lux d: 07 Dec
1867 in Boevange, Lux v: Boevange, Lux r: bd

8 WITRY, Peter b: 13 Aug 1862 in Boevange, Lux r: b

8 WITRY, Margaretha b: 22 Feb 1865 in Boevange, Lux d: 20
Nov 1943 in Grevenknapp, Lux o: Day laborer r: b c: 5

+ seq: 107.01 WELTER, Nicolas b: 14 May 1866 in Boevange, Lux w: 29 May 1889 in Boevange, Lux o: Mason o: Day laborer r: m f: Nicolas Welter m: Margaretha Zangerle c: 5

8 WITRY, Johanna (Marie) b: 01 Dec 1866 in Boevange, Lux a: Leonie-Anna Wittry v: Mersch, Lux v: McLean Co., ND i: Immigrated to USA in 1902 o: No profession r: b c: 4

+ seq: 107.02 KERZMANN, John b: 10 Aug 1862 in Mersch, Lux d: 28 Feb 1930 in McLean Co., ND w: 21 Feb 1892 in Mersch, Lux h: Kerzmann 1 v: Mersch, Lux v: McLean Co., ND i: Immigrated to USA in 1902 o: Day laborer r: m f: Mathias Kerzmann m: Mary Pickels c: 4

8 WITRY, Johann-Peter b: 11 May 1869 in Boevange, Lux d: 24 Sep 1934 in Rochester, MN v: Minneapolis, MN i: Emigrated to the USA in 1902 i: Arrived on the La Champagne from LeHavre o: Laborer o: Mersch, Lux r: bx c: 4

+ seq: 108 KRAUS, Theresa b: 08 Mar 1875 in Mersch, Lux d: 22 Aug 1925 in Minneapolis, MN w: 31 Jan 1899 in Mersch, Lux v: Minneapolis, MN v: Mersch, Lux i: Emigrated to the USA in 1902 o: No profession r: x r: mx f: Mathias Kraus m: Marie Fegen c: 4

8 WITRY, Anna b: 26 Jul 1871 in Boevange, Lux r: b

8 [1] WITRY, Catherine b: 01 Aug 1874 in Boevange, Lux d: 14 Aug 1950 in Mersch, Lux h: Kremer v: Mersch, Lux o: No profession r: b c: 6

+ seq: 119.00.50 WEBER, Johann-Peter b: 08 Feb 1866 in Hamm, Lux d: 17 Jul 1896 in Mersch, Lux w: 16 Jul 1896 in Mersch, Lux a: Johann-Baptiste Weber o: Doorman o: Mechanic r: d r: m f: Johann-Peter Weber m: Barbara Koob

* 2nd Husband of [1] WITRY, Catherine:

+ seq: 119.01 KREMER, Peter b: 03 Jan 1869 d: 04 Dec 1934 in Mersch, Lux w: 06 Mar 1898 in Reims, France h: Kremer v: Mersch, Lux o: Laborer o: Machinist c: 6

8 WITRY, Josefine b: 04 Jul 1877 in Boevange, Lux d: 18 Feb 1878 in Boevange, Lux v: Boevange, Lux r: bd

107.01

8 WITRY, Margaretha b: 22 Feb 1865 in Boevange, Lux d: 20 Nov 1943 in Grevenknapp, Lux o: Day laborer r: b c: 5

+ seq: 107.01 WELTER, Nicolas b: 14 May 1866 in Boevange, Lux w: 29 May 1889 in Boevange, Lux o: Mason o: Day laborer r: m f: Nicolas Welter m: Margaretha Zangerle c: 5

9 WELTER, Anne v: Mersch, Lux
9 WELTER, Johann-Peter b: 10 Feb 1892 in Grevenmacher, Lux
  o: Postman r: b c: 1
+ seq: 107.01.30 BRUCK, Maria b: 27 Mar 1894 in Burmerange,
  Lux w: 09 Jan 1918 in Boevange, Lux o: No profession r: m
  f: Johann Bruck m: Anna Grethen c: 1
9 WELTER, Johann b: 07 Jul 1893 in Boevange, Lux o:
  Excavator r: b
+ seq: 107.01.60 MULLER, Catharina b: 29 Nov 1893 in Befort,
  Lux w: 17 Sep 1920 in Boevange, Lux r: m f: Theodore
  Muller m: Susanna Rausch
9 WELTER, Nicolas b: 27 Feb 1895 in Boevange, Lux d: 29 Oct
  1933 r: b
9 WELTER, Johann-Emil b: 10 May 1896 in Boevange, Lux r: b

107.01.30
9 WELTER, Johann-Peter b: 10 Feb 1892 in Grevenmacher, Lux
  o: Postman r: b c: 1
+ seq: 107.01.30 BRUCK, Maria b: 27 Mar 1894 in Burmerange,
  Lux w: 09 Jan 1918 in Boevange, Lux o: No profession r: m
  f: Johann Bruck m: Anna Grethen c: 1
10 WELTER, Eugen b: 11 Apr 1912 in Metz, France

107.02
8 WITRY, Johanna (Marie) b: 01 Dec 1866 in Boevange, Lux a:
  Leonie-Anna Wittry v: Mersch, Lux v: McLean Co., ND i:
  Immigrated to USA in 1902 o: No profession r: b c: 4
+ seq: 107.02 KERZMANN, John b: 10 Aug 1862 in Mersch, Lux
  d: 28 Feb 1930 in McLean Co., ND w: 21 Feb 1892 in Mersch,
  Lux h: Kerzmann 1 v: Mersch, Lux v: McLean Co., ND i:
  Immigrated to USA in 1902 o: Day laborer r: m f: Mathias
  Kerzmann m: Mary Pickels c: 4
9 KERZMANN, Peter b: Abt. 1888
9 KERZMANN, Anton J. b: 20 Sep 1888 in Luxembourg, Lux
9 KERZMANN, Marie-Elise (Mary) b: 19 Nov 1892 in Mersch,
  Lux r: b
9 KERZMANN, Katherine b: 02 Feb 1896 in Mersch, Lux r: b

108
8 WITRY, Johann-Peter b: 11 May 1869 in Boevange, Lux d: 24
  Sep 1934 in Rochester, MN v: Minneapolis, MN i: Emigrated

to the USA in 1902 i: Arrived on the La Champagne from LeHavre o: Laborer o: Mersch, Lux r: bx c: 4

+ seq: 108 KRAUS, Theresa b: 08 Mar 1875 in Mersch, Lux d: 22 Aug 1925 in Minneapolis, MN w: 31 Jan 1899 in Mersch, Lux v: Minneapolis, MN v: Mersch, Lux i: Emigrated to the USA in 1902 o: No profession r: x r: mx f: Mathias Kraus m: Marie Fegen c: 4

9 WITRY, Margaretha b: 21 Apr 1900 in Mersch, Lux d: 04 Apr 1973 in Minneapolis, MN Cause of death: Stroke i: Emigrated to the U.S. with parents r: bx c: 1

+ seq: 108.01 KARDONG, Matthew J. b: 24 Feb 1897 in Minneapolis, MN d: 14 Feb 1976 in Hennepin County, MN Cause of death: Alzheimer's w: 08 Jun 1921 in Minneapolis, MN v: Minneapolis, MN c: 1

9 WITRY, Theophile-Joseph b: 08 Sep 1901 in Mersch, Lux d: 08 Sep 1901 in Mersch, Lux r: bd

9 WITRY, Joseph-John b: 03 May 1904 in Minneapolis, MN d: 22 Apr 1960 in Minneapolis, MN v: Minneapolis, MN c: 3

+ seq: 109 MILLER, Pearl-Barbara b: 28 Apr 1899 in Minneapolis, MN d: 29 Oct 1981 in Robbinsdale, MN w: 07 Jul 1928 in Minneapolis, MN v: Minneapolis, MN c: 3

9 WITRY, Aloys b: 1913 in Minneapolis, MN d: 12 Jan 1916 in Minneapolis, MN Cause of death: Pneumonia v: Minneapolis, MN

108.01

9 WITRY, Margaretha b: 21 Apr 1900 in Mersch, Lux d: 04 Apr 1973 in Minneapolis, MN Cause of death: Stroke i: Emigrated to the U.S. with parents r: bx c: 1

+ seq: 108.01 KARDONG, Matthew J. b: 24 Feb 1897 in Minneapolis, MN d: 14 Feb 1976 in Hennepin County, MN Cause of death: Alzheimer's w: 08 Jun 1921 in Minneapolis, MN v: Minneapolis, MN c: 1

10KARDONG, Donald M. b: 09 Mar 1922 in Minneapolis, MN d: 24 Jul 1949 in Sherburne County, MN Cause of death: Accidental drowning

109

9 WITRY, Joseph-John b: 03 May 1904 in Minneapolis, MN d: 22 Apr 1960 in Minneapolis, MN v: Minneapolis, MN c: 3

+ seq: 109 MILLER, Pearl-Barbara b: 28 Apr 1899 in

Minneapolis, MN d: 29 Oct 1981 in Robbinsdale, MN w: 07
Jul 1928 in Minneapolis, MN v: Minneapolis, MN c: 3
10 WITRY, Joseph-John (Joe) b: 14 Jul 1929 in Minneapolis, MN
v: Brooklyn Center, MN o: Accountant c: 4
+ seq: 110 GROTH, Eunice-Ruth b: 20 Dec 1927 in Steen, MN
w: 14 May 1955 in Luverne, MN v: Brooklyn Center, MN o:
Nurse o: Accountant c: 4
10[1] WITRY, Richard-Aloys b: 14 Oct 1930 in Minneapolis, MN
v: Minneapolis, MN o: Retail foods c: 4
+ seq: 114 HEALEY, Joan-Rita b: 01 Jun 1934 in Minneapolis,
MN w: 20 Jun 1953 in Minneapolis, MN v: Minneapolis, MN
c: 4
* 2nd Wife of [1] WITRY, Richard-Aloys:
+ seq: 117 BURNS-RAKOWSKI, Darlene-Beverly b: 09 Dec
1927 in Minneapolis, MN w: 19 Aug 1972 in Minneapolis, MN
v: Minneapolis, MN
10 WITRY, Charles-Lee b: 26 Apr 1934 in Minneapolis, MN v:
Brooklyn Center, MN o: Used-car runner o: Cost accountant c:
3
+ seq: 118 JENSON, Darlene-Rae b: 04 Sep 1937 in
Minneapolis, MN w: 15 Sep 1956 in Minneapolis, MN v:
Brooklyn Center, MN c: 3

110
10 WITRY, Joseph-John (Joe) b: 14 Jul 1929 in Minneapolis, MN
v: Brooklyn Center, MN o: Accountant c: 4
+ seq: 110 GROTH, Eunice-Ruth b: 20 Dec 1927 in Steen, MN
w: 14 May 1955 in Luverne, MN v: Brooklyn Center, MN o:
Nurse o: Accountant c: 4
11[1] WITRY, Gregory-Joseph b: 27 Oct 1957 in Minneapolis,
MN v: Barberton, OH o: Manager of a fast food store c: 3
+ seq: 111 FELTON, Jill-Ann b: 18 Nov 1957 in Sheboygan, WI
w: 23 Jun 1979 in Brooklyn Park, MN v: Sheboygan, WI c: 1
* 2nd Wife of [1] WITRY, Gregory-Joseph:
+ seq: 112 HUMPHREY, Kimberly-Skye b: 03 Jul 1959 in
Gravette, AR w: 04 Aug 1987 in St. Paul, MN v: Barberton,
OH c: 2
11 WITRY, Barbara-Jean b: 29 Nov 1958 in Minneapolis, MN v:
Batavia, IL o: Pharmacist c: 3
+ seq: 112.01 SEKELSKY, Mark-David b: 23 Jul 1957 in
Ironwood, MI w: 15 Aug 1987 in Brooklyn Park, MN v:

Batavia, IL o: Manager of a fast food business c: 3
11 WITRY, Wayne-William b: 07 Jan 1961 in Minneapolis, MN
   v: Brooklyn Center, MN o: Military o: Postal carrier
11 WITRY, James-Leslie b: 17 Oct 1962 in Minneapolis, MN v:
   Buffalo, MN o: Military o: Truck driver c: 2
  + seq: 113 FOSTERVOLD, Kari-Lise b: 07 May 1961 in
     Minneapolis, MN w: 19 Aug 1989 in Minneapolis, MN v:
     Buffalo, MN c: 2

111

11 [1] WITRY, Gregory-Joseph b: 27 Oct 1957 in Minneapolis,
   MN v: Barberton, OH o: Manager of a fast food store c: 3
  + seq: 111 FELTON, Jill-Ann b: 18 Nov 1957 in Sheboygan, WI
     w: 23 Jun 1979 in Brooklyn Park, MN v: Sheboygan, WI c: 1
12 WITRY, Elizabeth-Grace b: 08 Nov 1981 in Edina, MN
  * 2nd Wife of [1] WITRY, Gregory-Joseph:
  + seq: 112 HUMPHREY, Kimberly-Skye b: 03 Jul 1959 in
     Gravette, AR w: 04 Aug 1987 in St. Paul, MN v: Barberton,
     OH c: 2
12 WITRY, Joshua-Lee b: 11 Apr 1988 in St. Louis Park, MN
12 WITRY, Benjamin-Joseph b: 28 Jun 1989 in St. Louis Park,
   MN

112.01

11 WITRY, Barbara-Jean b: 29 Nov 1958 in Minneapolis, MN v:
   Batavia, IL o: Pharmacist c: 3
  + seq: 112.01 SEKELSKY, Mark-David b: 23 Jul 1957 in
     Ironwood, MI w: 15 Aug 1987 in Brooklyn Park, MN v:
     Batavia, IL o: Manager of a fast food business c: 3
12 SEKELSKY, Andrew b: Abt. 1982
12 SEKELSKY, Adam-Joseph b: 21 Nov 1990 in West Palm
   Beach, FL
12 SEKELSKY, Sara-Ruth b: 22 Jan 1994 in Aurora, IL

113

11 WITRY, James-Leslie b: 17 Oct 1962 in Minneapolis, MN v:
   Buffalo, MN o: Military o: Truck driver c: 2
  + seq: 113 FOSTERVOLD, Kari-Lise b: 07 May 1961 in
     Minneapolis, MN w: 19 Aug 1989 in Minneapolis, MN v:
     Buffalo, MN c: 2
12 WITRY, Zachary-James b: 17 Sep 1990 in Minneapolis, MN

12 WITRY, Travis-Clare-Fostervold b: 16 Nov 1993 in Edina, MN

114
10[1] WITRY, Richard-Aloys b: 14 Oct 1930 in Minneapolis, MN
v: Minneapolis, MN o: Retail foods c: 4
+ seq: 114 HEALEY, Joan-Rita b: 01 Jun 1934 in Minneapolis,
MN w: 20 Jun 1953 in Minneapolis, MN v: Minneapolis, MN
c: 4
11 WITRY, Patricia-Jo b: 03 Jun 1954 in Minneapolis, MN v:
Blaine, MN o: Hotel management c: 2
+ seq: 114.01 QUARBERG, Mark-James b: 28 Aug 1954 in
Minneapolis, MN w: 15 Oct 1976 in Minneapolis, MN v:
Blaine, MN c: 2
11 WITRY, David-Michael b: 18 Apr 1956 in Minneapolis, MN v:
Kansas City, MO o: Airplane mechanic c: 1
+ seq: 115 ALEXANDER, Denise-Virginia b: 07 Oct 1954 in
Waterloo, IA w: 27 Dec 1987 in Minneapolis, MN v: Kansas
City, MO c: 1
11 WITRY, Thomas-William b: 07 Dec 1957 in Minneapolis, MN
v: Minneapolis, MN o: Singer o: Actor o: Model
+ seq: 116 O'NEILL, Mellissa-Ellen b: 21 Sep 1959 in
Robbinsdale, MN w: 19 Sep 1986 in Minneapolis, MN v:
Minneapolis, MN
11 WITRY, Robert-Allen b: 30 Nov 1958 in Minneapolis, MN v:
Minneapolis, MN o: Machine operator o: Disc jockey
* 2nd Wife of [1] WITRY, Richard-Aloys:
+ seq: 117 BURNS-RAKOWSKI, Darlene-Beverly b: 09 Dec
1927 in Minneapolis, MN w: 19 Aug 1972 in Minneapolis, MN
v: Minneapolis, MN

114.01
11 WITRY, Patricia-Jo b: 03 Jun 1954 in Minneapolis, MN v:
Blaine, MN o: Hotel management c: 2
+ seq: 114.01 QUARBERG, Mark-James b: 28 Aug 1954 in
Minneapolis, MN w: 15 Oct 1976 in Minneapolis, MN v:
Blaine, MN c: 2
12 QUARBERG, Therese-Nicole b: 09 Oct 1990 in Minneapolis,
MN
12 QUARBERG, Jonathan-Richard b: 02 Jul 1993 in Minneapolis,
MN

115

11 WITRY, David-Michael b: 18 Apr 1956 in Minneapolis, MN v:
  Kansas City, MO o: Airplane mechanic c: 1
+ seq: 115 ALEXANDER, Denise-Virginia b: 07 Oct 1954 in
  Waterloo, IA w: 27 Dec 1987 in Minneapolis, MN v: Kansas
  City, MO c: 1
12 WITRY, Christopher-Michael b: 17 Oct 1987 in Denver, CO

118

10 WITRY, Charles-Lee b: 26 Apr 1934 in Minneapolis, MN v:
  Brooklyn Center, MN o: Used-car runner o: Cost accountant c:
  3
+ seq: 118 JENSON, Darlene-Rae b: 04 Sep 1937 in
  Minneapolis, MN w: 15 Sep 1956 in Minneapolis, MN v:
  Brooklyn Center, MN c: 3
11 WITRY, Cynthia-Lea b: 15 Aug 1959 in Minneapolis, MN v:
  New Brighton, MN o: Mother c: 2
+ seq: 118.01 RHEA, Bruce-Kevin b: 21 Feb 1963 in
  Minneapolis, MN w: 21 Jan 1984 in Minneapolis, MN v: New
  Brighton, MN c: 2
11 WITRY, William-Ray b: 22 Sep 1960 in Minneapolis, MN d:
  06 Feb 1975 in Minneapolis, MN Cause of death: Accident v:
  Minneapolis, MN
11 WITRY, Scott-Charles b: 03 Aug 1963 in Minneapolis, MN v:
  Savage, MN o: Computer consultant o: Computer programmer
  c: 3
+ seq: 119 BOOMGAARDEN, Lynn-Marie b: 02 May 1955 in
  Tacoma, WA w: 02 Sep 1989 in Minneapolis, MN v: Savage,
  MN c: 3

118.01

11 WITRY, Cynthia-Lea b: 15 Aug 1959 in Minneapolis, MN v:
  New Brighton, MN o: Mother c: 2
+ seq: 118.01 RHEA, Bruce-Kevin b: 21 Feb 1963 in
  Minneapolis, MN w: 21 Jan 1984 in Minneapolis, MN v: New
  Brighton, MN c: 2
12 RHEA, Brenda-Kathleen b: 24 Jul 1984 in Minneapolis, MN c:
  2
13 RHEA, Grace-Kathleen b: 06 Oct 2005 in Minneapolis, MN
13 RHEA, Bethany-Lea b: 06 Oct 2005 in Minneapolis, MN
12 RHEA, Tina-Marie b: 26 Jan 1987 in Minneapolis, MN

11 WITRY, Scott-Charles b: 03 Aug 1963 in Minneapolis, MN v: Savage, MN o: Computer consultant o: Computer programmer c: 3
+ seq: 119 BOOMGAARDEN, Lynn-Marie b: 02 May 1955 in Tacoma, WA w: 02 Sep 1989 in Minneapolis, MN v: Savage, MN c: 3
12 WITRY, Kirsten-Nichole b: 19 Feb 1991 in Minneapolis, MN
12 WITRY, Danielle-Marie b: 02 Jul 1992 in Minneapolis, MN
12 WITRY, Jason-William-Leon b: 14 Oct 1994 in Minneapolis, MN

119.00.50

8 [1] WITRY, Catherine b: 01 Aug 1874 in Boevange, Lux d: 14 Aug 1950 in Mersch, Lux h: Kremer v: Mersch, Lux o: No profession r: b c: 6
+ seq: 119.00.50 WEBER, Johann-Peter b: 08 Feb 1866 in Hamm, Lux d: 17 Jul 1896 in Mersch, Lux w: 16 Jul 1896 in Mersch, Lux a: Johann-Baptiste Weber o: Doorman o: Mechanic r: d r: m f: Johann-Peter Weber m: Barbara Koob
* 2nd Husband of [1] WITRY, Catherine:
+ seq: 119.01 KREMER, Peter b: 03 Jan 1869 d: 04 Dec 1934 in Mersch, Lux w: 06 Mar 1898 in Reims, France h: Kremer v: Mersch, Lux o: Laborer o: Machinist c: 6
9 KREMER, Antoine-Pierre b: 29 Jun 1899 in Mersch, Lux r: b
9 KREMER, Nicolas b: 24 Feb 1900 in Mersch, Lux d: 05 May 1969 in Dippach, Lux i: Married - 3 children r: b
9 KREMER, Johanna (Leanne) b: 24 Oct 1901 in Mersch, Lux d: 1981 v: Germany i: Married - 4 children r: b
9 KREMER, Peter-Heinrich (Henri) b: 20 Mar 1906 in Mersch, Lux d: 04 Jun 1988 in Ettelbruck, Lux h: No. 31 Lankhek v: Mersch, Lux r: b
9 KREMER, Marie-Antonia b: 20 Dec 1908 in Mersch, Lux r: b
9 KREMER, Leonie b: 28 Nov 1913 in Mersch, Lux d: 15 Feb 1933 in Mersch, Lux r: b c: 1
+ seq: 119.01.50 w: Abt. 1930 c: 1

119.01.50

9 KREMER, Leonie b: 28 Nov 1913 in Mersch, Lux d: 15 Feb 1933 in Mersch, Lux r: b c: 1
+ seq: 119.01.50 w: Abt. 1930 c: 1

10 KREMER, Liliane b: 29 Nov 1932

119.02

6 WITRY, Anna-Marie b: 07 Mar 1777 in Reuland, Lux d: 11
Mar 1837 in Roodt, Lux a: Peters a: Schneider h: Schneider v:
Roodt, Lux o: No profession r: bd c: 5
+ seq: 119.02 GEORGE, Johann b: 10 Jan 1772 in Roodt, Lux d:
14 Apr 1837 in Roodt, Lux w: 30 Dec 1801 in Betzdorf, Lux
a: Schneider h: Schneider v: Roodt, Lux o: Plowman o: Day
laborer o: Farmer r: d r: m f: Jacob George m: Anna-
Margaretha Wagner c: 5
7 GEORGE, Johann b: 11 Jul 1802 in Roodt, Lux r: b
7 GEORGE, Anna b: 30 Jan 1805 in Roodt, Lux r: b
7 GEORGE, Theodor b: 06 Feb 1808 in Roodt, Lux r: b
7 [1] GEORGE, Margaretha b: 25 Mar 1811 in Roodt, Lux d: 24
Oct 1868 in Roodt, Lux v: Roodt, Lux o: Day laborer r: bd c:
1
+ seq: 119.03 WAGNER, Mathias b: Abt. 1800 w: Abt. 1825 v:
Roodt, Lux o: Day laborer c: 1
* 2nd Husband of [1] GEORGE, Margaretha:
+ seq: 119.04 KIEFER, Franz b: Abt. 1800 w: Abt. 1826 v:
Roodt, Lux
7 GEORGE, Catherine b: 30 Nov 1814 in Roodt, Lux r: b

119.03

7 [1] GEORGE, Margaretha b: 25 Mar 1811 in Roodt, Lux d: 24
Oct 1868 in Roodt, Lux v: Roodt, Lux o: Day laborer r: bd c:
1
+ seq: 119.03 WAGNER, Mathias b: Abt. 1800 w: Abt. 1825 v:
Roodt, Lux o: Day laborer c: 1
8 WAGNER, Johann b: Abt. 1830 in Roodt, Lux v: Roodt, Lux
o: Day laborer
* 2nd Husband of [1] GEORGE, Margaretha:
+ seq: 119.04 KIEFER, Franz b: Abt. 1800 w: Abt. 1826 v:
Roodt, Lux

119.05

4 [1] WITRY, Marie-Franzisca-Xaveria (Severa) b: 26 Feb 1702
in Schrondweiler, Lux a: Thies h: Peffer v: Niederglabach, Lux
r: b c: 8
+ seq: 119.05 PEFFER, Adam b: Abt. 1697 in Niederglabach,

Lux d: 16 Aug 1754 in Niederglabach, Lux w: 1722 h: Peffer
v: Niederglabach, Lux o: Farmer r: d f: Jean Peffer m:
Marguerite Mehlen c: 8

5 PEFFER, Heinrich b: 06 Feb 1723 in Niederglabach, Lux r: b
+ seq: 119.06 JORDAN, Elisabeth b: Abt. 1735 in Brandenbourg,
Lux w: 04 Feb 1773 in Brandenbourg, Lux

5 PEFFER, Johann b: 14 Jun 1725 in Niederglabach, Lux r: b

5 PEFFER, Johann b: 07 Dec 1727 in Niederglabach, Lux r: b

5 PEFFER, Nicolas b: 23 Oct 1729 in Niederglabach, Lux d: 30
Nov 1798 in Niederglabach, Lux v: Glabach, Lux r: b
+ seq: 119.07 HAMES, Apollonia b: Abt. 1734 in Senningen,
Lux d: 24 Sep 1815 in Niederglabach, Lux w: 19 Nov 1754 in
Nommern, Lux v: Glabach, Lux r: m

5 PEFFER, Peter b: 07 Feb 1734 in Niederglabach, Lux r: b
+ seq: 119.08 ATTEN, Margaretha b: 1732 in Bissen, Lux d:
Bef. 1778 w: 22 Jan 1764 in Nommern, Lux r: m f: Martin
Atten m: Eve Wiltgen

5 PEFFER, Angela b: 24 Aug 1738 in Niederglabach, Lux r: b

5 PEFFER, Johann b: 29 Mar 1741 in Niederglabach, Lux r: b

5 PEFFER, Dominic b: 21 Jul 1743 in Niederglabach, Lux d: 11
Apr 1813 in Gilsdorf, Lux r: b
+ seq: 119.09 SINTGEN, Margaretha b: Abt. 1755 in Gilsdorf,
Lux d: 22 Feb 1821 in Diekirch, Lux w: 08 Jan 1775 in
Nommern, Lux r: m f: Adam Sintgen m: Angela Gillen

* 2nd Husband of [1] WITRY, Marie-Franzisca-Xaveria (Severa):
+ seq: 119.10 HAMES, Corneille b: 1700 in Senningen, Lux d:
12 Jan 1789 in Niederglabach, Lux w: 19 Nov 1754 in
Nommern, Lux v: Niederglabach, Lux r: d r: m

120

4 [3] WITRY, Nicolas b: 11 Jun 1708 in Schrondweiler, Lux d:
Aft. 1780 v: Beidweiler, Lux v: Bergem, Lux o: Laborer o:
Farmer r: b c: 11
+ seq: 120 PIERE, Anna b: 02 Apr 1724 in Rumelange, Lux d:
Abt. 1763 in Schiffelange, Lux w: Abt. 1744 in Bergem, Lux a:
Fischbach v: Bergem, Lux r: b r: x f: Jacques (Jacob) Piere m:
Margaretha (Anna-Marie) Weinand c: 10

5 WITRY, Johann b: 26 Feb 1745 in Bergem, Lux i: Confirmed
r: b

5 WITRY, Jean b: 12 Apr 1746 in Bergem, Lux d: 28 Dec 1792
in Bergem, Lux a: Brymmeyer h: Brymmeyer v: Bergem, Lux

o: Farmer r: bdx c: 9

+ seq: 121 LAUX, Marie-Catherine b: 21 Oct 1743 in Bergem,
  Lux d: 22 Dec 1833 in Bergem, Lux w: 27 Jan 1765 in Kayl,
  Lux h: Brimmeyer v: Bergem, Lux o: Farmer r: bd r: mx f:
  Pierre Laux m: Jeanne Welfringer c: 9

5 WITRY, Anna b: 14 Jan 1748 in Bergem, Lux i: Confirmed r:
  b

5 [1] WITRY, Nicolas b: 14 Mar 1750 in Bergem, Lux d: 17 Jul
  1804 in Beidweiler, Lux a: Diedesch h: Diedesch v:
  Beidweiler, Lux i: Confirmed o: Farmer r: bd c: 13

+ seq: 156 KUHNEN, Marie-Catherine b: 19 Oct 1750 in
  Beidweiler, Lux d: 03 May 1786 in Beidweiler, Lux w: 17 Dec
  1774 in Beidweiler, Lux a: Diedesch h: Diedesch v:
  Beidweiler, Lux i: Confirmed r: bd r: m f: Mathias Kuhnen
  m: Susanne Diedesch c: 6

* 2nd Wife of [1] WITRY, Nicolas:

+ seq: 228 HUSS, Elisabeth b: 09 Feb 1765 in Biwer, Lux d: 28
  Feb 1857 in Beidweiler, Lux w: 26 Jun 1786 in Beidweiler, Lux
  a: Weidich h: Diedesch v: Bergem, Lux v: Beidweiler, Lux o:
  Farmer r: d r: m f: Nicolas Huss m: Margaretha (Catherine)
  Moosbach c: 7

5 WITRY, Michel b: 12 May 1752 in Bergem, Lux i: Confirmed
  r: b

5 WITRY, Peter b: 03 Mar 1754 in Bergem, Lux i: Confirmed r:
  b

5 WITRY, Margaretha b: 14 Jul 1756 in Bergem, Lux h:
  Scheurengs v: Mondercange, Lux o: Farmer r: b c: 10

+ seq: 308.03 DONDELINGER, Michel b: Abt. 1750 in
  Mondercange, Lux d: 01 Jun 1839 in Bergem, Lux w: Abt.
  1774 a: Scheurengs h: Scheurengs v: Mondercange, Lux o:
  Farmer c: 10

5 [2] WITRY, Magdalena b: 14 Oct 1758 in Bergem, Lux d: 21
  Apr 1823 in Strassem, Lux h: Schneider-Meyers v: Strassem,
  Lux r: bd c: 6

+ seq: 308.07 SCHMITT, Johann b: Abt. 1755 in Strassem, Lux
  d: 20 Nov 1802 in Strassem, Lux w: 26 Feb 1781 in Bertrange,
  Lux h: Schneider-Meyers v: Strassem, Lux o: Innkeeper o:
  Farmer r: d r: m f: Nicolas Schmitt m: Marie Dondelinger c: 6

* 2nd Husband of [2] WITRY, Magdalena:

+ seq: 308.08 SCHINTGEN, Nicolas b: Abt. 1780 in
  Mondercange, Lux w: 11 Jan 1804 in Bertrange, Lux v:

Strassem, Lux o: Farmer r: m f: Johann Schintgen m: Marie
Lantgen
5 WITRY, Jacob b: 10 Aug 1760 in Bergem, Lux r: b
5 WITRY, Theodor b: 23 Sep 1762 in Bergem, Lux r: b
* 2nd Wife of [3] WITRY, Nicolas:
+ seq: 309 HYMBERT, Marie b: Abt. 1740 in Kayl, Lux w: 27
Jan 1765 in Schiffelange, Lux v: Bergem, Lux r: x c: 1
5 WITRY, Nicolas b: Abt. 1766 in Schiffelange, Lux v:
Dudelange, Lux o: Farmer c: 1
+ seq: 310 WEISGERBER, Margaretha b: Abt. 1765 w: Abt.
1790 v: Dudelange, Lux c: 1

121
5 WITRY, Jean b: 12 Apr 1746 in Bergem, Lux d: 28 Dec 1792
in Bergem, Lux a: Brymmeyer h: Brymmeyer v: Bergem, Lux
o: Farmer r: bdx c: 9
+ seq: 121 LAUX, Marie-Catherine b: 21 Oct 1743 in Bergem,
Lux d: 22 Dec 1833 in Bergem, Lux w: 27 Jan 1765 in Kayl,
Lux h: Brimmeyer v: Bergem, Lux o: Farmer r: bd r: mx f:
Pierre Laux m: Jeanne Welfringer c: 9
6 WITRY, Peter b: Abt. 1766 in Bergem, Lux
+ seq: 122 DONDELINGER, Catherine b: Abt. 1775 w: Abt.
1798 in Mondercange, Lux
6 WITRY, Willebrord b: 20 May 1767 in Bergem, Lux d: 16 Dec
1792 in Bergem, Lux a: Brimmeyer h: Brimmeyer v: Bergem,
Lux o: Farmer r: bd c: 1
+ seq: 123 DICKES, Margaretha b: Abt. 1770 in Bergem, Lux
w: 11 May 1791 in Schiffelange, Lux h: Brimmeyer v:
Bergem, Lux r: m f: Jacob Dickes m: Anna-Marie Hoff c: 1
6 WITRY, Margaretha b: 04 Oct 1769 in Bergem, Lux v:
Mondercange, Lux r: b
6 WITRY, Marie-Catherine b: 04 May 1772 in Bergem, Lux v:
Bergem, Lux r: b
6 WITRY, Johann b: 10 Mar 1774 in Bergem, Lux r: b
6 [1] WITRY, Jean b: 15 Dec 1775 in Bergem, Lux d: 12 May
1832 in Bergem, Lux a: Hansen h: No. 4/24 v: Bergem, Lux o:
Laborer o: Farmer r: bd c: 18
+ seq: 124 OLINGER, Anna-Catherine b: 1773 in Bergem, Lux
d: 29 Oct 1807 in Bergem, Lux w: Abt. 1795 in Schiffelange,
Lux h: No. 4 v: Bergem, Lux o: Farmer r: d f: Johann Wester
m: Angelique Kiersch c: 5

* 2nd Wife of [1] WITRY, Jean:
+ seq: 133 WESTER, Catherine b: Abt. 1783 in Bergem, Lux d: 03 Sep 1838 in Bergem, Lux w: 25 Jan 1809 in Mondercange, Lux h: No. 24 v: Bergem, Lux o: Housekeeper o: Farmer r: d r: m f: Nicolas-Jean Wester m: Angelica Kirsch c: 13
6 WITRY, Michel t: Mayor b: 14 Nov 1778 in Bergem, Lux d: 16 Aug 1849 in Boevange, Lux v: Boevange, Lux o: Farmer r: b c: 6
+ seq: 140 MATHEY, Catherine b: 21 Jun 1773 in Boevange, Lux d: 05 May 1843 in Boevange, Lux w: 1802 v: Boevange, Lux o: Farmer f: Michel Mathey m: Marie-Catherine Olinger c: 6
6 WITRY, Johann b: 19 Apr 1781 in Bergem, Lux d: 11 Mar 1837 in Strassem, Lux a: Deusch h: Deusch v: Strassem, Lux o: Weaver o: Farmer o: Laborer r: bd c: 10
+ seq: 142 NEPPER, Susanne b: 20 Feb 1780 in Strassem, Lux d: 13 Feb 1847 in Strassem, Lux w: 11 Feb 1806 in Strassem, Lux h: Deusch v: Strassem, Lux o: Property owner o: Farmer r: m f: Peter Nepper m: Margaretha Schroeder c: 10
6 WITRY, Pierre b: 02 Feb 1784 in Bergem, Lux d: 10 Feb 1862 in Bergem, Lux a: Farmer v: Eschweiler, Lux v: Bergem, Lux o: Day laborer r: bd c: 10
+ seq: 148 SCHINTGEN, Jeanette (Anna) b: 06 Mar 1786 in Bergem, Lux d: 06 Jun 1873 in Bergem, Lux w: 08 Nov 1809 in Mondercange, Lux v: Eschweiler, Lux v: Bergem, Lux o: Farmer r: d r: m f: Nicolas Schintgen m: Christine Steichen c: 10

123
6 WITRY, Willebrord b: 20 May 1767 in Bergem, Lux d: 16 Dec 1792 in Bergem, Lux a: Brimmeyer h: Brimmeyer v: Bergem, Lux o: Farmer r: bd c: 1
+ seq: 123 DICKES, Margaretha b: Abt. 1770 in Bergem, Lux w: 11 May 1791 in Schiffelange, Lux h: Brimmeyer v: Bergem, Lux r: m f: Jacob Dickes m: Anna-Marie Hoff c: 1
7 WITRY, Marie-Catherine b: 05 Jun 1792 in Bergem, Lux r: b

124
6 [1] WITRY, Jean b: 15 Dec 1775 in Bergem, Lux d: 12 May 1832 in Bergem, Lux a: Hansen h: No. 4/24 v: Bergem, Lux o: Laborer o: Farmer r: bd c: 18

+ seq: 124 OLINGER, Anna-Catherine b: 1773 in Bergem, Lux
  d: 29 Oct 1807 in Bergem, Lux w: Abt. 1795 in Schiffelange,
  Lux h: No. 4 v: Bergem, Lux o: Farmer r: d f: Johann Wester
  m: Angelique Kiersch c: 5

7 WITRY, Nicolas b: 15 Jul 1798 in Bergem, Lux v: Bergem,
  Lux o: Farmer r: b

7 WITRY, Marie-Catherine b: 10 May 1801 in Bergem, Lux d:
  14 Jan 1802 in Bergem, Lux v: Bergem, Lux o: No profession
  r: bd

7 WITRY, Heinrich b: 26 Feb 1803 in Bergem, Lux d: 05 Feb
  1826 in Wickrange, Lux v: Wickrange, Lux o: Farmer r: bd c:
  1

+ seq: 125 DECKER, Catherine b: 22 Feb 1804 in Mondercange,
  Lux d: 09 Sep 1847 in Wickrange, Lux w: 08 May 1825 in
  Mondercange, Lux v: Wickrange, Lux o: No profession r: m
  f: Theodore Decker m: Anne Gehlen c: 1

7 WITRY, Jean b: 24 Apr 1805 in Bergem, Lux d: 14 Sep 1837
  in Bergem, Lux v: Bergem, Lux o: Laborer o: Farmer r: bd c:
  1

+ seq: 126 BERENS, Jeanette b: 09 May 1804 in Bergem, Lux
  d: 01 Apr 1855 in Bergem, Lux w: 10 Feb 1836 in
  Mondercange, Lux v: Bergem, Lux o: No profession r: d r: m
  f: Jean Berens m: Marie-Catherine Groff c: 1

7 WITRY, Marie-Catherine b: 21 Oct 1807 in Bergem, Lux d: 19
  May 1878 in Bettembourg, Lux v: Bettembourg, Lux o:
  Housemaid r: bd c: 4

+ seq: 132.05 DENNEMEYER, Nicolas b: 30 Dec 1798 in
  Bettembourg, Lux d: 30 Apr 1881 w: 22 Feb 1830 in
  Bettembourg, Lux v: Bettembourg, Lux o: Farmer r: m f:
  Johann Dennemeyer m: Anna Majerus c: 4

* 2nd Wife of [1] WITRY, Jean:

+ seq: 133 WESTER, Catherine b: Abt. 1783 in Bergem, Lux d:
  03 Sep 1838 in Bergem, Lux w: 25 Jan 1809 in Mondercange,
  Lux h: No. 24 v: Bergem, Lux o: Housekeeper o: Farmer r: d
  r: m f: Nicolas-Jean Wester m: Angelica Kirsch c: 13

7 WITRY, Marie (Angelica) b: 02 Feb 1809 in Luxembourg, Lux
  d: 23 Jul 1837 o: No profession r: b

+ seq: 133.01 JACOBS, Peter b: 12 Sep 1811 in Bergem, Lux w:
  09 Mar 1835 in Mondercange, Lux o: Day laborer r: m f:
  Johann Jacobs m: Hoffmann

7 WITRY, Margaretha b: 18 Apr 1810 in Luxembourg, Lux d: 29

Jan 1882 o: No profession r: b

+ seq: 133.02 SPEYER, Peter b: 12 Nov 1810 in Bettembourg,
  Lux w: 15 Jan 1835 in Mondercange, Lux r: m f: Bernard
  Speyer m: Marie

7 WITRY, Jeanette b: 19 Jun 1811 in Bergem, Lux d: 20 Jun
  1811 in Bergem, Lux v: Bergem, Lux o: No profession r: bd

7 WITRY, Nicolas b: 24 Jun 1812 in Bergem, Lux d: 24 Jun
  1812 in Bergem, Lux v: Bergem, Lux o: No profession r: bd

7 WITRY, Peter b: 21 Jul 1813 in Bergem, Lux d: 22 Feb 1838 in
  Bergem, Lux v: Bergem, Lux o: Farmer r: bd

7 WITRY, Marie-Catherine b: 06 Apr 1815 in Bergem, Lux d: 30
  Apr 1825 v: Wormeldange, Lux r: b

7 WITRY, Marie-Catherine b: 29 Nov 1815 in Bergem, Lux d:
  30 Apr 1825 in Bergem, Lux v: Bergem, Lux o: No profession
  r: bd

7 WITRY, Catherine b: 10 Sep 1816 in Bergem, Lux r: b

7 WITRY, Johann b: 16 Sep 1817 in Bergem, Lux d: 29 Dec
  1818 in Bergem, Lux v: Bergem, Lux r: bd

7 WITRY, Marie-Catherine b: 11 Sep 1819 in Bergem, Lux d: 30
  Apr 1825 in Bergem, Lux r: bd

7 WITRY, Anna-Catherine b: 10 Jan 1822 in Bergem, Lux v:
  Bergem, Lux o: No profession r: b

+ seq: 133.03 ROLLIN, Jean-Francois b: 02 Dec 1811 in
  Fillieres, France w: 03 Dec 1840 in Mondercange, Lux o:
  Farmer r: m f: Joseph-Nicolas Rollin m: Renee Colligunn

7 WITRY, Bernard b: 11 Feb 1824 in Bergem, Lux d: 17 Aug
  1830 in Bergem, Lux h: No. 24 v: Bergem, Lux o: No
  profession r: bd

7 WITRY, Johann b: 19 Apr 1826 in Bergem, Lux d: 29 Mar
  1888 in Bergem, Lux v: Bergem, Lux o: Farmer r: bd c: 9

+ seq: 134 MATHEY, Barbara b: 10 Nov 1824 in Bettembourg,
  Lux d: 06 Feb 1866 in Bergem, Lux w: 26 Nov 1849 in
  Bettembourg, Lux a: Mathes v: Bergem, Lux o: No profession
  r: m f: Pierre Mathey m: Madeleine Georges c: 9

125

7 WITRY, Heinrich b: 26 Feb 1803 in Bergem, Lux d: 05 Feb
  1826 in Wickrange, Lux v: Wickrange, Lux o: Farmer r: bd c:
  1

+ seq: 125 DECKER, Catherine b: 22 Feb 1804 in Mondercange,
  Lux d: 09 Sep 1847 in Wickrange, Lux w: 08 May 1825 in

Mondercange, Lux v: Wickrange, Lux o: No profession r: m
f: Theodore Decker m: Anne Gehlen c: 1

8 WITRY, Anna b: 28 Oct 1825 in Wickrange, Lux d: 07 May
1841 in Wickrange, Lux v: Wickrange, Lux o: No profession r:
bd

+ seq: 125.01 KIRSCH, Jean-Pierre w: Abt. 1840 v: Wickrange,
Lux

126

7 WITRY, Jean b: 24 Apr 1805 in Bergem, Lux d: 14 Sep 1837
in Bergem, Lux v: Bergem, Lux o: Laborer o: Farmer r: bd c:
1

+ seq: 126 BERENS, Jeanette b: 09 May 1804 in Bergem, Lux d:
01 Apr 1855 in Bergem, Lux w: 10 Feb 1836 in Mondercange,
Lux v: Bergem, Lux o: No profession r: d r: m f: Jean Berens
m: Marie-Catherine Groff c: 1

8 WITRY, Jean-Nicolas b: 10 Nov 1836 in Bergem, Lux d: 18
Feb 1902 in Bergem, Lux h: Hentges v: Bergem, Lux v:
Dippach, Lux o: Landowner o: Farmer r: bd c: 10

+ seq: 127 BERENS, Marie-Therese b: 09 Oct 1829 in Boevange,
Lux d: 21 May 1899 in Bergem, Lux w: 30 May 1855 in
Mondercange, Lux h: Hentges v: Bergem, Lux v: Dippach, Lux
o: Housekeeper o: Farmer r: d r: m c: 10

127

8 WITRY, Jean-Nicolas b: 10 Nov 1836 in Bergem, Lux d: 18
Feb 1902 in Bergem, Lux h: Hentges v: Bergem, Lux v:
Dippach, Lux o: Landowner o: Farmer r: bd c: 10

+ seq: 127 BERENS, Marie-Therese b: 09 Oct 1829 in Boevange,
Lux d: 21 May 1899 in Bergem, Lux w: 30 May 1855 in
Mondercange, Lux h: Hentges v: Bergem, Lux v: Dippach, Lux
o: Housekeeper o: Farmer r: d r: m c: 10

9 WITRY, Johann-Nicolas b: 16 Mar 1856 in Bergem, Lux d: 04
Sep 1901 in Bergem, Lux v: Bergem, Lux o: Farmer r: bd

9 WITRY, Jean-Jacques b: 13 Apr 1858 in Bergem, Lux d: 12
Feb 1921 in Dippach, Lux v: Dippach, Lux o: Farmer r: bd c:
8

+ seq: 128 BERENS, Marie-Josefine b: 27 Nov 1855 in Dippach,
Lux d: 15 Oct 1903 in Dippach, Lux w: 04 Feb 1885 in
Dippach, Lux v: Dippach, Lux o: No profession r: d r: m f:
Peter Berents m: Catherine Berens c: 8

9 WITRY, Nicolas-Emil b: 10 Apr 1860 in Bergem, Lux d: 17 Sep 1915 in San Nicolas de los Arroyos, Argentina Cause of death: influenza v: San Nicolas de los Arroyos, Argentina i: Emigrated to Argentina o: Port construction o: Agricultural engineer r: bx c: 10

+ seq: 128.01 MURTAGH, Catalina d: 25 Jul 1951 in San Nicolas de los Arroyos, Argentina w: 05 May 1892 in Buenos Aires, Argentina v: San Nicolas de los Arroyos, Argentina f: William Murtagh m: Rosa Fox y Murray c: 10

9 WITRY, Johann-Baptist b: 08 Mar 1862 in Bergem, Lux d: 1897 h: 77 rue St Jacques v: Nancy, France o: Baker r: b c: 1

+ seq: 128.26 ROUSSEAU, Zoe-Marie-Josephine b: 28 May 1861 in Nancy, France w: 29 Dec 1884 in Nancy, France h: 77 rue St Jacques v: Nancy, France o: No profession r: m f: Christophe-Paul Rousseau m: Rose-Marie-Poussardin c: 1

9 WITRY, Henri b: 15 Feb 1864 in Bergem, Lux d: 1948 in Bergem, Lux v: Bergem, Lux o: Landowner o: Farmer r: b c: 6

+ seq: 129 NEPPER, Marie-Catherine b: 18 Jan 1867 in Wolkrange, Lux d: 17 Dec 1913 in Bergem, Lux w: 24 Aug 1897 in Mondercange, Lux v: Bergem, Lux o: No profession r: m f: Pierre Nepper m: Josephine Bonhomme c: 6

9 WITRY, Marie-Josefine b: 03 Apr 1866 in Bergem, Lux r: b

9 WITRY, Jean-Pierre-Leon b: 03 Nov 1866 in Bergem, Lux d: 16 Oct 1917 in Schweich, Lux v: Schweich, Lux o: Farmer r: d

+ seq: 132.04.01 JUNGERS, Elisabeth (Elise) b: 04 Jun 1861 in Schweich, Lux w: 11 Jun 1895 in Beckerich, Lux v: Schweich, Lux o: No profession r: m f: Jacques Jungers m: Marie Salentiny

9 WITRY, Nicolas-Gustav (Auguste) b: 23 Sep 1868 in Bergem, Lux d: 16 Apr 1884 r: b

9 WITRY, Johann-Peter b: 04 Jul 1870 in Bergem, Lux d: 11 Sep 1903 in Grevenmacher, Lux h: Dardenhacheuer v: Grevenmacher, Lux o: Pastry chef r: bd c: 2

+ seq: 132.04.02 LETHAL, Anne-Marie b: 08 Dec 1872 in Grevenmacher, Lux w: 29 Aug 1899 in Mondercange, Lux h: Dardenhacheuer v: Grevenmacher, Lux o: No profession r: m c: 2

9 WITRY, Johann-Baptist-Nicolas b: 14 May 1873 in Bergem, Lux r: b

9 WITRY, Jean-Jacques b: 13 Apr 1858 in Bergem, Lux d: 12 Feb 1921 in Dippach, Lux v: Dippach, Lux o: Farmer r: bd c: 8

+ seq: 128 BERENS, Marie-Josefine b: 27 Nov 1855 in Dippach, Lux d: 15 Oct 1903 in Dippach, Lux w: 04 Feb 1885 in Dippach, Lux v: Dippach, Lux o: No profession r: d r: m f: Peter Berents m: Catherine Berens c: 8

10 WITRY, Johann-Baptist-Alphonse b: 23 Nov 1885 in Dippach, Lux r: b

10 WITRY, Johann-Nicolas b: 02 May 1887 in Dippach, Lux d: 09 Aug 1906 in Dippach, Lux v: Dippach, Lux o: No profession r: bd

10 WITRY, Anne-Leonie b: 02 Feb 1889 in Dippach, Lux d: 10 Feb 1923 in Dippach, Lux v: Dippach, Lux o: No profession r: b

10 WITRY, Marie-Josefine b: 01 Nov 1890 in Dippach, Lux d: 19 Dec 1890 in Dippach, Lux r: b

10 WITRY, Marie-Anne (Marianne) b: 03 Jul 1892 in Dippach, Lux d: 29 Sep 1907 in Dippach, Lux v: Dippach, Lux o: No profession r: bd

10 WITRY, Marie-Marguerite b: 05 Jul 1894 in Dippach, Lux r: b

10 WITRY, Anne-Therese b: 14 Oct 1896 in Dippach, Lux r: b

10 WITRY, Victor b: 19 Aug 1898 in Dippach, Lux o: Farmer r: b c: 5

+ seq: 128.00.05 EPPE, Anne b: 05 May 1902 in Udange, Belgium w: Abt. 1925 c: 5

128.00.05

10 WITRY, Victor b: 19 Aug 1898 in Dippach, Lux o: Farmer r: b c: 5

+ seq: 128.00.05 EPPE, Anne b: 05 May 1902 in Udange, Belgium w: Abt. 1925 c: 5

11 WITRY, Marcel b: 30 Sep 1937 in Dippach, Lux v: Selange, Belgium c: 2

+ seq: 128.00.10 SCHOLTUS, Lucie b: 27 Jun 1942 w: 1964 in Selange, Belgium v: Selange, Belgium c: 2

11 WITRY, Alphonse b: 24 Mar 1936 in Dippach, Lux d: 27 Oct 2006 v: Dippach, Lux o: Farmer c: 4

+ seq: 128.00.20 FELLER, Francoise (Francie) b: 27 Jun 1944 w: Abt. 1970 v: Dippach, Lux o: Farmer f: Edouard Feller m:

Catherine Hemmering c: 4

11 WITRY, Marie-Therese b: 07 Aug 1939 v: Roodt, Lux c: 2
+ seq: 128.00.35 KREMER, Joseph (Josy) b: 03 Jul 1937 w:
   Abt. 1965 in Roodt-Eisch, Lux v: Roodt, Lux c: 2
11 WITRY, Jean-Pierre b: Abt. 1941
+ seq: 128.00.60 FELLER, Marie-Josee w: Abt. 1965 f: Feller
   m: Sciltz
11 WITRY, Florent b: Abt. 1944
+ seq: 128.00.70 FELLER, Christiane w: Abt. 1970 f: Feller m:
   Steimenz

128.00.10

11 WITRY, Marcel b: 30 Sep 1937 in Dippach, Lux v: Selange,
   Belgium c: 2
+ seq: 128.00.10 SCHOLTUS, Lucie b: 27 Jun 1942 w: 1964 in
   Selange, Belgium v: Selange, Belgium c: 2
12 WITRY, Evelyne b: 28 Apr 1967 c: 2
+ seq: 128.00.15 BERNA w: Abt. 1995 c: 2
12 WITRY, Alain b: 16 Sep 1974 c: 1
+ seq: 128.00.17 SCHMIT, Nathalie w: Abt. 2000 c: 1

128.00.15

12 WITRY, Evelyne b: 28 Apr 1967 c: 2
+ seq: 128.00.15 BERNA w: Abt. 1995 c: 2
13 BERNA, Allison b: 04 Feb 1999
13 BERNA, Tom b: 02 Jun 2000

128.00.17

12 WITRY, Alain b: 16 Sep 1974 c: 1
+ seq: 128.00.17 SCHMIT, Nathalie w: Abt. 2000 c: 1
13 WITRY, Emma

128.00.20

11 WITRY, Alphonse b: 24 Mar 1936 in Dippach, Lux d: 27 Oct
   2006 v: Dippach, Lux o: Farmer c: 4
+ seq: 128.00.20 FELLER, Francoise (Francie) b: 27 Jun 1944
   w: Abt. 1970 v: Dippach, Lux o: Farmer f: Edouard Feller m:
   Catherine Hemmering c: 4
12 WITRY, Pierre b: 13 Oct 1975 o: Volunteer fireman o: Farmer
12 WITRY, Victorine (Vicky) b: 31 Dec 1976
+ seq: 128.00.22 KRIPPELER, Marco w: Abt. 2000

12 WITRY, Catherine (Ketty) b: 26 May 1979
 + seq: 128.00.25 HANSEN, Laurent w: 31 Jul 2003
12 WITRY, Monique b: 08 Mar 1981 c: 2
 + seq: 128.00.30 THILL, Josy w: 29 Aug 2002 c: 2

128.00.30
12 WITRY, Monique b: 08 Mar 1981 c: 2
 + seq: 128.00.30 THILL, Josy w: 29 Aug 2002 c: 2
13 THILL, Sara b: 04 Jun 2004
13 THILL, Emma b: 17 Aug 2006

128.00.35
11 WITRY, Marie-Therese b: 07 Aug 1939 v: Roodt, Lux c: 2
 + seq: 128.00.35 KREMER, Joseph (Josy) b: 03 Jul 1937 w:
    Abt. 1965 in Roodt-Eisch, Lux v: Roodt, Lux c: 2
12 KREMER, Nadine b: 19 Nov 1967 c: 2
 + seq: 128.00.40 w: Abt. 1990 c: 2
12 KREMER, Isabelle b: 28 Jun 1969 c: 4
 + seq: 128.00.50 RASQUE, Jean-Claude w: 16 Dec 1989 c: 4

128.00.40
12 KREMER, Nadine b: 19 Nov 1967 c: 2
 + seq: 128.00.40 w: Abt. 1990 c: 2
13 KREMER, Anton(Andy) b: 05 Jul 1993
13 KREMER, Dany b: 19 Sep 1997

128.00.50
12 KREMER, Isabelle b: 28 Jun 1969 c: 4
 + seq: 128.00.50 RASQUE, Jean-Claude w: 16 Dec 1989 c: 4
13 RASQUE, Nina b: 07 Jun 1992
13 RASQUE, Victor b: 04 Nov 1993
13 RASQUE, Karin b: 16 Feb 1995
13 RASQUE, Arno b: 05 Feb 1998

128.01
 9 WITRY, Nicolas-Emil b: 10 Apr 1860 in Bergem, Lux d: 17
    Sep 1915 in San Nicolas de los Arroyos, Argentina Cause of
    death: influenza v: San Nicolas de los Arroyos, Argentina i:
    Emigrated to Argentina o: Port construction o: Agricultural
    engineer r: bx c: 10
 + seq: 128.01 MURTAGH, Catalina d: 25 Jul 1951 in San

Nicolas de los Arroyos, Argentina w: 05 May 1892 in Buenos
Aires, Argentina v: San Nicolas de los Arroyos, Argentina f:
William Murtagh m: Rosa Fox y Murray c: 10
10 WITRY, Maria-Theresa b: 12 Dec 1892 in Villarica, Paraguay
    d: 1959 c: 3
+ seq: 128.02 ONDARCUHU, Jose d: 1943 w: Abt. 1915 c: 3
10 WITRY, Clara-Josefina b: 20 Nov 1894 in San Nicolas de los
    Arroyos, Argentina d: 1934 o: Teacher c: 1
+ seq: 128.05 MARES, Aristobulo w: Abt. 1920 v: Villa
    Constitution, Argentina c: 1
10 WITRY, Emilio-Carlos b: 09 May 1896 in San Nicolas de los
    Arroyos, Argentina d: 1958 o: Court clerk c: 1
+ seq: 128.07 GOMEZ, Alicia w: Abt. 1920 c: 1
10 WITRY, Juan-Jose b: 06 May 1898 d: 1918
10 WITRY, Alfredo-Leon b: 20 Mar 1900 d: 14 Jul 1951 i:
    Member of Aden o: Farm manager c: 3
+ seq: 128.12 BARRERA, Maria-Carmen d: 14 Jul 1951 w: 09
    Nov 1935 c: 3
10 WITRY, Alberto-Alfonso b: 17 May 1902 d: 23 Mar 1967 o:
    Banker c: 3
+ seq: 128.20 FERNANDEZ SALAS, Elvia w: 06 Feb 1933 c: 3
10 WITRY, Hector-Francisco b: 11 May 1905
+ seq: 128.23 ARABUARENA, Etelvina w: Abt. 1930
10 WITRY, Rodolfo-Nicolas b: 30 Jul 1907 d: 23 Jul 1953 o:
    Pharmacist
10 WITRY, Blanca-Rosa b: 30 Aug 1909 d: 11 Sep 1941 o:
    University professor
10 WITRY, Horacio-Raul b: 06 Aug 1913 v: Santiago, Chili o:
    Customs clerk
+ seq: 128.24 CONCHA CONTRERAS, Victoria w: Abt. 1940
    v: Santiago, Chili

128.02
10 WITRY, Maria-Theresa b: 12 Dec 1892 in Villarica, Paraguay
    d: 1959 c: 3
+ seq: 128.02 ONDARCUHU, Jose d: 1943 w: Abt. 1915 c: 3
11 ONDARCUHU, Ana-Maria d: 13 Apr 1984
11 ONDARCUHU, Luis-Maria v: San Nicolas de los Arroyos,
    Argentina
+ seq: 128.03 w: Abt. 1945 v: san Nicolas de los Arroyos,
    Argentina

11 ONDARCUHU, Pedro E. v: Parana, Argentina
+ seq: 128.04 w: Abt. 1945 v: Parana, Argentina

128.05
10 WITRY, Clara-Josefina b: 20 Nov 1894 in San Nicolas de los
   Arroyos, Argentina d: 1934 o: Teacher c: 1
+ seq: 128.05 MARES, Aristobulo w: Abt. 1920 v: Villa
   Constitution, Argentina c: 1
11 MARES, Maria-Clara i: Villa Constitucion, Argentina
+ seq: 128.06 CALZOLARI w: Abt. 1950 i: Villa Constitucion,
   Argentina

128.07
10 WITRY, Emilio-Carlos b: 09 May 1896 in San Nicolas de los
   Arroyos, Argentina d: 1958 o: Court clerk c: 1
+ seq: 128.07 GOMEZ, Alicia w: Abt. 1920 c: 1
11 WITRY, Emilio-Carlos v: Florida, Argentina c: 3
+ seq: 128.08 w: Abt. 1950 v: Florida, Argentina c: 3

128.08
11 WITRY, Emilio-Carlos v: Florida, Argentina c: 3
+ seq: 128.08 w: Abt. 1950 v: Florida, Argentina c: 3
12 WITRY, Elizabeth
+ seq: 128.09 w: Abt. 1980
12 WITRY, Unknown
+ seq: 128.10 w: Abt. 1980
12 WITRY, Jorge-Nicolas c: 1
+ seq: 128.11 w: Abt. 1980 c: 1

128.11
12 WITRY, Jorge-Nicolas c: 1
+ seq: 128.11 w: Abt. 1980 c: 1
13 WITRY, Facundo

128.12
10 WITRY, Alfredo-Leon b: 20 Mar 1900 d: 14 Jul 1951 i:
   Member of Aden o: Farm manager c: 3
+ seq: 128.12 BARRERA, Maria-Carmen d: 14 Jul 1951 w: 09
   Nov 1935 c: 3
11 WITRY, Maria del Carmen b: 23 Mar 1937 v: Buenos Aires,
   Argentina c: 5

+ seq: 128.13 ZINGONI, Horacio W. w: 11 Nov 1959 v: Buenos Aires, Argentina c: 5

11 WITRY, Maria-Josefa b: 08 Jun 1940 v: Buenos Aires, Argentina c: 3
+ seq: 128.17 FOGG w: 03 Dec 1966 v: Buenos Aires, Argentina c: 3

11 WITRY, Manuel-Alejo b: 02 Apr 1943 d: 18 May 1987 v: Rosario, Argentina c: 1
+ seq: 128.19 ROUILLON, Ivonne w: Abt. 1970 v: Rosario, Argentina i: President of the Way Foundation, combatting infantile malnutrition c: 1

128.13

11 WITRY, Maria del Carmen b: 23 Mar 1937 v: Buenos Aires, Argentina c: 5
+ seq: 128.13 ZINGONI, Horacio W. w: 11 Nov 1959 v: Buenos Aires, Argentina c: 5

12 ZINGONI, Martin-Alfredo b: 24 Oct 1960 o: Agricultural engineer c: 3
+ seq: 128.14 BUZON, Alejandra w: 1991 c: 3

12 ZINGONI, Maria-Paula b: 23 Jul 1962 o: Bachelor of the history of the arts c: 4
+ seq: 128.15 BARBIERI, Carlos w: Abt. 1985 c: 4

12 ZINGONI, Ignacio-Jose b: 24 Mar 1965 o: Financial analyst

12 ZINGONI, Maria-Ines b: 01 Aug 1966 o: Systems analyst c: 3
+ seq: 128.16 WADE, Tristan w: Abt. 1990 c: 3

12 ZINGONI, Magdalena-Maria b: 21 Feb 1973 o: Agricultural production engineer

128.14

12 ZINGONI, Martin-Alfredo b: 24 Oct 1960 o: Agricultural engineer c: 3
+ seq: 128.14 BUZON, Alejandra w: 1991 c: 3

13 ZINGONI, Bautista

13 ZINGONI, Candelaria

13 ZINGONI, Felipe

128.15

12 ZINGONI, Maria-Paula b: 23 Jul 1962 o: Bachelor of the history of the arts c: 4
+ seq: 128.15 BARBIERI, Carlos w: Abt. 1985 c: 4

13BARBIERI, Carla b: 11 Nov
13BARBIERI, Francisco b: 18 Apr
13BARBIERI, Mercedes b: 21 Jun
13BARBIERI, Horacio b: 24 Jun

128.16

12ZINGONI, Maria-Ines b: 01 Aug 1966 o: Systems analyst c: 3
+ seq: 128.16 WADE, Tristan w: Abt. 1990 c: 3
13WADE, Sol b: 07 Sep 1992
13WADE, Marcos b: 11 Sep 1995
13WADE, Alejo b: 11 May 1997

128.17

11WITRY, Maria-Josefa b: 08 Jun 1940 v: Buenos Aires,
    Argentina c: 3
+ seq: 128.17 FOGG w: 03 Dec 1966 v: Buenos Aires,
    Argentina c: 3
12FOGG, Veronica
+ seq: 128.18 IMBROSCIANO w: Abt. 1995
12FOGG, Tomas
12FOGG, Sebastian

128.19

11WITRY, Manuel-Alejo b: 02 Apr 1943 d: 18 May 1987 v:
    Rosario, Argentina c: 1
+ seq: 128.19 ROUILLON, Ivonne w: Abt. 1970 v: Rosario,
    Argentina i: President of the Way Foundation, combatting
    infantile malnutrition c: 1
12WITRY, Manuel-Alejo b: 27 Jan i: Polo player

128.20

10WITRY, Alberto-Alfonso b: 17 May 1902 d: 23 Mar 1967 o:
    Banker c: 3
+ seq: 128.20 FERNANDEZ SALAS, Elvia w: 06 Feb 1933 c: 3
11WITRY, Alberto-Eduardo d: 24 Apr 1988
11WITRY, Elvia
+ seq: 128.21 CHURRUPIT w: 1965
11WITRY, Cristina v: Fort Lauderdale, FL
+ seq: 128.22 SUAREZ w: Abt. 1965 v: Fort Lauderdale, FL

128.26

9 WITRY, Johann-Baptist b: 08 Mar 1862 in Bergem, Lux d:
  1897 h: 77 rue St Jacques v: Nancy, France o: Baker r: b c: 1
+ seq: 128.26 ROUSSEAU, Zoe-Marie-Josephine b: 28 May
  1861 in Nancy, France w: 29 Dec 1884 in Nancy, France h: 77
  rue St Jacques v: Nancy, France o: No profession r: m f:
  Christophe-Paul Rousseau m: Rose-Marie-Poussardin c: 1
10WITRY, Marie-Marthe b: 02 Jul 1888 in Nancy, France r: b

129

9 WITRY, Henri b: 15 Feb 1864 in Bergem, Lux d: 1948 in
  Bergem, Lux v: Bergem, Lux o: Landowner o: Farmer r: b c:
  6
+ seq: 129 NEPPER, Marie-Catherine b: 18 Jan 1867 in
  Wolkrange, Lux d: 17 Dec 1913 in Bergem, Lux w: 24 Aug
  1897 in Mondercange, Lux v: Bergem, Lux o: No profession r:
  m f: Pierre Nepper m: Josephine Bonhomme c: 6
10WITRY, Marie-Therese b: 17 Oct 1898 in Bergem, Lux d: 26
  Jan 1899 in Bergem, Lux r: bd
10WITRY, Marie-Therese-Josephine (Josephine) b: 12 Dec 1899
  in Bergem, Lux d: 06 Oct 1986 in Esch-sur-Alzette, Lux v:
  Bergem, Lux o: No profession r: b c: 3
+ seq: 130 WITRY, Jules b: 04 Sep 1892 in Merl, Lux d: 1980 in
  Bergem, Lux w: 26 Feb 1927 in Mondercange, Lux v: Bergem,
  Lux i: Both are descendents of the family tree o: Landowner o:
  Farmer o: Distiller r: b f: Viktor Witry m: Barbara-Eugenie
  Bonifas c: 3
10WITRY, Marie-Henriette-Therese b: 22 Apr 1902 in Bergem,
  Lux d: 02 Jul 1993 in Bofferding, Lux v: Dudelange, Lux r: b
  c: 2
+ seq: 132.02 SCHANEN, Joseph b: 1901 d: 03 Jun 1991 in
  Dudelange, Lux w: 1929 v: Dudelange, Lux c: 2
10WITRY, Anna Maria (Maria) b: 30 Jul 1903 in Bergem, Lux d:
  08 Feb 1987 in Rumelange, Lux r: b c: 2
+ seq: 132.03 LINSTER, Robert b: Abt. 1900 w: Abt. 1930 c: 2
10WITRY, Hortense-Marie-Catherine b: 10 Nov 1905 in Bergem,
  Lux d: 13 Jan 1982 in Ettelbruck, Lux r: b c: 1
+ seq: 132.04 PUTZ, Nicolas b: Abt. 1905 w: Abt. 1930 c: 1
10WITRY, Anna-Marie-Marguerite (Margarite) b: 17 Jul 1911 in
  Bergem, Lux d: 1995 in Bergem, Lux v: Bergem, Lux r: b

10 WITRY, Marie-Therese-Josefine (Josephine) b: 12 Dec 1899 in Bergem, Lux d: 1986 in Bergem, Lux v: Bergem, Lux o: No profession c: 3

+ seq: 130 WITRY, Jules b: 04 Sep 1892 in Merl, Lux d: 1980 in Bergem, Lux w: 26 Feb 1927 in Mondercange, Lux v: Bergem, Lux i: Both are descendents of the family tree o: Landowner o: Farmer o: Distiller r: b f: Viktor Witry m: Barbara-Eugenie Bonifas c: 3

11 WITRY, Heinrich-Eugene-Arnold (Arnold) b: 07 Apr 1928 in Bergem, Lux d: 1981 in Bergem, Lux Cause of death: heart attack v: Bergem, Lux o: Farmer c: 3

+ seq: 131 WILHELM, Henriette b: 04 Mar 1940 w: Abt. 1966 v: Bergem, Lux c: 3

11 WITRY, Victor-Pierre-Paul (Paul) b: 02 Mar 1939 in Merl, Lux v: Luxembourg, Lux v: Bergem, Lux i: Retired o: Master butcher c: 1

+ seq: 132 BOURGMEYER, Josette b: Abt. 1940 w: Abt. 1965 c: 1

11 WITRY, Jeanne-Therese-Marie-Josee (Marie-Josee) b: 21 Aug 1930 in Bergem, Lux c: 1

+ seq: 132.01 DEMUTH, Eduard b: 20 Oct 1928 in Altrier, Lux d: 07 Feb 1992 in Altrier, Lux w: 30 Mar 1959 in Altrier, Lux v: Altrier, Lux o: Farmer c: 1

11 WITRY, Heinrich-Eugene-Arnold (Arnold) b: 07 Apr 1928 in Bergem, Lux d: 1981 in Bergem, Lux Cause of death: heart attack v: Bergem, Lux o: Farmer c: 3

+ seq: 131 WILHELM, Henriette b: 04 Mar 1940 w: Abt. 1966 v: Bergem, Lux c: 3

12 WITRY, Marc b: 20 Jan 1967 in Bergem, Lux v: Bergem, Lux o: Farmer

12 WITRY, Fernande b: 01 Apr 1968 in Bergem, Lux v: Grevels, Lux o: Salesperson c: 2

+ seq: 131.00.01 SCHARTZ, Jean-Pierre (Jemp) b: 25 Jun 1964 in Grevels, Lux w: 22 Aug 1991 in Bergem, Lux v: Grevels, Lux c: 2

12 WITRY, Josee b: 01 Apr 1968 in Bergem, Lux v: Belvaux, Lux o: Pharmacist c: 1

+ seq: 131.01 SCHNEIDER, Michel b: 12 May 1967 in Esch-sur-

Alzette, Lux w: 27 Jun 1996 in Bergem, Lux v: Belvaux, Lux
o: Electronics c: 1

131.00.01

12 WITRY, Fernande b: 01 Apr 1968 in Bergem, Lux v: Grevels,
Lux o: Salesperson c: 2

+ seq: 131.00.01 SCHARTZ, Jean-Pierre (Jemp) b: 25 Jun 1964
in Grevels, Lux w: 22 Aug 1991 in Bergem, Lux v: Grevels,
Lux c: 2

13 SCHARTZ, Carole b: 24 Mar 1993 in Esch-sur-Alzette, Lux
13 SCHARTZ, Christophe b: 16 Jul 1995 in Ettelbruck, Lux

131.01

12 WITRY, Josee b: 01 Apr 1968 in Bergem, Lux v: Belvaux, Lux
o: Pharmacist c: 1

+ seq: 131.01 SCHNEIDER, Michel b: 12 May 1967 in Esch-sur-
Alzette, Lux w: 27 Jun 1996 in Bergem, Lux v: Belvaux, Lux
o: Electronics c: 1

13 SCHNEIDER, Ines b: 20 Aug 1998

132

11 WITRY, Victor-Pierre-Paul (Paul) b: 02 Mar 1939 in Merl, Lux
v: Luxembourg, Lux v: Bergem, Lux i: Retired o: Master
butcher c: 1

+ seq: 132 BOURGMEYER, Josette b: Abt. 1940 w: Abt. 1965
c: 1

12 WITRY, Danielle b: 29 Jan 1971 in Bergem, Lux o:
Pharmaceutical secretary

132.01

11 WITRY, Jeanne-Therese-Marie-Josee (Marie-Josee) b: 21 Aug
1930 in Bergem, Lux c: 1

+ seq: 132.01 DEMUTH, Eduard b: 20 Oct 1928 in Altrier, Lux
d: 07 Feb 1992 in Altrier, Lux w: 30 Mar 1959 in Altrier, Lux
v: Altrier, Lux o: Farmer c: 1

12 DEMUTH, Carlo b: 13 Oct 1961 in Altrier, Lux v: Junglinster,
Lux o: Garage owner

132.02

10 WITRY, Marie-Henriette-Therese b: 22 Apr 1902 in Bergem,
Lux d: 02 Jul 1993 in Bofferding, Lux v: Dudelange, Lux r: b

c: 2
+ seq: 132.02 SCHANEN, Joseph b: 1901 d: 03 Jun 1991 in
Dudelange, Lux w: 1929 v: Dudelange, Lux c: 2
11 SCHANEN, Fernand b: 1929 in Dudelange, Lux v:
Luxembourg, Lux c: 2
+ seq: 132.02.01 SCHWEITZER, Nicole w: Abt. 1955 v:
Luxembourg, Lux c: 2
11 SCHANEN, Marcelle b: 1930 v: Luxembourg, Lux c: 2
+ seq: 132.02.02 HEISTEN, Jean-Joseph w: Abt. 1955 v:
Luxembourg, Lux c: 2

132.02.01

11 SCHANEN, Fernand b: 1929 in Dudelange, Lux v:
Luxembourg, Lux c: 2
+ seq: 132.02.01 SCHWEITZER, Nicole w: Abt. 1955 v:
Luxembourg, Lux c: 2
12 SCHANEN, Gilles b: 1958
12 SCHANEN, Luc b: 1964

132.02.02

11 SCHANEN, Marcelle b: 1930 v: Luxembourg, Lux c: 2
+ seq: 132.02.02 HEISTEN, Jean-Joseph w: Abt. 1955 v:
Luxembourg, Lux c: 2
12 HEISTEN, Rene
12 HEISTEN, Georges

132.03

10 WITRY, Anna Maria (Maria) b: 30 Jul 1903 in Bergem, Lux d:
08 Feb 1987 in Rumelange, Lux r: b c: 2
+ seq: 132.03 LINSTER, Robert b: Abt. 1900 w: Abt. 1930 c: 2
11 LINSTER, Gaby d: Dec 1944
11 LINSTER, Arthur

132.04

10 WITRY, Hortense-Marie-Catherine b: 10 Nov 1905 in Bergem,
Lux d: 13 Jan 1982 in Ettelbruck, Lux r: b c: 1
+ seq: 132.04 PUTZ, Nicolas b: Abt. 1905 w: Abt. 1930 c: 1
11 PUTZ, Marian b: May 1931 d: 12 Mar 1971 v: Bridel, Lux c:
1
+ seq: 132.04.00 DONCKEL, Pierre w: Abt. 1960 v: Bridel, Lux
o: Commanding officer of gendarmerie c: 1

132.04.00

11 PUTZ, Marian b: May 1931 d: 12 Mar 1971 v: Bridel, Lux c: 1

+ seq: 132.04.00 DONCKEL, Pierre w: Abt. 1960 v: Bridel, Lux o: Commanding officer of gendarmerie c: 1

12 DONCKEL, Pierre-Alain (Alain) v: Bridel

132.04.02

9 WITRY, Johann-Peter b: 04 Jul 1870 in Bergem, Lux d: 11 Sep 1903 in Grevenmacher, Lux h: Dardenhacheuer v: Grevenmacher, Lux o: Pastry chef r: bd c: 2

+ seq: 132.04.02 LETHAL, Anne-Marie b: 08 Dec 1872 in Grevenmacher, Lux w: 29 Aug 1899 in Mondercange, Lux h: Dardenhacheuer v: Grevenmacher, Lux o: No profession r: m c: 2

10 WITRY, Therese-Katharina b: 24 Aug 1900 in Grevenmacher, Lux r: b

10 WITRY, Mathias-Johann-Peter b: 26 May 1902 in Grevenmacher, Lux r: b

132.05

7 WITRY, Marie-Catherine b: 21 Oct 1807 in Bergem, Lux d: 19 May 1878 in Bettembourg, Lux v: Bettembourg, Lux o: Housemaid r: bd c: 4

+ seq: 132.05 DENNEMEYER, Nicolas b: 30 Dec 1798 in Bettembourg, Lux d: 30 Apr 1881 w: 22 Feb 1830 in Bettembourg, Lux v: Bettembourg, Lux o: Farmer r: m f: Johann Dennemeyer m: Anna Majerus c: 4

8 DENNEMEYER, Jean d: 17 Aug 1904

8 DENNEMEYER, Jean-Nicolas b: 07 Jan 1837 in Bettembourg, Lux d: 05 Apr 1878 r: b

8 DENNEMEYER, Johann-Peter b: 14 Mar 1841 in Bettembourg, Lux d: 20 Jul 1854 r: b

8 DENNEMEYER, Nicolas b: 06 Apr 1848 in Bettembourg, Lux r: b

134

7 WITRY, Johann b: 19 Apr 1826 in Bergem, Lux d: 29 Mar 1888 in Bergem, Lux v: Bergem, Lux o: Farmer r: bd c: 9

+ seq: 134 MATHEY, Barbara b: 10 Nov 1824 in Bettembourg,

Lux d: 06 Feb 1866 in Bergem, Lux w: 26 Nov 1849 in
Bettembourg, Lux a: Mathes v: Bergem, Lux o: No profession
r: m f: Pierre Mathey m: Madeleine Georges c: 9

8 WITRY, Johann-Peter b: 05 Jan 1850 in Bettembourg, Lux d:
30 Aug 1867 in Bergem, Lux v: Bergem, Lux o: Farmer r: bd

8 WITRY, Eugen b: 23 May 1851 in Bergem, Lux d: 20 Jan 1856
in Bergem, Lux v: Bergem, Lux o: No profession r: bd

8 WITRY, Johann-Nicolas b: 30 Nov 1852 in Bergem, Lux d: 24
Sep 1905 in Rodange, Lux r: b

8 WITRY, Pierre b: 17 Aug 1854 in Bergem, Lux d: 10 Jun 1917
in Bergem, Lux v: Bergem, Lux o: Farmer o: Property owner
r: bd c: 3

+ seq: 134.01 SCHMITT, Marie b: 05 Jul 1863 in Hellange, Lux
d: 27 Jun 1895 w: 14 Jan 1890 in Mondercange, Lux v:
Bergem, Lux o: No profession r: m f: Johann Schmit m:
Catherine Breistroff c: 3

8 WITRY, Michel b: 07 Jan 1856 in Bergem, Lux d: 14 May
1925 in Bergem, Lux v: Bergem, Lux o: Land owner o: Farmer
r: b c: 7

+ seq: 135 WITRY, Marie (Margaretha) b: 30 Mar 1856 in
Bergem, Lux d: 25 May 1931 in Bergem, Lux w: 29 Jul 1879 in
Mondercange, Lux v: Bergem, Lux i: Both are descendents of
the family tree o: No profession r: b r: m f: Peter Witry m:
Margaretha Muller c: 7

8 WITRY, Peter-Eugen b: 18 Jan 1858 in Bergem, Lux d: 16 Sep
1894 in Chicago, IL v: Chicago, IL i: Emigrated to the U. S. r:
bd

+ seq: 139.03 ENSWEILER, Susanna w: 20 Aug 1881 in
Chicago, IL

8 WITRY, Jean b: 25 Mar 1860

8 WITRY, Anna-Margaretha (Maria) b: 28 Sep 1861 in Bergem,
Lux d: 27 Nov 1953 v: Leudelange, Lux o: No profession r: b
c: 3

+ seq: 139.04 JACQUE, Nicolas b: 06 Aug 1856 in Leudelange,
Lux w: Abt. 1880 v: Leudelange, Lux o: Farmer r: m c: 3

8 WITRY, Marie-Josefine b: 13 Mar 1865 in Bergem, Lux d: 14
Aug 1877 in Bergem, Lux v: Bergem, Lux o: No profession r:
bd

134.01

8 WITRY, Pierre b: 17 Aug 1854 in Bergem, Lux d: 10 Jun 1917

in Bergem, Lux v: Bergem, Lux o: Farmer o: Property owner
r: bd c: 3

+ seq: 134.01 SCHMITT, Marie b: 05 Jul 1863 in Hellange, Lux
d: 27 Jun 1895 w: 14 Jan 1890 in Mondercange, Lux v:
Bergem, Lux o: No profession r: m f: Johann Schmit m:
Catherine Breistroff c: 3

9 WITRY, Berthe (Barbe) b: 02 Jan 1891 in Bergem, Lux r: b

9 WITRY, Eugenie b: 17 Dec 1892 in Bergem, Lux v: Bergem,
Lux o: No profession r: b c: 2

+ seq: 134.02 HILGER, Jean b: 04 Apr 1889 in Hondelange,
Belgium d: 18 Feb 1938 w: 19 Dec 1913 in Mondercange, Lux
v: Bergem, Lux o: Forester r: m f: Jacques Hilger m:
Marguerite Bernard c: 2

9 WITRY, Camille b: 04 Feb 1895 in Bergem, Lux d: 19 Apr
1895 in Bergem, Lux r: bd

134.02

9 WITRY, Eugenie b: 17 Dec 1892 in Bergem, Lux v: Bergem,
Lux o: No profession r: b c: 2

+ seq: 134.02 HILGER, Jean b: 04 Apr 1889 in Hondelange,
Belgium d: 18 Feb 1938 w: 19 Dec 1913 in Mondercange, Lux
v: Bergem, Lux o: Forester r: m f: Jacques Hilger m:
Marguerite Bernard c: 2

10HILGER, Maria-Margaretha (Marie) b: 25 May 1914 in
Bergem, Lux r: b

10HILGER, Joseph b: 20 Apr 1916 in Bergem, Lux r: b

135

8 WITRY, Michel b: 07 Jan 1856 in Bergem, Lux d: 14 May
1925 in Bergem, Lux v: Bergem, Lux o: Land owner o: Farmer
r: b c: 7

+ seq: 135 WITRY, Marie (Margaretha) b: 30 Mar 1856 in
Bergem, Lux d: 25 May 1931 in Bergem, Lux w: 29 Jul 1879 in
Mondercange, Lux v: Bergem, Lux i: Both are descendents of
the family tree o: No profession r: b r: m f: Peter Witry m:
Margaretha Muller c: 7

9 WITRY, Marie-Susanne-Valerie b: 21 Jul 1880 in Bergem, Lux
d: 11 Jun 1885 in Bergem, Lux v: Bergem, Lux r: b

9 WITRY, Alfred-Pierre b: 06 Apr 1882 in Bergem, Lux d: 14
Jul 1969 in Hamm, Lux v: Esch-sur-Alzette, Lux o: Architect
r: b c: 1

+ seq: 136 KLEBER, Marie-Louise b: 17 Sep 1896 in Knutange, Lux d: 04 Apr 1971 in Esch-sur-Alzette, Lux w: 08 Aug 1923 in Ottange, France v: Esch-sur-Alzette, Lux o: No profession f: Francois-Marcellin Kleber m: Adele Langers c: 1

9 WITRY, Henri-Lucien b: 26 Apr 1884 in Bergem, Lux d: 09 Apr 1930 v: Esch-sur-Alzette o: Farmer o: Auto mechanic o: Teamster r: b c: 3

+ seq: 139 REPELE, Marie b: Abt. 1885 w: 14 Feb 1917 in Esch-sur-Alzette, Lux v: Esch-sur-Alzette o: No profession r: m f: Cesar-August Repele m: Johanna Becker c: 3

9 WITRY, Michael-Nicolas-Leonard b: 03 Apr 1886 in Bergem, Lux d: 23 Feb 1890 in Bergem, Lux v: Bergem, Lux r: b

9 WITRY, Marie-Berthe-Valerie b: 06 Mar 1888 in Bergem, Lux d: 12 Mar 1891 in Bergem, Lux v: Bergem, Lux r: b

9 WITRY, Marie-Leonora b: 31 May 1891 in Bergem, Lux

+ seq: 139.01 VANDYCK, Victor b: Abt. 1885 w: 17 Jan 1924

9 WITRY, Marie-Suzanne-Valerie (Valerie) b: 04 May 1897 in Bergem, Lux d: 08 Jul 1983 in Esch-sur-Alzette, Lux o: No profession r: b c: 5

+ seq: 139.02 LECLERC, Victor-Joseph b: 05 Feb 1901 in Esch-sur-Alzette, Lux d: 06 Oct 1978 w: 18 Jun 1923 in Esch-sur-Alzette o: Farmer r: m f: Dominique Leclerc m: Mathilde Remlinger c: 5

136

9 WITRY, Alfred-Pierre b: 06 Apr 1882 in Bergem, Lux d: 14 Jul 1969 in Hamm, Lux v: Esch-sur-Alzette, Lux o: Architect r: b c: 1

+ seq: 136 KLEBER, Marie-Louise b: 17 Sep 1896 in Knutange, Lux d: 04 Apr 1971 in Esch-sur-Alzette, Lux w: 08 Aug 1923 in Ottange, France v: Esch-sur-Alzette, Lux o: No profession f: Francois-Marcellin Kleber m: Adele Langers c: 1

10 WITRY, Marcel-Alfred b: 27 Jul 1925 in Ottange, France v: Luxembourg, Lux o: Board of directors o: Licensed engineer c: 2

+ seq: 137 SCHWACHTGEN, Gertrude (Tuddie) b: 26 Aug 1927 in Luxembourg, Lux w: 05 Aug 1954 in Luxembourg, Lux v: Luxembourg, Lux o: High school teacher o: Doctor of Science c: 2

137

10 WITRY, Marcel-Alfred b: 27 Jul 1925 in Ottange, France v: Luxembourg, Lux o: Board of directors o: Licensed engineer c: 2

+ seq: 137 SCHWACHTGEN, Gertrude (Tuddie) b: 26 Aug 1927 in Luxembourg, Lux w: 05 Aug 1954 in Luxembourg, Lux v: Luxembourg, Lux o: High school teacher o: Doctor of Science c: 2

11 WITRY, Claude b: 10 Jul 1957 in Luxembourg, Lux v: Luxembourg, Lux i: Wrote article on rates of interest o: Executive secretary o: Lawyer c: 3

+ seq: 138 FEYEREISEN, Marthe b: 18 Sep 1959 in Luxembourg, Lux w: 20 Jul 1989 in Luxembourg, Lux v: Luxembourg, Lux o: Court advocate o: Lawyer c: 3

11 WITRY, Tom b: 30 Apr 1960 in Esch-sur-Alzette, Lux d: 21 Mar 1961 in Esch-sur-Alzette, Lux v: Esch-sur-Alzette, Lux

138

11 WITRY, Claude b: 10 Jul 1957 in Luxembourg, Lux v: Luxembourg, Lux i: Wrote article on rates of interest o: Executive secretary o: Lawyer c: 3

+ seq: 138 FEYEREISEN, Marthe b: 18 Sep 1959 in Luxembourg, Lux w: 20 Jul 1989 in Luxembourg, Lux v: Luxembourg, Lux o: Court advocate o: Lawyer c: 3

12 WITRY, Max b: 12 Sep 1991 in Luxembourg, Lux

12 WITRY, Tom b: 25 Aug 1994 in Luxembourg, Lux

12 WITRY, Nina b: 21 Sep 1999 in Luxembourg, Lux

139

9 WITRY, Henri-Lucien b: 26 Apr 1884 in Bergem, Lux d: 09 Apr 1930 v: Esch-sur-Alzette o: Farmer o: Auto mechanic o: Teamster r: b c: 3

+ seq: 139 REPELE, Marie b: Abt. 1885 w: 14 Feb 1917 in Esch-sur-Alzette, Lux v: Esch-sur-Alzette o: No profession r: m f: Cesar-August Repele m: Johanna Becker c: 3

10 WITRY, Marie-Victorine b: 10 Nov 1918 in Esch-sur-Alzette r: b

10 WITRY, Maria-Lucie-Valerie b: 22 Aug 1920 in Esch-sur-Alzette r: b

10 WITRY, Victor b: 24 Jul 1922 in Esch-sur-Alzette r: b

139.02

9 WITRY, Marie-Suzanne-Valerie (Valerie) b: 04 May 1897 in Bergem, Lux d: 08 Jul 1983 o: No profession c: 5

+ seq: 139.02 LECLERC, Victor-Joseph b: 05 Feb 1901 in Esch-sur-Alzette, Lux d: 06 Oct 1978 w: 18 Jun 1923 in Esch-sur-Alzette o: Farmer r: m f: Dominique Leclerc m: Mathilde Remlinger c: 5

10LECLERC, Dominique-Victor b: 02 May 1924 d: 10 Dec 1982

10LECLERC, Marie-Mathilde-Valerie b: 25 Jul 1925 d: 12 Jan 1988

10LECLERC, Marie-Louise-Victorine b: 17 Oct 1926

10LECLERC, Marie-Lucie-Albertine b: 19 Aug 1928 d: 07 May 1960

10LECLERC, Theodore-Charles b: 29 Apr 1930 in Esch-sur-Alzette, Lux v: Esch-sur-Alzette, Lux o: Tailor o: Storekeeper c: 2

+ seq: 139.02.01 QUIRING, Marianne b: 11 Mar 1938 w: Abt. 1960 v: Esch-sur-Alzette, Lux c: 2

139.02.01

10LECLERC, Theodore-Charles b: 29 Apr 1930 in Esch-sur-Alzette, Lux v: Esch-sur-Alzette, Lux o: Tailor o: Storekeeper c: 2

+ seq: 139.02.01 QUIRING, Marianne b: 11 Mar 1938 w: Abt. 1960 v: Esch-sur-Alzette, Lux c: 2

11LECLERC, Alain b: 17 Feb 1962

11LECLERC, Simone b: 07 Jul 1966

139.04

8 WITRY, Anna-Margaretha (Maria) b: 28 Sep 1861 in Bergem, Lux d: 27 Nov 1953 v: Leudelange, Lux o: No profession r: b c: 3

+ seq: 139.04 JACQUE, Nicolas b: 06 Aug 1856 in Leudelange, Lux w: Abt. 1880 v: Leudelange, Lux o: Farmer r: m c: 3

9 JACQUE, Marie-Victorine b: 09 Apr 1886 in Leudelange, Lux r: b

9 JACQUE, Nicolas b: 22 Oct 1889 in Leudelange, Lux r: b

9 JACQUE, Michel Emile (Emil) b: 06 Nov 1891 in Leudelange, Lux r: b

6 WITRY, Michel t: Mayor b: 14 Nov 1778 in Bergem, Lux d:
16 Aug 1849 in Boevange, Lux v: Boevange, Lux o: Farmer r:
b c: 6

+ seq: 140 MATHEY, Catherine b: 21 Jun 1773 in Boevange,
Lux d: 05 May 1843 in Boevange, Lux w: 1802 v: Boevange,
Lux o: Farmer f: Michel Mathey m: Marie-Catherine Olinger
c: 6

7 WITRY, Barbara b: 10 Nov 1803 in Boevange, Lux d: 19 Sep
1844 in Huncherange, Lux h: Schrei Ehnmann v: Mondercange,
Lux o: Housemaid r: d

+ seq: 140.01 STEICHEN, Peter b: 15 Feb 1807 in Noertzange,
Lux d: 27 Jul 1857 in Huncherange, Lux w: 26 May 1830 in
Bettembourg, Lux h: Schrei Ehnmann v: Mondercange, Lux
o: Farmer r: mx f: Johann Steichen m: Margaretha Goersch

7 WITRY, Elisabeth b: 16 Aug 1806 in Boevange, Lux d: Apr
1869 v: Hondelange, Bel r: b c: 1

+ seq: 140.06 WOUTERS, Pierre w: 1835 v: Hondelange, Bel c:
1

7 [1] WITRY, Michel b: 27 Nov 1808 in Boevange, Lux d: 1855
v: Koerich, Lux o: Herder r: b c: 5

+ seq: 141 LUN, Christine b: Abt. 1810 w: Abt. 1835 v:
Koerich, Lux o: No profession c: 1

* 2nd Wife of [1] WITRY, Michel:

+ seq: 141.02 SOUVIGNIER, Catherine b: in Almeroth, Bel w:
1836 c: 4

7 WITRY, Peter b: 21 Mar 1811 in Boevange, Lux d: 12 Jan
1812 in Boevange, Lux v: Boevange, Lux r: bd

7 WITRY, Nicolas b: 18 Mar 1813 in Boevange, Lux d: 20 May
1887 v: Boevange, Lux r: b c: 7

+ seq: 141.19 LENGER, Anne-Marie b: in Marnach, Lux d: 19
Nov 1902 w: 06 Dec 1849 v: Boevange, Lux c: 7

7 WITRY, Helene (Madeleine) b: 13 Jan 1816 in Boevange, Lux
d: 02 Mar 1881 r: b

+ seq: 141.26 SOUVIGNIER, Jean-Nicolas w: Abt. 1840

140.06

7 WITRY, Elisabeth b: 16 Aug 1806 in Boevange, Lux d: Apr
1869 v: Hondelange, Bel r: b c: 1

+ seq: 140.06 WOUTERS, Pierre w: 1835 v: Hondelange, Bel c:
1

8 WOUTERS, Emile b: 1838 d: 1898 c: 2
+ seq: 140.12 MUSCHANG, Barbe b: in Hondelange, Bel w:
   1876 c: 2

140.12

8 WOUTERS, Emile b: 1838 d: 1898 c: 2
+ seq: 140.12 MUSCHANG, Barbe b: in Hondelange, Bel w:
   1876 c: 2
9 WOUTERS, Eudalie b: Mar 1879 in Brussels, Belgium
9 WOUTERS, Aline b: 1886 d: 1893

141

7 [1] WITRY, Michel b: 27 Nov 1808 in Boevange, Lux d: 1855
   v: Koerich, Lux o: Herder r: b c: 5
+ seq: 141 LUN, Christine b: Abt. 1810 w: Abt. 1835 v:
   Koerich, Lux o: No profession c: 1
8 WITRY, Marie b: 01 Aug 1837 in Koerich, Lux d: 29 Aug
   1907 v: Schouweiler, Lux o: No profession r: d c: 7
+ seq: 141.01 SCHOEDGEN, Peter b: 20 Aug 1831 in Koerich,
   Lux w: 14 Mar 1865 in Dippach, Lux v: Schouweiler, Lux o:
   Day laborer o: Swineherd r: m c: 7
* 2nd Wife of [1] WITRY, Michel:
+ seq: 141.02 SOUVIGNIER, Catherine b: in Almeroth, Bel w:
   1836 c: 4
8 WITRY, Catherine b: 1837 d: Feb 1917 c: 1
+ seq: 141.03 LENGER, Francois d: Feb 1917 w: Abt. 1855 c: 1
8 WITRY, Nicolas b: 1839 d: 06 May 1883 v: Almeroth,
   Belgium c: 2
+ seq: 141.08 GENGLER, Marie w: 1873 v: Almeroth, Belgium
   c: 2
8 WITRY, Eudalie b: 08 Feb 1842 d: 07 Jun 1917 v: Musson,
   Belgium c: 5
+ seq: 141.13 JACQUES, Joseph b: 11 Oct 1840 d: Jan 1918 w:
   Abt. 1865 v: Musson, Belgium c: 5
8 WITRY, Edouard b: 16 Jun 1844 d: 12 Jun 1920 v: Almeroth,
   Belgium

141.01

8 WITRY, Marie b: 01 Aug 1837 in Koerich, Lux d: 29 Aug
   1907 v: Schouweiler, Lux o: No profession r: d c: 7
+ seq: 141.01 SCHOEDGEN, Peter b: 20 Aug 1831 in Koerich,

Lux w: 14 Mar 1865 in Dippach, Lux v: Schouweiler, Lux o:
Day laborer o: Swineherd r: m c: 7
9 SCHOEDGEN, Catherine b: 22 Apr 1866 in Schouweiler, Lux
d: 19 Feb 1870 in Schouweiler, Lux r: bd
9 SCHOEDGEN, Mathias b: 13 Mar 1868 in Schouweiler, Lux r:
b
9 SCHOEDGEN, Maria b: 30 Nov 1870 in Schouweiler, Lux r: b
9 SCHOEDGEN, Barbara b: 19 Feb 1872 in Schouweiler, Lux r:
b
9 SCHOEDGEN, Catharina b: 16 Nov 1874 in Schouweiler, Lux
r: b
9 SCHOEDGEN, Nikolas b: 11 Feb 1877 in Schouweiler, Lux r:
b
9 SCHOEDGEN, Peter b: 18 Mar 1879 in Schouweiler, Lux v:
Schouweiler, Lux o: Cobbler r: b
+ seq: 141.01.50 DIDIER, Barbe b: 15 Nov 1892 in Sprinkange,
Lux w: 05 Feb 1908 in Dippach, Lux o: No profession r: m f:
Nicolas Didier m: Elisabeth Wirth

141.03
8 WITRY, Catherine b: 1837 d: Feb 1917 c: 1
+ seq: 141.03 LENGER, Francois d: Feb 1917 w: Abt. 1855 c: 1
9 LENGER, Anatol b: 1858 in Habay, Bel c: 2
+ seq: 141.04 PARISSE, Marie w: Abt. 1880 c: 2

141.04
9 LENGER, Anatol b: 1858 in Habay, Bel c: 2
+ seq: 141.04 PARISSE, Marie w: Abt. 1880 c: 2
10LENGER, Francois c: 1
+ seq: 141.05 w: Abt. 1910 c: 1
10LENGER, Marie c: 1
+ seq: 141.07 STOFFEL, Jean-Nicolas w: Abt. 1910 c: 1

141.05
10LENGER, Francois c: 1
+ seq: 141.05 w: Abt. 1910 c: 1
11LENGER, Odette
+ seq: 141.06 BECKERS, Joseph w: Abt. 1940

141.07
10LENGER, Marie c: 1

+ seq: 141.07 STOFFEL, Jean-Nicolas w: Abt. 1910 c: 1
11 STOFFEL, Rene

141.08

8 WITRY, Nicolas b: 1839 d: 06 May 1883 v: Almeroth,
 Belgium c: 2
+ seq: 141.08 GENGLER, Marie w: 1873 v: Almeroth, Belgium
 c: 2
9 WITRY, Albert b: 23 Nov 1873 d: 02 Nov 1922 v: Almeroth,
 Belgium c: 4
+ seq: 141.09 ORIGER, Anne b: 13 Oct 1879 in Autelbas,
 Belgium w: Abt. 1900 v: Almeroth, Belgium i: Both are
 descendents of the family tree f: Francois Origer m: Marie
 Witry c: 4
9 WITRY, Joseph b: 16 Jun 1877 d: 17 Feb 1929 v: Nobressart,
 Belgium c: 2
+ seq: 141.12 WEYLAND, Clotilde w: 1909 v: Nobressart,
 Belgium c: 2

141.09

9 WITRY, Albert b: 23 Nov 1873 d: 02 Nov 1922 v: Almeroth,
 Belgium c: 4
+ seq: 141.09 ORIGER, Anne b: 13 Oct 1879 in Autelbas,
 Belgium w: Abt. 1900 v: Almeroth, Belgium i: Both are
 descendents of the family tree f: Francois Origer m: Marie
 Witry c: 4
10 WITRY, Octavie b: 10 May 1904 v: Rodange, Lux
+ seq: 141.10 BUCHET, Oscar w: Abt. 1930 v: Rodange, Lux
10 WITRY, Georges b: 22 Jun 1906 v: Almeroth, Belgium c: 1
+ seq: 141.10.50 HANKENNE, Marguerite c: 1
10 WITRY, Victor b: 16 Aug 1908 v: Almeroth, Belgium
10 WITRY, Sylvie b: 04 Feb 1910 c: 2
+ seq: 141.11 JACQUES, Victor b: in Niederfeulen, Lux w: Abt.
 1930 c: 2

141.10.50

10 WITRY, Georges b: 22 Jun 1906 v: Almeroth, Belgium c: 1
+ seq: 141.10.50 HANKENNE, Marguerite c: 1
11 WITRY, Nicole c: 1
+ seq: 141.10.60 WITRY, Marc b: 20 Dec 1935 w: Abt. 1965 f:
 Victor Witry m: Julie Capus c: 1

141.10.60

11 WITRY, Nicole c: 1
+ seq: 141.10.60 WITRY, Marc b: 20 Dec 1935 w: Abt. 1965 f:
   Victor Witry m: Julie Capus c: 1
12 WITRY, Pierre b: 09 Apr 1969 v: Waremme, Belgium c: 2
+ seq: 141.10.70 w: Abt. 1998 c: 2

141.10.70

12 WITRY, Pierre b: 09 Apr 1969 v: Waremme, Belgium c: 2
+ seq: 141.10.70 w: Abt. 1998 c: 2
13 WITRY, Alix b: 09 May 2000
13 WITRY, Arthur b: 02 Jul 2002

141.11

10 WITRY, Sylvie b: 04 Feb 1910 c: 2
+ seq: 141.11 JACQUES, Victor b: in Niederfeulen, Lux w: Abt.
   1930 c: 2
11 JACQUES, Albert b: 03 May 1935
11 JACQUES, Francois b: 28 Sep 1937

141.12

9 WITRY, Joseph b: 16 Jun 1877 d: 17 Feb 1929 v: Nobressart,
  Belgium c: 2
+ seq: 141.12 WEYLAND, Clotilde w: 1909 v: Nobressart,
   Belgium c: 2
10 WITRY, Mimi b: 14 Feb 1910
10 WITRY, Andree b: 04 Feb 1912

141.13

8 WITRY, Eudalie b: 08 Feb 1842 d: 07 Jun 1917 v: Musson,
  Belgium c: 5
+ seq: 141.13 JACQUES, Joseph b: 11 Oct 1840 d: Jan 1918 w:
   Abt. 1865 v: Musson, Belgium c: 5
9 JACQUES, Fortunat b: 03 Sep 1867 in Musson, Belgium v:
  Boulaide, Lux c: 3
+ seq: 141.14 FOURMAN, Therese b: 05 May 1876 w: Abt.
   1905 v: Boulaide, Lux c: 3
9 JACQUES, Firmin b: 1869 in Musson, Belgium d: 1915 in
  Musson, Belgium
9 JACQUES, Felicien b: 1871
9 JACQUES, Amant d: Apr 1938 c: 2

+   seq: 141.18 SINNER, Aline w: 1918 c: 2
9 JACQUES, Narcisse d: 1901

141.14

9 JACQUES, Fortunat b: 03 Sep 1867 in Musson, Belgium v: Boulaide, Lux c: 3
+   seq: 141.14 FOURMAN, Therese b: 05 May 1876 w: Abt. 1905 v: Boulaide, Lux c: 3
10JACQUES, Ferdnand b: 05 Aug 1907 in Boulaide, Lux c: 1
+   seq: 141.15 VAN VERWECK, Joanne w: 04 Jan 1934 c: 1
10JACQUES, Emile b: 11 Feb 1909 in Boulaide, Lux c: 2
+   seq: 141.16 JUNGELS, Josephine w: 1936 c: 2
10JACQUES, Germaine b: 10 May 1911 in Boulaide, Lux c: 1
+   seq: 141.17 EICHHORN, Emilie w: 1933 c: 1

141.15

10JACQUES, Ferdnand b: 05 Aug 1907 in Boulaide, Lux c: 1
+   seq: 141.15 VAN VERWECK, Joanne w: 04 Jan 1934 c: 1
11JACQUES, Claude b: 18 Oct 1935

141.16

10JACQUES, Emile b: 11 Feb 1909 in Boulaide, Lux c: 2
+   seq: 141.16 JUNGELS, Josephine w: 1936 c: 2
11JACQUES, Marie-Therese b: Mar 1937
11JACQUES, Micheline-Auriel b: 1939

141.17

10JACQUES, Germaine b: 10 May 1911 in Boulaide, Lux c: 1
+   seq: 141.17 EICHHORN, Emilie w: 1933 c: 1
11EICHHORN, Liette b: 26 Jun 1934

141.18

9 JACQUES, Amant d: Apr 1938 c: 2
+   seq: 141.18 SINNER, Aline w: 1918 c: 2
10JACQUES, Helene b: 06 Dec 1919
10JACQUES, Therese b: 06 Dec 1919

141.19

7 WITRY, Nicolas b: 18 Mar 1813 in Boevange, Lux d: 20 May 1887 v: Boevange, Lux r: b c: 7
+   seq: 141.19 LENGER, Anne-Marie b: in Marnach, Lux d: 19

Nov 1902 w: 06 Dec 1849 v: Boevange, Lux c: 7

8 WITRY, Arthur b: 29 Sep 1850 d: 02 Dec 1938 in Voneche,
  Belgium v: Voneche, Belgium c: 2
+ seq: 141.20 LEONARD, Marie w: 25 May 1887 v: Voneche,
  Belgium c: 2

8 WITRY, Victor b: 17 Jan 1852 v: Boevange, Lux

8 WITRY, Francois b: 14 Jan 1856 d: 22 Oct 1937 in Floreffe

8 WITRY, Marie b: 10 Dec 1857 v: Autelbas, Belgium c: 4
+ seq: 141.22 ORIGER, Francois b: 31 May 1845 d: 08 Apr
  1939 in Autelbas, Belgium w: 31 Dec 1878 v: Autelbas,
  Belgium c: 4

8 WITRY, Albert b: 13 Jan 1860 d: 22 Jan 1934 v: Differt,
  Belgium c: 2
+ seq: 141.25 BOSSELER, Marguerite b: 29 Jun 1866 in
  Buvange, Lux d: 12 Jan 1946 in Differt, Belgium w: Oct 1893
  v: Differt, Belgium c: 2

8 WITRY, Auguste-Paul b: 17 Mar 1862 in Lintgen, Lux v:
  Clemency, Lux o: Captain of 10th artillery regiment c: 1
+ seq: 141.25.50 LEFEBVRE, Marie-Josephe b: Abt. 1858 in
  Mardebius, Lux w: Abt. 1880 c: 1

8 WITRY, Josephine b: 03 Feb 1865

141.20

8 WITRY, Arthur b: 29 Sep 1850 d: 02 Dec 1938 in Voneche,
  Belgium v: Voneche, Belgium c: 2
+ seq: 141.20 LEONARD, Marie w: 25 May 1887 v: Voneche,
  Belgium c: 2

9 WITRY, August b: 15 Mar 1889 in Voneche, Belgium d: 20
  Feb 1924 in Brussels, Belgium

9 WITRY, Victor b: 16 Oct 1890 in Voneche, Belgium c: 3
+ seq: 141.21 CAPUS, Julie b: 10 Nov 1896 w: 20 Feb 1929 c:
  3

141.21

9 WITRY, Victor b: 16 Oct 1890 in Voneche, Belgium c: 3
+ seq: 141.21 CAPUS, Julie b: 10 Nov 1896 w: 20 Feb 1929 c:
  3

10 WITRY, Auguste b: 16 Apr 1930 v: Beauraing, Belgium

10 WITRY, Alixe b: 22 Feb 1932

10 WITRY, Marc b: 20 Dec 1935 c: 1
+ seq: 141.10.60 WITRY, Nicole w: Abt. 1965 f: Georges Witry

m: Marguerite Hankenne c: 1

141.22

8 WITRY, Marie b: 10 Dec 1857 v: Autelbas, Belgium c: 4
+ seq: 141.22 ORIGER, Francois b: 31 May 1845 d: 08 Apr
   1939 in Autelbas, Belgium w: 31 Dec 1878 v: Autelbas,
   Belgium c: 4
9 ORIGER, Anne b: 13 Oct 1879 in Autelbas, Belgium v:
   Almeroth, Belgium c: 4
+ seq: 141.09 WITRY, Albert b: 23 Nov 1873 d: 02 Nov 1922
   w: Abt. 1900 v: Almeroth, Belgium i: Both are descendents of
   the family tree f: Nicolas Witry m: Marie Gengler c: 4
9 ORIGER, Camille b: 28 May 1881 in Autelbas, Belgium
9 ORIGER, Arthur b: 23 Jun 1883 in Autelbas, Belgium v:
   Boevange, Lux c: 3
+ seq: 141.23 SINNER, Eugenie b: 01 Feb 1895 w: 04 Jun 1919
   v: Boevange, Lux c: 3
9 ORIGER, Sylvie b: 25 May 1885 in Autelbas, Belgium v:
   Grossbivange, Lux c: 2
+ seq: 141.24 KERSCHEN, Leon w: Abt. 1910 v: Grossbivange,
   Lux c: 2

141.23

9 ORIGER, Arthur b: 23 Jun 1883 in Autelbas, Belgium v:
   Boevange, Lux c: 3
+ seq: 141.23 SINNER, Eugenie b: 01 Feb 1895 w: 04 Jun 1919
   v: Boevange, Lux c: 3
10ORIGER, Marie b: 28 Aug 1920 in Buvange, Belgium
10ORIGER, Francois b: 13 Mar 1922 in Buvange, Belgium
10ORIGER, Andree b: 11 Dec 1925 in Buvange, Belgium

141.24

9 ORIGER, Sylvie b: 25 May 1885 in Autelbas, Belgium v:
   Grossbivange, Lux c: 2
+ seq: 141.24 KERSCHEN, Leon w: Abt. 1910 v: Grossbivange,
   Lux c: 2
10KERSCHEN, Paul b: 06 May 1911 in Grossbivange, Lux
10KERSCHEN, Alphonse b: 25 Apr 1913 in Grossbivange, Lux

141.25

8 WITRY, Albert b: 13 Jan 1860 d: 22 Jan 1934 v: Differt,

Belgium c: 2

+ seq: 141.25 BOSSELER, Marguerite b: 29 Jun 1866 in Buvange, Lux d: 12 Jan 1946 in Differt, Belgium w: Oct 1893 v: Differt, Belgium c: 2

9 WITRY, Rene b: Dec 1898 v: Differt, Belgium

9 WITRY, Joseph b: 1903

141.25.50

8 WITRY, Auguste-Paul b: 17 Mar 1862 in Lintgen, Lux v: Clemency, Lux o: Captain of 10th artillery regiment c: 1

+ seq: 141.25.50 LEFEBVRE, Marie-Josephe b: Abt. 1858 in Mardebius, Lux w: Abt. 1880 c: 1

9 WITRY, Paul-Auguste-Henri b: 23 May 1881 in Brouch, Lux

142

6 WITRY, Johann b: 19 Apr 1781 in Bergem, Lux d: 11 Mar 1837 in Strassem, Lux a: Deusch h: Deusch v: Strassem, Lux o: Weaver o: Farmer o: Laborer r: bd c: 10

+ seq: 142 NEPPER, Susanne b: 20 Feb 1780 in Strassem, Lux d: 13 Feb 1847 in Strassem, Lux w: 11 Feb 1806 in Strassem, Lux h: Deusch v: Strassem, Lux o: Property owner o: Farmer r: m f: Peter Nepper m: Margaretha Schroeder c: 10

7 WITRY, Margaretha b: 02 Jun 1806 in Strassem, Lux a: Nepper i: Illegitimate r: b

7 WITRY, Peter t: Mayor b: 30 Jun 1807 in Strassem, Lux d: 15 Sep 1870 in Strassem, Lux v: Strassem, Lux o: Horse breeder o: Property owner o: Carpenter o: Farmer r: bd c: 9

+ seq: 143 ENSCH, Anna b: 06 May 1817 in Bettange, Lux d: 31 Mar 1876 in Strassem, Lux w: 27 Jul 1842 in Bertrange, Lux v: Strassem, Lux o: Property owner o: Farmer r: m f: Bernhard Ensch m: Marie Liber c: 9

7 WITRY, Babette (Barbara) b: 20 May 1809 in Strassem, Lux r: b

+ seq: 147.01 THEIS, Johann b: 15 Nov 1806 in Hellange, Lux w: 04 Feb 1834 in Frisange, Lux o: Farmer r: m f: Franz Theis m: Anna-Margaretha Keyl

7 WITRY, Stillborn Girl b: 27 Feb 1811 in Strassem, Lux d: 27 Feb 1811 in Strassem, Lux v: Strassem, Lux r: b

7 WITRY, Margaretha b: 08 Feb 1812 in Strassem, Lux h: Gastgrund v: Mamer, Lux o: Farmer o: Miller r: b c: 9

+ seq: 147.02 TOUSSAINT, Michel b: 23 May 1810 in Mamer,

Lux d: 06 Sep 1879 in Mamer, Lux w: 18 May 1835 in Mamer, Lux h: Gastgrund v: Mamer, Lux o: Plowman o: Innkeeper o: Farmer o: Miller r: bd r: m f: Nicolas Toussaint m: Catherine Franck c: 9

7 WITRY, Marie b: 21 Dec 1814 in Strassem, Lux v: Capellen, Lux v: Strassem, Lux o: No profession r: b c: 9

+ seq: 147.03 EWERT, Nicolas b: 07 Dec 1812 in Mamer, Lux w: 22 Jan 1840 in Strassem, Lux v: Capellen, Lux v: Strassem, Lux o: Farmer r: m f: Johann Ewert m: Marie Gudenkauf c: 9

7 WITRY, Anna-Margaretha b: 14 Mar 1817 in Strassem, Lux d: 27 Mar 1817 in Strassem, Lux v: Strassem, Lux r: bd

7 WITRY, Catherine b: 04 Mar 1818 in Strassem, Lux d: 07 Jun 1905 in Strassem, Lux v: Strassem, Lux o: No profession r: bd

7 [1] WITRY, Barbara b: 10 Dec 1820 in Strassem, Lux d: 25 Dec 1891 in Dudelange, Lux v: Luxembourg, Lux o: Merchant r: bd c: 2

+ seq: 147.04 HERGES, Johann Philipp Lambert b: 26 Jun 1808 in Luxembourg, Lux d: 14 Jul 1845 in Luxembourg, Lux w: 08 Mar 1841 in Luxembourg, Lux v: Luxembourg, Lux o: Wine trader r: m f: Philipp Herges m: Anna-Marie Gonsal

* 2nd Husband of [1] WITRY, Barbara:

+ seq: 147.05 ZAHN, Dominic b: 01 Aug 1804 in Luxembourg, Lux d: 27 Dec 1891 in Dudelange, Lux w: 20 May 1846 in Luxembourg, Lux v: Luxembourg, Lux o: Merchant r: mx f: Carl Zahn m: Marie-Anna Wickning c: 2

7 WITRY, Margaretha b: 26 May 1824 in Strassem, Lux h: Schutzen v: Kehlen, Lux o: Farmer r: b c: 10

+ seq: 147.06 HOFFMANN, Johann b: 08 Oct 1815 in Kehlen, Lux w: 19 Mar 1849 in Kehlen, Lux h: Schutzen v: Kehlen, Lux o: Guard o: Doctor o: Farmer r: b r: m f: Nicolas Hoffmann m: Anna-Marie Reiser c: 10

143

7 WITRY, Peter t: Mayor b: 30 Jun 1807 in Strassem, Lux d: 15 Sep 1870 in Strassem, Lux v: Strassem, Lux o: Horse breeder o: Property owner o: Carpenter o: Farmer r: bd c: 9

+ seq: 143 ENSCH, Anna b: 06 May 1817 in Bettange, Lux d: 31 Mar 1876 in Strassem, Lux w: 27 Jul 1842 in Bertrange, Lux v: Strassem, Lux o: Property owner o: Farmer r: m f: Bernhard Ensch m: Marie Liber c: 9

8 WITRY, Marie b: 08 Jun 1843 in Strassem, Lux v: Eich, Lux

o: No profession r: b c: 6

+ seq: 143.01 GREIVELDINGER, Nicolas b: 02 Aug 1844 in
Eich, Lux w: 24 Jan 1872 in Strassem, Lux v: Eich, Lux o:
Butcher r: m f: Theodor Greiveldinger m: Magdalena Larosch
c: 6

8 WITRY, Michel b: 14 Jul 1845 in Strassem, Lux d: 23 Jun
1917 in Strassem, Lux v: Strassem, Lux o: Property owner o:
Farmer o: Private forester r: bd c: 2

+ seq: 143.50 GROFF, Susanna b: 01 Feb 1853 in Strassem, Lux
d: Bef. 1917 w: 18 Jul 1888 in Strassem, Lux o: No profession
r: m f: Pascale Groff m: Maria Buch c: 2

8 WITRY, Johann-Wilhelm b: 28 Nov 1847 in Strassem, Lux d:
04 Jun 1893 in Strassem, Lux v: Strassem, Lux o: Farmer r: bd
c: 6

+ seq: 144 GENGLER, Catherine b: 29 Dec 1857 in Niederpallen,
Lux w: 31 Aug 1880 in Strassem, Lux v: Strassem, Lux o: No
profession r: m f: Michel Gengler m: Anna Kirsch c: 6

8 WITRY, Susanne b: 12 Jan 1850 in Strassem, Lux d: 07 Mar
1909 in Burange, Lux v: Burange, Lux o: Housekeeper o:
Property owner r: bd c: 9

+ seq: 144.01 PHILIPPART, Frederic b: 24 Feb 1840 in Burange,
Lux w: 06 Apr 1876 in Strassem, Lux o: Farmer o: Retired r:
m f: Johann-Anton Philippart m: Anna Olinger c: 9

8 WITRY, Viktor b: 21 Jan 1852 in Strassem, Lux d: 23 Jul 1919
in Merl, Lux v: Merl, Lux o: Landowner o: Farmer o: Horse
breeder r: b c: 9

+ seq: 145 BONIFAS, Barbara-Eugenie b: 13 Nov 1859 in Merl,
Lux d: 1936 in Merl, Lux w: 03 Mar 1886 in Hollerich, Lux v:
Merl, Lux o: No profession r: m f: Johann-Peter Bonifas m:
Susanne Steichen c: 9

8 WITRY, Barbara b: 28 Jan 1854 in Strassem, Lux v:
Luxembourg, Lux r: bd c: 2

+ seq: 146.03 ZAHN, Dominic b: 30 Dec 1848 in Luxembourg,
Lux d: in Bef 1902 w: 07 Jan 1880 in Luxembourg, Lux v:
Luxembourg, Lux i: Both are descendents of the family tree o:
Assistant teamster o: Merchant o: Laborer f: Dominic Zahn m:
Barbara Witry c: 2

8 WITRY, Johann-Peter b: 15 May 1856 in Strassem, Lux d: 09
Mar 1925 v: Strassem, Lux o: Property owner o: Farmer r: b
c: 4

+ seq: 147 SCHMIT, Marie-Clementine (Clementine) b: 23 Nov

in Paris, France w: 28 Aug 1901 in Strassem, Lux v: Strassem, Lux o: No profession o: Folksinger r: m f: Jean Schmit m: Marguerite Guillon c: 4

8 WITRY, Johann-Edward b: 01 Jun 1858 in Strassem, Lux d: 24 Mar 1859 in Strassem, Lux v: Strassem, Lux o: No profession r: bd

8 WITRY, Marie-Solina b: 20 Jul 1860 in Strassem, Lux r: b

143.01

8 WITRY, Marie b: 08 Jun 1843 in Strassem, Lux v: Eich, Lux o: No profession r: b c: 6

+ seq: 143.01 GREIVELDINGER, Nicolas b: 02 Aug 1844 in Eich, Lux w: 24 Jan 1872 in Strassem, Lux v: Eich, Lux o: Butcher r: m f: Theodor Greiveldinger m: Magdalena Larosch c: 6

9 GREIVELDINGER, Theodor b: 24 Nov 1872 in Eich, Lux r: b

9 GREIVELDINGER, Leonie b: 04 Jun 1874 in Eich, Lux r: b

9 GREIVELDINGER, Susanna-Eugenie b: 09 Jun 1876 in Eich, Lux r: b

9 GREIVELDINGER, Barbara-Rosalie b: 22 Aug 1878 in Eich, Lux r: b

9 GREIVELDINGER, Margaretha b: 03 Jul 1881 in Eich, Lux r: b

9 GREIVELDINGER, Theodor b: 23 Jan 1884 in Eich, Lux r: b

143.50

8 WITRY, Michel b: 14 Jul 1845 in Strassem, Lux d: 23 Jun 1917 in Strassem, Lux v: Strassem, Lux o: Property owner o: Farmer o: Private forester r: bd c: 2

+ seq: 143.50 GROFF, Susanna b: 01 Feb 1853 in Strassem, Lux d: Bef. 1917 w: 18 Jul 1888 in Strassem, Lux o: No profession r: m f: Pascale Groff m: Maria Buch c: 2

9 WITRY, Jacob-Victor b: 1874 in Strassem, Lux d: 14 Sep 1900 in Strassem, Lux v: Strassem, Lux o: Day laborer r: d

9 WITRY, Leonie b: 1882 in Strassem, Lux d: 23 Jun 1917 in Strassem, Lux v: Strassem, Lux o: No profession r: d

+ seq: 143.70 FELLER, Joseph b: Abt. 1891 w: Abt. 1915 v: Strassem, Lux o: Foreman

144

8 WITRY, Johann-Wilhelm b: 28 Nov 1847 in Strassem, Lux d:

04 Jun 1893 in Strassem, Lux v: Strassem, Lux o: Farmer r: bd
c: 6

+ seq: 144 GENGLER, Catherine b: 29 Dec 1857 in Niederpallen,
Lux w: 31 Aug 1880 in Strassem, Lux v: Strassem, Lux o: No
profession r: m f: Michel Gengler m: Anna Kirsch c: 6

9 WITRY, Emil-Valentine b: 29 Aug 1881 in Strassem, Lux v:
Leudelange, Lux o: Farmer r: b c: 1

+ seq: 144.00 SCHMIT, Catharina b: 30 Apr 1880 in Leudelange,
Lux w: 17 Apr 1907 in Esch-sur-Alzette v: Leudelange, Lux o:
No profession r: m f: Nicolas Schmit m: Elisabeth Folschette
c: 1

9 WITRY, Maria b: 29 Jul 1883 in Strassem, Lux v:
Luxembourg, Lux o: No profession r: b

+ seq: 144.00.50 STEICHEN, Paul b: 30 Jan 1878 in Bettemburg,
Lux w: 17 May 1905 in Luxembourg, Lux o: Property owner
o: Farmer r: m f: Mathias Steichen m: Maria Hintgen

9 WITRY, Julie-Josephine b: 14 Aug 1885 in Strassem, Lux r: b

9 WITRY, Viktor b: 30 Sep 1887 in Strassem, Lux d: 01 Nov
1887 in Strassem, Lux v: Strassem, Lux o: Distiller o: Farmer
r: bd

9 WITRY, Alfred b: 24 Aug 1889 in Strassem, Lux r: b

9 WITRY, Jean-Pierre b: 25 Nov 1891 in Strassem, Lux r: b

144.00

9 WITRY, Emil-Valentine b: 29 Aug 1881 in Strassem, Lux v:
Leudelange, Lux o: Farmer r: b c: 1

+ seq: 144.00 SCHMIT, Catharina b: 30 Apr 1880 in Leudelange,
Lux w: 17 Apr 1907 in Esch-sur-Alzette v: Leudelange, Lux
o: No profession r: m f: Nicolas Schmit m: Elisabeth
Folschette c: 1

10 WITRY, Nicolas b: 01 Feb 1908 in Leudelange, Lux r: b

144.01

8 WITRY, Susanne b: 12 Jan 1850 in Strassem, Lux d: 07 Mar
1909 in Burange, Lux v: Burange, Lux o: Housekeeper o:
Property owner r: bd c: 9

+ seq: 144.01 PHILIPPART, Frederic b: 24 Feb 1840 in Burange,
Lux w: 06 Apr 1876 in Strassem, Lux o: Farmer o: Retired r:
m f: Johann-Anton Philippart m: Anna Olinger c: 9

9 PHILIPPART, Leonie-Barbara b: 13 Apr 1877 in Burange, Lux
d: 29 Jan 1882 in Burange, Lux r: bd

9 PHILIPPART, Michel-Alphonse b: 29 Jul 1878 in Burange, Lux d: 18 Feb 1883 in Burange, Lux r: bd

9 PHILIPPART, Anna-Magdalena b: 11 Jul 1880 in Burange, Lux o: No profession r: b

+ seq: 144.50 LEITGEN, Philippe b: 08 Jul 1864 in Burange, Lux w: 07 Jun 1905 in Dudelange, Lux o: Farmer r: m f: Johann Leitgen m: Margaretha Nilles

9 PHILIPPART, Regina-Bertha b: 1881 in Burange, Lux d: 20 Jan 1882 in Burange, Lux r: d

9 PHILIPPART, Maria-Leonie b: 23 Nov 1882 in Burange, Lux r: b

9 PHILIPPART, Victor b: 18 Jan 1884 in Burange, Lux r: b

9 PHILIPPART, Pauline b: 23 Apr 1885 in Burange, Lux d: 06 Nov 1918 in Burange, Lux r: bd

9 PHILIPPART, Leonie b: 05 Aug 1887 in Burange, Lux o: No profession r: b

+ seq: 144.70 WEBER, Mathias b: 08 Jun 1887 in Dudelange w: 22 Apr 1918 in Dudelange, Lux o: Locksmith r: m f: Jakob Weber m: Katharina Pauly

9 PHILIPPART, Regina-Bertha b: 1889 d: 09 Apr 1890 in Burange, Lux r: d

145

8 WITRY, Viktor b: 21 Jan 1852 in Strassem, Lux d: 23 Jul 1919 in Merl, Lux v: Merl, Lux o: Landowner o: Farmer o: Horse breeder r: b c: 9

+ seq: 145 BONIFAS, Barbara-Eugenie b: 13 Nov 1859 in Merl, Lux d: 1936 in Merl, Lux w: 03 Mar 1886 in Hollerich, Lux v: Merl, Lux o: No profession r: m f: Johann-Peter Bonifas m: Susanne Steichen c: 9

9 WITRY, Boy b: 23 Oct 1886 in Merl, Lux d: 23 Oct 1886 in Merl, Lux r: bd

9 WITRY, Susanne-Celestine b: 13 Sep 1887 in Merl, Lux r: bd

9 WITRY, Nicolas-Theophile b: 05 Apr 1889 in Merl, Lux d: 1912 in Merl, Lux v: Merl, Lux o: Farmer r: b

9 WITRY, Boy b: 08 May 1890 in Merl, Lux d: 08 May 1890 in Merl, Lux r: bd

9 WITRY, Susanne-Valerie b: 21 May 1891 in Merl, Lux d: 25 Oct 1891 in Merl, Lux r: bd

9 WITRY, Jules b: 04 Sep 1892 in Merl, Lux d: 1980 in Bergem, Lux v: Bergem, Lux o: Landowner o: Farmer o: Distiller r: b

c: 3

+ seq: 130 WITRY, Marie-Therese-Josephine (Josephine) b: 12
Dec 1899 in Bergem, Lux d: 06 Oct 1986 in Esch-sur-Alzette,
Lux w: 26 Feb 1927 in Mondercange, Lux v: Bergem, Lux i:
Both are descendents of the family tree o: No profession r: b f:
Henri Witry m: Marie-Catherine Nepper c: 3

9 WITRY, Irma-Eugenie-Josephine b: 31 Aug 1893 in Merl, Lux
v: Merl, Lux o: No profession r: b c: 1

+ seq: 145.01 ROSS, Johann-Peter b: 07 Aug 1887 in
Luxembourg, Lux w: 21 Feb 1916 in Luxembourg, Lux o:
Innkeeper r: m f: Johann Ross m: Margaretha Wintersdorff c:
1

+ seq: 145.02 SCHMITT, Pierre w: Abt. 1940 c: 1

9 WITRY, Paul-Jean-Pierre b: 19 Nov 1895 in Merl, Lux d: 1962
in Merl, Lux

9 WITRY, Leon-Nicolas b: 09 Nov 1897 in Merl, Lux d: 1979 in
Merl, Lux v: Merl, Lux o: Horse breeder o: Farmer c: 2

+ seq: 146 JACQUE, Albertine b: 1900 in Holzem, Lux d: 1966
in Merl, Lux w: Abt. 1925 v: Merl, Lux c: 2

145.01

9 WITRY, Irma-Eugenie-Josephine b: 31 Aug 1893 in Merl, Lux
v: Merl, Lux o: No profession r: b c: 1

+ seq: 145.01 ROSS, Johann-Peter b: 07 Aug 1887 in
Luxembourg, Lux w: 21 Feb 1916 in Luxembourg, Lux o:
Innkeeper r: m f: Johann Ross m: Margaretha Wintersdorff c:
1

10ROSS, Margot-Eugenie b: 30 Sep 1920 in Luxembourg, Lux d:
01 Feb 2001 in Luxembourg, Lux r: b c: 1

+ seq: 145.02 SCHMITT, Pierre w: Abt. 1940 c: 1

145.02

10ROSS, Margot-Eugenie b: 30 Sep 1920 in Luxembourg, Lux d:
01 Feb 2001 in Luxembourg, Lux r: b c: 1

+ seq: 145.02 SCHMITT, Pierre w: Abt. 1940 c: 1

11SCHMITT, Girl

+ seq: 145.03 WIRION w: Abt. 1970

146

9 WITRY, Leon-Nicolas b: 09 Nov 1897 in Merl, Lux d: 1979 in
Merl, Lux v: Merl, Lux o: Horse breeder o: Farmer c: 2

+ seq: 146 JACQUE, Albertine b: 1900 in Holzem, Lux d: 1966 in Merl, Lux w: Abt. 1925 v: Merl, Lux c: 2
10 WITRY, Irene-Eugenie b: 24 Nov 1925 in Merl, Lux v: Luxembourg, Lux c: 1
+ seq: 146.01 WEIS, Camille d: 18 Aug 2000 in Luxembourg, Lux w: Abt. 1950 v: Luxembourg, Lux o: Director of a dairy near Ettelbruck o: Licensed agricultural engineer c: 1
10 WITRY, Gaston b: 26 Aug 1929 in Merl, Lux d: 1974 in Merl, Lux v: Luxembourg, Lux i: Built various EEC buildings in Luxembourg i: Built first skyscraper (26 stories) in Luxembourg Ville o: Master architect

146.01

10 WITRY, Irene-Eugenie b: 24 Nov 1925 in Merl, Lux v: Luxembourg, Lux c: 1
+ seq: 146.01 WEIS, Camille d: 18 Aug 2000 in Luxembourg, Lux w: Abt. 1950 v: Luxembourg, Lux o: Director of a dairy near Ettelbruck o: Licensed agricultural engineer c: 1
11 WEIS, Denise v: Luxembourg, Lux c: 1
+ seq: 146.02 REUTER, Jean w: Abt. 1980 v: Luxembourg, Lux c: 1

146.02

11 WEIS, Denise v: Luxembourg, Lux c: 1
+ seq: 146.02 REUTER, Jean w: Abt. 1980 v: Luxembourg, Lux c: 1
12 REUTER, George o: Student in Paris

146.03

8 WITRY, Barbara b: 28 Jan 1854 in Strassem, Lux v: Luxembourg, Lux r: bd c: 2
+ seq: 146.03 ZAHN, Dominic b: 30 Dec 1848 in Luxembourg, Lux d: in Bef 1902 w: 07 Jan 1880 in Luxembourg, Lux v: Luxembourg, Lux i: Both are descendents of the family tree o: Assistant teamster o: Merchant o: Laborer f: Dominic Zahn m: Barbara Witry c: 2
9 ZAHN, Victor b: Abt. 1880 in Dudelange, Lux d: 05 Mar 1902 in Dudelange, Lux r: d
9 [1] ZAHN, Philippe-Marie-Dominick b: 14 Jan 1882 in Luxembourg, Lux v: Luxembourg, Lux o: Teacher o: Glazier
+ seq: 146.03.50 WOLFF, Susanna b: 13 Jul 1885 in

Luxembourg, Lux d: 17 Oct 1918 in Luxembourg, Lux w: 21
Sep 1908 in Luxembourg, Lux v: Luxembourg, Lux o: No
profession r: m f: Friedrich (Franz) Wolff m: Margaretha Roes
* 2nd Wife of [1] ZAHN, Philippe-Marie-Dominick:
+ seq: 146.03.70 WELSCH, Elisabetha b: 02 Feb 1893 in
Wintersdorf, Germany w: 15 Apr 1922 in Luxembourg, Lux v:
Luxembourg, Lux o: Cook r: m f: Michel Welsch m:
Elisabetha Welsch

147

8 WITRY, Johann-Peter b: 15 May 1856 in Strassem, Lux d: 09
Mar 1925 v: Strassem, Lux o: Property owner o: Farmer r: b
c: 4
+ seq: 147 SCHMIT, Marie-Clementine (Clementine) b: 23 Nov
in Paris, France w: 28 Aug 1901 in Strassem, Lux v: Strassem,
Lux o: No profession o: Folksinger r: m f: Jean Schmit m:
Marguerite Guillon c: 4
9 WITRY, Margaretha-Caroline (Caroline) b: 05 Jun 1902 in
Strassem, Lux d: 29 Jul 1997 in Luxembourg, Lux r: b
9 WITRY, Johann-Camille b: 25 May 1905 in Strassem, Lux d:
31 May 1905 in Strassem, Lux r: bd
9 WITRY, Edouard-Johann-Peter b: 14 Feb 1907 in Strassem,
Lux r: b
9 WITRY, Johann-Julius b: 23 Sep 1909 in Strassem, Lux r: b

147.02

7 WITRY, Margaretha b: 08 Feb 1812 in Strassem, Lux h:
Gastgrund v: Mamer, Lux o: Farmer o: Miller r: b c: 9
+ seq: 147.02 TOUSSAINT, Michel b: 23 May 1810 in Mamer,
Lux d: 06 Sep 1879 in Mamer, Lux w: 18 May 1835 in
Mamer, Lux h: Gastgrund v: Mamer, Lux o: Plowman o:
Innkeeper o: Farmer o: Miller r: bd r: m f: Nicolas Toussaint
m: Catherine Franck c: 9
8 TOUSSAINT, Susanne b: 23 Mar 1836 in Mamer, Lux r: b
8 TOUSSAINT, Catherine b: 07 May 1838 in Mamer, Lux r: b
8 TOUSSAINT, Barbara b: 19 Mar 1840 in Mamer, Lux r: b
8 TOUSSAINT, Marie b: 29 Nov 1842 in Mamer, Lux r: b
8 TOUSSAINT, Margaretha b: 18 Feb 1846 in Mamer, Lux r: b
8 TOUSSAINT, Nicolas b: 22 Apr 1848 in Mamer, Lux d: 10
Dec 1880 in Mamer, Lux v: Mamer, Lux o: Farmer r: bd
8 TOUSSAINT, Alphonse b: 23 Jul 1850 in Mamer, Lux v:

Mamer, Lux o: No profession r: b

8 TOUSSAINT, Johann b: 04 Sep 1852 in Mamer, Lux d: 02 Sep 1880 in Mamer, Lux v: Mamer, Lux o: Farmer r: bd

8 TOUSSAINT, Victor b: 17 Apr 1855 in Mamer, Lux r: b

147.03

7 WITRY, Marie b: 21 Dec 1814 in Strassem, Lux v: Capellen, Lux v: Strassem, Lux o: No profession r: b c: 9

+ seq: 147.03 EWERT, Nicolas b: 07 Dec 1812 in Mamer, Lux w: 22 Jan 1840 in Strassem, Lux v: Capellen, Lux v: Strassem, Lux o: Farmer r: m f: Johann Ewert m: Marie Gudenkauf c: 9

8 EWERT, Josefine b: 23 Jan 1838 in Schrassig, Lux

8 EWERT, Susanne b: 02 Apr 1839 in Strassem, Lux r: b

8 EWERT, Barbe b: 20 Jun 1842 in Capellen, Lux r: b

8 EWERT, Nicolas b: 14 Jul 1844 in Capellen, Lux r: b

8 EWERT, Anne b: 23 Mar 1847 in Capellen, Lux r: b

8 EWERT, Marguerite b: 08 Sep 1849 in Capellen, Lux r: b

8 EWERT, Nicolas b: 05 Apr 1853 in Capellen, Lux r: b

8 EWERT, Anne-Marguerite b: 23 Mar 1856 in Capellen, Lux r: b

8 EWERT, Jean-Baptiste b: 11 Oct 1859 in Capellen, Lux r: b

147.04

7 [1] WITRY, Barbara b: 10 Dec 1820 in Strassem, Lux d: 25 Dec 1891 in Dudelange, Lux v: Luxembourg, Lux o: Merchant r: bd c: 2

+ seq: 147.04 HERGES, Johann Philipp Lambert b: 26 Jun 1808 in Luxembourg, Lux d: 14 Jul 1845 in Luxembourg, Lux w: 08 Mar 1841 in Luxembourg, Lux v: Luxembourg, Lux o: Wine trader r: m f: Philipp Herges m: Anna-Marie Gonsal

* 2nd Husband of [1] WITRY, Barbara:

+ seq: 147.05 ZAHN, Dominic b: 01 Aug 1804 in Luxembourg, Lux d: 27 Dec 1891 in Dudelange, Lux w: 20 May 1846 in Luxembourg, Lux v: Luxembourg, Lux o: Merchant r: mx f: Carl Zahn m: Marie-Anna Wickning c: 2

8 ZAHN, V b: 1847

8 ZAHN, Dominic b: 30 Dec 1848 in Luxembourg, Lux v: Luxembourg, Lux o: Merchant c: 1

+ seq: 146.03 WITRY, Barbara b: 28 Jan 1854 in Strassem, Lux w: 07 Jan 1880 in Luxembourg, Lux v: Luxembourg, Lux i:

Both are descendents of the family tree r: bd f: Peter Witry m: Anna Ensch c: 1

147.06

7 WITRY, Margaretha b: 26 May 1824 in Strassem, Lux h: Schutzen v: Kehlen, Lux o: Farmer r: b c: 10
+ seq: 147.06 HOFFMANN, Johann b: 08 Oct 1815 in Kehlen, Lux w: 19 Mar 1849 in Kehlen, Lux h: Schutzen v: Kehlen, Lux o: Guard o: Doctor o: Farmer r: b r: m f: Nicolas Hoffmann m: Anna-Marie Reiser c: 10
8 HOFFMANN, Anna b: 18 Aug 1850 in Kehlen, Lux d: 18 Aug 1850 in Kehlen, Lux v: Kehlen, Lux r: bd
8 HOFFMANN, Anna b: 06 Oct 1851 in Kehlen, Lux r: b
8 HOFFMANN, Michel b: 29 Nov 1853 in Kehlen, Lux d: 28 Oct 1859 in Kehlen, Lux h: Schutzen v: Kehlen, Lux r: bd
8 HOFFMANN, Anna-Marie b: 23 Apr 1856 in Kehlen, Lux r: b
8 HOFFMANN, Catherine b: 13 Jan 1859 in Kehlen, Lux d: 13 Jan 1859 in Kehlen, Lux h: Schutzen v: Kehlen, Lux r: bd
8 HOFFMANN, Catherine b: 16 Apr 1860 in Kehlen, Lux r: b
8 HOFFMANN, Michel b: 08 Sep 1862 in Kehlen, Lux r: b
8 HOFFMANN, Barbara b: 02 Feb 1865 in Kehlen, Lux r: b
8 HOFFMANN, Marie b: 06 Mar 1868 in Kehlen, Lux r: b
8 HOFFMANN, Nicolas b: 06 Mar 1868 in Kehlen, Lux d: 06 Mar 1868 in Kehlen, Lux h: Schutzen v: Kehlen, Lux r: d

148

6 WITRY, Pierre b: 02 Feb 1784 in Bergem, Lux d: 10 Feb 1862 in Bergem, Lux a: Farmer v: Eschweiler, Lux v: Bergem, Lux o: Day laborer r: bd c: 10
+ seq: 148 SCHINTGEN, Jeanette (Anna) b: 06 Mar 1786 in Bergem, Lux d: 06 Jun 1873 in Bergem, Lux w: 08 Nov 1809 in Mondercange, Lux v: Eschweiler, Lux v: Bergem, Lux o: Farmer r: d r: m f: Nicolas Schintgen m: Christine Steichen c: 10
7 WITRY, Nicolas b: 21 Jun 1810 in Bergem, Lux d: 03 Aug 1810 in Bergem, Lux v: Bergem, Lux o: No profession r: bd
7 WITRY, Nicolas b: 24 Nov 1811 in Esch-sur-Alzette, Lux r: b
7 WITRY, Magdalena (Helena) b: 03 Dec 1813 in Eschweiler, Lux d: 15 Apr 1857 in Bergem, Lux v: Bergem, Lux o: No profession r: bd c: 6
+ seq: 148.01 BERENS, Johann-Jacob b: 30 May 1810 in

Bergem, Lux d: 20 Sep 1865 in Bergem, Lux w: 19 May 1836 in Mondercange, Lux v: Bergem, Lux o: Blacksmith o: Innkeeper r: bd r: m f: Johann Berens m: Marie-Catherine Groff c: 6

7 WITRY, Johann-Peter b: 09 Nov 1815 in Esch-sur-Alzette, Lux d: 15 Aug 1873 in Oelenberg, France i: Ordained in Trier cathedral o: Chaplain o: Trappist monk r: b

7 WITRY, Heinrich b: 24 Nov 1817 in Esch-sur-Alzette, Lux d: 09 Nov 1890 in Bergem, Lux v: Mondercange, Lux o: Farmer r: b

+ seq: 149 MULLER, Margaretha b: 23 May 1819 in Bergem, Lux d: 07 Oct 1894 w: 02 Mar 1848 in Mondercange, Lux v: Mondercange, Lux o: No profession r: b r: m f: Johann Muller m: Margaretha

7 WITRY, Elise b: 22 Nov 1819

7 WITRY, Marie b: 10 Jan 1822 in Brehan-la-Cour, France d: 19 Jun 1900 in Bergem, Lux o: No profession r: d

7 WITRY, Peter b: 10 May 1824 in Bergem, Lux d: 09 Jun 1897 in Bergem, Lux v: Bergem, Lux o: Farmer r: b c: 1

+ seq: 150 MULLER, Margaretha b: 26 Oct 1833 in Bergem, Lux d: 08 Mar 1857 in Bergem, Lux w: 05 Feb 1856 in Mondercange, Lux v: Bergem, Lux o: No profession r: b r: m f: Peter Muller m: Marguerite Wester c: 1

7 WITRY, Magdalena (Helene) b: 30 May 1828 in Bergem, Lux d: 12 Sep 1902 in Bergem, Lux o: No profession r: bd c: 3

+ seq: 150.01 SCHMIT, Nicolas b: 06 Dec 1830 in Altweis, Lux d: 14 Jan 1899 w: 16 May 1866 in Mondercange, Lux o: Farmer r: m f: Theodore Schmit m: Anne-Marie Muller c: 3

7 WITRY, Heinrich b: 03 Jan 1833 in Bergem, Lux d: 06 Jun 1920 in Bergem, Lux a: Kirsch h: Kirsch, Petesch v: Bergem, Lux o: Farmer o: Pensioner r: bd c: 11

+ seq: 151 KIRSCH, Marie-Anna b: 18 Jul 1838 in Bergem, Lux d: 27 Mar 1906 in Bergem, Lux w: 05 Jun 1867 in Mondercange, Lux h: Kirsch, Petesch v: Bergem, Lux o: Farmer r: d r: m f: Valentin (Anton) Kirsch m: Margaretha Nicolay c: 11

148.01

7 WITRY, Magdalena (Helena) b: 03 Dec 1813 in Eschweiler, Lux d: 15 Apr 1857 in Bergem, Lux v: Bergem, Lux o: No profession r: bd c: 6

+ seq: 148.01 BERENS, Johann-Jacob b: 30 May 1810 in
   Bergem, Lux d: 20 Sep 1865 in Bergem, Lux w: 19 May 1836
   in Mondercange, Lux v: Bergem, Lux o: Blacksmith o:
   Innkeeper r: bd r: m f: Johann Berens m: Marie-Catherine
   Groff c: 6
8 BERENS, Anne-Marie d: 11 Feb 1888
+ seq: 148.02 SCHUSTER, Adam d: 04 Dec 1877 w: 1871 f:
   Jean-Pierre Schuster m: Theis
8 BERENS, Jean-Nicolas b: 22 Dec 1839
8 BERENS, Jean-Jacques
8 BERENS, Henri b: 27 Aug 1844
8 BERENS, Francois b: 15 Dec 1847 i: Emigrated to America
8 BERENS, Francesca b: 06 Mar 1855 i: Emigrated to America

150

7 WITRY, Peter b: 10 May 1824 in Bergem, Lux d: 09 Jun 1897
   in Bergem, Lux v: Bergem, Lux o: Farmer r: b c: 1
+ seq: 150 MULLER, Margaretha b: 26 Oct 1833 in Bergem, Lux
   d: 08 Mar 1857 in Bergem, Lux w: 05 Feb 1856 in
   Mondercange, Lux v: Bergem, Lux o: No profession r: b r: m
   f: Peter Muller m: Marguerite Wester c: 1
8 WITRY, Marie (Margaretha) b: 30 Mar 1856 in Bergem, Lux
   d: 25 May 1931 in Bergem, Lux v: Bergem, Lux o: No
   profession r: b c: 7
+ seq: 135 WITRY, Michel b: 07 Jan 1856 in Bergem, Lux d: 14
   May 1925 in Bergem, Lux w: 29 Jul 1879 in Mondercange, Lux
   v: Bergem, Lux i: Both are descendents of the family tree o:
   Land owner o: Farmer r: b r: m f: Johann Witry m: Barbara
   Mathey c: 7

150.01

7 WITRY, Magdalena (Helene) b: 30 May 1828 in Bergem, Lux
   d: 29 Sep 1902 o: No profession r: bd c: 3
+ seq: 150.01 SCHMIT, Nicolas b: 06 Dec 1830 in Altweis, Lux
   d: 14 Jan 1899 w: 16 May 1866 in Mondercange, Lux o:
   Farmer r: m f: Theodore Schmit m: Anne-Marie Muller c: 3
8 SCHMIT, Anne-Marie b: 29 Nov 1867 d: 17 Dec 1867
8 SCHMIT, Helene-Marie b: 01 Mar 1869 d: 05 Mar 1869
8 SCHMIT, Marie b: 19 Mar 1871 d: 05 Apr 1871

7 WITRY, Heinrich b: 03 Jan 1833 in Bergem, Lux d: 06 Jun 1920 in Bergem, Lux a: Kirsch h: Kirsch, Petesch v: Bergem, Lux o: Farmer o: Pensioner r: bd c: 11

+ seq: 151 KIRSCH, Marie-Anna b: 18 Jul 1838 in Bergem, Lux d: 27 Mar 1906 in Bergem, Lux w: 05 Jun 1867 in Mondercange, Lux h: Kirsch, Petesch v: Bergem, Lux o: Farmer r: d r: m f: Valentin (Anton) Kirsch m: Margaretha Nicolay c: 11

8 WITRY, Joseph-Heinrich-Anton b: 13 Mar 1868 in Bergem, Lux d: 04 May 1868 in Bergem, Lux v: Bergem, Lux o: No profession r: bd

8 WITRY, Catherine b: 16 May 1869 in Bergem, Lux d: 1953 o: No profession r: b c: 10

+ seq: 151.01 JACOBY, Adam-Aloysius b: 15 Sep 1863 w: 03 Feb 1891 r: m c: 10

8 WITRY, Joseph-Nicolas (Adolph) b: 22 May 1870 in Bergem, Lux d: 19 Aug 1935 in Moesdorf, Lux r: b

8 WITRY, Joseph b: 29 Aug 1871 in Bergem, Lux d: 21 Jan 1872 in Bergem, Lux v: Bergem, Lux r: bd

8 WITRY, Marie b: 02 Nov 1872 in Bergem, Lux d: 23 Jun 1907 in Bergem, Lux v: Bergem, Lux o: No profession r: bd c: 2

+ seq: 151.02 TIX, Nicolas b: 23 Feb 1877 in Esch-sur-Alzette d: 1961 w: 12 Dec 1899 in Esch-sur-Alzette v: Bergem, Lux v: Haumecourt, France o: Oiler o: Railroad official r: m f: Michel Tix m: Maria Schuntgen c: 2

8 WITRY, Marie (Mathilde) (Leonie) b: 28 Sep 1874 in Bergem, Lux d: 30 Mar 1928 r: b

8 WITRY, Stephan-Alphonse-Joseph (Alphons) b: 16 Apr 1876 in Bergem, Lux d: 08 Jan 1963 v: Bergem, Lux o: Laborer o: Railroad official o: Railroad worker r: b c: 6

+ seq: 152 STOCKLAUSEN, Marie-Jeannette b: 04 Mar 1882 d: 1953 w: 29 Dec 1905 in Bergem, Lux v: Bergem, Lux o: No profession r: m f: Jacob Stocklausen m: Madeleine Clos c: 6

8 WITRY, Heinrich-Alexander b: 08 Mar 1878 in Bergem, Lux d: 1956 v: Bergem, Lux o: Land owner r: b

8 WITRY, Josephine b: 16 Mar 1879 in Bergem, Lux d: 01 Mar 1918 in Bergem, Lux r: bd

8 WITRY, Virginia b: 26 Nov 1880 in Bergem, Lux d: 1954 r: b

8 WITRY, Mathilde b: 28 Aug 1882 in Bergem, Lux d: 27 Nov 1936 in Bergem, Lux r: b

151.01

8 WITRY, Catherine b: 16 May 1869 in Bergem, Lux d: 1953 o: No profession r: b c: 10

+ seq: 151.01 JACOBY, Adam-Aloysius b: 15 Sep 1863 w: 03 Feb 1891 r: m c: 10

9 JACOBY, Joseph

9 JACOBY, Yvonne

9 JACOBY, Leon

9 JACOBY, Charles

9 JACOBY, Henriette

9 JACOBY, Albert

9 JACOBY, Adolphe

9 JACOBY, Leonie

9 JACOBY, Aloys

9 JACOBY, Arthur

151.02

8 WITRY, Marie b: 02 Nov 1872 in Bergem, Lux d: 23 Jun 1907 in Bergem, Lux v: Bergem, Lux o: No profession r: bd c: 2

+ seq: 151.02 TIX, Nicolas b: 23 Feb 1877 in Esch-sur-Alzette d: 1961 w: 12 Dec 1899 in Esch-sur-Alzette v: Bergem, Lux v: Haumecourt, France o: Oiler o: Railroad official r: m f: Michel Tix m: Maria Schuntgen c: 2

9 TIX, Aloys b: 1902 in Bergem, Lux d: 1960

9 TIX, Michel-Victor-Alexandre b: 16 Jun 1907 in Bergem, Lux r: b

152

8 WITRY, Stephan-Alphonse-Joseph (Alphons) b: 16 Apr 1876 in Bergem, Lux d: 08 Jan 1963 v: Bergem, Lux o: Laborer o: Railroad official o: Railroad worker r: b c: 6

+ seq: 152 STOCKLAUSEN, Marie-Jeannette b: 04 Mar 1882 d: 1953 w: 29 Dec 1905 in Bergem, Lux v: Bergem, Lux o: No profession r: m f: Jacob Stocklausen m: Madeleine Clos c: 6

9 WITRY, Jacques-Joseph (Josy) b: 06 Apr 1901 in Bergem, Lux d: 04 Nov 1971 in Greiveldange, Lux v: Rumelange, Lux o: Railroad employee r: b c: 1

+ seq: 153 SCHLESSER, Marguerite-Yvonne b: 30 May 1910 in Oberkorn, Lux d: 2001 w: 26 May 1928 in Rumelange, Lux v: Rumelange, Lux f: Jean Schlesser m: Helene Block c: 1

9 WITRY, Lucien b: 16 Mar 1907 in Bergem, Lux d: 14 Dec

1909 in Bergem, Lux v: Bergem, Lux r: bd
9 WITRY, Victorine-Anna b: 17 Apr 1908 in Bergem, Lux d:
1972 v: Grenoble, France r: b c: 3
+ seq: 153.03 RIVOIRE, Charles b: 1903 in Grenoble, France d:
1981 w: Abt. 1930 v: Grenoble, France c: 3
9 WITRY, Nicolas-Alphonse b: 07 Oct 1909 in Bergem, Lux d:
20 Jan 1914 in Bergem, Lux v: Bergem, Lux r: b
9 WITRY, Marie-Matilde (Maria) b: 13 Jun 1911 in Bergem, Lux
d: 1989 v: Pontpierre, Lux r: b c: 2
+ seq: 153.04 MORANG, Joseph b: 1911 in Steinbrucken, Lux d:
1979 w: Abt. 1935 v: Pontpierre, Lux c: 2
9 [1] WITRY, Emile-Arthur b: 28 Feb 1913 in Bergem, Lux d:
1982 in Bettembourg, Lux r: bd c: 1
+ seq: 154 HOSS, Anna b: 1912 in Bettembourg, Lux d: 1955 w:
Abt. 1940 c: 1
* 2nd Wife of [1] WITRY, Emile-Arthur:
+ seq: 155 BREVER, Marie b: 1923 w: Abt. 1945

153

9 WITRY, Jacques-Joseph (Josy) b: 06 Apr 1901 in Bergem, Lux
d: 04 Nov 1971 in Greiveldange, Lux v: Rumelange, Lux o:
Railroad employee c: 1
+ seq: 153 SCHLESSER, Marguerite-Yvonne b: 30 May 1910 in
Oberkorn, Lux d: 2001 w: 26 May 1928 in Rumelange, Lux v:
Rumelange, Lux f: Jean Schlesser m: Helene Block c: 1
10 WITRY, Leonie-Anna b: 26 Jul 1932 v: Rumelange, Lux c: 1
+ seq: 153.01 TERZER, Aloyse b: 26 Apr 1929 w: 15 Sep 1950
in Rumelange, Lux v: Rumelange, Lux o: Employee of
ARBED c: 1

153.01

10 WITRY, Leonie-Anna b: 26 Jul 1932 v: Rumelange, Lux c: 1
+ seq: 153.01 TERZER, Aloyse b: 26 Apr 1929 w: 15 Sep 1950
in Rumelange, Lux v: Rumelange, Lux o: Employee of
ARBED c: 1
11 TERZER, Josiane b: 30 Sep 1956 in Rumelange, Lux v:
Tetange, France o: Emloyee of International Bank of
Luxembourg c: 1
+ seq: 153.02 THILL, Eloi b: 22 Jul 1955 in Esch-sur-Alzette,
Lux w: 05 Apr 1976 in Rumelange, Lux v: Tetange, France o:
Employee of International Bank of Luxembourg c: 1

153.02

11 TERZER, Josiane b: 30 Sep 1956 in Rumelange, Lux v:
Tetange, France o: Emloyee of International Bank of
Luxembourg c: 1
+ seq: 153.02 THILL, Eloi b: 22 Jul 1955 in Esch-sur-Alzette,
Lux w: 05 Apr 1976 in Rumelange, Lux v: Tetange, France o:
Employee of International Bank of Luxembourg c: 1
12 THILL, Nathalie b: 13 Sep 1977 in Esch-sur-Alzette, Lux v:
Bissen, Lux o: Teacher
+ seq: 153.02.01 KESSELER, Claude b: 10 Feb 1971 in
Ettelbruck, Lux w: 21 May 2004 in Kayl, Lux v: Bissen, Lux
o: Newspaper reporter f: Joseph Kesseler m: Milly Glaesener

153.03

9 WITRY, Victorine b: 16 Apr 1908 in Bergem, Lux d: 1972 v:
Grenoble, France c: 3
+ seq: 153.03 RIVOIRE, Charles b: 1903 in Grenoble, France d:
1981 w: Abt. 1930 v: Grenoble, France c: 3
10 RIVOIRE, Henri b: 1931 d: 1986
10 RIVOIRE, Paulette b: 1932
10 RIVOIRE, Jean-Paul b: 1947

153.04

9 WITRY, Maria b: 13 Jun 1911 in Bergem, Lux d: 1989 v:
Pontpierre, Lux c: 2
+ seq: 153.04 MORANG, Joseph b: 1911 in Steinbrucken, Lux
d: 1979 w: Abt. 1935 v: Pontpierre, Lux c: 2
10 MORANG, Francois b: 1936 d: 1983
10 MORANG, Albert b: 1938

154

9 [1] WITRY, Emile b: 28 Feb 1913 in Bergem, Lux d: 1982 in
Bettembourg, Lux c: 1
+ seq: 154 HOSS, Anna b: 1912 in Bettembourg, Lux d: 1955
w: Abt. 1940 c: 1
10 WITRY, Fernand b: 1946
* 2nd Wife of [1] WITRY, Emile:
+ seq: 155 BREVER, Marie b: 1923 w: Abt. 1945

156

5 [1] WITRY, Nicolas b: 14 Mar 1750 in Bergem, Lux d: 17 Jul

1804 in Beidweiler, Lux a: Diedesch h: Diedesch v:
Beidweiler, Lux i: Confirmed o: Farmer r: bd c: 13
+ seq: 156 KUHNEN, Marie-Catherine b: 19 Oct 1750 in
  Beidweiler, Lux d: 03 May 1786 in Beidweiler, Lux w: 17 Dec
  1774 in Beidweiler, Lux a: Diedesch h: Diedesch v:
  Beidweiler, Lux i: Confirmed r: bd r: m f: Mathias Kuhnen
  m: Susanne Diedesch c: 6
6 WITRY, Valentin b: 02 Oct 1775 in Beidweiler, Lux d: 26 Sep
  1826 in Beidweiler, Lux a: Diedesch h: Diedesch v:
  Beidweiler, Lux o: Day laborer o: Farmer r: bd c: 14
+ seq: 157 MEYERS, Catherine b: 07 Jul 1782 in Biwer, Lux d:
  27 Apr 1831 in Fischbach, Lux w: 27 Apr 1796 in Rodenbourg,
  Lux h: Diedesch v: Beidweiler, Lux o: Day laborer o: Farmer
  r: bd r: m f: Peter Meyers m: Helene-Magdalena Kuhnen c: 14
6 WITRY, Stillborn Boy b: 01 Jul 1779 in Beidweiler, Lux d: 01
  Jul 1779 in Beidweiler, Lux h: Diedesch v: Beidweiler, Lux r:
  b
6 WITRY, Marie b: 25 Aug 1780 in Beidweiler, Lux d: 25 Aug
  1780 in Beidweiler, Lux h: Diedesch v: Beidweiler, Lux r: d
6 WITRY, Elisabeth b: 11 Jan 1783 in Beidweiler, Lux d: 04 Feb
  1783 in Beidweiler, Lux h: Diedesch v: Beidweiler, Lux r: bd
6 WITRY, Stillborn Boy b: 21 Jun 1784 in Beidweiler, Lux d: 21
  Jun 1784 in Beidweiler, Lux h: Diedesch v: Beidweiler, Lux r:
  bd
6 WITRY, Boy b: 29 Apr 1786 in Beidweiler, Lux d: 01 May
  1786 in Beidweiler, Lux h: Diedesch v: Beidweiler, Lux r: bd
* 2nd Wife of [1] WITRY, Nicolas:
+ seq: 228 HUSS, Elisabeth b: 09 Feb 1765 in Biwer, Lux d: 28
  Feb 1857 in Beidweiler, Lux w: 26 Jun 1786 in Beidweiler, Lux
  a: Weidich h: Diedesch v: Bergem, Lux v: Beidweiler, Lux o:
  Farmer r: d r: m f: Nicolas Huss m: Margaretha (Catherine)
  Moosbach c: 7
6 WITRY, Michel b: 31 Jul 1787 in Beidweiler, Lux d: 10 Mar
  1790 in Beidweiler, Lux h: Diedesch v: Beidweiler, Lux o: No
  profession r: bd
6 WITRY, Nicolas b: 07 Aug 1789 in Beidweiler, Lux d: 21 Mar
  1871 in Herborn, Lux h: No. 24 v: Herborn, Lux i: Wounded
  by lance in mouth and neck in Leipsig i: Awarded with the Lily
  i: Discharge from French Dragoons, served 1809-1814 o:
  Soldier o: Forest warden o: Farmer r: bdx c: 13
+ seq: 229 KUHNEN, Catherine b: 04 Sep 1799 in Herborn, Lux

d: 08 May 1878 in Herborn, Lux w: 19 Jan 1818 in Rodenbourg, Lux a: Kohn h: No. 24 v: Herborn, Lux o: No profession r: bd r: m f: Johann Kuhnen m: Elisabeth Baden c: 13

6 WITRY, Marie-Catherine b: 29 Sep 1792 in Beidweiler, Lux d: 14 Mar 1796 in Beidweiler, Lux h: Diedesch v: Beidweiler, Lux o: No profession r: bd

6 WITRY, Jacob b: 05 Oct 1794 in Beidweiler, Lux d: 21 Sep 1795 in Beidweiler, Lux h: Diedesch v: Beidweiler, Lux o: No profession r: bd

6 WITRY, Johann b: 04 Mar 1797 in Beidweiler, Lux d: 09 Mar 1865 in Beidweiler, Lux h: Hames v: Beidweiler, Lux i: Discharge from militia o: Day laborer o: Farmer r: bd c: 5

+ seq: 292 MEYERS, Barbara b: 19 Apr 1800 in Dickweiler, Lux d: 24 Feb 1874 in Beidweiler, Lux w: 21 Apr 1830 in Rodenbourg, Lux v: Beidweiler, Lux o: Farmer r: d r: m f: Nicolas Meyers m: Catherine Poos c: 5

6 WITRY, Valentin b: Abt. 1800 in Beidweiler, Lux d: 11 Mar 1803 in Beidweiler, Lux h: Diedesch v: Beidweiler, Lux o: No profession r: d

6 WITRY, Peter b: 02 May 1802 in Beidweiler, Lux d: 03 Mar 1847 in Osweiler, Lux v: Osweiler, Lux o: Laborer o: Farmer r: bd c: 3

+ seq: 300 NEU, Catherine b: 09 Nov 1810 in Osweiler, Lux w: 22 Feb 1838 in Rosport, Lux v: Osweiler, Lux o: No profession r: b r: m f: Peter Neu m: Susanne Neu c: 3

157

6 WITRY, Valentin b: 02 Oct 1775 in Beidweiler, Lux d: 26 Sep 1826 in Beidweiler, Lux a: Diedesch h: Diedesch v: Beidweiler, Lux o: Day laborer o: Farmer r: bd c: 14

+ seq: 157 MEYERS, Catherine b: 07 Jul 1782 in Biwer, Lux d: 27 Apr 1831 in Fischbach, Lux w: 27 Apr 1796 in Rodenbourg, Lux h: Diedesch v: Beidweiler, Lux o: Day laborer o: Farmer r: bd r: m f: Peter Meyers m: Helene-Magdalena Kuhnen c: 14

7 [1] WITRY, Elisabeth b: 11 Aug 1799 in Beidweiler, Lux d: 17 May 1835 in Beidweiler, Lux v: Herborn, Lux v: Beidweiler, Lux o: Day laborer o: Farmer r: b c: 2

+ seq: 157.01 TOURNER, Nicolas b: 02 Apr 1793 in Lenningen, Lux d: 06 Sep 1833 in Beidweiler, Lux w: 15 Sep 1823 in Rodenbourg, Lux v: Beidweiler, Lux o: Tailor r: d r: m f: Peter Tourner m: Magdalena Peyzant c: 2

* 2nd Husband of [1] WITRY, Elisabeth:
+ seq: 157.02 KUHNEN, Johann b: 01 Mar 1805 in Herborn, Lux
  d: 08 Mar 1852 in Herborn, Lux w: 25 Mar 1835 in
  Rodenbourg, Lux a: Kinn a: Schaut v: Beidweiler, Lux o:
  Rural guard o: Linen weaver r: d r: m f: Mathias Kuhnen m:
  Anna Schummer
7 WITRY, Elisabeth b: 05 Oct 1801 in Beidweiler, Lux d: 03
  Mar 1870 in Beidweiler, Lux h: Zirden v: Beidweiler, Lux o:
  Day laborer r: bd c: 10
+ seq: 157.03 STREFF, Johann b: 02 Mar 1802 in Rammeldange,
  Lux w: 15 Dec 1824 in Rodenbourg, Lux h: Zirden v:
  Beidweiler, Lux o: Day laborer o: Linen weaver r: m f:
  Theodor Streff m: Anna Feischten c: 10
7 [2] WITRY, Michel b: 29 Mar 1804 in Beidweiler, Lux d: 13
  May 1871 in Beidweiler, Lux v: Beidweiler, Lux o: Day laborer
  o: Farmer r: bd c: 2
+ seq: 158 GOELLER, Susanne b: 12 Mar 1785 in Bass-Rentgen,
  France w: 07 May 1831 in Fischbach, Lux v: Beidweiler, Lux
  f: Theodor Goeller m: Margaretha Neu
* 2nd Wife of [2] WITRY, Michel:
+ seq: 159 HUVELER, Barbara (Catharina) b: 24 Feb 1814 in
  Erpeldange, Lux w: 07 May 1849 in Rodenbourg, Lux a:
  Gregorius a: Schmitt v: Beidweiler, Lux o: Day laborer r: m f:
  Anton Huveler m: Catherine Seffer c: 2
7 WITRY, Reinhard b: 21 May 1806 in Beidweiler, Lux d: 12
  Jun 1872 in Dalheim, Lux a: Rene Witry v: Beidweiler, Lux i:
  Retired on state pension o: Machinist o: Day laborer o: Farmer
  r: bd c: 5
+ seq: 161 REGENWETTER, Anna-Marie b: 23 Jun 1807 in
  Angelsberg, Lux w: 13 Jan 1833 in Fischbach, Lux v:
  Beidweiler, Lux o: No profession r: b r: m f: Peter
  Regenwetter m: Marie-Catherine Binsfeld c: 5
7 WITRY, Margaretha b: 18 May 1808 in Beidweiler, Lux d: 05
  Mar 1862 in Rollingen, Lux v: Rollingen, Lux i: At her death,
  her husband didn't know the names of her parents o: No
  profession r: bd c: 5
+ seq: 161.01 KUGENER, Mathias b: 14 Mar 1808 in Lutgen,
  Lux w: 23 Jul 1835 in Mersch, Lux v: Rollingen, Lux o:
  Cobbler r: m f: Wilhelm Kugener m: Agnes Fischbach c: 5
7 WITRY, Anna b: 24 Jul 1810 in Beidweiler, Lux d: 24 Jun
  1858 in Beaufort, Lux v: Beaufort, Lux o: No profession r: bd

c: 3

+ seq: 161.03 EIFFES, Mathias b: 02 Aug 1823 in Beaufort, Lux
w: 10 Feb 1848 in Beaufort, Lux v: Beaufort, Lux o: Linen
weaver r: b r: m f: Johann Eiffes m: Johanna (Hanna) Charle
c: 3

7 WITRY, Johann b: 20 Sep 1812 in Beidweiler, Lux r: b

7 WITRY, Nicolas b: 09 Oct 1814 in Beidweiler, Lux d: 26 Feb
1841 in Rollingen, Lux h: Ruth v: Rollingen, Lux i: Served in
militia o: Tailor r: bd c: 2

+ seq: 162 RUTH, Marie-Magdalena b: 31 Mar 1813 in Mersch,
Lux w: 29 Mar 1838 in Mersch, Lux v: Rollingen, Lux o:
Seamstress r: b r: m f: Theodor Ruth m: Marie-Catherine
Duchene c: 2

7 WITRY, Barbara b: 01 Feb 1817 in Beidweiler, Lux d: 17 Apr
1846 in Beidweiler, Lux h: Diedesch v: Beidweiler, Lux o: No
profession r: bd

7 WITRY, Catherine b: 22 Mar 1819 in Beidweiler, Lux d: 20
Apr 1887 in Bech, Lux h: Hans h: Zehns v: Bech, Lux o: No
profession r: bd c: 4

+ seq: 164.01 FIXMER, Wilhelm b: 13 Jun 1811 in Bech, Lux w:
28 Nov 1848 in Bech, Lux h: Zehns h: Hans v: Bech, Lux o:
Road maintainer o: Rural guard o: Border guard r: m f: Johann
Fixmer m: Catherine Federspiel c: 8

7 [3] WITRY, Peter b: 30 Jun 1821 in Beidweiler, Lux d: 13 Aug
1888 in Beidweiler, Lux v: Beidweiler, Lux o: Thatcher o: Day
Laborer o: Linen weaver r: bd c: 6

+ seq: 165 GILLES, Barbara b: Abt. 1820 in Schuttrange, Lux w:
Abt. 1845 a: Gregorius v: Beidweiler, Lux o: Midwife

* 2nd Wife of [3] WITRY, Peter:

+ seq: 166 STIREN, Margaretha b: 25 Feb 1821 in Heffingen,
Lux d: 19 Mar 1877 in Beidweiler, Lux w: 23 Dec 1847 in
Rodenbourg, Lux v: Beidweiler, Lux o: Cobbler o: Day laborer
o: Seamstress r: d r: m f: Nicolas Stiren m: Elisabeth Peckes
c: 6

7 WITRY, Johann b: 04 Sep 1823 in Beidweiler, Lux d: 16 Nov
1823 in Beidweiler, Lux h: Diedesch v: Beidweiler, Lux r: bd

7 WITTRY, Jacob b: 08 Oct 1824 in Beidweiler, Lux d: 30 Apr
1906 in Aurora, IL a: Witry v: Big Woods, IL v: Beidweiler,
Lux i: Emigrated to Aurora, IL i: Discharge from militia i:
Arrived in New York on the Vulture with wife and two children
o: Servant o: Day laborer o: Farmer r: bdx c: 8

+ seq: 167 SCHONS, Magdalena b: 08 Mar 1827 in Olingen, Lux
  d: 08 Sep 1888 in Aurora, IL Cause of death: Heart illness w: 21
  May 1851 in Rodenbourg, Lux v: Big Woods, IL v: Beidweiler,
  Lux i: Emigrated to Aurora, IL o: Farmer r: bd r: m f: Peter
  Schons m: Margaretha Stoos c: 8
7 WITRY, Mathias b: 15 Jan 1827 in Beidweiler, Lux d: 22 Jan
  1880 in Beidweiler, Lux h: Diedesch v: Beidweiler, Lux o:
  Master tailor r: bd c: 9
+ seq: 214 LASCHETTE, Anna b: 26 Dec 1824 in Beaufort, Lux
  d: 14 Apr 1893 in Beidweiler, Lux w: 06 Feb 1850 in
  Rodenbourg, Lux h: Diedesch v: Beidweiler, Lux o:
  Seamstress r: d r: m f: Michel Laschette m: Anna-Marie
  Wagner c: 9

157.01

7 [1] WITRY, Elisabeth b: 11 Aug 1799 in Beidweiler, Lux d: 17
  May 1835 in Beidweiler, Lux v: Herborn, Lux v: Beidweiler,
  Lux o: Day laborer o: Farmer r: b c: 2
+ seq: 157.01 TOURNER, Nicolas b: 02 Apr 1793 in Lenningen,
  Lux d: 06 Sep 1833 in Beidweiler, Lux w: 15 Sep 1823 in
  Rodenbourg, Lux v: Beidweiler, Lux o: Tailor r: d r: m f:
  Peter Tourner m: Magdalena Peyzant c: 2
8 TOURNER, Mathias b: 01 Jul 1828 in Beidweiler, Lux r: b
8 TOURNER, Nicolas b: 10 Jan 1832 in Beidweiler, Lux d: 04
  Jun 1875 in Beidweiler, Lux v: Beidweiler, Lux o: House
  servant o: Farm servant r: bd
* 2nd Husband of [1] WITRY, Elisabeth:
+ seq: 157.02 KUHNEN, Johann b: 01 Mar 1805 in Herborn, Lux
  d: 08 Mar 1852 in Herborn, Lux w: 25 Mar 1835 in
  Rodenbourg, Lux a: Kinn a: Schaut v: Beidweiler, Lux o:
  Rural guard o: Linen weaver r: d r: m f: Mathias Kuhnen m:
  Anna Schummer

157.03

7 WITRY, Elisabeth b: 05 Oct 1801 in Beidweiler, Lux d: 03
  Mar 1870 in Beidweiler, Lux h: Zirden v: Beidweiler, Lux o:
  Day laborer r: bd c: 10
+ seq: 157.03 STREFF, Johann b: 02 Mar 1802 in Rammeldange,
  Lux w: 15 Dec 1824 in Rodenbourg, Lux h: Zirden v:
  Beidweiler, Lux o: Day laborer o: Linen weaver r: m f:
  Theodor Streff m: Anna Feischten c: 10

8 STREFF, Elisabeth b: 17 Dec 1824 in Beidweiler, Lux o: No profession r: b

+ seq: 157.04 HANSEN, Nicolas b: 04 Apr 1829 in Gonderange, Lux w: 21 Feb 1854 in Rodenbourg, Lux o: Carpenter r: m f: Nicolas Hansen m: Margaretha Weimaskirch

8 STREFF, Michel b: 25 Aug 1826 in Beidweiler, Lux d: 11 Apr 1837 in Beidweiler, Lux v: Beidweiler, Lux o: No profession r: bd

8 STREFF, Reinhard b: 07 Dec 1828 in Beidweiler, Lux v: Beidweiler, Lux o: Day laborer r: b

+ seq: 157.05 EVEN, Marie b: 27 Feb 1827 in Betzdorf, Lux w: 27 Aug 1851 in Rodenbourg, Lux o: No profession r: m f: Michel Even m: Elisabeth Baden

8 STREFF, Margaretha b: 13 Jan 1831 in Beidweiler, Lux v: Beidweiler, Lux o: No profession r: b

+ seq: 157.06 MENY, Peter b: 14 Oct 1833 in Ehlange, Lux w: 04 Feb 1863 in Rodenbourg, Lux v: Beidweiler, Lux o: Day laborer o: Cobbler r: m f: Peter Meny m: Margaretha Marschal

8 STREFF, Margaretha b: 19 Apr 1833 in Beidweiler, Lux r: b

8 STREFF, Philipp b: 22 Jul 1835 in Beidweiler, Lux r: b

8 STREFF, Peter b: 08 Apr 1838 in Beidweiler, Lux o: Carpenter r: b

+ seq: 157.07 EISCHEN, Catherine b: 19 Jul 1843 in Hemsthal, Lux w: 24 Aug 1864 in Rodenbourg, Lux o: No profession r: m f: Johann Eischen m: Maria Hastert

8 STREFF, Marie b: 19 Dec 1840 in Beidweiler, Lux r: b

8 STREFF, Franz b: 13 Nov 1842 in Beidweiler, Lux d: 14 Nov 1842 in Beidweiler, Lux v: Beidweiler, Lux o: No profession r: bd

8 STREFF, Nicolas b: 21 Feb 1844 in Beidweiler, Lux d: 01 Mar 1849 in Beidweiler, Lux o: No profession r: bd

158

7 [1] WITRY, Michel b: 29 Mar 1804 in Beidweiler, Lux d: 13 May 1871 in Beidweiler, Lux v: Beidweiler, Lux o: Day laborer o: Farmer r: bd c: 2

+ seq: 158 GOELLER, Susanne b: 12 Mar 1785 in Bass-Rentgen, France w: 07 May 1831 in Fischbach, Lux v: Beidweiler, Lux f: Theodor Goeller m: Margaretha Neu

* 2nd Wife of [1] WITRY, Michel:

+ seq: 159 HUVELER, Barbara (Catharina) b: 24 Feb 1814 in
Erpeldange, Lux w: 07 May 1849 in Rodenbourg, Lux a:
Gregorius a: Schmitt v: Beidweiler, Lux o: Day laborer r: m f:
Anton Huveler m: Catherine Seffer c: 2
8 WITRY, Catherine b: 31 Jul 1850 in Beidweiler, Lux h:
Diedesch v: Beidweiler, Lux o: Day laborer c: 5
+ seq: 159.01 NILLES, Peter b: 11 Feb 1840 in Junglinster, Lux
d: 25 Jun 1909 in Beidweiler, Lux w: 15 May 1877 in
Rodenbourg, Lux h: Diedesch v: Beidweiler, Lux o: Day
laborer r: d r: m f: Peter Nilles m: Catherine Reckinger c: 5
8 WITRY, Mathias b: 11 Feb 1853 in Beidweiler, Lux v:
Godbrange, Lux o: Farmer o: Carpenter r: b c: 5
+ seq: 160 FEDERSPIEL, Maria b: 29 Dec 1854 in Godbrange,
Lux w: 17 Aug 1882 in Junglinster, Lux v: Godbrange, Lux o:
Day laborer r: m f: Hubert Federspiel m: Elisabeth Kieffer c: 5

159.01

8 WITRY, Catherine b: 31 Jul 1850 in Beidweiler, Lux h:
Diedesch v: Beidweiler, Lux o: Day laborer c: 5
+ seq: 159.01 NILLES, Peter b: 11 Feb 1840 in Junglinster, Lux
d: 25 Jun 1909 in Beidweiler, Lux w: 15 May 1877 in
Rodenbourg, Lux h: Diedesch v: Beidweiler, Lux o: Day
laborer r: d r: m f: Peter Nilles m: Catherine Reckinger c: 5
9 NILLES, Nicolas b: 14 Jul 1878 in Beidweiler, Lux d: 30 Apr
1902 in Beidweiler, Lux o: Laborer r: bd
9 NILLES, Franzisca b: 18 Oct 1879 in Beidweiler, Lux r: b
9 NILLES, Josefine b: 18 Oct 1879 in Beidweiler, Lux r: b c: 1
10 NILLES, Emil b: 16 May 1910 in Beidweiler, Lux r: b
9 NILLES, Michel b: 1885 in Beidweiler, Lux
9 NILLES, Celestine b: 10 May 1895 in Beidweiler, Lux r: b

160

8 WITRY, Mathias b: 11 Feb 1853 in Beidweiler, Lux v:
Godbrange, Lux o: Farmer o: Carpenter r: b c: 5
+ seq: 160 FEDERSPIEL, Maria b: 29 Dec 1854 in Godbrange,
Lux w: 17 Aug 1882 in Junglinster, Lux v: Godbrange, Lux o:
Day laborer r: m f: Hubert Federspiel m: Elisabeth Kieffer c: 5
9 WITRY, Katharina b: 24 Oct 1884 in Godbrange, Lux r: b
9 WITRY, Susanna b: 08 Nov 1886 in Godbrange, Lux o: Maid
r: b c: 4
+ seq: 160.20 GREISCHER, Michel b: 21 Jan 1879 in Christnach,

Lux w: 27 May 1913 in Waldbillig, Lux o: Farmer r: m f:
Wilhelm Greischer m: Catherine Dohan c: 4

9 WITRY, Peter b: 03 Sep 1888 in Godbrange, Lux o: Laborer r:
b

9 WITRY, Edouard b: 25 May 1891 in Godbrange, Lux d: 19
Aug 1920 in Luxembourg, Lux o: Substitute teacher r: b

9 WITRY, Johann b: 20 Mar 1894 in Godbrange, Lux o: Tailor
r: b

+ seq: 160.50 WAGNER, Susanna b: 19 Jul 1899 in Godbrange,
Lux w: 08 Dec 1923 in Junglinster, Lux o: No profession r: m
f: Peter Wagner m: Elisabeth Meisenburg

160.20

9 WITRY, Susanna b: 08 Nov 1886 in Godbrange, Lux o: Maid
r: b c: 4

+ seq: 160.20 GREISCHER, Michel b: 21 Jan 1879 in Christnach,
Lux w: 27 May 1913 in Waldbillig, Lux o: Farmer r: m f:
Wilhelm Greischer m: Catherine Dohan c: 4

10GREISCHER, Catherine b: 24 Jul 1914 in Christnach, Lux r: b

10GREISCHER, Maria b: 19 Jul 1915 in Christnach, Lux r: b

10GREISCHER, Peter b: 28 Oct 1917 in Christnach, Lux r: b

10GREISCHER, Eugenie b: 08 Aug 1920 in Christnach, Lux r: b

161

7 WITRY, Reinhard b: 21 May 1806 in Beidweiler, Lux d: 12
Jun 1872 in Dalheim, Lux a: Rene Witry v: Beidweiler, Lux i:
Retired on state pension o: Machinist o: Day laborer o: Farmer
r: bd c: 5

+ seq: 161 REGENWETTER, Anna-Marie b: 23 Jun 1807 in
Angelsberg, Lux w: 13 Jan 1833 in Fischbach, Lux v:
Beidweiler, Lux o: No profession r: b r: m f: Peter
Regenwetter m: Marie-Catherine Binsfeld c: 5

8 WITRY, Susanne b: 30 Nov 1833 in Beidweiler, Lux

8 WITRY, Margaretha b: 10 May 1835 in Beidweiler, Lux r: b

8 WITRY, Marie b: 18 Aug 1837 in Beidweiler, Lux r: b

8 WITRY, Anna b: 30 May 1839 in Beidweiler, Lux r: b

8 WITRY, Catherine b: 22 Jun 1841 in Wiltz, Lux r: b

161.01

7 WITRY, Margaretha b: 18 May 1808 in Beidweiler, Lux d: 05
Mar 1862 in Rollingen, Lux v: Rollingen, Lux i: At her death,

her husband didn't know the names of her parents o: No
profession r: bd c: 5
+ seq: 161.01 KUGENER, Mathias b: 14 Mar 1808 in Lutgen,
   Lux w: 23 Jul 1835 in Mersch, Lux v: Rollingen, Lux o:
   Cobbler r: m f: Wilhelm Kugener m: Agnes Fischbach c: 5
8 KUGENER, Lambert b: 29 May 1837 in Rollingen, Lux d: 19
   Feb 1875 in Rollingen, Lux v: Rollingen, Lux o: Cobbler r: bd
+ seq: 161.02 GLODT, Marie b: 19 May 1834 in Betrange, Lux
   w: 25 Sep 1862 in Mersch, Lux o: No profession r: m f:
   Ludwig Glodt m: Margaretha Even
8 KUGENER, Peter b: 10 Aug 1839 in Rollingen, Lux r: b
8 KUGENER, Mathias b: 20 Nov 1841 in Rollingen, Lux r: b
8 KUGENER, Theodor b: 27 Jul 1844 in Rollingen, Lux r: b
8 KUGENER, Peter b: 30 Jun 1847 in Rollingen, Lux r: b

161.03
7 WITRY, Anna b: 24 Jul 1810 in Beidweiler, Lux d: 24 Jun
   1858 in Beaufort, Lux v: Beaufort, Lux o: No profession r: bd
   c: 3
+ seq: 161.03 EIFFES, Mathias b: 02 Aug 1823 in Beaufort, Lux
   w: 10 Feb 1848 in Beaufort, Lux v: Beaufort, Lux o: Linen
   weaver r: b r: m f: Johann Eiffes m: Johanna (Hanna) Charle
   c: 3
8 EIFFES, Anna b: 11 Dec 1848 in Beaufort, Lux o: No
   profession r: b
+ seq: 161.04 LICK, Mathias b: 29 May 1855 in Oettingen,
   France w: 20 Jan 1879 in Beaufort, Lux v: Oettingen, France
   o: Day laborer r: m f: Mathias Lick m: Anna Frisch
8 EIFFES, Anna-Marie b: 15 May 1851 in Beaufort, Lux d: 12
   Apr 1853 in Beaufort, Lux v: Beaufort, Lux o: No profession r:
   bd
8 EIFFES, Johann b: 10 May 1855 in Beaufort, Lux d: 23 Jun
   1857 in Beaufort, Lux v: Beaufort, Lux o: No profession r: bd

162
7 WITRY, Nicolas b: 09 Oct 1814 in Beidweiler, Lux d: 26 Feb
   1841 in Rollingen, Lux h: Ruth v: Rollingen, Lux i: Served in
   militia o: Tailor r: bd c: 2
+ seq: 162 RUTH, Marie-Magdalena b: 31 Mar 1813 in Mersch,
   Lux w: 29 Mar 1838 in Mersch, Lux v: Rollingen, Lux o:
   Seamstress r: b r: m f: Theodor Ruth m: Marie-Catherine

Duchene c: 2

8 [1] WITRY, Theodor t: Knight of the Crown of Oak b: 06 Mar
 1839 in Rollingen, Lux d: 16 Jan 1910 in Luxembourg, Lux h:
 2 Wasser v: Luxembourg, Lux i: Wrote article on the teaching
 of art o: Professor in the Athenaeum o: Head Secretary of
 Federal Unit r: bd

+ seq: 163 MICHAELIS, Marie b: 27 Jul 1835 in Luxembourg,
 Lux w: 09 Jun 1870 in Luxembourg, Lux h: 2 Wasser v:
 Luxembourg, Lux o: No profession r: m f: Theodor Michaelis
 m: Magdalena Klein

* 2nd Wife of [1] WITRY, Theodor:

+ seq: 164 GRUBER, Francoise-Antoinette-Julie b: 25 Apr 1844
 in Luxembourg, Lux w: 09 May 1889 in Luxembourg, Lux v:
 Luxembourg, Lux o: No profession r: m f: Anton Gruber m:
 Isabelle-Caroline-Josephine Probst

8 WITRY, Magdalena b: 21 Apr 1841 in Rollingen, Lux r: b c: 1

9 WITRY, Theodor-Michel b: 12 Nov 1871 in Rollingen, Lux v:
 Trier, Germany o: Coroner

+ seq: 164.00.50 TRAUSCH, Janine-Delphine b: 13 Feb 1876 in
 Luxembourg, Lux w: 14 Feb 1905 in Luxembourg, Lux o: No
 profession r: m f: Theodor Trausch m: Katharina Hardt

164.01

7 WITRY, Catherine b: 22 Mar 1819 in Beidweiler, Lux d: 20
 Apr 1887 in Bech, Lux h: Hans h: Zehns v: Bech, Lux o: No
 profession r: bd c: 4

+ seq: 164.01 FIXMER, Wilhelm b: 13 Jun 1811 in Bech, Lux
 w: 28 Nov 1848 in Bech, Lux h: Zehns h: Hans v: Bech, Lux
 o: Road maintainer o: Rural guard o: Border guard r: m f:
 Johann Fixmer m: Catherine Federspiel c: 8

8 FIXMER, Jean b: 06 Nov 1849 in Bech, Lux d: 06 Nov 1849 in
 Bech, Lux r: bd

8 FIXMER, Susanne b: 09 Nov 1850 in Bech, Lux d: 01 Jun
 1851 in Bech, Lux r: bd

8 FIXMER, Elisabeth b: 24 Dec 1854 in Bech, Lux r: b

+ seq: 164.10 THILL, Pierre b: Abt. 1851 w: Abt. 1880

8 FIXMER, Catherine b: 24 Mar 1857 in Bech, Lux r: b

+ seq: 164.20 BAUM, Jean b: Abt. 1854 w: Abt. 1880

165

7 [1] WITRY, Peter b: 30 Jun 1821 in Beidweiler, Lux d: 13 Aug

1888 in Beidweiler, Lux v: Beidweiler, Lux o: Thatcher o: Day
Laborer o: Linen weaver r: bd c: 6
+ seq: 165 GILLES, Barbara b: Abt. 1820 in Schuttrange, Lux w:
Abt. 1845 a: Gregorius v: Beidweiler, Lux o: Midwife
* 2nd Wife of [1] WITRY, Peter:
+ seq: 166 STIREN, Margaretha b: 25 Feb 1821 in Heffingen,
Lux d: 19 Mar 1877 in Beidweiler, Lux w: 23 Dec 1847 in
Rodenbourg, Lux v: Beidweiler, Lux o: Cobbler o: Day laborer
o: Seamstress r: d r: m f: Nicolas Stiren m: Elisabeth Peckes
c: 6
8 WITRY, Barbara b: 23 Oct 1848 in Beidweiler, Lux d: 01 Nov
1916 in Beidweiler, Lux v: Beidweiler, Lux o: Day laborer r: b
c: 6
+ seq: 166.01 KOERNER, Adam b: 09 May 1835 in Farschweiler
Kreis, Germany d: Bef. 1885 w: 22 Jan 1867 in Rodenbourg,
Lux v: Beidweiler, Lux o: Day laborer r: m f: Mathias Koerner
m: Barbara Schichel c: 6
8 WITRY, Elisabeth (Elise) b: 11 Apr 1850 in Beidweiler, Lux h:
Hoehl v: Beidweiler, Lux o: Day laborer o: Midwife o: Baker
r: b c: 6
+ seq: 166.02 FLAMMANG, Peter b: 09 Jan 1854 in Boudler,
Lux d: 20 Jul 1903 in Beidweiler, Lux w: 26 Nov 1879 in
Rodenbourg, Lux h: Hoehl v: Beidweiler, Lux o: Day laborer
o: Master tailor o: Blacksmith r: m f: Peter Flammang m:
Barbara Kieffer c: 6
8 WITRY, Johann b: 08 May 1852 in Beidweiler, Lux i:
Emigrated to France and the U. S. r: b
8 WITRY, Mathias b: 24 Jun 1856 in Beidweiler, Lux d: 17 Apr
1926 in Walferdange, Lux v: Walferdange, Lux o: Painter to
the Grand Duke Adolphe o: Artist o: Royal administrator r: b
c: 3
+ seq: 166.02.01 BACKES, Margareta b: 23 Sep 1860 in Clausen,
Lux d: 04 Jul 1932 in Bonnevoie, Lux w: 11 Sep 1894 v:
Walferdange, Lux f: Nilolaus Backes m: Maria Jones c: 3
8 WITRY, Peter b: 12 Nov 1858 in Beidweiler, Lux d: 25 Apr
1927 h: 1 Stadthausplatz v: Esch-sur-Alzette, Lux v:
Differdange, Lux o: Rural Guard r: b c: 6
+ seq: 166.03 PAULUS, Caroline b: 04 Mar 1866 in Esch-sur-
Alzette, Lux d: 27 May 1944 w: 02 Sep 1887 in Esch-sur-
Alzette, Lux v: Esch-sur-Alzette, Lux v: Differdange, Lux o:
No profession c: 6

8 WITRY, Franz b: 15 Jul 1861 in Beidweiler, Lux d: 28 Feb 1867 in Beidweiler, Lux v: Beidweiler, Lux o: No profession r: bd

166.01

8 WITRY, Barbara b: 23 Oct 1848 in Beidweiler, Lux d: 01 Nov 1916 in Beidweiler, Lux v: Beidweiler, Lux o: Day laborer r: b c: 6

+ seq: 166.01 KOERNER, Adam b: 09 May 1835 in Farschweiler Kreis, Germany d: Bef. 1885 w: 22 Jan 1867 in Rodenbourg, Lux v: Beidweiler, Lux o: Day laborer r: m f: Mathias Koerner m: Barbara Schichel c: 6

9 KOERNER, Nicolas b: 03 Nov 1867 in Beidweiler, Lux r: b

9 KOERNER, Nicolas-Emil b: 21 Jan 1870 in Beidweiler, Lux r: b

9 KOERNER, Johann b: 22 Dec 1872 in Beidweiler, Lux o: Day laborer r: b

9 KOERNER, Peter b: 13 Apr 1875 in Beidweiler, Lux r: b

9 KOERNER, Mathias b: 07 Sep 1878 in Beidweiler, Lux r: b

9 WITRY, Johanna (Jeanne) b: 22 Aug 1885 in Beidweiler, Lux o: No profession r: b

+ seq: 166.01.50 USELDINGER, Wilhelm b: 17 Oct 1881 in Dalheim, Lux w: 13 Oct 1906 in Rodenbourg, Lux o: Master house painter r: m f: Nicolas Uscheldinger m: Catharina Feidt

166.02

8 WITRY, Elisabeth (Elise) b: 11 Apr 1850 in Beidweiler, Lux h: Hoehl v: Beidweiler, Lux o: Day laborer o: Midwife o: Baker r: b c: 6

+ seq: 166.02 FLAMMANG, Peter b: 09 Jan 1854 in Boudler, Lux d: 20 Jul 1903 in Beidweiler, Lux w: 26 Nov 1879 in Rodenbourg, Lux h: Hoehl v: Beidweiler, Lux o: Day laborer o: Master tailor o: Blacksmith r: m f: Peter Flammang m: Barbara Kieffer c: 6

9 FLAMMANG, Marie b: 08 Feb 1881 in Beidweiler, Lux r: b

9 FLAMMANG, Catherine b: 19 Feb 1883 in Beidweiler, Lux o: Midwife r: b

+ seq: 166.02.00 SCHMIT, Johann b: 25 Jan 1869 in Landsweiler, France d: 20 Jul 1903 in Beidweiler, Lux w: 28 Jan 1903 in Rodenbourg, Lux o: Day laborer r: d r: m f: Nicolas Schmidt m: Elisabetha Doerr

9 FLAMMANG, Marie b: 13 Nov 1885 in Beidweiler, Lux r: b
9 FLAMMANG, Mathias b: 22 Jan 1889 in Beidweiler, Lux r: b
9 FLAMMANG, Catherine-Justine b: 11 Feb 1891 in Beidweiler,
  Lux r: b
9 FLAMMANG, Emil b: 08 Oct 1895 in Beidweiler, Lux r: b

166.02.01
8 WITRY, Mathias b: 24 Jun 1856 in Beidweiler, Lux d: 17 Apr
  1926 in Walferdange, Lux v: Walferdange, Lux o: Painter to
  the Grand Duke Adolphe o: Artist o: Royal administrator r: b
  c: 3
+ seq: 166.02.01 BACKES, Margareta b: 23 Sep 1860 in
  Clausen, Lux d: 04 Jul 1932 in Bonnevoie, Lux w: 11 Sep
  1894 v: Walferdange, Lux f: Nilolaus Backes m: Maria Jones
  c: 3
9 WITRY, Maria b: 07 Jul 1895 in Walferdange, Lux
+ seq: 166.02.02 w: Abt. 1920 in Germany
9 WITRY, Jacob b: 21 Oct 1896 in Walferdange, Lux d: 31 May
  1923 in Walferdange, Lux
9 WITRY, Gregoire b: 15 Feb 1899 in Walferdange, Lux d: 14
  Feb 1967 in Luxembourg, Lux v: Bonnevoie, Lux o: Train
  conductor c: 1
+ seq: 166.02.03 LUTGEN, Susanne b: 05 Nov 1905 in Colmar,
  Lux d: 22 May 1969 in Ettelbruck, Lux w: 04 Nov 1932 in
  Walferdange, Lux f: Michel Lutgen m: Angelika Lesch c: 1

166.02.03
9 WITRY, Gregoire b: 15 Feb 1899 in Walferdange, Lux d: 14
  Feb 1967 in Luxembourg, Lux v: Bonnevoie, Lux o: Train
  conductor c: 1
+ seq: 166.02.03 LUTGEN, Susanne b: 05 Nov 1905 in Colmar,
  Lux d: 22 May 1969 in Ettelbruck, Lux w: 04 Nov 1932 in
  Walferdange, Lux f: Michel Lutgen m: Angelika Lesch c: 1
10WITRY, Jeanne-Margerite (Janine) b: 06 Nov 1937 in
  Hollarich, Lux v: Clemency, Lux c: 2
+ seq: 166.02.04 SALES, Pierre-Joseph-Henri (Jos) b: 19 Dec
  1932 in Hamm, Lux d: 02 Apr 1989 in Walferdange, Lux w:
  19 Jun 1959 in Bonnevoie, Lux v: Walferdange, Lux c: 2

166.02.04
10WITRY, Jeanne-Margerite (Janine) b: 06 Nov 1937 in

Hollarich, Lux v: Clemency, Lux c: 2
+ seq: 166.02.04 SALES, Pierre-Joseph-Henri (Jos) b: 19 Dec
   1932 in Hamm, Lux d: 02 Apr 1989 in Walferdange, Lux w:
   19 Jun 1959 in Bonnevoie, Lux v: Walferdange, Lux c: 2
11 SALES, Jean-Louis b: 11 Aug 1960 in Luxembourg, Lux v:
   Luxembourg, Lux o: Licensed engineer c: 2
+ seq: 166.02.05 HAMES, Monique b: 27 Aug 1962 w: 1990 v:
11 SALES, Andre b: 22 Jul 1963 in Luxembourg, Lux v:
   Bereldange, Lux o: Works for the city of Luxembourg

166.02.05
11 SALES, Jean-Louis b: 11 Aug 1960 in Luxembourg, Lux v:
   Luxembourg, Lux o: Licensed engineer c: 2
+ seq: 166.02.05 HAMES, Monique b: 27 Aug 1962 w: 1990 v:
   Luxembourg, Lux c: 2
12 SALES, Yan b: 06 Jul 1991 in Luxembourg, Lux
12 SALES, Max b: 22 Feb 1994 in Luxembourg, Lux

166.03
8 WITRY, Peter b: 12 Nov 1858 in Beidweiler, Lux d: 25 Apr
   1927 h: 1 Stadthausplatz v: Esch-sur-Alzette, Lux v:
   Differdange, Lux o: Official o: Rural Guard r: b c: 6
+ seq: 166.03 PAULUS, Caroline b: 04 Mar 1866 in Esch-sur-
   Alzette, Lux d: 27 May 1944 w: 02 Sep 1887 in Esch-sur-
   Alzette, Lux v: Esch-sur-Alzette, Lux v: Differdange, Lux o:
   No profession c: 6
9 WITRY, Mathias-Marcel-Julius b: 23 Jul 1888 in Esch-sur-
   Alzette, Lux d: 06 May 1925 in Differdange, Lux v:
   Differdange, Lux o: Electrician o: Painter to the Grand Duke
   Adolphe o: Artist r: b
+ seq: 166.03.50 SAND, Amelie b: 23 Oct 1889 in
   Niederkerschen, Lux w: 18 Apr 1923 in Luxembourg, Lux o:
   No profession r: m f: Franz Sand m: Maria Brandenburger
9 WITRY, Maria-Augusta b: 23 Jan 1890 in Esch-sur-Alzette,
   Lux r: b
9 WITRY, Maria-Anna-Caroline b: 28 Feb 1891 in Esch-sur-
   Alzette, Lux d: 05 Mar 1891 in Esch-sur-Alzette, Lux r: bd
9 WITRY, Josephine-Augusta-Hilda b: 02 Aug 1892 in Esch-sur-
   Alzette, Lux d: 1981 in Differdange, Lux r: b
9 WITRY, Theodore-Mathias-Vincenz b: 05 Apr 1894 in Esch-
   sur-Alzette, Lux d: 16 Jan 1963 o: Technical manager r: b

9 WITRY, Nicolas-Marie-Camille b: 22 Jul 1899 in Differdange,
Lux d: 01 Jun 1975 in Differdange, Lux v: Differdange, Lux o:
Steel wire drawer o: Lathe foreman c: 1
+ seq: 166.04 LOGELIN, Leonie b: 11 Nov 1901 in Differdange,
Lux d: 05 Jun 1942 w: Abt. 1925 o: Merchant c: 1

166.04

9 WITRY, Nicolas-Marie-Camille b: 22 Jul 1899 in Differdange,
Lux d: 01 Jun 1975 in Differdange, Lux v: Differdange, Lux o:
Steel wire drawer o: Lathe foreman c: 1
+ seq: 166.04 LOGELIN, Leonie b: 11 Nov 1901 in Differdange,
Lux d: 05 Jun 1942 w: Abt. 1925 o: Merchant c: 1
10 WITRY, Carola-Catherine-Marie-Madelaine b: 02 Nov 1927 in
Differdange, Lux v: Huldange, Lux o: Merchant c: 1
+ seq: 166.05 PUTZ, Edouard-Pierre b: 27 Dec 1926 in Esch-sur-
Alzette, Lux d: 24 Mar 2003 in Huldange, Lux w: Abt. 1945 in
Huldange, Lux v: Huldange, Lux i: European champion for
working dogs o: Expert dog trainer c: 1

166.05

10 WITRY, Carola-Catherine-Marie-Madelaine b: 02 Nov 1927 in
Differdange, Lux v: Huldange, Lux o: Merchant c: 1
+ seq: 166.05 PUTZ, Edouard-Pierre b: 27 Dec 1926 in Esch-sur-
Alzette, Lux d: 24 Mar 2003 in Huldange, Lux w: Abt. 1945 in
Huldange, Lux v: Huldange, Lux i: European champion for
working dogs o: Expert dog trainer c: 1
11 PUTZ, Nicole-Barbe b: 24 Apr 1947 c: 2
+ seq: 166.20 LEYERS, Camille d: 07 Feb 1996 w: Abt. 1965
o: Policeman c: 2

166.20

11 PUTZ, Nicole-Barbe b: 24 Apr 1947 c: 2
+ seq: 166.20 LEYERS, Camille d: 07 Feb 1996 w: Abt. 1965
o: Policeman c: 2
12 LEYERS, Albertine-Barbara (Babsi) b: 10 Jan 1967 o:
Bookkeeper c: 2
+ seq: 166.30 STRENG, Romain w: Abt. 1996 o: Fire fighter c:
2
12 LEYERS, Carol-Nicolas b: 10 Nov 1969 c: 1
+ seq: 166.40 JUNGERS, Sonja w: Abt. 2001 c: 1

166.30

12LEYERS, Albertine-Barbara (Babsi) b: 10 Jan 1967 o: Bookkeeper c: 2
+ seq: 166.30 STRENG, Romain w: Abt. 1996 o: Fire fighter c: 2
13STRENG, Laura b: 29 Apr 1998
13STRENG, Yannick b: 16 Feb 2001

166.40

12LEYERS, Carol-Nicolas b: 10 Nov 1969 c: 1
+ seq: 166.40 JUNGERS, Sonja w: Abt. 2001 c: 1
13LEYERS, Nastasja-Nicole b: 10 Jan 2003

167

7 WITTRY, Jacob b: 08 Oct 1824 in Beidweiler, Lux d: 30 Apr 1906 in Aurora, IL a: Witry v: Big Woods, IL v: Beidweiler, Lux i: Emigrated to Aurora, IL i: Discharge from militia i: Arrived in New York on the Vulture with wife and two children o: Servant o: Day laborer o: Farmer r: bdx c: 8
+ seq: 167 SCHONS, Magdalena b: 08 Mar 1827 in Olingen, Lux d: 08 Sep 1888 in Aurora, IL Cause of death: Heart illness w: 21 May 1851 in Rodenbourg, Lux v: Big Woods, IL v: Beidweiler, Lux i: Emigrated to Aurora, IL o: Farmer r: bd r: m f: Peter Schons m: Margaretha Stoos c: 8
8 WITTRY, Margaretha b: 27 Aug 1851 in Beidweiler, Lux d: 16 Sep 1864 in Aurora, IL v: Aurora, IL r: b
8 WITTRY, Michel b: 11 Jul 1853 in Beidweiler, Lux d: 15 Apr 1919 in Aurora, IL v: Aurora, IL o: Machinist at CB&Q Railroad r: bx c: 6
+ seq: 168 WELTER, Agnes b: 02 Aug 1859 d: 27 Jun 1941 in Aurora, IL w: 02 Apr 1877 v: Aurora, IL c: 6
8 WITTRY, Anna b: 25 May 1856 in Aurora, IL d: 13 Jan 1940 v: Big Rock, IL c: 9
+ seq: 172.37 PLAIN, John W. b: 30 Nov 1852 d: 08 Jul 1929 w: 30 Oct 1878 v: Big Rock, IL c: 9
8 WITTRY, Henry b: 20 Jun 1858 in Aurora, IL d: 19 Mar 1911 in Aurora, IL Cause of death: arteriosclerosis v: Kaneville, IL c: 11
+ seq: 173 MOLITOR, Margaret b: 08 Mar 1861 in Dacada, WI d: 16 Jul 1944 w: 17 Jan 1882 v: Kaneville, IL f: Peter Molitor m: Mary Thill c: 11

8 WITTRY, John b: 20 Sep 1860 in Aurora, IL d: 15 Oct 1943 in Aurora, IL h: 747 Liberty v: Big Rock, IL o: Farmer c: 8

+ seq: 182 WITTRY, Barbara b: 27 Apr 1864 in Ernzen, Lux d: 30 Mar 1933 in Aurora, IL w: 18 Feb 1886 in Aurora, IL a: Witry h: 747 Liberty v: Big Rock, IL i: Emigrated to Aurora, IL r: b f: Paul Wittry m: Marie Weber c: 8

8 WITTRY, Nick b: 28 Feb 1862 in Aurora, IL d: 30 Oct 1935 v: Kaneville, IL o: Farmer c: 6

+ seq: 203 DOCKENDORF, Lena b: 13 Jan 1866 in Michelau, Lux d: 07 May 1948 in Kaneville, IL w: 14 Apr 1885 v: Kaneville, IL r: d f: Nicolaus Dockendorf m: Magdalena c: 6

8 WITTRY, Adam b: 18 May 1864 in Aurora, IL d: 10 Sep 1940 in Aurora, IL v: Aurora, IL i: Elected VP of German Settlers in Aurora i: Alderman of 7th Ward i: President of American-Luxembourger Club o: Machinist at W W Mach Co r: x c: 5

+ seq: 208 HUSS, Mary S. b: 15 May 1867 in Chicago, IL d: 23 Jul 1946 in Aurora, IL w: 14 May 1889 in Aurora, IL v: Aurora, IL f: Peter Huss c: 5

8 WITTRY, Lena b: 07 Oct 1867 in Aurora, IL d: 03 Feb 1909 v: Chicago, IL

+ seq: 213.01 REITZ, August W. b: 06 Oct 1868 d: 19 May 1937 w: 11 Feb 1892 v: Chicago, IL

168

8 WITTRY, Michel b: 11 Jul 1853 in Beidweiler, Lux d: 15 Apr 1919 in Aurora, IL v: Aurora, IL o: Machinist at CB&Q Railroad r: bx c: 6

+ seq: 168 WELTER, Agnes b: 02 Aug 1859 d: 27 Jun 1941 in Aurora, IL w: 02 Apr 1877 v: Aurora, IL c: 6

9 WITTRY, Nickolas M. b: 19 Jan 1878 d: 28 Apr 1960 v: Aurora, IL o: Machinist at CB&Q Railroad c: 4

+ seq: 169 MEARS, Elizabeth b: 04 Dec 1878 d: 08 Oct 1965 w: 09 Sep 1903 v: Aurora, IL c: 4

9 WITTRY, Elizabeth b: 15 Apr 1880 d: 08 May 1957 v: Aurora, IL c: 8

+ seq: 171.01 SPANG, Peter J. b: 28 Jan 1877 in Aurora, IL d: 23 Sep 1941 in Aurora, IL w: 10 Nov 1903 in Aurora, IL v: Aurora, IL r: x f: John Spang m: Mary Stevens c: 8

9 WITTRY, Henry b: 20 Jun 1882 d: 23 Jun 1956 v: Aurora, IL o: Machinist at CB&Q Railroad c: 3

+ seq: 172 DRAUDT, Mary b: 24 Sep 1884 d: 26 Apr 1965 w:

08 Jul 1908 in Aurora, IL v: Aurora, IL r: x f: Peter Draudt c: 3

9 WITTRY, Anna b: 16 Mar 1885 d: 20 Jul 1974 v: Aurora, IL c: 2

+ seq: 172.21 THEIS, Nicholas A. b: 23 Aug 1884 d: 08 Oct 1953 w: Abt. 1910 v: Aurora, IL f: John Theis m: Catherine Clemens c: 2

9 WITTRY, Mary M. b: 03 Jun 1888 in Aurora, IL d: 03 Aug 1932 in Aurora, IL v: Aurora, IL o: Worked at Aurora Cotton Mills c: 3

+ seq: 172.24 FRIEDERS, John-Aloysius b: 17 Jan 1891 in Aurora, IL d: 22 Jul 1957 in Aurora, IL w: Abt. 1915 v: Aurora, IL f: Michael-Nicholas Frieders m: Magdalena (Lena) Molitor c: 3

9 WITTRY, Theresa-Mary b: 09 Mar 1893 in Aurora, IL d: 26 Nov 1895 in Aurora, IL v: Aurora, IL r: x

+ seq: 172.36 LIES, Peter-Paul b: 15 Dec 1892 in Sugar Grove, IL d: 13 Dec 1982 in Aurora, IL w: 01 Apr 1918 in Aurora, IL v: Aurora, IL f: Peter Lies m: Magdalena Frieders

169

9 WITTRY, Nickolas M. b: 19 Jan 1878 d: 28 Apr 1960 v: Aurora, IL o: Machinist at CB&Q Railroad c: 4

+ seq: 169 MEARS, Elizabeth b: 04 Dec 1878 d: 08 Oct 1965 w: 09 Sep 1903 v: Aurora, IL c: 4

10 WITTRY, Margaret b: 15 Dec 1905 d: 20 Jun 1990 in Burlingame, CA v: Burlingame, CA

+ seq: 169.01 DAVIDSON, James b: 23 Nov 1899 d: 01 Sep 1986 in Burlingame, CA w: Abt. 1930 v: Burlingame, CA o: Pharmacist

10[1] WITTRY, Alois b: 02 May 1908 d: 04 Oct 1974 in Florida v: Aurora, IL

+ seq: 170 TELLISON, Dorothy b: 23 Feb 1915 w: Abt. 1940 v: Aurora, IL

* 2nd Wife of [1] WITTRY, Alois:

+ seq: 171 JOHNSON, Ione b: 28 Nov 1901 d: 19 Dec 1981 w: Abt. 1960 v: Aurora, IL o: Bookkeeper

10 WITTRY, Marie b: 10 Jul 1911 d: 11 Jul 1911

10 WITTRY, Charles b: 15 Aug 1914 d: 05 Jun 1954

171.01

9 WITTRY, Elizabeth b: 15 Apr 1880 d: 08 May 1957 v: Aurora, IL c: 8

+ seq: 171.01 SPANG, Peter J. b: 28 Jan 1877 in Aurora, IL d: 23 Sep 1941 in Aurora, IL w: 10 Nov 1903 in Aurora, IL v: Aurora, IL r: x f: John Spang m: Mary Stevens c: 8

10 SPANG, John b: 29 Jul 1904 d: 08 Jul 1953 c: 4

+ seq: 171.02 STULL, Hildegarde b: 17 Aug 1904 d: 26 Jan 1989 w: Abt. 1926 c: 4

10 SPANG, Mary b: 07 Jun 1905 d: 13 Aug 1981 c: 1

+ seq: 171.23 ANDERSON, Carl b: 23 Nov 1904 d: 17 Nov 1965 w: Abt. 1935 c: 1

10 SPANG, Agnes b: 29 Oct 1906 d: 10 Jun 1975 c: 4

+ seq: 171.29 KOHLEY, Ralph b: 14 May 1905 d: 04 Feb 1973 w: Abt. 1929 c: 4

10 SPANG, Henry b: 02 Sep 1910 d: 16 Apr 1958

+ seq: 171.39 BYERS, Eva b: 07 Apr 1914 w: Abt. 1940

10 SPANG, Ann b: 19 Jul 1912 d: 30 Apr 1958 c: 3

+ seq: 171.40 TANNENBAUM, George b: 25 May 1910 w: Abt. 1931 c: 3

10 SPANG, Ursula (Sally) b: 31 Mar 1916 v: Aurora, IL c: 3

+ seq: 171.47 OBERMAN, John P. b: 10 Mar 1912 d: 10 Feb 1993 in Aurora, IL w: Abt. 1940 v: Aurora, IL c: 3

10 SPANG, Theresa b: 14 Feb 1919 d: 23 Apr 1980 c: 4

+ seq: 171.51 HIGHT, Charles b: 11 Feb 1914 d: 10 Jun 1973 w: Abt. 1940 c: 4

10 SPANG, Margaret b: 19 Jul 1920 d: 20 May 1968 c: 2

+ seq: 171.57 ERATH, Harry b: 21 Aug 1919 w: Abt. 1943 c: 2

171.02

10 SPANG, John b: 29 Jul 1904 d: 08 Jul 1953 c: 4

+ seq: 171.02 STULL, Hildegarde b: 17 Aug 1904 d: 26 Jan 1989 w: Abt. 1926 c: 4

11 SPANG, Gerald b: 26 Dec 1927 v: Batavia, IL c: 6

+ seq: 171.03 GASPAR, Donna b: 04 Sep 1931 w: Abt. 1950 v: Batavia, IL c: 6

11 SPANG, Choral b: 22 Feb 1930 v: Aurora, IL c: 6

+ seq: 171.09 WATGEN, Robert b: 05 Sep 1931 w: Abt. 1951 v: Aurora, IL c: 6

11 SPANG, Joan b: 14 Mar 1931 v: Millington, IL c: 4

+ seq: 171.16 KANE, Ted b: Abt. 1930 w: Abt. 1950 v:

Millington, IL c: 4

11 SPANG, Thomas b: 25 Sep 1932 d: 11 May 1999 in Batavia, IL
v: Batavia, IL i: Board member of Catholic school and charity
organizations i: Scout leader and 4-H leader o: Barber Greene
c: 6

+ seq: 171.18 FEUERBORN, Joan F. b: 22 Apr 1931 w: 18 Jun
1955 in Batavia, IL v: Batavia, IL c: 6

171.03

11 SPANG, Gerald b: 26 Dec 1927 v: Batavia, IL c: 6

+ seq: 171.03 GASPAR, Donna b: 04 Sep 1931 w: Abt. 1950 v:
Batavia, IL c: 6

12 SPANG, Mark b: 12 Nov 1951 c: 2

+ seq: 171.04 TILLIS, Cheryl b: 02 Jun 1957 w: Abt. 1980 c: 2

12 [1] SPANG, Kim b: 26 Sep 1953

+ seq: 171.05 BURGHOLZER, Kim b: 25 Nov 1956 w: Abt.
1980

* 2nd Wife of [1] SPANG, Kim:

+ seq: 171.06 FOWLER, Anne b: 08 Feb 1959 w: Abt. 1985

12 SPANG, Brian J. b: 23 May 1957 c: 1

+ seq: 171.07 KELLY, Geraldine b: 21 Feb 1956 w: Abt. 1980
c: 1

12 SPANG, Tracy b: 18 Nov 1959 c: 1

+ seq: 171.08 JOY, Peter-Douglas b: 30 Jan 1958 w: Abt. 1985
c: 1

12 SPANG, Nicholas b: 13 Apr 1964

12 SPANG, Lisa b: 15 Sep 1966

171.04

12 SPANG, Mark b: 12 Nov 1951 c: 2

+ seq: 171.04 TILLIS, Cheryl b: 02 Jun 1957 w: Abt. 1980 c: 2

13 SPANG, Justin-Arthur b: 04 Jun 1981

13 SPANG, Nathan-Christopher b: 12 Dec 1984

171.07

12 SPANG, Brian J. b: 23 May 1957 c: 1

+ seq: 171.07 KELLY, Geraldine b: 21 Feb 1956 w: Abt. 1980
c: 1

13 SPANG, Matthew b: 06 Jun 1984

171.08

12 SPANG, Tracy b: 18 Nov 1959 c: 1
+ seq: 171.08 JOY, Peter-Douglas b: 30 Jan 1958 w: Abt. 1985
  c: 1
13 JOY, Hannah-Elizabeth b: 26 Jul 1988

171.09

11 SPANG, Choral b: 22 Feb 1930 v: Aurora, IL c: 6
+ seq: 171.09 WATGEN, Robert b: 05 Sep 1931 w: Abt. 1951
  v: Aurora, IL c: 6
12 WATGEN, Thomas b: 17 Feb 1952 c: 2
+ seq: 171.10 BELLER, Linda b: 26 May 1952 w: Abt. 1975 c:
  2
12 WATGEN, Dennis b: 04 Dec 1952 c: 3
+ seq: 171.11 SCHINDLBECK, Joyce b: 12 Jul 1954 w: Abt.
  1975 c: 3
12 WATGEN, Katherine b: 31 Oct 1953 c: 2
+ seq: 171.12 BERENYI, Richard b: 24 Nov 1948 w: Abt. 1980
  c: 2
12 WATGEN, Deborah b: 23 Sep 1954 c: 4
+ seq: 171.13 SOLECKI, Michael b: 07 May 1954 w: Abt. 1976
  c: 4
12 WATGEN, Donald b: 26 Feb 1955 c: 3
+ seq: 171.14 CRAWFORD, Susan b: 22 Jun 1955 d: 04 Sep
  1990 w: Abt. 1980 c: 3
12 WATGEN, William b: 26 Dec 1957
+ seq: 171.15 RETTERER, Wendy b: Abt. 1960 w: Abt. 1985

171.10

12 WATGEN, Thomas b: 17 Feb 1952 c: 2
+ seq: 171.10 BELLER, Linda b: 26 May 1952 w: Abt. 1975 c:
  2
13 WATGEN, James b: 02 Jun 1978
13 WATGEN, Sarah-Jane b: 29 Mar 1982

171.11

12 WATGEN, Dennis b: 04 Dec 1952 c: 3
+ seq: 171.11 SCHINDLBECK, Joyce b: 12 Jul 1954 w: Abt.
  1975 c: 3
13 WATGEN, Jacob b: Abt. 1977
13 WATGEN, Nicholas b: 15 Nov 1979

13 WATGEN, Shannon b: 12 Mar 1981

171.12

12 WATGEN, Katherine b: 31 Oct 1953 c: 2
+ seq: 171.12 BERENYI, Richard b: 24 Nov 1948 w: Abt. 1980
  c: 2
13 BERENYI, Timothy b: 28 Jul 1981
13 BERENYI, Catherine b: 08 Nov 1982

171.13

12 WATGEN, Deborah b: 23 Sep 1954 c: 4
+ seq: 171.13 SOLECKI, Michael b: 07 May 1954 w: Abt. 1976
  c: 4
13 SOLECKI, Michelle b: 15 Feb 1979
13 SOLECKI, Marci-Ann b: 17 Dec 1981
13 SOLECKI, Daniel b: 28 Mar 1983
13 SOLECKI, Joseph b: 15 Mar 1987

171.14

12 WATGEN, Donald b: 26 Feb 1955 c: 3
+ seq: 171.14 CRAWFORD, Susan b: 22 Jun 1955 d: 04 Sep
  1990 w: Abt. 1980 c: 3
13 WATGEN, Kara b: 04 Sep 1980
13 WATGEN, Krystan b: 12 Sep 1983
13 WATGEN, Adam b: Abt. 1985

171.16

11 SPANG, Joan b: 14 Mar 1931 v: Millington, IL c: 4
+ seq: 171.16 KANE, Ted b: Abt. 1930 w: Abt. 1950 v:
  Millington, IL c: 4
12 KANE, Candace b: 22 Aug 1953
+ seq: 171.17 WHITFIELD, Robert b: Abt. 1950 w: Abt. 1975
12 KANE, Sherry b: Abt. 1955
12 KANE, Susan b: Abt. 1955
12 KANE, Sandra b: Abt. 1955

171.18

11 SPANG, Thomas b: 25 Sep 1932 d: 11 May 1999 in Batavia, IL
  v: Batavia, IL i: Board member of Catholic school and charity
  organizations i: Scout leader and 4-H leader o: Barber Greene
  c: 6

+ seq: 171.18 FEUERBORN, Joan F. b: 22 Apr 1931 w: 18 Jun
    1955 in Batavia, IL v: Batavia, IL c: 6
12 SPANG, John T. b: 25 Mar 1958 v: Batavia, IL c: 1
+ seq: 171.19 SLOCUM, Debra b: 10 Nov 1960 w: Abt. 1981 v:
    Batavia, IL c: 1
12 SPANG, Mary C. b: 13 Jan 1960 v: Sugar Grove, IL c: 3
+ seq: 171.20 ALBRECHT, Michael b: 21 Sep 1959 w: Abt.
    1981 v: Sugar Grove, IL c: 3
12 SPANG, David b: 14 Sep 1961 v: Batavia, IL c: 3
+ seq: 171.21 HORA, Jill b: 03 May 1962 w: Abt. 1982 v:
    Batavia, IL c: 3
12 SPANG, Laura H. b: 16 Oct 1963 v: Batavia, IL
12 SPANG, Diane b: 26 Oct 1967 v: North Aurora, IL c: 2
+ seq: 171.22 APPEL, Bryan b: 01 Sep 1964 w: Abt. 1990 v:
    North Aurora, IL c: 2
12 SPANG, Gregory b: 10 Jun 1971 v: Chicago, IL

171.19
12 SPANG, John T. b: 25 Mar 1958 v: Batavia, IL c: 1
+ seq: 171.19 SLOCUM, Debra b: 10 Nov 1960 w: Abt. 1981 v:
    Batavia, IL c: 1
13 SPANG, Jessica-Rose b: 05 Jan 1983

171.20
12 SPANG, Mary C. b: 13 Jan 1960 v: Sugar Grove, IL c: 3
+ seq: 171.20 ALBRECHT, Michael b: 21 Sep 1959 w: Abt.
    1981 v: Sugar Grove, IL c: 3
13 ALBRECHT, Patrick-Michael b: 15 Jun 1983
13 ALBRECHT, Michelle b: 12 Apr 1985
13 ALBRECHT, Daniel-Thomas b: 10 Oct 1987

171.21
12 SPANG, David b: 14 Sep 1961 v: Batavia, IL c: 3
+ seq: 171.21 HORA, Jill b: 03 May 1962 w: Abt. 1982 v:
    Batavia, IL c: 3
13 SPANG, Christi b: 17 Feb 1984
13 SPANG, Kelly b: 06 Aug 1986
13 SPANG, Eric-John b: 11 Mar 1991

171.22
12 SPANG, Diane b: 26 Oct 1967 v: North Aurora, IL c: 2

+ seq: 171.22 APPEL, Bryan b: 01 Sep 1964 w: Abt. 1990 v:
    North Aurora, IL c: 2
13 APPEL, Davis
13 APPEL, Rose

171.23
10 SPANG, Mary b: 07 Jun 1905 d: 13 Aug 1981 c: 1
+ seq: 171.23 ANDERSON, Carl b: 23 Nov 1904 d: 17 Nov
    1965 w: Abt. 1935 c: 1
11 ANDERSON, Phyllis-Corrine b: 20 Mar 1939 c: 3
+ seq: 171.24 MEYER, Jerry b: 19 Apr 1936 w: Abt. 1959 c: 3

171.24
11 ANDERSON, Phyllis-Corrine b: 20 Mar 1939 c: 3
+ seq: 171.24 MEYER, Jerry b: 19 Apr 1936 w: Abt. 1959 c: 3
12 [1] MEYER, Lianne-Kay b: 26 Jan 1960 c: 2
+ seq: 171.25 HALLING, David b: 17 Feb 1959 w: Abt. 1979 c:
    2
* 2nd Husband of [1] MEYER, Lianne-Kay:
+ seq: 171.26 SPENCER, John b: Abt. 1955 d: 09 Jul 1981 w:
    Abt. 1985
12 MEYER, Gregory-John b: 18 Mar 1961 c: 1
+ seq: 171.27 WEISTROFFER, Jane b: 11 Sep 1958 w: Abt.
    1986 c: 1
12 MEYER, Dawn-Corrine b: 19 Jun 1964 c: 1
+ seq: 171.28 JARKA, Tim b: Jun 1962 w: Abt. 1987 c: 1

171.25
12 [1] MEYER, Lianne-Kay b: 26 Jan 1960 c: 2
+ seq: 171.25 HALLING, David b: 17 Feb 1959 w: Abt. 1979 c:
    2
13 HALLING, Joshua-Spencer b: 20 Nov 1980
13 HALLING, Cory-David b: 14 Jun 1985
* 2nd Husband of [1] MEYER, Lianne-Kay:
+ seq: 171.26 SPENCER, John b: Abt. 1955 d: 09 Jul 1981 w:
    Abt. 1985

171.27
12 MEYER, Gregory-John b: 18 Mar 1961 c: 1
+ seq: 171.27 WEISTROFFER, Jane b: 11 Sep 1958 w: Abt.
    1986 c: 1

13MEYER, Amanda-Marie b: 07 Aug 1989

171.28
12MEYER, Dawn-Corrine b: 19 Jun 1964 c: 1
+ seq: 171.28 JARKA, Tim b: Jun 1962 w: Abt. 1987 c: 1
13JARKA, Zarchary-Alan b: 27 Nov 1989

171.29
10SPANG, Agnes b: 29 Oct 1906 d: 10 Jun 1975 c: 4
+ seq: 171.29 KOHLEY, Ralph b: 14 May 1905 d: 04 Feb 1973
    w: Abt. 1929 c: 4
11KOHLEY, Donald J. b: 07 Feb 1931 v: Huntley, IL c: 4
+ seq: 171.30 DIEHL, Katherine J. (Kathleen) b: 23 Aug 1932
    w: 11 Apr 1953 v: Huntley, IL c: 4
11KOHLEY, Louise b: 19 Mar 1932 v: Aurora, IL
+ seq: 171.35 ZIMAN, John G. b: 09 Oct 1928 d: 19 Feb 1986
    w: 10 Sep 1955 v: Aurora, IL
11KOHLEY, Richard J. b: 30 Aug 1936 in Naperville, IL d: 26
    Aug 2001 in Woodstock, IL v: Huntley, IL c: 3
+ seq: 171.36 MIELKE, Karen b: 24 Oct 1941 d: 12 Oct 1995
    w: 26 Nov 1965 in Naperville, IL v: Huntley, IL c: 3
11KOHLEY, Kenneth R. (Ken) b: 08 Jun 1939 v: Garden Prairie,
    IL c: 3
+ seq: 171.38 MESSMER, Susan C. (Sue) b: 05 Mar 1943 w: 21
    Mar 1964 v: Garden Prairie, IL c: 3

171.30
11KOHLEY, Donald J. b: 07 Feb 1931 v: Huntley, IL c: 4
+ seq: 171.30 DIEHL, Katherine J. (Kathleen) b: 23 Aug 1932
    w: 11 Apr 1953 v: Huntley, IL c: 4
12KOHLEY, Karen L. b: 30 Mar 1954 v: Elgin, IL c: 2
+ seq: 171.31 OSTRANDER, Mark R. b: 09 Mar 1954 w: 04 Oct
    1975 v: Elgin, IL c: 2
12KOHLEY, Donna K. b: 14 Jun 1955 v: Huntley, IL c: 2
+ seq: 171.32 KALSOW, Thomas N. b: 19 Jul 1954 w: 11 Jun
    1977 v: Huntley, IL c: 2
12KOHLEY, Thomas K. b: 25 Sep 1957 v: Dundee, IL c: 3
+ seq: 171.33 KUNDE, Becky S. b: 31 Mar 1963 w: 24 Aug
    1991 v: Dundee, IL c: 3
12KOHLEY, Sandra L. b: 03 Nov 1958 v: Maple Park, IL c: 2
+ seq: 171.34 DEUTSCH, Michael J. b: 09 Sep 1958 w: 14 Aug

1993 v: Maple Park, IL c: 2

171.31

12KOHLEY, Karen L. b: 30 Mar 1954 v: Elgin, IL c: 2
+ seq: 171.31 OSTRANDER, Mark R. b: 09 Mar 1954 w: 04 Oct
   1975 v: Elgin, IL c: 2
13OSTRANDER, Melissa R. b: 19 Dec 1979 v: Chicago, IL
13OSTRANDER, Sara E. b: 03 Mar 1983 v: Chicago, IL

171.32

12KOHLEY, Donna K. b: 14 Jun 1955 v: Huntley, IL c: 2
+ seq: 171.32 KALSOW, Thomas N. b: 19 Jul 1954 w: 11 Jun
   1977 v: Huntley, IL c: 2
13KALSOW, Jason T. b: 18 Jul 1983 v: Stevens Point, WI
13KALSOW, Bradley R. A. b: 20 Feb 1986 v: Stevens Point, WI

171.33

12KOHLEY, Thomas K. b: 25 Sep 1957 v: Dundee, IL c: 3
+ seq: 171.33 KUNDE, Becky S. b: 31 Mar 1963 w: 24 Aug
   1991 v: Dundee, IL c: 3
13KOHLEY, Katelyn M. b: 29 Jan 1993 in Dundee, IL
13KOHLEY, Emily E. b: 24 Mar 1995 in Dundee, IL
13KOHLEY, Jacob T. b: 20 Jun 1997 in Dundee, IL

171.34

12KOHLEY, Sandra L. b: 03 Nov 1958 v: Maple Park, IL c: 2
+ seq: 171.34 DEUTSCH, Michael J. b: 09 Sep 1958 w: 14 Aug
   1993 v: Maple Park, IL c: 2
13STRISSEL, Kyle D. b: 18 May 1984 v: Maple Park, IL
13STRISSEL, Colt A. b: 08 Oct 1986 v: Maple Park, IL

171.36

11KOHLEY, Richard J. b: 30 Aug 1936 in Naperville, IL d: 26
   Aug 2001 in Woodstock, IL v: Huntley, IL c: 3
+ seq: 171.36 MIELKE, Karen b: 24 Oct 1941 d: 12 Oct 1995
   w: 26 Nov 1965 in Naperville, IL v: Huntley, IL c: 3
12KOHLEY, Paula b: 30 Nov 1968 in Woodstock, IL v:
   Woodstock, IL
12KOHLEY, Nancy b: 20 Jul 1970 in Woodstock, IL v:
   Woodstock, IL c: 2
+ seq: 171.37 EHRKE, Robert b: 17 Jul 1971 w: 22 May 1993

v: Woodstock, IL c: 2

12KOHLEY, Laura b: 27 Dec 1977 in Woodstock, IL d: 26 Nov 2006 in Woodstock, IL Cause of death: blood clot on the lung v: Woodstock, IL
+ seq: 171.37.50 FARLEY

171.37

12KOHLEY, Nancy b: 20 Jul 1970 in Woodstock, IL v: Woodstock, IL c: 2
+ seq: 171.37 EHRKE, Robert b: 17 Jul 1971 w: 22 May 1993 v: Woodstock, IL c: 2
13EHRKE, Kaylee-Rose b: 27 Dec 2003 in Woodstock, IL
13EHRKE, Lindsey-Nicole b: 09 Sep 2006 in Woodstock, IL

171.38

11KOHLEY, Kenneth R. (Ken) b: 08 Jun 1939 v: Garden Prairie, IL c: 3
+ seq: 171.38 MESSMER, Susan C. (Sue) b: 05 Mar 1943 w: 21 Mar 1964 v: Garden Prairie, IL c: 3
12KOHLEY, Maggie b: 13 Oct 1968 v: Garden Prairie, IL c: 1
13KOHLEY, Evan b: 21 Jul 1991
12KOHLEY, Peter-Timothy b: 23 Oct 1970 in Aurora, IL d: 09 Nov 1991 in Rockford, IL Cause of death: Automobile accident v: Garden Prairie, IL o: U. S. Air Force
12KOHLEY, Christopher b: 05 Jan 1976 v: Garden Prairie, IL

171.40

10SPANG, Ann b: 19 Jul 1912 d: 30 Apr 1958 c: 3
+ seq: 171.40 TANNENBAUM, George b: 25 May 1910 w: Abt. 1931 c: 3
11TANNENBAUM, Raymond b: 17 Aug 1932 c: 2
+ seq: 171.41 ARBOGAST, Grace b: 01 Jun 1931 w: Abt. 1955 c: 2
11[1] TANNENBAUM, Robert b: 13 Jul 1933 c: 5
+ seq: 171.42 SCHIRDELLY, Erma b: Abt. 1930 w: Abt. 1952 c: 4
* 2nd Wife of [1] TANNENBAUM, Robert:
+ seq: 171.45 Sandy b: 30 Oct 1948 w: Abt. 1968 c: 1
11TANNENBAUM, James b: 08 May 1940 d: 21 Jun 1987 c: 2
+ seq: 171.46 ALBRIGHT, Jean b: Abt. 1945 w: Abt. 1970 c: 2

171.41

11 TANNENBAUM, Raymond b: 17 Aug 1932 c: 2
+ seq: 171.41 ARBOGAST, Grace b: 01 Jun 1931 w: Abt. 1955
  c: 2
12 TANNENBAUM, Scott b: 18 Apr 1960
12 TANNENBAUM, Deborah b: 05 Aug 1962

171.42

11 [1] TANNENBAUM, Robert b: 13 Jul 1933 c: 5
+ seq: 171.42 SCHIRDELLY, Erma b: Abt. 1930 w: Abt. 1952
  c: 4
12 TANNENBAUM, Robert-Earl b: 02 Nov 1954 c: 2
+ seq: 171.43 BRITT, Brenda b: Abt. 1960 w: Abt. 1985 c: 2
12 TANNENBAUM, Kris-Lee b: 25 Dec 1955 c: 3
+ seq: 171.44 FETZER, Barbara b: Abt. 1955 w: Abt. 1978 c: 3
12 TANNENBAUM, Bradley b: 17 Nov 1956
12 TANNENBAUM, Greg-Harry b: 08 Jun 1957
* 2nd Wife of [1] TANNENBAUM, Robert:
+ seq: 171.45 Sandy b: 30 Oct 1948 w: Abt. 1968 c: 1
12 TANNENBAUM, Michael b: 04 Jul 1969

171.43

12 TANNENBAUM, Robert-Earl b: 02 Nov 1954 c: 2
+ seq: 171.43 BRITT, Brenda b: Abt. 1960 w: Abt. 1985 c: 2
13 TANNENBAUM, Boy b: 05 Aug 1986
13 TANNENBAUM, Girl b: 28 Nov 1987

171.44

12 TANNENBAUM, Kris-Lee b: 25 Dec 1955 c: 3
+ seq: 171.44 FETZER, Barbara b: Abt. 1955 w: Abt. 1978 c: 3
13 TANNENBAUM, Girl b: 11 Aug 1980
13 TANNENBAUM, Boy b: 11 Oct 1981
13 TANNENBAUM, Kris-Earl b: 05 Aug 1983

171.46

11 TANNENBAUM, James b: 08 May 1940 d: 21 Jun 1987 c: 2
+ seq: 171.46 ALBRIGHT, Jean b: Abt. 1945 w: Abt. 1970 c: 2
12 TANNENBAUM, Kerri b: Abt. 1975
12 TANNENBAUM, Patrick J. b: Abt. 1975

171.47

10SPANG, Ursula (Sally) b: 31 Mar 1916 v: Aurora, IL c: 3
+ seq: 171.47 OBERMAN, John P. b: 10 Mar 1912 d: 10 Feb
1993 in Aurora, IL w: Abt. 1940 v: Aurora, IL c: 3
11OBERMAN, Diane b: 27 Apr 1942 v: Aurora, IL c: 2
+ seq: 171.48 ORLAND, Clinton (Clint) b: 06 Nov 1936 w: Abt.
1963 v: Aurora, IL c: 2
11OBERMAN, Sharon b: 10 Aug 1946 v: Aurora, IL c: 2
+ seq: 171.49 SICKLES, Ronald b: 18 Jan 1945 w: Abt. 1968 v:
Aurora, IL c: 2
11OBERMAN, Cecelia b: 16 Aug 1948 v: Batavia, IL c: 1
+ seq: 171.50 ANDERSON, Dean b: 30 Dec 1947 w: Abt. 1970
v: Batavia, IL c: 1

171.48

11OBERMAN, Diane b: 27 Apr 1942 v: Aurora, IL c: 2
+ seq: 171.48 ORLAND, Clinton (Clint) b: 06 Nov 1936 w: Abt.
1963 v: Aurora, IL c: 2
12ORLAND, Timothy b: 13 Mar 1966
12ORLAND, Kimberly b: 02 Mar 1967

171.49

11OBERMAN, Sharon b: 10 Aug 1946 v: Aurora, IL c: 2
+ seq: 171.49 SICKLES, Ronald b: 18 Jan 1945 w: Abt. 1968 v:
Aurora, IL c: 2
12SICKLES, Joseph P. b: 10 Mar 1971
12SICKLES, Sarah-Elizabeth b: 02 Mar 1981

171.50

11OBERMAN, Cecelia b: 16 Aug 1948 v: Batavia, IL c: 1
+ seq: 171.50 ANDERSON, Dean b: 30 Dec 1947 w: Abt. 1970
v: Batavia, IL c: 1
12ANDERSON, Stephanie b: 18 Jul 1974

171.51

10SPANG, Theresa b: 14 Feb 1919 d: 23 Apr 1980 c: 4
+ seq: 171.51 HIGHT, Charles b: 11 Feb 1914 d: 10 Jun 1973
w: Abt. 1940 c: 4
11HIGHT, Kathleen b: 14 Apr 1942 c: 3
+ seq: 171.52 LONSWAY, John b: 07 Jan 1941 w: Abt. 1965 c:
3

11HIGHT, William-George b: 25 Mar 1943 v: North Ridgeville, OH c: 3
+ seq: 171.54 COLE, Sherry-Lee b: 28 Jun 1946 w: Abt. 1968 v: North Ridgeville, OH c: 3
11HIGHT, Charles-Peter b: 04 Apr 1946 c: 2
+ seq: 171.55 Jean b: Abt. 1950 w: Abt. 1975 c: 2
11HIGHT, Cynthia b: 16 Mar 1954
+ seq: 171.56 RUDIGIER, Bruce b: 08 Aug 1949 w: Abt. 1980

171.52

11HIGHT, Kathleen b: 14 Apr 1942 c: 3
+ seq: 171.52 LONSWAY, John b: 07 Jan 1941 w: Abt. 1965 c: 3
12LONSWAY, Patrick-John b: 05 Jan 1966
+ seq: 171.53 MACKENZIE, Karen-Sue b: 16 Mar 1967 w: Abt. 1990
12LONSWAY, Mark b: 04 May 1967
12LONSWAY, David b: 08 Nov 1974

171.54

11HIGHT, William-George b: 25 Mar 1943 v: North Ridgeville, OH c: 3
+ seq: 171.54 COLE, Sherry-Lee b: 28 Jun 1946 w: Abt. 1968 v: North Ridgeville, OH c: 3
12HIGHT, Rebecca-Eileen b: 19 Jul 1970
12HIGHT, Jennifer-Ann b: 04 Apr 1972
12HIGHT, Kimberly-Sue b: 06 Sep 1976

171.55

11HIGHT, Charles-Peter b: 04 Apr 1946 c: 2
+ seq: 171.55 Jean b: Abt. 1950 w: Abt. 1975 c: 2
12HIGHT, Andrew b: Abt. 1980
12HIGHT, Jeffrey b: Abt. 1980

171.57

10SPANG, Margaret b: 19 Jul 1920 d: 20 May 1968 c: 2
+ seq: 171.57 ERATH, Harry b: 21 Aug 1919 w: Abt. 1943 c: 2
11ERATH, Thomas J. b: 17 Nov 1945 c: 2
+ seq: 171.58 WILSON, Rose-Mary b: Abt. 1945 w: Abt. 1967 c: 2
11ERATH, John b: 17 May 1951

171.58

11ERATH, Thomas J. b: 17 Nov 1945 c: 2
+ seq: 171.58 WILSON, Rose-Mary b: Abt. 1945 w: Abt. 1967
    c: 2
12ERATH, Timothy J. b: 31 Aug 1969
12ERATH, Laura b: Abt. 1970

172

9 WITTRY, Henry b: 20 Jun 1882 d: 23 Jun 1956 v: Aurora, IL
    o: Machinist at CB&Q Railroad c: 3
+ seq: 172 DRAUDT, Mary b: 24 Sep 1884 d: 26 Apr 1965 w:
    08 Jul 1908 in Aurora, IL v: Aurora, IL r: x f: Peter Draudt c:
    3
10WITTRY, Margaret L. b: 23 Feb 1909 d: 02 Jun 1940 v:
    Aurora, IL c: 3
+ seq: 172.01 SCHRAMER, Ralph M. b: 17 Aug 1906 d: 29 Jul
    1990 w: Abt. 1928 v: Aurora, IL o: Insurance salesman o:
    Scoutmaster c: 3
10WITTRY, Agnes M. b: 11 Mar 1911 d: 02 Dec 1913 in Aurora,
    IL Cause of death: Spinal meningitis v: Aurora, IL r: d
10WITTRY, Dorothy H. b: 25 Sep 1913 v: Aurora, IL o:
    Violinist c: 1
+ seq: 172.19 PILLATSCH, Herman b: 18 May 1907 d: 23 Aug
    1968 w: Abt. 1940 v: Aurora, IL c: 1

172.01

10WITTRY, Margaret L. b: 23 Feb 1909 d: 02 Jun 1940 v:
    Aurora, IL c: 3
+ seq: 172.01 SCHRAMER, Ralph M. b: 17 Aug 1906 d: 29 Jul
    1990 w: Abt. 1928 v: Aurora, IL o: Insurance salesman o:
    Scoutmaster c: 3
11[1] SCHRAMER, Robert G. b: 05 Dec 1930 in Aurora, IL v:
    Tierra Verde, FL c: 5
+ seq: 172.02 STANEK, Rose-Mary b: 15 Jun 1926 w: Abt.
    1952 v: Tierra Verde, FL c: 5
* 2nd Wife of [1] SCHRAMER, Robert G.:
+ seq: 172.08 KEENAN, Karen-Elliot b: 14 Jan 1941 w: Abt.
    1965
11SCHRAMER, Daniel F. b: 10 Oct 1933 in Aurora, IL d: 24 Jun
    1998 in Bay Pines, FL v: Tierra Verde, FL o: Owner of TV
    store o: Air traffic controller c: 4

+ seq: 172.09 WALKER, Charlotte b: 31 Aug 1935 w: Abt.
1955 v: Tierra Verde, FL c: 4

11 SCHRAMER, David T. b: 10 Oct 1933 in Aurora, IL v: Green
Cove Springs, FL c: 3

+ seq: 172.15 PEIFFER, Patricia b: 03 Jul 1936 w: 01 Sep 1956
v: Green Cove Springs, FL c: 3

172.02

11 [2] SCHRAMER, Robert G. b: 05 Dec 1930 in Aurora, IL v:
Tierra Verde, FL c: 5

+ seq: 172.02 STANEK, Rose-Mary b: 15 Jun 1926 w: Abt.
1952 v: Tierra Verde, FL c: 5

12 [1] SCHRAMER, Gayle-Ann b: 04 Sep 1953

+ seq: 172.03 SEVERSON, Steven-Ransom b: Abt. 1950 w:
Abt. 1975

* 2nd Husband of [1] SCHRAMER, Gayle-Ann:

+ seq: 172.04 MITCHELL, Donald b: Abt. 1950 w: Abt. 1975

12 SCHRAMER, Gary R. b: 13 Jul 1955

12 SCHRAMER, Gwen M. b: 30 Nov 1957 c: 2

+ seq: 172.05 CRABBE, Kerry b: 29 Jul 1956 w: Abt. 1980 c: 2

12 SCHRAMER, Gill b: 29 Nov 1964 c: 1

+ seq: 172.06 VIERECKL, Rudolph b: 04 Dec 1959 w: Abt.
1985 c: 1

12 SCHRAMER, Gina b: 29 Nov 1964 c: 1

+ seq: 172.07 NOWICKI, Michael b: 05 Jun 1961 w: Abt. 1984
c: 1

* 2nd Wife of [2] SCHRAMER, Robert G.:

+ seq: 172.08 KEENAN, Karen-Elliot b: 14 Jan 1941 w: Abt.
1965

172.05

12 SCHRAMER, Gwen M. b: 30 Nov 1957 c: 2

+ seq: 172.05 CRABBE, Kerry b: 29 Jul 1956 w: Abt. 1980 c: 2

13 CRABBE, Elissa b: 08 Oct 1981

13 CRABBE, Kera b: 27 Apr 1984

172.06

12 SCHRAMER, Gill b: 29 Nov 1964 c: 1

+ seq: 172.06 VIERECKL, Rudolph b: 04 Dec 1959 w: Abt.
1985 c: 1

13 VIERECKL, Ashle-Rose b: 12 Oct 1987

172.07

12 SCHRAMER, Gina b: 29 Nov 1964 c: 1
+ seq: 172.07 NOWICKI, Michael b: 05 Jun 1961 w: Abt. 1984
   c: 1
13 NOWICKI, Michael-John b: 29 Sep 1985

172.09

11 SCHRAMER, Daniel F. b: 10 Oct 1933 in Aurora, IL d: 24 Jun
   1998 in Bay Pines, FL v: Tierra Verde, FL o: Owner of TV
   store o: Air traffic controller c: 4
+ seq: 172.09 WALKER, Charlotte b: 31 Aug 1935 w: Abt.
   1955 v: Tierra Verde, FL c: 4
12[1] SCHRAMER, Kathleen M. b: 16 Dec 1956 v: Oswego, IL
   c: 1
+ seq: 172.10 CHALLY, Gerald b: Abt. 1950 w: Abt. 1980
* 2nd Husband of [1] SCHRAMER, Kathleen M.:
+ seq: 172.11 KRANT, David b: 02 Nov 1947 w: Abt. 1982 c: 1
12[2] SCHRAMER, Sharon K. b: 18 Sep 1958 v: Greenback, TN
   c: 3
+ seq: 172.12 HETTINGER, George b: Abt. 1950 w: Abt. 1975
   c: 1
* 2nd Husband of [2] SCHRAMER, Sharon K.:
+ seq: 172.13 SAMUELSON, Robert b: 02 Dec 1962 w: Abt.
   1985 c: 2
12 SCHRAMER, Donna-Louise b: 17 Feb 1960 v: Tampa, FL
12 SCHRAMER, Dianne-Lois b: 18 Jan 1963 v: Naperville, IL
+ seq: 172.14 DION, George V. b: Abt. 1960 w: 01 Jun 1991 v:
   Batavia, IL

172.10

12[1] SCHRAMER, Kathleen M. b: 16 Dec 1956 v: Oswego, IL
   c: 1
+ seq: 172.10 CHALLY, Gerald b: Abt. 1950 w: Abt. 1980
* 2nd Husband of [1] SCHRAMER, Kathleen M.:
+ seq: 172.11 KRANT, David b: 02 Nov 1947 w: Abt. 1982 c: 1
13 KRANT, Melissa-Ruth b: 21 Nov 1986

172.12

12[1] SCHRAMER, Sharon K. b: 18 Sep 1958 v: Greenback, TN
   c: 3
+ seq: 172.12 HETTINGER, George b: Abt. 1950 w: Abt. 1975

c: 1

13 HETTINGER, Ryan b: 22 Jun 1976

* 2nd Husband of [1] SCHRAMER, Sharon K.:

+ seq: 172.13 SAMUELSON, Robert b: 02 Dec 1962 w: Abt.
    1985 c: 2

13 SAMUELSON, Girl b: 19 Jan 1988

13 SAMUELSON, Daniel-Alan b: 16 Mar 1991

172.15

11 SCHRAMER, David T. b: 10 Oct 1933 in Aurora, IL v: Green
    Cove Springs, FL c: 3

+ seq: 172.15 PEIFFER, Patricia b: 03 Jul 1936 w: 01 Sep 1956
    v: Green Cove Springs, FL c: 3

12 SCHRAMER, Margaret L. b: 18 Dec 1960

+ seq: 172.16 FOSTER, Jayce b: 27 Jan 1959 w: 28 Feb 1981

12 SCHRAMER, Carolyn-Kay b: 11 Sep 1963 c: 1

+ seq: 172.17 TROSINE, Kevin E. b: 31 Mar 1964 w: 15 Oct
    1988 c: 1

12 SCHRAMER, Merri-Kay b: 14 Feb 1965 c: 2

+ seq: 172.18 SULLIVAN, John b: 25 Mar 1962 w: 08 Dec 1984
    c: 2

172.17

12 SCHRAMER, Carolyn-Kay b: 11 Sep 1963 c: 1

+ seq: 172.17 TROSINE, Kevin E. b: 31 Mar 1964 w: 15 Oct
    1988 c: 1

13 TROSINE, Lucas-David b: 22 Mar 1991

172.18

12 SCHRAMER, Merri-Kay b: 14 Feb 1965 c: 2

+ seq: 172.18 SULLIVAN, John b: 25 Mar 1962 w: 08 Dec 1984
    c: 2

13 SULLIVAN, Alexandra b: 28 Jul 1986

13 SULLIVAN, Riley-Joseph b: 04 Feb 1991

172.19

10 WITTRY, Dorothy H. b: 25 Sep 1913 v: Aurora, IL o:
    Violinist c: 1

+ seq: 172.19 PILLATSCH, Herman b: 18 May 1907 d: 23 Aug
    1968 w: Abt. 1940 v: Aurora, IL c: 1

11 PILLATSCH, Mary-Agnes b: 22 Dec 1947 c: 1

+ seq: 172.20 RUPPERT, Edwin b: 03 Mar 1946 w: Abt. 1975
c: 1

172.20

11 PILLATSCH, Mary-Agnes b: 22 Dec 1947 c: 1
+ seq: 172.20 RUPPERT, Edwin b: 03 Mar 1946 w: Abt. 1975
c: 1
12 RUPERT, William A. b: 26 Aug 1980

172.21

9 WITTRY, Anna b: 16 Mar 1885 d: 20 Jul 1974 v: Aurora, IL
c: 2
+ seq: 172.21 THEIS, Nicholas A. b: 23 Aug 1884 d: 08 Oct
1953 w: Abt. 1910 v: Aurora, IL f: John Theis m: Catherine
Clemens c: 2
10 THEIS, John J. b: 21 Sep 1915 d: 12 Jul 2000 in Aurora, IL v:
Aurora, IL c: 2
+ seq: 172.22 ZMUDA, Lucille b: 11 Feb 1926 d: 11 Sep 1994
w: Abt. 1951 v: Aurora, IL c: 2
10 THEIS, Carl N. b: 25 Feb 1928 in Aurora, IL d: 07 Oct 2005 in
Aurora, IL v: Aurora, IL

172.22

10 THEIS, John J. b: 21 Sep 1915 d: 12 Jul 2000 in Aurora, IL v:
Aurora, IL c: 2
+ seq: 172.22 ZMUDA, Lucille b: 11 Feb 1926 d: 11 Sep 1994
w: Abt. 1951 v: Aurora, IL c: 2
11 THEIS, James E. b: 27 Aug 1953 c: 2
+ seq: 172.23 HOWARD, Tamara b: 19 Apr 1960 w: Abt. 1983
c: 2
11 THEIS, Laura J. b: 14 Sep 1956

172.23

11 THEIS, James E. b: 27 Aug 1953 c: 2
+ seq: 172.23 HOWARD, Tamara b: 19 Apr 1960 w: Abt. 1983
c: 2
12 THEIS, Michael-John b: 14 Jan 1985
12 THEIS, Nathaniel

172.24

9 WITTRY, Mary M. b: 03 Jun 1888 in Aurora, IL d: 03 Aug

1932 in Aurora, IL v: Aurora, IL o: Worked at Aurora Cotton
Mills c: 3
+ seq: 172.24 FRIEDERS, John-Aloysius b: 17 Jan 1891 in
Aurora, IL d: 22 Jul 1957 in Aurora, IL w: Abt. 1915 v:
Aurora, IL f: Michael-Nicholas Frieders m: Magdalena (Lena)
Molitor c: 3
10FRIEDERS, Herman-Joseph b: 22 Mar 1919 in Aurora, IL d:
03 Feb 2001 in Geneva, IL v: Aurora, IL o: Supervisor at
Austin-Western c: 3
+ seq: 172.25 MEYER, Ruth-Catherine b: 20 Jun 1921 in
Mendota, IL w: 27 Feb 1943 in Aurora, IL v: Aurora, IL c: 3
10FRIEDERS, Leona (Anna-Marie) b: 19 Apr 1922 in Aurora, IL
d: 25 Nov 1997 in Aurora, IL v: Aurora, IL o: Worked at Dick's
Vending Service c: 2
+ seq: 172.29 PIRON, Ervin R. (Bud) b: 16 Oct 1916 in Aurora,
IL d: 26 Mar 1976 in Aurora, IL w: 24 Jun 1944 in Aurora, IL
v: Aurora, IL c: 2
10FRIEDERS, Anastasia (Sue or Stacey) b: 25 Oct 1923 in
Aurora, IL d: 18 Dec 1963 in Aurora, IL v: Aurora, IL c: 2
+ seq: 172.33 ANDERSON, William-Fred b: 08 Jun 1921 d: Jul
1985 w: 12 Oct 1946 in Aurora, IL v: Aurora, IL c: 2

172.25
10FRIEDERS, Herman-Joseph b: 22 Mar 1919 in Aurora, IL d:
03 Feb 2001 in Geneva, IL v: Aurora, IL o: Supervisor at
Austin-Western c: 3
+ seq: 172.25 MEYER, Ruth-Catherine b: 20 Jun 1921 in
Mendota, IL w: 27 Feb 1943 in Aurora, IL v: Aurora, IL c: 3
11FRIEDERS, Lawrence-Joseph b: 21 Oct 1946 in Aurora, IL v:
Aurora, IL c: 2
+ seq: 172.26 WILLIAMS, Patricia-Ann b: 01 Dec 1948 in
Chicago, IL w: 28 Aug 1971 in Evergreen Park, IL v: Aurora,
IL c: 2
11FRIEDERS, Mary-Catherine b: 15 Sep 1952 in Aurora, IL v:
Naperville, IL c: 2
+ seq: 172.27 CONNORS, Michael-Jeffrey b: 08 Jul 1949 in
Lynn, MA w: 06 Oct 1973 in Aurora, IL v: Naperville, IL c: 2
11FRIEDERS, John-Joseph b: 11 Aug 1959 in Aurora, IL v:
Oswego, IL c: 2
+ seq: 172.28 SWORDS, Suzanne b: 25 Jul 1958 w: 11 Jul 1987
v: Oswego, IL c: 2

172.26

11 FRIEDERS, Lawrence-Joseph b: 21 Oct 1946 in Aurora, IL v: Aurora, IL c: 2

+ seq: 172.26 WILLIAMS, Patricia-Ann b: 01 Dec 1948 in Chicago, IL w: 28 Aug 1971 in Evergreen Park, IL v: Aurora, IL c: 2

12 FRIEDERS, Lydia-Jean b: 07 Mar 1977 in Oak Park, IL

+ seq: 172.26.01 LESNIAK, David w: Abt. 2000 v: Aurora, IL

12 FRIEDERS, Joel-Robert b: 07 Nov 1979 in Oak Park, IL v: Aurora, IL

172.27

11 FRIEDERS, Mary-Catherine b: 15 Sep 1952 in Aurora, IL v: Naperville, IL c: 2

+ seq: 172.27 CONNORS, Michael-Jeffrey b: 08 Jul 1949 in Lynn, MA w: 06 Oct 1973 in Aurora, IL v: Naperville, IL c: 2

12 CONNORS, Michelle-Catherine b: 22 Nov 1976 in Naperville, IL v: Naperville, IL

12 CONNORS, James-Michael b: 08 Jan 1979 in Naperville, IL v: Naperville, IL

172.28

11 FRIEDERS, John-Joseph b: 11 Aug 1959 in Aurora, IL v: Oswego, IL c: 2

+ seq: 172.28 SWORDS, Suzanne b: 25 Jul 1958 w: 11 Jul 1987 v: Oswego, IL c: 2

12 FRIEDERS, Jordan-Joseph b: 26 Jul 1992 v: Oswego, IL

12 FRIEDERS, Grant-Mike b: 26 Mar 1996 v: Oswego, IL

172.29

10 FRIEDERS, Leona (Anna-Marie) b: 19 Apr 1922 in Aurora, IL d: 25 Nov 1997 in Aurora, IL v: Aurora, IL o: Worked at Dick's Vending Service c: 2

+ seq: 172.29 PIRON, Ervin R. (Bud) b: 16 Oct 1916 in Aurora, IL d: 26 Mar 1976 in Aurora, IL w: 24 Jun 1944 in Aurora, IL v: Aurora, IL c: 2

11 PIRON, Patricia-Ann b: 12 Apr 1945 in Aurora, IL v: Naperville, IL c: 2

+ seq: 172.30 BURSON, Douglas-Robert (Doug) b: 16 Mar 1945 in Aurora, IL w: 23 May 1970 in Aurora, IL v: Naperville, IL c: 2

11PIRON, Carol-Lee b: 30 Dec 1946 in Aurora, IL v: Polo, IL c:
3
+ seq: 172.31 EUBANKS, Kenneth-Eugene b: 23 Sep 1939 in
Milledgeville, IL w: 08 Oct 1966 in Aurora, IL v: Polo, IL c:
3

172.30
11PIRON, Patricia-Ann b: 12 Apr 1945 in Aurora, IL v:
Naperville, IL c: 2
+ seq: 172.30 BURSON, Douglas-Robert (Doug) b: 16 Mar 1945
in Aurora, IL w: 23 May 1970 in Aurora, IL v: Naperville, IL
c: 2
12BURSON, Douglas-Paul b: 25 Nov 1971 in Naperville, IL v:
Aurora, IL
12BURSON, Amy E. b: 16 Feb 1974 in Naperville, IL v:
Naperville, IL

172.31
11PIRON, Carol-Lee b: 30 Dec 1946 in Aurora, IL v: Polo, IL c:
3
+ seq: 172.31 EUBANKS, Kenneth-Eugene b: 23 Sep 1939 in
Milledgeville, IL w: 08 Oct 1966 in Aurora, IL v: Polo, IL c:
3
12EUBANKS, Laura-Marie b: 04 Apr 1967 in Dixon, Il v:
Milledgeville, IL c: 1
+ seq: 172.32 WAGENKNECHT, Gary w: 12 Jun 1993 v:
Milledgeville, IL c: 1
12EUBANKS, Henry-Michael (Hank) b: 15 Mar 1969 in Freeport,
IL
12EUBANKS, Lisa-Lynn b: 13 Apr 1972 in Dixon, IL v:
Chicago, IL

172.32
12EUBANKS, Laura-Marie b: 04 Apr 1967 in Dixon, Il v:
Milledgeville, IL c: 1
+ seq: 172.32 WAGENKNECHT, Gary w: 12 Jun 1993 v:
Milledgeville, IL c: 1
13WAGENKNECHT, Kayla-Ashley b: 27 Jul 1996

172.33
10FRIEDERS, Anastasia (Sue or Stacey) b: 25 Oct 1923 in

Aurora, IL d: 18 Dec 1963 in Aurora, IL v: Aurora, IL c: 2
+ seq: 172.33 ANDERSON, William-Fred b: 08 Jun 1921 d: Jul
   1985 w: 12 Oct 1946 in Aurora, IL v: Aurora, IL c: 2
11 ANDERSON, Linda-Sue b: 09 Oct 1948 in Aurora, IL c: 3
+ seq: 172.34 WYATT, Michael-Vickery b: 24 Jan 1943 in
   Windsor, Ontario, Canada w: 27 Nov 1971 in Aurora, IL c: 3
11 ANDERSON, Cynthia-Ann b: 30 Jul 1954 in Aurora, IL c: 2
+ seq: 172.35 CARLSON, Geoffrey-Alan b: 11 Nov 1952 in
   Sycamore, IL w: 29 Sep 1979 in Sycamore, IL c: 2

172.34

11 ANDERSON, Linda-Sue b: 09 Oct 1948 in Aurora, IL c: 3
+ seq: 172.34 WYATT, Michael-Vickery b: 24 Jan 1943 in
   Windsor, Ontario, Canada w: 27 Nov 1971 in Aurora, IL c: 3
12 WYATT, Jennifer-Ann b: 15 Jun 1972 in Naperville, IL
12 WYATT, Melissa-Anastasia b: 26 Jun 1973 in Columbus, OH
12 WYATT, Bethany-Therese b: 12 Jul 1978 in Columbus, OH

172.35

11 ANDERSON, Cynthia-Ann b: 30 Jul 1954 in Aurora, IL c: 2
+ seq: 172.35 CARLSON, Geoffrey-Alan b: 11 Nov 1952 in
   Sycamore, IL w: 29 Sep 1979 in Sycamore, IL c: 2
12 CARLSON, Benjamin-Geoffrey b: 20 Apr 1982 in Sycamore,
   IL
12 CARLSON, Sarah-Ann b: 12 Dec 1986

172.37

8 WITTRY, Anna b: 25 May 1856 in Aurora, IL d: 13 Jan 1940
   v: Big Rock, IL c: 9
+ seq: 172.37 PLAIN, John W. b: 30 Nov 1852 d: 08 Jul 1929
   w: 30 Oct 1878 v: Big Rock, IL c: 9
9 PLAIN, Jacob b: 20 Dec 1879 d: 27 Jan 1886
9 PLAIN, Michael W. b: 09 May 1881 d: 01 Oct 1959 c: 4
+ seq: 172.38 PUNG, Anna b: 24 Sep 1882 d: 14 Jan 1916 w:
   Abt. 1907 c: 4
9 PLAIN, Peter J. b: 27 Jul 1882 d: 20 Nov 1954 c: 2
+ seq: 172.47 SCHUSTER, Helen b: 07 Jul 1889 d: 16 Nov 1970
   w: Abt. 1914 c: 2
9 PLAIN, Henry J. b: 11 May 1884 d: 28 Nov 1970
9 PLAIN, Magdalene b: 04 Nov 1885 d: 01 Nov 1969
9 PLAIN, Barbara b: 16 Mar 1889 d: 20 Jan 1980 v: Aurora, IL

c: 4

+ seq: 172.53 REINES, Frank H. b: 12 Dec 1881 d: 15 Jan 1972
w: Abt. 1911 v: Aurora, IL c: 4

9 PLAIN, Margaret b: 11 Sep 1890 d: 14 Mar 1961

9 PLAIN, Adam J. b: 30 Sep 1892 d: 27 Nov 1975

9 PLAIN, Nicholas b: 18 Mar 1894 d: 23 Aug 1894

172.38

9 PLAIN, Michael W. b: 09 May 1881 d: 01 Oct 1959 c: 4

+ seq: 172.38 PUNG, Anna b: 24 Sep 1882 d: 14 Jan 1916 w:
Abt. 1907 c: 4

10PLAIN, Alvin-Arnold b: 07 Jan 1910 d: 12 Feb 1995

10PLAIN, Gilbert-John b: 27 Feb 1911 c: 4

+ seq: 172.39 SWAN, Felice-Bancroft b: 21 Feb 1918 w: Abt.
1940 c: 4

10PLAIN, Esther-Anne b: 06 Jan 1913

10PLAIN, Jacob-Peter b: 23 Dec 1914 d: 17 Apr 1996 in
Bakersfield, CA c: 2

+ seq: 172.44 MUNNERLYN, Lou-Dean b: 29 Jun 1919 d: 16
May 1991 w: Abt. 1945 c: 2

172.39

10PLAIN, Gilbert-John b: 27 Feb 1911 c: 4

+ seq: 172.39 SWAN, Felice-Bancroft b: 21 Feb 1918 w: Abt.
1940 c: 4

11PLAIN, Karen E. b: 01 May 1944 c: 2

+ seq: 172.40 SWITZER, Robert b: 29 Jan 1940 w: Abt. 1970 c:
2

11PLAIN, Margaret E. b: 05 Nov 1945

+ seq: 172.41 BROWN, Max b: 30 Nov 1943 w: Abt. 1970

11PLAIN, John M. b: 21 Dec 1947

+ seq: 172.42 MATHIS, Jeanne b: 22 Jun 1940 w: Abt. 1970

11PLAIN, Janet B. b: 04 May 1954

+ seq: 172.43 STANLEY, Gregory b: 27 Jan 1953 w: Abt. 1980

172.40

11PLAIN, Karen E. b: 01 May 1944 c: 2

+ seq: 172.40 SWITZER, Robert b: 29 Jan 1940 w: Abt. 1970 c:
2

12SWITZER, Elizabeth-Stephanie b: 28 Mar 1972

12SWITZER, Elinor-Natalie b: 06 Aug 1975

172.44

10PLAIN, Jacob-Peter b: 23 Dec 1914 d: 17 Apr 1996 in
  Bakersfield, CA c: 2
+ seq: 172.44 MUNNERLYN, Lou-Dean b: 29 Jun 1919 d: 16
  May 1991 w: Abt. 1945 c: 2
11PLAIN, Gail-Marie b: 25 Mar 1951
+ seq: 172.45 JONES, Thomas A. b: 24 May 1946 w: Abt. 1975
11PLAIN, Michael D. b: 16 Aug 1953 d: 03 Jan 1985
+ seq: 172.46 VIEBIG, Gail b: Abt. 1960 w: 07 Apr 1984

172.47

9 PLAIN, Peter J. b: 27 Jul 1882 d: 20 Nov 1954 c: 2
+ seq: 172.47 SCHUSTER, Helen b: 07 Jul 1889 d: 16 Nov 1970
  w: Abt. 1914 c: 2
10[1] PLAIN, Ruth-Helen b: 30 Jul 1917 c: 1
+ seq: 172.48 SCHASSOW, Wayburn b: Abt. 1910 w: Abt. 1940
* 2nd Husband of [1] PLAIN, Ruth-Helen:
+ seq: 172.49 MARTIN, Albert b: Abt. 1915 w: Abt. 1945 c: 1
10PLAIN, Clarence-Peter b: 14 Jan 1924 d: 28 Dec 1971
+ seq: 172.52 Dorothy b: Abt. 1930 d: 29 Apr 1976 w: Abt.
  1955

172.48

10[1] PLAIN, Ruth-Helen b: 30 Jul 1917 c: 1
+ seq: 172.48 SCHASSOW, Wayburn b: Abt. 1910 w: Abt. 1940
* 2nd Husband of [1] PLAIN, Ruth-Helen:
+ seq: 172.49 MARTIN, Albert b: Abt. 1915 w: Abt. 1945 c: 1
11MARTIN, Helen M. b: 30 Aug 1950 c: 3
+ seq: 172.50 KING, Jimmy b: Abt. 1945 w: Abt. 1970 c: 3

172.50

11MARTIN, Helen M. b: 30 Aug 1950 c: 3
+ seq: 172.50 KING, Jimmy b: Abt. 1945 w: Abt. 1970 c: 3
12KING, Shawna H. b: 22 Jun 1971 c: 1
+ seq: 172.51 GUEST, Guy b: Abt. 1965 w: 10 Feb 1990 c: 1
12KING, Misty-Dawn b: 21 Mar 1979
12KING, Meghan-Renee b: 16 Oct 1982

172.51

12KING, Shawna H. b: 22 Jun 1971 c: 1
+ seq: 172.51 GUEST, Guy b: Abt. 1965 w: 10 Feb 1990 c: 1

13 GUEST, Hannah-Marie b: 15 Aug 1990

172.53

9 PLAIN, Barbara b: 16 Mar 1889 d: 20 Jan 1980 v: Aurora, IL
  c: 4
+ seq: 172.53 REINES, Frank H. b: 12 Dec 1881 d: 15 Jan 1972
  w: Abt. 1911 v: Aurora, IL c: 4
10[1] REINES, Raymond R. b: 17 May 1914 d: 24 Jan 1988 v:
  Naperville, IL c: 4
+ seq: 172.54 BRENNAN, Geraldine b: 21 Sep 1921 d: 28 Apr
  1962 w: 11 Oct 1952 v: Maple Park, IL c: 4
* 2nd Wife of [1] REINES, Raymond R.:
+ seq: 172.58 ADAMS, Anne-Mary b: 20 Nov 1928 in
  Naperville, IL d: 22 Mar 2005 in St. Charles, IL w: 25 Jul
  1970 in St. Charles, IL v: Naperville, IL o: Caterer o:
  Township assessor f: Burness Adams m: Marion Kearns c: 3
10 REINES, Virginia E. b: 30 Jan 1917 in Virgil, IL d: 05 Jan
  1993 in Aurora, IL Cause of death: Shot in the head in her home
  by a burglar v: Aurora, IL o: Bookkeeper c: 2
+ seq: 172.59 JOHANNESSEN, Howard E. b: 10 Aug 1919 d:
  22 May 1968 w: 25 Nov 1952 v: Aurora, IL c: 2
10 REINES, Regina F. b: 07 Sep 1921 d: 10 Sep 1994 in Aurora,
  IL v: Aurora, IL
+ seq: 172.63 THEIS, William J. b: 08 Jul 1915 w: 24 Nov 1949
  v: Aurora, IL
10 REINES, Francis E. (Fritz) b: 09 Dec 1922 v: Aurora, IL

172.54

10[1] REINES, Raymond R. b: 17 May 1914 d: 24 Jan 1988 v:
  Naperville, IL c: 4
+ seq: 172.54 BRENNAN, Geraldine b: 21 Sep 1921 d: 28 Apr
  1962 w: 11 Oct 1952 v: Maple Park, IL c: 4
11 REINES, Mary-Kathleen b: 03 Sep 1953 v: St. Charles, IL c: 2
+ seq: 172.55 HAUSER, Mark J. b: 30 May 1954 w: 04 Oct
  1975 v: St. Charles, IL c: 2
11 REINES, Robert-Raymond (Bob) b: 16 Sep 1955 v: Sycamore,
  IL
+ seq: 172.56 WINTHERS, Linda-Marie b: 21 Nov 1957 w: 21
  Sep 1991 v: Sycamore, IL
11 REINES, Patricia-Marie b: 15 Apr 1958 v: St. Charles, IL
11 REINES, Therese-Mary b: 11 Nov 1960 v: Geneva, IL c: 3

+ seq: 172.57 AUGUSTINE, Todd b: 11 Jul 1960 w: 25 Apr
  1987 v: Geneva, IL c: 3
* 2nd Wife of [1] REINES, Raymond R.:
+ seq: 172.58 ADAMS, Anne-Mary b: 20 Nov 1928 in
  Naperville, IL d: 22 Mar 2005 in St. Charles, IL w: 25 Jul
  1970 in St. Charles, IL v: Naperville, IL o: Caterer o:
  Township assessor f: Burness Adams m: Marion Kearns c: 3

172.55

11REINES, Mary-Kathleen b: 03 Sep 1953 v: St. Charles, IL c: 2
+ seq: 172.55 HAUSER, Mark J. b: 30 May 1954 w: 04 Oct
  1975 v: St. Charles, IL c: 2
12HAUSER, Ryan-Jacob b: 16 Oct 1979
12HAUSER, Eric-Bennett b: 07 Mar 1983

172.57

11REINES, Therese-Mary b: 11 Nov 1960 v: Geneva, IL c: 3
+ seq: 172.57 AUGUSTINE, Todd b: 11 Jul 1960 w: 25 Apr
  1987 v: Geneva, IL c: 3
12AUGUSTINE, Jacob-William b: 24 Mar 1989
12AUGUSTINE, Matthew-Todd b: 07 Apr 1991
12AUGUSTINE, Alexandra-Rae b: 01 Oct 1993

172.59

10REINES, Virginia E. b: 30 Jan 1917 in Virgil, IL d: 05 Jan
  1993 in Aurora, IL Cause of death: Shot in the head in her home
  by a burglar v: Aurora, IL o: Bookkeeper c: 2
+ seq: 172.59 JOHANNESSEN, Howard E. b: 10 Aug 1919 d:
  22 May 1968 w: 25 Nov 1952 v: Aurora, IL c: 2
11[1] JOHANNESSEN, Karen M. b: 19 Feb 1957 v: Hanover
  Park, IL c: 2
+ seq: 172.60 KIERES, Michael b: 27 Apr 1952 w: Abt. 1974 c:
  2
* 2nd Husband of [1] JOHANNESSEN, Karen M.:
+ seq: 172.61 BRENNER, Craig (Cian) w: Abt. 1985 v: Hanover
  Park, IL
11JOHANNESSEN, Barbara S. b: 02 Dec 1958 v: Lodi, WI
+ seq: 172.62 BAILEY, John w: Abt. 1980 v: Lodi, WI

172.60

11[1] JOHANNESSEN, Karen M. b: 19 Feb 1957 v: Hanover

Park, IL c: 2
+ seq: 172.60 KIERES, Michael b: 27 Apr 1952 w: Abt. 1974 c: 2
12 KIERES, Jennifer-Joan b: 09 Jan 1975
12 KIERES, Jacqueline-Diane b: 09 May 1976
* 2nd Husband of [1] JOHANNESSEN, Karen M.:
+ seq: 172.61 BRENNER, Craig (Cian) w: Abt. 1985 v: Hanover Park, IL

173
8 WITTRY, Henry b: 20 Jun 1858 in Aurora, IL d: 19 Mar 1911 in Aurora, IL Cause of death: arteriosclerosis v: Kaneville, IL c: 11
+ seq: 173 MOLITOR, Margaret b: 08 Mar 1861 in Dacada, WI d: 16 Jul 1944 w: 17 Jan 1882 v: Kaneville, IL f: Peter Molitor m: Mary Thill c: 11
9 WITTRY, Barbara M. b: 22 Oct 1882 d: 20 Jun 1949 v: Aurora, IL c: 3
+ seq: 173.01 WEDDIGE, Frederick (Fred) J. b: 16 Dec 1881 in Hanover, Germany d: 25 Nov 1965 w: 26 Nov 1908 v: Aurora, IL o: Liquor distributor f: Heinrich-Christian Weddige m: Amalia c: 3
9 WITTRY, Adam H. b: 11 Jun 1884 d: 14 Mar 1968 in Illinois v: Maple Park, IL o: Grain elevator manager
+ seq: 174 POBSTMAN, Mary b: 24 Mar 1887 d: 22 Jul 1973 w: 22 Nov 1922 v: Maple Park, IL
9 WITTRY, John H. b: 25 Apr 1886 in Aurora, IL d: 06 Oct 1920 o: Miller
9 WITTRY, Henry A. b: 06 Feb 1888 d: 06 Nov 1889
9 WITTRY, Anna M. b: 12 Feb 1890 d: 29 Apr 1960 v: Maple Park, IL
+ seq: 174.01 GORMLEY, Thomas b: 08 Apr 1877 d: 17 Nov 1950 w: 16 Oct 1935 v: Maple Park, IL
9 WITTRY, Clara M. b: 10 Feb 1892 d: 05 Nov 1932 in Aurora, IL o: Maid
9 WITTRY, Jennie M. b: 06 May 1894 d: 01 Dec 1895
9 WITTRY, Margaret M. b: 22 Nov 1896 in Sugar Grove, IL d: 08 Apr 1989 in DeKalb, IL v: DeKalb, IL o: Homemaker c: 2
+ seq: 174.02 POBSTMAN, James b: 27 Dec 1892 in Cortland, IL d: 08 Mar 1969 in Elburn, IL w: 31 Jan 1924 in Aurora, IL v: DeKalb, IL o: Farmer c: 2

9 WITTRY, Peter H. b: 12 Jan 1899 d: 31 Oct 1980 in Aurora, IL
v: Aurora, IL o: Salesman for International Harvester Co. o:
Service Supervisor for International Harvester Co. c: 2
+ seq: 175 SMITH, Olive L. b: 29 Apr 1900 d: 28 May 1975 in
Aurora, IL w: 28 Jun 1928 v: Aurora, IL c: 2
9 WITTRY, George H. b: 13 Jul 1901 d: 21 Oct 1967 in Aurora,
IL v: Aurora, IL o: Salesman c: 3
+ seq: 180 LEIDER, Josephine b: 19 Dec 1904 d: 29 Jan 1995 in
Torrance, CA w: 30 Jan 1932 v: Aurora, IL f: Leider m:
Schawl c: 3
9 WITTRY, May A. b: 28 Aug 1904 d: 15 Feb 1981 v: Falls
Church, VA
+ seq: 181.02 BURKEL, John B. b: 01 Feb 1912 d: 22 Jan 1998
in Falls Church, VA Cause of death: Cardiopulmonary arrest
w: 12 Aug 1936 v: Falls Church, VA o: U. S. Army
Intelligence officer in WW II o: Attorney o: Intelligence
analyst

173.01
9 WITTRY, Barbara M. b: 22 Oct 1882 d: 20 Jun 1949 v:
Aurora, IL c: 3
+ seq: 173.01 WEDDIGE, Frederick (Fred) J. b: 16 Dec 1881 in
Hanover, Germany d: 25 Nov 1965 w: 26 Nov 1908 v:
Aurora, IL o: Liquor distributor f: Heinrich-Christian Weddige
m: Amalia c: 3
10 WEDDIGE, Paul H. b: 22 Oct 1911 in Aurora, IL d: 20 Jul
1957 in Powers Lake, WI v: Aurora, IL o: Liquor distributor c:
3
+ seq: 173.02 HENRICKSON, Christine V. b: 13 Nov 1911 d:
20 Mar 1984 w: 11 Nov 1936 v: Aurora, IL c: 3
10 WEDDIGE, Martha-Elisabeth b: 02 Jul 1915 d: 13 Feb 2004 v:
Aurora, IL
10 WEDDIGE, Esther-Mary b: 15 May 1918 d: 27 Aug 1918

173.02
10 WEDDIGE, Paul H. b: 22 Oct 1911 in Aurora, IL d: 20 Jul
1957 in Powers Lake, WI v: Aurora, IL o: Liquor distributor c:
3
+ seq: 173.02 HENRICKSON, Christine V. b: 13 Nov 1911 d:
20 Mar 1984 w: 11 Nov 1936 v: Aurora, IL c: 3
11 [1] WEDDIGE, Carol-Mae b: 25 Sep 1937 c: 3

+ seq: 173.03 GRATTAFIORI, Alan-Bruce b: 23 Aug 1938 w:
    29 Nov 1958 c: 2
* 2nd Husband of [1] WEDDIGE, Carol-Mae:
+ seq: 173.07 HUNTER, Jason-Donald b: 13 Oct 1929 w: 12
    Aug 1970 c: 1
* 3rd Husband of [1] WEDDIGE, Carol-Mae:
+ seq: 173.08 CLARK, David-Thomas b: 04 Feb 1932 w: 06 Feb
    1988
11 WEDDIGE, Pauline-Marie b: 03 Jun 1939 c: 4
+ seq: 173.09 MERTES, Edward-James b: 29 Mar 1939 w: 23
    Aug 1958 c: 4
11 WEDDIGE, David-Paul b: 28 Mar 1941 in Aurora, IL c: 3
+ seq: 173.13 HUTCHINSON, Sally-Lee b: 18 Aug 1942 w: 28
    Jun 1960 c: 3

173.03

11 [2] WEDDIGE, Carol-Mae b: 25 Sep 1937 c: 3
+ seq: 173.03 GRATTAFIORI, Alan-Bruce b: 23 Aug 1938 w:
    29 Nov 1958 c: 2
12 [1] GRATTAFIORI, Cynthia-Marie (Cindy) b: 20 Jan 1960 c: 4
+ seq: 173.04 EASTERDAY, Geoffrey L. b: Abt. 1955 w: 19
    Apr 1980 c: 1
* 2nd Husband of [1] GRATTAFIORI, Cynthia-Marie (Cindy):
+ seq: 173.05 STROHMENGER, Brian-Robert b: 12 Jul 1963 w:
    Abt. 1983 c: 3
12 GRATTAFIORI, Michael-Alan b: 27 Jun 1962 c: 2
+ seq: 173.06 KREUL, Diane-Lee b: 14 Feb 1965 w: 14 Feb
    1985 c: 2
* 2nd Husband of [2] WEDDIGE, Carol-Mae:
+ seq: 173.07 HUNTER, Jason-Donald b: 13 Oct 1929 w: 12
    Aug 1970 c: 1
12 HUNTER, Christy-Jayne b: 24 Nov 1973
* 3rd Husband of [2] WEDDIGE, Carol-Mae:
+ seq: 173.08 CLARK, David-Thomas b: 04 Feb 1932 w: 06 Feb
    1988

173.04

12 [1] GRATTAFIORI, Cynthia-Marie (Cindy) b: 20 Jan 1960 c: 4
+ seq: 173.04 EASTERDAY, Geoffrey L. b: Abt. 1955 w: 19
    Apr 1980 c: 1
13 GRATTAFIORI, Paula-Mae b: 08 Sep 1983

* 2nd Husband of [1] GRATTAFIORI, Cynthia-Marie (Cindy):
+ seq: 173.05 STROHMENGER, Brian-Robert b: 12 Jul 1963 w:
   Abt. 1983 c: 3
13 STROHMENGER, Paula-Marie b: 1983
13 STROHMENGER, Amy-Marie b: 22 Aug 1985
13 STROHMENGER, Andrea-Marie b: 22 Aug 1985

173.06
12 GRATTAFIORI, Michael-Alan b: 27 Jun 1962 c: 2
+ seq: 173.06 KREUL, Diane-Lee b: 14 Feb 1965 w: 14 Feb
   1985 c: 2
13 GRATTAFIORI, Adam-John b: 18 Nov 1989 d: 18 Nov 1989
13 GRATTAFIORI, Anthony-Micheal b: 20 Apr 1991

173.09
11 WEDDIGE, Pauline-Marie b: 03 Jun 1939 c: 4
+ seq: 173.09 MERTES, Edward-James b: 29 Mar 1939 w: 23
   Aug 1958 c: 4
12 MERTES, Susan-Marie b: 08 Nov 1959 c: 2
+ seq: 173.10 NITSCHKE, Robert D. b: 24 Feb 1959 w: 14 Mar
   1981 c: 2
12 MERTES, James-Arthur b: 06 Nov 1961 c: 2
+ seq: 173.11 DINEEN, Susan b: 31 Jul 1961 w: 14 Nov 1987
   c: 2
12 MERTES, Jean-Christine b: 13 Jan 1963 c: 3
+ seq: 173.12 JOHNSON, Ronald L. b: 15 Aug 1956 w: 18 Dec
   1982 c: 3
12 MERTES, Daniel-Edward b: 19 Dec 1969

173.10
12 MERTES, Susan-Marie b: 08 Nov 1959 c: 2
+ seq: 173.10 NITSCHKE, Robert D. b: 24 Feb 1959 w: 14 Mar
   1981 c: 2
13 NITSCHKE, Sara-Jean b: 13 Sep 1982
13 NITSCHKE, Valerie-Marie b: 15 Mar 1984

173.11
12 MERTES, James-Arthur b: 06 Nov 1961 c: 2
+ seq: 173.11 DINEEN, Susan b: 31 Jul 1961 w: 14 Nov 1987
   c: 2
13 MERTES, Nicholas-James b: 26 Jan 1989

13 MERTES, Matthew-Kyle b: 13 Jan 1990

173.12

12 MERTES, Jean-Christine b: 13 Jan 1963 c: 3
+ seq: 173.12 JOHNSON, Ronald L. b: 15 Aug 1956 w: 18 Dec 1982 c: 3
13 JOHNSON, David-Scott b: 25 Aug 1985
13 JOHNSON, Kristin-Jean b: 08 Sep 1987
13 JOHNSON, Kelly-Marie b: 04 Nov 1989

173.13

11 WEDDIGE, David-Paul b: 28 Mar 1941 in Aurora, IL c: 3
+ seq: 173.13 HUTCHINSON, Sally-Lee b: 18 Aug 1942 w: 28 Jun 1960 c: 3
12 WEDDIGE, David-Kent b: 18 Jan 1961 c: 2
+ seq: 173.14 DE COSMO, Maria b: 16 Mar 1964 w: 21 Jun 1986 in Aurora, IL c: 2
12 WEDDIGE, Diana-Lynn b: 25 Apr 1962 c: 2
+ seq: 173.15 MICHELS, William-John b: 21 Apr 1961 w: 14 Jul 1986 c: 2
12 WEDDIGE, Michael-Paul b: 06 Jan 1970 v: San Luis Obispo, CA o: Calpoly
+ seq: 173.16 MOORE, Kristi b: in Tennessee w: 28 Jun 2004 in Yosemite Park, CA v: San Luis Obispo, CA i: Calpoly

173.14

12 WEDDIGE, David-Kent b: 18 Jan 1961 c: 2
+ seq: 173.14 DE COSMO, Maria b: 16 Mar 1964 w: 21 Jun 1986 in Aurora, IL c: 2
13 WEDDIGE, Christopher-Paul b: 29 Jan 1990
13 WEDDIGE, Michelle-Lynn b: 14 Sep 1991

173.15

12 WEDDIGE, Diana-Lynn b: 25 Apr 1962 c: 2
+ seq: 173.15 MICHELS, William-John b: 21 Apr 1961 w: 14 Jul 1986 c: 2
13 MICHELS, Kevin-Christopher b: 17 May 1988
13 MICHELS, Joshua-David b: 05 May 1990

174.02

9 WITTRY, Margaret M. b: 22 Nov 1896 in Sugar Grove, IL d:

08 Apr 1989 in DeKalb, IL v: DeKalb, IL o: Homemaker c: 2

+ seq: 174.02 POBSTMAN, James b: 27 Dec 1892 in Cortland,
   IL d: 08 Mar 1969 in Elburn, IL w: 31 Jan 1924 in Aurora, IL
   v: DeKalb, IL o: Farmer c: 2

10 POBSTMAN, Lorraine b: 07 Feb 1926 in Elburn, IL v: Elburn,
   IL o: Bookkeeper c: 1

+ seq: 174.03 WHITE, Francis (Bud) b: 22 Aug 1922 in Elburn,
   IL w: 04 May 1946 in Maple Park, IL v: Elburn, IL o: Farmer
   c: 1

10 POBSTMAN, Dorothy E. b: 04 Aug 1927 v: Sycamore, IL c: 4

+ seq: 174.05 HIPPS, Harold b: 11 Jan 1928 d: 14 May 2002 w:
   Abt. 1955 v: Port Arthur, LA c: 4

174.03

10 POBSTMAN, Lorraine b: 07 Feb 1926 in Elburn, IL v: Elburn,
   IL o: Bookkeeper c: 1

+ seq: 174.03 WHITE, Francis (Bud) b: 22 Aug 1922 in Elburn,
   IL w: 04 May 1946 in Maple Park, IL v: Elburn, IL o: Farmer
   c: 1

11 WHITE, Mary-Frances b: 04 Jun 1958 in St. Charles. IL v:
   Lake Charles, LA o: Reference librarian c: 1

+ seq: 174.04 SHERWOOD, Edwin-Douglas b: 03 Mar 1949 in
   Port Arthur, LA w: 04 Nov 1989 in Port Arthur, LA v: Lake
   Charles, LA o: Salesman c: 1

174.04

11 WHITE, Mary-Frances b: 04 Jun 1958 in St. Charles. IL v:
   Lake Charles, LA o: Reference librarian c: 1

+ seq: 174.04 SHERWOOD, Edwin-Douglas b: 03 Mar 1949 in
   Port Arthur, LA w: 04 Nov 1989 in Port Arthur, LA v: Lake
   Charles, LA o: Salesman c: 1

12 SHERWOOD, William-Bennen b: 16 Oct 1992 in Lake Charles,
   LA v: Port Arthur, LA

174.05

10 POBSTMAN, Dorothy E. b: 04 Aug 1927 v: Sycamore, IL c: 4

+ seq: 174.05 HIPPS, Harold b: 11 Jan 1928 d: 14 May 2002 w:
   Abt. 1955 v: Port Arthur, LA c: 4

11 HIPPS, Elizabeth-Ann b: 28 Jul 1957 c: 2

+ seq: 174.06 RUSSIE, Daniel b: 24 Apr 1956 w: Abt. 1978 c: 2

11 HIPPS, David-James b: 30 Jan 1959

11 HIPPS, Rebecca-Sue b: 04 Apr 1961 v: Grand Prairie, TX c: 2
+ seq: 174.07 POWELL, Kenneth b: 24 Sep 1959 w: Abt. 1983
   v: Grand Prairie, TX c: 2
11 [1] HIPPS, Margaret-Marie b: 20 Feb 1963 c: 2
+ seq: 174.08 NORDMAN, Alan b: 12 Sep 1963 w: Abt. 1985
   c: 1
* 2nd Husband of [1] HIPPS, Margaret-Marie:
+ seq: 174.09 DOHNALIK, Wayne-Martin b: 14 Oct 1962 w:
   Abt. 1989 c: 1

174.06
11 HIPPS, Elizabeth-Ann b: 28 Jul 1957 c: 2
+ seq: 174.06 RUSSIE, Daniel b: 24 Apr 1956 w: Abt. 1978 c: 2
12 RUSSIE, Matthew-John b: 31 Mar 1980
12 RUSSIE, Carolyn-Ann b: 24 Sep 1992

174.07
11 HIPPS, Rebecca-Sue b: 04 Apr 1961 v: Grand Prairie, TX c: 2
+ seq: 174.07 POWELL, Kenneth b: 24 Sep 1959 w: Abt. 1983
   v: Grand Prairie, TX c: 2
12 POWELL, William-Joseph b: 13 Jul 1985
12 POWELL, Elizabeth-Marie b: 18 Oct 1986

174.08
11 [1] HIPPS, Margaret-Marie b: 20 Feb 1963 c: 2
+ seq: 174.08 NORDMAN, Alan b: 12 Sep 1963 w: Abt. 1985
   c: 1
12 NORDMAN, Andrew b: 14 Jul 1988
* 2nd Husband of [1] HIPPS, Margaret-Marie:
+ seq: 174.09 DOHNALIK, Wayne-Martin b: 14 Oct 1962 w:
   Abt. 1989 c: 1
12 DOHNALIK, Megan-Marie b: 09 Mar 1990

175
9 WITTRY, Peter H. b: 12 Jan 1899 d: 31 Oct 1980 in Aurora, IL
   v: Aurora, IL o: Salesman for International Harvester Co. o:
   Service Supervisor for International Harvester Co. c: 2
+ seq: 175 SMITH, Olive L. b: 29 Apr 1900 d: 28 May 1975 in
   Aurora, IL w: 28 Jun 1928 v: Aurora, IL c: 2
10 WITTRY, John-Peter (Jack) t: Brigadeer General, U. S. Air
   Force b: 06 Sep 1929 in Aurora, IL v: Hurricane, UT o:

Aeronautical Engineer c: 6
+ seq: 176 ERNST, Theresa-Marie b: 01 Nov 1930 in St. Charles
 Co., MO w: 29 Dec 1951 in St. Charles, MO v: Hurricane, UT
 f: Lawrence-Johannes (John) Ernst m: Josephine-Mathilda
 Diedrich c: 6
10WITTRY, Rose-Mary b: 07 Oct 1932 v: West Chicago, IL o:
 Account Clerk
+ seq: 179.01 SCHRAMER, James M. b: 19 Sep 1925 w: 28 Jun
 1969 v: West Chicago, IL o: Agricultural research associate
 with Campbell Soup Co.

176

10WITTRY, John-Peter (Jack) t: Brigadeer General, U. S. Air
 Force b: 06 Sep 1929 in Aurora, IL v: Hurricane, UT o:
 Aeronautical Engineer c: 6
+ seq: 176 ERNST, Theresa-Marie b: 01 Nov 1930 in St. Charles
 Co., MO w: 29 Dec 1951 in St. Charles, MO v: Hurricane, UT
 f: Lawrence-Johannes (John) Ernst m: Josephine-Mathilda
 Diedrich c: 6
11WITTRY, Stephen-Paul b: 03 Dec 1952 in Dayton, OH v:
 Crosby, TX o: Vice-President of Foley's Department Stores
+ seq: 177 CONTRERAS, Karen b: 25 Aug 1957 w: 06 Sep
 1982 in Houston, TX v: Crosby, TX
11WITTRY, Kathryn-Mary b: 08 Aug 1954 in Dayton, OH v:
 Colorado Springs, CO o: School administrator c: 3
+ seq: 177.01 CHRISTY, Kent-Reynolds b: 30 Jun 1952 w: 29
 Dec 1973 v: Colorado Springs, CO c: 3
11WITTRY, Susan-Ann b: 10 Aug 1955 in Dayton, OH v:
 Dayton, OH o: School administrator c: 1
+ seq: 177.02 WALKER, Kim-Bradley b: 12 Oct 1954 w: 30
 Dec 1986 v: Dayton, OH c: 1
11WITTRY, Michael-Gerard b: 24 Nov 1956 in Dayton, OH v:
 Colorado Springs, CO o: Paramedic o: Fire fighter c: 2
+ seq: 178 WILLIAMS, Beatrice-Dene (Bea) b: 14 Oct 1960 w:
 06 Dec 1980 in Colorado Springs, CO v: Colorado Springs, CO
 c: 2
11WITTRY, Jeanne-Marie b: 03 Nov 1960 in Ypsilanti, MI v:
 Colorado Springs, CO o: Secretary c: 2
+ seq: 178.01 ALDERMAN, George-Henry (Rock) b: 22 Sep
 1954 w: 15 Jan 1983 v: Colorado Springs, CO c: 2
11WITTRY, John-Paul b: 02 Jul 1963 in Colorado Springs, CO v:

Mountain View, CA o: Animal health technologist c: 2
+ seq: 179 DODSON, Donna-Lee w: 09 Aug 1986 in Colorado
   Springs, CO v: Mountain View, CA c: 2

177.01

11 WITTRY, Kathryn-Mary b: 08 Aug 1954 in Dayton, OH v:
   Colorado Springs, CO o: School administrator c: 3
+ seq: 177.01 CHRISTY, Kent-Reynolds b: 30 Jun 1952 w: 29
   Dec 1973 v: Colorado Springs, CO c: 3
12 CHRISTY, Karen-Lynne b: 09 May 1978 in Colorado Springs,
   CO
12 CHRISTY, Brian-Reynolds b: 15 Nov 1980 in Colorado
   Springs, CO
12 CHRISTY, David-Scott b: 16 Nov 1982 in Colorado Springs,
   CO

177.02

11 WITTRY, Susan-Ann b: 10 Aug 1955 in Dayton, OH v:
   Dayton, OH o: School administrator c: 1
+ seq: 177.02 WALKER, Kim-Bradley b: 12 Oct 1954 w: 30
   Dec 1986 v: Dayton, OH c: 1
12 WALKER, Averi-Marie b: 11 Sep 1990

178

11 WITTRY, Michael-Gerard b: 24 Nov 1956 in Dayton, OH v:
   Colorado Springs, CO o: Paramedic o: Fire fighter c: 2
+ seq: 178 WILLIAMS, Beatrice-Dene (Bea) b: 14 Oct 1960 w:
   06 Dec 1980 in Colorado Springs, CO v: Colorado Springs, CO
   c: 2
12 WITTRY, Jesse-Michael b: 18 Jul 1981 in Colorado Springs,
   CO
12 WITTRY, Matthew-Arlis b: 20 Sep 1984 in Colorado Springs,
   CO

178.01

11 WITTRY, Jeanne-Marie b: 03 Nov 1960 in Ypsilanti, MI v:
   Colorado Springs, CO o: Secretary c: 2
+ seq: 178.01 ALDERMAN, George-Henry (Rock) b: 22 Sep
   1954 w: 15 Jan 1983 v: Colorado Springs, CO c: 2
12 ALDERMAN, David-Michael b: 20 Aug 1984 in Colorado
   Springs, CO

12 ALDERMAN, Kathryn-Macall (Katie) b: 03 Feb 1987 in Colorado Springs, CO

179

11 WITTRY, John-Paul b: 02 Jul 1963 in Colorado Springs, CO v: Mountain View, CA o: Animal health technologist c: 2
+ seq: 179 DODSON, Donna-Lee w: 09 Aug 1986 in Colorado Springs, CO v: Mountain View, CA c: 2
12 WITTRY, Chloe-Noel b: 06 Jan 1989
12 WITTRY, Lewis-Evan b: 02 Mar 1991

180

9 WITTRY, George H. b: 13 Jul 1901 d: 21 Oct 1967 in Aurora, IL v: Aurora, IL o: Salesman c: 3
+ seq: 180 LEIDER, Josephine b: 19 Dec 1904 d: 29 Jan 1995 in Torrance, CA w: 30 Jan 1932 v: Aurora, IL f: Leider m: Schawl c: 3
10 WITTRY, Robert-J. (Brother-Dominic) t: Benedictine Monk b: 11 Sep 1934 in Aurora, IL v: Aurora, IL
10 WITTRY, Richard G. b: 11 Sep 1934 in Aurora, IL v: Torrance, CA o: Lawyer with FAA
10 WITTRY, Frank J. b: 09 Feb 1936 in Aurora, IL v: Naperville, IL o: Computer programmer c: 3
+ seq: 181 HAUFLE, Helen-Jane b: 20 Dec 1945 in Chicago, IL w: 24 Jul 1965 v: Naperville, IL o: Realtor c: 3

181

10 WITTRY, Frank J. b: 09 Feb 1936 in Aurora, IL v: Naperville, IL o: Computer programmer c: 3
+ seq: 181 HAUFLE, Helen-Jane b: 20 Dec 1945 in Chicago, IL w: 24 Jul 1965 v: Naperville, IL o: Realtor c: 3
11 WITTRY, David-Joseph b: 21 Dec 1966 in Aurora, IL v: Taipei, Taiwan o: Teacher of high school computer science c: 2
+ seq: 181.01.01 CHANG, Shu-mei (Jody) b: 17 Oct 1967 in Taichung City, Taiwan w: 14 Jul 1996 in Naperville, IL v: Taipei, Taiwan o: Apparel designer f: Ming-Lang Chang m: Shomei Lin c: 2
11 WITTRY, Daniel-George b: 09 Jul 1968 v: Oswego, IL o: Oracle database administrator c: 3
+ seq: 181.01.02 TOLEDO, Tannia-Cecile b: 02 Jan 1967 in Guayaquil, Ecuador w: 30 Oct 2000 in Evergreen, CO v:

Oswego, IL f: Victor-Raul Toledo m: Gladys-Mercedes
Rendon c: 3

11 WITTRY, Steven-Francis (Steve) b: 04 Sep 1969 in Rockford,
IL v: Naperville, IL o: Real estate c: 1
+ seq: 181.01.03 OTTEN, Carol b: 24 Nov 1963 in Jackson, MI
w: 07 Oct 2000 v: Naperville, IL f: Ralph-Friedrich Otten m:
Ethel-May Wilson c: 1

181.01.01

11 WITTRY, David-Joseph b: 21 Dec 1966 in Aurora, IL v:
Taipei, Taiwan o: Teacher of high school computer science c: 2
+ seq: 181.01.01 CHANG, Shu-mei (Jody) b: 17 Oct 1967 in
Taichung City, Taiwan w: 14 Jul 1996 in Naperville, IL v:
Taipei, Taiwan o: Apparel designer f: Ming-Lang Chang m:
Shomei Lin c: 2
12 WITTRY, Kaylin-Helen b: 12 Mar 2000 in Irvine, CA v:
Taipei, Taiwan
12 WITTRY, Darren-Joseph b: 14 Feb 2002 in Irvine, CA v:
Taipei, Taiwan

181.01.02

11 WITTRY, Daniel-George b: 09 Jul 1968 v: Oswego, IL o:
Oracle database administrator c: 3
+ seq: 181.01.02 TOLEDO, Tannia-Cecile b: 02 Jan 1967 in
Guayaquil, Ecuador w: 30 Oct 2000 in Evergreen, CO v:
Oswego, IL f: Victor-Raul Toledo m: Gladys-Mercedes
Rendon c: 3
12 TOLEDO, Juan-Martin b: 23 Jun 1993 in Guayaquil, Ecuador
12 TOLEDO, Daniel-Alejandro b: 16 Oct 1998 in Cuenca, Ecuador
12 WITTRY, Emma-Jane b: 15 Aug 2001 in Lakewood, CO

181.01.03

11 WITTRY, Steven-Francis (Steve) b: 04 Sep 1969 in Rockford,
IL v: Naperville, IL o: Real estate c: 1
+ seq: 181.01.03 OTTEN, Carol b: 24 Nov 1963 in Jackson, MI
w: 07 Oct 2000 v: Naperville, IL f: Ralph-Friedrich Otten m:
Ethel-May Wilson c: 1
12 WITTRY, Lauren-Marie b: 20 Apr 2003 in Naperville, IL v:
Naperville, IL

182

8 WITTRY, John b: 20 Sep 1860 in Aurora, IL d: 15 Oct 1943 in Aurora, IL h: 747 Liberty v: Big Rock, IL o: Farmer c: 8

+ seq: 182 WITTRY, Barbara b: 27 Apr 1864 in Ernzen, Lux d: 30 Mar 1933 in Aurora, IL w: 18 Feb 1886 in Aurora, IL a: Witry h: 747 Liberty v: Big Rock, IL i: Emigrated to Aurora, IL r: b f: Paul Wittry m: Marie Weber c: 8

9 WITTRY, Lena M. b: 08 Dec 1886 in Sugar Grove, IL d: 23 Jun 1973 in Elburn, IL Cause of death: Lingering illness following a fall v: Aurora, IL o: Church laundry o: Seamstress c: 4

+ seq: 182.01 FLORENCE, Edward P. b: 05 Jan 1884 in Baker, IL d: 18 Dec 1919 in Big Rock, IL Cause of death: Shot in hunting accident w: 22 Jan 1913 in Aurora, IL v: Big Rock, IL o: Farmer f: John Florence m: Emilie Grandgeorge c: 4

9 WITTRY, Laura-Lena b: 21 Apr 1888 in Sugar Grove, IL d: 10 Dec 1961 in Aurora, IL v: Aurora, IL o: Farmer c: 5

+ seq: 182.09 KONEN, Michael P. (Mike) b: 18 May 1889 d: 09 Jan 1956 in Aurora, IL w: 08 Jan 1913 in Aurora, IL v: Aurora, IL o: Farmer c: 5

9 WITTRY, John B. b: 09 Jun 1890 in Aurora, IL d: 24 Dec 1979 in Oakland, CA v: Oakland, CA o: Auto mechanic c: 3

+ seq: 183 IRWIN, Mary b: 26 Sep 1891 d: 21 Dec 1950 in Oakland, CA w: Abt. 1915 v: Oakland, CA f: Irwin m: Tally c: 3

9 WITTRY, Michael-Robert b: 06 Jun 1893 in Aurora, IL d: 10 Jan 1974 in San Diego, CA v: San Diego, CA o: City employee

+ seq: 190 FISHER, Louise b: 27 Apr 1895 d: 02 Aug 1962 in San Diego, CA w: Abt. 1920 v: San Diego, CA f: Fisher m: Jansz

9 WITTRY, Nickolaus J. b: 11 Oct 1896 in Aurora, IL d: 05 Dec 1971 in Pomona, CA v: Pomona, CA o: Owner of Pomona Pump Co.

+ seq: 191 SCHAUB, Gladys b: 14 Dec 1894 in Plainfield, IL d: 25 Jul 1982 in Pomona, CA w: Abt. 1920 v: Pomona CA f: Ludwig Schaub m: Mary Ziegler

9 WITTRY, Albert-Adam (Al) b: 05 Apr 1898 in Big Rock, IL d: 17 Sep 1967 in Aurora, IL Cause of death: Lung cancer v: Aurora, IL o: Customer service agent o: Draftsman c: 4

+ seq: 192 KNEIPPER, Margaret-Elizabeth b: 08 Feb 1902 in Pinckneyville, IL d: 15 Sep 1988 in Peoria, IL Cause of death:

Pneumonia w: 22 Sep 1925 in Aurora, IL v: Aurora, IL o:
Bookkeeper f: Nicholas (Nick) Kneipper m: Elizabeth Lorenz
c: 4

9 WITTRY, Ferdinand-Jacob (Fred) b: 20 Dec 1900 in Aurora, IL
d: 30 Aug 1986 in Pomona, CA v: Malibu, CA c: 2

+ seq: 197 WEHDEN, Lillian-Elizabeth (Lew) b: 27 Oct 1900 d:
04 Aug 1986 in Pomona, CA w: 21 Oct 1925 v: Malibu, CA
c: 2

9 WITTRY, Louisa H. b: 10 Oct 1910 in Aurora, IL d: 19 May
1915 in Aurora, IL v: Aurora, IL

182.01

9 WITTRY, Lena M. b: 08 Dec 1886 in Sugar Grove, IL d: 23
Jun 1973 in Elburn, IL Cause of death: Lingering illness
following a fall v: Aurora, IL o: Church laundry o: Seamstress
c: 4

+ seq: 182.01 FLORENCE, Edward P. b: 05 Jan 1884 in Baker, IL
d: 18 Dec 1919 in Big Rock, IL Cause of death: Shot in hunting
accident w: 22 Jan 1913 in Aurora, IL v: Big Rock, IL o:
Farmer f: John Florence m: Emilie Grandgeorge c: 4

10 FLORENCE, Barbara L. b: 05 Jun 1914 in Big Rock, IL d: 14
May 2001 in Peoria, IL Cause of death: cardiac arrest v: Peoria,
IL o: Bookkeeper

+ seq: 182.02 THEIS, John W. b: 06 May 1914 in West Chicago,
IL d: 13 May 2004 in Peoria, IL w: 24 Jan 1959 in Aurora, IL
v: Peoria, IL o: Farmer

10 FLORENCE, Emily H. b: 09 Sep 1915 in Big Rock, IL d: 22
Jan 1994 in Aurora, IL v: Aurora, IL o: Secretary c: 7

+ seq: 182.03 SABO, Julius A. (Juke) b: 04 Jul 1911 d: 12 Dec
1982 in Aurora, IL w: 24 Jun 1939 in Aurora, IL v: Aurora, IL
o: Electronics c: 7

10 FLORENCE, John E. b: 07 Sep 1917 in Big Rock, IL d: 27 Sep
2007 in Orlando, FL Cause of death: Infection v: Orlando, FL
o: Real estate appraiser o: Peat production o: Pilot c: 2

+ seq: 182.07 DAETWYLER, Peggy b: 01 Jun 1920 in Orlando,
FL d: 13 Mar 1998 in Orlando, FL w: Abt. 1946 in Orlando, FL
v: Orlando, FL c: 2

10 FLORENCE, Edward J. b: 08 Apr 1919 in Big Rock, IL d: 14
Oct 1920 in Aurora, IL v: Aurora, IL

182.03

10FLORENCE, Emily H. b: 09 Sep 1915 in Big Rock, IL d: 22 Jan 1994 in Aurora, IL v: Aurora, IL o: Secretary c: 7

+ seq: 182.03 SABO, Julius A. (Juke) b: 04 Jul 1911 d: 12 Dec 1982 in Aurora, IL w: 24 Jun 1939 in Aurora, IL v: Aurora, IL o: Electronics c: 7

11SABO, Judith M. b: 07 Apr 1940 in Aurora, IL v: North Aurora, IL o: Fermi Lab technician

11SABO, Mary-Ellen b: 08 Dec 1941 in Aurora, IL v: Aurora, CO o: Teacher c: 2

+ seq: 182.04 WITTMAN, Thomas V. b: 14 Feb 1944 w: 10 Jan 1976 in Columbus, OH v: Aurora, CO o: Business manager o: Accountant c: 2

11SABO, Barbara-Ann b: 01 Jun 1943 in Aurora, IL v: North Aurora, IL o: Medical record transcriber

11SABO, Clara-Leonette b: 15 Mar 1947 in Aurora, IL v: Elgin, IL o: Post office employee

11SABO, Monica-Margaret t: Partner in Arthur Anderson b: 31 Dec 1948 in Aurora, IL v: Dundee, IL o: Certified public accountant o: Financial consultant c: 2

+ seq: 182.05 MORGANSTEIN, Sanford (Sandy) b: 08 Dec 1943 in Bronx, NY w: 06 Jun 1970 in Aurora, IL v: Dundee, IL o: Inventor o: Electronic engineering c: 2

11SABO, Sarah-Jo b: 31 Mar 1952 in Aurora, IL v: Elgin, IL o: Medical transcriber c: 2

+ seq: 182.06 ORIZONDO, Frank b: 30 Apr 1946 w: 27 Aug 1977 in Elgin, IL v: Elgin, IL o: Salesman c: 2

11SABO, Edward-Francis b: 13 Oct 1953 in Aurora, IL v: Columbus, OH o: McDonalds

182.04

11SABO, Mary-Ellen b: 08 Dec 1941 in Aurora, IL v: Aurora, CO o: Teacher c: 2

+ seq: 182.04 WITTMAN, Thomas V. b: 14 Feb 1944 w: 10 Jan 1976 in Columbus, OH v: Aurora, CO o: Business manager o: Accountant c: 2

12WITTMAN, Gregory-Martin b: 07 May 1978 v: Aurora, CO o: Accountant

12WITTMAN, Christopher-Michael b: 19 Nov 1979 v: Topeka, KS

182.05

11SABO, Monica-Margaret t: Partner in Arthur Anderson b: 31
Dec 1948 in Aurora, IL v: Dundee, IL o: Certified public
accountant o: Financial consultant c: 2

+ seq: 182.05 MORGANSTEIN, Sanford (Sandy) b: 08 Dec
1943 in Bronx, NY w: 06 Jun 1970 in Aurora, IL v: Dundee,
IL o: Inventor o: Electronic engineering c: 2

12MORGANSTEIN, Jace-Grant (Jace) b: 10 Mar 1990 in
Hoffman Estates, IL v: Dundee, IL

12MORGANSTEIN, Tyler-Cole b: 15 Oct 1992 v: Dundee, IL

182.06

11SABO, Sarah-Jo b: 31 Mar 1952 in Aurora, IL v: Elgin, IL o:
Medical transcriber c: 2

+ seq: 182.06 ORIZONDO, Frank b: 30 Apr 1946 w: 27 Aug
1977 in Elgin, IL v: Elgin, IL o: Salesman c: 2

12ORIZONDO, Amy-Josephine b: 02 Aug 1979 v: Margate, FL
o: X-ray technician

+ seq: 182.06.01 MCGUFFIN, Craig w: 24 May 2003 in
Sycamore, IL v: Margate, FL o: X-ray technician

12ORIZONDO, Emily-Rose b: 30 Sep 1983

182.07

10FLORENCE, John E. b: 07 Sep 1917 in Big Rock, IL d: 27 Sep
2007 in Orlando, FL Cause of death: Infection v: Orlando, FL
o: Real estate appraiser o: Peat production o: Pilot c: 2

+ seq: 182.07 DAETWYLER, Peggy b: 01 Jun 1920 in Orlando,
FL d: 13 Mar 1998 in Orlando, FL w: Abt. 1946 in Orlando, FL
v: Orlando, FL c: 2

11FLORENCE, Marcia-Duncan b: 22 Mar 1954 in Orlando, FL v:
St. Petersburg, FL c: 1

+ seq: 182.08 HAZELWOOD, Richard b: 05 Mar 1949 w: Abt.
1980 v: St. Petersburg, FL o: Microbiologist c: 1

11FLORENCE, Joanne-Wittry b: 23 Apr 1955 in Orlando, FL v:
Orlando, FL o: Caterer o: Cake decorator

+ seq: 182.08.01 HOWARD, Ronald-Gene (Ron) b: 06 May 1955
in Orlando, FL w: 14 Jun 2002 in North Captiva Island, FL v:
Orlando, FL f: Varner Howard m: Agnew Abernathy

182.08

11FLORENCE, Marcia-Duncan b: 22 Mar 1954 in Orlando, FL v:

St. Petersburg, FL c: 1

+ seq: 182.08 HAZELWOOD, Richard b: 05 Mar 1949 w: Abt.
  1980 v: St. Petersburg, FL o: Microbiologist c: 1

12 HAZELWOOD, Ian-Richard b: 01 Nov 1982

182.09

9 WITTRY, Laura-Lena b: 21 Apr 1888 in Sugar Grove, IL d: 10
  Dec 1961 in Aurora, IL v: Aurora, IL o: Farmer c: 5

+ seq: 182.09 KONEN, Michael P. (Mike) b: 18 May 1889 d: 09
  Jan 1956 in Aurora, IL w: 08 Jan 1913 in Aurora, IL v:
  Aurora, IL o: Farmer c: 5

10 KONEN, John M. b: 21 Feb 1914 in Aurora, IL d: 25 Jun 1952
  in Aurora, IL v: Aurora, IL c: 2

+ seq: 182.10 MEZAN, Frances b: 07 Jul 1918 d: 27 Jan 1997 in
  Aurora, IL w: 25 Nov 1937 v: Geneva, IL c: 2

10 KONEN, Paul P. b: 29 Mar 1915 in Aurora, IL d: 03 Nov 1921
  in Aurora, IL

10 KONEN, Dorothy M. b: 24 Apr 1916 in Sugar Grove, IL d: 15
  Dec 1995 in Aurora, IL v: Aurora, IL c: 7

+ seq: 182.14 STULL, Emil W. b: 29 Oct 1906 in Aurora, IL d:
  15 Sep 1991 in Aurora, IL w: 18 Aug 1937 in Aurora, IL v:
  Aurora, IL c: 7

10[1] KONEN, Verdell-Barbara b: 06 Aug 1923 in Kaneville, IL
  d: 27 Mar 1996 in Aurora, IL v: Aurora, IL o: Furniture
  refinisher c: 11

+ seq: 182.25 CARLSON, Clarence (Cal) E. b: 11 Apr 1911 in
  Batavia, IL d: 23 Oct 1959 in Aurora, IL w: 30 Jun 1945 in
  Batavia, IL v: Aurora, IL f: Nils-Addick Carlson m: Augusta-
  Wilhelmina Anderson c: 11

* 2nd Husband of [1] KONEN, Verdell-Barbara:

+ seq: 182.38.50 HANKINS, Robert-Eugene b: 28 Jan 1938 w:
  1954

10 KONEN, Stillborn Boy b: 24 Aug 1930 d: 24 Aug 1930

182.10

10 KONEN, John M. b: 21 Feb 1914 in Aurora, IL d: 25 Jun 1952
  in Aurora, IL v: Aurora, IL c: 2

+ seq: 182.10 MEZAN, Frances b: 07 Jul 1918 d: 27 Jan 1997 in
  Aurora, IL w: 25 Nov 1937 v: Geneva, IL c: 2

11 KONEN, Donald M. b: 06 Mar 1939 v: Centralia, IL c: 2

+ seq: 182.11 JONES, Betty-Ann b: 08 Jun 1937 w: 11 May

1963 v: Geneva, IL c: 2

11KONEN, Gilbert-James b: 13 Apr 1944 in Aurora, IL d: 23 Dec 1974 in Aurora, IL v: Aurora, IL c: 1

+ seq: 182.13 ADKINS, Theresa b: Abt. 1945 w: Abt. 1970 v: Aurora, IL c: 1

182.11

11KONEN, Donald M. b: 06 Mar 1939 v: Centralia, IL c: 2

+ seq: 182.11 JONES, Betty-Ann b: 08 Jun 1937 w: 11 May 1963 v: Geneva, IL c: 2

12KONEN, John-Irvin b: 07 Dec 1967 v: Aurora, IL c: 1

+ seq: 182.12 PELLEGRINO, Diane b: 08 Aug 1956 w: 11 Nov 1989 v: Aurora, IL c: 1

12KONEN, Michael-Charles b: 25 Oct 1972

+ seq: 182.12.05 HASS, Megan-Marie b: 01 Nov 1976 w: 09 May 2003 v: Aurora, IL

182.12

12KONEN, John-Irvin b: 07 Dec 1967 v: Aurora, IL c: 1

+ seq: 182.12 PELLEGRINO, Diane b: 08 Aug 1956 w: 11 Nov 1989 v: Aurora, IL c: 1

13KONEN, Ashley-Danielle b: 11 Nov 1990

182.13

11KONEN, Gilbert-James b: 13 Apr 1944 in Aurora, IL d: 23 Dec 1974 in Aurora, IL v: Aurora, IL c: 1

+ seq: 182.13 ADKINS, Theresa b: Abt. 1945 w: Abt. 1970 v: Aurora, IL c: 1

12KONEN, Jeremy b: Feb 1974

182.14

10KONEN, Dorothy M. b: 24 Apr 1916 in Sugar Grove, IL d: 15 Dec 1995 in Aurora, IL v: Aurora, IL c: 7

+ seq: 182.14 STULL, Emil W. b: 29 Oct 1906 in Aurora, IL d: 15 Sep 1991 in Aurora, IL w: 18 Aug 1937 in Aurora, IL v: Aurora, IL c: 7

11STULL, Dianne M. b: 12 Feb 1939 in Aurora, IL v: Columbus, OH o: Homemaker o: Artist c: 4

+ seq: 182.15 EFSIC, Edward J. b: 30 Apr 1939 w: 27 Jan 1962 in Aurora, IL v: Columbus, OH o: Manager o: Engineer c: 4

11STULL, Laura-Li (Laurie) b: 07 Feb 1940 in Aurora, IL v:

Aurora, IL
+ seq: 182.18 MARZUKI, Henry, Jr. b: 08 Jan 1932 w: 02 Jan
1960 v: Aurora, IL
11STULL, Nicholas P. b: 14 Jan 1944 in Aurora, IL v: Aurora, IL
c: 4
+ seq: 182.19 MATYAS, Marsha L. b: 28 Oct 1945 w: 30 Apr
1966 v: Aurora, IL c: 4
11STULL, Dorothy-Ann b: 16 Feb 1946 in Aurora, IL v:
Sandwich, IL
+ seq: 182.21 SUCIK, John M. b: 11 Oct 1935 in Aurora, IL d:
21 Mar 2003 in Sandwich, IL Cause of death: cancer w: 12 Sep
1970 v: Sandwich, IL o: State of Illinois Employment Services
f: Jacob Sucik m: Verinica Okapal
11STULL, Margaret-Mary (Margie) b: 16 Apr 1948 in Aurora, IL
v: Earlville, IL o: Manager of a nursery c: 2
+ seq: 182.22 GEORGE, Robert-Kent (Bob) b: 30 Mar 1947 w:
08 Apr 1967 v: Earlville, IL o: Manager of a nursery c: 2
11STULL, Gary-Michael b: 07 Dec 1955 in Aurora, IL v: Aurora,
IL c: 2
+ seq: 182.23 MODAFF, Janet b: 31 Aug 1956 w: 28 May 1977
v: Aurora, IL c: 2
11STULL, Michael-John b: 02 Jul 1960 in Aurora, IL c: 1
+ seq: 182.24 COLLLINS, Teri w: Abt. 1992 c: 1

182.15
11STULL, Dianne M. b: 12 Feb 1939 in Aurora, IL v: Columbus,
OH o: Homemaker o: Artist c: 4
+ seq: 182.15 EFSIC, Edward J. b: 30 Apr 1939 w: 27 Jan 1962
in Aurora, IL v: Columbus, OH o: Manager o: Engineer c: 4
12EFSIC, Ellen-Rose b: 02 Jan 1963 in Urbana, IL v: Houston,
TX o: Arts c: 1
+ seq: 182.16 LEGG, Scott-Eric b: 15 Jan 1955 w: 16 Feb 1991
v: Houston, TX o: Law clerk c: 1
12[1] EFSIC, Maria-Elena b: 22 Jun 1964 in Urbana, IL v:
Columbus, OH c: 1
+ seq: 182.17 SPOERRI, Stefan b: 13 May 1961 in Manhattan,
NY w: 20 Jun 1986 in Manhattan, NY v: Columbus, OH c: 1
* 2nd Husband of [1] EFSIC, Maria-Elena:
+ seq: 182.17.01 VAN BOEKEL, Lambertus (Berry) b: in
Holland w: 30 Jun 2000
12EFSIC, Edward-John b: 14 Aug 1965 in Urbana, IL v: Live

Oak, TX i: Officer in U. S. Air Force o: Physicist c: 1
+ seq: 182.17.50 WILSON, Barbara (Barb) w: 03 Jun 1992 in
   San Antonio, TX c: 1
12 EFSIC, Matthew-Emil b: 20 Jan 1968 in Columbus, OH v:
   Manhattan, NY o: Navigator

182.16
12 EFSIC, Ellen-Rose b: 02 Jan 1963 in Urbana, IL v: Houston,
   TX o: Arts c: 1
+ seq: 182.16 LEGG, Scott-Eric b: 15 Jan 1955 w: 16 Feb 1991
   v: Houston, TX o: Law clerk c: 1
13 LEGG, Clare-Madelyn b: 17 Aug 1995

182.17
12 [1] EFSIC, Maria-Elena b: 22 Jun 1964 in Urbana, IL v:
   Columbus, OH c: 1
+ seq: 182.17 SPOERRI, Stefan b: 13 May 1961 in Manhattan,
   NY w: 20 Jun 1986 in Manhattan, NY v: Columbus, OH c: 1
13 SPOERRI, Emil-Johann b: 12 Mar 1987 in Manhattan, NY
* 2nd Husband of [1] EFSIC, Maria-Elena:
+ seq: 182.17.01 VAN BOEKEL, Lambertus (Berry) b: in
   Holland w: 30 Jun 2000

182.17.50
12 EFSIC, Edward-John b: 14 Aug 1965 in Urbana, IL v: Live
   Oak, TX i: Officer in U. S. Air Force o: Physicist c: 1
+ seq: 182.17.50 WILSON, Barbara (Barb) w: 03 Jun 1992 in
   San Antonio, TX c: 1
13 EFSIC, Joni c: 1
+ seq: 182.17.60 PATTERSON, Doug w: Abt. 2000 c: 1

182.17.60
13 EFSIC, Joni c: 1
+ seq: 182.17.60 PATTERSON, Doug w: Abt. 2000 c: 1
14 PATTERSON, Kamden b: 05 Dec 2005

182.19
11 STULL, Nicholas P. b: 14 Jan 1944 in Aurora, IL v: Aurora, IL
   c: 4
+ seq: 182.19 MATYAS, Marsha L. b: 28 Oct 1945 w: 30 Apr
   1966 v: Aurora, IL c: 4

12STULL, Jennifer L. b: 22 Jul 1967
12STULL, John W. b: 03 Sep 1968
12STULL, Anthony P. b: 01 Mar 1971
12STULL, Nicholas b: 11 Dec 1972 c: 3
+ seq: 182.20 STEVENS, Vicki w: Abt. 1994 c: 3

182.20
12STULL, Nicholas b: 11 Dec 1972 c: 3
+ seq: 182.20 STEVENS, Vicki w: Abt. 1994 c: 3
13STULL, Nicholas-Alexander b: 27 Dec 1995
13STULL, Samantha-Nicole b: 09 Jun 1998
13STULL, Mackenzie-Nicole b: 19 Sep 2001

182.22
11STULL, Margaret-Mary (Margie) b: 16 Apr 1948 in Aurora, IL
   v: Earlville, IL o: Manager of a nursery c: 2
+ seq: 182.22 GEORGE, Robert-Kent (Bob) b: 30 Mar 1947 w:
   08 Apr 1967 v: Earlville, IL o: Manager of a nursery c: 2
12GEORGE, Ami-Sue b: 04 Jul 1971 c: 1
+ seq: 182.22.01 CLARK, Steven b: 06 Mar 1961 w: 1999 c: 1
12GEORGE, James R. b: 28 Oct 1980

182.22.01
12GEORGE, Ami-Sue b: 04 Jul 1971 c: 1
+ seq: 182.22.01 CLARK, Steven b: 06 Mar 1961 w: 1999 c: 1
13CLARK, Chase-Alexander b: 28 Apr 2001

182.23
11STULL, Gary-Michael b: 07 Dec 1955 in Aurora, IL v: Aurora,
   IL c: 2
+ seq: 182.23 MODAFF, Janet b: 31 Aug 1956 w: 28 May 1977
   v: Aurora, IL c: 2
12STULL, Katherine M. (Katie) b: 04 Aug 1979
12STULL, Emily L. b: 29 Apr 1983

182.24
11STULL, Michael-John b: 02 Jul 1960 in Aurora, IL c: 1
+ seq: 182.24 COLLLINS, Teri w: Abt. 1992 c: 1
12STULL, Michael-John (Mac) b: 23 Mar 1994

10[6] KONEN, Verdell-Barbara b: 06 Aug 1923 in Kaneville, IL
   d: 27 Mar 1996 in Aurora, IL v: Aurora, IL o: Furniture
   refinisher c: 11
+ seq: 182.25 CARLSON, Clarence (Cal) E. b: 11 Apr 1911 in
   Batavia, IL d: 23 Oct 1959 in Aurora, IL w: 30 Jun 1945 in
   Batavia, IL v: Aurora, IL f: Nils-Addick Carlson m: Augusta-
   Wilhelmina Anderson c: 11
11[1] CARLSON, Michael-Edward b: 14 Jun 1946 in Aurora, IL
   v: Texas c: 4
+ seq: 182.26 STRICKLAND, Kitina-Jean (Kitty) b: 04 Apr
   1952 in Jerome, ID w: 14 Feb 1970 v: Texas f: Clair-Leroy
   Strickland m: Agnes-Cecellia Pyne c: 4
* 2nd Wife of [1] CARLSON, Michael-Edward:
+ seq: 182.29 UNDERHILL, June b: Abt. 1950 w: Abt. 1975
11[2] CARLSON, Peggy-Ann b: 16 Dec 1947 in Aurora, IL v:
   Belvidere, IL c: 4
+ seq: 182.30 THIELE, John-Lee b: 11 Jun 1948 w: 13 Aug
   1966 v: Aurora, IL c: 4
* 2nd Husband of [2] CARLSON, Peggy-Ann:
+ seq: 182.34 WILDER, John-Paul (Al) b: 04 Jun 1942 w: 05
   Sep 1989 v: Belvidere, IL
11 CARLSON, Raymond-Allen b: 04 Aug 1949 in Aurora, IL v:
   Sandwich, IL c: 3
+ seq: 182.35 HOLMES, Patricia-Alice b: 22 Aug 1958 in
   Aurora, IL w: 02 Aug 1981 v: Sandwich, IL c: 3
11[3] CARLSON, James-Alan b: 21 Jul 1950 in Aurora, IL v:
   Helmar, IL c: 2
+ seq: 182.36 KOHLER, Kathy L. b: 07 Dec 1950 in Louisiana
   d: 08 Jul 1976 in Aurora, IL w: 06 Jun 1970 v: Aurora, IL
* 2nd Wife of [3] CARLSON, James-Alan:
+ seq: 182.37 CASEY, Antoinette-Lynn b: 18 Nov 1959 in
   Aurora, IL w: 27 Feb 1982 v: Helmar, IL c: 2
11 CARLSON, Sally-Ann b: 01 Feb 1952 in Aurora, IL v:
   Belvidere, IL c: 2
+ seq: 182.38 FRYE, Roger-Neal b: 18 Mar 1947 w: 14 May
   1969 v: Belvidere, IL c: 2
11 CARLSON, John-Bernard b: 08 Jul 1953 in Aurora, IL v:
   Texas
* 2nd Husband of [6] KONEN, Verdell-Barbara:
+ seq: 182.38.50 HANKINS, Robert-Eugene b: 28 Jan 1938 w:

1954

11 HANKINS, Robert-Eugene-Carlson b: 31 Dec 1954 in Aurora,
IL v: Aurora, IL c: 2

+ seq: 182.39 GARZA, Emma-Lee b: 21 Sep 1956 in Aurora, IL
w: 25 Nov 1978 v: Aurora, IL c: 2

11 [4] HANKINS, Mary-Joan-Carlson b: 19 Jan 1956 in Aurora, IL
v: Rockford, IL c: 1

+ seq: 182.40 BENSON, David-Bruce b: Abt. 1950 w: 14 Jun
1978 v: Aurora, IL c: 1

* 2nd Husband of [4] HANKINS, Mary-Joan-Carlson:

+ seq: 182.41 SWARTOUT, Seldon-James (Sol) b: 15 Nov 1935
w: 25 May 1991 v: Rockford, IL

11 HANKINS, Carol-Ann-Carlson b: 25 Dec 1957 in Aurora, IL
v: Aurora, IL c: 1

+ seq: 182.42 MCDANIEL, Philip b: 10 May 1960 w: Apr 1977
v: Aurora, IL c: 1

11 [5] HANKINS, Eugene-Leonard-Carlson b: 07 May 1959 in
Aurora, IL v: Florida c: 2

+ seq: 182.43 GOSSET, Kyle-Marlin b: 30 Jun 1960 w: 14 Feb
1977 c: 1

* 2nd Wife of [5] HANKINS, Eugene-Leonard-Carlson:

+ seq: 182.44 ROSELLI, Debra-Ann b: 02 Jul 1958 w: 10 Oct
1981 v: Florida c: 1

11 HANKINS, Clare-Anne-Carlson b: 13 May 1960 in Aurora, IL
v: Flanagan, IL c: 4

+ seq: 182.45 RITLI, Charles-George, Jr. b: 13 Oct 1959 in
Naples, FL w: 09 Dec 1978 v: Flanagan, IL c: 4

182.26

11 [3] CARLSON, Michael-Edward b: 14 Jun 1946 in Aurora, IL
v: Texas c: 4

+ seq: 182.26 STRICKLAND, Kitina-Jean (Kitty) b: 04 Apr
1952 in Jerome, ID w: 14 Feb 1970 v: Texas f: Clair-Leroy
Strickland m: Agnes-Cecellia Pyne c: 4

12 CARLSON, Jeffery-Paul b: 15 Jul 1970 in Aurora, IL v:
Puyallup, WA

12 CARLSON, Joanna-Marie b: 12 May 1972 in Aurora, IL v:
Vernal, UT c: 4

+ seq: 182.27 BATTY, Brent-Dee b: 25 Jun 1964 in Vernal, UT
w: 23 Jun 1989 in Vernal, UT v: Vernal, UT f: Vern Batty m:
Kathleen-Elaine Allred c: 5

12[1] CARLSON, Joseph-Michael b: 12 Aug 1973 in Aurora, IL
  v: Youngstown, OH c: 2
+ seq: 182.27.10 SZAKACS, Amanda-Renee b: 03 Jul 1980 in
  Geneva, OH w: 25 Aug 2000 in Youngstown, OH c: 1
* 2nd Wife of [1] CARLSON, Joseph-Michael:
+ seq: 182.27.20 BRANCHO, Ann b: 11 Oct 1973 in
  Youngstown, OH w: Abt. 2001 v: Youngstown, OH c: 1
12[2] CARLSON, Kira-Lynn b: 30 May 1975 in Aurora, IL v:
  Delta, CO c: 3
+ seq: 182.28 GROSS, Jason-Larry b: 22 May 1973 in Vernal,
  UT w: 07 Dec 1991 in Jensen, UT f: Larry Gross m: Karen
  Peterson c: 2
* 2nd Husband of [2] CARLSON, Kira-Lynn:
+ seq: 182.28.10 MCINTYRE, Chip-Dio b: 28 Aug 1973 in
  Craig, CO w: 07 Nov 1997 in Craig, CO v: Delta, CO c: 1
* 2nd Wife of [3] CARLSON, Michael-Edward:
+ seq: 182.29 UNDERHILL, June b: Abt. 1950 w: Abt. 1975

182.27
12CARLSON, Joanna-Marie b: 12 May 1972 in Aurora, IL v:
  Vernal, UT c: 4
+ seq: 182.27 BATTY, Brent-Dee b: 25 Jun 1964 in Vernal, UT
  w: 23 Jun 1989 in Vernal, UT v: Vernal, UT f: Vern Batty m:
  Kathleen-Elaine Allred c: 5
13BATTY, Darcey-Rae b: 29 Jan 1990 in Vernal, UT
13BATTY, Wayne-Ross b: 10 Jun 1991 in Vernal, UT
13BATTY, Ashlee-Dawn b: 25 Mar 1992 in Vernal, UT
13BATTY, Alexis-Jean b: 25 Mar 1992 in Vernal, UT

182.27.10
12[1] CARLSON, Joseph-Michael b: 12 Aug 1973 in Aurora, IL
  v: Youngstown, OH c: 2
+ seq: 182.27.10 SZAKACS, Amanda-Renee b: 03 Jul 1980 in
  Geneva, OH w: 25 Aug 2000 in Youngstown, OH c: 1
13CARLSON, Dylan-Gene b: 22 Nov 2000 in Ohio
* 2nd Wife of [1] CARLSON, Joseph-Michael:
+ seq: 182.27.20 BRANCHO, Ann b: 11 Oct 1973 in
  Youngstown, OH w: Abt. 2001 v: Youngstown, OH c: 1
13CARLSON, Kaylyn-Marie b: 06 Jun 2001 in Youngstown, OH

182.28

12[1] CARLSON, Kira-Lynn b: 30 May 1975 in Aurora, IL v: Delta, CO c: 3

+ seq: 182.28 GROSS, Jason-Larry b: 22 May 1973 in Vernal, UT w: 07 Dec 1991 in Jensen, UT f: Larry Gross m: Karen Peterson c: 2

13 GROSS, Shelby-Nicole b: 11 Oct 1992 in Roosevelt, UT

13 GROSS, Christopher-Jason b: 22 Nov 1994 in Roosevelt, UT

* 2nd Husband of [1] CARLSON, Kira-Lynn:

+ seq: 182.28.10 MCINTYRE, Chip-Dio b: 28 Aug 1973 in Craig, CO w: 07 Nov 1997 in Craig, CO v: Delta, CO c: 1

13 MCINTYRE, McKinley-Faith b: 07 Mar 2000 in Steamboat Springs, CO

182.30

11[1] CARLSON, Peggy-Ann b: 16 Dec 1947 in Aurora, IL v: Belvidere, IL c: 4

+ seq: 182.30 THIELE, John-Lee b: 11 Jun 1948 w: 13 Aug 1966 v: Aurora, IL c: 4

12 THEILE, Jon-Charles b: 24 Aug 1967

12 THEILE, Michael-Paul b: 21 Sep 1968 c: 1

+ seq: 182.31 Anita w: Abt. 1990 c: 1

12 THEILE, Dorian-Lee b: 10 Jun 1970 c: 1

+ seq: 182.32 w: Abt. 1995 c: 1

12 THEILE, Lynn-Marie b: 05 Jan 1976 c: 1

+ seq: 182.33 w: Abt. 2000 c: 1

* 2nd Husband of [1] CARLSON, Peggy-Ann:

+ seq: 182.34 WILDER, John-Paul (Al) b: 04 Jun 1942 w: 05 Sep 1989 v: Belvidere, IL

182.31

12 THEILE, Michael-Paul b: 21 Sep 1968 c: 1

+ seq: 182.31 Anita w: Abt. 1990 c: 1

13 THEILE, Christina-Marie

182.32

12 THEILE, Dorian-Lee b: 10 Jun 1970 c: 1

+ seq: 182.32 w: Abt. 1995 c: 1

13 THEILE, Todd-Anthony

182.33

12 THEILE, Lynn-Marie b: 05 Jan 1976 c: 1
+ seq: 182.33 w: Abt. 2000 c: 1
13 THEILE, Shaa-Marie

182.35

11 CARLSON, Raymond-Allen b: 04 Aug 1949 in Aurora, IL v:
   Sandwich, IL c: 3
+ seq: 182.35 HOLMES, Patricia-Alice b: 22 Aug 1958 in
   Aurora, IL w: 02 Aug 1981 v: Sandwich, IL c: 3
12 CARLSON, Drew-Clarence b: 03 Sep 1983 in Aurora, IL v:
   Aurora, IL
12 CARLSON, Shayna-Frances b: 24 Apr 1985 in Aurora, IL v:
   Aurora, IL
12 CARLSON, Bethany-Holmes b: 20 Jul 1987 in Aurora, IL d:
   20 Jul 1987 in Aurora, IL v: Aurora, IL

182.36

11 [1] CARLSON, James-Alan b: 21 Jul 1950 in Aurora, IL v:
   Helmar, IL c: 2
+ seq: 182.36 KOHLER, Kathy L. b: 07 Dec 1950 in Louisiana
   d: 08 Jul 1976 in Aurora, IL w: 06 Jun 1970 v: Aurora, IL
* 2nd Wife of [1] CARLSON, James-Alan:
+ seq: 182.37 CASEY, Antoinette-Lynn b: 18 Nov 1959 in
   Aurora, IL w: 27 Feb 1982 v: Helmar, IL c: 2
12 CARLSON, James-Alan b: 13 Oct 1983 in St. Charles, IL
12 CARLSON, Travis-Edward b: 29 Jul 1985 in St. Charles, IL

182.38

11 CARLSON, Sally-Ann b: 01 Feb 1952 in Aurora, IL v:
   Belvidere, IL c: 2
+ seq: 182.38 FRYE, Roger-Neal b: 18 Mar 1947 w: 14 May
   1969 v: Belvidere, IL c: 2
12 FRYE, Laura-Barbara b: 09 May 1974
12 FRYE, Krystal-Elizabeth b: 21 Feb 1983 in Rockford, IL

182.39

11 HANKINS, Robert-Eugene-Carlson b: 31 Dec 1954 in Aurora,
   IL v: Aurora, IL c: 2
+ seq: 182.39 GARZA, Emma-Lee b: 21 Sep 1956 in Aurora, IL
   w: 25 Nov 1978 v: Aurora, IL c: 2

12HANKINS, Elise-Maria b: 10 Jul 1983 in Aurora, IL
12HANKINS, Samuel-Robert b: 27 Aug 1985 in Aurora, IL

182.40

11[1] HANKINS, Mary-Joan-Carlson b: 19 Jan 1956 in Aurora, IL
v: Rockford, IL c: 1
+ seq: 182.40 BENSON, David-Bruce b: Abt. 1950 w: 14 Jun
1978 v: Aurora, IL c: 1
12BENSON, Christopher-Raymond b: 08 Oct 1979
* 2nd Husband of [1] HANKINS, Mary-Joan-Carlson:
+ seq: 182.41 SWARTOUT, Seldon-James (Sol) b: 15 Nov 1935
w: 25 May 1991 v: Rockford, IL

182.42

11HANKINS, Carol-Ann-Carlson b: 25 Dec 1957 in Aurora, IL
v: Aurora, IL c: 1
+ seq: 182.42 MCDANIEL, Philip b: 10 May 1960 w: Apr 1977
v: Aurora, IL c: 1
12MCDANIELS, Jessica-Ann b: 07 Sep 1977

182.43

11[1] HANKINS, Eugene-Leonard-Carlson b: 07 May 1959 in
Aurora, IL v: Florida c: 2
+ seq: 182.43 GOSSET, Kyle-Marlin b: 30 Jun 1960 w: 14 Feb
1977 c: 1
12MCHALE, Amy-Kristine b: 09 Sep 1977
* 2nd Wife of [1] HANKINS, Eugene-Leonard-Carlson:
+ seq: 182.44 ROSELLI, Debra-Ann b: 02 Jul 1958 w: 10 Oct
1981 v: Florida c: 1
12HANKINS, Amy-Christina

182.45

11HANKINS, Clare-Anne-Carlson b: 13 May 1960 in Aurora, IL
v: Flanagan, IL c: 4
+ seq: 182.45 RITLI, Charles-George, Jr. b: 13 Oct 1959 in
Naples, FL w: 09 Dec 1978 v: Flanagan, IL c: 4
12RITLI, Fawn-Marie b: 23 Nov 1979 in Killeen, FL
12RITLI, Charles-George III b: 18 Sep 1986
12RITLI, Destiny-Katherine b: 29 Sep 1990 in Aurora, IL
12RITLI, Alexander-Louigi

183

9 WITTRY, John B. b: 09 Jun 1890 in Aurora, IL d: 24 Dec 1979 in Oakland, CA v: Oakland, CA o: Auto mechanic c: 3

+ seq: 183 IRWIN, Mary b: 26 Sep 1891 d: 21 Dec 1950 in Oakland, CA w: Abt. 1915 v: Oakland, CA f: Irwin m: Tally c: 3

10WITTRY, Donald J. b: 15 Apr 1921 d: 12 Oct 1987 in Richmond, CA v: Richmond, CA o: School principal c: 2

+ seq: 184 DINWIDDIE, Diane b: 09 Aug 1924 w: Abt. 1950 v: Richmond, CA c: 2

10WITTRY, Edmund-Robert b: 17 Jan 1927 d: 19 Aug 1987 v: Clinton, TN o: Atomic physicist c: 3

+ seq: 185 BRENNAN, Celestine (Cel) b: Abt. 1930 w: Abt. 1955 v: Clinton, TN c: 3

10WITTRY, Raymond-Irwin b: 17 Jan 1927 d: 16 Jan 1978 v: San Mateo, CA o: Electric wire salesman c: 4

+ seq: 188 MURPHY, Shannon-Aileen b: 01 Dec 1933 d: 02 Feb 1996 in Walnut Creek, CA w: Abt. 1953 v: San Mateo, CA f: Murphy m: Brennan c: 4

10WITTRY, Donald J. b: 15 Apr 1921 d: 12 Oct 1987 in Richmond, CA v: Richmond, CA o: School principal c: 2

+ seq: 184 DINWIDDIE, Diane b: 09 Aug 1924 w: Abt. 1950 v: Richmond, CA c: 2

11WITTRY, Vaughan-John b: 07 Mar 1952 in Berkeley, CA v: Monterey, CA o: Physician

11WITTRY, Charmian-Anne (Cherie) b: 28 Jun 1953 in Berkeley, CA o: Commercial realtor c: 2

+ seq: 184.01 GEYTON, Donald-Patrick (Don) b: 05 Jan 1952 in Wayandotte, MI d: Oct 2006 in San Mateo, CA Cause of death: colon cancer w: Abt. 1985 v: San Mateo, CA o: Electronic technician f: James-Michael Geyton m: Elizabeth-Mae Marchell c: 2

11WITTRY, Charmian-Anne (Cherie) b: 28 Jun 1953 in Berkeley, CA o: Commercial realtor c: 2

+ seq: 184.01 GEYTON, Donald-Patrick (Don) b: 05 Jan 1952 in Wayandotte, MI d: Oct 2006 in San Mateo, CA Cause of death: colon cancer w: Abt. 1985 v: San Mateo, CA o: Electronic technician f: James-Michael Geyton m: Elizabeth-Mae Marchell c: 2

12GEYTON, Dior-Yvonne b: 21 Jul 1988 in Redwood City, CA

12GEYTON, Bryce-Vaughn b: 06 Oct 1989 in Redwood City, CA

185

10WITTRY, Edmund-Robert b: 17 Jan 1927 d: 19 Aug 1987 v: Clinton, TN o: Atomic physicist c: 3

+ seq: 185 BRENNAN, Celestine (Cel) b: Abt. 1930 w: Abt. 1955 v: Clinton, TN c: 3

11WITTRY, Randal-Joseph (Randy) b: 04 Feb 1957 v: Coronado, CA c: 2

+ seq: 186 DRUM, Melissa b: 1957 in Monterey, CA w: 14 Aug 1982 in Williamsburg, VA v: Coronado, CA c: 2

11[1] WITTRY, Edmund B. b: 23 Aug 1959 in Livermore, CA v: Denver, CO o: Representative for Oasis LifeSciences o: Consultant for product design c: 3

+ seq: 187 BROWN, Lynne B. b: 22 Oct 1960 w: 10 Jun 1988 in Denver, CO v: Denver, CO c: 2

* 2nd Wife of [1] WITTRY, Edmund B.:

+ seq: 187.00.50 Chris w: 29 Jul 2006 in Denver, CO c: 1

11WITTRY, Nannon K. b: 16 Jan 1961 c: 2

+ seq: 187.01 ROOSA, Jack b: Abt. 1955 w: 01 Mar 1986 c: 2

186

11WITTRY, Randal-Joseph (Randy) b: 04 Feb 1957 v: Coronado, CA c: 2

+ seq: 186 DRUM, Melissa b: 1957 in Monterey, CA w: 14 Aug 1982 in Williamsburg, VA v: Coronado, CA c: 2

12WITTRY, Beth-Celestine b: Feb 1986

12WITTRY, Scott b: Dec 1987

187

11[1] WITTRY, Edmund B. b: 23 Aug 1959 in Livermore, CA v: Denver, CO o: Representative for Oasis LifeSciences o: Consultant for product design c: 3

+ seq: 187 BROWN, Lynne B. b: 22 Oct 1960 w: 10 Jun 1988 in Denver, CO v: Denver, CO c: 2

12WITTRY, Connor b: 28 Oct 1990 in Phoenix, AZ

12WITTRY, Brennan b: 27 Oct 1993 in Philadelphia, PA

* 2nd Wife of [1] WITTRY, Edmund B.:

+ seq: 187.00.50 Chris w: 29 Jul 2006 in Denver, CO c: 1
12WITTRY, Melanie b: 1993

187.01
11WITTRY, Nannon K. b: 16 Jan 1961 c: 2
+ seq: 187.01 ROOSA, Jack b: Abt. 1955 w: 01 Mar 1986 c: 2
12ROOSA, Kathleen b: Sep 1988
12ROOSA, Danielle b: 04 Jul 1995 in Phoenix, AZ

188
10WITTRY, Raymond-Irwin b: 17 Jan 1927 d: 16 Jan 1978 v:
　　San Mateo, CA o: Electric wire salesman c: 4
+ seq: 188 MURPHY, Shannon-Aileen b: 01 Dec 1933 d: 02 Feb
　　1996 in Walnut Creek, CA w: Abt. 1953 v: San Mateo, CA f:
　　Murphy m: Brennan c: 4
11WITTRY, Heather-Aileen b: 05 Mar 1954
11WITTRY, Lisa-Marie b: 10 Feb 1955 v: St. Charles, IL
11WITTRY, Diedra-Ann b: 06 Apr 1957 v: Oakland, CA
11WITTRY, Robert-Irwin b: 13 Jun 1959 v: Windsor, CA o:
　　Contracting Superintendant c: 2
+ seq: 189 BUCKLEY, Janet-Marie b: Abt. 1960 w: Abt. 1985
　　in Santa Rosa, CA v: Windsor, CA o: Teacher c: 2

189
11WITTRY, Robert-Irwin b: 13 Jun 1959 v: Windsor, CA o:
　　Contracting Superintendant c: 2
+ seq: 189 BUCKLEY, Janet-Marie b: Abt. 1960 w: Abt. 1985
　　in Santa Rosa, CA v: Windsor, CA o: Teacher c: 2
12WITTRY, Chelsey-Anne b: 24 Oct 1992
12WITTRY, Jennifer-Marie b: 29 Dec 1994

192
9 WITTRY, Albert-Adam (Al) b: 05 Apr 1898 in Big Rock, IL d:
　　17 Sep 1967 in Aurora, IL Cause of death: Lung cancer v:
　　Aurora, IL o: Customer service agent o: Draftsman c: 4
+ seq: 192 KNEIPPER, Margaret-Elizabeth b: 08 Feb 1902 in
　　Pinckneyville, IL d: 15 Sep 1988 in Peoria, IL Cause of death:
　　Pneumonia w: 22 Sep 1925 in Aurora, IL v: Aurora, IL o:
　　Bookkeeper f: Nicholas (Nick) Kneipper m: Elizabeth Lorenz
　　c: 4
10WITTRY, Shirley M. b: 06 Aug 1927 in Aurora, IL d: 06 Aug

1927 in Aurora, IL

10WITTRY, Urban C. b: 06 Aug 1927 in Aurora, IL d: 12 Aug 1927 in Aurora, IL

10WITTRY, David-Albert b: 20 Feb 1930 in Aurora, IL v: Los Angeles, CA o: Floral designer

10WITTRY, Eugene-Joseph (Gene) t: Election Commissioner b: 04 Jan 1932 in Aurora, IL v: Peoria, IL o: Teacher o: Amateur genealogist o: Computer systems development manager c: 5

+ seq: 193 LINK, Nancy-Ann b: 18 Aug 1934 in Dubuque, IA w: 02 Oct 1954 in Elgin, IL v: Peoria, IL o: Bookkeeper f: Albert-James Link m: Delphine-Elizabeth (Del) Herkes c: 5

193

10WITTRY, Eugene-Joseph (Gene) b: 04 Jan 1932 in Aurora, IL v: Peoria, IL o: Computer systems development manager t: Election Commissioner o: Teacher c: 5

+ seq: 193 LINK, Nancy-Ann b: 18 Aug 1934 in Dubuque, IA w: 02 Oct 1954 in Elgin, IL v: Peoria, IL f: Albert-James Link m: Delphine-Elizabeth (Del) Herkes c: 5

11WITTRY, Stephen-Albert (Steve) b: 09 Nov 1955 in Aurora, IL v: Lawrenceville GA o: Systems consultant t: Project manager o: Industrial engineer c: 4

+ seq: 194 BURKE, Kathleen-Marie (Kathy) b: 22 May 1956 in Madison, WI w: 24 Apr 1976 in Morton, IL v: Lawrenceville, GA o: Office Manager o: School counselor f: Lawrence-Patrick Burke m: Margaret-Mary Moriarty c: 4

11WITTRY, Mark-David b: 09 Jul 1957 in Aurora, IL v: St. Louis, MO o: Nuclear physician o: Radialogist o: Computer programmer

11WITTRY, Mary-Elizabeth (Mary-Beth) b: 21 Jun 1959 in Aurora, IL v: Shrewsbury, MO o: Director of music

11WITTRY, Philip-John (Phil) b: 06 Jan 1963 in Peoria, IL v: Terrace Park, OH c: 2

+ seq: 196 MOORE, Kelly-Jo b: 21 Dec 1966 in Chillicothe, OH w: 26 Oct 1991 in Jackson, OH v: Terrace Park, OH f: Jimmie-Lee Moore m: Dianne-Ruth Rowe c: 2

11WITTRY, Susan-Anne (Susie) b: 01 Feb 1965 in Peoria, IL v: Evanston, IL t: Vice-president and CFO of Element 79 o: Human Services Manager

+ seq: 196.01 RASHID, Jeffrey-Michael (Jeff) b: 07 Jun 1965 in Peoria, IL w: 24 Nov 2000 in Evanston, IL v: Evanston, IL o:

Graphic Designer f: Ameel-George Rashid m: Joyce Arlene Lahne

194

11 WITTRY, Stephen-Albert (Steve) t: Project manager b: 09 Nov 1955 in Aurora, IL v: Lawrenceville GA o: Industrial engineer o: Computer systems engineer o: Systems consultant c: 4

+ seq: 194 BURKE, Kathleen-Marie (Kathy) b: 22 May 1956 in Madison, WI w: 24 Apr 1976 in Morton, IL v: Lawrenceville, GA o: School counselor o: Realtor o: Office Manager f: Lawrence-Patrick Burke m: Margaret-Mary Moriarty c: 4

12 WITTRY, Eric-Stephen b: 13 Dec 1977 in Peoria, IL v: Lawrenceville, GA o: Systems consultant

12 WITTRY, Shanna-Nicole b: 09 Feb 1979 in Peoria, IL v: Gainesville, GA c: 1

+ seq: 194.01 MALONE, Timothy-Mark b: 14 May 1974 in Gulfport, MI w: 19 Aug 2000 in Atlanta, GA v: Gainesville, GA o: Finance f: Mark-Elliott Malone m: Sara-Katherine Riley c: 1

12 WITTRY, Jennifer-Lynn (Jenny) b: 10 Feb 1980 in Peoria, IL v: Lawrenceville, GA o: Systems consultant

+ seq: 195 ROBERTSON, Christian-James (Chris) b: 31 Oct 1980 in Ypsilanti, MI w: 28 Jan 2006 in Lilburn, GA v: Lawrenceville, GA i: Served in US Marine Corps in Iraq o: Police officer f: James-Cecil Robertson m: Mary-Louise Schmid

12 WITTRY, Evan-Ryan b: 29 Dec 1982 in Peoria, IL v: Lawrenceville, GA o: Systems consultant

+ seq: 195.50 INGRAM, Kristin-Michelle b: 03 Jan 1983 in Albany, GA w: 20 May 2006 in Vienna, GA v: Lawrenceville, GA f: Mark-Murphy Ingram m: Michelle-Moncrief Sheppard

194.01

12 WITTRY, Shanna-Nicole b: 09 Feb 1979 in Peoria, IL v: Gainesville, GA c: 1

+ seq: 194.01 MALONE, Timothy-Mark b: 14 May 1974 in Gulfport, MI w: 19 Aug 2000 in Atlanta, GA v: Gainesville, GA o: Finance f: Mark-Elliott Malone m: Sara-Katherine Riley c: 1

13 MALONE, Madison-Lee b: 19 Jun 2006 in Atlanta, GA v: Gainesville, GA

196

11 WITTRY, Philip-John (Phil) b: 06 Jan 1963 in Peoria, IL v: Terrace Park, OH o: Data base engineer c: 2

+ seq: 196 MOORE, Kelly-Jo b: 21 Dec 1966 in Chillicothe, OH w: 26 Oct 1991 in Jackson, OH v: Terrace Park, OH o: Computer systems development manager f: Jimmie-Lee Moore m: Dianne-Ruth Rowe c: 2

12 WITTRY, Andrew-Stephen (Andy) b: 06 Aug 1994 in Cincinnati, OH v: Terrace Park, OH

12 WITTRY, Gretchen-Nicole b: 17 Nov 1996 in Cincinnati, OH v: Terrace Park, OH

197

9 WITTRY, Ferdinand-Jacob (Fred) b: 20 Dec 1900 in Aurora, IL d: 30 Aug 1986 in Pomona, CA v: Malibu, CA c: 2

+ seq: 197 WEHDEN, Lillian-Elizabeth (Lew) b: 27 Oct 1900 d: 04 Aug 1986 in Pomona, CA w: 21 Oct 1925 v: Malibu, CA c: 2

10 WITTRY, Delmar L. b: 11 Jul 1928 d: 25 Mar 1968 v: San Diego, CA c: 3

+ seq: 198 DOUGLAS, Patricia-Kay b: 29 Jul 1930 d: 06 Jun 2003 w: 14 Aug 1949 v: San Diego, CA c: 3

10 WITTRY, Delbert F. b: 11 Jul 1928 d: 18 Jan 1989 v: Malibu, CA c: 4

+ seq: 201 KIEFER, Patricia-Mae b: 26 Jun 1929 w: 05 Jun 1949 v: Port Hueneme, CA v: Malibu, CA c: 4

198

10 WITTRY, Delmar L. b: 11 Jul 1928 d: 25 Mar 1968 v: San Diego, CA c: 3

+ seq: 198 DOUGLAS, Patricia-Kay b: 29 Jul 1930 d: 06 Jun 2003 w: 14 Aug 1949 v: San Diego, CA c: 3

11 WITTRY, Sandra-Lynn (Sandi) b: 31 Aug 1950 in Upland, CA v: Santee, CA c: 2

+ seq: 198.01 HILL, Gary-Dee b: 12 Nov 1947 w: 25 Oct 1969 in Lancaster, CA v: Santee, CA c: 2

11 WITTRY, James-Douglas b: 10 May 1953 in Glendale, CA v: San Clemente, CA c: 2

+ seq: 199 BUNKELMAN, Susan-Denise b: 14 Apr 1953 w: Abt. 1980 v: San Clemente, CA o: Realtor at Prudential California Realty c: 2

11WITTRY, Glen-Louis b: 25 Mar 1959 in Palmdale, CA v:
Santee, CA c: 2
+ seq: 200 COHEN, Ellen-Andrea b: 07 Jul 1961 w: Abt. 1981
v: Santee, CA c: 2

198.01

11WITTRY, Sandra-Lynn (Sandi) b: 31 Aug 1950 in Upland, CA
v: Santee, CA c: 2
+ seq: 198.01 HILL, Gary-Dee b: 12 Nov 1947 w: 25 Oct 1969
in Lancaster, CA v: Santee, CA c: 2
12HILL, Matthew-Glen b: 09 Jul 1971 v: Santee, CA c: 2
+ seq: 198.02 SIMMONS, Tanya M. b: 15 Mar 1977 w: 21 Apr
2001 v: Santee, CA c: 2
12HILL, Pamela-Dee b: 27 Oct 1976 v: Murietta, CA
+ seq: 198.03 KAARG, Jason P. b: 16 Aug 1976 w: 17 Nov
2001 v: Murietta, CA

198.02

12HILL, Matthew-Glen b: 09 Jul 1971 v: Santee, CA c: 2
+ seq: 198.02 SIMMONS, Tanya M. b: 15 Mar 1977 w: 21 Apr
2001 v: Santee, CA c: 2
13HILL, Kelci-Dawn b: 11 Aug 2001
13HILL, Kalyn-Lorraine b: 16 Feb 2003

199

11WITTRY, James-Douglas b: 10 May 1953 in Glendale, CA v:
San Clemente, CA c: 2
+ seq: 199 BUNKELMAN, Susan-Denise b: 14 Apr 1953 w:
Abt. 1980 v: San Clemente, CA o: Realtor at Prudential
California Realty c: 2
12WITTRY, Wesley-James b: 04 Jan 1982
12WITTRY, Waylon-Robert b: 22 Sep 1984

200

11WITTRY, Glen-Louis b: 25 Mar 1959 in Palmdale, CA v:
Santee, CA c: 2
+ seq: 200 COHEN, Ellen-Andrea b: 07 Jul 1961 w: Abt. 1981
v: Santee, CA c: 2
12WITTRY, Janelle-Patricia b: 21 May 1983
12WITTRY, Brandon-Gary b: 05 Jun 1991

10WITTRY, Delbert F. b: 11 Jul 1928 d: 18 Jan 1989 v: Malibu,
CA c: 4
+ seq: 201 KIEFER, Patricia-Mae b: 26 Jun 1929 w: 05 Jun 1949
v: Port Hueneme, CA v: Malibu, CA c: 4
11WITTRY, Catherine-Patricia (Cathy) b: 10 Apr 1950 in San
Bernadino, CA c: 2
+ seq: 201.01 MCMAHAN, Robert-Bruce b: 31 May 1947 w: 26
Sep 1975 f: Walter-Carl McMahan m: Frankie Craig c: 2
11[1] WITTRY, Debra-Christine b: 01 Mar 1953 in San
Bernadino, CA c: 4
+ seq: 201.02 MCDANIEL, James-Lee b: 05 Mar 1943 w: 30
Nov 1970 c: 1
* 2nd Husband of [1] WITTRY, Debra-Christine:
+ seq: 201.04 MERCER, John-Allan b: 01 Jun 1948 w: 25 Aug
1973 c: 3
11WITTRY, Jonathan-Marc (Jon) b: 28 Feb 1958 in Covina, CA
v: Deer Park, WA o: Spur of the Moment Equestrian Center c:
4
+ seq: 202 SETH, Karen-Lee b: 23 Feb 1952 w: 27 Jun 1981 v:
Deer Park, WA o: Spur of the Moment Equestrian Center c: 4
11[2] WITTRY, Anne-Michelle b: 14 Apr 1961 in Santa Monica,
CA v: Port Hueneme, CA
+ seq: 202.01 WAIND, Patrick-Allen b: 28 Dec 1953 w: 07 Apr
1990 v: Port Hueneme, CA
* 2nd Husband of [2] WITTRY, Anne-Michelle:
+ seq: 202.02 DEPAOLO, David-John b: 02 Oct 1959 w: 23 Jan
1999

201.01

11WITTRY, Catherine-Patricia (Cathy) b: 10 Apr 1950 in San
Bernadino, CA c: 2
+ seq: 201.01 MCMAHAN, Robert-Bruce b: 31 May 1947 w: 26
Sep 1975 f: Walter-Carl McMahan m: Frankie Craig c: 2
12MCMAHAN, Brian-Robert b: 14 Nov 1977
12MCMAHAN, Brigitte-Megan b: 24 Jun 1980

201.02

11[1] WITTRY, Debra-Christine b: 01 Mar 1953 in San
Bernadino, CA c: 4
+ seq: 201.02 MCDANIEL, James-Lee b: 05 Mar 1943 w: 30

Nov 1970 c: 1

12 MCDANIEL, Dawn-Leanne b: 28 Sep 1971 a: Dawn-Leanne
Mercer c: 2

+ seq: 201.03 BARRON, Daniel-David b: 17 Sep 1970 w: 16
May 1998 c: 2

* 2nd Husband of [1] WITTRY, Debra-Christine:

+ seq: 201.04 MERCER, John-Allan b: 01 Jun 1948 w: 25 Aug
1973 c: 3

12 MERCER, John-Jacob b: 28 Aug 1974

12 MERCER, Joseph-Michael b: 29 Oct 1976

12 MERCER, Joshua-James b: 30 Dec 1979

201.03

12 MCDANIEL, Dawn-Leanne b: 28 Sep 1971 a: Dawn-Leanne
Mercer c: 2

+ seq: 201.03 BARRON, Daniel-David b: 17 Sep 1970 w: 16
May 1998 c: 2

13 BARRON, Sonrisa-Christine b: 23 Nov 1998 in Olympia, WA

13 BARRON, Elias-DeSpain b: 02 Mar 2001

202

11 WITTRY, Jonathan-Marc (Jon) b: 28 Feb 1958 in Covina, CA
v: Deer Park, WA o: Spur of the Moment Equestrian Center c:
4

+ seq: 202 SETH, Karen-Lee b: 23 Feb 1952 w: 27 Jun 1981 v:
Deer Park, WA o: Spur of the Moment Equestrian Center c: 4

12 WITTRY, Taylor-Ann b: 02 Feb 1984

12 WITTRY, Jonathan-Marc b: 28 Jun 1985

12 WITTRY, Payton-Elaine b: 27 Mar 1988

12 WITTRY, Hagen-Patricia b: 27 Jun 1991

203

8 WITTRY, Nick b: 28 Feb 1862 in Aurora, IL d: 30 Oct 1935 v:
Kaneville, IL o: Farmer c: 6

+ seq: 203 DOCKENDORF, Lena b: 13 Jan 1866 in Michelau,
Lux d: 07 May 1948 in Kaneville, IL w: 14 Apr 1885 v:
Kaneville, IL r: d f: Nicolaus Dockendorf m: Magdalena c: 6

9 WITTRY, Jacob (Jake) b: 16 Jan 1886 d: 20 Feb 1975 in
Aurora, IL v: Aurora, IL o: Farmer c: 2

+ seq: 204 KAMMES, Josephine b: 12 Mar 1890 d: 06 Sep 1974
in Aurora, IL w: Abt. 1912 v: Aurora, IL c: 2

9 WITTRY, Lena b: 08 Oct 1887 d: 12 Jun 1973 v: Maple Park, IL c: 1

+ seq: 204.27 FREDERICK, Roy b: 27 Jan 1887 d: 08 Oct 1983 w: Abt. 1920 v: Maple Park, IL c: 1

9 WITTRY, Mike N. b: 04 Mar 1890 d: 15 Mar 1954 v: Chicago, IL c: 1

+ seq: 205 ZEBEL, Vita b: 28 Dec 1895 d: 08 Jun 1970 w: Abt. 1925 v: Chicago, IL c: 1

9 WITTRY, Christ b: 06 Aug 1892 d: 29 Nov 1908

9 WITTRY, Henry b: 02 Nov 1895 d: 17 Oct 1978 in Illinois v: Warrenville, IL c: 1

+ seq: 206 HANKES, Eva b: 14 May 1897 d: 11 Apr 1975 in Illinois w: Abt. 1925 v: Warrenville, IL c: 1

9 WITTRY, Julia b: 07 May 1906 d: 28 Feb 1913

204

9 WITTRY, Jacob (Jake) b: 16 Jan 1886 d: 20 Feb 1975 in Aurora, IL v: Aurora, IL o: Farmer c: 2

+ seq: 204 KAMMES, Josephine b: 12 Mar 1890 d: 06 Sep 1974 in Aurora, IL w: Abt. 1912 v: Aurora, IL c: 2

10 WITTRY, Julia b: 23 Jan 1914 d: 09 Sep 1990 in Aurora, IL v: Aurora, IL c: 11

+ seq: 204.01 HUSS, Henry (Hank) b: 09 May 1911 d: 02 Apr 1977 in Aurora, IL w: 23 Jan 1933 v: Aurora, IL o: Painter c: 11

10 WITTRY, Alice L. b: 08 Nov 1918 d: 22 Dec 1974 in Aurora, IL v: Shorewood, IL c: 4

+ seq: 204.21 EVANS, Robert J. (Bob) b: 15 Jan 1919 in Aurora, IL d: 11 Nov 1995 in Shorewood, IL w: Abt. 1941 v: Shorewood, IL o: Chief engineer o: Toolmaker f: Leonard Evans m: Eva Kneipper c: 4

204.01

10 WITTRY, Julia b: 23 Jan 1914 d: 09 Sep 1990 in Aurora, IL v: Aurora, IL c: 11

+ seq: 204.01 HUSS, Henry (Hank) b: 09 May 1911 d: 02 Apr 1977 in Aurora, IL w: 23 Jan 1933 v: Aurora, IL o: Painter c: 11

11 HUSS, Donna-Mae b: 24 Mar 1936 in Aurora, IL v: Hinkley, IL c: 9

+ seq: 204.02 GARY, Eugene D. b: 30 Aug 1934 w: 24 Apr

1954 v: Hinkley, IL o: Restaurant owner c: 9

11[1] HUSS, Richard-Henry b: 28 Apr 1937 in Aurora, IL d: 20
     Aug 2002 in Wheatland, WY v: Glendo, WY c: 3

+ seq: 204.11 FREDERICKSON, Judy b: Abt. 1940 w: Abt.
     1963 c: 3

* 2nd Wife of [1] HUSS, Richard-Henry:

+ seq: 204.11.01 Cleo w: Abt. 1980

* 3rd Wife of [1] HUSS, Richard-Henry:

+ seq: 204.11.02 PRISCILLA w: Abt. 1990 v: Glendo, WY

11 HUSS, Mona-Marie b: 21 Jun 1942 v: Batavia, IL c: 3

+ seq: 204.12 ADAM, David b: 08 May 1940 w: Abt. 1962 v:
     Batavia, IL c: 3

11 HUSS, Edwin L. (Ed) b: 09 Sep 1943 v: Aurora, IL c: 3

+ seq: 204.14 PILCH, Judith E. (Judie) b: 10 Aug 1939 w: 29
     Mar 1969 v: Aurora, IL c: 3

11 HUSS, Thomas J. (Tom) b: 27 Mar 1944 v: Sarasota, FL c: 3

+ seq: 204.15 BOCKMAN, Pam b: 27 Jun 1947 w: Abt. 1975 v:
     Sarasota, FL c: 3

11 HUSS, Anna-Jean (Ann) b: 30 Nov 1948 v: Fresno, CA c: 4

+ seq: 204.16 HANKES, John D. (Jack) b: 15 Aug 1947 w: 27
     Dec 1969 v: Fresno, CA c: 4

11 HUSS, Kathy-Jo (Kathryn) b: 01 Feb 1950 v: Aurora, IL c: 2

+ seq: 204.17 TIERNEY, Michael T. (Mike) b: 14 Aug 1947 w:
     15 Nov 1969 v: Aurora, IL c: 2

11 HUSS, Henry J. (Harry) b: 23 Nov 1951 v: Corona, CA

11 HUSS, Margaret-Marie (Margie) b: 01 Nov 1952 v: Aurora, IL
     c: 3

+ seq: 204.18 WEITEN, Ronald (Ron) b: 22 Feb 1945 w: 10 Jun
     1972 v: Aurora, IL c: 3

11 HUSS, Bernadine b: 05 Nov 1956 v: Sugar Grove, IL c: 2

+ seq: 204.19 DE KING, Brad b: Abt. 1950 w: Abt. 1980 v:
     Sugar Grove, IL c: 2

11 HUSS, Joseph R. (Joe) b: 15 Nov 1957 v: Wheaton, IL c: 3

+ seq: 204.20 HEATON, Eileen b: 11 Mar 1957 w: 16 Jun 1979
     v: Wheaton, IL c: 3

204.02

11 HUSS, Donna-Mae b: 24 Mar 1936 in Aurora, IL v: Hinkley,
     IL c: 9

+ seq: 204.02 GARY, Eugene D. b: 30 Aug 1934 w: 24 Apr
     1954 v: Hinkley, IL o: Restaurant owner c: 9

12GARY, Arthur-Bernard b: 29 Mar 1955 in Aurora, IL c: 1
+ seq: 204.03 POTTS, Brenda b: Abt. 1960 w: 04 Nov 1989 c: 1
12GARY, Dean-Edward b: 25 Mar 1956 in Aurora, IL c: 4
+ seq: 204.04 RECKMEYER, Pamela b: 14 Jun 1955 w: 14 May
   1976 c: 4
12GARY, Gwen-Helene b: 06 Feb 1957 c: 2
+ seq: 204.05 BOCKMAN, Patrick b: 17 Mar 1954 w: 04 Sep
   1975 c: 2
12GARY, James-Kenneth b: 22 Feb 1958 c: 2
+ seq: 204.06 DESMOND, Judith b: 28 Oct 1959 w: 15 Mar
   1980 c: 2
12GARY, Marianne N. b: 19 Jul 1959 c: 2
+ seq: 204.07 MCCORMICK, Daniel b: 01 Aug 1955 w: 06 Jun
   1981 c: 2
12GARY, Phillip Q. b: 01 Jun 1960 c: 2
+ seq: 204.08 NORTHRUP, Sherri b: 21 Mar 1963 w: 06 Jun
   1985 c: 2
12GARY, Stephan-Thomas b: 12 Aug 1961
12GARY, Vincent-William b: 30 Jul 1962 c: 2
+ seq: 204.09 SPEARS, Cindy b: 13 Jul 1958 w: 06 Sep 1987 c:
   2
12GARY, Donald-Gene b: 31 Jul 1965 c: 2
+ seq: 204.10 DONKA, Joy L. b: 01 Feb 1965 w: 17 Aug 1987
   c: 2

204.03
12GARY, Arthur-Bernard b: 29 Mar 1955 in Aurora, IL c: 1
+ seq: 204.03 POTTS, Brenda b: Abt. 1960 w: 04 Nov 1989 c: 1
13GARY, Andrew-William b: 26 Apr 1993

204.04
12GARY, Dean-Edward b: 25 Mar 1956 in Aurora, IL c: 4
+ seq: 204.04 RECKMEYER, Pamela b: 14 Jun 1955 w: 14 May
   1976 c: 4
13GARY, Jason b: 10 Jun 1978
13GARY, Jeremey b: 24 Apr 1979
13GARY, Michael b: 25 Jun 1982
13GARY, Chris b: 24 Dec 1983

204.05
12GARY, Gwen-Helene b: 06 Feb 1957 c: 2

+ seq: 204.05 BOCKMAN, Patrick b: 17 Mar 1954 w: 04 Sep 1975 c: 2
13BOCKMAN, Timothy b: 12 Jan 1985
13BOCKMAN, Stephanie b: 11 Aug 1986

204.06

12GARY, James-Kenneth b: 22 Feb 1958 c: 2
+ seq: 204.06 DESMOND, Judith b: 28 Oct 1959 w: 15 Mar 1980 c: 2
13GARY, Jennifer M. b: 01 Sep 1980
13GARY, Brian b: 25 Jun 1982

204.07

12GARY, Marianne N. b: 19 Jul 1959 c: 2
+ seq: 204.07 MCCORMICK, Daniel b: 01 Aug 1955 w: 06 Jun 1981 c: 2
13MCCORMICK, Colissa A. b: 23 May 1982
13MCCORMICK, Kaley A. b: 27 Apr 1985

204.08

12GARY, Phillip Q. b: 01 Jun 1960 c: 2
+ seq: 204.08 NORTHRUP, Sherri b: 21 Mar 1963 w: 06 Jun 1985 c: 2
13GARY, Kelli-Ann b: 20 Feb 1987
13GARY, Christa-Page b: 25 Dec 1988

204.09

12GARY, Vincent-William b: 30 Jul 1962 c: 2
+ seq: 204.09 SPEARS, Cindy b: 13 Jul 1958 w: 06 Sep 1987 c: 2
13GARY, Courtney-Ann b: 28 Sep 1988
13GARY, Kevin-James b: 06 Jun 1991

204.10

12GARY, Donald-Gene b: 31 Jul 1965 c: 2
+ seq: 204.10 DONKA, Joy L. b: 01 Feb 1965 w: 17 Aug 1987 c: 2
13GARY, Nathan-Donka b: 05 Oct 1985
13GARY, Mathew b: 13 Dec 1988

204.11

11[1] HUSS, Richard-Henry b: 28 Apr 1937 in Aurora, IL d: 20
   Aug 2002 in Wheatland, WY v: Glendo, WY c: 3
 + seq: 204.11 FREDERICKSON, Judy b: Abt. 1940 w: Abt.
   1963 c: 3
12 HUSS, Elizabeth-Ann (Liz) b: 11 Dec 1965 v: Elgin, IL
12 HUSS, Katharine-Kristina (Kathy) b: 06 Nov 1968 v: Illinois
12 HUSS, Susannah-Ruth (Sue) b: 22 Jan 1972 v: Austin, TX
 * 2nd Wife of [1] HUSS, Richard-Henry:
 + seq: 204.11.01 Cleo w: Abt. 1980
 * 3rd Wife of [1] HUSS, Richard-Henry:
 + seq: 204.11.02 PRISCILLA w: Abt. 1990 v: Glendo, WY

204.12

11 HUSS, Mona-Marie b: 21 Jun 1942 v: Batavia, IL c: 3
 + seq: 204.12 ADAM, David b: 08 May 1940 w: Abt. 1962 v:
   Batavia, IL c: 3
12 ADAM, Daniel b: 18 Jul 1963 c: 2
 + seq: 204.13 NAIL, Lea b: Abt. 1965 w: 25 May 1991 c: 2
12 ADAM, Timothy (Tim) b: 27 Jul 1964
 + seq: 204.13.01 RAVINDRAN, Kay b: 20 Dec 1965 w: Abt.
   1990
12 ADAM, Heather b: 09 Aug 1969 c: 1
 + seq: 204.13.02 RUFFALO, Ken b: 05 Jan 1970 w: 05 Jul 1994
   c: 1

204.13

12 ADAM, Daniel b: 18 Jul 1963 c: 2
 + seq: 204.13 NAIL, Lea b: Abt. 1965 w: 25 May 1991 c: 2
13 ADAM, Mich b: 30 Dec 1991
13 ADAM, Samantha b: 12 Sep 1994

204.13.02

12 ADAM, Heather b: 09 Aug 1969 c: 1
 + seq: 204.13.02 RUFFALO, Ken b: 05 Jan 1970 w: 05 Jul 1994
   c: 1
13 RUFFALO, Anna b: 24 Jun 1998

204.14

11 HUSS, Edwin L. (Ed) b: 09 Sep 1943 v: Aurora, IL c: 3
 + seq: 204.14 PILCH, Judith E. (Judie) b: 10 Aug 1939 w: 29

Mar 1969 v: Aurora, IL c: 3
12 HUSS, Jacob A. b: 25 Jun 1970 c: 1
+ seq: 204.14.01 Lida b: 09 Jun 1963 w: 23 Apr 1998 c: 1
12 HUSS, Gregg b: Abt. 1975
12 HUSS, Benjamin (Ben) b: 31 Jan 1978

204.14.01
12 HUSS, Jacob A. b: 25 Jun 1970 c: 1
+ seq: 204.14.01 Lida b: 09 Jun 1963 w: 23 Apr 1998 c: 1
13 HUSS, Josephine b: 24 Jan 2000 in Aurora, IL

204.15
11 HUSS, Thomas J. (Tom) b: 27 Mar 1944 v: Sarasota, FL c: 3
+ seq: 204.15 BOCKMAN, Pam b: 27 Jun 1947 w: Abt. 1975 v:
    Sarasota, FL c: 3
12 HUSS, Shannon b: 21 Dec 1976
12 HUSS, Kenyan b: 25 Sep 1978
12 HUSS, Jordan b: Sep 1984

204.16
11 HUSS, Anna-Jean (Ann) b: 30 Nov 1948 v: Fresno, CA c: 4
+ seq: 204.16 HANKES, John D. (Jack) b: 15 Aug 1947 w: 27
    Dec 1969 v: Fresno, CA c: 4
12 HANKES, Amy b: 09 Apr 1971
+ seq: 204.16.01 GONZALEZ, Hector w: 25 Sep 1997
12 HANKES, Kristen b: 07 Dec 1973
+ seq: 204.16.02 CROCKER, Gary w: 16 Aug 1997
12 HANKES, Nicholas b: 11 Jul 1977 c: 3
+ seq: 204.16.03 WHITECOTTON, Kristie b: 07 Feb 1975 w:
    03 May 1997 c: 3
12 HANKES, Aaron b: 22 May 1980 c: 1
+ seq: 204.16.04 GORDINAIRE, Nicole w: 29 Dec 2001 c: 1

204.16.03
12 HANKES, Nicholas b: 11 Jul 1977 c: 3
+ seq: 204.16.03 WHITECOTTON, Kristie b: 07 Feb 1975 w:
    03 May 1997 c: 3
13 WHITECOTTON, Kaeley b: 25 Sep 1995
13 HANKES, Devyn-Daniel b: 29 Jan 1998
13 HANKES, Amber-Nicole b: 30 Jan 2001

204.16.04

12HANKES, Aaron b: 22 May 1980 c: 1
+ seq: 204.16.04 GORDINAIRE, Nicole w: 29 Dec 2001 c: 1
13HANKES, Madison b: 03 Jun 2002

204.17

11HUSS, Kathy-Jo (Kathryn) b: 01 Feb 1950 v: Aurora, IL c: 2
+ seq: 204.17 TIERNEY, Michael T. (Mike) b: 14 Aug 1947 w:
    15 Nov 1969 v: Aurora, IL c: 2
12TIERNEY, Joelle (Jody) b: 01 May 1970
+ seq: 204.17.01 PFAFF, Bruce b: 04 Jun 1962 w: 12 Aug 1999
12TIERNEY, Daniel (Dan) b: 27 Jun 1973
+ seq: 204.17.02 ALLEN, Kathie b: 12 Dec 1974 w: 11 Jan 2002

204.18

11HUSS, Margaret-Marie (Margie) b: 01 Nov 1952 v: Aurora, IL
    c: 3
+ seq: 204.18 WEITEN, Ronald (Ron) b: 22 Feb 1945 w: 10 Jun
    1972 v: Aurora, IL c: 3
12WEITEN, Ericka b: 26 Jul 1974
+ seq: 204.18.01 FICKER, John b: in Charlotte, NC w: 11 Aug
    2001
12WEITEN, Kari b: 18 May 1977 c: 1
+ seq: 204.18.02 w: Abt. 1995 c: 1
12WEITEN, Jeffrey (Jeff) b: 26 Dec 1978

204.18.02

12WEITEN, Kari b: 18 May 1977 c: 1
+ seq: 204.18.02 w: Abt. 1995 c: 1
13WEITEN, Nathan-Lee b: 22 Jan 1998

204.19

11HUSS, Bernadine b: 05 Nov 1956 v: Sugar Grove, IL c: 2
+ seq: 204.19 DE KING, Brad b: Abt. 1950 w: Abt. 1980 v:
    Sugar Grove, IL c: 2
12DE KING, Brianne b: 02 Jan 1982
12DE KING, Brant b: 21 Nov 1985

204.20

11HUSS, Joseph R. (Joe) b: 15 Nov 1957 v: Wheaton, IL c: 3
+ seq: 204.20 HEATON, Eileen b: 11 Mar 1957 w: 16 Jun 1979

v: Wheaton, IL c: 3
12HUSS, Lisa b: 08 Feb 1980
12HUSS, Joseph (Joe) b: 08 Aug 1981
12HUSS, Rebecca-Lynn b: 21 May 1984

204.21

10WITTRY, Alice L. b: 08 Nov 1918 d: 22 Dec 1974 in Aurora,
  IL v: Shorewood, IL c: 4
+ seq: 204.21 EVANS, Robert J. (Bob) b: 15 Jan 1919 in Aurora,
  IL d: 11 Nov 1995 in Shorewood, IL w: Abt. 1941 v:
  Shorewood, IL o: Chief engineer o: Toolmaker f: Leonard
  Evans m: Eva Kneipper c: 4
11EVANS, James b: 15 Feb 1943 v: Aurora, IL c: 4
+ seq: 204.22 MEYER, Susan N. (Sue) b: 22 Jun 1943 w: Abt.
  1965 v: Aurora, IL f: Glenn Meyer m: Violet c: 4
11EVANS, Donald L. b: 27 Nov 1945 v: Washington, IL o:
  Planning manager c: 3
+ seq: 204.24 DE VOUS, Margaret-Lucille (Lucie) b: 30 Nov
  1949 w: 1972 v: Washington, IL c: 3
11EVANS, Mary-Louise b: 04 Oct 1948 d: 28 Mar 2002 in
  Plainfield, IL
11[1] EVANS, Ronald (Randy) b: 04 Oct 1950 c: 2
+ seq: 204.25 CHEFNER, Rose b: Abt. 1950 w: Abt. 1970 c: 1
* 2nd Wife of [1] EVANS, Ronald (Randy):
+ seq: 204.26 Sue b: 15 Feb 1948 w: Abt. 1977 c: 1

204.22

11EVANS, James b: 15 Feb 1943 v: Aurora, IL c: 4
+ seq: 204.22 MEYER, Susan N. (Sue) b: 22 Jun 1943 w: Abt.
  1965 v: Aurora, IL f: Glenn Meyer m: Violet c: 4
12EVANS, Jayme-Susan b: 12 Jan 1967 d: 19 Jul 1998 in
  Columbus, WI Cause of death: Auto accident v: Aurora, IL o:
  Assistant publisher c: 1
+ seq: 204.23 CARLSON, John E. b: 31 Dec 1965 in Oak Park,
  IL d: 19 Jul 1998 in Columbus, WI Cause of death: Auto
  accident w: Abt. 1990 v: Aurora, IL o: Sales representative f:
  John Carlson m: Gloria c: 1
12EVANS, Todd-James b: 03 Jun 1968 v: Big Rock, IL
12EVANS, Karlin-Ann (Kari) b: 12 Apr 1972 v: Aurora, IL
12EVANS, Angiene-Alice (Angie) b: 15 Apr 1975 v: St. Charles,
  IL

+ seq: 204.23.10 VAN FLEET w: Abt. 2000

204.23

12EVANS, Jayme-Susan b: 12 Jan 1967 d: 19 Jul 1998 in Columbus, WI Cause of death: Auto accident v: Aurora, IL o: Assistant publisher c: 1
+ seq: 204.23 CARLSON, John E. b: 31 Dec 1965 in Oak Park, IL d: 19 Jul 1998 in Columbus, WI Cause of death: Auto accident w: Abt. 1990 v: Aurora, IL o: Sales representative f: John Carlson m: Gloria c: 1
13CARLSON, Ian-James

204.24

11EVANS, Donald L. b: 27 Nov 1945 v: Washington, IL o: Planning manager c: 3
+ seq: 204.24 DE VOUS, Margaret-Lucille (Lucie) b: 30 Nov 1949 w: 1972 v: Washington, IL c: 3
12EVANS, Patrick-Sebastian b: 19 Feb 1973 v: Hudson, IL
12EVANS, Kristin-Marie b: 03 Nov 1974 v: Bloomington, IL
+ seq: 204.24.10 TECHMANSKI w: Abt. 2000 v: Chicago, IL
12EVANS, Jill-Elizabeth b: 05 Jun 1976 v: Chicago, IL

204.25

11[1] EVANS, Ronald (Randy) b: 04 Oct 1950 c: 2
+ seq: 204.25 CHEFNER, Rose b: Abt. 1950 w: Abt. 1970 c: 1
12EVANS, Shawn b: 19 Oct 1972
* 2nd Wife of [1] EVANS, Ronald (Randy):
+ seq: 204.26 Sue b: 15 Feb 1948 w: Abt. 1977 c: 1
12EVANS, Randy-Scott b: 04 Apr 1979 v: Lake Villa, IL

204.27

9 WITTRY, Lena b: 08 Oct 1887 d: 12 Jun 1973 v: Maple Park, IL c: 1
+ seq: 204.27 FREDERICK, Roy b: 27 Jan 1887 d: 08 Oct 1983 w: Abt. 1920 v: Maple Park, IL c: 1
10FREDERICK, William b: 18 Dec 1921 v: Chicago, IL o: Designer metalsmith

205

9 WITTRY, Mike N. b: 04 Mar 1890 d: 15 Mar 1954 v: Chicago, IL c: 1

+ seq: 205 ZEBEL, Vita b: 28 Dec 1895 d: 08 Jun 1970 w: Abt. 1925 v: Chicago, IL c: 1

10WITTRY, Kathleen b: 20 Jun 1932 c: 1

+ seq: 205.01 STIMAC, Frank b: Abt. 1930 w: Abt. 1952 c: 1

205.01

10WITTRY, Kathleen b: 20 Jun 1932 c: 1

+ seq: 205.01 STIMAC, Frank b: Abt. 1930 w: Abt. 1952 c: 1

11STIMAC, Sharon-Kathleen b: 30 Apr 1954

206

9 WITTRY, Henry b: 02 Nov 1895 d: 17 Oct 1978 in Illinois v: Warrenville, IL c: 1

+ seq: 206 HANKES, Eva b: 14 May 1897 d: 11 Apr 1975 in Illinois w: Abt. 1925 v: Warrenville, IL c: 1

10WITTRY, Roy-Jacob b: 09 Feb 1931 v: Grand Junction, CO o: Precinct Extrusions c: 6

+ seq: 207 FOSTER, Barbara-Joan b: 09 Nov 1932 w: 13 Aug 1952 in San Diego, CA v: Grand Junction, CO o: Librarian f: Arthur Foster m: Grace Dueringer c: 6

207

10WITTRY, Roy-Jacob b: 09 Feb 1931 v: Grand Junction, CO o: Precinct Extrusions c: 6

+ seq: 207 FOSTER, Barbara-Joan b: 09 Nov 1932 w: 13 Aug 1952 in San Diego, CA v: Grand Junction, CO o: Librarian f: Arthur Foster m: Grace Dueringer c: 6

11WITTRY, Theresa-Marie b: 06 Mar 1953 in Aurora, IL v: Montgomery, IL c: 2

+ seq: 207.01 MCQUEEN, Joseph A. b: 17 May 1952 w: 03 Nov 1973 v: Montgomery, IL c: 2

11[1] WITTRY, Elizabeth-Jane b: 04 Apr 1954 in Aurora, IL v: Genoa City, WI c: 3

+ seq: 207.03 WENCKUS b: Abt. 1950 w: Abt. 1970 c: 2

* 2nd Husband of [1] WITTRY, Elizabeth-Jane:

+ seq: 207.06 ARTERBURN, Dale E. b: 30 Jan 1953 w: 05 Jun 1982 v: Burlington, WI c: 1

11WITTRY, Michael-Henry b: 08 May 1955 in Aurora, IL v: Wheatridge, CO

+ seq: 207.07 ROBLES, Susan (Sue) b: 05 Apr 1955 w: 30 Nov 1991 v: Wheatridge, CO o: Thrift store manager

11 WITTRY, Marianne-Grace b: 29 Apr 1956 in Aurora, IL v: Clifton, CO c: 1
+ seq: 207.08 LOPEZ, Phillip b: 15 Apr 1927 w: 13 Mar 1980 v: Clifton, CO c: 1
11 WITTRY, Christine-Eva b: 22 Nov 1960 in Aurora, IL v: Woodland Hills, CO c: 1
+ seq: 207.10 LAYMAN, Richard-Lee b: 11 Sep 1959 w: 11 Sep 1981 v: Woodland Hills, CO f: Layman m: Endicott c: 1
11 [2] WITTRY, Karen-Annette b: 28 May 1963 in Aurora, IL v: Cortland, IL
+ seq: 207.11 WAGNER b: Abt. 1960 w: Abt. 1985
* 2nd Husband of [2] WITTRY, Karen-Annette:
+ seq: 207.12 HUNTER, Christopher-Leland b: 31 Dec 1958 in Detroit, MI w: 19 Jun 1987 in St. Charles, IL v: Cortland, IL

207.01

11 WITTRY, Theresa-Marie b: 06 Mar 1953 in Aurora, IL v: Montgomery, IL c: 2
+ seq: 207.01 MCQUEEN, Joseph A. b: 17 May 1952 w: 03 Nov 1973 v: Montgomery, IL c: 2
12 MCQUEEN, Angelica-Michelle b: 28 Mar 1974 v: Davis Junction, IL c: 3
+ seq: 207.02 SCHOPP, Troy b: 01 Dec 1969 w: 09 Apr 1994 v: Davis Junction, IL c: 3
12 MCQUEEN, Jacqueline-Evette b: 05 May 1976 v: Las Vegas, NV

207.02

12 MCQUEEN, Angelica-Michelle b: 28 Mar 1974 v: Davis Junction, IL c: 3
+ seq: 207.02 SCHOPP, Troy b: 01 Dec 1969 w: 09 Apr 1994 v: Davis Junction, IL c: 3
13 MCQUEEN, William-Gage b: 22 Nov 1992
13 SCHOPP, Dylan-Troy Schopp b: 15 Feb 1994
13 SCHOPP, Christopher-Drake b: 19 Feb 1999

207.03

11 [1] WITTRY, Elizabeth-Jane b: 04 Apr 1954 in Aurora, IL v: Genoa City, WI c: 3
+ seq: 207.03 WENCKUS b: Abt. 1950 w: Abt. 1970 c: 2
12 WENCKUS, Neal-Richard b: 28 Jun 1972 v: Aurora, IL c: 2

+ seq: 207.04 ESTRUP, Jennifer b: 20 Jul 1972 w: 22 Aug 1998
    v: Aurora, IL c: 2
12 WENCKUS, Jennifer-Ann b: 01 Jun 1973 v: Aurora, IL c: 1
+ seq: 207.05 BUCHMEIER w: Abt. 1995 c: 1
* 2nd Husband of [1] WITTRY, Elizabeth-Jane:
+ seq: 207.06 ARTERBURN, Dale E. b: 30 Jan 1953 w: 05 Jun
    1982 v: Burlington, WI c: 1
12 ARTERBURN, Matthew-John b: 27 Jul 1986

207.04
12 WENCKUS, Neal-Richard b: 28 Jun 1972 v: Aurora, IL c: 2
+ seq: 207.04 ESTRUP, Jennifer b: 20 Jul 1972 w: 22 Aug 1998
    v: Aurora, IL c: 2
13 WENCHUS, Samantha b: 26 May 2001
13 WENCHUS, Steven-Neal b: 05 Apr 2005

207.05
12 WENCKUS, Jennifer-Ann b: 01 Jun 1973 v: Aurora, IL c: 1
+ seq: 207.05 BUCHMEIER w: Abt. 1995 c: 1
13 BUCHMEIER, Ariel-Jean b: 19 Jul 1997

207.08
11 WITTRY, Marianne-Grace b: 29 Apr 1956 in Aurora, IL v:
    Clifton, CO c: 1
+ seq: 207.08 LOPEZ, Phillip b: 15 Apr 1927 w: 13 Mar 1980
    v: Clifton, CO c: 1
12 LOPEZ, Crystal-Ann b: 05 May 1980 v: Clifton, CO c: 2
+ seq: 207.09 SMITH, Steven-Patrick b: 23 Apr 1978 w: 24 Jul
    1999 v: Clifton, CO c: 2

207.09
12 LOPEZ, Crystal-Ann b: 05 May 1980 v: Clifton, CO c: 2
+ seq: 207.09 SMITH, Steven-Patrick b: 23 Apr 1978 w: 24 Jul
    1999 v: Clifton, CO c: 2
13 SMITH, Brooke-Taylor b: 27 Aug 1999
13 SMITH, Zander-Donovan b: 13 Mar 2003

207.10
11 WITTRY, Christine-Eva b: 22 Nov 1960 in Aurora, IL v:
    Woodland Hills, CO c: 1
+ seq: 207.10 LAYMAN, Richard-Lee b: 11 Sep 1959 w: 11 Sep

1981 v: Woodland Hills, CO f: Layman m: Endicott c: 1
12LAYMAN, Amanda-June b: 14 Mar 1985

208

8 WITTRY, Adam b: 18 May 1864 in Aurora, IL d: 10 Sep 1940
in Aurora, IL v: Aurora, IL i: Elected VP of German Settlers in
Aurora i: Alderman of 7th Ward i: President of American-
Luxembourger Club o: Machinist at W W Mach Co r: x c: 5
+ seq: 208 HUSS, Mary S. b: 15 May 1867 in Chicago, IL d: 23
Jul 1946 in Aurora, IL w: 14 May 1889 in Aurora, IL v:
Aurora, IL f: Peter Huss c: 5
9 WITTRY, Emma-Barbara b: 15 Mar 1890 in Aurora, IL d: 24
Mar 1969 in Aurora, IL v: Aurora, IL c: 4
+ seq: 208.01 WEBER, Ferdinand-Nicholas (Ferry) b: 06 Dec
1890 d: 23 Nov 1959 in Aurora, IL w: 18 Jun 1913 v: Aurora,
IL o: Movie industry f: Peter M. Weber m: Susan Bonefas c:
4
9 WITTRY, Rose-Catherine b: 08 Aug 1891 d: 25 Apr 1940 o:
Operator at J. C. Ruth c: 1
+ seq: 208.15 REIDER, William F. b: 14 Aug 1893 w: Abt. 1920
c: 1
9 WITTRY, Paul-Peter (Hi) b: 25 Mar 1893 in Aurora, IL d: 18
Aug 1942 v: Aurora, IL o: Pipefitter at CB&Q Railroad o:
Tavern keeper
+ seq: 209 NALLINGER, Mary-Weiler b: 05 Jun 1901 d: Abt.
1990 w: Dec 1941 v: Aurora, IL
9 WITTRY, Dorothy M. b: 06 Feb 1894 d: 11 Jun 1935 v:
Aurora, IL c: 3
+ seq: 209.01 LANHAM, Robert H. b: 17 Nov 1898 d: 17 Jan
1953 w: Abt. 1925 v: Aurora, IL c: 3
9 [1] WITTRY, Elmer-John b: 28 May 1904 d: 24 Jul 1950 v:
Chicago, IL o: Advertising executive c: 2
+ seq: 210 FLANNIGAN, Alice b: 03 Mar 1904 d: 12 Aug 1945
w: Abt. 1930 v: Chicago, IL
* 2nd Wife of [1] WITTRY, Elmer-John:
+ seq: 211 O'CONNOR, Kathryn b: Abt. 1915 w: Abt. 1945 v:
St. Louis, MO c: 2

208.01

9 WITTRY, Emma-Barbara b: 15 Mar 1890 in Aurora, IL d: 24
Mar 1969 in Aurora, IL v: Aurora, IL c: 4

+ seq: 208.01 WEBER, Ferdinand-Nicholas (Ferry) b: 06 Dec 1890 d: 23 Nov 1959 in Aurora, IL w: 18 Jun 1913 v: Aurora, IL o: Movie industry f: Peter M. Weber m: Susan Bonefas c: 4

10 WEBER, Carl W. b: 16 May 1914 d: 28 May 2002 in Sun City, AZ v: Sun City, AZ c: 3

+ seq: 208.02 BERNBROCK, Mary A. b: 09 Dec 1914 w: 15 Oct 1938 v: Sun City, AZ c: 3

10 WEBER, Marian-Susan b: 24 Oct 1916 in Aurora, IL d: 25 May 2007 in Naples, FL v: Naples, FL c: 1

+ seq: 208.06 HAWKING, J. Wilfrid (Bill) b: 24 Apr 1915 d: 16 Nov 2000 in Naples, FL w: 02 Sep 1939 v: Naples, FL c: 1

10 WEBER, Ruthe-Rose b: 12 Apr 1922 d: 05 Feb 2005 in Naples, FL v: Aurora, IL

10 WEBER, Dorothy-June (June) b: 05 Jun 1924 d: Bef. 2007 in Naples, FL v: Naples, FL c: 4

+ seq: 208.09.01 JOHNSEN, Donald B. b: 22 Jun 1923 d: 13 Oct 2005 in Naples, FL w: 21 Oct 1950 v: Naples, FL c: 4

208.02

10 WEBER, Carl W. b: 16 May 1914 d: 28 May 2002 in Sun City, AZ v: Sun City, AZ c: 3

+ seq: 208.02 BERNBROCK, Mary A. b: 09 Dec 1914 w: 15 Oct 1938 v: Sun City, AZ c: 3

11 WEBER, Elwyn-James (Jim) b: 15 Jul 1941 c: 2

+ seq: 208.03 PEDERSON, Ingrid b: 04 Apr 1944 w: Abt. 1968 c: 2

11 WEBER, William (Bill) C. b: 10 Jun 1950 v: St. Louis Park, MN c: 2

+ seq: 208.04 HOCKSTEIN, Linda b: 07 Jul 1948 w: Abt. 1980 v: St. Louis Park, MN c: 2

11 WEBER, Caryl A. b: 05 Sep 1953 v: Edna, MN c: 2

+ seq: 208.05 MORGAN, Randy b: 25 Nov 1953 w: Abt. 1980 v: Edna, MN c: 2

208.03

11 WEBER, Elwyn-James (Jim) b: 15 Jul 1941 c: 2

+ seq: 208.03 PEDERSON, Ingrid b: 04 Apr 1944 w: Abt. 1968 c: 2

12 WEBER, Kathleen-Gabrielle b: 07 Aug 1971 v: Atlanta, GA

12 WEBER, Jennifer b: 28 Oct 1975 v: Chicago, IL

+ seq: 208.03.05 STEVENS, Scott w: Abt. 2000 v: Chicago, IL

208.04

11 WEBER, William (Bill) C. b: 10 Jun 1950 v: St. Louis Park, MN c: 2

+ seq: 208.04 HOCKSTEIN, Linda b: 07 Jul 1948 w: Abt. 1980 v: St. Louis Park, MN c: 2

12 WEBER, Charles-William b: 19 Dec 1984 o: Miami University Student

12 WEBER, Audrey-Lynne b: 23 Sep 1986

208.05

11 WEBER, Caryl A. b: 05 Sep 1953 v: Edna, MN c: 2

+ seq: 208.05 MORGAN, Randy b: 25 Nov 1953 w: Abt. 1980 v: Edna, MN c: 2

12 MORGAN, Margaret-Ann (Rita) b: 10 Sep 1982 o: Notre Dame Student

12 MORGAN, Thomas-Weber b: 03 Jul 1984 o: Student at Boston College

208.06

10 WEBER, Marian-Susan b: 24 Oct 1916 in Aurora, IL d: 25 May 2007 in Naples, FL v: Naples, FL c: 1

+ seq: 208.06 HAWKING, J. Wilfrid (Bill) b: 24 Apr 1915 d: 16 Nov 2000 in Naples, FL w: 02 Sep 1939 v: Naples, FL c: 1

11 HAWKING, John F. b: 14 Apr 1941 in Aurora, IL v: Naples, FL c: 3

+ seq: 208.07 HANKES, Suzon b: 12 Apr 1941 w: Abt. 1963 v: Naples, FL c: 3

208.07

11 HAWKING, John F. b: 14 Apr 1941 in Aurora, IL v: Naples, FL c: 3

+ seq: 208.07 HANKES, Suzon b: 12 Apr 1941 w: Abt. 1963 v: Naples, FL c: 3

12 HAWKING, Karen-Elizabeth b: 10 Jul 1965 in Aurora, IL d: 22 Jun 2005 in Palo Alto, CA v: Palo Alto, CA c: 1

+ seq: 208.08 LAWSON, Robert-John (Bob) b: 26 Jun 1964 w: Abt. 1988 in Aurora, IL v: Palo Alto, CA c: 1

12 HAWKING, Brian-John b: 20 May 1967 v: Tampa, FL c: 1

+ seq: 208.08.50 GAMON, Mitzilyn w: 05 Nov 2005 in Tampa,

FL v: Tampa, FL c: 1

12HAWKING, Michael-John (Robby) b: 02 Mar 1969 v: Lutz, FL c: 2

+ seq: 208.09 REPASS, Robin-Renee w: 19 Feb 2000 in Indiana v: Lutz, FL c: 2

208.08

12HAWKING, Karen-Elizabeth b: 10 Jul 1965 in Aurora, IL d: 22 Jun 2005 in Palo Alto, CA v: Palo Alto, CA c: 1

+ seq: 208.08 LAWSON, Robert-John (Bob) b: 26 Jun 1964 w: Abt. 1988 in Aurora, IL v: Palo Alto, CA c: 1

13LAWSON, Elizabeth-Sue b: 17 Oct 1990 in Esen Prairie, MN v: Palo Alto, CA

208.08.50

12HAWKING, Brian-John b: 20 May 1967 v: Tampa, FL c: 1

+ seq: 208.08.50 GAMON, Mitzilyn w: 05 Nov 2005 in Tampa, FL v: Tampa, FL c: 1

13HAWKING, Lillie E b: 22 Jun 2006 in Tampa, FL v: Tampa, FL

208.09

12HAWKING, Michael-John (Robby) b: 02 Mar 1969 v: Lutz, FL c: 2

+ seq: 208.09 REPASS, Robin-Renee w: 19 Feb 2000 in Indiana v: Lutz, FL c: 2

13HAWKING, Grant M. b: 06 Jan 2004 v: Lutz, FL

13HAWKING, Logan K. b: 26 Sep 2005 v: lutz, FL

208.09.01

10WEBER, Dorothy-June (June) b: 05 Jun 1924 d: Bef. 2007 in Naples, FL v: Naples, FL c: 4

+ seq: 208.09.01 JOHNSEN, Donald B. b: 22 Jun 1923 d: 13 Oct 2005 in Naples, FL w: 21 Oct 1950 v: Naples, FL c: 4

11[1] JOHNSEN, Mary-Sue b: 10 Aug 1951 c: 4

+ seq: 208.10 BORLAND, Kevin b: Abt. 1950 w: Abt. 1975 c: 2

* 2nd Husband of [1] JOHNSEN, Mary-Sue:

+ seq: 208.11 SILVER, Robert b: 20 Jun 1951 w: Abt. 1982 c: 2

11JOHNSEN, Debra-Anne b: 02 Oct 1952 c: 3

+ seq: 208.12 SWAIDAN, George b: 13 Jan 1950 w: Abt. 1980

c: 3

11 JOHNSEN, Jane-Ellen b: 26 Feb 1954 c: 3
+ seq: 208.13 BARBIERE, Lawrence b: 06 Mar 1951 w: Abt. 1980 c: 3

11 JOHNSEN, Joyce-Anne b: 08 Feb 1957 c: 3
+ seq: 208.14 NORTH, John L. (Jack) b: 28 Feb 1955 w: Abt. 1980 c: 3

208.10

11 [1] JOHNSEN, Mary-Sue b: 10 Aug 1951 c: 4
+ seq: 208.10 BORLAND, Kevin b: Abt. 1950 w: Abt. 1975 c: 2

12 BORLAND, Kerry-Jane b: 28 Sep 1977
12 BORLAND, Patrick-Bennett b: 22 Oct 1979
* 2nd Husband of [1] JOHNSEN, Mary-Sue:
+ seq: 208.11 SILVER, Robert b: 20 Jun 1951 w: Abt. 1982 c: 2
12 SILVER, Helen-Elizabeth b: 22 Mar 1984
12 SILVER, Emily-Susan b: 09 Oct 1985

208.12

11 JOHNSEN, Debra-Anne b: 02 Oct 1952 c: 3
+ seq: 208.12 SWAIDAN, George b: 13 Jan 1950 w: Abt. 1980 c: 3

12 SWAIDAN, Matthew-Johnsen b: 12 Aug 1982
12 SWAIDAN, Michael-Joseph b: 21 Sep 1984
12 SWAIDAN, Molly-Elizabeth b: 30 May 1986

208.13

11 JOHNSEN, Jane-Ellen b: 26 Feb 1954 c: 3
+ seq: 208.13 BARBIERE, Lawrence b: 06 Mar 1951 w: Abt. 1980 c: 3

12 BARBIERE, Katherine-Linda b: 20 Jul 1984
12 BARBIERE, Emily-Weber b: 26 Jul 1986
12 BARBIERE, James-Johnsen b: 07 Jul 1989

208.14

11 JOHNSEN, Joyce-Anne b: 08 Feb 1957 c: 3
+ seq: 208.14 NORTH, John L. (Jack) b: 28 Feb 1955 w: Abt. 1980 c: 3

12 NORTH, Casey-Jens b: 03 Mar 1983
12 NORTH, Jenna-Elizabeth b: 06 Aug 1984

12NORTH, Kelly-Lynn b: 07 Dec 1985

208.15
9 WITTRY, Rose-Catherine b: 08 Aug 1891 d: 25 Apr 1940 o: Operator at J. C. Ruth c: 1
+ seq: 208.15 REIDER, William F. b: 14 Aug 1893 w: Abt. 1920 c: 1
10REIDER, William A. b: 17 Oct 1928
+ seq: 208.16 LEPLEY, Helene b: Abt. 1930 w: Abt. 1955

209.01
9 WITTRY, Dorothy M. b: 06 Feb 1894 d: 11 Jun 1935 v: Aurora, IL c: 3
+ seq: 209.01 LANHAM, Robert H. b: 17 Nov 1898 d: 17 Jan 1953 w: Abt. 1925 v: Aurora, IL c: 3
10LANHAM, Rita-Helene b: 29 Mar 1927 v: Camp Hill, PA c: 2
+ seq: 209.02 KRANTZ, Eugene b: Abt. 1920 d: 23 Dec 1992 w: 19 May 1945 v: Camp Hill, PA c: 2
10LANHAM, Doris-Mae b: 12 Apr 1929 d: 17 Apr 1995 v: Golden, CO
10LANHAM, Robert-Francis b: 03 Oct 1930 v: Fairfax, VA c: 2
+ seq: 209.04 MCWAIN, Jacquelyn b: 13 Nov 1934 w: Abt. 1955 v: Fairfax, VA c: 2

209.02
10LANHAM, Rita-Helene b: 29 Mar 1927 v: Camp Hill, PA c: 2
+ seq: 209.02 KRANTZ, Eugene b: Abt. 1920 d: 23 Dec 1992 w: 19 May 1945 v: Camp Hill, PA c: 2
11KRANTZ, Maretta b: 30 Jul 1946 c: 4
+ seq: 209.03 SCHMIDT, Donald E. b: 27 Oct 1946 w: 28 Aug 1970 c: 4
11KRANTZ, Gina b: 04 Apr 1948 v: Farmingdale, NJ

209.03
11KRANTZ, Maretta b: 30 Jul 1946 c: 4
+ seq: 209.03 SCHMIDT, Donald E. b: 27 Oct 1946 w: 28 Aug 1970 c: 4
12SCHMIDT, Kiera-Don-Mar b: 25 Apr 1975
12SCHMIDT, Heath-Don-Mar b: 22 Aug 1976
12SCHMIDT, Kendra-Don-Mar b: 05 Apr 1979 d: 08 Apr 1979
12SCHMIDT, Adam-Don-Mar b: 06 Aug 1980

209.04

10LANHAM, Robert-Francis b: 03 Oct 1930 v: Fairfax, VA c: 2
+ seq: 209.04 MCWAIN, Jacquelyn b: 13 Nov 1934 w: Abt.
   1955 v: Fairfax, VA c: 2
11LANHAM, Michael-Charles b: 19 Oct 1956
11LANHAM, Paul-Joseph b: 26 Aug 1958 v: St. Louis, MO
+ seq: 209.05 MCCULLOH, Lori A. b: Abt. 1965 w: 29 Jun
   1991 in St. Louis, MO v: St. Louis, MO

210

10WITTRY, Elmer-John (John) b: 25 Nov 1947 v: Waukesha, WI
   o: Finance manager c: 3
+ seq: 212 STEPENSKE, Marilyn F. b: 25 Nov 1947 w: 27 Jun
   1970 in Fontana, WI v: Waukesha, WI c: 3
11WITTRY, Michael-John b: 29 Apr 1973 v: Minoqua, WI o:
   Realtor
11WITTRY, Matthew-Denis b: 30 Jul 1974
11WITTRY, Peter-Arthur b: 14 Apr 1983

212

10WITTRY, Elmer-John (John) b: 25 Nov 1947 v: Waukesha, WI
   o: Finance manager c: 3
+ seq: 212 STEPENSKE, Marilyn F. b: 25 Nov 1947 w: 27 Jun
   1970 in Fontana, WI v: Waukesha, WI c: 3
11WITTRY, Michael-John b: 29 Apr 1973 v: Minoqua, WI o:
   Realtor
11WITTRY, Matthew-Denis b: 30 Jul 1974
11WITTRY, Peter-Arthur b: 14 Apr 1983

213

10WITTRY, Dennis-Joseph b: 12 Oct 1950 v: Elgin, IL c: 2
+ seq: 213 TRACEY, Deborah b: Abt. 1950 w: Abt. 1975 v:
   Elgin, IL c: 2
11WITTRY, Patrick-John b: 07 Sep 1979
11WITTRY, Brendan-Colin b: 27 Apr 1982

214

7 WITRY, Mathias b: 15 Jan 1827 in Beidweiler, Lux d: 22 Jan
   1880 in Beidweiler, Lux h: Diedesch v: Beidweiler, Lux o:
   Master tailor r: bd c: 9
+ seq: 214 LASCHETTE, Anna b: 26 Dec 1824 in Beaufort, Lux

d: 14 Apr 1893 in Beidweiler, Lux w: 06 Feb 1850 in Rodenbourg, Lux h: Diedesch v: Beidweiler, Lux o: Seamstress r: d r: m f: Michel Laschette m: Anna-Marie Wagner c: 9

8 WITRY, Johann b: 20 Jan 1851 in Beidweiler, Lux d: 24 Jun 1851 in Beidweiler, Lux h: Diedesch v: Beidweiler, Lux r: bd

8 WITRY, Georg b: 18 Jun 1852 in Beidweiler, Lux h: Trapen v: Bech, Lux o: Farmer o: Day laborer r: b c: 3

+ seq: 215 LUDWIGS, Catherine b: 25 Dec 1846 in Bech, Lux d: 21 Oct 1879 in Bech, Lux w: 18 Jan 1876 in Bech, Lux h: Trapen v: Bech, Lux o: Farmer r: d r: m f: Franz Ludwigs m: Marie Dahn c: 3

8 WITRY, Madeleine b: 17 Aug 1854 in Beidweiler, Lux h: Oppert v: Bertrange, Lux o: No profession r: b c: 8

+ seq: 215.50 FRIES, Pierre b: 10 Jan 1858 in Bertrange, Lux w: 07 Feb 1881 in Bertrange, Lux h: Oppert v: Bertrange, Lux o: Day laborer r: m m: Barbe Fries c: 8

8 WITRY, Peter b: 26 Nov 1857 in Beidweiler, Lux d: 29 Apr 1872 in Biwer, Lux h: Weidich v: Biwer, Lux o: Day laborer o: Servant r: bd

8 WITRY, Marie b: 21 Dec 1859 in Beidweiler, Lux r: b c: 1

+ seq: 215.70 w: Abt. 1885 c: 1

8 WITRY, Nicolas b: 05 Dec 1861 in Beidweiler, Lux d: 08 Mar 1865 in Beidweiler, Lux v: Beidweiler, Lux o: No profession r: bd

8 WITRY, Peter b: 29 Sep 1863 in Beidweiler, Lux h: Diedesch v: Beidweiler, Lux o: Farmer o: Day laborer r: b c: 4

+ seq: 216 OLINGER, Marie-Anna b: 27 Oct 1863 in Graulinster, Lux w: 20 Jan 1892 in Rodenbourg, Lux h: Diedesch v: Beidweiler, Lux o: No profession r: m f: Johann Olinger m: Elisabeth Ernster c: 4

8 WITRY, Johann-Peter b: 10 Jun 1866 in Beidweiler, Lux d: Mar 1925 in Bertrange, Lux v: Bertrange, Lux o: Day laborer o: Merchant r: b c: 7

+ seq: 218.01 BLEY, Angelika b: 18 Dec 1872 in Bertrange, Lux d: 06 Jul 1937 in Bertrange, Lux w: Abt. 1892 a: Blei v: Bertrange, Lux o: No profession c: 7

8 WITRY, Jacob b: 05 Jul 1868 in Beidweiler, Lux d: 1946 in Bertrange, Lux v: Bertrange, Lux v: Strassem, Lux o: Day laborer o: Master manufacturer o: Merchant r: b c: 11

+ seq: 219 HEUSCHLING, Anna b: 22 Oct 1874 in Ehlange, Lux

d: 1945 in Bertrange, Lux w: 07 Jan 1895 in Reckange, Lux v:
Bertrange, Lux v: Strassem, Lux o: No profession r: m f:
Nikolas Heuschling m: Maria Frieden c: 11

215

8 WITRY, Georg b: 18 Jun 1852 in Beidweiler, Lux h: Trapen v:
 Bech, Lux o: Farmer o: Day laborer r: b c: 3
+ seq: 215 LUDWIGS, Catherine b: 25 Dec 1846 in Bech, Lux
 d: 21 Oct 1879 in Bech, Lux w: 18 Jan 1876 in Bech, Lux h:
 Trapen v: Bech, Lux o: Farmer r: d r: m f: Franz Ludwigs
 m: Marie Dahn c: 3
9 WITRY, Magdalena b: 02 Dec 1876 in Bech, Lux v: Bech, Lux
 o: No profession r: b
+ seq: 215.10 HECK, Jacques b: 18 Jul 1874 in Holzthum, Lux
 d: in Echternach, Lux w: 10 May 1901 in Bech, Lux v: Bech,
 Lux o: Excavator r: m f: Johann Heck m: Anna Zimmer
9 WITRY, Elisabetha b: 27 Jun 1884 in Bech, Lux d: 11 Feb
 1889 in Bech, Lux r: bd
9 WITRY, Stillborn Boy b: 21 Oct 1879 in Bech, Lux

215.50

8 WITRY, Madeleine b: 17 Aug 1854 in Beidweiler, Lux h:
 Oppert v: Bertrange, Lux o: No profession r: b c: 8
+ seq: 215.50 FRIES, Pierre b: 10 Jan 1858 in Bertrange, Lux w:
 07 Feb 1881 in Bertrange, Lux h: Oppert v: Bertrange, Lux o:
 Day laborer r: m m: Barbe Fries c: 8
9 FRIES, Marie b: 13 Apr 1880 in Bertrange, Lux d: 20 Aug
 1881 in Bertrange, Lux r: bd
9 FRIES, Johann b: 11 Mar 1882 in Bertrange, Lux o: Forge
 worker r: b
+ seq: 215.55 HOFFMANN, Catharina b: 05 Dec 1877 in
 Angelsberg, Lux w: 04 Apr 1904 in Bertrange, Lux o:
 Housemaid r: m f: Johann-Peter Hoffmann m: Margaretha
 Coster
9 FRIES, Jean-Auguste b: 31 Mar 1884 in Bertrange, Lux d: 04
 Feb 1889 in Bertrange, Lux r: bd
9 FRIES, Leonard b: 11 Dec 1886 in Bertrange, Lux r: b
9 FRIES, Susanna b: 13 Oct 1888 in Bertrange, Lux r: b
9 FRIES, Johann-Peter b: 15 Sep 1890 in Bertrange, Lux d: 09
 Sep 1911 in Bertrange, Lux o: Laborer r: bd
9 [1] FRIES, Helena b: 31 May 1895 in Bertrange, Lux o: No

profession r: b c: 2
+ seq: 215.60 BEMTGEN, Johann-Joseph b: 30 Jan 1894 in
   Bertrange, Lux d: 21 Jul 1915 in Bertrange, Lux w: 07 Jun
   1915 in Bertrange, Lux o: Railroad conductor o: Brakeman r:
   d r: m f: Johann-Peter Bemtgen m: Elisabeth (Elise) Andring
   c: 1
* 2nd Husband of [1] FRIES, Helena:
+ seq: 215.65 BEMTGEN, Johann-Peter b: 06 Jan 1898 in
   Bertrange, Lux w: 07 Sep 1917 in Bertrange, Lux o: Brakeman
   o: Deliveryman o: Crew worker r: m f: Johann-Peter Bemtgen
   m: Elisabeth (Elise) Andring c: 1
9 FRIES, Anna b: 06 Jul 1897 in Bertrange, Lux d: 17 Sep 1897
   in Bertrange, Lux r: bd

215.60
9 [1] FRIES, Helena b: 31 May 1895 in Bertrange, Lux o: No
   profession r: b c: 7
+ seq: 215.60 BEMTGEN, Johann-Joseph b: 30 Jan 1894 in
   Bertrange, Lux d: 21 Jul 1915 in Bertrange, Lux w: 07 Jun
   1915 in Bertrange, Lux o: Railroad conductor o: Brakeman r: d
   r: m f: Jean-Pierre Bemtgen m: Elisabeth (Elise) Andring c: 1
10BEMTGEN, Magdalena-Josephine b: 30 Dec 1915 in Bertrange,
   Lux d: 13 Dec 2003 r: b
+ seq: 215.62 WENMACHER, Jos w: 02 Mar 1935
* 2nd Husband of [1] FRIES, Helena:
+ seq: 215.65 BEMTGEN, Johann-Peter b: 06 Jan 1898 in
   Bertrange, Lux d: 14 Mar 1975 in Luxembourg, Lux w: 07 Sep
   1917 in Bertrange, Lux o: Brakeman o: Deliveryman o: Crew
   worker r: m f: Jean-Pierre Bemtgen m: Elisabeth (Elise)
   Andring c: 6
10[2] BEMTGEN, Adolf b: 17 Dec 1919 in Bertrange, Lux d: 21
   Apr 1985 r: b
+ seq: 215.65.20 KOCH, Philomene d: 06 Dec 1957 w: 02 Jul
   1948
* 2nd Wife of [2] BEMTGEN, Adolf:
+ seq: 215.65.40 KIRSCH, Margot w: 13 Aug 1959
10BEMTGEN, Peter-Albert b: 15 Jan 1918 d: 19 Sep 1991
+ seq: 215.65.60 WEYER, Catherine w: 1948
10BEMTGEN, Alice b: 26 Jan 1925
+ seq: 215.65.70 GEIMER, Jacques b: 16 Apr 1916 d: 10 Jun
   1982 w: 26 Dec 1945

10BEMTGEN, Nico c: 3
+ seq: 215.65.80 JOST, Marie-France w: Abt. 1960 c: 3
10BEMTGEN, Annette
10BEMTGEN, Paul c: 2
+ seq: 215.65.90 GABY w: Abt. 1960 c: 2

215.65.80
10BEMTGEN, Nico c: 3
+ seq: 215.65.80 JOST, Marie-France w: Abt. 1960 c: 3
11BEMTGEN, Pit
11BEMTGEN, Ben
11BEMTGEN, Tessy

215.65.90
10BEMTGEN, Paul c: 2
+ seq: 215.65.90 GABY w: Abt. 1960 c: 2
11BEMTGEN, Stephane
11BEMTGEN, Laurent

215.70
8 WITRY, Marie b: 21 Dec 1859 in Beidweiler, Lux r: b c: 1
+ seq: 215.70 w: Abt. 1885 c: 1
9 WITRY, Maria b: 05 Mar 1886 in Bertrange, Lux d: 14 Apr
1886 in Bertrange, Lux r: bd

216
8 WITRY, Peter b: 29 Sep 1863 in Beidweiler, Lux h: Diedesch
v: Beidweiler, Lux o: Farmer o: Day laborer r: b c: 4
+ seq: 216 OLINGER, Marie-Anna b: 27 Oct 1863 in Graulinster,
Lux w: 20 Jan 1892 in Rodenbourg, Lux h: Diedesch v:
Beidweiler, Lux o: No profession r: m f: Johann Olinger m:
Elisabeth Ernster c: 4
9 WITRY, Anna b: 23 Jan 1893 in Beidweiler, Lux o: No
profession r: b c: 5
+ seq: 216.50 BEMTGEN, Jean b: 19 Sep 1889 in Bertrange, Lux
w: 08 Feb 1916 in Bertrange, Lux o: Brakeman o: Crew worker
r: m f: Jean-Pierre Bemtgen m: Elisabeth (Elise) Andring c: 5
9 WITRY, Elisabeth (Elise) b: 30 Mar 1896 in Beidweiler, Lux d:
07 Jul 1918 in Bertrange, Lux r: bd
9 WITRY, Johann (Jean) b: 25 Feb 1903 in Beidweiler, Lux d:
Jan 1985 h: Diedesch v: Beidweiler, Lux r: b c: 4

+ seq: 217 MENNE, Anne b: 22 Jan 1906 d: 13 Feb 1997 in
Beidweiler, Lux w: Abt. 1935 h: Diedesch v: Beidweiler, Lux
c: 4
9 WITRY, Johann-Peter b: 08 May 1898 in Beidweiler, Lux v:
Strassem, Lux o: Laborer r: b
+ seq: 218.00.50 VEYDER, Elise b: 13 Feb 1901 in Strassem,
Lux w: 10 Oct 1923 in Strassem, Lux v: Strassem, Lux o: No
profession r: m f: Edouard Veyder m: Lucie Stanen

216.50
9 WITRY, Anna b: 23 Jan 1893 in Beidweiler, Lux o: No
profession r: b c: 5
+ seq: 216.50 BEMTGEN, Jean b: 19 Sep 1889 in Bertrange, Lux
w: 08 Feb 1916 in Bertrange, Lux o: Brakeman o: Crew
worker r: m f: Jean-Pierre Bemtgen m: Elisabeth (Elise)
Andring c: 5
10BEMTGEN, Johann-Peter b: 16 Dec 1916 d: 26 Dec 1972 in
Liege, Belgium
10BEMTGEN, Maria b: 02 Mar 1920 in Bertrange, Lux d: 11 Jan
2003 in Luxembourg, Lux r: b
10BEMTGEN, Josef b: 15 Mar 1922 in Bertrange, Lux r: b
10BEMTGEN, Johann b: 07 Jun 1923 in Bertrange, Lux d: 26 Jun
1923 in Bertrange, Lux r: bd
10BEMTGEN, Susanne b: 21 Sep 1925 d: 21 Nov 1998 in
Rodange, Lux

217
9 WITRY, Johann (Jean) b: 25 Feb 1903 in Beidweiler, Lux d:
Jan 1985 h: Diedesch v: Beidweiler, Lux r: b c: 4
+ seq: 217 MENNE, Anne b: 22 Jan 1906 d: 13 Feb 1997 in
Beidweiler, Lux w: Abt. 1935 h: Diedesch v: Beidweiler, Lux
c: 4
10WITRY, Rudi b: 18 Dec 1931 in Beidweiler, Lux v:
Bonnevoie, Lux c: 1
+ seq: 217.01 HINTERLANG, Leny b: 14 Feb 1930 w: Abt.
1955 v: Bonnevoie, Lux c: 1
10WITRY, Marcel b: 11 Jan 1933 in Beidweiler, Lux v:
Oberanven, Lux
+ seq: 217.03 KLEES, Valerie b: 15 Nov 1933 w: Abt. 1955 v:
Oberanven, Lux
10WITRY, Georges b: 02 Dec 1936 in Beidweiler, Lux v:

Frisange, Lux c: 1

+ seq: 217.04 WOHL, Aloysia b: 12 May 1940 w: Abt. 1960 v:
   Frisange, Lux c: 1

10 WITRY, Nicolas (Nic) b: 08 Aug 1941 in Beidweiler, Lux h:
   Diedesch v: Beidweiler, Lux o: Painter c: 2

+ seq: 218 FLAMMANG, Josette b: 01 Aug 1950 in Scheidgen,
   Lux w: Abt. 1970 h: Diedesch v: Beidweiler, Lux c: 2

217.01

10 WITRY, Rudi b: 18 Dec 1931 in Beidweiler, Lux v:
   Bonnevoie, Lux c: 1

+ seq: 217.01 HINTERLANG, Leny b: 14 Feb 1930 w: Abt.
   1955 v: Bonnevoie, Lux c: 1

11 WITRY, Viviane b: 17 Jan 1956 c: 2

+ seq: 217.02 WAGNER, Romain w: Abt. 1980 c: 2

217.02

11 WITRY, Viviane b: 17 Jan 1956 c: 2

+ seq: 217.02 WAGNER, Romain w: Abt. 1980 c: 2

12 WAGNER, Tyrone

12 WAGNER, Kim

217.04

10 WITRY, Georges b: 02 Dec 1936 in Beidweiler, Lux v:
   Frisange, Lux c: 1

+ seq: 217.04 WOHL, Aloysia b: 12 May 1940 w: Abt. 1960 v:
   Frisange, Lux c: 1

11 WITRY, Romain b: 29 Dec 1962 c: 1

+ seq: 217.05 MICHAELY, Geraldine b: 19 Nov 1971 w: Abt.
   1995 c: 1

217.05

11 WITRY, Romain b: 29 Dec 1962 c: 1

+ seq: 217.05 MICHAELY, Geraldine b: 19 Nov 1971 w: Abt.
   1995 c: 1

12 WITRY, Chiara b: 02 Jun 1999

218

10 WITRY, Nicolas (Nic) b: 08 Aug 1941 in Beidweiler, Lux h:
   Diedesch v: Beidweiler, Lux o: Painter c: 2

+ seq: 218 FLAMMANG, Josette b: 01 Aug 1950 in Scheidgen,

Lux w: Abt. 1970 h: Diedesch v: Beidweiler, Lux c: 2

11 WITRY, Yolande b: 13 Apr 1969 in Luxembourg, Lux v: Echternach, Lux

11 WITRY, Pascal b: 22 Aug 1970 in Luxembourg, Lux v: Differdange, Lux

218.01

8 WITRY, Johann-Peter b: 10 Jun 1866 in Beidweiler, Lux d: Mar 1925 in Bertrange, Lux v: Bertrange, Lux o: Day laborer o: Merchant r: b c: 7

+ seq: 218.01 BLEY, Angelika b: 18 Dec 1872 in Bertrange, Lux d: 06 Jul 1937 in Bertrange, Lux w: Abt. 1892 a: Blei v: Bertrange, Lux o: No profession c: 7

9 WITRY, Helene b: 30 Dec 1895 in Bertrange, Lux d: 23 Apr 1972 in Schiffelange, Lux r: b

9 WITRY, Jacques b: 20 Sep 1897 in Bertrange, Lux d: 26 Nov 1974 in Bettembourg, Lux v: Bertrange, Lux o: Engineer o: Laborer o: Railroad employee r: b c: 4

+ seq: 218.02 QUINTUS, Josefine b: 06 Mar 1893 in Mamer, Lux d: 30 Oct 1973 in Bettembourg, Lux w: 11 Jul 1919 in Bertrange, Lux o: Housemaid r: m f: Peter Quintus m: Maria Bauer c: 4

9 WITRY, Marie b: 16 Apr 1899 in Bertrange, Lux d: 08 Feb 1981 in Bertrange, Lux r: b

9 WITRY, Margaretha b: 17 Nov 1901 in Bertrange, Lux d: 27 Nov 1901 in Bertrange, Lux r: bd

9 WITRY, Susanne b: 11 Jan 1905 in Bertrange, Lux d: 15 Mar 1905 in Bertrange, Lux r: bd

9 WITRY, Maria-Anna b: 19 Mar 1907 in Bertrange, Lux d: 08 May 1907 in Bertrange, Lux r: bd

9 WITRY, Juliette-Helene b: 09 Oct 1908 in Bertrange, Lux d: 08 Nov 1908 in Bertrange, Lux r: bd

218.02

9 WITRY, Jacques b: 20 Sep 1897 in Bertrange, Lux d: 26 Nov 1974 in Bettembourg, Lux v: Bertrange, Lux o: Engineer o: Laborer o: Railroad employee r: b c: 4

+ seq: 218.02 QUINTUS, Josefine b: 06 Mar 1893 in Mamer, Lux d: 30 Oct 1973 in Bettembourg, Lux w: 11 Jul 1919 in Bertrange, Lux o: Housemaid r: m f: Peter Quintus m: Maria Bauer c: 4

10WITRY, Ernest b: 15 Apr 1920 in Hollerich, Lux d: 20 Jul 1952 in Remich, Lux v: Luxembourg, Lux o: Railroad employee c: 1
+ seq: 218.03 BELLION, Germaine b: 01 Mar 1919 in Luxembourg, Lux w: Abt. 1945 v: Luxembourg, Lux c: 1
10WITRY, Josef b: 16 Sep 1923 in Bertrange, Lux d: 18 Sep 1943 in Russia o: Railroad employee r: b
10WITRY, Roger b: 17 Nov 1929 in Bertrange, Lux v: Bettembourg, Lux o: Railroad, employee c: 3
+ seq: 218.04 MANGERICH, Marguerite b: 27 Nov 1933 in Haller, Lux d: 21 Sep 2007 in Esch-sur-Alzette, Lux w: 16 Oct 1954 in Haller, Lux v: Bettembourg, Lux c: 3
10WITRY, Laure b: 19 Sep 1934 in Bettembourg, Lux

218.03
10WITRY, Ernest b: 15 Apr 1920 in Hollarich, Lux d: 20 Jul 1952 in Remich, Lux v: Luxembourg, Lux o: Railroad employee c: 1
+ seq: 218.03 BELLION, Germaine b: 01 Mar 1919 in Luxembourg, Lux w: Abt. 1945 v: Luxembourg, Lux c: 1
11WITRY, Josette b: 18 Jul 1948 in Luxembourg, Lux

218.04
10WITRY, Roger b: 17 Nov 1929 in Bertrange, Lux v: Bettembourg, Lux o: Railroad, employee c: 3
+ seq: 218.04 MANGERICH, Marguerite b: 27 Nov 1933 in Haller, Lux d: 21 Sep 2007 in Esch-sur-Alzette, Lux w: 16 Oct 1954 in Haller, Lux v: Bettembourg, Lux c: 3
11WITRY, Jacqueline b: 18 Dec 1956 in Bettembourg, Lux v: Trier, Germany o: Lux bureau employee
+ seq: 218.04.50 MARCHAL, Jean w: Abt. 1980
11WITRY, Andre b: 26 Apr 1960 in Bettembourg, Lux v: Dudelange, Lux o: Electrical engineer c: 3
+ seq: 218.05 KOLBACH, Sylvie b: 07 Dec 1962 in Dudelange, Lux w: 29 Jun 1984 in Dudelange, Lux v: Schiffelange, Lux c: 3
11WITRY, Pascal b: 07 Mar 1969 in Bettembourg, Lux v: Trier, Germany o: Freelance journalist
+ seq: 218.05.50 WYRWIK, Claudia w: Abt. 1995

218.05

11 WITRY, Andre b: 26 Apr 1960 in Bettembourg, Lux v:
Dudelange, Lux o: Electrical engineer c: 3
+ seq: 218.05 KOLBACH, Sylvie b: 07 Dec 1962 in Dudelange,
Lux w: 29 Jun 1984 in Dudelange, Lux v: Schiffelange, Lux
c: 3
12 WITRY, Stella b: 23 Mar 1987 in Luxembourg, Lux v:
Schiffelange, Lux
12 WITRY, Amanda b: 20 Aug 1989 in Esch-sur-Alzette, Lux v:
Schiffelange, Lux
12 WITRY, Denis b: 28 May 1991 in Luxembourg, Lux v:
Schiffelange, Lux

219

8 WITRY, Jacob b: 05 Jul 1868 in Beidweiler, Lux d: 1946 in
Bertrange, Lux v: Bertrange, Lux v: Strassem, Lux o: Day
laborer o: Master manufacturer o: Merchant r: b c: 11
+ seq: 219 HEUSCHLING, Anna b: 22 Oct 1874 in Ehlange, Lux
d: 1945 in Bertrange, Lux w: 07 Jan 1895 in Reckange, Lux v:
Bertrange, Lux v: Strassem, Lux o: No profession r: m f:
Nikolas Heuschling m: Maria Frieden c: 11
9 WITRY, Jean-Pierre b: 25 Nov 1891 in Strassem, Lux d: 1958
+ seq: 220 GLANGE, Marguerite b: Abt. 1895 w: Abt. 1920
9 WITRY, Maria b: 25 Nov 1895 in Brouch, Lux d: 23 Oct 1983
v: Bertrange, Lux o: No profession r: b c: 9
+ seq: 220.01 FABER, Bernard b: 08 Dec 1893 in Kopstal, Lux
w: 18 Apr 1921 in Bertrange, Lux v: Bertrange, Lux o: Laborer
r: m f: Theodor Faber m: Catherine Marson c: 9
9 WITRY, Pierre b: 13 Jun 1900 in Strassem, Lux d: 29 Mar
1977 in Luxembourg, Lux v: Bertrange, Lux o: Ironworks in
Rodange r: b c: 4
+ seq: 221 MORETTE, Madeleine b: 15 Feb 1904 in Sandweiler,
Lux d: 25 Dec 1986 in Luxembourg, Lux w: Abt. 1925 v:
Bertrange, Lux c: 4
9 WITRY, Elisabeth b: 03 Dec 1901 in Strassem, Lux d: 11 Mar
1920 in Strassem, Lux r: bd
9 WITRY, Virginie (Marie) b: 03 Dec 1901 in Strassem, Lux o:
No profession c: 3
+ seq: 225.03 MORES, Nicolaus b: 19 Apr 1896 in Folscheid,
Lux o: Cabin worker f: Nicolaus Mores m: Marie Reisen c: 3
9 WITRY, Mathias b: 05 Aug 1904 in Strassem, Lux d: 26 Apr

1976 in Esch-sur-Alzette, Lux r: b
+ seq: 226 GLANGE, Anna b: Abt. 1910 w: Abt. 1935 v:
   Bertrange, Lux
9 WITRY, Catherine (Ketty) b: 24 Feb 1906 in Strassem, Lux d:
   10 Mar 1920 in Bertrange, Lux o: No profession r: bd
9 WITRY, Jean b: 02 Feb 1908 in Strassem, Lux d: 30 May 1992
   v: Mondercange, Lux r: b c: 1
+ seq: 227 BOLLIG, Sanny b: Abt. 1910 w: Abt. 1930 v:
   Mondercange, Lux c: 1
9 WITRY, Suzanne b: 14 Sep 1909 in Strassem, Lux d: 16 Apr
   1976 in Vianden, Lux r: b c: 1
+ seq: 227.01 KLOSEN, Franz (Metty) b: 12 Nov 1907 in
   Bertrange, Lux d: 13 Dec 1965 in Bertrange, Lux w: Abt. 1933
   c: 1
9 WITRY, Eugenie b: 27 May 1911 in Bertrange, Lux d: 05 Mar
   2001 in Howald, Lux v: Bertrange, Lux r: b c: 2
+ seq: 227.06 HOETT, Pierre b: Abt. 1905 w: Abt. 1929 c: 2
9 WITRY, Jacques b: 04 Feb 1914 in Bertrange, Lux d: 1925 r: b

220.01

9 WITRY, Maria b: 25 Nov 1895 in Brouch, Lux v: Bertrange,
   Lux o: No profession r: b c: 9
+ seq: 220.01 FABER, Bernard b: 08 Dec 1893 in Kopstal, Lux
   w: 18 Apr 1921 in Bertrange, Lux v: Bertrange, Lux o:
   Laborer r: m f: Theodor Faber m: Catherine Marson c: 9
10FABER, Anna b: 19 Sep 1915 in Bertrange, Lux r: b
10FABER, Nicolas b: 26 Dec 1919 d: 04 Aug 1994 v: Bertrange,
   Lux
10FABER, Marcel b: 13 Mar 1922
10FABER, J. P. b: Abt. 1925 d: 01 Oct 1993
10FABER, Rene b: 05 Aug 1927 v: Mondercange, Lux
+ seq: 220.02 BRAKONIER w: Abt. 1955
10FABER, Cecile b: 14 Aug 1930 v: Bertrange, Lux
+ seq: 220.03 HEINERSCHEID w: Abt. 1955 v: Bertrange, Lux
10FABER, Georgette b: 05 Apr 1932 v: Messancy, Belgium
10FABER, Suzanne b: 09 Oct 1933
10FABER, Maisy b: 07 Oct 1937 v: Edmonton, Alberta, Canada
+ seq: 220.04 NEY w: Abt. 1960 v: Edmonton, Alberta, Canada

221

9 WITRY, Pierre b: 19 Jun 1900 in Strassem, Lux d: 29 Mar

1977 in Luxembourg, Lux v: Bertrange, Lux o: Ironworks in
Rodange c: 4
+ seq: 221 MORETTE, Madeleine b: 15 Feb 1904 in Sandweiler,
Lux d: 25 Dec 1986 in Luxembourg, Lux w: Abt. 1925 v:
Bertrange, Lux c: 4
10WITRY, Emile b: 27 Feb 1927 in Bertrange, Lux v:
Leudelange, Lux o: Arbed ironworks c: 1
+ seq: 222 LUCIUS, Sisy b: 12 Feb 1929 in Leudelange, Lux w:
Abt. 1955 v: Leudelange, Lux c: 1
10WITRY, Jean-Pierre b: 23 Sep 1930 in Bertrange, Lux v:
Bascharage, Lux o: Arbed ironworks c: 2
+ seq: 223 ANDRING, Marie-Louise b: 25 Apr 1935 in
Bertrange, Lux d: 10 Jul 1997 in Bascharage, Lux Cause of
death: Cancer w: 31 May 1955 v: Bascharage, Lux c: 2
10WITRY, Caroline b: 07 Jul 1932 in Bertrange, Lux v:
Sandweiler, Lux c: 1
+ seq: 224.02 THOLL, Gaston b: 26 Aug 1932 in Sandweiler,
Lux w: Abt. 1952 v: Sandweiler, Lux c: 1
10WITRY, Jacques b: 16 Oct 1937 in Bertrange, Lux v:
Schouweiler, Lux o: Arbed ironworks c: 2
+ seq: 225 LUCIUS, Susanne b: 14 Feb 1938 in Soleuvre, Lux d:
26 Oct 2003 Cause of death: Cancer w: Abt. 1958 v:
Schouweiler, Lux c: 2

222

10WITRY, Emile b: 27 Feb 1927 in Bertrange, Lux v:
Leudelange, Lux o: Arbed ironworks c: 1
+ seq: 222 LUCIUS, Sisy b: 12 Feb 1929 in Leudelange, Lux w:
Abt. 1955 v: Leudelange, Lux c: 1
11WITRY, Yvette b: 23 Jun 1957 in Luxembourg, Lux v:
Heisdorf, Lux c: 1
+ seq: 222.01 ANDRING, Rene b: 31 May 1957 in Luxembourg,
Lux w: Abt. 1983 v: Heisdorf, Lux c: 1

222.01

11WITRY, Yvette b: 23 Jun 1957 in Luxembourg, Lux v:
Heisdorf, Lux c: 1
+ seq: 222.01 ANDRING, Rene b: 31 May 1957 in Luxembourg,
Lux w: Abt. 1983 v: Heisdorf, Lux c: 1
12ANDRING, Gilles b: 18 Nov 1986 in Luxembourg, Lux

223

10 WITRY, Jean-Pierre b: 23 Sep 1930 in Bertrange, Lux v: Bascharage, Lux o: Arbed ironworks c: 2
+ seq: 223 ANDRING, Marie-Louise b: 25 Apr 1935 in Bertrange, Lux d: 10 Jul 1997 in Bascharage, Lux Cause of death: Cancer w: 31 May 1955 v: Bascharage, Lux c: 2
11 WITRY, Joseph (Josy) b: 23 Jul 1956 in Luxembourg, Lux v: Grosbous, Lux o: Luxembourg railroad c: 1
+ seq: 224 WARLIES, Alexa b: 28 Dec 1961 in Steinfort, Lux w: Abt. 1985 v: Grosbous, Lux c: 1
11 WITRY, Patrick b: 09 Nov 1966 in Luxembourg, Lux v: Bascharage, Lux o: Auto mechanic c: 1
+ seq: 224.01 KABER, Joelle b: in Linger, Lux w: 02 Aug 1997 v: Bascharage, Lux c: 1

224

11 WITRY, Joseph (Josy) b: 23 Jul 1956 in Luxembourg, Lux v: Grosbous, Lux o: Luxembourg railroad c: 1
+ seq: 224 WARLIES, Alexa b: 28 Dec 1961 in Steinfort, Lux w: Abt. 1985 v: Grosbous, Lux c: 1
12 WITRY, Romain b: 12 Mar 1990 in Luxembourg, Lux

224.01

11 WITRY, Patrick b: 09 Nov 1966 in Luxembourg, Lux v: Bascharage, Lux o: Auto mechanic c: 1
+ seq: 224.01 KABER, Joelle b: in Linger, Lux w: 02 Aug 1997 v: Bascharage, Lux c: 1
12 WITRY, Ben b: 31 Oct 2000

224.02

10 WITRY, Caroline b: 07 Jul 1932 in Bertrange, Lux v: Sandweiler, Lux c: 1
+ seq: 224.02 THOLL, Gaston b: 26 Aug 1932 in Sandweiler, Lux w: Abt. 1952 v: Sandweiler, Lux c: 1
11 THOLL, Jean-Marie b: 24 Jun 1953 in Luxembourg, Lux

225

10 WITRY, Jacques b: 16 Oct 1937 in Bertrange, Lux v: Schouweiler, Lux o: Arbed ironworks c: 2
+ seq: 225 LUCIUS, Susanne b: 14 Feb 1938 in Soleuvre, Lux d: 26 Oct 2003 Cause of death: Cancer w: Abt. 1958 v:

Schouweiler, Lux c: 2

11[1] WITRY, Marie-Paule b: 26 Sep 1960 in Esch-sur-Alzette,
   Lux v: Hivange, Lux c: 1
 + seq: 225.01 HAAS, Fernand b: 16 Aug 1958 in Esch-sur-
   Alzette, Lux w: Abt. 1983 v: Hivange, Lux c: 1
 * 2nd Husband of [1] WITRY, Marie-Paule:
 + seq: 225.01.50 MICHAELIS, Mich w: Abt. 1985
11 WITRY, Claudine b: 10 Apr 1965 in Esch-sur-Alzette, Lux v:
   Dahlem, Lux c: 2
 + seq: 225.02 HESS, Claude b: 09 Mar 1964 in Differdange, Lux
   w: Abt. 1988 v: Dahlem, Lux c: 2

225.01

11[1] WITRY, Marie-Paule b: 26 Sep 1960 in Esch-sur-Alzette,
   Lux v: Hivange, Lux c: 1
 + seq: 225.01 HAAS, Fernand b: 16 Aug 1958 in Esch-sur-
   Alzette, Lux w: Abt. 1983 v: Hivange, Lux c: 1
12 HAAS, Michel b: 22 Mar 1986 in Luxembourg, Lux
 * 2nd Husband of [1] WITRY, Marie-Paule:
 + seq: 225.01.50 MICHAELIS, Mich w: Abt. 1985

225.02

11 WITRY, Claudine b: 10 Apr 1965 in Esch-sur-Alzette, Lux v:
   Dahlem, Lux c: 2
 + seq: 225.02 HESS, Claude b: 09 Mar 1964 in Differdange, Lux
   w: Abt. 1988 v: Dahlem, Lux c: 2
12 HESS, Pit b: 17 Jan 1990 in Luxembourg, Lux
12 HESS, Rick b: 08 Mar 1992 in Luxembourg, Lux

225.03

 9 WITRY, Virginie (Marie) b: 03 Dec 1901 in Strassem, Lux o:
   No profession c: 3
 + seq: 225.03 MORES, Nicolaus b: 19 Apr 1896 in Folscheid,
   Lux o: Cabin worker f: Nicolaus Mores m: Marie Reisen c: 3
10 MORES, Anna b: 04 Dec 1921 v: Reckange, Lux
 + seq: 225.04 FOGOLIN, Arthur w: Abt. 1945
10 MORES, Jean b: 14 Aug 1926 d: 26 Jun 1994
10 MORES, Simone b: 17 Jul 1934 v: Bascharage, Lux
 + seq: 225.05 SCHUEREN w: Abt. 1960 v: Bascharage, Lux

227

9 WITRY, Jean b: 02 Feb 1908 in Strassem, Lux d: 30 May 1992
  v: Mondercange, Lux c: 1
+ seq: 227 BOLLIG, Sanny b: Abt. 1910 w: Abt. 1930 v:
  Mondercange, Lux c: 1
10 WITRY, Egide b: 14 Aug 1932 v: Bertrange, Lux c: 3
+ seq: 227.00.01 BIVER, Yvonne b: 06 Jul 1939 w: Abt. 1960
  v: Bertrange, Lux c: 3

227.00.01

10 WITRY, Egide b: 14 Aug 1932 v: Bertrange, Lux c: 3
+ seq: 227.00.01 BIVER, Yvonne b: 06 Jul 1939 w: Abt. 1960
  v: Bertrange, Lux c: 3
11 WITRY, Josiane b: 29 Dec 1961 v: Kleinbettingen, Lux c: 3
+ seq: 227.00.02 LORDONG, Jean-Pierre w: Abt. 1980 v:
  Kleinbettingen, Lux c: 3
11 WITRY, Luc b: 21 Apr 1971 d: 25 Nov 1995 Cause of death:
  Auto accident
11 WITRY, Jacqueline b: 03 Aug 1964 c: 2
+ seq: 227.00.03 ZIMMER, Georges w: Abt. 1995 c: 2

227.00.02

11 WITRY, Josiane b: 29 Dec 1961 v: Kleinbettingen, Lux c: 3
+ seq: 227.00.02 LORDONG, Jean-Pierre w: Abt. 1980 v:
  Kleinbettingen, Lux c: 3
12 LORDONG, Caroline b: 01 Sep 1983
12 LORDONG, Christine b: 25 Jun 1986
12 LORDONG, Joe b: 06 Dec 1989

227.00.03

11 WITRY, Jacqueline b: 03 Aug 1964 c: 2
+ seq: 227.00.03 ZIMMER, Georges w: Abt. 1995 c: 2
12 ZIMMER, Bob b: 07 Sep 1996
12 ZIMMER, Frank b: 23 Mar 1995

227.01

9 WITRY, Suzanne b: 14 Sep 1909 in Strassem, Lux d: 16 Apr
  1976 in Vianden, Lux c: 1
+ seq: 227.01 KLOSEN, Franz (Metty) b: 12 Nov 1907 in
  Bertrange, Lux d: 13 Dec 1965 in Bertrange, Lux w: Abt. 1933
  c: 1

10KLOSEN, Joseph-Jacques-Mathias (Josy) b: 03 Jun 1935 in
  Bertrange, Lux v: Esch-sur-Alzette, Lux c: 3
+ seq: 227.02 BAUER, Fernande w: Abt. 1960 c: 3

227.02

10KLOSEN, Joseph-Jacques-Mathias (Josy) b: 03 Jun 1935 in
  Bertrange, Lux v: Esch-sur-Alzette, Lux c: 3
+ seq: 227.02 BAUER, Fernande w: Abt. 1960 c: 3
11KLOSEN, Paul b: 1963 o: Professor of microbiology at
  University of Heidelburg
+ seq: 227.03 TERAO, Eriko w: Abt. 1990
11KLOSEN, Georges b: 1965 c: 2
+ seq: 227.04 GUDENDORF, Simone w: Abt. 1990 c: 2
11KLOSEN, Michel b: 1971
+ seq: 227.05 WEIRICH, Viviane w: Abt. 1995

227.04

11KLOSEN, Georges b: 1965 c: 2
+ seq: 227.04 GUDENDORF, Simone w: Abt. 1990 c: 2
12KLOSEN, Laure
12KLOSEN, Gilles

227.06

9 WITRY, Eugenie b: 27 May 1911 in Bertrange, Lux d: 05 Mar
  2001 in Howald, Lux v: Bertrange, Lux r: b c: 2
+ seq: 227.06 HOETT, Pierre b: Abt. 1905 w: Abt. 1929 c: 2
10HOETT, Raymond b: 22 Feb 1931 v: Soleuvre, Lux c: 1
+ seq: 227.06.01 NEY, Tilly w: Abt. 1955 c: 1
10HOETT, Yvonne b: 07 May 1934 v: Howald, Lux
+ seq: 227.07 DIEDERICH, Georges w: Abt. 1955 v: Howald,
  Lux o: Railroad employee

227.06.01

10HOETT, Raymond b: 22 Feb 1931 v: Soleuvre, Lux c: 1
+ seq: 227.06.01 NEY, Tilly w: Abt. 1955 c: 1
11HOETT, Celestine

229

6 WITRY, Nicolas b: 07 Aug 1789 in Beidweiler, Lux d: 21 Mar
  1871 in Herborn, Lux h: No. 24 v: Herborn, Lux i: Wounded
  by lance in mouth and neck in Leipsig i: Awarded with the Lily

i: Discharge from French Dragoons, served 1809-1814 o:
Soldier o: Forest warden o: Farmer r: bdx c: 13
+ seq: 229 KUHNEN, Catherine b: 04 Sep 1799 in Herborn, Lux
  d: 08 May 1878 in Herborn, Lux w: 19 Jan 1818 in Rodenbourg,
  Lux a: Kohn h: No. 24 v: Herborn, Lux o: No profession r: bd
  r: m f: Johann Kuhnen m: Elisabeth Baden c: 13
7 WITRY, Elisabeth b: 06 Dec 1818 in Herborn, Lux d: 30 Jun
  1886 in Herborn, Lux v: Herborn, Lux o: No profession r: bd
  c: 7
+ seq: 229.01 MOOS, Jacob b: 20 Jun 1817 in Mittendorf, Lux w:
  23 Feb 1846 in Mompach, Lux v: Herborn, Lux o: Blacksmith
  o: Farmer r: m f: Mathias Moos m: Anna-Catherine
  Schommers c: 7
7 WITRY, Johann b: 11 Nov 1820 in Herborn, Lux d: 07 Oct
  1882 in Gilzem, Germany v: Gilzem, Germany o: Blacksmith
  o: Day laborer o: Farmer r: b c: 4
+ seq: 230 LICHTER, Susanna (Anna) b: 03 Jun 1826 in Gilzem,
  Germany d: 23 May 1857 in Gilzem, Germany w: 30 Jan 1850
  in Gilzem, Germany v: Gilzem, Germany i: Children lived with
  her parents after her death r: d r: m f: Stephan Lichter m: Anna
  Reuter c: 4
7 [1] WITRY, Michel b: 12 Aug 1822 in Herborn, Lux v:
  Herborn, Lux i: Emigrated to the U. S., probably Iowa r: b c: 2
+ seq: 262 KARPES, Lucia b: Abt. 1930 w: Abt. 1860 v:
  Herborn, Lux c: 1
* 2nd Wife of [1] WITRY, Michel:
+ seq: 263 KOHL, Barbara b: Abt. 1830 w: Abt. 1867 v:
  Herborn, Lux c: 1
7 WITRY, Marie b: 16 Jul 1824 in Herborn, Lux d: 27 Nov 1826
  in Herborn, Lux h: No. 24 v: Herborn, Lux o: No profession r:
  bd
7 WITRY, Peter b: 16 Jul 1826 in Herborn, Lux d: 05 Jul 1882 in
  Herborn, Lux v: Herborn, Lux o: Farmer o: Carpenter o: Day
  laborer r: bd
7 WITTRY, Paul b: 21 Mar 1828 in Herborn, Lux d: 31 Oct 1897
  in Aurora, IL Cause of death: Stomach cancer a: Witry v:
  Ernzen, Lux i: Emigrated to Aurora, IL i: Discharge from
  militia i: Emigrated to the U.S. o: Wheelwright o: Carpenter o:
  Farmer r: bdx c: 3
+ seq: 271 WEBER, Marie b: 03 Mar 1824 in Ernzen, Lux d: 08
  Jun 1879 in Ernzen, Lux w: 07 Jul 1858 in Fels, Lux v: Ernzen,

Lux o: No profession r: bd r: mx f: Michel Weber m: Anna-Marie Goedert c: 3

7 WITRY, Marie-Anna b: 24 Feb 1830 in Herborn, Lux d: 02 Apr 1830 in Herborn, Lux h: No. 24 v: Herborn, Lux o: No profession r: bd

7 WITRY, Elisabeth b: 18 Apr 1831 in Herborn, Lux d: 25 Jul 1847 in Herborn, Lux h: No. 24 v: Herborn, Lux o: No profession r: bd

7 WITRY, Barbara b: 07 May 1833 in Herborn, Lux d: 13 Dec 1902 in Rosport, Lux v: Rosport, Lux o: No profession r: bd c: 5

+ seq: 283.03 THINNES, Pierre b: 17 Jan 1832 in Rosport, Lux d: 16 Jan 1907 in Rosport, Lux w: 01 Feb 1864 in Rosport, Lux v: Rosport, Lux o: Master bricklayer r: d r: m f: Michel Thinnes m: Marie Schmitt c: 5

7 WITRY, Peter b: 16 Mar 1835 in Herborn, Lux d: 16 Jan 1901 in Herborn, Lux v: Herborn, Lux o: Day laborer o: Carpenter o: Craftsman r: b c: 8

+ seq: 284 WEISGERBER, Anna b: 04 Oct 1841 in Herborn, Lux w: 09 Jan 1867 in Mompach, Lux v: Herborn, Lux o: No profession r: b r: m f: Johann Weisgerber m: Elisabeth Baden c: 8

7 [2] WITRY, Nicolas b: 09 Apr 1837 in Herborn, Lux d: 17 Feb 1914 in Waterloo, IA Cause of death: Pneumonia h: Kuhnen v: Breda, IA v: Herborn, Lux i: Emigrated to the U. S. o: Mason o: Farmer o: Wagon maker r: bdx c: 2

+ seq: 285 COOPER, Mary b: 1840 d: 09 Sep 1875 in Breda, IA w: 10 Jul 1873 in Dubuque, IA v: Breda, IA c: 2

* 2nd Wife of [2] WITRY, Nicolas:

+ seq: 286 SALMEN, Sophia b: 1834 d: 06 Oct 1906 in Iowa w: 28 Jan 1876 in Dubuque, IA v: Breda, IA v: Carroll, IA

* 3rd Wife of [2] WITRY, Nicolas:

+ seq: 287 ENGELBRECHT, Mary b: Abt. 1850 w: Dec 1913 v: Breda, IA

7 WITRY, Catherine b: 15 Jun 1839 in Herborn, Lux d: Abt. 1912 h: Kuhnen v: Waterloo, IA v: Herborn, Lux i: Emigrated to the U. S. r: b c: 7

+ seq: 287.01 BLITSCH, Jacob b: Abt. 1840 w: Abt. 1868 v: Waterloo, IA v: Herborn, Lux o: Cabinet maker c: 7

7 WITRY, Dominic b: 19 Oct 1841 in Herborn, Lux d: 23 Oct 1912 in Waterloo, IA h: Kuhnen v: Waterloo, IA v: Herborn,

Lux i: Emigrated to the U.S. o: Grocer r: bdx c: 3
+ seq: 288 POTT, Margaretha b: 10 Oct 1844 d: 14 Aug 1924 in
  Waterloo, IA w: 16 Feb 1869 v: Waterloo, IA c: 3

229.01

7 WITRY, Elisabeth b: 06 Dec 1818 in Herborn, Lux d: 30 Jun
  1886 in Herborn, Lux v: Herborn, Lux o: No profession r: bd
  c: 7
+ seq: 229.01 MOOS, Jacob b: 20 Jun 1817 in Mittendorf, Lux
   w: 23 Feb 1846 in Mompach, Lux v: Herborn, Lux o:
   Blacksmith o: Farmer r: m f: Mathias Moos m: Anna-
   Catherine Schommers c: 7
8 MOOS, Nicolas b: 11 Dec 1846 in Herborn, Lux d: 17 Dec
  1846 in Herborn, Lux v: Herborn, Lux o: No profession r: bd
8 MOOS, Catherine b: 07 Feb 1848 in Herborn, Lux v: Herborn,
  Lux o: No profession r: b c: 3
+ seq: 229.02 GOEDERT, Michel b: 07 Jan 1847 in Herborn,
   Lux w: 24 Jan 1887 in Herborn, Lux v: Herborn, Lux o:
   Blacksmith o: Blacksmith r: b r: m f: Domnik Goedert m:
   Susanna Fahr c: 3
8 MOOS, Johann b: 15 Nov 1849 in Herborn, Lux r: b
8 MOOS, Margaretha b: 06 Jun 1852 in Herborn, Lux i:
  Emigrated to Waterloo, IA r: b c: 1
+ seq: 229.06 CONRAD, Bernard b: in Luxembourg, Lux w: 22
   Apr 1884 in Waterloo, IA i: Emigrated to Waterloo, IA f:
   Matthew Conrad m: Clara Bedel c: 1
8 MOOS, Marie b: 07 Sep 1854 in Herborn, Lux r: b c: 1
+ seq: 229.38 CONTER, Dominique w: 28 May 1891 in
   Mompach, Lux c: 1
8 MOOS, Marie b: 22 May 1860 in Herborn, Lux d: 07 Aug 1887
  in Herborn, Lux v: Herborn, Lux o: No profession r: bd c: 1
+ seq: 229.38.01 w: Abt. 1880 c: 1
8 MOOS, Barbara b: 21 May 1863 in Herborn, Lux d: 08 Jan
  1866 in Herborn, Lux v: Herborn, Lux o: No profession r: bd

229.02

8 MOOS, Catherine b: 07 Feb 1848 in Herborn, Lux v: Herborn,
  Lux o: No profession r: b c: 3
+ seq: 229.02 GOEDERT, Michel b: 07 Jan 1847 in Herborn,
   Lux w: 24 Jan 1887 in Herborn, Lux v: Herborn, Lux o:
   Blacksmith o: Blacksmith r: b r: m f: Domnik Goedert m:

Susanna Fahr c: 3

9 GOEDERT, Peter b: 01 Dec 1887 in Herborn, Lux d: 06 May
1953 in Herborn, Lux v: Herborn, Lux o: Farmer r: b c: 3

+ seq: 229.03 KAISER, Barbara-Eugenie b: 16 Oct 1884 in
Mertert, Lux d: 12 Mar 1971 in Luxembourg, Lux w: 12 Jan
1914 in Mompach, Lux v: Herborn, Lux o: No profession f:
Nicolas Kaiser m: Maria Petry c: 3

9 GOEDERT, Felix-Jacob b: 21 Nov 1889 in Herborn, Lux d: 17
Jan 1890 in Herborn, Lux v: Herborn, Lux o: No profession r:
bd

9 GOEDERT, Anna-Maria b: 11 Sep 1891 in Herborn, Lux r: b

229.03

9 GOEDERT, Peter b: 01 Dec 1887 in Herborn, Lux d: 06 May
1953 in Herborn, Lux v: Herborn, Lux o: Farmer r: b c: 3

+ seq: 229.03 KAISER, Barbara-Eugenie b: 16 Oct 1884 in
Mertert, Lux d: 12 Mar 1971 in Luxembourg, Lux w: 12 Jan
1914 in Mompach, Lux v: Herborn, Lux o: No profession f:
Nicolas Kaiser m: Maria Petry c: 3

10GOEDERT, Michel b: 25 Aug 1915 d: 09 Mar 1950 in
Herborn, Lux o: Farmer

10GOEDERT, Nicolas-Felix b: 19 Nov 1916 in Herborn, Lux v:
Herborn, Lux o: Farmer c: 3

+ seq: 229.05 GEVELINGER, Agnese b: 08 Oct 1921 in
Beidweiler, Lux d: 30 Dec 1983 in Echternach, Lux w: 14 Feb
1953 o: No profession f: Jean Gevelinger m: Margueritte
Kieffer c: 3

10GOEDERT, Jean b: 1918 in Herborn, Lux d: 1918 in Herborn,
Lux

229.05

10GOEDERT, Nicolas-Felix b: 19 Nov 1916 in Herborn, Lux v:
Herborn, Lux o: Farmer c: 3

+ seq: 229.05 GEVELINGER, Agnese b: 08 Oct 1921 in
Beidweiler, Lux d: 30 Dec 1983 in Echternach, Lux w: 14 Feb
1953 o: No profession f: Jean Gevelinger m: Margueritte
Kieffer c: 3

11GOEDERT, Eugenie b: 10 Jan 1954 in Echternach, Lux o: No
profession

11GOEDERT, Lucien b: 04 Oct 1955 in Echternach, Lux d: 06
Oct 1988 in Herborn, Lux o: Farmer

11 GOEDERT, Marie-Paule b: 21 Aug 1962 in Echternach, Lux v: Echternach, Lux o: Bank employee
+ seq: 229.05.01 ZAPPONE, Marco b: 13 Sep 1967 in Bettembourg, Lux w: 12 Oct 2002 in Echtenach, Lux v: Echternach, Lux o: Railroad employee f: Rene Zaponne m: Leontine Weins

229.06

8 MOOS, Margaretha b: 06 Jun 1852 in Herborn, Lux i: Emigrated to Waterloo, IA r: b c: 1
+ seq: 229.06 CONRAD, Bernard b: in Luxembourg, Lux w: 22 Apr 1884 in Waterloo, IA i: Emigrated to Waterloo, IA f: Matthew Conrad m: Clara Bedel c: 1
9 [1] CONRAD, Robert-Louis b: 20 Nov 1897 in Riceville, IA d: 25 Jan 1935 v: Raymond, IA o: Mechanic c: 7
+ seq: 229.07 NATHEM, Frances b: Abt. 1901 d: 03 May 1922 in North Washington, IA w: 05 Oct 1921 in North Washington, IA c: 1
* 2nd Wife of [1] CONRAD, Robert-Louis:
+ seq: 229.09 WITTRY, Mary-Elizabeth b: 02 Jul 1902 in Breda, IA d: 19 Jul 1995 in Raymond, IA w: 22 Sep 1925 in Mount Carmel, IA v: Raymond, IA i: Both are descendents of the family tree o: Homemaker f: Jacob Witry m: Anna Wirtz c: 6

229.07

9 [1] CONRAD, Robert-Louis b: 20 Nov 1897 in Riceville, IA d: 25 Jan 1935 v: Raymond, IA o: Mechanic c: 7
+ seq: 229.07 NATHEM, Frances b: Abt. 1901 d: 03 May 1922 in North Washington, IA w: 05 Oct 1921 in North Washington, IA c: 1
10 CONRAD, Frances-Loretta b: 03 May 1922 in North Washington, IA d: 07 Feb 1974 in Phoenix, AZ v: Phoenix, AZ o: Seamstress
+ seq: 229.08 Hollar, Donald-Michael b: 04 Jun 1921 in Waterloo, IA d: 08 Aug 2001 w: 20 Jun 1944 in Waterloo, IA v: Phoenix, AZ o: Aero-space worker
* 2nd Wife of [1] CONRAD, Robert-Louis:
+ seq: 229.09 WITTRY, Mary-Elizabeth b: 02 Jul 1902 in Breda, IA d: 19 Jul 1995 in Raymond, IA w: 22 Sep 1925 in Mount Carmel, IA v: Raymond, IA i: Both are descendents of the family tree o: Homemaker f: Jacob Witry m: Anna Wirtz c: 6

10CONRAD, Robert-Bernard (Bud) b: 26 Sep 1926 in Raymond,
   IA v: Raymond, IA o: Carpenter c: 2
 + seq: 229.10 BROWN, Clarice-Mae b: 04 Jan 1928 in Waterloo,
   IA d: 02 May 1994 in Iowa City, IA w: 07 Jun 1952 in
   Raymond, IA v: Raymond, IA o: Homemaker c: 2
10CONRAD, Marie-Ann b: 22 Aug 1927 in Raymond, IA d: 01
   Apr 2007 in Raymond, IA v: Raymond, IA o: Homemaker c: 4
 + seq: 229.13 SACHS, Merle-Walter b: 30 Dec 1926 in Lakota,
   IA d: 10 May 1988 in Raymond, IA w: 18 Jul 1953 in
   Raymond, IA v: Raymond, IA o: John Deere c: 4
10CONRAD, Louis-Robert b: 17 Dec 1928 in Raymond, IA v:
   Raymond, IA o: Construction c: 2
 + seq: 229.18 HEMMER, Teresa-Ann b: 02 Dec 1937 in
   Gilbertville, IA w: 25 Jun 1960 in Gilbertville, IA v:
   Raymond, IA o: Homemaker c: 2
10CONRAD, Anita-Margaret b: 20 Feb 1930 in Raymond, IA v:
   Raymond, IA o: Homemaker c: 4
 + seq: 229.21 RUSSELL, Milo-French (Frenchy) b: 13 Apr 1928
   in Cedar Falls, IA w: 06 Aug 1949 in Raymond, IA v:
   Raymond, IA o: Tool designer c: 4
10CONRAD, William-Nicholas (Bill) b: 08 Jul 1932 in Raymond,
   IA v: Washburn, IA o: ICRR c: 5
 + seq: 229.28 SMITH, Carole-Delight b: 28 Dec 1934 in
   Brandon, IA w: 23 Apr 1957 in Raymond, IA v: Washburn, IA
   o: Homemaker c: 5
10[2] CONRAD, James-Leo (Jim) b: 19 Dec 1934 in Raymond,
   IA v: Washburn, IA o: John Deere c: 4
 + seq: 229.35 BEARBOWER, Patricia-May b: 29 Oct 1934 in
   Independence, IA d: 13 Dec 1995 in Waterloo, IA w: 21 Jan
   1961 in Waterloo, IA v: Washburn, IA o: Homemaker c: 4
 * 2nd Wife of [2] CONRAD, James-Leo (Jim):
 + seq: 229.37.02 FOLLAN, Marva N. b: 24 Jan 1938 in
   Jefferson, IA w: 27 Dec 2003 in Des Moines, IA

229.10
10CONRAD, Robert-Bernard (Bud) b: 26 Sep 1926 in Raymond,
   IA v: Raymond, IA o: Carpenter c: 2
 + seq: 229.10 BROWN, Clarice-Mae b: 04 Jan 1928 in Waterloo,
   IA d: 02 May 1994 in Iowa City, IA w: 07 Jun 1952 in
   Raymond, IA v: Raymond, IA o: Homemaker c: 2
11CONRAD, Robert-Louis b: 07 Jul 1954 in Waterloo, IA v:

Washburn, IA o: Construction worker c: 2
+ seq: 229.11 SCHARES, Betty-Jean b: 29 Jun 1956 in
   Gilbertville, IA w: 01 May 1978 in Gilbertville, IA v:
   Washburn, IA o: Nurse c: 2
11[1] CONRAD, David-Eugene b: 19 Aug 1958 in Waterloo, IA
   v: Waterloo, IA o: Construction worker c: 1
+ seq: 229.12 RIGGLE, Carla-Rae b: 20 Jan 1962 w: 07 Jun
   1980 in La Porte City, IA v: Fayetteville, AR o: Homemaker
   c: 1
* 2nd Wife of [1] CONRAD, David-Eugene:
+ seq: 229.12.02 MCGREW, Mary b: 30 Jan 1956 in Waterloo,
   IA w: 30 Dec 1999 in Waterloo, IA v: Waterloo, IA o:
   Homemaker

229.11

11CONRAD, Robert-Louis b: 07 Jul 1954 in Waterloo, IA v:
   Washburn, IA o: Construction worker c: 2
+ seq: 229.11 SCHARES, Betty-Jean b: 29 Jun 1956 in
   Gilbertville, IA w: 01 May 1978 in Gilbertville, IA v:
   Washburn, IA o: Nurse c: 2
12CONRAD, Angela-Jo b: 27 Feb 1982 in Waterloo, IA o:
   Student
12CONRAD, Michelle-Ann b: 13 Apr 1984 in Waterloo, IA o:
   Student

229.12

11[1] CONRAD, David-Eugene b: 19 Aug 1958 in Waterloo, IA
   v: Waterloo, IA o: Construction worker c: 1
+ seq: 229.12 RIGGLE, Carla-Rae b: 20 Jan 1962 w: 07 Jun
   1980 in La Porte City, IA v: Fayetteville, AR o: Homemaker
   c: 1
12CONRAD, Jamie-Lynn b: 09 Nov 1980 in Waterloo, IA v:
   Fayetteville, AR o: Sales
+ seq: 229.12.01 BLAIR, Thomas b: 18 Feb 1971 in Fayetteville,
   AR w: 12 Feb 2001 in Fayetteville, AR o: Self employed
* 2nd Wife of [1] CONRAD, David-Eugene:
+ seq: 229.12.02 MCGREW, Mary b: 30 Jan 1956 in Waterloo,
   IA w: 30 Dec 1999 in Waterloo, IA v: Waterloo, IA o:
   Homemaker

229.13

10CONRAD, Marie-Ann b: 22 Aug 1927 in Raymond, IA d: 01 Apr 2007 in Raymond, IA v: Raymond, IA o: Homemaker c: 4

+ seq: 229.13 SACHS, Merle-Walter b: 30 Dec 1926 in Lakota, IA d: 10 May 1988 in Raymond, IA w: 18 Jul 1953 in Raymond, IA v: Raymond, IA o: John Deere c: 4

11SACHS, Suzanne-Marie b: 27 May 1954 in Waterloo, IA v: Colleyville, TX o: Insurance agent c: 2

+ seq: 229.14 BROWN, Lansing-James, Jr. b: 15 Apr 1949 in Willmington, NC w: 21 Jul 1973 in Raymond, IA v: Colleyville, TX o: Real estate agent c: 2

11SACHS, Mary-Kay b: 06 Jun 1956 in Waterloo, IA v: Raymond, IA o: Seamstress c: 2

+ seq: 229.15 KANE, Randy-Guerdon b: 21 May 1956 in Waterloo, IA w: 15 Sep 1979 in Raymond, IA v: Raymond, IA o: Nestle Co. c: 2

11SACHS, Kathleen-Jo b: 23 Dec 1958 in Waterloo, IA v: Gilbertville, IA o: GMAC c: 2

+ seq: 229.16 FRAMPTON, Steven-David b: 18 Nov 1959 in Dubuque, IA w: 03 Oct 1981 in Raymond, IA v: Gilbertville, IA o: Accountant c: 2

11SACHS, Lori-Jean b: 16 Mar 1964 in Waterloo, IA v: Jesup, IA o: Homemaker c: 3

+ seq: 229.17 CORKERY, Lawrence-Patrick b: 28 May 1964 in Waterloo, IA w: 08 Nov 1986 in Raymond, IA v: Jesup, IA o: Recycling engineer c: 3

229.14

11SACHS, Suzanne-Marie b: 27 May 1954 in Waterloo, IA v: Colleyville, TX o: Insurance agent c: 2

+ seq: 229.14 BROWN, Lansing-James, Jr. b: 15 Apr 1949 in Willmington, NC w: 21 Jul 1973 in Raymond, IA v: Colleyville, TX o: Real estate agent c: 2

12BROWN, Heather-Ann b: 26 May 1974 in Waterloo, IA v: Fort Worth, TX o: Clerical c: 1

+ seq: 229.14.01 LUHMAN, Edward-Frederick (Buddy) IV b: 28 Apr 1974 in Bedford, TX w: 02 Oct 1999 in Colleyville, TX v: Fort Worth, TX o: Design engineer c: 1

12BROWN, Kimberly-Kay b: 18 Feb 1977 in Rochester, MN v: Flower Mound, TX o: Flight attendant c: 1

+ seq: 229.14.02 SHARP, Ronald J. b: 06 Aug 1971 in Dallas,

TX w: 21 Sep 2002 in Dallas, TX c: 1

229.14.01
12BROWN, Heather-Ann b: 26 May 1974 in Waterloo, IA v: Fort
   Worth, TX o: Clerical c: 1
+ seq: 229.14.01 LUHMAN, Edward-Frederick (Buddy) IV b: 28
   Apr 1974 in Bedford, TX w: 02 Oct 1999 in Colleyville, TX v:
   Fort Worth, TX o: Design engineer c: 1
13LUHMAN, Hunter-Ryan b: 11 Feb 2003

229.14.02
12BROWN, Kimberly-Kay b: 18 Feb 1977 in Rochester, MN v:
   Flower Mound, TX o: Flight attendant c: 1
+ seq: 229.14.02 SHARP, Ronald J. b: 06 Aug 1971 in Dallas,
   TX w: 21 Sep 2002 in Dallas, TX c: 1
13SHARP, Caden-James b: 06 May 2004 in Bedford, TX

229.15
11SACHS, Mary-Kay b: 06 Jun 1956 in Waterloo, IA v:
   Raymond, IA o: Seamstress c: 2
+ seq: 229.15 KANE, Randy-Guerdon b: 21 May 1956 in
   Waterloo, IA w: 15 Sep 1979 in Raymond, IA v: Raymond, IA
   o: Nestle Co. c: 2
12KANE, Kristen-Marie b: 12 Jan 1985 in Waterloo, IA o:
   Student
12KANE, Emily-Ann b: 24 Nov 1987 in Waterloo, IA o: Student

229.16
11SACHS, Kathleen-Jo b: 23 Dec 1958 in Waterloo, IA v:
   Gilbertville, IA o: GMAC c: 2
+ seq: 229.16 FRAMPTON, Steven-David b: 18 Nov 1959 in
   Dubuque, IA w: 03 Oct 1981 in Raymond, IA v: Gilbertville,
   IA o: Accountant c: 2
12FRAMPTON, Jenna-Ann b: 11 Sep 1987 in Waterloo, IA o:
   Student
12FRAMPTON, Collin-David b: 11 Jan 1990 in Waterloo, IA o:
   Student

229.17
11SACHS, Lori-Jean b: 16 Mar 1964 in Waterloo, IA v: Jesup, IA
   o: Homemaker c: 3

+ seq: 229.17 CORKERY, Lawrence-Patrick b: 28 May 1964 in
   Waterloo, IA w: 08 Nov 1986 in Raymond, IA v: Jesup, IA o:
   Recycling engineer c: 3
12 CORKERY, John-Walter b: 27 Aug 1990 in Waterloo, IA o:
   Student
12 CORKERY, Ross-Lawrence b: 06 Dec 1991 in Waterloo, IA o:
   Student
12 CORKERY, Lee-Sachs b: 15 Dec 1993 in Waterloo, IA

229.18

10 CONRAD, Louis-Robert b: 17 Dec 1928 in Raymond, IA v:
   Raymond, IA o: Construction c: 2
+ seq: 229.18 HEMMER, Teresa-Ann b: 02 Dec 1937 in
   Gilbertville, IA w: 25 Jun 1960 in Gilbertville, IA v:
   Raymond, IA o: Homemaker c: 2
11 CONRAD, Roxane-Marie b: 06 May 1963 in Waterloo, IA v:
   Moor Park, CA o: Homemaker c: 1
+ seq: 229.19 HARMS, Daniel-Wade b: 21 Nov 1964 in
   Wellsberg, IA w: 13 Feb 1987 in Raymond, IA v: Moor Park,
   CA o: Chemist c: 1
11 CONRAD, Joseph-Louis (Joe) b: 27 Mar 1969 in Waterloo, IA
   v: Raymond, IA o: Construction worker c: 1
+ seq: 229.20 WEBER, Kristine-Kay b: 03 Jan 1971 in Waterloo,
   IA w: 01 Oct 1994 in Waterloo, IA v: Cedar Falls, IA c: 1

229.19

11 CONRAD, Roxane-Marie b: 06 May 1963 in Waterloo, IA v:
   Moor Park, CA o: Homemaker c: 1
+ seq: 229.19 HARMS, Daniel-Wade b: 21 Nov 1964 in
   Wellsberg, IA w: 13 Feb 1987 in Raymond, IA v: Moor Park,
   CA o: Chemist c: 1
12 HARMS, Ashley-Elizabeth b: 20 Mar 1996 in Midland, MI

229.20

11 CONRAD, Joseph-Louis (Joe) b: 27 Mar 1969 in Waterloo, IA
   v: Raymond, IA o: Construction worker c: 1
+ seq: 229.20 WEBER, Kristine-Kay b: 03 Jan 1971 in Waterloo,
   IA w: 01 Oct 1994 in Waterloo, IA v: Cedar Falls, IA c: 1
12 CONRAD, Cody-Allen b: 24 May 1994 in Waterloo, IA

229.21

10CONRAD, Anita-Margaret b: 20 Feb 1930 in Raymond, IA v: Raymond, IA o: Homemaker c: 4

+ seq: 229.21 RUSSELL, Milo-French (Frenchy) b: 13 Apr 1928 in Cedar Falls, IA w: 06 Aug 1949 in Raymond, IA v: Raymond, IA o: Tool designer c: 4

11RUSSELL, Steven-James b: 25 Jul 1953 in Waterloo, IA v: Independence, IA o: John Deere c: 2

+ seq: 229.22 NELSON, Pamela (Pam) b: 21 Jun 1955 in Preston, MN w: 09 Nov 1973 in Barclay, IA v: Independence, IA o: Homemaker c: 2

11[1] RUSSELL, Michael-William b: 28 Jul 1955 in Waterloo, IA v: Elk Run Heights, IA o: John Deere c: 1

+ seq: 229.23 BROWN, Sally b: 04 Dec 1956 in Waterloo, IA w: 12 Jul 1976 in Waterloo, IA v: Waterloo, IA o: Banking c: 1

* 2nd Wife of [1] RUSSELL, Michael-Williaw:

+ seq: 229.24 RASKA, Kathryn-Helen b: 31 Aug 1953 in Waterloo, IA w: 23 Sep 1995 in Raymond, IA v: Elk Run Heights, IA o: Sales

11[2] RUSSELL, Julia-Ann b: 10 Jan 1957 in Waterloo, IA v: Dewar, IA o: County government employee c: 1

+ seq: 229.25 WIDDEL, John (Jack) b: 21 Mar 1950 in Waterloo, IA w: 10 Sep 1977 in Nashua, IA v: Dunkerton, IA o: Cabinet maker c: 1

* 2nd Husband of [2] RUSSELL, Julia-Ann:

+ seq: 229.26 PROTSMAN, Ron-Wayne b: 02 Jun 1950 in Lansing, IA w: 15 Nov 1997 in Waterloo, IA v: Dewar, IA o: John Deere

11RUSSELL, Timothy-Milo b: 06 Jun 1968 in Waterloo, IA v: Fresno, CA o: Cabinet maker c: 2

+ seq: 229.27 WOOLSEY, Jamie b: 13 Dec 1967 in Waterloo, IA w: 11 Jan 1989 in Waterloo, IA v: Fresno, CA o: Teacher c: 2

229.22

11RUSSELL, Steven-James b: 25 Jul 1953 in Waterloo, IA v: Independence, IA o: John Deere c: 2

+ seq: 229.22 NELSON, Pamela (Pam) b: 21 Jun 1955 in Preston, MN w: 09 Nov 1973 in Barclay, IA v: Independence, IA o: Homemaker c: 2

12RUSSELL, Shawn b: 31 May 1974 in Waterloo, IA v: Independence, IA o: Laborer

12RUSSELL, Stacy b: 20 Oct 1976 in Waterloo, IA v: Independence, IA o: MCI c: 1
+ seq: 229.22.01 JENKINS, Johnny F. b: 04 Nov 1975 in Knoxville,TN w: 04 Sep 1999 in Independence, IA v: Independence, IA o: Machinist c: 1

229.22.01
12RUSSELL, Stacy b: 20 Oct 1976 in Waterloo, IA v: Independence, IA o: MCI c: 1
+ seq: 229.22.01 JENKINS, Johnny F. b: 04 Nov 1975 in Knoxville,TN w: 04 Sep 1999 in Independence, IA v: Independence, IA o: Machinist c: 1
13JENKINS, Johnny W. b: 28 Dec 2003 in Knoxville, TN d: 09 Jan 2004 in Knoxville, TN

229.23
11[1] RUSSELL, Michael-William b: 28 Jul 1955 in Waterloo, IA v: Elk Run Heights, IA o: John Deere c: 1
+ seq: 229.23 BROWN, Sally b: 04 Dec 1956 in Waterloo, IA w: 12 Jul 1976 in Waterloo, IA v: Waterloo, IA o: Banking c: 1
12RUSSELL, Jodi-Elizabeth b: 07 Oct 1978 in Waterloo, IA o: Student
* 2nd Wife of [1] RUSSELL, Michael-Williaw:
+ seq: 229.24 RASKA, Kathryn-Helen b: 31 Aug 1953 in Waterloo, IA w: 23 Sep 1995 in Raymond, IA v: Elk Run Heights, IA o: Sales

229.25
11[1] RUSSELL, Julia-Ann b: 10 Jan 1957 in Waterloo, IA v: Dewar, IA o: County government employee c: 1
+ seq: 229.25 WIDDEL, John (Jack) b: 21 Mar 1950 in Waterloo, IA w: 10 Sep 1977 in Nashua, IA v: Dunkerton, IA o: Cabinet maker c: 1
12WIDDEL, Erica b: 24 May 1982 in Waterloo, IA v: Elk Run Heights, IA o: Hospital worker c: 1
+ seq: 229.25.10 w: Abt. 1998 c: 1
* 2nd Husband of [1] RUSSELL, Julia-Ann:
+ seq: 229.26 PROTSMAN, Ron-Wayne b: 02 Jun 1950 in Lansing, IA w: 15 Nov 1997 in Waterloo, IA v: Dewar, IA o: John Deere

229.25.10

12 WIDDEL, Erica b: 24 May 1982 in Waterloo, IA v: Elk Run Heights, IA o: Hospital worker c: 1
+ seq: 229.25.10 w: Abt. 1998 c: 1
13 WIDDEL, Hanna-Nicole b: 19 Oct 1999 in Waterloo, IA

229.27

11 RUSSELL, Timothy-Milo b: 06 Jun 1968 in Waterloo, IA v: Fresno, CA o: Cabinet maker c: 2
+ seq: 229.27 WOOLSEY, Jamie b: 13 Dec 1967 in Waterloo, IA w: 11 Jan 1989 in Waterloo, IA v: Fresno, CA o: Teacher c: 2
12 RUSSELL, Brendan-Michael b: 16 Aug 1989 in Waterloo, IA o: Student
12 RUSSELL, Caitlyn-Breanne b: 29 Sep 1992 in Fresno, CA o: Student

229.28

10 CONRAD, William-Nicholas (Bill) b: 08 Jul 1932 in Raymond, IA v: Washburn, IA o: ICRR c: 5
+ seq: 229.28 SMITH, Carole-Delight b: 28 Dec 1934 in Brandon, IA w: 23 Apr 1957 in Raymond, IA v: Washburn, IA o: Homemaker c: 5
11 CONRAD, Anthony-William b: 18 Oct 1957 in Waterloo, IA v: Evansdale, IA o: Horticulturist c: 2
+ seq: 229.29 DEHECK, Kelly-Jane b: 17 Feb 1960 in Dubuque, IA w: 03 Jun 1977 in Waterloo, IA v: Evansdale, IA o: Horticulture therapist c: 2
11 CONRAD, Denise-Marie b: 14 Jun 1959 in Waterloo, IA v: Washburn, IA o: Seamstress
+ seq: 229.30 GLENNY, William-Charles (Bill) b: 10 May 1956 in Waterloo, IA w: 02 Jun 1979 in Washburn, IA v: Washburn, IA o: Pipefitter/welder
11 CONRAD, Diane-Carole b: 28 Jul 1960 in Waterloo, IA v: Downey, IA o: Homemaker c: 2
+ seq: 229.32 ELLIOTT, Michael-LeRoy b: 06 Aug 1959 in Payola, KS w: 12 May 1990 in Iowa City, IA v: Downey, IA o: Welder c: 2
11 CONRAD, Craig-Alan b: 27 Aug 1965 in Waterloo, IA v: Washburn, IA o: Mechanic c: 2
+ seq: 229.33 PEDERSON, Justine-Marie b: 03 Feb 1964 in Waterloo, IA w: 10 Sep 1988 in Eagle Center, IA v:

Washburn, IA o: Auto parts specialist c: 2

11 CONRAD, Debra-Ann (Deb) b: 26 Oct 1970 in Waterloo, IA v: Freemont, NE o: Retirement administrator c: 1

+ seq: 229.34 HILL, Chad-Mason b: 07 Feb 1971 in Fort Dodge, IA w: 06 Nov 1999 in Gilbertville, IA v: Freemont, NE o: Computer programmer c: 1

229.29

11 CONRAD, Anthony-William b: 18 Oct 1957 in Waterloo, IA v: Evansdale, IA o: Horticulturist c: 2

+ seq: 229.29 DEHECK, Kelly-Jane b: 17 Feb 1960 in Dubuque, IA w: 03 Jun 1977 in Waterloo, IA v: Evansdale, IA o: Horticulture therapist c: 2

12 CONRAD, Nichole-Lynn b: 16 Feb 1977 in Waterloo, IA v: Waterloo, IA o: Nursing student c: 2

+ seq: 229.29.01 GUENTHER, Timothy-Burton (Tim) b: 28 Apr 1977 in Waterloo, IA w: 07 Dec 2002 in Waterloo, IA v: Waterloo, IA o: Self-employed salesman c: 2

12 CONRAD, Holly-Ann b: 28 Dec 1984 in Waterloo, IA v: Waterloo, IA o: Works at Lincoln Savings Bank in Cedar Falls, IA

+ seq: 229.29.50 GOLDSMITH, Cory b: 24 Sep 1984 in Waterloo, IA w: 09 Sep 2006 in Waterloo, IA v: Waterloo, IA o: Student teacher f: Mike Goldsmith m: Debbie

229.29.01

12 CONRAD, Nichole-Lynn b: 16 Feb 1977 in Waterloo, IA v: Waterloo, IA o: Nursing student c: 2

+ seq: 229.29.01 GUENTHER, Timothy-Burton (Tim) b: 28 Apr 1977 in Waterloo, IA w: 07 Dec 2002 in Waterloo, IA v: Waterloo, IA o: Self-employed salesman c: 2

13 GUENTHER, Quinton-Timothy b: 22 Apr 1998 in Waterloo, IA

13 GUENTHER, Alex-Anthony b: 12 Mar 2004

229.32

11 CONRAD, Diane-Carole b: 28 Jul 1960 in Waterloo, IA v: Downey, IA o: Homemaker c: 2

+ seq: 229.32 ELLIOTT, Michael-LeRoy b: 06 Aug 1959 in Payola, KS w: 12 May 1990 in Iowa City, IA v: Downey, IA o: Welder c: 2

12 ELLIOTT, Haily-Ann b: 29 Oct 1991 in Iowa City, IA o:

Student

12ELLIOTT, Mariah-Savannah b: 06 Mar 1995 in Iowa City, IA
o: Student

229.33

11CONRAD, Craig-Alan b: 27 Aug 1965 in Waterloo, IA v:
Washburn, IA o: Mechanic c: 2
+ seq: 229.33 PEDERSON, Justine-Marie b: 03 Feb 1964 in
Waterloo, IA w: 10 Sep 1988 in Eagle Center, IA v:
Washburn, IA o: Auto parts specialist c: 2
12CONRAD, Kayla-Marie b: 11 Oct 1991 in Waterloo, IA v:
Washburn, IA o: Student
12CONRAD, Nicholas-Alan b: 14 Feb 1994 in Waterloo, IA v:
Washburn, IA o: Student

229.34

11CONRAD, Debra-Ann (Deb) b: 26 Oct 1970 in Waterloo, IA v:
Freemont, NE o: Retirement administrator c: 1
+ seq: 229.34 HILL, Chad-Mason b: 07 Feb 1971 in Fort Dodge,
IA w: 06 Nov 1999 in Gilbertville, IA v: Freemont, NE o:
Computer programmer c: 1
12HILL, Mason-Conrad b: 25 Jan 2006 in Ames, IA

229.35

10[1] CONRAD, James-Leo (Jim) b: 19 Dec 1934 in Raymond,
IA v: Washburn, IA o: John Deere c: 4
+ seq: 229.35 BEARBOWER, Patricia-May b: 29 Oct 1934 in
Independence, IA d: 13 Dec 1995 in Waterloo, IA w: 21 Jan
1961 in Waterloo, IA v: Washburn, IA o: Homemaker c: 4
11CONRAD, Jeffrey-James b: 23 Oct 1961 in Waterloo, IA v:
McComb, IL o: Teacher
11CONRAD, Christine-Marie b: 25 Dec 1962 in Waterloo, IA v:
Waterloo, IA o: Homemaker o: Social worker c: 4
+ seq: 229.36 HARMS, Barton-Eugene b: 08 May 1961 in
Waterloo, IA w: 13 Jul 1985 in Gilbertville, IA v: Waterloo,
IA o: Insurance agent c: 4
11CONRAD, Gregory-Joseph b: 20 Oct 1964 in Waterloo, IA v:
West Burlington, IA o: Electrical maintenance c: 1
+ seq: 229.37 BARTELLS, Robin-Rae b: 15 Jan 1962 in
Oelwein, IA w: 16 Aug 1986 in Waterloo, IA v: West
Burlington, IA o: Secretary c: 1
11CONRAD, Andrew-Patrick b: 22 Sep 1968 in Waterloo, IA v:

Waterloo, IA o: Program associate
+ seq: 229.37.01 RUNYAN, Angela-Marie b: 08 Oct 1970 in Des
   Moines, IA w: 11 Oct 1997 in Des Moines, IA v: Waterloo, IA
   o: Social worker
* 2nd Wife of [1] CONRAD, James-Leo (Jim):
+ seq: 229.37.02 FOLLAN, Marva N. b: 24 Jan 1938 in
   Jefferson, IA w: 27 Dec 2003 in Des Moines, IA

229.36
11 CONRAD, Christine-Marie b: 25 Dec 1962 in Waterloo, IA v:
   Waterloo, IA o: Homemaker o: Social worker c: 4
+ seq: 229.36 HARMS, Barton-Eugene b: 08 May 1961 in
   Waterloo, IA w: 13 Jul 1985 in Gilbertville, IA v: Waterloo,
   IA o: Insurance agent c: 4
12 HARMS, Andrea-Elizabeth b: 30 Dec 1986 in Cedar Rapids, IA
   d: 11 Mar 1987 in Cedar Rapids, IA
12 HARMS, Tyler-Anthony b: 03 Jul 1989 in Cedar Rapids, IA v:
   Waterloo, IA o: Student
12 HARMS, Emelia-Rae b: 22 Jan 1993 in Waterloo, IA v:
   Waterloo, IA o: Student
12 HARMS, Courtney-Kathryn b: 20 Oct 1995 in Waterloo, IA v:
   Waterloo, IA o: Student

229.37
11 CONRAD, Gregory-Joseph b: 20 Oct 1964 in Waterloo, IA v:
   West Burlington, IA o: Electrical maintenance c: 1
+ seq: 229.37 BARTELLS, Robin-Rae b: 15 Jan 1962 in
   Oelwein, IA w: 16 Aug 1986 in Waterloo, IA v: West
   Burlington, IA o: Secretary c: 1
12 CONRAD, David-James b: 17 Dec 1986 in Waterloo, IA o:
   Student

229.38
8 MOOS, Marie b: 07 Sep 1854 in Herborn, Lux r: b c: 1
+ seq: 229.38 CONTER, Dominique w: 28 May 1891 in
   Mompach, Lux c: 1
9 CONTER, Jakob b: 31 Aug 1881 in Herborn, Lux

229.38.01
8 MOOS, Marie b: 22 May 1860 in Herborn, Lux d: 07 Aug 1887
   in Herborn, Lux v: Herborn, Lux o: No profession r: bd c: 1

+ seq: 229.38.01 w: Abt. 1880 c: 1
9 MOOS, Jacob b: 30 Aug 1881 in Mompach, Lux r: b

230
7 WITRY, Johann b: 11 Nov 1820 in Herborn, Lux d: 07 Oct
1882 in Gilzem, Germany v: Gilzem, Germany o: Blacksmith
o: Day laborer o: Farmer r: b c: 4
+ seq: 230 LICHTER, Susanna (Anna) b: 03 Jun 1826 in Gilzem,
Germany d: 23 May 1857 in Gilzem, Germany w: 30 Jan 1850
in Gilzem, Germany v: Gilzem, Germany i: Children lived
with her parents after her death r: d r: m f: Stephan Lichter m:
Anna Reuter c: 4
8 WITRY, Anna b: 20 Apr 1851 in Gilzem, Germany i: Born
crippled r: b
8 WITRY, Katharina b: 23 Nov 1852 in Gilzem, Germany r: b c:
6
+ seq: 230.01 MARMANN, Mathias b: 1852 w: Abt. 1880 c: 6
8 WITRY, Jacob b: 10 Oct 1854 in Gilzem, Germany d: 03 Oct
1932 Cause of death: Chronic myocarditis and arteriosclerosis
v: Mount Carmel, IA i: Called "Rotenbart" due to red beard i:
Landed from ship Waesland, worked for uncle Nick to repay for
tickets i: Emigrated to U. S. i: Heavy-footed dancer and good
singer o: Farmer o: Deliveryman r: b c: 10
+ seq: 231 WIRTZ, Anna b: 04 Feb 1865 in Echternach, Lux d:
17 Dec 1942 in Breda, IA Cause of death: Hypertension and
cardivascular arteriosclerosis w: 24 Dec 1888 in Trier,
Germany v: Mount Carmel, IA i: Both were living in
Niedervise, Germany when they met i: Emigrated with husband
o: Servant o: Farmer f: Nicklaus Wirtz m: Susanna Stukert c:
10
8 WITRY, Peter b: 14 May 1857 in Gilzem, Germany d: 31 Aug
1857 in Gilzem, Germany v: Dubuque, IA i: Emigrated to the
U.S. o: No profession r: bd

230.01
8 WITRY, Katharina b: 23 Nov 1852 in Gilzem, Germany r: b c:
6
+ seq: 230.01 MARMANN, Mathias b: 1852 w: Abt. 1880 c: 6
9 MARMANN, Peter M. b: Abt. 1889 d: 1921
+ seq: 230.02 LEHNEN, Marie b: Abt. 1895 w: 1921
9 MARMANN, Elizabeth b: Abt. 1891 d: 1909

+ seq: 230.03 APPEL, Carl b: Abt. 1885 w: Abt. 1909
9 MARMANN, Katharina b: Abt. 1892
+ seq: 230.04 STUBERT, Christophe b: Abt. 1880 w: Abt. 1914
9 MARMANN, Appolonia b: Abt. 1893
9 MARMANN, Susanna b: 1890 d: 1968 c: 4
+ seq: 230.05 JARDIN, Josef b: 1881 d: 1956 w: Abt. 1915 c: 4
9 MARMANN, Bernhard

230.05
9 MARMANN, Susanna b: 1890 d: 1968 c: 4
+ seq: 230.05 JARDIN, Josef b: 1881 d: 1956 w: Abt. 1915 c: 4
10JARDIN, Thomas b: 1921
10JARDIN, Josef b: 1924 d: 1942
10JARDIN, Katharina b: 1926 c: 1
+ seq: 230.06 ESCH, Willi b: 1920 w: Abt. 1950 c: 1
10JARDIN, Fritz b: 1932

230.06
10JARDIN, Katharina b: 1926 c: 1
+ seq: 230.06 ESCH, Willi b: 1920 w: Abt. 1950 c: 1
11ESCH, Hannelore b: 1954 c: 3
+ seq: 230.07 ZENDER, Edgar b: 1950 w: Abt. 1975 c: 3

230.07
11ESCH, Hannelore b: 1954 c: 3
+ seq: 230.07 ZENDER, Edgar b: 1950 w: Abt. 1975 c: 3
12ZENDER, Florian b: 1980 v: Trier, Germany
12ZENDER, Pia b: 1983
12ZENDER, David b: 1987

231
8 WITRY, Jacob b: 10 Oct 1854 in Gilzem, Germany d: 03 Oct
   1932 Cause of death: Chronic myocarditis and arteriosclerosis
   v: Mount Carmel, IA i: Called "Rotenbart" due to red beard i:
   Landed from ship Waesland, worked for uncle Nick to repay for
   tickets i: Emigrated to U. S. i: Heavy-footed dancer and good
   singer o: Farmer o: Deliveryman r: b c: 10
+ seq: 231 WIRTZ, Anna b: 04 Feb 1865 in Echternach, Lux d:
   17 Dec 1942 in Breda, IA Cause of death: Hypertension and
   cardivascular arteriosclerosis w: 24 Dec 1888 in Trier,
   Germany v: Mount Carmel, IA i: Both were living in

Niedervise, Germany when they met i: Emigrated with husband
o: Servant o: Farmer f: Nicklaus Wirtz m: Susanna Stukert c:
10

9 WITTRY, Sophia-Suzanne b: 19 Nov 1889 in Breda, IA d: 21
Jul 1977 v: Richmond, CA o: Seamstress c: 11
+ seq: 231.01 KOEHNE, William (Bill) b: 19 Oct 1881 in
Heiden, Germany d: 08 Mar 1966 in Richmond, CA w: 01 Mar
1916 in Breda, IA v: Richmond, CA o: Builder o: Contractor
c: 11

9 [1] WITTRY, Nicholas-Martin t: Officer of Soil Conservation
Commission b: 30 Jan 1891 in Breda, IA d: 17 Mar 1981 in
Maple River, IA v: Maple River, IA o: Farmer c: 6
+ seq: 232 RETTENMAIER, Anna-Magdalena b: 02 Oct 1891
d: 07 May 1922 w: 23 Sep 1916 v: Maple River, IA o: Farmer
c: 3

* 2nd Wife of [1] WITTRY, Nicholas-Martin:
+ seq: 234 FENDRICHS, Ella-Hannah b: 25 Nov 1890 d: 20 Oct
1978 in Iowa w: 28 Apr 1924 v: Mt. Carmel, IA c: 3

9 WITTRY, John b: 28 Sep 1892 in Breda, IA d: 01 Aug 1979 in
Marshall, MN v: Marshall, MN c: 2
+ seq: 237 PAPE, Mayme b: 13 Oct 1882 d: 01 May 1943 w: 13
Feb 1917 v: Marshall, MN c: 2

9 WITTRY, Jacob J. (Jake) b: 05 Aug 1894 in Mount Carmel, IA
d: 19 Aug 1966 in Breda, IA v: Carroll, IA i: US Army in WWI
o: Farmer o: Farmer's insurance salesman c: 7
+ seq: 240 NIELAND, Anna-Catherine (Ann) b: 30 May 1899 in
Carroll, IA d: 12 May 1984 in Breda, IA w: 06 Sep 1921 in
Breda, IA v: Carroll, IA f: John-Henry Nieland m: Anna
Koester c: 7

9 WITTRY, Clara b: 31 Mar 1896 in Breda, IA d: 02 Jun 1991 v:
Marshall, MN c: 5
+ seq: 240.22 PAPE, John b: 09 Jun 1885 d: 13 Feb 1965 w: 18
Sep 1917 v: Marshall, MN c: 5

9 WITTRY, Joseph-Nicholas (Joe) b: 19 Aug 1899 in Breda, IA
d: 22 Jan 1987 v: Carroll, IA o: Barber c: 3
+ seq: 241 WILBERDING, Rose-Elizabeth b: 19 Feb 1908 in
Little Rock, IA d: 06 Nov 1982 in Iowa w: 13 Jun 1933 v:
Carroll, IA c: 3

9 WITTRY, Mary-Elizabeth b: 02 Jul 1902 in Breda, IA d: 19 Jul
1995 in Raymond, IA v: Raymond, IA o: Homemaker c: 6
+ seq: 229.09 CONRAD, Robert-Louis b: 20 Nov 1897 in

Riceville, IA d: 25 Jan 1935 w: 22 Sep 1925 in Mount Carmel,
IA v: Raymond, IA i: Both are descendents of the family tree
o: Mechanic f: Bernard Conrad m: Margaretha Moos c: 7
9 WITTRY, Bernard-Anthony (Barney) b: 13 Jan 1904 in Breda,
IA d: 06 Nov 1977 in Breda, IA v: Breda, IA o: Farmer c: 6
+ seq: 248 SNYDER, Magdalene M. b: 28 Feb 1909 in Breda, IA
d: 27 Sep 1988 in Breda, IA w: 07 Feb 1928 v: Breda, IA c: 6
9 WITTRY, Andrew-Nicholas b: 13 May 1906 in Mount Carmel,
IA d: 20 May 1997 in Carroll, IA v: Carroll, IA o: Salesman
for Moorman's Feed Co. o: Dairy farmer o: Dealer for Schettler
Seed Co. c: 5
+ seq: 260 WOLTERMAN, Leola b: 03 Dec 1911 in Breda, IA
d: 07 Aug 1986 in Mount Carmel, IA w: 03 Jan 1933 in Breda,
IA v: Carroll, IA o: Homemaker c: 5
9 WITTRY, Mary-Ann (Girlie) b: 21 Jun 1908 in Breda, IA d: 05
Dec 1991 v: Seaforth, MN c: 11
+ seq: 261.11 BERNARDY, Mathew-Frank b: 20 Nov 1907 d:
02 Jan 1995 w: 30 Apr 1935 v: Seaforth, MN o: Farmer o:
Salesman of electric engines c: 11

231.01
9 WITTRY, Sophia-Suzanne b: 19 Nov 1889 in Breda, IA d: 21
Jul 1977 v: Richmond, CA o: Seamstress c: 11
+ seq: 231.01 KOEHNE, William (Bill) b: 19 Oct 1881 in Heiden,
Germany d: 08 Mar 1966 in Richmond, CA w: 01 Mar 1916 in
Breda, IA v: Richmond, CA o: Builder o: Contractor c: 11
10KOEHNE, Bernard-Edward b: 21 Dec 1916 in Breda, IA d: 24
Jan 1978 v: Richmond, CA
10KOEHNE, Harold-Jacob b: 29 Oct 1918 in Breda, IA d: Jan
1988 in Richmond, CA o: Deliveryman c: 2
+ seq: 231.02 RAMOS, Isabel b: 13 Oct 1920 d: 19 Sep 1978 in
Richmond, CA w: 25 May 1947 c: 2
10[1] KOEHNE, Juvent-Joseph (Jovie) b: 01 Jun 1920 in Breda,
IA o: Porterville, CA c: 1
+ seq: 231.05 FREDERIKS, Margaret b: 15 Dec 1922 w: 11 Nov
1950 c: 1
* 2nd Wife of [1] KOEHNE, Juvent-Joseph (Jovie):
+ seq: 231.06 WALL, Sallie-Cornwall b: 12 Mar 1917 w: 01 Mar
1975 v: Porterville, CA
10KOEHNE, Marianne-Elizabeth b: 30 Sep 1922 in Breda, IA v:
Healdsburg, CA c: 4

+ seq: 231.07 TAPPARO, John A. b: 09 Aug 1920 in Healdsburg,
  CA d: 02 Dec 2002 w: 15 Oct 1945 v: Healdsburg, CA c: 4

10KOEHNE, Paul-Anton b: 01 Apr 1924 in Breda, IA d: 19 Jul
  1969

+ seq: 231.14 RAMIREZ, Dolores b: 08 Jun 1931 d: Abt. 1970
  w: 11 Mar 1961

10KOEHNE, Magdalen-Mary (Maggie) b: 18 Jul 1926 in
  Minnesota d: 10 Aug 2005 in Castro Valley, CA Cause of death:
  cancer c: 3

+ seq: 231.15 JOY, Robert-Charles b: 29 Oct 1923 d: 15 Dec
  1986 w: 02 Mar 1946 c: 3

10KOEHNE, Adelaide-Agnes (Addie) b: 28 Jun 1928 in
  Minnesota v: Hayward, CA c: 8

+ seq: 231.21 THURSTON-II, John-Roy b: 15 Sep 1926 d: 07
  Mar 1993 w: 04 Sep 1948 v: Hayward, CA c: 8

10[2] KOEHNE, Joseph-William (Joe) b: 17 Mar 1930 in
  Minnesota v: El Sobrante, CA c: 10

+ seq: 231.29 MARTIN, Dorotha-Eleanor (Dot) b: 19 Jul 1930 d:
  03 Jul 1985 w: 15 Apr 1951 c: 5

* 2nd Wife of [2] KOEHNE, Joseph-William (Joe):

+ seq: 231.35 ROTH, Auldene-Schaeffer b: 08 Jun 1944 d: 08
  Dec 2002 w: 16 Nov 1986 v: El Sobrante, CA c: 5

10KOEHNE, Catherine-Ann (Katie) b: 08 Oct 1932 in Minnesota
  v: Richmond, CA c: 5

+ seq: 231.38 CRENSHAW, Billy-Ray b: 03 Oct 1934 w: 20 Nov
  1955 v: Richmond, CA c: 5

10KOEHNE, John-James b: 03 Aug 1934 in Lismore, MN d: 30
  Aug 2007 in Pinole, CA v: Pinole, CA o: U S Army - staff
  sergeant o: Warehouseman at United Grocers and Safeway o:
  Worked for Harris Digital c: 5

+ seq: 231.45 FELICIANO, Judith-Mae (July) b: 07 Apr 1940 d:
  19 Nov 2002 in Pinole, CA w: 16 May 1959 v: Pinole, CA c: 5

10KOEHNE, William-Peter (Bill) b: 21 Sep 1936 in Lismore, IA
  d: 12 Feb 2002 c: 3

+ seq: 231.49 MARTIN, Frances-Barrera-Graap (Fran) b: 07 Oct
  1930 d: 09 Dec 2001 w: 01 Dec 1962 c: 3

231.02

10KOEHNE, Harold-Jacob b: 29 Oct 1918 in Breda, IA d: Jan
  1988 in Richmond, CA o: Deliveryman c: 2

+ seq: 231.02 RAMOS, Isabel b: 13 Oct 1920 d: 19 Sep 1978 in

Richmond, CA w: 25 May 1947 c: 2
11[1] KOEHNE, Gerald-Michael b: 09 Apr 1950 c: 3
+ seq: 231.03 BARNETT, Lois-Arlene b: 19 Mar 1950 w: 19
 Jun 1971 c: 3
* 2nd Wife of [1] KOEHNE, Gerald-Michael:
+ seq: 231.03.50 BLEDSOE, Karen w: Abt. 2005
11 KOEHNE, Diane-Renee b: 25 Nov 1952 c: 2
+ seq: 231.04 CLARK, Stephen b: 24 Nov 1954 w: 22 Jan 1983
 c: 2

231.03

11[1] KOEHNE, Gerald-Michael b: 09 Apr 1950 c: 3
+ seq: 231.03 BARNETT, Lois-Arlene b: 19 Mar 1950 w: 19
 Jun 1971 c: 3
12 KOEHNE, Michael-David b: 09 Feb 1974
12 KOEHNE, Julie-Ann b: 12 Apr 1976
12 KOEHNE, Arlene-Isabel b: 01 Aug 1979
* 2nd Wife of [1] KOEHNE, Gerald-Michael:
+ seq: 231.03.50 BLEDSOE, Karen w: Abt. 2005

231.04

11 KOEHNE, Diane-Renee b: 25 Nov 1952 c: 2
+ seq: 231.04 CLARK, Stephen b: 24 Nov 1954 w: 22 Jan 1983
 c: 2
12 CLARK, Rebecca-Katherine b: 20 Aug 1986
12 CLARK, Kenneth-Robert b: 03 Aug 1990

231.05

10[1] KOEHNE, Juvent-Joseph b: 01 Jun 1920 in Breda, IA c: 1
+ seq: 231.05 FREDERIKS, Margaret b: 15 Dec 1922 w: 11 Nov
 1950 c: 1
11 KOEHNE, Paula-Marie b: 22 Apr 1957
* 2nd Wife of [1] KOEHNE, Juvent-Joseph:
+ seq: 231.06 WALL, Sallie-Cornwall b: 12 Mar 1917 w: 01
 Mar 1975

231.07

10 KOEHNE, Marianne-Elizabeth b: 30 Sep 1922 in Breda, IA v:
 Healdsburg, CA c: 4
+ seq: 231.07 TAPPARO, John A. b: 09 Aug 1920 in
 Healdsburg, CA d: 02 Dec 2002 w: 15 Oct 1945 v:

Healdsburg, CA c: 4

11 TAPPARO, William-Victor b: 29 May 1948 c: 2
+ seq: 231.08 POTTER, Beatrice b: 23 Nov 1949 w: 04 Oct
   1969 c: 2

11 TAPPARO, Ronald-John b: 04 Jan 1952 c: 2
+ seq: 231.11 LODRAGA, Judy b: 22 Jul 1952 w: 15 Aug 1975
   c: 2

11 TAPPARO, John-Anton b: 17 Oct 1954 c: 3
+ seq: 231.12 BAUMUNK, Geri-Bolloman b: 21 Jan 1952 w: 05
   Mar 1977 c: 3

11 TAPPARO, Michael-Edward (Mickey) b: 26 May 1956 c: 2
+ seq: 231.13 CLEMENTS, Melody b: 28 Feb 1958 w: 24 Jul
   1981 c: 2

231.08

11 TAPPARO, William-Victor b: 29 May 1948 c: 2
+ seq: 231.08 POTTER, Beatrice b: 23 Nov 1949 w: 04 Oct
   1969 c: 2

12 TAPPARO, Troy b: 26 Dec 1970 c: 1
+ seq: 231.09 CHRISTIAN, Sara b: 11 Mar 1974 w: 06 Feb
   1993 c: 1

12 TAPPARO, Brian b: 22 Jul 1972 c: 2
+ seq: 231.10 SCHLICK, Pamela b: 1972 w: 20 Apr 1991 c: 2

231.09

12 TAPPARO, Troy b: 26 Dec 1970 c: 1
+ seq: 231.09 CHRISTIAN, Sara b: 11 Mar 1974 w: 06 Feb
   1993 c: 1

13 TAPPARO, Brittany-Renee b: 01 Aug 1996

231.10

12 TAPPARO, Brian b: 22 Jul 1972 c: 2
+ seq: 231.10 SCHLICK, Pamela b: 1972 w: 20 Apr 1991 c: 2

13 TAPPARO, Alyssa b: 25 May 1992

13 TAPPARO, Brian b: 25 Aug 1994

231.11

11 TAPPARO, Ronald-John b: 04 Jan 1952 c: 2
+ seq: 231.11 LODRAGA, Judy b: 22 Jul 1952 w: 15 Aug 1975
   c: 2

12 TAPPARO, Joseph b: 24 Apr 1982

12TAPPARO, Benjamin b: 25 Jan 1985

231.12
11TAPPARO, John-Anton b: 17 Oct 1954 c: 3
+ seq: 231.12 BAUMUNK, Geri-Bolloman b: 21 Jan 1952 w: 05
  Mar 1977 c: 3
12BAUMUNK, Jennifer b: 04 Feb 1971
12BAUMUNK, Stefanie b: 13 Jan 1974
12TAPPARO, Nicholas b: 18 Apr 1981

231.13
11TAPPARO, Michael-Edward (Mickey) b: 26 May 1956 c: 2
+ seq: 231.13 CLEMENTS, Melody b: 28 Feb 1958 w: 24 Jul
  1981 c: 2
12TAPPARO, Michael-Edward b: 28 Mar 1985
12TAPPARO, Matthew-James b: 05 May 1987

231.15
10KOEHNE, Magdalen-Mary (Maggie) b: 18 Jul 1926 in
  Minnesota d: 10 Aug 2005 in Castro Valley, CA Cause of death:
  cancer c: 3
+ seq: 231.15 JOY, Robert-Charles b: 29 Oct 1923 d: 15 Dec
  1986 w: 02 Mar 1946 c: 3
11[1] JOY, Randall-Paul b: 22 May 1948
+ seq: 231.16 KINMAN, Kathleen b: 1951 w: 26 Jul 1969
* 2nd Wife of [1] JOY, Randall-Paul:
+ seq: 231.17 FRALEY, Diane b: 20 Jan 1949 w: 24 Sep 1973
* 3rd Wife of [1] JOY, Randall-Paul:
+ seq: 231.18 THOMAS, Linda b: 1948 w: 1990
11JOY, Gary-Alan b: 25 Jun 1949 d: 18 May 1973
11[2] JOY, Sharon-Ann b: 14 Sep 1951 c: 2
+ seq: 231.19 DUNN, James b: 30 Apr 1951 d: 03 May 1984 w:
  30 Jan 1977 c: 2
* 2nd Husband of [2] JOY, Sharon-Ann:
+ seq: 231.20 LEMAY, Richard Francis (Dick) b: 1951 w: 1992

231.19
11[1] JOY, Sharon-Ann b: 14 Sep 1951 c: 2
+ seq: 231.19 DUNN, James b: 30 Apr 1951 d: 03 May 1984 w:
  30 Jan 1977 c: 2
12DUNN, Olivia-Loraine b: 20 Mar 1978 c: 1

+ seq: 231.19.01 HENDRICKSON, Daren b: 31 Jan 1966 w: 20 May 2000 c: 1

12 DUNN, Matthew-Tobias b: 12 Oct 1979

* 2nd Husband of [1] JOY, Sharon-Ann:

+ seq: 231.20 LEMAY, Richard Francis (Dick) b: 1951 w: 1992

231.19.01

12 DUNN, Olivia-Loraine b: 20 Mar 1978 c: 1

+ seq: 231.19.01 HENDRICKSON, Daren b: 31 Jan 1966 w: 20 May 2000 c: 1

13 HENDRICKSON, Amber b: 14 Mar 2002

231.21

10 KOEHNE, Adelaide-Agnes (Addie) b: 28 Jun 1928 in Minnesota v: Hayward, CA c: 8

+ seq: 231.21 THURSTON-II, John-Roy b: 15 Sep 1926 d: 07 Mar 1993 w: 04 Sep 1948 v: Hayward, CA c: 8

11 THURSTON, John-Roy III b: 04 Jun 1949 c: 2

+ seq: 231.22 EDWARDS, Judy b: 20 Dec 1950 w: 30 Oct 1976 c: 2

11 THURSTON, Janice-Lea b: 06 Nov 1950 c: 2

+ seq: 231.23 DILBECK, William-Michael b: 07 Jun 1952 w: 30 Jun 1973 c: 2

11 THURSTON, Michael-Steven b: 29 Sep 1954

11 THURSTON, Patricia-Ann b: 22 Oct 1955 c: 3

+ seq: 231.24 DURYEE, Donald-Guy b: 07 Jul 1952 w: 05 Jul 2002 c: 3

11 THURSTON, James-William b: 08 Feb 1957 c: 2

+ seq: 231.25 LANTEIGNE, Michele b: 07 Jul 1961 w: 09 Jul 1977 c: 2

11 [1] THURSTON, Joseph-Bernard b: 14 Sep 1958 c: 5

+ seq: 231.26 KING, Leslie b: 09 Sep 1960 w: 25 Feb 1979 c: 2

* 2nd Wife of [1] THURSTON, Joseph-Bernard:

+ seq: 231.27 BUTCHER, Tammy b: 1958 w: 25 Feb 1989 c: 3

* 3rd Wife of [1] THURSTON, Joseph-Bernard:

+ seq: 231.27.50 PADILLA, Brenda w: Abt. 2005

11 THURSTON, Steven b: 09 Dec 1959 c: 3

+ seq: 231.28 MOORE, Sheila b: 20 Aug 1962 w: 10 Nov 1984 c: 3

11 THURSTON, Cindy-Lou b: 06 Jan 1962

+ seq: 231.28.01 STANFIELD, Jim b: 12 Jul 1951 w: 16 May

1999 in Mobile, AL

231.22
11 THURSTON, John-Roy III b: 04 Jun 1949 c: 2
+ seq: 231.22 EDWARDS, Judy b: 20 Dec 1950 w: 30 Oct 1976
   c: 2
12 THURSTON, Jennifer-Blanche b: 19 Dec 1979
12 THURSTON, John-Edward b: 11 Mar 1982

231.23
11 THURSTON, Janice-Lea b: 06 Nov 1950 c: 2
+ seq: 231.23 DILBECK, William-Michael b: 07 Jun 1952 w: 30
   Jun 1973 c: 2
12 DILBECK, Michelle-Lee b: 13 Sep 1975
12 DILBECK, Michael b: 05 Mar 1977

231.24
11 THURSTON, Patricia-Ann b: 22 Oct 1955 c: 3
+ seq: 231.24 DURYEE, Donald-Guy b: 07 Jul 1952 w: 05 Jul
   2002 c: 3
12 DURYEE, Adelaide-Estelle b: 30 Jul 2003
12 DURYEE, Sophie-Louise b: 30 Jul 2003
12 DURYEE, Guy-Donald b: 30 Jul 2003

231.25
11 THURSTON, James-William b: 08 Feb 1957 c: 2
+ seq: 231.25 LANTEIGNE, Michele b: 07 Jul 1961 w: 09 Jul
   1977 c: 2
12 THURSTON, Patricia-Jeanne b: 22 Mar 1979 c: 3
+ seq: 231.25.01 MARTINEZ, Enrique b: Dec 1978 w: 10 Jan
   1998 c: 3
12 THURSTON, Amanda-Jeanne b: 04 Apr 1980 c: 1
+ seq: 231.25.50 w: Abt. 1997 c: 1

231.25.01
12 THURSTON, Patricia-Jeanne b: 22 Mar 1979 c: 3
+ seq: 231.25.01 MARTINEZ, Enrique b: Dec 1978 w: 10 Jan
   1998 c: 3
13 MARTINEZ, John-Drake b: 07 Dec 1997
13 MARTINEZ, Brianna-Lee b: 11 Aug 2000 d: 21 Jul 2004
Cause of death: Drowning in a swimming pool

13MARTINEZ, Magdalena-Trinity b: 21 Jul 2004

231.25.50
12THURSTON, Amanda-Jeanne b: 04 Apr 1980 c: 1
+ seq: 231.25.50 w: Abt. 1997 c: 1
13HUMPHREY, Miranda-Lee b: 05 Sep 1998

231.26
11[1] THURSTON, Joseph-Bernard b: 14 Sep 1958 c: 5
+ seq: 231.26 KING, Leslie b: 09 Sep 1960 w: 25 Feb 1979 c: 2
12THURSTON, Christopher-Joseph b: 01 Feb 1987
12THURSTON, Nicholas-Robert b: 23 Dec 1988
 * 2nd Wife of [1] THURSTON, Joseph-Bernard:
+ seq: 231.27 BUTCHER, Tammy b: 1958 w: 25 Feb 1989 c: 3
12THURSTON, Joel b: 16 Mar 1985
12THURSTON, Sierra b: 18 Apr 1986
12THURSTON, Jeremy-Bernard b: 06 Jul 1993
 * 3rd Wife of [1] THURSTON, Joseph-Bernard:
+ seq: 231.27.50 PADILLA, Brenda w: Abt. 2005

231.28
11THURSTON, Steven b: 09 Dec 1959 c: 3
+ seq: 231.28 MOORE, Sheila b: 20 Aug 1962 w: 10 Nov 1984
   c: 3
12THURSTON, Matthew-Steven b: 11 Feb 1987
12THURSTON, Thomas-Garrett b: 29 Jun 1989
12THURSTON, Andrew-William b: 1991

231.29
10[1] KOEHNE, Joseph-William (Joe) b: 17 Mar 1930 in
   Minnesota v: El Sobrante, CA c: 10
+ seq: 231.29 MARTIN, Dorotha-Eleanor (Dot) b: 19 Jul 1930 d:
   03 Jul 1985 w: 15 Apr 1951 c: 5
11KOEHNE, Debra-Ann b: 05 Jul 1952 c: 4
+ seq: 231.30 ROSSI, Ralph b: 14 Aug 1951 w: 02 Jun 1973 c: 4
11KOEHNE, Thomas-Paul b: 26 Feb 1955 c: 1
+ seq: 231.31 PIMENTAL, Lori b: 16 Dec 1956 w: 31 Jan 1976
   c: 1
11KOEHNE, Margaret-Suzanne (Peggy) b: 29 May 1958 c: 2
+ seq: 231.32 READING, Joseph b: 1958 w: 10 Jul 1993 c: 2
11KOEHNE, Josephine-Nuel b: 17 Jan 1961 c: 4

+ seq: 231.33 BRYANT, John b: 25 Jul 1961 w: 07 Jan 1984 c: 4

11KOEHNE, Ethel-Marie b: 22 Oct 1964 c: 2

+ seq: 231.34 HUTTON, Timothy b: 1964 w: 1993 c: 2

* 2nd Wife of [1] KOEHNE, Joseph-William (Joe):

+ seq: 231.35 ROTH, Auldene-Schaeffer b: 08 Jun 1944 d: 08 Dec 2002 w: 16 Nov 1986 v: El Sobrante, CA c: 5

11JACOBSEN, Ronald b: 14 Aug 1962

11JACOBSEN, Eric-Roth b: 18 Feb 1964 c: 1

+ seq: 231.36 FLORES, Adrienne b: Abt. 1964 w: Abt. 1980 c: 1

11JACOBSEN, De-Anne b: 27 Apr 1965 c: 1

+ seq: 231.37 MORGAN, Art b: Abt. 1965 w: 03 Jul 1981 c: 1

11JACOBSEN, Laura b: 05 Oct 1966

11JACOBSEN, Noelle b: 21 Dec 1969 c: 2

+ seq: 231.37.01 THOMPSON, John w: Abt. 1990 c: 2

231.30

11KOEHNE, Debra-Ann b: 05 Jul 1952 c: 4

+ seq: 231.30 ROSSI, Ralph b: 14 Aug 1951 w: 02 Jun 1973 c: 4

12ROSSI, Jennifer b: 10 Jan 1976

12ROSSI, Amy b: 28 Dec 1978

12ROSSI, Matthew-Ralph b: 04 Jun 1981

12ROSSI, Kathryn b: 26 Feb 1983

231.31

11KOEHNE, Thomas-Paul b: 26 Feb 1955 c: 1

+ seq: 231.31 PIMENTAL, Lori b: 16 Dec 1956 w: 31 Jan 1976 c: 1

12KOEHNE, Jason-Edward b: 13 Jan 1984

231.32

11KOEHNE, Margaret-Suzanne (Peggy) b: 29 May 1958 c: 2

+ seq: 231.32 READING, Joseph b: 1958 w: 10 Jul 1993 c: 2

12READING, Dorothy-Helen (Dori) b: 24 Jul 1987

12READING, Andrew-Joseph-Lloyd b: 22 Aug 1989

231.33

11KOEHNE, Josephine-Nuel b: 17 Jan 1961 c: 4

+ seq: 231.33 BRYANT, John b: 25 Jul 1961 w: 07 Jan 1984 c: 4

12BRYANT, Kristen-Koehne b: 22 Jul 1984 c: 1

+ seq: 231.33.50 w: Abt. 2000 c: 1
12BRYANT, John-Henry b: 13 Jun 1987
12BRYANT, Joshua-Joseph b: 15 May 1989
12BRYANT, Nathaniel-Albert b: 18 Oct 1997

231.33.50
12BRYANT, Kristen-Koehne b: 22 Jul 1984 c: 1
+ seq: 231.33.50 w: Abt. 2000 c: 1
13BRYANT, Kiley b: Jul 2004

231.34
11KOEHNE, Ethel-Marie b: 22 Oct 1964 c: 2
+ seq: 231.34 HUTTON, Timothy b: 1964 w: 1993 c: 2
12HUTTON, Ashley-Marie b: 02 Jan 1994
12HUTTON, Emily-Patricia b: 15 May 1997

231.36
11JACOBSEN, Eric-Roth b: 18 Feb 1964 c: 1
+ seq: 231.36 FLORES, Adrienne b: Abt. 1964 w: Abt. 1980 c:
  1
12JACOBSEN, Daniel b: 13 May 1982

231.37
11JACOBSEN, De-Anne b: 27 Apr 1965 c: 1
+ seq: 231.37 MORGAN, Art b: Abt. 1965 w: 03 Jul 1981 c: 1
12MORGAN, Melissa b: 06 Dec 1982

231.37.01
11JACOBSEN, Noelle b: 21 Dec 1969 c: 2
+ seq: 231.37.01 THOMPSON, John w: Abt. 1990 c: 2
12THOMPSON, Justin b: 15 Apr
12THOMPSON, Kaytin b: 17 Mar

231.38
10KOEHNE, Catherine-Ann (Katie) b: 08 Oct 1932 in Minnesota
  v: Richmond, CA c: 5
+ seq: 231.38 CRENSHAW, Billy-Ray b: 03 Oct 1934 w: 20
  Nov 1955 v: Richmond, CA c: 5
11CRENSHAW, Joan-Marie b: 14 Dec 1957 c: 2
+ seq: 231.39 JONES, Thorro P. b: 19 Jun 1955 w: 26 Jul 1980
  c: 2

11 CRENSHAW, Richard-Louis (Ricky) b: 29 Aug 1959 c: 2
+ seq: 231.40 PARELLA, Lisa K. b: 29 Feb 1960 w: 08 Feb 1986 c: 2
11 CRENSHAW, Mary-Linda b: 04 Sep 1960 c: 2
+ seq: 231.41 PHELPS, Larry-Dwane b: 15 Sep 1951 w: 27 Apr 1991 c: 2
11 CRENSHAW, Brenda-Kay b: 16 Feb 1962 c: 1
+ seq: 231.42 COGGINS, Christopher-Scott b: 04 Mar 1967 w: 10 Oct 1992 c: 1
11 [1] CRENSHAW, Sara-Jane (Sally) b: 12 Mar 1965 v: Concord, CA c: 4
+ seq: 231.43 COUSER, Scott b: 17 Nov 1962 w: 23 May 1987 c: 2
* 2nd Husband of [1] CRENSHAW, Sara-Jane (Sally):
+ seq: 231.44 VILLALPANDO, Jose b: 05 Aug 1967 w: Abt. 1992 v: Concord, CA c: 2

231.39
11 CRENSHAW, Joan-Marie b: 14 Dec 1957 c: 2
+ seq: 231.39 JONES, Thorro P. b: 19 Jun 1955 w: 26 Jul 1980 c: 2
12 JONES, Amanda-Sophia b: 20 Apr 1985
12 JONES, Kathy-Marie b: 02 Apr 1987

231.40
11 CRENSHAW, Richard-Louis (Ricky) b: 29 Aug 1959 c: 2
+ seq: 231.40 PARELLA, Lisa K. b: 29 Feb 1960 w: 08 Feb 1986 c: 2
12 CRENSHAW, Dustin-Harold b: 08 Sep 1988
12 CRENSHAW, Derek-Frank b: 09 Oct 1991

231.41
11 CRENSHAW, Mary-Linda b: 04 Sep 1960 c: 2
+ seq: 231.41 PHELPS, Larry-Dwane b: 15 Sep 1951 w: 27 Apr 1991 c: 2
12 PHELPS, Shawna-Rene b: 21 Feb 1979 c: 1
13 PHELPS, Brenden-Ray b: 08 Apr 1999
12 PHELPS, Jennifer-Ann b: 19 Nov 1981

231.42
11 CRENSHAW, Brenda-Kay b: 16 Feb 1962 c: 1

+ seq: 231.42 COGGINS, Christopher-Scott b: 04 Mar 1967 w:
10 Oct 1992 c: 1
12COGGINS, Cabe-Talon b: 15 Nov 2003

231.43
11[1] CRENSHAW, Sara-Jane (Sally) b: 12 Mar 1965 v:
Concord, CA c: 4
+ seq: 231.43 COUSER, Scott b: 17 Nov 1962 w: 23 May 1987
c: 2
12COUSER, Daniel-Raymond b: 17 Nov 1987
12COUSER, Rachel-Frances b: 05 Oct 1989
* 2nd Husband of [1] CRENSHAW, Sara-Jane (Sally):
+ seq: 231.44 VILLALPANDO, Jose b: 05 Aug 1967 w: Abt.
1992 v: Concord, CA c: 2
12VILLALPANDO, Zackery-Paul b: 17 Dec 1994
12VILLALPANDO, Katelynn-Marie b: 07 Dec 1995

231.45
10KOEHNE, John-James b: 03 Aug 1934 in Lismore, MN d: 30
Aug 2007 in Pinole, CA v: Pinole, CA o: U S Army - staff
sergeant o: Warehouseman at United Grocers and Safeway o:
Worked for Harris Digital c: 5
+ seq: 231.45 FELICIANO, Judith-Mae (July) b: 07 Apr 1940 d:
19 Nov 2002 in Pinole, CA w: 16 May 1959 v: Pinole, CA c: 5
11KOEHNE, Dennis-Edward b: 30 Jul 1960 v: Los Angeles
11KOEHNE, Robert-Allen b: 25 Mar 1962 v: Fairfield, CA c: 2
+ seq: 231.46 GARCIA, Melinda b: 23 Mar 1960 w: 02 Aug
1986 v: Fairfield, CA c: 2
11KOEHNE, Scott-Anthony b: 16 Dec 1963 v: Rodeo, CA c: 2
+ seq: 231.47 GOMEZ, Dolores-Ginny (Lola) b: 22 Jan 1960 w:
12 Dec 1987 v: Rodeo, CA c: 2
11KOEHNE, Mark-Andrew b: 07 May 1967 v: Boston, MA
+ seq: 231.47.01 BARKER, Christine b: 02 Dec 1970 w: Abt.
1995 v: Boston, MA
11KOEHNE, Stephanie-Ann b: 09 May 1968 v: El Sobrante, CA
c: 2
+ seq: 231.48 JENSEN, John-Alfred b: 08 May 1953 w: 05 Aug
1989 v: El Sobrante, CA c: 2

231.46
11KOEHNE, Robert-Allen b: 25 Mar 1962 v: Fairfield, CA c: 2

+ seq: 231.46 GARCIA, Melinda b: 23 Mar 1960 w: 02 Aug
  1986 v: Fairfield, CA c: 2
12KOEHNE, Jessica-Sophia b: 26 Oct 1991 v: Fairfield, CA
12KOEHNE, Samantha-Rose b: 11 May 1995 v: Fairfield, CA

231.47
11KOEHNE, Scott-Anthony b: 16 Dec 1963 v: Rodeo, CA c: 2
+ seq: 231.47 GOMEZ, Dolores-Ginny (Lola) b: 22 Jan 1960 w:
  12 Dec 1987 v: Rodeo, CA c: 2
12KOEHNE, Aaron-Scott b: 17 Feb 1990 v: Rodeo, CA
12KOEHNE, Jordon-Anthony (Jordy) b: 01 Jun 1991 v: Rodeo,
  CA

231.48
11KOEHNE, Stephanie-Ann b: 09 May 1968 v: El Sobrante, CA
  c: 2
+ seq: 231.48 JENSEN, John-Alfred b: 08 May 1953 w: 05 Aug
  1989 v: El Sobrante, CA c: 2
12JENSEN, Jack-Richard b: 07 Feb 1991 v: El Sobrante, CA
12JENSEN, Drake-Irvin b: 10 Dec 1992 v: El Sobrante, CA

231.49
10KOEHNE, William-Peter (Bill) b: 21 Sep 1936 in Lismore, IA
  d: 12 Feb 2002 c: 3
+ seq: 231.49 MARTIN, Frances-Barrera-Graap (Fran) b: 07 Oct
  1930 d: 09 Dec 2001 w: 01 Dec 1962 c: 3
11[1] GRAAP, Frances-Marie b: 05 May 1949 c: 2
+ seq: 231.50 ALDEN, William b: Aug 1949 w: 25 Jul 1967 c:
  1
* 2nd Husband of [1] GRAAP, Frances-Marie:
+ seq: 231.51 JONES, David b: 07 Nov 1948 w: Jun 1973 c: 1
* 3rd Husband of [1] GRAAP, Frances-Marie:
+ seq: 231.52 O'STEEN, Chester b: 01 Mar 1942 w: 14 Mar
  1977
11GRAAP, Nancy-Ellen b: 03 Apr 1950 c: 2
+ seq: 231.53 LEE, Mick-Potter b: 29 Aug 1949 w: 29 Aug 1970
  c: 2
11KOEHNE, Terry-William b: 26 Dec 1964 v: San Ramon, CA
  c: 2
+ seq: 231.54 CARSON, Christine-Michele b: 13 Jun 1967 w:
  19 Jun 1993 v: San Ramon, CA c: 2

231.50

11[1] GRAAP, Frances-Marie b: 05 May 1949 c: 2
+ seq: 231.50 ALDEN, William b: Aug 1949 w: 25 Jul 1967 c: 1

12 ALDEN, Denise b: 25 Jul 1970
 * 2nd Husband of [1] GRAAP, Frances-Marie:
+ seq: 231.51 JONES, David b: 07 Nov 1948 w: Jun 1973 c: 1
12 JONES, Michael-David b: 08 Oct 1973
 * 3rd Husband of [1] GRAAP, Frances-Marie:
+ seq: 231.52 O'STEEN, Chester b: 01 Mar 1942 w: 14 Mar 1977

231.53

11 GRAAP, Nancy-Ellen b: 03 Apr 1950 c: 2
+ seq: 231.53 LEE, Mick-Potter b: 29 Aug 1949 w: 29 Aug 1970 c: 2

12 LEE, Daniel-Clinton-Paul b: 19 Jan 1976
12 LEE, Lynette-Nicole b: 09 Jan 1980

231.54

11 KOEHNE, Terry-William b: 26 Dec 1964 v: San Ramon, CA c: 2
+ seq: 231.54 CARSON, Christine-Michele b: 13 Jun 1967 w: 19 Jun 1993 v: San Ramon, CA c: 2
12 KOEHNE, Trevor-Carson b: 08 Mar 1998
12 KOEHNE, Rachael-Catherine b: 21 May 2001

232

9 [1] WITTRY, Nicholas-Martin t: Officer of Soil Conservation Commission b: 30 Jan 1891 in Breda, IA d: 17 Mar 1981 in Maple River, IA v: Maple River, IA o: Farmer c: 6
+ seq: 232 RETTENMAIER, Anna-Magdalena b: 02 Oct 1891 d: 07 May 1922 w: 23 Sep 1916 v: Maple River, IA o: Farmer c: 3
10 WITTRY, Louis b: 17 Sep 1917 d: 24 Apr 1919
10 WITTRY, Carl J. b: 24 Mar 1919 in Mount Carmel, IA d: 01 May 1945 in Okinawa Cause of death: Killed in battle v: Mt. Carmel, IA o: Soldier o: Musician
+ seq: 233 NIELAND, Marie-Tarcissa b: 23 Mar 1921 d: 07 Jul 1999 in Carroll, IA w: 26 Dec 1942 v: Mt. Carmel, IA f: Frank-Joseph Nieland m: Mary-Anna Naberhaus

10WITTRY, Marie b: 30 May 1921 v: Carroll, IA c: 6
+ seq: 233.01 GLASS, Robert (Bob) b: 30 Jun 1917 in Halbur,
   IA d: 28 Sep 1999 in Carroll, IA w: 27 Aug 1947 v: Carroll,
   IA c: 6
* 2nd Wife of [1] WITTRY, Nicholas-Martin:
+ seq: 234 FENDRICHS, Ella-Hannah b: 25 Nov 1890 d: 20 Oct
   1978 in Iowa w: 28 Apr 1924 v: Mt. Carmel, IA c: 3
10WITTRY, Lawrence b: 25 Dec 1927 in Maple River, IA d: 07
   Jan 2003 in Carroll, IA v: Carroll, IA o: Director for Glidden
   REC o: Director of Corn Belt Power Cooperative c: 4
+ seq: 235 NAGL, Lucille b: 02 Jul 1926 d: 12 Sep 1994 w: 06
   Sep 1950 v: Carroll, IA c: 4
10WITTRY, Rita-Ann b: 23 May 1931 v: Breda, IA c: 8
+ seq: 236.02 VENNER, Paul b: 20 Apr 1927 w: 24 Jan 1951 v:
   Breda, IA c: 8
10WITTRY, Anita-Mae b: 23 May 1931 in Carroll, IA v: Carroll,
   IA o: Parish secretary c: 7
+ seq: 236.11 TEGELS, Joseph M. (Joe) b: 09 Apr 1929 in
   Ulmer, IA d: 11 Sep 2000 in Carroll, IA w: 18 Apr 1953 in
   Maple River, IA v: Carroll, IA i: Served in U.S. Army during
   WWII o: U. S. Postal worker f: Joe Tegels m: Clara Julich c:
   7

233.01
10WITTRY, Marie b: 30 May 1921 v: Carroll, IA c: 6
+ seq: 233.01 GLASS, Robert (Bob) b: 30 Jun 1917 in Halbur,
   IA d: 28 Sep 1999 in Carroll, IA w: 27 Aug 1947 v: Carroll,
   IA c: 6
11[1] GLASS, William (Billy) b: 11 Jun 1948 c: 4
+ seq: 233.02 TRENT, Beverly b: 03 Feb 1948 w: 06 Feb 1968
* 2nd Wife of [1] GLASS, William (Billy):
+ seq: 233.03 MCCARTHY, Wanda b: 01 Jan 1950 w: 13 Mar
   1982 c: 3
* 3rd Wife of [1] GLASS, William (Billy):
+ seq: 233.04 STARK, Tara b: Abt. 1950 w: Abt. 1990 c: 1
11GLASS, Mary-Ellen b: 10 Apr 1951 c: 2
+ seq: 233.05 DOYLE, Keith b: 03 Mar 1942 w: 31 Aug 1974
   c: 2
11[2] GLASS, Jean-Marie b: 11 Jun 1953 c: 1
+ seq: 233.06 BLOMMEL, David b: Abt. 1953 w: 24 Nov 1973
* 2nd Husband of [2] GLASS, Jean-Marie:

+ seq: 233.07 ZUMBURGE, Fred b: 25 Jun 1949 w: 08 May 1982 c: 1

11 GLASS, Jon-Laurence b: 08 Dec 1955 c: 3

+ seq: 233.08 PALMER, Marian-Lee b: 28 Oct 1957 w: 06 Jun 1978 c: 3

11[3] GLASS, Steven-Paul b: 06 Oct 1958 c: 4

+ seq: 233.09 ERICKSON, Billye-Jo b: 05 Jan 1959 w: 19 Jul 1980 c: 2

* 2nd Wife of [3] GLASS, Steven-Paul:

+ seq: 233.10 JUSTICE, Leneatha b: Abt. 1960 w: Abt. 1990 c: 2

11 GLASS, Louis-Joseph b: 09 Jul 1960 v: Hay Springs, NE c: 3

+ seq: 233.11 GREEN, Kelly b: 24 Sep 1960 w: 05 Sep 1981 v: Hay Springs, NE c: 3

233.02

11[1] GLASS, William (Billy) b: 11 Jun 1948 c: 4

+ seq: 233.02 TRENT, Beverly b: 03 Feb 1948 w: 06 Feb 1968

* 2nd Wife of [1] GLASS, William (Billy):

+ seq: 233.03 MCCARTHY, Wanda b: 01 Jan 1950 w: 13 Mar 1982 c: 3

12 MCCARTHY, Scott b: 05 May 1970 d: 15 Feb 1985

12 MCCARTHY, Aaron b: 29 Jul 1971 d: 29 May 1988

12 MCCARTHY, Brandy b: 30 Jul 1973

* 3rd Wife of [1] GLASS, William (Billy):

+ seq: 233.04 STARK, Tara b: Abt. 1950 w: Abt. 1990 c: 1

12 GLASS, Lauren-Elizabeth b: 1991

233.05

11 GLASS, Mary-Ellen b: 10 Apr 1951 c: 2

+ seq: 233.05 DOYLE, Keith b: 03 Mar 1942 w: 31 Aug 1974 c: 2

12 DOYLE, Regan-Marie b: 1987

12 DOYLE, Kameron-Ann b: 1990

233.06

11[1] GLASS, Jean-Marie b: 11 Jun 1953 c: 1

+ seq: 233.06 BLOMMEL, David b: Abt. 1953 w: 24 Nov 1973

* 2nd Husband of [1] GLASS, Jean-Marie:

+ seq: 233.07 ZUMBURGE, Fred b: 25 Jun 1949 w: 08 May 1982 c: 1

12ZUMBURGE, Lacey-Marie b: 03 Mar 1985

233.08
11GLASS, Jon-Laurence b: 08 Dec 1955 c: 3
 + seq: 233.08 PALMER, Marian-Lee b: 28 Oct 1957 w: 06 Jun
    1978 c: 3
12GLASS, Christine-Catherine b: 04 Dec 1986
12GLASS, Jonathan-Palmer b: 1989
12GLASS, Caroline-Jane b: 1992

233.09
11[1] GLASS, Steven-Paul b: 06 Oct 1958 c: 4
 + seq: 233.09 ERICKSON, Billye-Jo b: 05 Jan 1959 w: 19 Jul
    1980 c: 2
12GLASS, Nicholas b: 17 Sep 1982
12GLASS, Megan-Marie b: 29 Jan 1985
 * 2nd Wife of [1] GLASS, Steven-Paul:
 + seq: 233.10 JUSTICE, Leneatha b: Abt. 1960 w: Abt. 1990 c:
    2
12GLASS, Katherine-Taylor b: 1995
12GLASS, Mitchell-Steven b: 10 Jun 1997

233.11
11GLASS, Louis-Joseph b: 09 Jul 1960 v: Hay Springs, NE c: 3
 + seq: 233.11 GREEN, Kelly b: 24 Sep 1960 w: 05 Sep 1981 v:
    Hay Springs, NE c: 3
12GLASS, Andrea-Lynn b: 24 Sep 1985
12GLASS, Emma-Lee b: 1988
12GLASS, Maxwell b: 1993

235
10WITTRY, Lawrence b: 25 Dec 1927 in Maple River, IA d: 07
    Jan 2003 in Carroll, IA v: Carroll, IA o: Director for Glidden
    REC o: Director of Corn Belt Power Cooperative c: 4
 + seq: 235 NAGL, Lucille b: 02 Jul 1926 d: 12 Sep 1994 w: 06
    Sep 1950 v: Carroll, IA c: 4
11WITTRY, Lois-Ann b: 02 Nov 1953 v: Oak Grove, MO c: 3
 + seq: 235.01 HILDMAN, Paul-Joseph b: 06 Dec 1949 w: 11 Jul
    1974 v: Oak Grove, MO f: John-Mathias Hildman m:
    Florence-Ann Hilbert c: 3
11WITTRY, Mary-Lynn b: 13 Apr 1960 d: 13 Apr 1960

11WITTRY, Lawrence (Larry) b: 24 Jan 1962 v: Carroll, IA c: 1
+ seq: 236 WEGMAN, Carol b: Abt. 1965 w: Abt. 1990 v:
Breda, IA c: 1
11WITTRY, Laurie b: 11 Feb 1965 v: Fort Collins, CO c: 3
+ seq: 236.01 HARVEY, Michael b: Abt. 1960 w: 23 Aug 1986
v: Fort Collins, CO c: 3

235.01
11WITTRY, Lois-Ann b: 02 Nov 1953 v: Oak Grove, MO c: 3
+ seq: 235.01 HILDMAN, Paul-Joseph b: 06 Dec 1949 w: 11 Jul
1974 v: Oak Grove, MO f: John-Mathias Hildman m:
Florence-Ann Hilbert c: 3
12HILDMAN, Tracy-Lee b: 13 Apr 1977
12HILDMAN, Kristy-Marie b: 16 Aug 1980
12HILDMAN, Daniel-Paul b: 11 Nov 1984

236
11WITTRY, Lawrence (Larry) b: 24 Jan 1962 v: Carroll, IA c: 1
+ seq: 236 WEGMAN, Carol b: Abt. 1965 w: Abt. 1990 v:
Breda, IA c: 1
12WITTRY, Nicholas b: 28 Aug 1988

236.01
11WITTRY, Laurie b: 11 Feb 1965 v: Fort Collins, CO c: 3
+ seq: 236.01 HARVEY, Michael b: Abt. 1960 w: 23 Aug 1986
v: Fort Collins, CO c: 3
12HARVEY, Steven-Michael b: 22 Jan 1995
12HARVEY, Michaela-Lucille b: 08 Oct 1997
12HARVEY, Lindsey-Marie b: 25 Jul 2000 in Fort Collins, CO

236.02
10WITTRY, Rita-Ann b: 23 May 1931 v: Breda, IA c: 8
+ seq: 236.02 VENNER, Paul b: 20 Apr 1927 w: 24 Jan 1951 v:
Breda, IA c: 8
11VENNER, Christy-Mae b: 04 Oct 1951 d: 20 Jan 2007 in
Missouri Valley, IA Cause of death: conjestive heart failure o:
Teacher c: 3
+ seq: 236.03 SMITH, Frank b: 04 Apr 1949 Cause of death:
Congestive heart failure w: 03 Jun 1973 v: Missouri Valley, IA
c: 3
11VENNER, James (Jimmy) b: 25 Dec 1953 v: Breda, IA c: 2

+ seq: 236.04 TANK, Becky b: 24 Jul 1956 w: 04 Oct 1975 v:
   Breda, IA c: 2

11[1] VENNER, Susan-Kaye b: 12 Sep 1955 d: 16 Oct 2006 in
   Byhalia, MS Cause of death: Ovarian cancer v: Byhalia, MS o:
   Florist c: 1

+ seq: 236.05 BARNETT, Dean b: Abt. 1955 w: 20 May 1974

* 2nd Husband of [1] VENNER, Susan-Kaye:

+ seq: 236.06 YARBROUGH, Joe b: 13 Jul 1944 w: 06 Jun
   1983 v: Byhalia, MS c: 1

11 VENNER, Elizabeth (Betty) b: 05 Dec 1956 v: Ames, IA

+ seq: 236.06.01 KURT, Tom b: 20 Oct 1952 w: 25 Nov 1994
   v: Ames, IA

11 VENNER, Thomas (Tom) b: 24 May 1958 v: Boone, IA c: 2

+ seq: 236.07 KNOBBE, Julie b: 17 Nov 1957 w: 26 Apr 1986
   v: Boone, IA c: 2

11 VENNER, Dale-Nick b: 27 Feb 1960 v: Clarence, IA c: 2

+ seq: 236.08 LARSON, Kimberly-Lynn b: 14 May 1962 w: 05
   Dec 1988 v: Clarence, IA c: 3

11 VENNER, Joan-Cecelia b: 07 Apr 1964 v: Cottage Grove, MN
   c: 3

+ seq: 236.09 FRAZIER, Jeffrey b: 09 Jan 1964 w: 19 Jun 1989
   v: Cottage Grove, MN c: 3

11 VENNER, Mark-James b: 08 Feb 1971 v: McCallsburg, IA

+ seq: 236.10 PRUISNER, Robin b: 11 Feb 1970 w: 01 Jul 1995
   v: McCallsburg, IA

236.03

11 VENNER, Christy-Mae b: 04 Oct 1951 d: 20 Jan 2007 in
   Missouri Valley, IA Cause of death: conjestive heart failure o:
   Teacher c: 3

+ seq: 236.03 SMITH, Frank b: 04 Apr 1949 Cause of death:
   Congestive heart failure w: 03 Jun 1973 v: Missouri Valley, IA
   c: 3

12 SMITH, Steve b: 01 Jun 1978 v: Council Bluffs, IA

+ seq: 236.03.01 POWERS, Elisabeth-Ann w: 13 Oct 2001 v:
   Council Bluffs, IA

12 SMITH, Stefanie b: 07 Jan 1982 v: Ames, IA

12 SMITH, Stuart b: 01 Nov 1983 v: Henderson, NV

236.04

11 VENNER, James (Jimmy) b: 25 Dec 1953 v: Breda, IA c: 2

+   seq: 236.04 TANK, Becky b: 24 Jul 1956 w: 04 Oct 1975 v:
    Breda, IA c: 2
12 VENNER, Justin b: 16 Jan 1978
12 VENNER, Jacqueline b: 15 Oct 1980

236.05

11 [1] VENNER, Susan-Kaye b: 12 Sep 1955 d: 16 Oct 2006 in
    Byhalia, MS Cause of death: Ovarian cancer v: Byhalia, MS o:
    Florist c: 1
+   seq: 236.05 BARNETT, Dean b: Abt. 1955 w: 20 May 1974
*   2nd Husband of [1] VENNER, Susan-Kaye:
+   seq: 236.06 YARBROUGH, Joe b: 13 Jul 1944 w: 06 Jun
    1983 v: Byhalia, MS c: 1
12 YARBROUGH, Kelly b: 19 May 1975 v: Tampa, FL
+   seq: 236.06.00 GEORGE, Cory w: 01 Jun 2002 v: Tampa, FL

236.07

11 VENNER, Thomas (Tom) b: 24 May 1958 v: Boone, IA c: 2
+   seq: 236.07 KNOBBE, Julie b: 17 Nov 1957 w: 26 Apr 1986
    v: Boone, IA c: 2
12 VENNER, John-Paul b: 15 May 1989
12 VENNER, Jacob-Thomas b: 20 Mar 1991

236.08

11 VENNER, Dale-Nick b: 27 Feb 1960 v: Clarence, IA c: 2
+   seq: 236.08 LARSON, Kimberly-Lynn b: 14 May 1962 w: 05
    Dec 1988 v: Clarence, IA c: 3
12 VENNER, Channelle-Nicole b: 05 Dec 1984
12 VENNER, Chane-Nicholas b: 27 Feb 1990

236.09

11 VENNER, Joan-Cecelia b: 07 Apr 1964 v: Cottage Grove, MN
    c: 3
+   seq: 236.09 FRAZIER, Jeffrey b: 09 Jan 1964 w: 19 Jun 1989
    v: Cottage Grove, MN c: 3
12 FRAZIER, Nicholas-Glenn b: 27 Nov 1992
12 FRAZIER, Ella-Mary b: 16 Jan 1995
12 FRAZIER, Rachel-Ann b: 16 Mar 1998

236.11

10 WITTRY, Anita-Mae b: 23 May 1931 in Carroll, IA v: Carroll,

IA o: Parish secretary c: 7
+ seq: 236.11 TEGELS, Joseph M. (Joe) b: 09 Apr 1929 in
   Ulmer, IA d: 11 Sep 2000 in Carroll, IA w: 18 Apr 1953 in
   Maple River, IA v: Carroll, IA i: Served in U.S. Army during
   WWII o: U. S. Postal worker f: Joe Tegels m: Clara Julich c:
   7
11 TEGELS, LuAnn b: 27 Apr 1954 in Carroll, IA v: Glidden, IA
   o: Department manager c: 3
+ seq: 236.12 VANDERHEIDEN, Randall (Randy) b: 28 Jan
   1953 w: 29 Dec 1972 v: Glidden, IA o: Auto transporter f:
   Leonard Vanderheiden m: Beverly Alcox c: 3
11 TEGELS, Robert-Joseph (Bob) b: 13 Jul 1955 in Carroll, IA v:
   Manchester, MO o: Telecommunications manager c: 2
+ seq: 236.15 BRINSON, Cathleen (Cathi) b: 29 Oct 1954 in
   Washington, DC w: 25 Oct 1980 in Forrestville, MD v:
   Manchester, MO o: Teacher's aide f: Emory Brinson m:
   Elizabeth Latwas c: 2
11 TEGELS, Richard-Raymond (Dick) b: 23 Nov 1956 in Carroll,
   IA v: Carroll, IA o: Dishwasher
11 TEGELS, Karen-Sue b: 27 Feb 1958 in Carroll, IA v: Fort
   Dodge, IA o: Office manager o: Legal assistant
+ seq: 236.16 WOOD, Robert (Bob) b: 06 Oct 1956 w: 10 Sep
   1977 in Carroll, IA v: Fort Dodge, IA o: Director of
   broadcasting/educational services f: Claude Wood m: Gladys
   Coppock
11 TEGELS, Kenneth-Patrick (Ken) b: 17 Mar 1961 in Carroll, IA
   v: Atlantic, IA o: Certified public accountant
+ seq: 236.17 OLSON, Kathryn (Kathy) b: 12 Aug 1962 in
   Beloit, WI w: 23 Jun 1984 in Dubuque, IA v: Atlantic, IA o:
   Teacher's aide f: Robert Olson m: Jan Herbst
11 TEGELS, Gerald-Glenn (Jerry) b: 09 Jun 1962 in Carroll, IA v:
   Ankeny, IA o: Chemical engineer c: 4
+ seq: 236.18 WEISE, Shelley b: 20 Aug 1962 in Carroll, IA w:
   08 Jun 1985 in Arcadia, IA v: Ankeny, IA f: Forrest Weise m:
   Virginia Greteman c: 4
11 TEGELS, Timothy-Donald (Tim) b: 10 Feb 1965 in Carroll, IA
   v: Omaha, NE o: Computer account executive c: 1
+ seq: 236.19 TIEFENTHALER, Jill b: 16 Aug 1968 in Carroll,
   IA w: 30 Nov 1991 in Carroll, IA v: Omaha, NE o: Executive
   secretary f: Merlin Tiefenthaler m: Marcia Rutten c: 1

236.12

11TEGELS, LuAnn b: 27 Apr 1954 in Carroll, IA v: Glidden, IA
o: Department manager c: 3
+ seq: 236.12 VANDERHEIDEN, Randall (Randy) b: 28 Jan
1953 w: 29 Dec 1972 v: Glidden, IA o: Auto transporter f:
Leonard Vanderheiden m: Beverly Alcox c: 3
12VANDERHEIDEN, Trenton-Paul b: 04 Apr 1974 in Ida Grove,
IA v: Davenport, IA o: Truck driver c: 4
+ seq: 236.13 HOLMES, Jennifer b: 12 Apr 1973 w: 22 Oct
1994 in Carroll, IA v: Davenport, IA f: Mike Dryden m:
Jackie c: 4
12VANDERHEIDEN, Carin-Ann b: 22 Jul 1976 in Fort Worth,
TX v: Kaiserslautern, Germany o: Homemaker c: 2
+ seq: 236.14 WALLACE, Thomas b: 07 Oct 1977 in Kentucky
w: 26 Apr 1997 in Glidden, IA v: Kaiserslautern, Germany o:
U. S. Air Force f: Thomas Wallace m: Kaye Rimmer c: 2
12VANDERHEIDEN, John-Joseph b: 03 Nov 1988 in Carroll, IA

236.13

12VANDERHEIDEN, Trenton-Paul b: 04 Apr 1974 in Ida Grove,
IA v: Davenport, IA o: Truck driver c: 4
+ seq: 236.13 HOLMES, Jennifer b: 12 Apr 1973 w: 22 Oct
1994 in Carroll, IA v: Davenport, IA f: Mike Dryden m:
Jackie c: 4
13VANDERHEIDEN, Abbey b: 21 May 1992
13VANDERHEIDEN, Sara b: 05 Oct 1994 in Lake City, IA
13VANDERHEIDEN, Clayton-Paul b: 08 Sep 1995 in Spencer,
IA
13VANDERHEIDEN, Bennett-Neil b: 21 Mar 1998

236.14

12VANDERHEIDEN, Carin-Ann b: 22 Jul 1976 in Fort Worth,
TX v: Kaiserslautern, Germany o: Homemaker c: 2
+ seq: 236.14 WALLACE, Thomas b: 07 Oct 1977 in Kentucky
w: 26 Apr 1997 in Glidden, IA v: Kaiserslautern, Germany o:
U. S. Air Force f: Thomas Wallace m: Kaye Rimmer c: 2
13WALLACE, Logan-Patrick-Thomas b: 12 Apr 1999 in
Kaiserslautern, Germany
13WALLACE, Alana-Marie b: 03 Mar 2000 in Kaiserslautern,
Germany

236.15

11 TEGELS, Robert-Joseph (Bob) b: 13 Jul 1955 in Carroll, IA v: Manchester, MO o: Telecommunications manager c: 2
+ seq: 236.15 BRINSON, Cathleen (Cathi) b: 29 Oct 1954 in Washington, DC w: 25 Oct 1980 in Forrestville, MD v: Manchester, MO o: Teacher's aide f: Emory Brinson m: Elizabeth Latwas c: 2
12 TEGELS, Emma-Lynn b: 24 Oct 1987 in Morristown, NJ
12 TEGELS, Alec-Scott b: 29 Jun 1990 in Morristown, NJ

236.18

11 TEGELS, Gerald-Glenn (Jerry) b: 09 Jun 1962 in Carroll, IA v: Ankeny, IA o: Chemical engineer c: 4
+ seq: 236.18 WEISE, Shelley b: 20 Aug 1962 in Carroll, IA w: 08 Jun 1985 in Arcadia, IA v: Ankeny, IA f: Forrest Weise m: Virginia Greteman c: 4
12 TEGELS, Ashley-Marie b: 17 Jun 1986 in Des Moines, IA
12 TEGELS, Austin-Joseph b: 22 Aug 1987 in Des Moines, IA
12 TEGELS, Chelsea-Leigh b: 07 Feb 1991 in Des Moines, IA
12 TEGELS, Tristan-Nichole b: 16 Feb 1993 in Des Moines, IA

236.19

11 TEGELS, Timothy-Donald (Tim) b: 10 Feb 1965 in Carroll, IA v: Omaha, NE o: Computer account executive c: 1
+ seq: 236.19 TIEFENTHALER, Jill b: 16 Aug 1968 in Carroll, IA w: 30 Nov 1991 in Carroll, IA v: Omaha, NE o: Executive secretary f: Merlin Tiefenthaler m: Marcia Rutten c: 1
12 TEGELS, Maxwell-Joseph b: 13 Jul 2001

237

9 WITTRY, John b: 28 Sep 1892 in Breda, IA d: 01 Aug 1979 in Marshall, MN v: Marshall, MN c: 2
+ seq: 237 PAPE, Mayme b: 13 Oct 1882 d: 01 May 1943 w: 13 Feb 1917 v: Marshall, MN c: 2
10 WITTRY, Winifred (Sister Esperance) b: 13 Jan 1920 h: Bethany Convent v: St. Paul, MN i: Received the habit o: Sister of St. Joseph of Carondelet o: Dean of women at St. Catherine College
10 WITTRY, Leonard J. b: 02 Jan 1923 d: 08 Sep 1998 in Marshall, MN v: Marshall, MN c: 5
+ seq: 238 VIAENE, Margaret A. b: 05 Apr 1925 w: 14 Nov

1944 v: Marshall, MN c: 5

238

10WITTRY, Leonard J. b: 02 Jan 1923 d: 08 Sep 1998 in
Marshall, MN v: Marshall, MN c: 5
+ seq: 238 VIAENE, Margaret A. b: 05 Apr 1925 w: 14 Nov
1944 v: Marshall, MN c: 5
11WITTRY, Shirley b: 01 Oct 1945 c: 3
+ seq: 238.01 SENDENS, Tom b: 01 Feb 1945 w: 06 Aug 1963
c: 3
11WITTRY, Mary-Ellen b: 30 Oct 1946 c: 4
+ seq: 238.02 MURRAY, Bruce b: 15 Oct 1945 w: 24 Nov 1964
c: 4
11WITTRY, Carol b: 26 May 1951 c: 2
+ seq: 238.03 WESKOTT, Denny b: 28 Sep 1948 w: 10 May
1975 c: 2
11WITTRY, Darlene b: 26 Feb 1956 c: 3
+ seq: 238.04 WIEBE, Thomas b: 26 May 1950 w: 21 Jun 1979
c: 3
11WITTRY, Thomas L. (Tom) b: 09 Oct 1961 v: Caledonia, MN
+ seq: 239 MALHAIUK, Julie M. b: Abt. 18 Oct 1960 w: 28
May 1983 v: Caledonia, MN

238.01

11WITTRY, Shirley b: 01 Oct 1945 c: 3
+ seq: 238.01 SENDENS, Tom b: 01 Feb 1945 w: 06 Aug 1963
c: 3
12SENDENS, Mike b: 26 Jul 1966
12SENDENS, Mark b: 26 Jan 1969
12SENDENS, Jim b: 29 Jan 1970

238.02

11WITTRY, Mary-Ellen b: 30 Oct 1946 c: 4
+ seq: 238.02 MURRAY, Bruce b: 15 Oct 1945 w: 24 Nov 1964
c: 4
12MURRAY, Jane-Marie b: 07 Mar 1965
12MURRAY, Catherine-Ann (Katie) b: 24 Sep 1966
12MURRAY, Mark b: 22 Dec 1968
12MURRAY, Ann b: 12 Dec 1971

238.03

11 WITTRY, Carol b: 26 May 1951 c: 2
+ seq: 238.03 WESKOTT, Denny b: 28 Sep 1948 w: 10 May
    1975 c: 2
12 WESKOTT, Carrie b: 19 Nov 1973
12 WESKOTT, John b: 25 Aug 1977

238.04

11 WITTRY, Darlene b: 26 Feb 1956 c: 3
+ seq: 238.04 WIEBE, Thomas b: 26 May 1950 w: 21 Jun 1979
    c: 3
12 WIEBE, Stacy b: 13 Oct 1972
12 WIEBE, Jenny b: 03 Jan 1979
12 WIEBE, Kris b: 04 Oct 1980

240

9 WITTRY, Jacob J. (Jake) b: 05 Aug 1894 in Mount Carmel, IA
   d: 19 Aug 1966 in Breda, IA v: Carroll, IA i: US Army in WWI
   o: Farmer o: Farmer's insurance salesman c: 7
+ seq: 240 NIELAND, Anna-Catherine (Ann) b: 30 May 1899 in
    Carroll, IA d: 12 May 1984 in Breda, IA w: 06 Sep 1921 in
    Breda, IA v: Carroll, IA f: John-Henry Nieland m: Anna
    Koester c: 7
10 WITTRY, Dorothy b: 03 Oct 1922 in Breda, IA d: 08 Dec 1922
   in Breda, IA
10 WITTRY, Leona-Monica (Leone) b: 12 Nov 1923 in Coon
   Rapids, IA v: Breda, IA o: Homemaker c: 5
+ seq: 240.01 BUELT, Leo-Frank b: 12 Feb 1922 in Templeton,
    IA d: 08 May 1984 in Breda, IA w: 22 Nov 1944 in Breda, IA
    v: Breda, IA i: US Air Force in WWII o: Partner in a hatchery
    and feed business f: Henry Buelt m: Elizabeth Soppe c: 5
10 WITTRY, Francis-Joseph b: 10 Jan 1925 in Breda, IA d: 10 Jan
   1925 in Breda, IA
10 MARY-DANIELLE, Pauline-Ann (Sr., FSPA) Wittry b: 12 Jan
   1926 in Breda, IA v: Manitowish Waters, WI i: Final vows o:
   Franciscan Sister of Perpetual Adoration
10 [1] WITTRY, Joan-Margaret b: 27 Nov 1927 in Coon Rapids,
   IA v: Rosemount, MN c: 12
+ seq: 240.09 KRAUS, Clarence-John b: 06 May 1924 d: 29 Jun
    1952 w: 14 Jun 1949 in Breda, IA i: US Army in WWII o:
    Farmer f: Joseph Kraus m: Elizabeth Meiners c: 2

* 2nd Husband of [1] WITTRY, Joan-Margaret:
+ seq: 240.12 HANNASCH, Jerome-Joseph (Jerry) b: 25 Jun
  1926 in Carroll, IA d: 26 Nov 1997 in Bellechester, MN w: 24
  Jul 1954 in Carroll, IA o: Salesman for 21st Century Genetics
  o: U. S. Army in WW II f: John-Bernard Hannasch m: Leota-
  Agnes Murphy c: 10
10WITTRY, Helen b: 08 Mar 1929 in Breda, IA d: 08 Mar 1929
  in Breda, IA
10WITTRY, Teresa b: 07 Mar 1930 in Breda, IA d: 07 Mar 1930
  in Breda, IA

240.01

10WITTRY, Leona-Monica (Leone) b: 12 Nov 1923 in Coon
  Rapids, IA v: Breda, IA o: Homemaker c: 5
+ seq: 240.01 BUELT, Leo-Frank b: 12 Feb 1922 in Templeton,
  IA d: 08 May 1984 in Breda, IA w: 22 Nov 1944 in Breda, IA
  v: Breda, IA i: US Air Force in WWII o: Partner in a hatchery
  and feed business f: Henry Buelt m: Elizabeth Soppe c: 5
11BUELT, Kathleen-Ann (Kay) b: 06 May 1947 in Carroll, IA v:
  Kent, WA o: Medical technologist
+ seq: 240.02 DAVIS, Don-Allen b: 29 Dec 1930 w: 17 Nov
  1979 in Seattle, WA v: Kent, WA o: Worked for Boeing f:
  Delmar-Pate Davis m: Hazel Triplett
11BUELT, Mary-Joan b: 31 Jul 1948 in Carroll, IA d: 17 Jul 1996
  in Omaha, NE v: Omaha, NE o: Homemaker c: 3
+ seq: 240.03 HALLER, Robert-John b: 15 Aug 1946 w: 28 Dec
  1968 in Omaha, NE v: Omaha, NE o: Used truck selesman f:
  Phillip Haller m: Jeanne c: 3
11BUELT, Rose-Marie b: 11 Oct 1950 in Carroll, IA v: Glendale,
  CA o: Licensed practical nurse c: 3
+ seq: 240.05 WIEDERIN, Andrew E. (Andy) b: 04 May 1947 in
  Mount Carmel, IA w: 04 Apr 1970 in Breda, IA v: Glendale,
  CA o: Electrical engineer f: David Wiederin m: Agnes Sturm
  c: 3
11BUELT, Leo-Donald (Lee) b: 11 May 1954 in Carroll, IA v:
  Exira, IA i: Sheep shearer and broker o: Sheep shearer and
  broker c: 3
+ seq: 240.07 FLYNN, Merrie-Ann b: 20 Nov 1954 w: 29 Jul
  1978 in Breda, IA v: Exira, IA o: Teacher of Spanish and
  computers f: Charles-Edward Flynn m: Elaine c: 3
11BUELT, Robert-Joseph b: 01 Jan 1959 in Carroll, IA v: Breda,

IA o: Used car salesman c: 2

+ seq: 240.08 DREY, Joan-Marie b: 12 Aug 1959 w: 19 Apr 1980 in Early, IA v: Breda, IA o: Secretary f: Joseph Drey m: Marian Berger c: 2

240.03

11 BUELT, Mary-Joan b: 31 Jul 1948 in Carroll, IA d: 17 Jul 1996 in Omaha, NE v: Omaha, NE o: Homemaker c: 3

+ seq: 240.03 HALLER, Robert-John b: 15 Aug 1946 w: 28 Dec 1968 in Omaha, NE v: Omaha, NE o: Used truck selesman f: Phillip Haller m: Jeanne c: 3

12 HALLER, Jennifer-Marie b: 17 Nov 1969 in Omaha, NE o: Tanning salon c: 1

+ seq: 240.04 WILKENS, Gary b: Abt. 1965 w: 03 Aug 1991 c: 1

12 HALLER, Laura-Ann b: 19 Jun 1977 v: Omaha, NE o: Telemarketer

+ seq: 240.04.01 STAPLETON, Timothy (Tim) w: Jun 2000 o: Sitel Corp.

12 HALLER, Jeffrey-Robert b: 04 Mar 1985 v: Omaha, NE

240.04

12 HALLER, Jennifer-Marie b: 17 Nov 1969 in Omaha, NE o: Tanning salon c: 1

+ seq: 240.04 WILKENS, Gary b: Abt. 1965 w: 03 Aug 1991 c: 1

13 HALLER, Cassandra-Lynn b: 13 Apr 1991

240.05

11 BUELT, Rose-Marie b: 11 Oct 1950 in Carroll, IA v: Glendale, CA o: Licensed practical nurse c: 3

+ seq: 240.05 WIEDERIN, Andrew E. (Andy) b: 04 May 1947 in Mount Carmel, IA w: 04 Apr 1970 in Breda, IA v: Glendale, CA o: Electrical engineer f: David Wiederin m: Agnes Sturm c: 3

12 WIEDERIN, Lisa-Ann b: 10 Aug 1971 in North Hollywood, CA v: Albuquerque, NM c: 2

+ seq: 240.06 EKNESS, Michael (Mike) b: 01 Jul 1971 in Wyoming w: 27 Apr 1996 in La Conada, CA v: Albuquerque, NM c: 2

12 WIEDERIN, Stacy-Kay b: 09 Mar 1977 in North Hollywood,

CA

12 WIEDERIN, Susan-Lynn b: 20 May 1982 in North Hollywood, CA

240.06

12 WIEDERIN, Lisa-Ann b: 10 Aug 1971 in North Hollywood, CA v: Albuquerque, NM c: 2
+ seq: 240.06 EKNESS, Michael (Mike) b: 01 Jul 1971 in Wyoming w: 27 Apr 1996 in La Conada, CA v: Albuquerque, NM c: 2
13 EKNESS, Courtney-Ann b: 19 Nov 1998
13 EKNESS, Joshua-Dean b: 07 Feb 2002

240.07

11 BUELT, Leo-Donald (Lee) b: 11 May 1954 in Carroll, IA v: Exira, IA i: Sheep shearer and broker o: Sheep shearer and broker c: 3
+ seq: 240.07 FLYNN, Merrie-Ann b: 20 Nov 1954 w: 29 Jul 1978 in Breda, IA v: Exira, IA o: Teacher of Spanish and computers f: Charles-Edward Flynn m: Elaine c: 3
12 BUELT, Austin-Lee b: 23 Dec 1979 in Iowa
12 BUELT, Brandon-John b: 11 Nov 1981 in Iowa o: Construction o: Sheep shearing
12 BUELT, Carrie-Ann b: 11 Nov 1982 in Iowa o: Student c: 2
+ seq: 240.07.01 MUELL, Richard-Kenneth (Rick) w: 26 Oct 2002 in Exira, IA c: 2

240.07.01

12 BUELT, Carrie-Ann b: 11 Nov 1982 in Iowa o: Student c: 2
+ seq: 240.07.01 MUELL, Richard-Kenneth (Rick) w: 26 Oct 2002 in Exira, IA c: 2
13 MUELL, Anastasia b: 09 Sep 2002
13 MUELL, Lane b: 28 Aug 2003 in Audubon, IA

240.08

11 BUELT, Robert-Joseph b: 01 Jan 1959 in Carroll, IA v: Breda, IA o: Used car salesman c: 2
+ seq: 240.08 DREY, Joan-Marie b: 12 Aug 1959 w: 19 Apr 1980 in Early, IA v: Breda, IA o: Secretary f: Joseph Drey m: Marian Berger c: 2
12 BUELT, Nicholas-John b: 09 Mar 1986 in Carroll, IA

12BUELT, Jacob-Robert b: 18 Dec 1992 in Carroll, IA

240.09
10[2] WITTRY, Joan-Margaret b: 27 Nov 1927 in Coon Rapids,
IA v: Rosemount, MN c: 12
+ seq: 240.09 KRAUS, Clarence-John b: 06 May 1924 d: 29 Jun
1952 w: 14 Jun 1949 in Breda, IA i: US Army in WWII o:
Farmer f: Joseph Kraus m: Elizabeth Meiners c: 2
11KRAUS, LeRoy-Joseph b: 31 Mar 1950 in Carroll, IA d: 02
Jun 1981 in Omaha, NE
11[1] KRAUS, Gerald-James b: 26 Oct 1951 in Carroll, IA v: Des
Moines, IA o: Legislative lobbyist for Homesteaders Life
Insurance Co. V.P. c: 3
+ seq: 240.10 HACKETT, Pamela (Pam) b: 23 Nov 1950 w: 19
Jun 1971 v: Des Moines, IA f: William Hackett m: Lucille c:
1
* 2nd Wife of [1] KRAUS, Gerald-James:
+ seq: 240.11 CHRISTIAN, Terri-Lynn w: 05 Jul 1998 in Sac
City, IA i: Singer by avocation o: Insurance sales c: 2
* 2nd Husband of [2] WITTRY, Joan-Margaret:
+ seq: 240.12 HANNASCH, Jerome-Joseph (Jerry) b: 25 Jun
1926 in Carroll, IA d: 26 Nov 1997 in Bellechester, MN w: 24
Jul 1954 in Carroll, IA o: Salesman for 21st Century Genetics
o: U. S. Army in WW II f: John-Bernard Hannasch m: Leota-
Agnes Murphy c: 10
11HANNASCH, Michael-John (Mike) b: 16 Apr 1955 in Carroll,
IA v: Bedford, TX o: Regional Manager of Dome Nutrition
Stores c: 3
+ seq: 240.13 BURDITT, Valerie-Kay b: 27 Jan 1959 in Fonda,
IA w: 14 Jun 1980 v: Bedford, TX o: Teacher's assistant f:
Orville Burditt m: Doris Carlson c: 3
11HANNASCH, Jane-Frances b: 08 Jul 1956 in Carroll, IA v:
Kelley, IA i: City council member o: Insurance c: 2
+ seq: 240.14 WALTER, Gary-Thomas b: 19 Dec 1956 in
Kirksville, MO w: 10 Jun 1978 v: Kelley, IA o: Warehouse
manager f: Thomas Walter m: Lucille Clark c: 2
11HANNASCH, Patrick-Henry (Pat) b: 16 Jan 1958 in Carroll, IA
d: 04 Mar 1978 in Carroll, IA

11HANNASCH, Thomas-William (Tom) b: 02 Apr 1959 in
Carroll, IA v: Apple Valley, MN o: Engineer for McGough
Companies, Minneapolis c: 2
+ seq: 240.15 BULLERMAN, Susan-Renee (Sue) b: 13 Sep 1962
in Calmar, IA w: 20 Sep 1986 v: Apple Valley, MN o:
Registered nurse f: Leonard Bullerman m: Irma Schmidt c: 2
11HANNASCH, Mark-Anthony b: 25 Jun 1960 in Carroll, IA v:
Cedar Falls, IA o: National supervisor for Professional Office
Services
+ seq: 240.16 CERNOHAUS, Sharon-Ann b: 06 Jul 1962 in
Hastings, MN w: 01 Sep 1984 v: Cedar Falls, IA o: Property
management VP o: Computer work for the Linder Company f:
Gerald Cernohaus m: Judy Reinardy
11HANNASCH, Richard-Joseph (Dick) b: 23 Aug 1961 in
Carroll, IA v: Huxley, IA o: Computer training author for
Principle Finance c: 2
+ seq: 240.17 LAMPE, Kay-Marie b: 22 May 1963 in Dubuque,
IA w: 18 Jul 1987 v: Huxley, IA o: Hazardous materials
specialist f: Tom Lampe m: Jane Schuster c: 2
11[3] HANNASCH, Mary-Ann b: 20 Aug 1962 in Carroll, IA v:
Prospect, CT o: Homemaker c: 6
+ seq: 240.18 MCCANN, Daniel-John (Dan) b: 19 Mar 1958 w:
13 Oct 1984
* 2nd Husband of [3] HANNASCH, Mary-Ann:
+ seq: 240.19 DONNELLY, Raymond-Patrick (Randy) b: 11 Sep
1963 w: 27 Jul 1996 v: Prospect, CT i: Served in US Marines
o: Sheet metal designer f: Raymond Donnelly m: Margaret
Maguire c: 6
11HANNASCH, Roch-James b: 15 Dec 1963 in Carroll, IA v:
Apple Valley, MN o: Production manager of Store Fixture
Manufacturing c: 5
+ seq: 240.20 DAHLING, Lori-Kristeen b: 06 Oct 1964 in Lake
City, MN w: 27 Jul 1985 v: Apple Valley, MN o: Day care
provider f: Charles Dahling m: Ardel Bakken c: 5
11HANNASCH, Teresa-Marie b: 23 Jan 1965 in Carroll, IA d: 06
Feb 1965 in Carroll, IA
11HANNASCH, James-John (Jim) b: 03 Aug 1966 in Carroll, IA
v: Savage, MN o: Accounting manager c: 2
+ seq: 240.21 PETERSON, Linda-Kay b: 10 Nov 1967 w: 18
May 1991 v: Savage, MN o: Computer programmer f: Daniel
Peterson m: Evelyn Burzlaff c: 2

240.10

11[1] KRAUS, Gerald-James b: 26 Oct 1951 in Carroll, IA v: Des Moines, IA o: Legislative lobbyist for Homesteaders Life Insurance Co. V.P. c: 3

+ seq: 240.10 HACKETT, Pamela (Pam) b: 23 Nov 1950 w: 19 Jun 1971 v: Des Moines, IA f: William Hackett m: Lucille c: 1

12 KRAUS, Justin-Jade b: 28 May 1975 in Des Moines, IA v: Cologne, MN o: Electrical Engineer, LSI

+ seq: 240.10.00 CHRISTIAN, Terri-Lynn b: 27 Oct 1955 w: 05 Jun 1998 in Sac City, IA

* 2nd Wife of [1] KRAUS, Gerald-James:

+ seq: 240.11 CHRISTIAN, Terri-Lynn w: 05 Jul 1998 in Sac City, IA i: Singer by avocation o: Insurance sales c: 2

12 COLE, Matthew-Aaron b: 09 Mar 1975 v: Ankeny, IA c: 3

+ seq: 240.11.01 STRAND, Susannah (Sanna) b: 01 Feb 1976 w: 24 Apr 1999 v: Ankeny, IA c: 3

12 COLE, Andrea-Michelle b: 02 Dec 1978 v: Marshalltown, IA c: 1

+ seq: 240.11.50 TROUTNER, Jeff w: Abt. 2000 v: Marshalltown, IA c: 1

240.11.01

12 COLE, Matthew-Aaron b: 09 Mar 1975 v: Ankeny, IA c: 3

+ seq: 240.11.01 STRAND, Susannah (Sanna) b: 01 Feb 1976 w: 24 Apr 1999 v: Ankeny, IA c: 3

13 COLE, James-Dixon b: 30 Jan 2001

13 COLE, Madelynn-Beth b: 30 Jan 2001

13 COLE, Hannah-Cheryl b: 30 Jan 2001

240.11.50

12 COLE, Andrea-Michelle b: 02 Dec 1978 v: Marshalltown, IA c: 1

+ seq: 240.11.50 TROUTNER, Jeff w: Abt. 2000 v: Marshalltown, IA c: 1

13 TROUTNER, Grace (Gracie) b: Abt. 2001

240.13

11 HANNASCH, Michael-John (Mike) b: 16 Apr 1955 in Carroll, IA v: Bedford, TX o: Regional Manager of Dome Nutrition Stores c: 3

+ seq: 240.13 BURDITT, Valerie-Kay b: 27 Jan 1959 in Fonda, IA w: 14 Jun 1980 v: Bedford, TX o: Teacher's assistant f: Orville Burditt m: Doris Carlson c: 3
12HANNASCH, Jacob-Michael b: 22 Sep 1984 in Sioux City, IA
12HANNASCH, Heather-Kay b: 03 Sep 1987 in Sioux City, IA
12HANNASCH, Jessica-Ann b: 22 Jan 1993 in Bedford, TX

240.14

11HANNASCH, Jane-Frances b: 08 Jul 1956 in Carroll, IA v: Kelley, IA i: City council member o: Insurance c: 2
+ seq: 240.14 WALTER, Gary-Thomas b: 19 Dec 1956 in Kirksville, MO w: 10 Jun 1978 v: Kelley, IA o: Warehouse manager f: Thomas Walter m: Lucille Clark c: 2
12WALTER, Benjamin-Thomas b: 26 Mar 1983 in Ames, IA
12WALTER, Dylan-Patrick b: 27 Feb 1986 in Ames, IA

240.15

11HANNASCH, Thomas-William (Tom) b: 02 Apr 1959 in Carroll, IA v: Apple Valley, MN o: Engineer for McGough Companies, Minneapolis c: 2
+ seq: 240.15 BULLERMAN, Susan-Renee (Sue) b: 13 Sep 1962 in Calmar, IA w: 20 Sep 1986 v: Apple Valley, MN o: Registered nurse f: Leonard Bullerman m: Irma Schmidt c: 2
12HANNASCH, Maria-Catherine b: 22 Oct 1989
12HANNASCH, John-Leonard b: 04 Apr 1991

240.17

11HANNASCH, Richard-Joseph (Dick) b: 23 Aug 1961 in Carroll, IA v: Huxley, IA o: Computer training author for Principle Finance c: 2
+ seq: 240.17 LAMPE, Kay-Marie b: 22 May 1963 in Dubuque, IA w: 18 Jul 1987 v: Huxley, IA o: Hazardous materials specialist f: Tom Lampe m: Jane Schuster c: 2
12HANNASCH, Margaret-Anne (Meg) b: 01 Sep 1996 in Ames, IA
12HANNASCH, Teresa-Marie-Lampe b: 30 Oct 1999 in Huxley, IA

240.18

11[1] HANNASCH, Mary-Ann b: 20 Aug 1962 in Carroll, IA v: Prospect, CT o: Homemaker c: 6

+ seq: 240.18 MCCANN, Daniel-John (Dan) b: 19 Mar 1958 w: 13 Oct 1984

* 2nd Husband of [1] HANNASCH, Mary-Ann:

+ seq: 240.19 DONNELLY, Raymond-Patrick (Randy) b: 11 Sep 1963 w: 27 Jul 1996 v: Prospect, CT i: Served in US Marines o: Sheet metal designer f: Raymond Donnelly m: Margaret Maguire c: 6

12 DONNELLY, Melissa-Marie b: 07 Jul 1992 a: McCann
12 DONNELLY, Rosemary-Elizabeth b: 18 May 1997
12 DONNELLY, Katelin-Casey b: 07 Dec 1998
12 DONNELLY, Casey-Morgan b: 13 Nov 2000
12 DONNELLY, Ryan-Patrick b: 28 May 2004
12 DONNELLY, Erin-Margaret b: 15 Jul 2006

240.20

11 HANNASCH, Roch-James b: 15 Dec 1963 in Carroll, IA v: Apple Valley, MN o: Production manager of Store Fixture Manufacturing c: 5

+ seq: 240.20 DAHLING, Lori-Kristeen b: 06 Oct 1964 in Lake City, MN w: 27 Jul 1985 v: Apple Valley, MN o: Day care provider f: Charles Dahling m: Ardel Bakken c: 5

12 HANNASCH, Brandon-Jerome b: 30 Sep 1988 in Edina, MN
12 HANNASCH, Amanda-Rochelle b: 14 Aug 1990 in Edina, MN d: 14 Aug 1990 in Farmington, MN
12 HANNASCH, Gabrielle-Pauline b: 10 Oct 1991 in Edina, MN
12 HANNASCH, Kyle-Charles b: 09 Aug 1994 in Edina, MN
12 HANNASCH, Michele-Jean b: 29 Dec 1995 in Edina, MN

240.21

11 HANNASCH, James-John (Jim) b: 03 Aug 1966 in Carroll, IA v: Savage, MN o: Accounting manager c: 2

+ seq: 240.21 PETERSON, Linda-Kay b: 10 Nov 1967 w: 18 May 1991 v: Savage, MN o: Computer programmer f: Daniel Peterson m: Evelyn Burzlaff c: 2

12 HANNASCH, Seth-Jacob b: 11 Sep 1994 in St. Paul, MN
12 HANNASCH, August-James b: 23 Nov 1997 in St. Paul, MN

240.22

9 WITTRY, Clara b: 31 Mar 1896 in Breda, IA d: 02 Jun 1991 v: Marshall, MN c: 5

+ seq: 240.22 PAPE, John b: 09 Jun 1885 d: 13 Feb 1965 w: 18

Sep 1917 v: Marshall, MN c: 5

10[1] PAPE, Annabella b: 04 Aug 1918 c: 7

+ seq: 240.23 SCHMIDT, Kenneth b: 19 Nov 1916 d: 04 Aug
   1962 w: 23 Nov 1937 c: 7

* 2nd Husband of [1] PAPE, Annabella:

+ seq: 240.33 TURBOS, Ray b: 03 Mar 1911 d: Feb 1991 w: 29
   Nov 1968

10PAPE, Margorie b: 16 Mar 1920 v: Marshall, MN c: 2

+ seq: 240.34 VERDECK, Francis b: 12 May 1914 d: 19 Jul
   1976 w: 31 Jan 1940 v: Marshall, MN c: 2

10[2] PAPE, Laverdos (Bud) b: 22 Feb 1922 v: Marshall, MN c:
   6

+ seq: 240.37 BLANCHETTE, Beatrice (Beedy) b: 24 Oct 1925
   w: 05 Jun 1945 v: Marshall, MN c: 6

* 2nd Wife of [2] PAPE, Laverdos (Bud):

+ seq: 240.42 FRANSEN, Leona b: 09 Jun 1922 w: 23 Aug 1980

10PAPE, Agnes b: 16 Jul 1935 d: 16 Jul 1935

10PAPE, Betty-Lou b: 19 Jan 1937 c: 7

+ seq: 240.43 HOFLOCK, Raymond (Ray) b: 14 May 1931 d:
   26 Jun 1986 w: 18 Sep 1952 c: 7

240.23

10[2] PAPE, Annabella b: 04 Aug 1918 c: 7

+ seq: 240.23 SCHMIDT, Kenneth b: 19 Nov 1916 d: 04 Aug
   1962 w: 23 Nov 1937 c: 7

11SCHMIDT, Genevieve b: 13 Oct 1938 v: Minneapolis, MN c:
   5

+ seq: 240.24 GJERDE, Kenneth b: 18 Feb 1934 w: 26 Oct 1957
   v: Minneapolis, MN c: 5

11SCHMIDT, Janice b: 06 Jan 1941 c: 3

+ seq: 240.26 DONAVAN, Pete b: 15 Nov 1935 w: 04 May
   1974 c: 3

11SCHMIDT, Marlene b: 09 Feb 1942 c: 2

+ seq: 240.27 GLOMSKI, Tom b: 07 Jan 1942 w: Abt. 1967 c:
   2

11SCHMIDT, Allen-Lee b: 15 Oct 1943 c: 4

+ seq: 240.28 ZWACH, Carol-Jean b: 23 Jun 1943 w: 20 Aug
   1963 c: 4

11SCHMIDT, JoAnn b: 03 Nov 1944 c: 2

+ seq: 240.29 STATTELMAN, Tom b: 16 Jan 1943 w: 07 Sep
   1963 c: 2

11[1] SCHMIDT, Gordon b: 18 May 1946 c: 3
+ seq: 240.30 DUGAN, Leann b: 23 Mar 1946 w: 04 May 1968
   c: 3
* 2nd Wife of [1] SCHMIDT, Gordon:
+ seq: 240.31 ALLEN, Guelda b: 19 Nov 1944 w: 24 Mar 1984
11SCHMIDT, Rosemary b: 11 Jun 1950 c: 4
+ seq: 240.32 BRAU, Leroy b: 28 Feb 1950 w: 05 Jul 1969 c: 4
* 2nd Husband of [2] PAPE, Annabella:
+ seq: 240.33 TURBOS, Ray b: 03 Mar 1911 d: Feb 1991 w: 29
   Nov 1968

240.24

11SCHMIDT, Genevieve b: 13 Oct 1938 v: Minneapolis, MN c:
   5
+ seq: 240.24 GJERDE, Kenneth b: 18 Feb 1934 w: 26 Oct 1957
   v: Minneapolis, MN c: 5
12GJERDE, Parris b: 09 Feb 1958
12GJERDE-JR., Kenneth b: 18 Feb 1959
+ seq: 240.25 Wendy b: Abt. 1960 w: Jun 1985
12GJERDE, Steve b: 06 Jul 1960
12GJERDE, Mark b: 08 Jan 1963
12GJERDE, Angela b: 03 Sep 1965

240.26

11SCHMIDT, Janice b: 06 Jan 1941 c: 3
+ seq: 240.26 DONAVAN, Pete b: 15 Nov 1935 w: 04 May
   1974 c: 3
12DONAVAN, Anne-Marie b: 25 Jun 1975
12DONAVAN, Mary-Jane b: 22 Dec 1976
12DONAVAN, Patricia-Ann b: 11 Nov 1979

240.27

11SCHMIDT, Marlene b: 09 Feb 1942 c: 2
+ seq: 240.27 GLOMSKI, Tom b: 07 Jan 1942 w: Abt. 1967 c:
   2
12GLOMSKI, Lori b: 11 Mar 1969
12GLOMSKI, Thomas b: 11 Jun 1970

240.28

11SCHMIDT, Allen-Lee b: 15 Oct 1943 c: 4
+ seq: 240.28 ZWACH, Carol-Jean b: 23 Jun 1943 w: 20 Aug

1963 c: 4
12SCHMIDT, Wade-Allen b: 10 Jun 1964
12SCHMIDT, Kelly b: 10 Oct 1966
12SCHMIDT, Greg b: 02 Feb 1968
12SCHMIDT, Dean b: 29 Jan 1974

240.29
11SCHMIDT, JoAnn b: 03 Nov 1944 c: 2
+ seq: 240.29 STATTELMAN, Tom b: 16 Jan 1943 w: 07 Sep
  1963 c: 2
12STATTELMAN, Wesley b: 23 Feb 1964
12STATTELMAN, Jesse b: 04 Jun 1965

240.30
11[1] SCHMIDT, Gordon b: 18 May 1946 c: 3
+ seq: 240.30 DUGAN, Leann b: 23 Mar 1946 w: 04 May 1968
  c: 3
12SCHMIDT, Denise b: 25 Dec 1969
12SCHMIDT, Janelle b: 08 Oct 1972
12SCHMIDT, Kenneth b: 18 Mar 1975
* 2nd Wife of [1] SCHMIDT, Gordon:
+ seq: 240.31 ALLEN, Guelda b: 19 Nov 1944 w: 24 Mar 1984

240.32
11SCHMIDT, Rosemary b: 11 Jun 1950 c: 4
+ seq: 240.32 BRAU, Leroy b: 28 Feb 1950 w: 05 Jul 1969 c: 4
12BRAU, Brian b: 19 Jun 1970
12BRAU, Stacey b: 28 Aug 1972
12BRAU, Stefanie b: 21 Mar 1974
12BRAU, Sara b: 13 Nov 1975

240.34
10PAPE, Margorie b: 16 Mar 1920 v: Marshall, MN c: 2
+ seq: 240.34 VERDECK, Francis b: 12 May 1914 d: 19 Jul
  1976 w: 31 Jan 1940 v: Marshall, MN c: 2
11VERDECK, Bonnie b: 12 Jul 1941
+ seq: 240.35 LARSON, Lloyd b: 28 Dec 1940 w: 19 Feb 1966
11VERDECK, Beverly b: 28 Oct 1946 c: 1
+ seq: 240.36 PETERSON, Mike b: 08 Sep 1946 w: 16 Jun 1966
  c: 1

240.36

11 VERDECK, Beverly b: 28 Oct 1946 c: 1

+ seq: 240.36 PETERSON, Mike b: 08 Sep 1946 w: 16 Jun 1966
  c: 1

12 PETERSON, Michelle b: 28 Mar 1968

240.37

10 [2] PAPE, Laverdos (Bud) b: 22 Feb 1922 v: Marshall, MN c:
  6

+ seq: 240.37 BLANCHETTE, Beatrice (Beedy) b: 24 Oct 1925
  w: 05 Jun 1945 v: Marshall, MN c: 6

11 [1] PAPE, Judith (Judy) b: 19 Aug 1946 c: 1

+ seq: 240.38 WILLS, Robert b: 09 Aug 1939 d: 01 Jul 1982 w:
  24 Feb 1968 c: 1

* 2nd Husband of [1] PAPE, Judith (Judy):

+ seq: 240.39 TAYLOR, Arthur b: 10 Apr 1943 w: 02 Dec 1983

11 PAPE, James-Allen b: 18 Oct 1949

11 PAPE, Robert-Lee b: 27 Mar 1955 d: 20 Aug 1977

11 PAPE, Timothy b: 12 Jan 1961 d: 30 Sep 1970

11 PAPE, Tammy b: 08 Dec 1961 c: 2

+ seq: 240.40 CORNO, James b: 26 Oct 1961 w: 21 Oct 1980 c:
  2

11 PAPE, Brenda b: 21 Mar 1963 c: 1

+ seq: 240.41 MIKEL, Steve b: 22 Dec 1962 w: 13 Aug 1984 c:
  1

* 2nd Wife of [2] PAPE, Laverdos (Bud):

+ seq: 240.42 FRANSEN, Leona b: 09 Jun 1922 w: 23 Aug 1980

240.38

11 [1] PAPE, Judith (Judy) b: 19 Aug 1946 c: 1

+ seq: 240.38 WILLS, Robert b: 09 Aug 1939 d: 01 Jul 1982 w:
  24 Feb 1968 c: 1

12 WILLS, Dawn b: 28 Sep 1969

* 2nd Husband of [1] PAPE, Judith (Judy):

+ seq: 240.39 TAYLOR, Arthur b: 10 Apr 1943 w: 02 Dec 1983

240.40

11 PAPE, Tammy b: 08 Dec 1961 c: 2

+ seq: 240.40 CORNO, James b: 26 Oct 1961 w: 21 Oct 1980 c:
  2

12 CORNO, Brandon b: 26 Jan 1981

12CORNO, Nicholas b: 21 Mar 1982

240.41
11PAPE, Brenda b: 21 Mar 1963 c: 1
+ seq: 240.41 MIKEL, Steve b: 22 Dec 1962 w: 13 Aug 1984 c:
   1
12MIKEL, Amanda b: 11 May 1985

240.43
10PAPE, Betty-Lou b: 19 Jan 1937 c: 7
+ seq: 240.43 HOFLOCK, Raymond (Ray) b: 14 May 1931 d:
   26 Jun 1986 w: 18 Sep 1952 c: 7
11HOFLOCK, Larry b: 14 Mar 1953
+ seq: 240.44 KUEHL, Cheryl b: 21 Feb 1958 w: 15 Jan 1977
11HOFLOCK, Gary b: 13 Jul 1954 c: 2
+ seq: 240.45 LABAT, Mary-Kay b: 25 Jan 1956 w: 01 Dec
   1973 c: 2
11HOFLOCK, Ronald b: 15 Mar 1956 c: 3
+ seq: 240.46 HAUGEN, Karen b: 30 Sep 1958 w: 20 Aug 1977
   c: 3
11HOFLOCK, Kevin b: 16 Apr 1959
+ seq: 240.47 VAN MOER, Nancy b: 24 Apr 1959 w: 15 Dec
   1978
11HOFLOCK, Todd b: 06 Jul 1963
+ seq: 240.48 SCHMITT, Melissa b: 31 Aug 1966 w: 20 Oct
   1984
11HOFLOCK, Wesley-David b: 28 Dec 1965
+ seq: 240.49 STATLER, Tamara b: 16 Sep 1966 w: 07 Jun
   1986
11HOFLOCK-JR., Raymond b: 19 Jul 1967

240.45
11HOFLOCK, Gary b: 13 Jul 1954 c: 2
+ seq: 240.45 LABAT, Mary-Kay b: 25 Jan 1956 w: 01 Dec
   1973 c: 2
12HOFLOCK, Brian b: 08 Mar 1974
12HOFLOCK, Christina-Kay b: 19 Sep 1977

240.46
11HOFLOCK, Ronald b: 15 Mar 1956 c: 3
+ seq: 240.46 HAUGEN, Karen b: 30 Sep 1958 w: 20 Aug 1977

c: 3

12 HOFLOCK, Jared b: 21 Aug 1982
12 HOFLOCK, Justin b: 02 Mar 1984
12 HOFLOCK, Jorden b: 14 Dec 1985

241

9 WITTRY, Joseph-Nicholas (Joe) b: 19 Aug 1899 in Breda, IA
  d: 22 Jan 1987 v: Carroll, IA o: Barber c: 3
+ seq: 241 WILBERDING, Rose-Elizabeth b: 19 Feb 1908 in
  Little Rock, IA d: 06 Nov 1982 in Iowa w: 13 Jun 1933 v:
  Carroll, IA c: 3
10 WITTRY, Marvin-Bernard b: 12 Dec 1934 in Carroll, IA v:
  Los Gatos, CA o: Consultant for G. E. c: 5
+ seq: 242 OSTERHOLT, Angela-Maria-Anna b: 13 Jul 1936 in
  San Francisco, CA w: 09 Jun 1956 in Cotati, CA v: Los Gatos,
  CA f: Anton-Bernard Osterholt m: Maria-Anna Feuerstein c:
  5
10 WITTRY, Janice-Mae b: 04 Sep 1937 in Carroll, IA v: Boone,
  IA c: 3
+ seq: 243.01 KANNE, Ralph b: 10 Jan 1937 in Carroll, IA w:
  27 Dec 1958 in Boone, IA v: Boone, IA c: 3
10 [1] WITTRY, Lyle-John b: 10 Jun 1942 v: Bentonville, AR c:
  2
+ seq: 244 SHAEFFER, Joan b: 02 Oct 1942 d: 21 Mar 1993 w:
  29 Aug 1964 v: Bentonville, AR f: John Winters Shaeffer m:
  Jean Louise Curtis c: 2
* 2nd Wife of [1] WITTRY, Lyle-John:
+ seq: 246 DENNIS, Connie b: Abt. 1942 d: 1995 w: 1994 v:
  Fayetteville, AR
* 3rd Wife of [1] WITTRY, Lyle-John:
+ seq: 247 CAMPBELL, Cynthia (Cindy) b: 24 Mar 1951 w: 01
  Mar 1996 in Fayetteville, AR

242

10 WITTRY, Marvin-Bernard b: 12 Dec 1934 in Carroll, IA v:
  Los Gatos, CA o: Consultant for G. E. c: 5
+ seq: 242 OSTERHOLT, Angela-Maria-Anna b: 13 Jul 1936 in
  San Francisco, CA w: 09 Jun 1956 in Cotati, CA v: Los Gatos,
  CA f: Anton-Bernard Osterholt m: Maria-Anna Feuerstein c:
  5
11 WITTRY, Karen-Anne b: 04 Apr 1958 in San Louis Obispo,

CA v: Black Forest, CO c: 2
+ seq: 242.01 ULEN, Charles-Howard (Chuck) b: 26 Oct 1955
   w: 21 Mar 1981 v: Black Forest, CO c: 2
11 WITTRY, Rosemarie-Lynn b: 04 Nov 1960 in Omaha, NE v:
   Yukon, OK c: 2
+ seq: 242.02 CASE, Patrick-Ernest (Pat) b: 22 Aug 1958 w: 12
   Dec 1981 v: Yukon, OR c: 2
11 WITTRY, Bryon-Joseph b: 10 Nov 1962 in San Jose, CA v:
   Sunnyvale, CA c: 2
+ seq: 242.03 COOLS, Karolien b: in Belgium w: 15 Jul 2000 c:
   2
11 WITTRY, David-Anthony b: 08 Apr 1965 in San Jose, CA v:
   Los Gatos, CA o: Manager of Togo
11 WITTRY, Steven-James b: 02 Aug 1967 in Los Gatos, CA v:
   San Jose, CA c: 4
+ seq: 243 BULDER, Regina-Wilhelmina b: 14 Aug 1968 in San
   Jose, CA w: 10 Mar 1990 v: San Jose, CA c: 4

242.01
11 WITTRY, Karen-Anne b: 04 Apr 1958 in San Louis Obispo,
   CA v: Black Forest, CO c: 2
+ seq: 242.01 ULEN, Charles-Howard (Chuck) b: 26 Oct 1955
   w: 21 Mar 1981 v: Black Forest, CO c: 2
12 ULEN, Scott-Alexander b: 30 Dec 1986 in San Jose, CA
12 ULEN, Michael-James b: 02 Feb 1991 in San Jose, CA

242.02
11 WITTRY, Rosemarie-Lynn b: 04 Nov 1960 in Omaha, NE v:
   Yukon, OK c: 2
+ seq: 242.02 CASE, Patrick-Ernest (Pat) b: 22 Aug 1958 w: 12
   Dec 1981 v: Yukon, OR c: 2
12 CASE, Angela-Marie b: 15 Apr 1991 in Oklahoma City, OK
12 CASE, Beverly-Ann b: 16 May 1995 in Oklahoma City, OK

242.03
11 WITTRY, Bryon-Joseph b: 10 Nov 1962 in San Jose, CA v:
   Sunnyvale, CA c: 2
+ seq: 242.03 COOLS, Karolien b: in Belgium w: 15 Jul 2000 c:
   2
12 WITTRY, Quinn-Cools b: 11 Jun 2002
12 WITTRY, Rhys-Cools b: 27 Jun 2004

11WITTRY, Steven-James b: 02 Aug 1967 in Los Gatos, CA v: San Jose, CA c: 4

+ seq: 243 BULDER, Regina-Wilhelmina b: 14 Aug 1968 in San Jose, CA w: 10 Mar 1990 v: San Jose, CA c: 4

12WITTRY, Erik-James b: 12 May 1992 in Ames, IA

12WITTRY, Sara-Elizabeth b: 09 Dec 1993 in San Jose, CA

12WITTRY, Emma-Lee b: 08 Dec 1997 in San Jose, CA

12WITTRY, Alexander-Antonius-Jacob b: 03 May 2001 in San Jose, CA

243.01

10WITTRY, Janice-Mae b: 04 Sep 1937 in Carroll, IA v: Boone, IA c: 3

+ seq: 243.01 KANNE, Ralph b: 10 Jan 1937 in Carroll, IA w: 27 Dec 1958 in Boone, IA v: Boone, IA c: 3

11KANNE, Roxanne-Maree b: 19 Oct 1959 c: 2

+ seq: 243.02 ROUSH, Kent b: 28 Feb 1960 w: 04 May 1988 c: 2

11KANNE, Jayne-Teresa b: 09 Oct 1962 c: 2

+ seq: 243.03 WELCH, Randy-Lynn b: 30 Jul 1962 w: 07 May 1990 c: 2

11KANNE, Michael-Joseph b: 23 Dec 1971 c: 2

+ seq: 243.04 MCBRIDE, Joy-Lynne b: 28 Oct 1973 w: 15 Jun 1996 in Boone, IA c: 2

243.02

11KANNE, Roxanne-Maree b: 19 Oct 1959 c: 2

+ seq: 243.02 ROUSH, Kent b: 28 Feb 1960 w: 04 May 1988 c: 2

12KANNE-ROUSH, Anne-Maree b: 12 Aug 1989

12KANNE-ROUSH, Kristine-Maree b: 23 Nov 1992

243.03

11KANNE, Jayne-Teresa b: 09 Oct 1962 c: 2

+ seq: 243.03 WELCH, Randy-Lynn b: 30 Jul 1962 w: 07 May 1990 c: 2

12WELCH, Madison-Kanne b: 18 Apr 1994

12WELCH, Erika-Rose b: 05 Sep 1997

243.04

11KANNE, Michael-Joseph b: 23 Dec 1971 c: 2
+ seq: 243.04 MCBRIDE, Joy-Lynne b: 28 Oct 1973 w: 15 Jun
1996 in Boone, IA c: 2
12KANNE, Charles-Anthony b: 04 May 2001 in Austin, MN
12KANNE, Ellen-Faith b: 31 Mar 2003

244

10[1] WITTRY, Lyle-John b: 10 Jun 1942 v: Bentonville, AR c:
2
+ seq: 244 SHAEFFER, Joan b: 02 Oct 1942 d: 21 Mar 1993 w:
29 Aug 1964 v: Bentonville, AR f: John Winters Shaeffer m:
Jean Louise Curtis c: 2
11WITTRY, Jill-Renee b: 01 Jul 1968 v: Bentonville, AR
11WITTRY, James-Nicolas (Jimmy) b: 24 Jan 1972 v: Florida
+ seq: 245 MOORE, Nicole b: 12 Sep 1974 w: 05 May 1996 in
Bentonville, AR
* 2nd Wife of [1] WITTRY, Lyle-John:
+ seq: 246 DENNIS, Connie b: Abt. 1942 d: 1995 w: 1994 v:
Fayetteville, AR
* 3rd Wife of [1] WITTRY, Lyle-John:
+ seq: 247 CAMPBELL, Cynthia (Cindy) b: 24 Mar 1951 w: 01
Mar 1996 in Fayetteville, AR

248

9 WITTRY, Bernard-Anthony (Barney) b: 13 Jan 1904 in Breda,
IA d: 06 Nov 1977 in Breda, IA v: Breda, IA o: Farmer c: 6
+ seq: 248 SNYDER, Magdalene M. b: 28 Feb 1909 in Breda, IA
d: 27 Sep 1988 in Breda, IA w: 07 Feb 1928 v: Breda, IA c: 6
10WITTRY, Della-Margery v: Manson, IA c: 6
+ seq: 248.01 NIELAND, Patrick-Edgar b: 17 Mar 1924 in Sac
County, IA d: 25 Jun 2004 in Manson, IA Cause of death:
Cancer w: 25 Aug 1948 v: Manson, IA o: Farmer f: Bernard A.
Nieland m: Mary-Ann Grote c: 6
10WITTRY, Dale-Matthew b: 06 Jan 1930 v: Carroll, IA i:
Compiled family tree o: Musician o: Factory worker, retired o:
Photographer c: 11
+ seq: 249 BAUMHOVER, Catherine-Mary b: 07 Jul 1934 w: 21
Jan 1954 v: Carroll, IA f: Bernard L. Baumhover m: Rose
Kanne c: 11
10WITTRY, John-Adrian b: 27 Mar 1931 v: Breda, IA c: 5

+ seq: 253 GEHLING, Marceal (Marri) b: 25 Jun 1935 w: 10 Apr 1956 v: Breda, IA f: William Gehling m: Agnes Staiert c: 5

10WITTRY, Romayne-Andrew (Romie) b: 10 Dec 1932 v: Carroll, IA

10WITTRY, Eugene-Irwin (Gene) b: 08 Jun 1934 in Carroll, IA d: 18 Oct 2007 in Breda, IA v: Breda, IA o: Farmer o: Operated plumbing business, cafe and tavern c: 4

+ seq: 256 PUDENZ, Joan b: 29 Sep 1934 w: 17 Jun 1954 in Mount Carmel, IA v: Breda, IA c: 4

10WITTRY, Kenneth-James b: 25 Mar 1942 v: Des Moines, IA o: Works in a prison c: 9

+ seq: 259 NELSON, Jane A b: 20 Jul 1944 w: 01 Aug 1964 v: Des. Moines, IA c: 9

248.01

10WITTRY, Della-Margery v: Manson, IA c: 6

+ seq: 248.01 NIELAND, Patrick-Edgar b: 17 Mar 1924 in Sac County, IA d: 25 Jun 2004 in Manson, IA Cause of death: Cancer w: 25 Aug 1948 v: Manson, IA o: Farmer f: Bernard A. Nieland m: Mary-Ann Grote c: 6

11[1] NIELAND, Allen-Patrick b: 25 Jun 1949 d: 14 Oct 1990 in Willilamsburg, IA v: Iowa City, IA o: Highway patrol pilot c: 4

+ seq: 248.02 AULTMAN, Bettideane b: 1949 w: 10 Jan 1970 c: 2

* 2nd Wife of [1] NIELAND, Allen-Patrick:

+ seq: 248.03 FREIE, Julie b: 17 Sep 1956 w: 03 Dec 1982 v: Iowa City, IA c: 2

11NIELAND, Daniel-Bernard (Dan) b: 29 Sep 1950 v: Fort Dodge, IA o: Telephone complex installer c: 3

+ seq: 248.04 BENNETT, Cindy b: 16 Jan 1951 w: 08 Nov 1969 v: Fort Dodge, IA c: 3

11NIELAND, Craig-Anthony b: 30 Mar 1953 c: 5

+ seq: 248.05 PELZ, Nikki-Louise b: 18 Mar 1954 w: 03 Dec 1971 c: 5

11[2] NIELAND, Douglas-Edward b: 05 May 1956 d: 14 Aug 2004 Cause of death: Cancer c: 4

+ seq: 248.06 TJEBBENS, Mary b: Abt. 1957 w: 1976 c: 2

* 2nd Wife of [2] NIELAND, Douglas-Edward:

+ seq: 248.07 WELDON, Mindy b: Abt. 1961 w: Abt. 1986 c: 2

11NIELAND, Sharon-Annette b: 27 Feb 1962 v: Manson, IA c: 2

+ seq: 248.08 JOHNSON, Craig b: 17 Aug 1957 w: 16 Jul 1983
   v: Manson, IA c: 2
11 NIELAND, Patricia-Ann (Trish) b: 20 Jan 1965 c: 2
+ seq: 248.09 WETZEL, Robert b: 31 Mar 1958 w: 19 Sep 1992
   c: 2

248.02

11 [1] NIELAND, Allen-Patrick b: 25 Jun 1949 d: 14 Oct 1990 in
   Willilamsburg, IA v: Iowa City, IA o: Highway patrol pilot c:
   4
+ seq: 248.02 AULTMAN, Bettideane b: 1949 w: 10 Jan 1970
   c: 2
12 NIELAND, Andrea b: 27 Sep 1972 c: 1
+ seq: 248.02.01 BRINLEY, Kenneth w: Jul 1998 c: 1
12 NIELAND, Jeanette b: 19 Dec 1974 c: 1
+ seq: 248.02.02 w: Abt. 2000 c: 1
* 2nd Wife of [1] NIELAND, Allen-Patrick:
+ seq: 248.03 FREIE, Julie b: 17 Sep 1956 w: 03 Dec 1982 v:
   Iowa City, IA c: 2
12 NIELAND, Eric-Allen b: 09 Sep 1986
12 NIELAND, Ryan-Patrick b: 28 Mar 1989

248.02.01

12 NIELAND, Andrea b: 27 Sep 1972 c: 1
+ seq: 248.02.01 BRINLEY, Kenneth w: Jul 1998 c: 1
13 BRINLEY, Courtney b: 20 Jul 2002

248.02.02

12 NIELAND, Jeanette b: 19 Dec 1974 c: 1
+ seq: 248.02.02 w: Abt. 2000 c: 1
13 NIELAND, Oscar-Joseph

248.04

11 NIELAND, Daniel-Bernard (Dan) b: 29 Sep 1950 v: Fort
   Dodge, IA o: Telephone complex installer c: 3
+ seq: 248.04 BENNETT, Cindy b: 16 Jan 1951 w: 08 Nov 1969
   v: Fort Dodge, IA c: 3
12 NIELAND, Chad-Anthony b: 21 Jul 1973 c: 2
+ seq: 248.04.01 ANDERSON, Melanie w: 28 Aug 1998 c: 2
12 NIELAND, Lisa b: 18 Jun 1980
12 NIELAND, Lindsay b: 29 Aug 1984

+ seq: 248.04.50 UNDERBERG, Gabriel w: 30 Sep 2006 in Fort Dodge, IA

248.04.01
12 NIELAND, Chad-Anthony b: 21 Jul 1973 c: 2
+ seq: 248.04.01 ANDERSON, Melanie w: 28 Aug 1998 c: 2
13 NIELAND, Ashley-Susan b: 21 Dec 1999
13 NIELAND, Allyson b: 19 Feb 2004

248.05
11 NIELAND, Craig-Anthony b: 30 Mar 1953 c: 5
+ seq: 248.05 PELZ, Nikki-Louise b: 18 Mar 1954 w: 03 Dec 1971 c: 5
12 NIELAND, Jennifer-Lee b: 05 May 1972 c: 1
+ seq: 248.05.00 w: Abt. 1993 c: 1
12 NIELAND, LeAnn b: 18 Mar 1975 c: 1
+ seq: 248.05.01 BANWART, Scott b: 1972 w: 13 Apr 1996 c: 1
12 NIELAND, Kimberly (Kim) b: 31 May 1980 c: 1
+ seq: 248.05.50 SMITH, Justin B. b: 17 Dec 1979 w: 02 Aug 2003 c: 1
12 NIELAND, Kelly-Josephine b: 31 May 1980
12 NIELAND, Mallory-Ann b: 09 Jan 1987

248.05.00
12 NIELAND, Jennifer-Lee b: 05 May 1972 c: 1
+ seq: 248.05.00 w: Abt. 1993 c: 1
13 NIELAND, Ian b: 21 Apr 1994

248.05.01
12 NIELAND, LeAnn b: 18 Mar 1975 c: 1
+ seq: 248.05.01 BANWART, Scott b: 1972 w: 13 Apr 1996 c: 1
13 BANWART, Grace-Elizabeth b: 07 Dec 2004

248.05.50
12 NIELAND, Kimberly (Kim) b: 31 May 1980 c: 1
+ seq: 248.05.50 SMITH, Justin B. b: 17 Dec 1979 w: 02 Aug 2003 c: 1
13 SMITH, Jackson-Blake b: 12 Nov 2004

248.06

11[1] NIELAND, Douglas-Edward b: 05 May 1956 d: 14 Aug
 2004 Cause of death: Cancer c: 4
+ seq: 248.06 TJEBBENS, Mary b: Abt. 1957 w: 1976 c: 2
12 NIELAND, Kori b: 04 Nov 1976
12 NIELAND, Anthony (Tony) b: 04 Dec 1978
 * 2nd Wife of [1] NIELAND, Douglas-Edward:
+ seq: 248.07 WELDON, Mindy b: Abt. 1961 w: Abt. 1986 c: 2
12 NIELAND, Kaylene (Katie) b: 07 Jul 1986
12 NIELAND, Kalene (Kalle) b: 10 Jun 1989

248.08

11 NIELAND, Sharon-Annette b: 27 Feb 1962 v: Manson, IA c: 2
+ seq: 248.08 JOHNSON, Craig b: 17 Aug 1957 w: 16 Jul 1983
 v: Manson, IA c: 2
12 JOHNSON, Laura-Kristine b: 11 Jul 1989
12 JOHNSON, Emma-Katherine b: 21 Feb 1995

248.09

11 NIELAND, Patricia-Ann (Trish) b: 20 Jan 1965 c: 2
+ seq: 248.09 WETZEL, Robert b: 31 Mar 1958 w: 19 Sep 1992
 c: 2
12 WETZEL, William-Robert (Will) b: 17 Feb 1999
12 WETZEL, Lucas-Alan b: 28 Aug 2000

249

10 WITTRY, Dale-Matthew b: 06 Jan 1930 v: Carroll, IA i:
 Compiled family tree o: Musician o: Factory worker, retired o:
 Photographer c: 11
+ seq: 249 BAUMHOVER, Catherine-Mary b: 07 Jul 1934 w:
 21 Jan 1954 v: Carroll, IA f: Bernard L. Baumhover m: Rose
 Kanne c: 11
11 WITTRY, Mary-Jo-Rose b: 24 Dec 1954 v: University City,
 MO o: Writer c: 4
+ seq: 249.01 MASON, James-Foster b: 19 May 1952 in Iowa
 Falls, IA w: 03 Sep 1976 v: University City, MO o: Engineer
 c: 4
11 WITTRY, Sandra-Mae (Sandy) b: 29 Jan 1957 v: Carroll, IA
 o: Nurse c: 2
+ seq: 249.02 CAYLOR, Jeffrey-Reed b: 08 Oct 1958 w: 10 Jul
 1982 v: Carroll, IA o: Chief of police c: 2

11 WITTRY, Dean-Patrick b: 01 Apr 1958 v: Des Moines, IA c: 2
+ seq: 250 DE PHILLIPS, Monica-Joanne b: 19 Feb 1959 w: 29
    May 1982 v: Des Moines, IA c: 2
11 WITTRY, Janet-Margaret b: 29 Aug 1959 v: Mt. Vernon, IA
    o: Lab technician c: 4
+ seq: 250.01 DIETRICH, Dennis-Allen b: 27 Aug 1957 w: 06
    Jun 1981 v: Mt. Vernon, IA o: Grocer c: 4
11 WITTRY, Susan-Marie b: 12 Aug 1960 v: Wall Lake, IA c: 3
+ seq: 250.02 NUETZMAN, Steven b: 28 Aug 1957 w: 20 Sep
    1980 v: Wall Lake, IA o: Coach o: Farmer c: 3
11 WITTRY, Richard-Gerald (Dick) b: 18 Oct 1961 v: Indianola,
    IA c: 2
+ seq: 251 CARPENTER, Rebecca (Becky) b: 25 May 1963 w:
    02 Sep 1983 v: Indianola, IA f: Jim Carpenter m: Betty
    Horner c: 2
11 WITTRY, Ann b: 14 Jan 1963 d: 14 Jan 1963
11 WITTRY, Mark-Paul b: 31 Jul 1964 v: Dubuque, IA
+ seq: 252 GALLUP, Cynthia-Elaine (Cyndi) b: 22 Aug 1962 w:
    16 May 1992 v: San Marcos, TX
11 WITTRY, Margaret-Joan (Margy) b: 27 Nov 1965 v: Kansas
    City, MO c: 2
+ seq: 252.01 ANDERSON, Kevin b: 26 Nov 1964 w: 22 Oct
    1988 v: Kansas City, MO c: 2
11 WITTRY, Judith-Mary (Judy) b: 21 May 1967 v: Woolstock,
    IA c: 3
+ seq: 252.02 WAGNER, Paul b: 05 May 1967 w: 29 Jun 1991
    v: Woolstock, IA c: 3
11 WITTRY, Timothy-Bernard (Tim) b: 21 Feb 1975 v: Carroll,
    IA i: Student at Briar Cliff o: Paralegal with Grete and Sidney
    Law Firm

249.01

11 WITTRY, Mary-Jo-Rose b: 24 Dec 1954 v: University City,
    MO o: Writer c: 4
+ seq: 249.01 MASON, James-Foster b: 19 May 1952 in Iowa
    Falls, IA w: 03 Sep 1976 v: University City, MO o: Engineer
    c: 4
12 MASON, Neal-Bernard b: 08 Mar 1982
12 MASON, John-Foster b: 18 May 1984 d: 16 Jul 1984 Cause of
    death: Sudden infant death syndrome
12 MASON, Anna-Louise b: 06 Feb 1986 d: 06 Feb 1986

12MASON, Eleonore-Anna b: 18 Sep 1987

249.02

11WITTRY, Sandra-Mae (Sandy) b: 29 Jan 1957 v: Carroll, IA
  o: Nurse c: 2
+ seq: 249.02 CAYLOR, Jeffrey-Reed b: 08 Oct 1958 w: 10 Jul
  1982 v: Carroll, IA o: Chief of police c: 2
12CAYLOR, Amy-Elizabeth b: 07 Dec 1985
12CAYLOR, Kristine-Anne b: 08 Jul 1987

250

11WITTRY, Dean-Patrick b: 01 Apr 1958 v: Des Moines, IA c: 2
+ seq: 250 DE PHILLIPS, Monica-Joanne b: 19 Feb 1959 w: 29
  May 1982 v: Des Moines, IA c: 2
12WITTRY, Caryn-Ann b: 05 Nov 1987
12WITTRY, Jayne-Ann b: 17 May 1990

250.01

11WITTRY, Janet-Margaret b: 29 Aug 1959 v: Mt. Vernon, IA
  o: Lab technician c: 4
+ seq: 250.01 DIETRICH, Dennis-Allen b: 27 Aug 1957 w: 06
  Jun 1981 v: Mt. Vernon, IA o: Grocer c: 4
12DIETRICH, Margaret-Ann (Micki) b: 02 Jan 1985
12DIETRICH, Nicholas-Owen b: 15 Mar 1986
12DIETRICH, Peter b: 07 Nov 1987
12DIETRICH, Joseph-Edward-August b: 19 Feb 1991

250.02

11WITTRY, Susan-Marie b: 12 Aug 1960 v: Wall Lake, IA c: 3
+ seq: 250.02 NUETZMAN, Steven b: 28 Aug 1957 w: 20 Sep
  1980 v: Wall Lake, IA o: Coach o: Farmer c: 3
12NUETZMAN, Matthew-Jack b: 05 Oct 1981
12NUETZMAN, Shawn-Michael b: 07 Oct 1984
12NUETZMAN, Holly-Sue b: 19 Apr 1992

251

11WITTRY, Richard-Gerald (Dick) b: 18 Oct 1961 v: Indianola,
  IA c: 2
+ seq: 251 CARPENTER, Rebecca (Becky) b: 25 May 1963 w:
  02 Sep 1983 v: Indianola, IA f: Jim Carpenter m: Betty
  Horner c: 2

12 WITTRY, Allyson-Marie b: 06 Sep 1989
12 WITTRY, Brooke-Lynn b: 26 Apr 1993

252.01

11 WITTRY, Margaret-Joan (Margy) b: 27 Nov 1965 v: Kansas City, MO c: 2
+ seq: 252.01 ANDERSON, Kevin b: 26 Nov 1964 w: 22 Oct 1988 v: Kansas City, MO c: 2
12 ANDERSON, Michael-Joseph b: 28 Mar 1994
12 ANDERSON, Jacob-Thomas b: 15 Oct 1996

252.02

11 WITTRY, Judith-Mary (Judy) b: 21 May 1967 v: Woolstock, IA c: 3
+ seq: 252.02 WAGNER, Paul b: 05 May 1967 w: 29 Jun 1991 v: Woolstock, IA c: 3
12 WAGNER, Amanda-Marie b: 18 Apr 1992
12 WAGNER, Adam-Joseph b: 30 Jun 1994
12 WAGNER, Kaitlyn-Rose b: 17 Dec 1999 in Ames, IA

253

10 WITTRY, John-Adrian b: 27 Mar 1931 v: Breda, IA c: 5
+ seq: 253 GEHLING, Marceal (Marri) b: 25 Jun 1935 w: 10 Apr 1956 v: Breda, IA f: William Gehling m: Agnes Staiert c: 5
11 WITTRY, Barbara-Kay b: 17 Jan 1957 v: Breda, IA c: 3
+ seq: 253.01 HOFFMAN, Mark b: 24 Jan 1955 w: 09 Aug 1979 v: Breda, IA c: 3
11 WITTRY, David-John (Dave) b: 12 Aug 1958 v: Breda, IA c: 3
+ seq: 254 BRENNER, Mary b: 28 Dec 1960 w: 07 Aug 1982 v: Breda, IA c: 3
11 WITTRY, Kevin-Patrick b: 13 Jul 1962 v: Jefferson, IA c: 3
+ seq: 255 PEARSON, Gail b: 03 Jun 1960 w: 02 May 1987 v: Jefferson, IA c: 3
11 WITTRY, Kristy-Agnes b: 22 Jul 1965 v: Boone, IA o: Asst. to director of mgt. services c: 2
+ seq: 255.01 EASTMAN, Robb-John b: 09 Dec 1961 w: 08 Apr 1989 v: Boone, IA o: Eastman Construction c: 2
11 WITTRY, Keith-Joseph b: 22 Jul 1965 v: Sac City, IA o: Photographer

253.01

11WITTRY, Barbara-Kay b: 17 Jan 1957 v: Breda, IA c: 3

+ seq: 253.01 HOFFMAN, Mark b: 24 Jan 1955 w: 09 Aug 1979
   v: Breda, IA c: 3

12HOFFMAN, Brianna-Kay b: 12 May 1983

12HOFFMAN, Karolina-Marie b: 28 Mar 1985

12HOFFMAN, Steven-Eugene b: 03 Nov 1986

254

11WITTRY, David-John (Dave) b: 12 Aug 1958 v: Breda, IA c:
   3

+ seq: 254 BRENNER, Mary b: 28 Dec 1960 w: 07 Aug 1982 v:
   Breda, IA c: 3

12WITTRY, Matthew-James b: 28 Apr 1984

12WITTRY, Michael (Mike) b: 14 Aug 1986 i: Majoring in
   Business Marketing and Business Management o: Student at
   Buena Vista University

12WITTRY, Beth-Nicole b: 05 Aug 1992

255

11WITTRY, Kevin-Patrick b: 13 Jul 1962 v: Jefferson, IA c: 3

+ seq: 255 PEARSON, Gail b: 03 Jun 1960 w: 02 May 1987 v:
   Jefferson, IA c: 3

12WITTRY, Marie-Louise b: 24 Feb 1988

12WITTRY, Jessica-Lee b: 04 Jan 1991

12WITTRY, Jacob-Nels b: 18 Apr 1997 in Boone, IA

255.01

11WITTRY, Kristy-Agnes b: 22 Jul 1965 v: Boone, IA o: Asst.
   to director of mgt. services c: 2

+ seq: 255.01 EASTMAN, Robb-John b: 09 Dec 1961 w: 08 Apr
   1989 v: Boone, IA o: Eastman Construction c: 2

12EASTMAN, Tyler-Jorden b: 29 Mar 1991

12EASTMAN, Erin-Nicole b: 05 Feb 1995

256

10WITTRY, Eugene-Irwin (Gene) b: 08 Jun 1934 v: Breda, IA c:
   4

+ seq: 256 PUDENZ, Joan b: 29 Sep 1934 w: 17 Jun 1954 v:
   Breda, IA c: 4

11WITTRY, Thomas B. (Tom) b: 03 Jul 1955 v: Breda, IA o:

Farmer c: 3

+ seq: 257 HEINRICHS, Sara b: 02 Sep 1955 w: 08 Oct 1983 v: Breda, IA c: 3

11 WITTRY, Peggy-Ann b: 07 Jun 1956 v: Carroll, IA o: Nurse c: 3

+ seq: 257.01 LEITING, Marc b: 26 May 1952 w: 14 Jun 1975 v: Carroll, IA c: 3

11 WITTRY, Debra-Kay b: 09 Aug 1959 c: 3

+ seq: 257.02 BRECKENRIDGE, Douglas-Lane b: 10 Mar 1956 w: 19 Aug 1979 c: 3

11 WITTRY, James-Dale (Jim) b: 26 Jun 1966 v: Des Moines, IA c: 3

+ seq: 258 STUHR, Jodi-Lynn b: Abt. 1965 w: Abt. 1990 v: Des Moines, IA c: 3

257

11 WITTRY, Thomas B. (Tom) b: 03 Jul 1955 v: Breda, IA o: Farmer c: 3

+ seq: 257 HEINRICHS, Sara b: 02 Sep 1955 w: 08 Oct 1983 v: Breda, IA c: 3

12 WITTRY, Ross-Thomas b: 10 Jun 1986

12 WITTRY, Rachel-Sara b: 10 Jun 1986

12 WITTRY, Roxanne b: 1987

257.01

11 WITTRY, Peggy-Ann b: 07 Jun 1956 v: Carroll, IA o: Nurse c: 3

+ seq: 257.01 LEITING, Marc b: 26 May 1952 w: 14 Jun 1975 v: Carroll, IA c: 3

12 LEITING, Melissa-Ann b: 15 Nov 1976

12 LEITING, Melanie-Rose b: 10 Jun 1979

12 LEITING, Megan-Michelle b: 05 Apr 1983

257.02

11 WITTRY, Debra-Kay b: 09 Aug 1959 c: 3

+ seq: 257.02 BRECKENRIDGE, Douglas-Lane b: 10 Mar 1956 w: 19 Aug 1979 c: 3

12 BRECKENRIDGE, Tiffany b: 30 Mar 1980

+ seq: 257.10 RICKBIEL, Eric w: 05 Jul 2002 in Des Moines, IA

12 BRECKENRIDGE, Aaron-Alexander b: 20 Sep 1981

12 BRECKENRIDGE, Laura-Ann b: 20 Nov 1983

258

11 WITTRY, James-Dale (Jim) b: 26 Jun 1966 v: Des Moines, IA
c: 3
+ seq: 258 STUHR, Jodi-Lynn b: Abt. 1965 w: Abt. 1990 v:
Des Moines, IA c: 3
12 WITTRY, Andrew-James b: 06 Mar 1998 in Des Moines, IA
12 WITTRY, Madalene b: 26 Mar 1999
12 WITTRY, Alyssa b: 11 Jun 2001

259

10 WITTRY, Kenneth-James b: 25 Mar 1942 v: Des Moines, IA
o: Works in a prison c: 9
+ seq: 259 NELSON, Jane A b: 20 Jul 1944 w: 01 Aug 1964 v:
Des. Moines, IA c: 9
11 WITTRY, Karman-Maria b: 04 May 1965 v: Des Moines, IA
o: Book editor c: 2
+ seq: 259.01 HOTCHKISS, Todd-Wesley b: Abt. 1960 w: Abt.
1990 o: Architect c: 2
11 WITTRY, Anthony-Joseph (Tony) b: 26 Oct 1966 v: San
Francisco, CA c: 2
+ seq: 259.01.50 CHAN, Sonya w: 25 Sep 2004 in Courtland, CA
c: 2
11 WITTRY, Christopher-John (Chris) b: 21 Feb 1968 v: Fort
Madison, IA o: Engineer c: 2
+ seq: 259.02 MARTINEZ, Cindy w: Abt. 1995 v: Fort Madison,
IA c: 2
11 WITTRY, Kandance-Ann (Kandy) b: 07 Oct 1969 v:
Marshalltown, IA o: Recreational activity
11 WITTRY, Melissa-Sue (Missy) b: 14 Feb 1975
11 WITTRY, Melanie-Jane (Mel) b: 13 Jul 1977 o: Electrical
engineer c: 1
+ seq: 259.10 DYKSTRA, Andres-George (Andy) w: 28 Aug
2004 c: 1
11 WITTRY, Benjamin-James (Benji) b: 23 Jan 1979 v: Ames, IA
o: History student
11 WITTRY, Nichole-Noel (Nikki) b: 13 Dec 1983
11 WITTRY, Alexander-Michael (Alex) b: 25 Jun 1985

259.01

11 WITTRY, Karman-Maria b: 04 May 1965 v: Des Moines, IA
o: Book editor c: 2

+ seq: 259.01 HOTCHKISS, Todd-Wesley b: Abt. 1960 w: Abt.
   1990 o: Architect c: 2
12 HOTCHKISS, Ruby-Kathryn b: 13 Sep 1997
12 HOTCHKISS, Theo-James b: 26 Aug 2000

259.01.50
11 WITTRY, Anthony-Joseph (Tony) b: 26 Oct 1966 v: San
   Francisco, CA c: 2
+ seq: 259.01.50 CHAN, Sonya w: 25 Sep 2004 in Courtland, CA
   c: 2
12 CHAN-WITTRY, Brendan-Lee b: 05 Apr 2006 in San
   Francisco, CA
12 CHAN-WITTRY, Derek L. b: 25 Sep 2007 in San Francisco,
   CA

259.02
11 WITTRY, Christopher-John (Chris) b: 21 Feb 1968 v: Fort
   Madison, IA o: Engineer c: 2
+ seq: 259.02 MARTINEZ, Cindy w: Abt. 1995 v: Fort
   Madison, IA c: 2
12 WITTRY, Cecelia b: 13 Feb 1999
12 WITTRY, Christipher-Jude b: 18 Feb 2002

259.10
11 WITTRY, Melanie-Jane (Mel) b: 13 Jul 1977 o: Electrical
   engineer c: 1
+ seq: 259.10 DYKSTRA, Andres-George (Andy) w: 28 Aug
   2004 c: 1
12 DYKSTRA, Carson b: 22 Oct 2007 in Naperville, IL

260
 9 WITTRY, Andrew-Nicholas b: 13 May 1906 in Mount Carmel,
   IA d: 20 May 1997 in Carroll, IA v: Carroll, IA o: Salesman
   for Moorman's Feed Co. o: Dairy farmer o: Dealer for Schettler
   Seed Co. c: 5
+ seq: 260 WOLTERMAN, Leola b: 03 Dec 1911 in Breda, IA
   d: 07 Aug 1986 in Mount Carmel, IA w: 03 Jan 1933 in Breda,
   IA v: Carroll, IA o: Homemaker c: 5
10 WITTRY, Arden-John (Art) b: 13 Apr 1933 in Mount Carmel,
   IA d: 05 Feb 1960 in Mount Carmel, IA Cause of death: Cancer
   i: Served in military from 1956 o: Truck driver

10 WITTRY, Ruth-Ann b: 17 Jun 1934 in Mount Carmel, IA v:
Hamlin, IA o: Housewife c: 5
+ seq: 260.01 BOCK, Howard-Paul b: 09 Feb 1932 in Raeville,
NE d: 13 Mar 2002 in Hamlin, IA w: 21 Nov 1953 in Mount
Carmel, IA v: Hamlin, IA o: Farmer f: Cornelius F. Bock m:
Mayme-Katherine Heithoff c: 5
10 WITTRY, Louis-Leroy b: 10 Apr 1937 in Carroll County, IA v:
Armstrong, IA o: Owned and operated grocery stores c: 4
+ seq: 261 STRACKE, Marie H. b: 10 Jan 1939 w: 11 Apr 1959
v: Armstrong, IA o: Ran a catering service c: 4
10 WITTRY, Vera-Mae b: 04 Nov 1938 in Mount Carmel, IA v:
Dedham, IA o: Bank Teller c: 7
+ seq: 261.03 DERNER, Eugene A. b: 19 Sep 1932 in Auburn,
IA w: 26 Sep 1959 in Mount Carmel, IA v: Dedham, IA f:
Arthur Derner m: Margerite Grote c: 7
10 WITTRY, Marcia-Lou b: 20 Sep 1940 in Carroll, IA v: Carroll,
IA c: 4
+ seq: 261.08 WIEDERIN, Eugene (Gene) b: 02 Jun 1940 in
Carroll, IA w: 20 Jan 1962 in Mount Carmel, IA v: Carroll, IA
i: Served in military from 1963 to 1965 o: Postal Clerk f: Carl
Wiederin m: Rosina Staiert c: 4

260.01
10 WITTRY, Ruth-Ann b: 17 Jun 1934 in Mount Carmel, IA v:
Hamlin, IA o: Housewife c: 5
+ seq: 260.01 BOCK, Howard-Paul b: 09 Feb 1932 in Raeville,
NE d: 13 Mar 2002 in Hamlin, IA w: 21 Nov 1953 in Mount
Carmel, IA v: Hamlin, IA o: Farmer f: Cornelius F. Bock m:
Mayme-Katherine Heithoff c: 5
11 [1] BOCK, Sharon-Kay b: 12 Apr 1955 in Carroll, IA v:
Overland Park, KS o: Marketing c: 3
+ seq: 260.02 BOND, Patrick b: Abt. 1955 w: 17 Jul 1976 in Des
Moines, IA
* 2nd Husband of [1] BOCK, Sharon-Kay:
+ seq: 260.03 MILLER, Frederick-George (Fred) b: 20 Jun 1950
w: 17 Apr 1982 in Audubon, IA v: Overland Park, KS c: 3
11 BOCK, Lori-Marie b: 28 May 1958 v: Jolley, IA o: Postmaster
c: 1
+ seq: 260.04 SCHAFFER, Dennis-Ray b: 09 Feb 1951 in Lake
City, IA w: 08 Mar 1980 in Audubon, IA v: Jolley, IA c: 1
11 BOCK, Susan-Eileen b: 30 Mar 1961 in Carroll, IA v:

Cambridge, IA o: CPA o: VP and controller of Iowa Cubs ball team c: 2

+ seq: 260.05 TOLLEFSON, Steven-Karl (Steve) b: 20 Jul 1960 in Virginia, WI w: 09 Jul 1983 in Audubon, IA v: Cambridge, IA o: Tax consultant c: 2

11 BOCK, Lisa-Ann b: 22 Jun 1965 in Carroll, IA v: Van Meter, IA o: Registered nurse c: 3

+ seq: 260.06 BENTON, Michael-Dean (Mike) b: 30 Jan 1965 in Audubon, IA w: 11 Nov 1989 in Audubon, IA v: Van Meter, IA o: Salesman c: 3

11 BOCK, Christopher-Paul b: 21 Sep 1974 in Carroll, IA v: Kankakee, IL o: Systems consultant c: 1

+ seq: 260.07 RENHOLEN, Wendy-Michelle b: 15 Jun 1975 in Cedar Rapida, IA w: 06 Sep 2003 in Marion, IA v: Kankakee, IL f: Robert RInholn m: Carolyn Emerson c: 1

260.02

11 [1] BOCK, Sharon-Kay b: 12 Apr 1955 in Carroll, IA v: Overland Park, KS o: Marketing c: 3

+ seq: 260.02 BOND, Patrick b: Abt. 1955 w: 17 Jul 1976 in Des Moines, IA

* 2nd Husband of [1] BOCK, Sharon-Kay:

+ seq: 260.03 MILLER, Frederick-George (Fred) b: 20 Jun 1950 w: 17 Apr 1982 in Audubon, IA v: Overland Park, KS c: 3

12 MILLER, Barbara-Ann b: 18 Jul 1982 in Sioux City, IA

12 MILLER, Robert-Thomas (Bob) b: 18 Mar 1985 in Des Moines, IA

12 MILLER, William-Howard (Bill) b: 19 Sep 1987 in Des Moines, IA

260.04

11 BOCK, Lori-Marie b: 28 May 1958 v: Jolley, IA o: Postmaster c: 1

+ seq: 260.04 SCHAFFER, Dennis-Ray b: 09 Feb 1951 in Lake City, IA w: 08 Mar 1980 in Audubon, IA v: Jolley, IA c: 1

12 SCHAFFER, Brent-Lee b: 13 Jun 1980 in Lake City, IA v: Manson, IA c: 1

+ seq: 260.04.01 FRYER, Kelly b: 24 Jan 1982 in Lake City, IA w: 12 Apr 2003 v: Manson, IA f: Dean Fryer m: Candance Melohn c: 1

260.04.01

12SCHAFFER, Brent-Lee b: 13 Jun 1980 in Lake City, IA v: Manson, IA c: 1

+ seq: 260.04.01 FRYER, Kelly b: 24 Jan 1982 in Lake City, IA w: 12 Apr 2003 v: Manson, IA f: Dean Fryer m: Candance Melohn c: 1

13SCHAFFER, Ashley-Kay b: 03 Aug 2006 in Fort Dodge, IA

260.05

11BOCK, Susan-Eileen b: 30 Mar 1961 in Carroll, IA v: Cambridge, IA o: CPA o: VP and controller of Iowa Cubs ball team c: 2

+ seq: 260.05 TOLLEFSON, Steven-Karl (Steve) b: 20 Jul 1960 in Virginia, WI w: 09 Jul 1983 in Audubon, IA v: Cambridge, IA o: Tax consultant c: 2

12TOLLEFSON, Cael-Andrew b: 21 Jul 2005 in Des Moines, IA

12TOLLEFSON, Katie-Jean b: 21 Jul 2005 in Des Moines, IA

260.06

11BOCK, Lisa-Ann b: 22 Jun 1965 in Carroll, IA v: Van Meter, IA o: Registered nurse c: 3

+ seq: 260.06 BENTON, Michael-Dean (Mike) b: 30 Jan 1965 in Audubon, IA w: 11 Nov 1989 in Audubon, IA v: Van Meter, IA o: Salesman c: 3

12BENTON, Marcus-Dean b: 17 Sep 1992 in Des Moines, IA

12BENTON, Spencer-Michael b: 09 Feb 1996 in Des Moines, IA

12BENTON, Isaac-Howard b: 03 Nov 1997 in Des Moines, IA

260.07

11BOCK, Christopher-Paul b: 21 Sep 1974 in Carroll, IA v: Kankakee, IL o: Systems consultant c: 1

+ seq: 260.07 RENHOLEN, Wendy-Michelle b: 15 Jun 1975 in Cedar Rapida, IA w: 06 Sep 2003 in Marion, IA v: Kankakee, IL f: Robert RInholn m: Carolyn Emerson c: 1

12BOCK, Jocelyn-Ann b: 19 Sep 2006 in Peoria, IL

261

10WITTRY, Louis-Leroy b: 10 Apr 1937 in Carroll County, IA v: Armstrong, IA o: Owned and operated grocery stores c: 4

+ seq: 261 STRACKE, Marie H. b: 10 Jan 1939 w: 11 Apr 1959 v: Armstrong, IA o: Ran a catering service c: 4

11 WITTRY, Linda-Louise b: 03 Sep 1960 v: Mason City, IA o:
  Employed by Principle Financial c: 2
 + seq: 261.01 MESSMORE, Gregory (Greg) b: 10 Apr 1960 w:
  23 Jun 1984 v: Mason City, IA o: Basketball coach o:
  Midwest Region, Inc. c: 2
11 WITTRY, Nancy-Kay b: 12 Sep 1962 in Carroll County, IA v:
  Ankeny, IA o: Employed at Principle Financial c: 2
 + seq: 261.02 TJARKS, Michael b: 26 Dec 1961 in Iowa Falls,
  IA w: 03 May 1986 in Iowa Falls, IA v: Ankeny, IA o: Vice
  President of Iowa Limestone c: 2
11 WITTRY, Karen-Ann b: 20 Dec 1963 in Carroll County, IA v:
  Springfield, TN o: Human Resources
 + seq: 261.02.01 SCHUMACHER, Greg b: 30 Dec 1962 in Iowa
  Falls, IA w: 11 Jul 1987 in Iowa Falls, IA v: Springfield, TN
  o: Food service manager
11 WITTRY, Mark-Alan b: 06 Apr 1967 in Carroll, IA v: Ankeny,
  IA o: Automobile Sales Manager c: 1
 + seq: 261.02.02 BREUER, Jaci b: 14 Mar 1975 in Fairmont,
  MN w: 01 Jun 1996 in Armstrong, IA c: 1

261.01
11 WITTRY, Linda-Louise b: 03 Sep 1960 v: Mason City, IA o:
  Employed by Principle Financial c: 2
 + seq: 261.01 MESSMORE, Gregory (Greg) b: 10 Apr 1960 w:
  23 Jun 1984 v: Mason City, IA o: Basketball coach o:
  Midwest Region, Inc. c: 2
12 MESSMORE, Haley b: 31 Aug 1992 in Mason City, IA
12 MESSMORE, Andrew-James (A. J.) b: 18 Feb 1988 in
  Waterloo, IA d: 29 Oct 1998 in Mason City, IA Cause of death:
  bone cancer v: Mason City, IA

261.02
11 WITTRY, Nancy-Kay b: 12 Sep 1962 in Carroll County, IA v:
  Ankeny, IA o: Employed at Principle Financial c: 2
 + seq: 261.02 TJARKS, Michael b: 26 Dec 1961 in Iowa Falls, IA
  w: 03 May 1986 in Iowa Falls, IA v: Ankeny, IA o: Vice
  President of Iowa Limestone c: 2
12 TJARKS, Aaron b: 05 Mar 1989
12 TJARKS, Avery (Auri) b: 20 Nov 1991

261.02.02

11 WITTRY, Mark-Alan b: 06 Apr 1967 in Carroll, IA v: Ankeny,
IA o: Automobile Sales Manager c: 1
+ seq: 261.02.02 BREUER, Jaci b: 14 Mar 1975 in Fairmont,
MN w: 01 Jun 1996 in Armstrong, IA c: 1
12 WITTRY, Christian b: 08 Apr 1998

261.03

10 WITTRY, Vera-Mae b: 04 Nov 1938 in Mount Carmel, IA v:
Dedham, IA o: Bank Teller c: 7
+ seq: 261.03 DERNER, Eugene A. b: 19 Sep 1932 in Auburn, IA
w: 26 Sep 1959 in Mount Carmel, IA v: Dedham, IA f: Arthur
Derner m: Margerite Grote c: 7
11 DERNER, Dale-Anthony b: 05 Jul 1960 in Carroll, IA v:
Dedham, IA o: Fire equipmant salesman c: 2
+ seq: 261.04 GRETTENBERG, Jeanean b: 27 Sep 1959 w: 23
Apr 1983 in Carroll, IA c: 2
11 DERNER, Janet-Marie b: 07 Jan 1962 in Carroll, IA v:
Creston, IA o: Supervisor in Bunn-O-Matic Corp. c: 2
+ seq: 261.05 SCHULTE, Dean-Edgar b: 05 Jul 1962 w: 21 Mar
1987 in Dedham, IA v: Creston, IA o: Safety and
environmental superintendent f: Gerald Schulte m: Peg Neil c:
2
11 DERNER, Carol-Ann b: 09 Apr 1963 in Carroll, IA v: Carroll,
IA o: Office manager c: 2
+ seq: 261.06 TIGGES, Mark-Alan b: 29 May 1963 in Carroll, IA
w: 21 Jul 1983 v: Carroll, IA o: Cafe owner f: Don Tigges m:
Marlene Rienart c: 2
11 DERNER, Mary-Jo b: 19 Mar 1965 in Carroll, IA v: Dedham,
IA o: Registered nurse c: 2
+ seq: 261.07 MIKKELSEN, Steve b: 02 Sep 1963 in Carroll, IA
w: 16 Apr 1988 in Dedham, IA v: Dedham, IA o: Salesman f:
Donald Mikkelsen m: Louise Gross c: 2
11 DERNER, John-Arthur b: 13 Jan 1968 v: Dedham, IA i:
Served in military from 1992 to 1997 o: Parts and Service
Manager
11 DERNER, Tony-Joe b: 23 Feb 1972 in Carroll, IA v: Dedham,
IA o: Heavy duty sales and service c: 2
+ seq: 261.07.01 DANNER, Lori-Ann b: 11 Dec 1973 in Carroll,
IA w: 19 Sep 1999 in Dedham, IA v: Dedham, IA o: Travel
agent o: Accountant c: 2

11DERNER, Pat-Alan b: 01 Nov 1973 in Carroll, IA v: Dedham,
   IA o: Electrician c: 2
+ seq: 261.07.02 TIGGES, Jennifer-Marie b: 16 May 1977 in
   Carroll, IA w: 15 Mar 1997 in Dedham, IA v: Dedham, IA f:
   Gary Tigges m: Lola Fischer c: 2

261.04
11DERNER, Dale-Anthony b: 05 Jul 1960 in Carroll, IA v:
   Dedham, IA o: Fire equipmant salesman c: 2
+ seq: 261.04 GRETTENBERG, Jeanean b: 27 Sep 1959 w: 23
   Apr 1983 in Carroll, IA c: 2
12DERNER, Callie-Bliss b: 24 Jan 1984 c: 1
12DERNER, Betsy-Ann b: 22 Aug 1988

261.05
11DERNER, Janet-Marie b: 07 Jan 1962 in Carroll, IA v:
   Creston, IA o: Supervisor in Bunn-O-Matic Corp. c: 2
+ seq: 261.05 SCHULTE, Dean-Edgar b: 05 Jul 1962 w: 21 Mar
   1987 in Dedham, IA v: Creston, IA o: Safety and
   environmental superintendent f: Gerald Schulte m: Peg Neil c:
   2
12SCHULTE, Alison-Marie b: 27 Jul 1986
12SCHULTE, Nicholas-Dean b: 10 Apr 1989

261.06
11DERNER, Carol-Ann b: 09 Apr 1963 in Carroll, IA v: Carroll,
   IA o: Office manager c: 2
+ seq: 261.06 TIGGES, Mark-Alan b: 29 May 1963 in Carroll,
   IA w: 21 Jul 1983 v: Carroll, IA o: Cafe owner f: Don Tigges
   m: Marlene Rienart c: 2
12TIGGES, Benjamin-Lee b: 06 Aug 1985
12TIGGES, Emily-Ann b: 12 Dec 1987

261.07
11DERNER, Mary-Jo b: 19 Mar 1965 in Carroll, IA v: Dedham,
   IA o: Registered nurse c: 2
+ seq: 261.07 MIKKELSEN, Steve b: 02 Sep 1963 in Carroll, IA
   w: 16 Apr 1988 in Dedham, IA v: Dedham, IA o: Salesman f:
   Donald Mikkelsen m: Louise Gross c: 2
12MIKKELSEN, Adam b: 20 Mar 1990 in Carroll, IA
12MIKKELSEN, Brittney b: 16 Feb 1995 in Carroll, IA

261.07.01

11DERNER, Tony-Joe b: 23 Feb 1972 in Carroll, IA v: Dedham,
  IA o: Heavy duty sales and service c: 2
 + seq: 261.07.01 DANNER, Lori-Ann b: 11 Dec 1973 in Carroll,
  IA w: 19 Sep 1999 in Dedham, IA v: Dedham, IA o: Travel
  agent o: Accountant c: 2
12DERNER, Abby-Elizabeth b: 21 Jan 1998
12DERNER, Kyle-John b: 27 Jan 2000

261.07.02

11DERNER, Pat-Alan b: 01 Nov 1973 in Carroll, IA v: Dedham,
  IA o: Electrician c: 2
 + seq: 261.07.02 TIGGES, Jennifer-Marie b: 16 May 1977 in
  Carroll, IA w: 15 Mar 1997 in Dedham, IA v: Dedham, IA f:
  Gary Tigges m: Lola Fischer c: 2
12DERNER, Jacob-Eugene b: 02 Sep 1998
12DERNER, Nathan-Edward b: 05 Apr 2001

261.08

10WITTRY, Marcia-Lou b: 20 Sep 1940 in Carroll, IA v: Carroll,
  IA c: 4
 + seq: 261.08 WIEDERIN, Eugene (Gene) b: 02 Jun 1940 in
  Carroll, IA w: 20 Jan 1962 in Mount Carmel, IA v: Carroll, IA
  i: Served in military from 1963 to 1965 o: Postal Clerk f: Carl
  Wiederin m: Rosina Staiert c: 4
11WIEDERIN, Douglas-Gerard b: 31 Jan 1964
 + seq: 261.09 BAUMHOVER, Laurie b: Abt. 1965 w: 23 Aug
  1986
11WIEDERIN, Steven-Gerard b: 05 Oct 1968
11WIEDERIN, Jodi-Mary b: 03 Sep 1969 in Carroll, IA v:
  Carroll, IA o: Sales-calidoucious for kids c: 2
 + seq: 261.10 BAYLISS, Terry b: 23 Jan 1967 in Carroll, IA w:
  05 May 1990 in Carroll, IA v: Carroll, IA o: Coordinator f:
  Eugene Bayliss m: Bernice c: 2
11WIEDERIN, Tom-Eugene b: 28 Apr 1973
 + seq: 261.10.01 REID, Stacy w: 15 Jun 2002 in Key West, FL

261.10

11WIEDERIN, Jodi-Mary b: 03 Sep 1969 in Carroll, IA v:
  Carroll, IA o: Sales-calidoucious for kids c: 2
 + seq: 261.10 BAYLISS, Terry b: 23 Jan 1967 in Carroll, IA w:

05 May 1990 in Carroll, IA v: Carroll, IA o: Coordinator f:
Eugene Bayliss m: Bernice c: 2
12BAYLISS, Nathan-Eugene b: 20 Apr 1993 in Carroll, IA
12BAYLISS, Madison-Jo b: 14 Jun 1997 in Carroll, IA

261.11

9 WITTRY, Mary-Ann (Girlie) b: 21 Jun 1908 in Breda, IA d: 05
Dec 1991 v: Seaforth, MN c: 11
+ seq: 261.11 BERNARDY, Mathew-Frank b: 20 Nov 1907 d:
02 Jan 1995 w: 30 Apr 1935 v: Seaforth, MN o: Farmer o:
Salesman of electric engines c: 11
10BERNARDY, Catherine-Ann (Kate) b: 27 Mar 1937 v: Tyler,
MN o: Head start home visitor c: 11
+ seq: 261.12 THOOFT, Ernest H. (Ernie) b: 22 Jun 1936 w: 30
Apr 1958 v: Tyler, MN o: Farmer c: 11
10BERNARDY, Jean-Marie b: 17 Sep 1938 v: Lynd, MN c: 7
+ seq: 261.21 THOOFT, Raymond-Jerome b: 22 May 1933 w:
15 Oct 1958 v: Lynd, MN c: 7
10BERNARDY, Jerome-Ambrose b: 12 Nov 1939 d: 03 Sep 1959
10BERNARDY, Robert-John b: 30 Sep 1941 v: Seaforth, MN c:
1
+ seq: 261.28 TREXLER, Linda b: 11 Apr 1947 w: 02 Jun 1975
v: Seaforth, MN c: 1
10BERNARDY, Patricia-Ann b: 12 Dec 1942 v: Kerkhoven, MN
o: Day care provider c: 6
+ seq: 261.29 GOBLIRSCH, Gerald-Bernard (Jerry) b: 02 May
1942 w: 14 May 1962 v: Kerkhoven, MN o: Retired
accountant c: 6
10BERNARDY, Marlene-Mary b: 20 Oct 1945 in Vesta, MN v:
Austin, TX c: 2
+ seq: 261.31 HEILING, Gerald-Michael (Gerry) b: 12 Apr 1945
in Redwood Falls, MN w: 20 Nov 1965 in Seaforth, MN v:
Austin, TX c: 2
10BERNARDY, Mary-Josephine (Mary Jo) b: 26 Dec 1946 v:
Janesville, MN o: Retired day care provider c: 2
+ seq: 261.32 POHLEN, Francis-George (Frank) b: 04 Feb 1941
w: 03 Feb 1967 v: Janesville, MN o: Retiree c: 2
10BERNARDY, Linda-Kathryn b: 08 Feb 1948 v: Prior Lake,
MN o: BC/BS Insurance writer c: 2
+ seq: 261.33 CHAPMAN, Thomas-John b: 20 Sep 1943 w: 25
Apr 1970 v: Prior Lake, MN c: 2

10BERNARDY, James-Mathew b: 03 Nov 1949 d: 11 Jan 2003
+ seq: 261.34 COULTER, Cindy-Fay b: 09 Jan 1957 w: 20 Jun
    1987 o: Nurse in nursing home
10BERNARDY, Thomas-Joseph b: 03 Nov 1949 v: Seaforth,
    MN
10BERNARDY, Ronald-Bernard b: 16 Jul 1952 v: Olivia, MN o:
    Auto mechanic c: 3
+ seq: 261.35 STRAND, Lynette-Sue b: 27 Apr 1955 w: 22 Jun
    1973 v: Olivia, MN c: 3

261.12

10BERNARDY, Catherine-Ann (Kate) b: 27 Mar 1937 v: Tyler,
    MN o: Head start home visitor c: 11
+ seq: 261.12 THOOFT, Ernest H. (Ernie) b: 22 Jun 1936 w: 30
    Apr 1958 v: Tyler, MN o: Farmer c: 11
11THOOFT, Richard-Allen b: 05 Feb 1959 v: Lakefield, MN o:
    Farmer c: 2
+ seq: 261.13 JOHNSON, Shirley b: 20 Jul 1956 w: 01 Jun 1985
    v: Lakefield, MN c: 2
11THOOFT, Jerome-Ernest b: 30 Jun 1960 v: St.Cloud, MN
11THOOFT, Douglas-John b: 27 Jun 1961 v: Hampton, MN o:
    State patrol trooper c: 2
+ seq: 261.14 LAMOTE, Brenda b: 08 Sep 1963 w: 06 Oct 1984
    v: Hampton, MN c: 2
11THOOFT, Janine-Louise b: 14 Aug 1962 c: 1
+ seq: 261.15 RASMUSSEN, Douglas b: 26 Aug 1960 w: 16
    Oct 1982 c: 1
11THOOFT, Edward-Patrick b: 23 Aug 1963 v: Milroy, MN c: 3
+ seq: 261.16 SANTO, Susan-Kay b: 22 Oct 1964 w: 06 Sep
    1986 v: Milroy, MN c: 3
11THOOFT, Karen-Marie b: 12 Jan 1965 v: Chanhassen, MN c:
    4
+ seq: 261.17 KRAEMER, John E. b: 02 Aug 1963 w: 30 Sep
    1989 v: Chanhassen, MN o: Electical engineer c: 4
11THOOFT, Thomas-Joseph b: 23 Dec 1965 v: Morris, MN o:
    Farmer c: 4
+ seq: 261.18 THOLEN, Susan (Sue) b: 10 Oct 1966 w: 12 May
    1990 v: Morris, MN c: 4
11THOOFT, Mary-Christina b: 23 Dec 1965 d: 24 Dec 1965
11THOOFT, Suzanne-Marie b: 20 Apr 1967 v: Milroy, MN c: 2
+ seq: 261.19 KIRSH, Robert b: 18 May 1966 w: 19 Aug 1989

v: Milroy, MN o: Auto body mechanic c: 2

11 THOOFT, Bruce-Francis b: 26 Oct 1969 v: Milroy, MN o:
City maintenance worker

11 THOOFT, Scott-Joseph b: 15 Dec 1970 v: Lynd, MN o:
Farmer c: 4

+ seq: 261.20 LOUWAGIE, Debbie b: 27 Dec 1971 w: 12 Sep
1992 v: Lynd, MN c: 4

261.13

11 THOOFT, Richard-Allen b: 05 Feb 1959 v: Lakefield, MN o:
Farmer c: 2

+ seq: 261.13 JOHNSON, Shirley b: 20 Jul 1956 w: 01 Jun 1985
v: Lakefield, MN c: 2

12 THOOFT, Alisa-Ann b: 09 Mar 1986

12 THOOFT, Anthony-Allen b: 01 Nov 1989

261.14

11 THOOFT, Douglas-John b: 27 Jun 1961 v: Hampton, MN o:
State patrol trooper c: 2

+ seq: 261.14 LAMOTE, Brenda b: 08 Sep 1963 w: 06 Oct 1984
v: Hampton, MN c: 2

12 THOOFT, Derek-Douglas b: 22 Jun 1991

12 THOOFT, Dylan-Joseph b: 01 Oct 1998

261.15

11 THOOFT, Janine-Louise b: 14 Aug 1962 c: 1

+ seq: 261.15 RASMUSSEN, Douglas b: 26 Aug 1960 w: 16
Oct 1982 c: 1

12 RASMUSSEN, Chelsey b: 12 May 1989

261.16

11 THOOFT, Edward-Patrick b: 23 Aug 1963 v: Milroy, MN c: 3

+ seq: 261.16 SANTO, Susan-Kay b: 22 Oct 1964 w: 06 Sep
1986 v: Milroy, MN c: 3

12 THOOFT, Danielle-Kay b: 28 May 1988

12 THOOFT, Ryan-Robert b: 16 Jul 1989

12 THOOFT, Andrew-Ernest b: 03 Mar 1991

261.17

11 THOOFT, Karen-Marie b: 12 Jan 1965 v: Chanhassen, MN c:
4

+ seq: 261.17 KRAEMER, John E. b: 02 Aug 1963 w: 30 Sep
   1989 v: Chanhassen, MN o: Electical engineer c: 4
12 THOOFT, Jared-Paul b: 08 Jun 1985 a: Adrian Welle
12 KRAEMER, Kassandra-Elizabeth b: 30 Aug 1990
12 KRAEMER, Jerome-Edward b: 19 Jun 1992
12 KRAEMER, Jacob-Ernest b: 04 Feb 1995

261.18

11 THOOFT, Thomas-Joseph b: 23 Dec 1965 v: Morris, MN o:
   Farmer c: 4
+ seq: 261.18 THOLEN, Susan (Sue) b: 10 Oct 1966 w: 12 May
   1990 v: Morris, MN c: 4
12 THOOFT, Travis-Joseph b: 30 Aug 1990
12 THOOFT, Megan b: 30 Aug 1991
12 THOOFT, Christina b: 13 Dec 1993
12 THOOFT, Jordan b: 05 Jun 1995

261.19

11 THOOFT, Suzanne-Marie b: 20 Apr 1967 v: Milroy, MN c: 2
+ seq: 261.19 KIRSH, Robert b: 18 May 1966 w: 19 Aug 1989
   v: Milroy, MN o: Auto body mechanic c: 2
12 KIRSH, Bridgit-Christina b: 17 Sep 1990
12 KIRSH, Brandon-Joseph b: 18 May 1992

261.20

11 THOOFT, Scott-Joseph b: 15 Dec 1970 v: Lynd, MN o:
   Farmer c: 4
+ seq: 261.20 LOUWAGIE, Debbie b: 27 Dec 1971 w: 12 Sep
   1992 v: Lynd, MN c: 4
12 THOOFT, Tanner-Dean b: 09 Mar 1996
12 THOOFT, Taylor-Ann b: 02 Jul 1998
12 THOOFT, Tara-Lynn b: 12 Jun 2001
12 THOOFT, Tucker b: 12 Aug 2003

261.21

10 BERNARDY, Jean-Marie b: 17 Sep 1938 v: Lynd, MN c: 7
+ seq: 261.21 THOOFT, Raymond-Jerome b: 22 May 1933 w:
   15 Oct 1958 v: Lynd, MN c: 7
11 THOOFT, Carol-Jean b: 28 Aug 1959 v: Milroy, MN o: Day
   care provider c: 6
+ seq: 261.22 GOBLISH, Stephen-Joseph (Steve) b: 03 Jun 1961

w: 24 Sep 1983 v: Milroy, MN o: Schwan's - Marshall c: 6

11 THOOFT, David-Joseph b: 22 Nov 1960 v: Lynd, MN o: Schwan's - Marshall c: 2

+ seq: 261.23 SEVERSON, Connie-Joann b: 10 Feb 1966 w: 13 Apr 1991 v: Lynd, MN c: 2

11 THOOFT, Dennis-John b: 15 Feb 1962 v: Lynd, MN c: 1

+ seq: 261.24 KRAUS, Mary-Jo b: 03 Aug 1966 w: 09 Sep 1989 v: Lynd, MN c: 1

11 THOOFT, Joan-Marie b: 08 Mar 1963 v: Tracy, MN o: Beautician c: 2

+ seq: 261.25 LAVOY, Gary b: 21 Jan 1966 w: 03 Sep 1994 v: Tracy, MN o: Farmer c: 2

11 THOOFT, Dean-Thomas b: 06 Jan 1965 v: Tracy, MN c: 3

+ seq: 261.26 ARNDT, Michelle-Kelly b: 29 Jan 1964 w: 03 Nov 1990 v: Tracy, MN c: 3

11 THOOFT, Kevin-Raymond b: 13 Mar 1969 v: St. Clair, MN o: Farmer o: Hog raiser o: Meat cutter c: 2

+ seq: 261.27 YOUNGERBERG, Kristin-Lee b: 06 Jun 1974 w: 27 Feb 1993 v: St. Clair, MN o: Licensed practical nurse c: 2

11 THOOFT, Brian-David b: 09 Nov 1978 v: Lynd, MN c: 1

+ seq: 261.27.01 FORTHMAN, Jill b: 14 May 1979 w: 14 Oct 2000 v: Lynd, MN c: 1

261.22

11 THOOFT, Carol-Jean b: 28 Aug 1959 v: Milroy, MN o: Day care provider c: 6

+ seq: 261.22 GOBLISH, Stephen-Joseph (Steve) b: 03 Jun 1961 w: 24 Sep 1983 v: Milroy, MN o: Schwan's - Marshall c: 6

12 GOBLISH, Adam-Stephan b: 06 Oct 1984

12 GOBLISH, Michael-John b: 31 Oct 1986

12 GOBLISH, Melissa-Jean b: 21 May 1988

12 GOBLISH, Amanda-Jo b: 19 Aug 1991

12 GOBLISH, Jordon-David b: 14 Mar 1997

12 GOBLISH, Kaittynn-Ann b: 08 Sep 2003

261.23

11 THOOFT, David-Joseph b: 22 Nov 1960 v: Lynd, MN o: Schwan's - Marshall c: 2

+ seq: 261.23 SEVERSON, Connie-Joann b: 10 Feb 1966 w: 13 Apr 1991 v: Lynd, MN c: 2

12 CASTLE, Danica-Lynn b: 18 Sep 1986

12THOOFT, Austin-Matthew b: 23 Mar 1992

261.24
11THOOFT, Dennis-John b: 15 Feb 1962 v: Lynd, MN c: 1
+ seq: 261.24 KRAUS, Mary-Jo b: 03 Aug 1966 w: 09 Sep 1989
   v: Lynd, MN c: 1
12THOOFT, Jessica-Ann b: 06 May 1996

261.25
11THOOFT, Joan-Marie b: 08 Mar 1963 v: Tracy, MN o:
   Beautician c: 2
+ seq: 261.25 LAVOY, Gary b: 21 Jan 1966 w: 03 Sep 1994 v:
   Tracy, MN o: Farmer c: 2
12LAVOY, Mathew-Raymond b: 26 Jan 1996
12LAVOY, Jennifer-Marie b: 11 Jan 1997

261.26
11THOOFT, Dean-Thomas b: 06 Jan 1965 v: Tracy, MN c: 3
+ seq: 261.26 ARNDT, Michelle-Kelly b: 29 Jan 1964 w: 03
   Nov 1990 v: Tracy, MN c: 3
12THOOFT, Zachariah-Dean b: 28 Jan 1993
12THOOFT, Lucas-Kelly b: 02 Aug 1995
12THOOFT, Joshua-Jordon b: 02 Feb 1997

261.27
11THOOFT, Kevin-Raymond b: 13 Mar 1969 v: St. Clair, MN o:
   Farmer o: Hog raiser o: Meat cutter c: 2
+ seq: 261.27 YOUNGERBERG, Kristin-Lee b: 06 Jun 1974 w:
   27 Feb 1993 v: St. Clair, MN o: Licensed practical nurse c: 2
12THOOFT, Ashley-Ann b: 05 Aug 1993
12THOOFT, Alleson-Lee b: 24 Mar 1995

261.27.01
11THOOFT, Brian-David b: 09 Nov 1978 v: Lynd, MN c: 1
+ seq: 261.27.01 FORTHMAN, Jill b: 14 May 1979 w: 14 Oct
   2000 v: Lynd, MN c: 1
12THOOFT, Brandon-William b: 02 Jul 2005 in Lynd, MN

261.28
10BERNARDY, Robert-John b: 30 Sep 1941 v: Seaforth, MN c:
   1

+ seq: 261.28 TREXLER, Linda b: 11 Apr 1947 w: 02 Jun 1975
   v: Seaforth, MN c: 1
11 BERNARDY, Vicky-Lynn b: 25 Sep 1980 o: U. S. Navy c: 1
+ seq: 261.28.01 MAIN, Thomas b: 17 Sep 1977 w: 05 Mar
   2001 c: 1

261.28.01
11 BERNARDY, Vicky-Lynn b: 25 Sep 1980 o: U. S. Navy c: 1
+ seq: 261.28.01 MAIN, Thomas b: 17 Sep 1977 w: 05 Mar
   2001 c: 1
12 MAIN, Lillith-Kennedy b: 19 Sep 2001

261.29
10 BERNARDY, Patricia-Ann b: 12 Dec 1942 v: Kerkhoven, MN
   o: Day care provider c: 6
+ seq: 261.29 GOBLIRSCH, Gerald-Bernard (Jerry) b: 02 May
   1942 w: 14 May 1962 v: Kerkhoven, MN o: Retired
   accountant c: 6
11 GOBLIRSCH, Randall-Joseph b: 13 Nov 1963
11 [1] GOBLIRSCH, Eric-Mathew b: 17 Nov 1965 v: Lawrence,
   KS
+ seq: 261.30 JOHNSTON, Wendy b: 08 Jun 1967 w: 12 May
   1986 o: U. S. Navy
* 2nd Wife of [1] GOBLIRSCH, Eric-Mathew:
+ seq: 261.30.01 COLLINS, Marget b: 03 Jul 1965 in Scotland
   w: 19 Aug 1988 in Greenock, Scotland v: Lawrence, KS
11 GOBLIRSCH, Steven-Gerald b: 24 Aug 1966 d: 24 Aug 1966
11 [2] GOBLIRSCH, Mark-Donovan b: 12 Apr 1968
+ seq: 261.30.02 GEISTFELD, Janna b: 12 Jun 1975 w: 26 Aug
   1995
* 2nd Wife of [2] GOBLIRSCH, Mark-Donovan:
+ seq: 261.30.03 ALTURA, Nina R. b: 26 Mar 1969 in
   Phillipines w: 31 Dec 2002 v: California
11 GOBLIRSCH, Julie-Rhonda b: 01 May 1969 v: Willmar, MN
11 GOBLIRSCH, Heidi-Lynette b: 06 Aug 1979 v: Lynd, MN
+ seq: 261.30.04 WINTER, Jeremy b: 26 Aug 1975 w: 07 Sep
   2002 v: Lynd, MN

261.31
10 BERNARDY, Marlene-Mary b: 20 Oct 1945 in Vesta, MN v:
   Austin, TX c: 2

+ seq: 261.31 HEILING, Gerald-Michael (Gerry) b: 12 Apr 1945 in Redwood Falls, MN w: 20 Nov 1965 in Seaforth, MN v: Austin, TX c: 2

11 HEILING, Ann-Marie b: 16 Feb 1967 in Minneapolis, MN v: Lacey, WA o: Medical doctor c: 2

+ seq: 261.31.01 SMITH-TOSOMEEN, Craig-Alan b: 09 Mar 1967 in Australia w: 23 Mar 1991 in Pine Island, MN v: Lacey, WA c: 2

11 HEILING, Barry-Todd b: 12 Sep 1968 in Minneapolis, MN o: U. S. Air Force in Germany

261.31.01

11 HEILING, Ann-Marie b: 16 Feb 1967 in Minneapolis, MN v: Lacey, WA o: Medical doctor c: 2

+ seq: 261.31.01 SMITH-TOSOMEEN, Craig-Alan b: 09 Mar 1967 in Australia w: 23 Mar 1991 in Pine Island, MN v: Lacey, WA c: 2

12 TOSOMEEN, Kai-Jakob b: 06 Jul 1997

12 TOSOMEEN, Mya-Joy b: 21 Jun 2001

261.32

10 BERNARDY, Mary-Josephine (Mary Jo) b: 26 Dec 1946 v: Janesville, MN o: Retired day care provider c: 2

+ seq: 261.32 POHLEN, Francis-George (Frank) b: 04 Feb 1941 w: 03 Feb 1967 v: Janesville, MN o: Retiree c: 2

11 POHLEN, Michael-Alois (Mike) b: 14 Jun 1967 v: Waseca, MN o: Factory maintenance c: 1

+ seq: 261.32.01 FITZLOFF, Lisa-Renae-Bauleke b: 09 May 1974 w: 02 Jun 2001 v: Waseca, MN c: 1

11 POHLEN, Kathryn-Lynn (Kathy) b: 11 May 1974 o: Carson Craft/Keyc-TV

261.32.01

11 POHLEN, Michael-Alois (Mike) b: 14 Jun 1967 v: Waseca, MN o: Factory maintenance c: 1

+ seq: 261.32.01 FITZLOFF, Lisa-Renae-Bauleke b: 09 May 1974 w: 02 Jun 2001 v: Waseca, MN c: 1

12 POHLEN, Mathew-John b: 21 Dec 2000

261.33

10 BERNARDY, Linda-Kathryn b: 08 Feb 1948 v: Prior Lake,

MN o: BC/BS Insurance writer c: 2
+ seq: 261.33 CHAPMAN, Thomas-John b: 20 Sep 1943 w: 25
Apr 1970 v: Prior Lake, MN c: 2
11CHAPMAN, Tawnya-Joanne b: 13 Jan 1973 c: 1
12CHAPMAN, Gerred-Quinn b: 22 Nov 1993
11CHAPMAN, Jennifer-Lynn b: 07 Nov 1975 v: New Market,
MN c: 2
+ seq: 261.33.50 MACK, Andrew b: 10 Oct 1981 w: 08 Nov
2003 v: New Market, MN c: 2

261.33.50
11CHAPMAN, Jennifer-Lynn b: 07 Nov 1975 v: New Market,
MN c: 2
+ seq: 261.33.50 MACK, Andrew b: 10 Oct 1981 w: 08 Nov
2003 v: New Market, MN c: 2
12CHAPMAN, Atreyn (Louis) b: 10 Apr 1998
12MACK, Stazia b: 11 Mar 2003

261.35
10BERNARDY, Ronald-Bernard b: 16 Jul 1952 v: Olivia, MN o:
Auto mechanic c: 3
+ seq: 261.35 STRAND, Lynette-Sue b: 27 Apr 1955 w: 22 Jun
1973 v: Olivia, MN c: 3
11BERNARDY, Staci-Ann b: 02 Jan 1979 v: Lynd, MN
+ seq: 261.36 HALBERSMA, Justin b: 27 Jan 1980 w: 29 Jun
2002 v: Lynd, MN
11BERNARDY, Angela-Jean b: 20 Apr 1981 d: 23 Aug 2003 v:
Rochester, MN
+ seq: 261.37 LUCKHARDT, Brian b: 21 Dec 1979 w: 23 Aug
2003 v: Rochester, MN
11BERNARDY, Adam-Ronald b: 25 Apr 1983

262
7 [1] WITRY, Michel b: 12 Aug 1822 in Herborn, Lux v:
Herborn, Lux i: Emigrated to the U. S., probably Iowa r: b c: 2
+ seq: 262 KARPES, Lucia b: Abt. 1930 w: Abt. 1860 v:
Herborn, Lux c: 1
8 WITRY, Nicholas (Little Nick) b: 1867
* 2nd Wife of [1] WITRY, Michel:
+ seq: 263 KOHL, Barbara b: Abt. 1830 w: Abt. 1867 v:
Herborn, Lux c: 1

8 WITTRY, Jacob b: 19 Sep 1868 in Herborn, Lux d: 18 Dec
  1940 in Butte, NE h: Holmberg or Wittry farm at Mankato v:
  Carroll, IA v: Butte, NE i: Said to have deserted from German
  army i: Inherited money from cousin, Louis Witry o: Farmer c:
  8
+ seq: 264 BAMBERG, Catherine b: 25 Mar 1871 in Rosport,
  Lux d: 29 Apr 1929 in Nebraska w: 19 Jul 1898 in Carroll, IA
  v: Butte, NE v: Carroll, IA c: 8

264

8 WITTRY, Jacob b: 19 Sep 1868 in Herborn, Lux d: 18 Dec
  1940 in Butte, NE h: Holmberg or Wittry farm at Mankato v:
  Carroll, IA v: Butte, NE i: Said to have deserted from German
  army i: Inherited money from cousin, Louis Witry o: Farmer c:
  8
+ seq: 264 BAMBERG, Catherine b: 25 Mar 1871 in Rosport,
  Lux d: 29 Apr 1929 in Nebraska w: 19 Jul 1898 in Carroll, IA
  v: Butte, NE v: Carroll, IA c: 8
9 WITTRY, Nicholas-Frank b: 30 May 1899 in Carroll, IA d: 18
  Jun 1963 in Lismore, MN c: 5
+ seq: 265 WILBERDING, Frances-Celia b: 10 Nov 1909 w: 03
  Feb 1931 in Butte, NE f: Ben Wilberding m: Anna Fehring c:
  5
9 WITTRY, Frank-Nicholas b: 14 Jul 1900 in Carroll, IA d: 08
  Sep 1929
9 WITTRY, Jacob b: 28 Aug 1902 in Carroll, IA d: 10 Dec 1944
  in Butte, NE o: Butcher
+ seq: 269 DE JARLIS, Helena b: 21 Aug 1902 d: Nov 1973 in
  Iowa w: 1935
9 WITTRY, Christian-Frank (Chris) b: 04 Feb 1904 in Carroll
  County IA d: 01 Jul 1983 in Butte, NE v: Butte, NE o: Farmer
  c: 4
+ seq: 270 REISER, Marie-Isabel b: 29 Dec 1912 d: 05 Jan 2004
  in Creighton, NE w: 1935 v: Creighton, NE v: Butte, NE c: 4
9 WITTRY, Clara b: 08 May 1905 in Carroll County IA c: 4
+ seq: 270.03 HOLMBERG, Arvid b: Abt. 1900 w: 26 Jan 1937
  c: 4
9 WITTRY, Sophia b: 25 Sep 1906 in Carroll County IA v:
  Jacksonville, FL v: Chicago, IL o: Nanny
+ seq: 270.03.25 WRETSTROM, Joseph b: 29 Sep 1915 d: 16
  Aug 1997 w: Abt. 1987

9 WITTRY, Elizabeth b: 14 Feb 1908 in Carroll County, IA d: 22 Jul 1991 in Orcharchie, OK v: Okarche, OK c: 3
+ seq: 270.04 WITTROCK, Anton (Tony) b: 09 Jul 1898 in Carroll County, IA d: 24 Aug 1976 in Kingfisher, OK w: 09 Apr 1934 in Butte, NE v: Okarche, OK o: Farmer f: Anton-Heinrich (Henry) Wittrock m: Anna Sprenger c: 3
9 WITTRY, Stillborn child b: 1909

265

9 WITTRY, Nicholas-Frank b: 30 May 1899 in Carroll, IA d: 18 Jun 1963 in Lismore, MN c: 5
+ seq: 265 WILBERDING, Frances-Celia b: 10 Nov 1909 w: 03 Feb 1931 in Butte, NE f: Ben Wilberding m: Anna Fehring c: 5
10 WITTRY, Edwin-Jacob (Sonny) b: 30 Dec 1931 in Butte, NE v: Lismore, MN c: 4
+ seq: 266 BUSS, Jan-Marie b: 13 Mar 1937 d: Dec 2003 w: 07 Mar 1957 in Barrington, MN v: Lismore, MN f: Chris Buss m: Marie Diddler c: 4
10 WITTRY, Doris-Elaine b: 17 Oct 1933 c: 6
+ seq: 267.01 BRAKE, Donald-Stephen b: 14 Dec 1932 w: Abt. 1952 c: 6
10 WITTRY, Arlene-Marie b: 14 Dec 1934 v: Lismore, MN c: 4
+ seq: 267.07 KNIPS, Earl-William b: 30 Dec 1931 w: Abt. 1955 v: Lismore, MN c: 4
10 WITTRY, Robert-Lee b: 14 Aug 1944 v: Lismore, MN c: 3
+ seq: 268 BALK, Kathy-Denyce b: 07 Jun 1951 w: Abt. 1970 v: Lismore, MN c: 3
10[1] WITTRY, Judith-Ann b: 29 Aug 1947 c: 1
+ seq: 268.01 STRAIGHT, Phillip-Nolan b: 03 Nov 1944 w: Abt. 1970 c: 1
* 2nd Husband of [1] WITTRY, Judith-Ann:
+ seq: 268.02 BAUER, James-Alan b: 1944 w: Abt. 1975

266

10 WITTRY, Edwin-Jacob (Sonny) b: 30 Dec 1931 in Butte, NE v: Lismore, MN c: 4
+ seq: 266 BUSS, Jan-Marie b: 13 Mar 1937 d: Dec 2003 w: 07 Mar 1957 in Barrington, MN v: Lismore, MN f: Chris Buss m: Marie Diddler c: 4
11 WITTRY, Lezlee-Marie b: 21 Jan 1958 c: 2

+ seq: 266.01 ROEMELING, Lawrence-Raymond b: 14 Jun 1955
w: Abt. 1980 c: 2
11WITTRY, Brett-Allan b: 06 Jun 1959 v: Lismore, MN
+ seq: 267 REUTER, Melissa-Sue b: 08 Aug 1962 d: 20 Aug
1998 in Spencer, IA Cause of death: Helicopter crash w: Abt.
1985 v: Lismore, MN o: Nurse
11WITTRY, Kevin-Michael b: 26 Apr 1962 v: Minneapolis, MN
11WITTRY, Jodi-Linn b: 11 Jul 1964

266.01

11WITTRY, Lezlee-Marie b: 21 Jan 1958 c: 2
+ seq: 266.01 ROEMELING, Lawrence-Raymond b: 14 Jun 1955
w: Abt. 1980 c: 2
12ROEMELING, Morgan-Marie b: 1985
12ROEMELING, Macey-Lynn b: 1986

267.01

10WITTRY, Doris-Elaine b: 17 Oct 1933 c: 6
+ seq: 267.01 BRAKE, Donald-Stephen b: 14 Dec 1932 w: Abt.
1952 c: 6
11BRAKE, Douglas-Joseph b: 25 Apr 1954 c: 3
+ seq: 267.02 YACKEL, Marie-Ann b: 27 Nov 1954 w: Abt.
1975 c: 3
11BRAKE, Debra-Jean b: 13 May 1955 c: 2
+ seq: 267.03 BROCKBERG, Jeffrey-Paul b: 20 Jan 1955 w:
Abt. 1980 c: 2
11BRAKE, Jeffrey-Dean b: 05 Jul 1956 c: 1
+ seq: 267.04 BRANDT, Marlene-Ann b: 18 Aug 1953 w: Abt.
1980 c: 1
11BRAKE, Steven-Don b: 21 Nov 1958 c: 2
+ seq: 267.05 DREALAN, Mary-Frances b: 25 Jun 1960 w: Abt.
1980 c: 2
11BRAKE, Jerry-David b: 20 Aug 1960 c: 2
+ seq: 267.06 THIER, Julie-Kathryn b: 30 Nov 1962 w: Abt.
1985 c: 2
11BRAKE, Sharon-Kay b: 01 Aug 1964

267.02

11BRAKE, Douglas-Joseph b: 25 Apr 1954 c: 3
+ seq: 267.02 YACKEL, Marie-Ann b: 27 Nov 1954 w: Abt.
1975 c: 3

12BRAKE, Angela-Sue b: 1979
12BRAKE, Kimberly-Ann b: 1982
12BRAKE, David-Joseph b: 1985

267.03
11BRAKE, Debra-Jean b: 13 May 1955 c: 2
+ seq: 267.03 BROCKBERG, Jeffrey-Paul b: 20 Jan 1955 w: Abt. 1980 c: 2
12BROCKBERG, JoAnn-Marie b: 1982
12BROCKBERG, Michael-Paul b: 1984

267.04
11BRAKE, Jeffrey-Dean b: 05 Jul 1956 c: 1
+ seq: 267.04 BRANDT, Marlene-Ann b: 18 Aug 1953 w: Abt. 1980 c: 1
12BRAKE, Meghan-Ann b: 1984

267.05
11BRAKE, Steven-Don b: 21 Nov 1958 c: 2
+ seq: 267.05 DREALAN, Mary-Frances b: 25 Jun 1960 w: Abt. 1980 c: 2
12BRAKE, Matthew-Steven b: 1984
12BRAKE, Bradley-James b: 1987

267.06
11BRAKE, Jerry-David b: 20 Aug 1960 c: 2
+ seq: 267.06 THIER, Julie-Kathryn b: 30 Nov 1962 w: Abt. 1985 c: 2
12BRAKE, Jared-David b: 1985
12BRAKE, Jordan-Lee b: 1987
267.07
10WITTRY, Arlene-Marie b: 14 Dec 1934 v: Lismore, MN c: 4
+ seq: 267.07 KNIPS, Earl-William b: 30 Dec 1931 w: Abt. 1955 v: Lismore, MN c: 4
11KNIPS, Kristi-Rae b: 23 Jun 1959 c: 2
+ seq: 267.08 REKER, Gary-Lee b: 30 Nov 1952 w: Abt. 1980 c: 2
11KNIPS, Kay-Marie b: 14 Dec 1961
11KNIPS, Ronald-Earl b: 16 Nov 1963
11KNIPS, Richard-Neal b: 18 Jul 1967

267.08

11 KNIPS, Kristi-Rae b: 23 Jun 1959 c: 2

+ seq: 267.08 REKER, Gary-Lee b: 30 Nov 1952 w: Abt. 1980
   c: 2

12 REKER, Kassandra-Lee b: 1984

12 REKER, Mitchell-Lee b: 1987

268

10 WITTRY, Robert-Lee b: 14 Aug 1944 v: Lismore, MN c: 3

+ seq: 268 BALK, Kathy-Denyce b: 07 Jun 1951 w: Abt. 1970
   v: Lismore, MN c: 3

11 WITTRY, Shawn-Alan b: 1972 v: Rushmore, MN

11 WITTRY, Bobbi-Michele b: 1974 v: Adrian, MN

11 WITTRY, Nicole-Denyce b: 1977 v: Lake Wilson, MN

+ seq: 268.00.50 PLATT, Jason w: Abt. 2000 v: Lake Wilson,
   MN

268.01

10 [1] WITTRY, Judith-Ann b: 29 Aug 1947 c: 1

+ seq: 268.01 STRAIGHT, Phillip-Nolan b: 03 Nov 1944 w:
   Abt. 1970 c: 1

11 STRAIGHT, Brenda-Nichole b: 1971

* 2nd Husband of [1] WITTRY, Judith-Ann:

+ seq: 268.02 BAUER, James-Alan b: 1944 w: Abt. 1975

270

9 WITTRY, Christian-Frank (Chris) b: 04 Feb 1904 in Carroll
   County IA d: 01 Jul 1983 in Butte, NE v: Butte, NE o: Farmer
   c: 4

+ seq: 270 REISER, Marie-Isabel b: 29 Dec 1912 d: 05 Jan 2004
   in Creighton, NE w: 1935 v: Creighton, NE v: Butte, NE c: 4

10 WITTRY, Robert-Christopher b: 07 Jul 1949 v: Blair, NE c: 5

+ seq: 270.01 GOERKE, Victoria J. (Vicki) b: 07 Mar 1952 w:
   1976 v: Blair, NE f: Victor Goerke m: Maxine Shearon c: 5

10 WITTRY, Barbara R. b: 16 Apr 1938 in Butte, NE v: St. Paul,
   NE i: High school valedictorian o: Hairstylist c: 2

+ seq: 270.02 MCINTYRE, Dan R. w: 22 Apr 1967 in Grand
   Island, NE v: St. Paul, NE o: Gen. Mgr of Howard-Greeley
   Rural Electric c: 2

10 WITTRY, Marilyn-Agnes b: 17 Dec 1943 in Butte, NE v:
   Wayne, NE c: 4

+ seq: 270.02.05 OTTE, Gerald-Ray b: 04 Aug 1943 in Wayne, NE w: 10 Oct 1964 in Butte, NE v: Wayne, NE c: 4

10 WITTRY, Catherine M. (Cathy) b: 22 Sep 1941 in Butte, NE v: Creighton, NE v: Wayne, NE o: Owner and manager of Salmen Hardware & Furnityre c: 4

+ seq: 270.02.30 SALMEN, Richard A. b: 18 Dec 1940 in Boyd County, NE w: 02 Jun 1962 in Butte, NE v: Creighton, NE o: Owner of Salmen Hardware & Furniture f: Chester Salmen m: Iola Cue c: 4

270.01

10 WITTRY, Robert-Christopher b: 07 Jul 1949 v: Blair, NE c: 5

+ seq: 270.01 GOERKE, Victoria J. (Vicki) b: 07 Mar 1952 w: 1976 v: Blair, NE f: Victor Goerke m: Maxine Shearon c: 5

11 WITTRY, Christopher b: 13 Aug 1978 in O'Neill, NE v: Blair, NE

+ seq: 270.01.01 HANSEN, Jennifer w: 16 Jun 2001 in St. Blair, NE

11 WITTRY, Justin b: 13 Mar 1981

11 WITTRY, Nicholas (Nick) b: 10 Feb 1983

11 WITTRY, Jennifer-Jean b: 15 May 1986

11 WITTRY, Lindsey-Marie b: 11 Nov 1990

270.02

10 WITTRY, Barbara R. b: 16 Apr 1938 in Butte, NE v: St. Paul, NE i: High school valedictorian o: Hairstylist c: 2

+ seq: 270.02 MCINTYRE, Dan R. w: 22 Apr 1967 in Grand Island, NE v: St. Paul, NE o: Gen. Mgr of Howard-Greeley Rural Electric c: 2

11 MCINTYRE, John F. b: 03 Oct 1968 in St. Paul, NE v: Omaha, NE i: Salutatorian of Creighton School of Business i: MBA o: Manager in several companies

11 MCINTYRE, Tom P. b: 29 Aug 1970 in St. Paul, NE i: Cum laude at Creighton School of Business o: Manger at ACE Hardware

270.02.05

10 WITTRY, Marilyn-Agnes b: 17 Dec 1943 in Butte, NE v: Wayne, NE c: 4

+ seq: 270.02.05 OTTE, Gerald-Ray b: 04 Aug 1943 in Wayne, NE w: 10 Oct 1964 in Butte, NE v: Wayne, NE c: 4

11OTTE, Julie-Ann b: 28 Oct 1965 in Wayne, NE c: 2
+ seq: 270.02.10 EDWARDS, Neil-Harley b: 04 Oct 1965 in
   Cleveland, OH w: 22 Jun 1996 in Norfolk, NE c: 2
11OTTE, Mark-Allen b: 12 Dec 1966 in Wakefield, NE c: 2
+ seq: 270.02.15 NORTHEY, Jill-Patricia b: 23 Apr 1965 in
   South Bend, IN w: 04 May 1996 in Bettendorf, IA c: 2
11OTTE, Coleen-Mary b: 17 May 1968 in Wakefield, NE c: 2
+ seq: 270.02.20 KYHN, Steven-Lloyd b: 09 May 1968 in Grand
   Island, NE w: 16 Nov 1991 in Lincoln, NE c: 2
11OTTE, Bowdie-Dean b: 28 Dec 1969 in Wayne, NE c: 2
+ seq: 270.02.25 PICK, Heather-Lee b: 18 Apr 1973 in Yankton,
   SD w: 02 Sep 1994 in Wayne, NE c: 2

270.02.10

11OTTE, Julie-Ann b: 28 Oct 1965 in Wayne, NE c: 2
+ seq: 270.02.10 EDWARDS, Neil-Harley b: 04 Oct 1965 in
   Cleveland, OH w: 22 Jun 1996 in Norfolk, NE c: 2
12EDWARDS, Nicholas-Neil-Harley b: 31 Dec 2002 in Norfolk,
   NE d: 04 Jan 2003 in Norfolk, NE Cause of death: trisomy 13
   syndrome
12EDWARDS, Kathlyne-Danielle b: 27 Jun 2005 in Norfolk, NE

270.02.15

11OTTE, Mark-Allen b: 12 Dec 1966 in Wakefield, NE c: 2
+ seq: 270.02.15 NORTHEY, Jill-Patricia b: 23 Apr 1965 in
   South Bend, IN w: 04 May 1996 in Bettendorf, IA c: 2
12OTTE, Megan-Lynn b: 09 Apr 1999 in Omaha, NE
12OTTE, Ryan-Wade b: 07 Mar 2001 in Omaha, NE

270.02.20

11OTTE, Coleen-Mary b: 17 May 1968 in Wakefield, NE c: 2
+ seq: 270.02.20 KYHN, Steven-Lloyd b: 09 May 1968 in Grand
   Island, NE w: 16 Nov 1991 in Lincoln, NE c: 2
12KYHN, Cody-Lloyd b: 02 Jan 1994 in Grand Island, NE
12KYHN, Lucas-Ray b: 27 Dec 1996 in Grand Island, NE

270.02.25

11OTTE, Bowdie-Dean b: 28 Dec 1969 in Wayne, NE c: 2
+ seq: 270.02.25 PICK, Heather-Lee b: 18 Apr 1973 in Yankton,
   SD w: 02 Sep 1994 in Wayne, NE c: 2
12OTTE, Blake-Jordan b: 15 Feb 1995 in Wayne, NE

12OTTE, Gage-Riley b: 08 Jul 2002 in Norfolk, NE

270.02.30

10WITTRY, Catherine M. (Cathy) b: 22 Sep 1941 in Butte, NE v:
Creighton, NE v: Wayne, NE o: Owner and manager of Salmen
Hardware & Furnityre c: 4

+ seq: 270.02.30 SALMEN, Richard A. b: 18 Dec 1940 in Boyd
County, NE w: 02 Jun 1962 in Butte, NE v: Creighton, NE o:
Owner of Salmen Hardware & Furniture f: Chester Salmen m:
Iola Cue c: 4

11[1] SALMEN, Richard C. b: 13 Mar 1963 in Wayne, NE v:
Olathe, KS i: Pilot's license i: MBA o: Air traffic controller o:
Financial consultant c: 2

+ seq: 270.02.35 PARTAKA, Barbara w: Apr 1983 in Creighton,
NE

* 2nd Wife of [1] SALMEN, Richard C.:

+ seq: 270.02.40 SHELDON, Lisa-Marie b: 30 Dec 1966 in
Kearney, NE w: 15 Aug 1987 v: Olathe, KS f: Carroll
Sheldon m: Helen Schuetz c: 2

11[2] SALMEN, Lisa-Catherine b: 29 Jul 1964 in Creighton, NE
v: Creighton, NE v: Lincoln, NE o: Cosmetologist c: 2

+ seq: 270.02.45 JOHNSTON, Todd w: 02 Oct 1988

* 2nd Husband of [2] SALMEN, Lisa-Catherine:

+ seq: 270.02.50 ARMSTRONG, Larry w: 26 Aug 1993

* 3rd Husband of [2] SALMEN, Lisa-Catherine:

+ seq: 270.02.55 BALLER, Michael b: 17 Sep 1968 in Creighton,
NE w: 24 Nov 1997 in Las Vegas, NV v: Creighton, NE v:
Lincoln, NE o: Businessman - Bobcat Mike o: Carpet layer c:
2

11SALMEN, David-Robert b: 09 Jun 1966 in Creighton, NE v:
Centre Hall, PA v: Washington D. C. o: Computer consultant

+ seq: 270.02.58 CRUTS, Cathy w: 21 Feb 2004

11[3] SALMEN, Amy-Marie b: 10 Aug 1972 in Creighton, NE v:
Wayne, NE i: MBA o: Asst. Dir. of Business Development c: 2

+ seq: 270.02.60 SMITH w: Abt. 1990

* 2nd Husband of [3] SALMEN, Amy-Marie:

+ seq: 270.02.65 THOMAS, Rodney b: 01 Oct 1966 w: 05 Apr
2002 v: Creighton, NE o: Advertising sales representative c: 2

270.02.35

11[1] SALMEN, Richard C. b: 13 Mar 1963 in Wayne, NE v:

Olathe, KS i: Pilot's license i: MBA o: Air traffic controller o: Financial consultant c: 2

+ seq: 270.02.35 PARTAKA, Barbara w: Apr 1983 in Creighton, NE

* 2nd Wife of [1] SALMEN, Richard C.:

+ seq: 270.02.40 SHELDON, Lisa-Marie b: 30 Dec 1966 in Kearney, NE w: 15 Aug 1987 v: Olathe, KS f: Carroll Sheldon m: Helen Schuetz c: 2

12SALMEN, Richard-James (RJ) b: 29 Jan 2002 in Olathe, KS
12SALMEN, Alexia-Marie b: 07 Sep 2004 in Olathe, KS

270.02.45

11[1] SALMEN, Lisa-Catherine b: 29 Jul 1964 in Creighton, NE v: Creighton, NE v: Lincoln, NE o: Cosmetologist c: 2

+ seq: 270.02.45 JOHNSTON, Todd w: 02 Oct 1988

* 2nd Husband of [1] SALMEN, Lisa-Catherine:

+ seq: 270.02.50 ARMSTRONG, Larry w: 26 Aug 1993

* 3rd Husband of [1] SALMEN, Lisa-Catherine:

+ seq: 270.02.55 BALLER, Michael b: 17 Sep 1968 in Creighton, NE w: 24 Nov 1997 in Las Vegas, NV v: Creighton, NE v: Lincoln, NE o: Businessman - Bobcat Mike o: Carpet layer c: 2

12BALLER, Brook-Michael b: 17 Jun 1997 in Creighton, NE
12BALLER, Drake-David b: 31 Oct 2001 in Lincoln, NE

270.02.60

11[1] SALMEN, Amy-Marie b: 10 Aug 1972 in Creighton, NE v: Wayne, NE i: MBA o: Asst. Dir. of Business Development c: 2

+ seq: 270.02.60 SMITH w: Abt. 1990

* 2nd Husband of [1] SALMEN, Amy-Marie:

+ seq: 270.02.65 THOMAS, Rodney b: 01 Oct 1966 w: 05 Apr 2002 v: Creighton, NE o: Advertising sales representative c: 2

12THOMAS, Cleopatra b: 02 Dec 2002 in Creighton, NE
12THOMAS, Josephine-Kennedy b: 22 Nov 2004 in Creighton, NE

270.03

9 WITTRY, Clara b: 08 May 1905 in Carroll County IA c: 4

+ seq: 270.03 HOLMBERG, Arvid b: Abt. 1900 w: 26 Jan 1937 c: 4

10HOLMBERG, Daryl b: 10 Dec 1938 in Stuart, NE d: 27 Dec

2003 v: Butte, NE o: Farmer

10[1] HOLMBERG, Darlene b: 22 Jul 1943 in Stuart, NE v:
O'Neill, NE o: Residential assistant
+ seq: 270.03.05 PELC, Gordon b: 24 Mar 1932 d: 16 Oct 2000
in O'Neill, NE w: 12 Jun 1990 v: O'Neill, NE
* 2nd Husband of [1] HOLMBERG, Darlene:
+ seq: 270.03.10 KRAFKA, Arnold b: 14 May 1939 in
Valoarausi, NE w: 04 Oct 2003 in Stromsberg, NE v: O'Neill,
NE
10HOLMBERG, Stanley b: 25 Mar 1945 in Stuart, NE d: 08 Dec
1967 Cause of death: accidental shooting
10HOLMBERG, Patrick b: 16 Jul 1947 in Stuart, NE v: Atkinson,
NE o: Farmer c: 3
+ seq: 270.03.15 LANGE, Marian b: 03 Jan 1951 w: 10 Jun
1973 in Butte, NE v: Atkinson, NE c: 3

270.03.15

10HOLMBERG, Patrick b: 16 Jul 1947 in Stuart, NE v: Atkinson,
NE o: Farmer c: 3
+ seq: 270.03.15 LANGE, Marian b: 03 Jan 1951 w: 10 Jun
1973 in Butte, NE v: Atkinson, NE c: 3
11HOLMBERG, Patricia b: 05 Dec 1973
11HOLMBERG, Michelle b: 17 Sep 1974 c: 1
+ seq: 270.03.20 TUTENDER w: Abt. 2000 c: 1
11HOLMBERG, Cathy b: 10 Oct 1976

270.03.20

11HOLMBERG, Michelle b: 17 Sep 1974 c: 1
+ seq: 270.03.20 TUTENDER w: Abt. 2000 c: 1
12TUTENDER, Sara

270.04

9 WITTRY, Elizabeth b: 14 Feb 1908 in Carroll County, IA d: 22
Jul 1991 in Orcharchie, OK v: Okarche, OK c: 3
+ seq: 270.04 WITTROCK, Anton (Tony) b: 09 Jul 1898 in
Carroll County, IA d: 24 Aug 1976 in Kingfisher, OK w: 09
Apr 1934 in Butte, NE v: Okarche, OK o: Farmer f: Anton-
Heinrich (Henry) Wittrock m: Anna Sprenger c: 3
10WITTROCK, Ralph v: Merced, CA o: Major
10WITTROCK, Marvin-Anthony v: North Carolina
+ seq: 270.05 SCHWARTZ, Mary-Ann w: Abt. 1965

10WITTROCK, LeRoy b: 12 Jan 1939 in Okarche, OK d: 11 Sep 1970 in Okarche, OK Cause of death: murder/suicide v: Okarche, OK o: Farmer c: 3
+ seq: 270.06 BRUGEON, Pat w: Abt. 1960 c: 3

270.06

10WITTROCK, LeRoy b: 12 Jan 1939 in Okarche, OK d: 11 Sep 1970 in Okarche, OK Cause of death: murder/suicide v: Okarche, OK o: Farmer c: 3
+ seq: 270.06 BRUGEON, Pat w: Abt. 1960 c: 3
11WITTROCK, Kelly
11WITTROCK, Allen-Thomas b: 02 Aug 1963 in Okarche, OK d: 11 Sep 1970 in Okarche, OK Cause of death: murder
11WITTROCK, Carol-Jean b: 23 Oct 1964 in Kingfisher, OK d: 11 Sep 1970 in Okarche, OK Cause of death: murder

271

7 WITTRY, Paul b: 21 Mar 1828 in Herborn, Lux d: 31 Oct 1897 in Aurora, IL Cause of death: Stomach cancer a: Witry v: Ernzen, Lux i: Emigrated to Aurora, IL i: Discharge from militia i: Emigrated to the U.S. o: Wheelwright o: Carpenter o: Farmer r: bdx c: 3
+ seq: 271 WEBER, Marie b: 03 Mar 1824 in Ernzen, Lux d: 08 Jun 1879 in Ernzen, Lux w: 07 Jul 1858 in Fels, Lux v: Ernzen, Lux o: No profession r: bd r: mx f: Michel Weber m: Anna-Marie Goedert c: 3
8 WITTRY, Marie-Magdalena (Lena) b: 18 May 1859 in Ernzen, Lux a: Witry v: Chicago, IL i: Emigrated to Aurora, IL c: 2
+ seq: 271.01 JADO, Michael (Mike) b: Abt. 1955 w: Abt. 1885 v: Chicago, IL c: 2
8 WITTRY, John-Baptist b: 31 Oct 1861 in Ernzen, Lux d: 25 May 1921 in Aurora, IL Cause of death: Tuberculosis and stomach cancer a: Witry v: Aurora, IL i: Emigrated to Aurora, IL o: Tailor r: b c: 8
+ seq: 272 JANSZ, Mary-Anna b: 15 Mar 1865 in Aurora, IL d: 27 Mar 1950 w: Abt. 1884 v: Aurora, IL c: 8
8 WITTRY, Barbara b: 27 Apr 1864 in Ernzen, Lux d: 30 Mar 1933 in Aurora, IL a: Witry h: 747 Liberty v: Big Rock, IL i: Emigrated to Aurora, IL r: b c: 8
+ seq: 182 WITTRY, John b: 20 Sep 1860 in Aurora, IL d: 15 Oct 1943 in Aurora, IL w: 18 Feb 1886 in Aurora, IL h: 747

Liberty v: Big Rock, IL o: Farmer f: Jacob Wittry m: Magdalena Schons c: 8

271.01

8 WITTRY, Marie-Magdalena (Lena) b: 18 May 1859 in Ernzen, Lux a: Witry v: Chicago, IL i: Emigrated to Aurora, IL c: 2
+ seq: 271.01 JADO, Michael (Mike) b: Abt. 1955 w: Abt. 1885 v: Chicago, IL c: 2
9 JADO, Paul b: 07 Sep d: 28 Jun 1969
9 JADO, Catherine C. b: 22 Aug d: 17 Jul 1973 c: 3
+ seq: 271.02 SITTER, Joseph w: Abt. 1910 c: 3

271.02

9 JADO, Catherine C. b: 22 Aug d: 17 Jul 1973 c: 3
+ seq: 271.02 SITTER, Joseph w: Abt. 1910 c: 3
10SITTER, Katherine b: 17 Oct 1912 c: 4
+ seq: 271.03 BURGIN, John w: Abt. 1935 c: 4
10SITTER, Bernadine b: 12 Aug 1914 c: 3
+ seq: 271.04 KUBACKI, Stanley w: Abt. 1935 c: 3
10SITTER, Gerald-Joseph b: 01 Jan 1918 c: 3
+ seq: 271.05 MURPHY, Lois b: 22 May 1921 d: 02 Dec 1993 w: Abt. 1945 Number of children

271.03

10SITTER, Katherine b: 17 Oct 1912 c: 4
+ seq: 271.03 BURGIN, John w: Abt. 1935 c: 4
11BURGIN, Mary-Kay b: 18 Jun 1938
11BURGIN, Jack b: 28 Oct 1941
11BURGIN, Barbara-Jean b: 05 Feb 1945
11BURGIN, Thomas b: 20 Mar

271.04

10SITTER, Bernadine b: 12 Aug 1914 c: 3
+ seq: 271.04 KUBACKI, Stanley w: Abt. 1935 c: 3
11KUBACKI, Ronald b: 24 Oct 1939
11KUBACKI, Susan b: 28 Aug 1946 d: 21 Jul 1970
11KUBACKI, Lee b: 17 Nov 1942

271.05

10SITTER, Gerald-Joseph b: 01 Jan 1918 c: 3
+ seq: 271.05 MURPHY, Lois b: 22 May 1921 d: 02 Dec 1993

w: Abt. 1945 c: 3
11 SITTER, Jerry b: 01 Jan
11 SITTER, Catherine-Marie (Kathy) b: 25 May 1949
11 SITTER, Patricia-Ann b: 09 Jun 1954

272

8 WITTRY, John-Baptist b: 31 Oct 1861 in Ernzen, Lux d: 25
   May 1921 in Aurora, IL Cause of death: Tuberculosis and
   stomach cancer a: Witry v: Aurora, IL i: Emigrated to Aurora,
   IL o: Tailor r: b c: 8
+ seq: 272 JANSZ, Mary-Anna b: 15 Mar 1865 in Aurora, IL d:
   27 Mar 1950 w: Abt. 1884 v: Aurora, IL c: 8
9 WITTRY, Barbara b: Abt. 1886 d: Abt. 1886
9 [1] WITTRY, Paul-Peter b: 13 Nov 1888 in Biwer, Lux d: 03
   Feb 1968 in Seattle, WA v: Seattle, WA v: Aurora, IL o:
   Machinist at Automatic c: 5
+ seq: 273 Marie b: Abt. 1880 w: Abt. 1915 in Biwer, Lux v:
   Aurora, IL
* 2nd Wife of [1] WITTRY, Paul-Peter:
+ seq: 274 ALLEN, Clara-Mary b: 01 Mar 1898 in Austin, MN
   d: 22 Sep 1937 in Seattle, WA w: 09 Aug 1920 v: Seattle, WA
   c: 4
* 3rd Wife of [1] WITTRY, Paul-Peter:
+ seq: 274.03 BAKER, Mary-Carolyn b: 02 Jul 1921 in
   Monrovia, CA d: Aug 1987 w: 1942 c: 1
9 WITTRY, John-Frank b: 14 May 1890 d: 05 Jan 1989 v:
   Aurora, IL i: Tailor c: 2
+ seq: 275 CLAUSON, Rose-Ella (Rosella) b: 16 Apr 1900 d: 28
   Feb 1988 w: Abt. 1920 v: Aurora, IL c: 2
9 WITTRY, Elizabeth M. b: 25 Jan 1894 d: 19 Dec 1947 c: 2
+ seq: 277.01 KELLEY, William H. b: Abt. 1890 d: 09 Nov
   1957 w: Abt. 1920 c: 2
9 WITTRY, Louise b: 27 Apr 1895 in Colorado d: 02 Aug 1962
   in San Diego, CA
9 WITTRY, Anthony J. b: 14 Aug 1898 d: 26 Dec 1998 in
   Rockford, IL v: Rockford, IL v: Aurora, IL o: Tsilor o:
   Salesman of dry cleaning and laundry equipment c: 1
+ seq: 278 CALLAHAN, Marcella b: 26 Jul 1903 d: 25 Nov
   2000 in Rockford, IL w: 30 Dec 1922 in Aurora, IL v:
   Rockford, IL v: Aurora, IL i: Reknowned storyteller o:
   Legislator c: 1

9 WITTRY, Herman-Joseph b: 25 Mar 1901 in Aurora, IL d: 02 Jan 1948 in Green Bay, Wi Cause of death: Auto accident i: Auto accident, returning from Green Bay, WI o: Accountant c: 2

+ seq: 279 FILBEY, Edna P. b: 31 Jan 1901 in Plano, IL d: 25 Dec 1947 in Green Bay, Wi Cause of death: Auto accident w: Abt. 1925 in Aurora, IL f: Oliver B. Filbey m: Mary-Elizabeth Worby c: 2

9 WITTRY, Alfred N. b: 22 Nov 1905 d: 13 Jan 1961 v: Aurora, IL c: 2

+ seq: 283 PFISTER, Lillian C. b: 1899 d: 1948 in Aurora, IL w: Abt. 1935 v: Aurora, IL c: 2

273

9 [1] WITTRY, Paul-Peter b: 13 Nov 1888 in Biwer, Lux d: 03 Feb 1968 in Seattle, WA v: Seattle, WA v: Aurora, IL o: Machinist at Automatic c: 5

+ seq: 273 Marie b: Abt. 1880 w: Abt. 1915 in Biwer, Lux v: Aurora, IL

* 2nd Wife of [1] WITTRY, Paul-Peter:

+ seq: 274 ALLEN, Clara-Mary b: 01 Mar 1898 in Austin, MN d: 22 Sep 1937 in Seattle, WA w: 09 Aug 1920 v: Seattle, WA c: 4

10 WITTRY, Mary-Clara b: 21 Jul 1923 in Deer Park, WA c: 1

+ seq: 274.01 BRINGEN w: 1945 c: 1

10 WITTRY, Frances C. b: 12 Nov 1932 in Aurora, IL v: Tacoma, WA

10 WITTRY, Theresa-Virginia (Terry) b: 01 Oct 1925 in Aurora, IL v: Temple City, CA

+ seq: 274.02 KNISLEY, Edward-Walton b: Abt. 1920 w: Jun 1945 v: Temple City, CA

10 WITTRY, Paul-Peter b: 25 May 1921 d: 10 Mar 1988 in Spokane, WA v: Anchorage, AK

* 3rd Wife of [1] WITTRY, Paul-Peter:

+ seq: 274.03 BAKER, Mary-Carolyn b: 02 Jul 1921 in Monrovia, CA d: Aug 1987 w: 1942 c: 1

10 WITTRY, Carolyn-Joyce b: 21 Sep 1946 in Arcadia, CA

274.01

10 WITTRY, Mary-Clara b: 21 Jul 1923 in Deer Park, WA c: 1

+ seq: 274.01 BRINGEN w: 1945 c: 1

11WITTRY, Paul-Peter b: 23 Nov 1945 v: Index, WA i: Taken into grandfather's family i: Legally adopted by grandfather

275

9 WITTRY, John-Frank b: 14 May 1890 d: 05 Jan 1989 v: Aurora, IL i: Tailor c: 2
+ seq: 275 CLAUSON, Rose-Ella (Rosella) b: 16 Apr 1900 d: 28 Feb 1988 w: Abt. 1920 v: Aurora, IL c: 2
10WITTRY, Donald-Laverne b: 28 Aug 1924 d: 04 Aug 1997 in Aurora, IL Cause of death: Pneumonia v: Aurora, IL o: Salesman for a card company
10WITTRY, John (Jack) Clausen b: 11 Nov 1928 v: North Aurora, IL c: 2
+ seq: 276 HAGERTY, Kathleen M. b: 03 Feb 1933 w: Abt. 1950 v: North Aurora, IL c: 2

276

10WITTRY, John (Jack) Clausen b: 11 Nov 1928 v: North Aurora, IL c: 2
+ seq: 276 HAGERTY, Kathleen M. b: 03 Feb 1933 w: Abt. 1950 v: North Aurora, IL c: 2
11WITTRY, Jack-Martin b: 16 Nov 1955 v: Aurora, IL c: 1
+ seq: 277 CHRISTOPHERSON, Phyllis b: 17 May 1955 w: Abt. 1980 v: Aurora, IL c: 1
11WITTRY, Timothy-Scott b: 05 Jan 1959 v: North Aurora, IL

277

11WITTRY, Jack-Martin b: 16 Nov 1955 v: Aurora, IL c: 1
+ seq: 277 CHRISTOPHERSON, Phyllis b: 17 May 1955 w: Abt. 1980 v: Aurora, IL c: 1
12WITTRY, Erin-Kay b: 19 Feb 1994 in Aurora, IL

277.01

9 WITTRY, Elizabeth M. b: 25 Jan 1894 d: 19 Dec 1947 c: 2
+ seq: 277.01 KELLEY, William H. b: Abt. 1890 d: 09 Nov 1957 w: Abt. 1920 c: 2
10KELLEY, William H. b: Abt. 1925 c: 5
+ seq: 277.02 Maryann b: Abt. 1930 w: Abt. 1955 c: 5
10KELLEY, Richard b: Abt. 1925
+ seq: 277.03 MCKAY, Margie b: Abt. 1930 w: Abt. 1955

277.02

10KELLEY, William H. b: Abt. 1925 c: 5

+ seq: 277.02 Maryann b: Abt. 1930 w: Abt. 1955 c: 5

11KELLEY, Gloria b: Abt. 1960

11KELLEY, Regina-Clare b: Abt. 1960

11KELLEY, Kevin-Shawn b: Abt. 1960

11KELLEY, Robert-Patrick-Erin b: Abt. 1960

11KELLEY, Willliam-Francis (Willie) b: Abt. 1960

278

9 WITTRY, Anthony J. b: 14 Aug 1898 d: 26 Dec 1998 in
Rockford, IL v: Rockford, IL v: Aurora, IL o: Tsilor o:
Salesman of dry cleaning and laundry equipment c: 1

+ seq: 278 CALLAHAN, Marcella b: 26 Jul 1903 d: 25 Nov
2000 in Rockford, IL w: 30 Dec 1922 in Aurora, IL v:
Rockford, IL v: Aurora, IL i: Reknowned storyteller o:
Legislator c: 1

10WITTRY, Mary-Lou b: 22 Apr 1927 c: 6

+ seq: 278.01 O'LEARY, Donald P. b: 01 Aug 1926 w: Abt.
1948 c: 6

278.01

10WITTRY, Mary-Lou b: 22 Apr 1927 c: 6

+ seq: 278.01 O'LEARY, Donald P. b: 01 Aug 1926 w: Abt.
1948 c: 6

11O'LEARY, Sheila b: 29 Jun 1950

11O'LEARY, Maureen b: 25 Sep 1952 c: 2

+ seq: 278.02 KOTELES, Gary T. b: 12 Jan 1952 w: Abt. 1980
c: 2

11O'LEARY, Aileen b: 25 Sep 1952 c: 2

+ seq: 278.03 SECKMAN, Michael b: 24 Jan 1947 w: 1975 c: 2

11O'LEARY, Clare b: 02 Jan 1955

11O'LEARY, Brigid b: 29 Apr 1960

11O'LEARY, Tara b: 17 Aug 1966

278.02

11O'LEARY, Maureen b: 25 Sep 1952 c: 2

+ seq: 278.02 KOTELES, Gary T. b: 12 Jan 1952 w: Abt. 1980
c: 2

12KOTELES, Michael-Thomas b: 24 Aug 1982

12KOTELES, Lauren-Ann b: 22 Jan 1985

278.03

11O'LEARY, Aileen b: 25 Sep 1952 c: 2
+ seq: 278.03 SECKMAN, Michael b: 24 Jan 1947 w: 1975 c: 2
12SECKMAN, John-Anthony b: 21 Dec 1980
12SECKMAN, David-Michael b: 21 May 1983

279

9 WITTRY, Herman-Joseph b: 25 Mar 1901 in Aurora, IL d: 02
Jan 1948 in Green Bay, Wi Cause of death: Auto accident i:
Auto accident, returning from Green Bay, WI o: Accountant c:
2
+ seq: 279 FILBEY, Edna P. b: 31 Jan 1901 in Plano, IL d: 25
Dec 1947 in Green Bay, Wi Cause of death: Auto accident w:
Abt. 1925 in Aurora, IL f: Oliver B. Filbey m: Mary-Elizabeth
Worby c: 2
10[1] WITTRY, Warren-Lee b: 24 May 1927 d: 15 Dec 1995 in
Washington, MO v: Washington, MO o: Archeologist c: 3
+ seq: 280 KLEPPE, Joan-Beth b: 16 Dec 1927 in Troy, MI w:
28 Jan 1950 in Madison, WI v: Troy, MI c: 3
* 2nd Wife of [1] WITTRY, Warren-Lee:
+ seq: 281.50 RADFORD, Carol S. w: Abt. 1965
10WITTRY, David-Beryle (Dave) b: 07 Feb 1929 in Mason City,
IA d: 05 May 2007 in Pasadena, CA Cause of death: pneumonia
v: Pasadena, CA o: Professor c: 5
+ seq: 282 DUBOIS, Mildred Elizabeth (Elizabeth) b: 12 Jul
1926 in Brandon, FL w: 01 Jul 1955 in Pasadena, CA v:
Pasadena, CA o: Homemaker o: Bookkeeper f: Earl Dubois
m: Etta c: 5

280

10[1] WITTRY, Warren-Lee b: 24 May 1927 d: 15 Dec 1995 in
Washington, MO v: Washington, MO o: Archeologist c: 3
+ seq: 280 KLEPPE, Joan-Beth b: 16 Dec 1927 in Troy, MI w:
28 Jan 1950 in Madison, WI v: Troy, MI c: 3
11WITTRY, Elissa A. b: 03 Jan 1951 v: Birmingham, MI
+ seq: 280.01 CZERKAS, Jan b: 23 Jun 1953 in Krakow, Poland
w: Abt. 1975 v: Birmingham, MI
11WITTRY, Steven L. b: 22 Mar 1952 v: Bryn Mawr, PA o:
Architect c: 2
+ seq: 281 BREDE, Nadia B. b: 21 Aug 1952 w: Abt. 1980 v:
Bryn Mawr, PA c: 2

11 WITTRY, David-Carl b: Jul 1963 in Royal Oak, MI v: Lake
   Orion, MI c: 2
+ seq: 281.01 BOHANEK, Therese b: 02 Jan 1965 w: 14 May
   1988 v: Lake Orion, MI c: 2
* 2nd Wife of [1] WITTRY, Warren-Lee:
+ seq: 281.50 RADFORD, Carol S. w: Abt. 1965

281

11 WITTRY, Steven L. b: 22 Mar 1952 v: Bryn Mawr, PA o:
   Architect c: 2
+ seq: 281 BREDE, Nadia B. b: 21 Aug 1952 w: Abt. 1980 v:
   Bryn Mawr, PA c: 2
12 WITTRY, David-Spencer b: 05 Mar 1990
12 WITTRY, Nathanial-Brede b: 19 May 1994

281.01

11 WITTRY, David-Carl b: Jul 1963 in Royal Oak, MI v: Lake
   Orion, MI c: 2
+ seq: 281.01 BOHANEK, Therese b: 02 Jan 1965 w: 14 May
   1988 v: Lake Orion, MI c: 2
12 WITTRY, Weston b: 05 Feb 1991
12 WITTRY, Addison b: 29 Dec 1994

282

10 WITTRY, David-Beryle (Dave) b: 07 Feb 1929 in Mason City,
   IA d: 05 May 2007 in Pasadena, CA Cause of death: pneumonia
   v: Pasadena, CA o: Professor c: 5
+ seq: 282 DUBOIS, Mildred Elizabeth (Elizabeth) b: 12 Jul
   1926 in Brandon, FL w: 01 Jul 1955 in Pasadena, CA v:
   Pasadena, CA o: Homemaker o: Bookkeeper f: Earl Dubois
   m: Etta c: 5
11 WITTRY, James-David (Jim) b: 22 Aug 1956 in Pasadena, CA
   v: Pasadena, CA o: Geologist c: 1
+ seq: 282.00.01 HALL, Nadine w: 28 Jun 1997 c: 1
11 WITTRY, Robert-Andrew (Rob) b: 16 Feb 1958 in Pasadena,
   CA v: Pasadena, CA o: Electrical engineer
11 WITTRY, Kristopher-Lee (Kris) b: 17 May 1960 in Pasadena,
   CA v: Pasadena, CA o: Geotechnical technician c: 2
+ seq: 282.01 LUGO, Sonya-Nancy b: 14 Jul 1960 in Los
   Angeles, CA w: 23 Sep 1989 in Pasadena, CA v: Pasadena,
   CA o: Editor of health magazine o: Administrative assistant at

a Christian school f: Lugo m: Magdalena Hernandez c: 2
11 WITTRY, Diane-Marie b: 11 Oct 1961 in Pasadena, CA v:
   West Orange, NJ o: Orchestra conductor
 + seq: 282.02 PECKHAM, Richard-Edward b: 19 May 1956 w:
   06 Jun 1999 in Beaumont, TX f: Jay-Roy Peckham
11 WITTRY, Linda-Beryle b: 12 Aug 1963 in Pasadena, CA v:
   Altadena, CA o: Educator

282.00.01
11 WITTRY, James-David (Jim) b: 22 Aug 1956 in Pasadena, CA
   v: Pasadena, CA o: Geologist c: 1
 + seq: 282.00.01 HALL, Nadine w: 28 Jun 1997 c: 1
12 WITTRY, Elaine-Grace b: 26 Mar 1998

282.01
11 WITTRY, Kristopher-Lee (Kris) b: 17 May 1960 in Pasadena,
   CA v: Pasadena, CA o: Geotechnical technician c: 2
 + seq: 282.01 LUGO, Sonya-Nancy b: 14 Jul 1960 in Los
   Angeles, CA w: 23 Sep 1989 in Pasadena, CA v: Pasadena,
   CA o: Editor of health magazine o: Administrative assistant at
   a Christian school f: Lugo m: Magdalena Hernandez c: 2
12 WITTRY, Kyle-David b: 03 Apr 1992 in Upland, CA
12 WITTRY, Amanda-Lydia (Mandy) b: 16 Aug 1996 in
   Pasadena, CA

283
9 WITTRY, Alfred N. b: 22 Nov 1905 d: 13 Jan 1961 v: Aurora,
   IL c: 2
 + seq: 283 PFISTER, Lillian C. b: 1899 d: 1948 in Aurora, IL
   w: Abt. 1935 v: Aurora, IL c: 2
10 WITTRY, Myrna b: Abt. 1940
 + seq: 283.01 GUESS, Robert b: Abt. 1935 w: Abt. 1965
10 WITTRY, Delores-Lilyan b: Abt. 1940 c: 3
 + seq: 283.02 GARRISON, Robert-Glen (Bobby) b: Abt. 1935
   w: Abt. 1965 f: Virgil Garrison m: Cleona-Mae Trotter c: 3

283.02
10 WITTRY, Delores-Lilyan b: Abt. 1940 c: 3
 + seq: 283.02 GARRISON, Robert-Glen (Bobby) b: Abt. 1935
   w: Abt. 1965 f: Virgil Garrison m: Cleona-Mae Trotter c: 3
11 GARRISON, Cary-Lynn b: Abt. 1970

11 GARRISON, Gary-Glen b: Abt. 1970
11 GARRISON, Brenda-Lee b: Abt. 1970

283.03

7 WITRY, Barbara b: 07 May 1833 in Herborn, Lux d: 13 Dec 1902 in Rosport, Lux v: Rosport, Lux o: No profession r: bd c: 5
+ seq: 283.03 THINNES, Pierre b: 17 Jan 1832 in Rosport, Lux d: 16 Jan 1907 in Rosport, Lux w: 01 Feb 1864 in Rosport, Lux v: Rosport, Lux o: Master bricklayer r: d r: m f: Michel Thinnes m: Marie Schmitt c: 5
8 THINNES, Michel b: 25 Dec 1864 in Rosport, Lux r: b
8 THINNES, Maria b: 18 Jan 1867 in Rosport, Lux r: b
8 THINNES, Johann b: 02 Nov 1868 in Rosport, Lux r: b
8 THINNES, Michel b: 10 Feb 1871 in Rosport, Lux r: b
8 THINNES, Catharina b: 08 Apr 1875 in Rosport, Lux r: b

284

7 WITRY, Peter b: 16 Mar 1835 in Herborn, Lux d: 16 Jan 1901 in Herborn, Lux v: Herborn, Lux o: Day laborer o: Carpenter o: Craftsman r: b c: 8
+ seq: 284 WEISGERBER, Anna b: 04 Oct 1841 in Herborn, Lux w: 09 Jan 1867 in Mompach, Lux v: Herborn, Lux o: No profession r: b r: m f: Johann Weisgerber m: Elisabeth Baden c: 8
8 WITRY, Nicolas (Nic) b: 11 Oct 1867 in Herborn, Lux d: 07 Oct 1944 in Herborn, Lux Cause of death: German mortar v: Herborn, Lux o: Carpenter r: b
8 WITRY, Catherine b: 08 Oct 1869 in Herborn, Lux d: 20 Aug 1923 in Rosport, Lux o: No profession r: bd c: 7
+ seq: 284.20 RAUSCH, Peter b: 31 May 1865 in Rosport, Lux d: 14 Dec 1912 in Rosport, Lux w: 28 Apr 1896 in Rosport, Lux o: Factory worker o: Day laborer r: d r: m f: Mathias Rausch m: Gertrude Thinnes c: 7
8 WITRY, Anna b: 02 Apr 1873 in Herborn, Lux h: Orteschhof h: Peteschhof v: Grevenmacher, Lux o: No profession r: b c: 8
+ seq: 284.50 MULLER, Johann Peter b: 28 Mar 1870 in Breinert, Lux w: 09 May 1900 in Grevenmacher, Lux h: Orteschhof h: Peteschhof v: Grevenmacher, Lux o: Laborer o: Farmer o: Laborer r: m f: Michel Muller m: Margaretha Bains c: 8
8 WITRY, Jacob b: 17 Sep 1874 in Herborn, Lux d: 13 May 1886

in Herborn, Lux v: Herborn, Lux o: No profession r: bd

8 WITRY, Margaretha b: 26 Jan 1878 in Herborn, Lux r: b

8 WITRY, Peter (Pierre) b: 11 Aug 1879 in Herborn, Lux d: 07
Oct 1944 in Herborn, Lux Cause of death: German mortar v:
Herborn, Lux o: Carpenter r: b

8 WITRY, Marie b: 18 Apr 1881 in Herborn, Lux d: 05 Jan 1884
in Herborn, Lux v: Herborn, Lux o: No profession r: bd

8 WITRY, Mathias b: 08 Aug 1883 in Herborn, Lux d: 25 May
1907 in Herborn, Lux v: Herborn, Lux o: No profession

284.20

8 WITRY, Catherine b: 08 Oct 1869 in Herborn, Lux d: 20 Aug
1923 in Rosport, Lux o: No profession r: bd c: 7

+ seq: 284.20 RAUSCH, Peter b: 31 May 1865 in Rosport, Lux d:
14 Dec 1912 in Rosport, Lux w: 28 Apr 1896 in Rosport, Lux
o: Factory worker o: Day laborer r: d r: m f: Mathias Rausch
m: Gertrude Thinnes c: 7

9 RAUSCH, Anna b: 05 Apr 1897 in Rosport, Lux r: b

9 RAUSCH, Peter-Johann b: 21 Sep 1898 in Rosport, Lux d: 14
Oct 1976 in Rosport, Lux v: Rosport, Lux o: Railroad worker
r: b

9 RAUSCH, Maria-Anna b: 14 May 1900 in Rosport, Lux r: b

9 RAUSCH, Catharina b: 06 Jul 1902 in Rosport, Lux r: b

9 RAUSCH, Georg b: 24 Apr 1904 in Rosport, Lux d: 10 Nov
1983 in Luxembourg, Lux r: b

9 RAUSCH, Franz b: 29 Jan 1906 in Rosport, Lux r: b

9 RAUSCH, Margaretha b: 30 Oct 1909 in Rosport, Lux d: 16
May 1973 in Luxembourg, Lux r: b

284.50

8 WITRY, Anna b: 02 Apr 1873 in Herborn, Lux h: Orteschhof
h: Peteschhof v: Grevenmacher, Lux o: No profession r: b c: 8

+ seq: 284.50 MULLER, Johann Peter b: 28 Mar 1870 in
Breinert, Lux w: 09 May 1900 in Grevenmacher, Lux h:
Orteschhof h: Peteschhof v: Grevenmacher, Lux o: Laborer
o: Farmer o: Laborer r: m f: Michel Muller m: Margaretha
Bains c: 8

9 MULLER, Margaretha b: 03 Jun 1901 in Grevenmacher, Lux r:
b

9 MULLER, Anna b: 17 May 1902 in Grevenmacher, Lux d: 30
Nov 1987 in Grevenmacher, Lux r: b

9 MULLER, Nikolas b: 25 Jun 1903 in Grevenmacher, Lux d: 15 Aug 1972 in Grevenmacher, Lux r: b

9 MULLER, Adam b: 03 Jul 1904 in Grevenmacher, Lux r: b

9 MULLER, Peter-Nicolas b: 25 Feb 1908 in Grevenmacher, Lux r: b

9 MULLER, Johann-Peter b: 29 May 1910 in Grevenmacher, Lux r: b

9 MULLER, Maria b: 11 Nov 1911 in Grevenmacher, Lux d: 16 Feb 1912 in Grevenmacher, Lux r: bd

9 MULLER, Franz b: 27 Feb 1907 in Grevenmacher, Lux r: b

285

7 [1] WITRY, Nicolas b: 09 Apr 1837 in Herborn, Lux d: 17 Feb 1914 in Waterloo, IA Cause of death: Pneumonia h: Kuhnen v: Breda, IA v: Herborn, Lux i: Emigrated to the U. S. o: Mason o: Farmer o: Wagon maker r: bdx c: 2

+   seq: 285 COOPER, Mary b: 1840 d: 09 Sep 1875 in Breda, IA w: 10 Jul 1873 in Dubuque, IA v: Breda, IA c: 2

8 WITRY, Mathias i: Died young

8 WITRY, Clara i: Died young

* 2nd Wife of [1] WITRY, Nicolas:

+   seq: 286 SALMEN, Sophia b: 1834 d: 06 Oct 1906 in Iowa w: 28 Jan 1876 in Dubuque, IA v: Breda, IA v: Carroll, IA

* 3rd Wife of [1] WITRY, Nicolas:

+   seq: 287 ENGELBRECHT, Mary b: Abt. 1850 w: Dec 1913 v: Breda, IA

287.01

7 WITRY, Catherine b: 15 Jun 1839 in Herborn, Lux d: Abt. 1912 h: Kuhnen v: Waterloo, IA v: Herborn, Lux i: Emigrated to the U. S. r: b c: 7

+   seq: 287.01 BLITSCH, Jacob b: Abt. 1840 w: Abt. 1868 v: Waterloo, IA v: Herborn, Lux o: Cabinet maker c: 7

8 BLITSCH, Dominic b: 26 Oct 1869

8 BLITSCH, Henry b: 06 Mar 1872

8 BLITSCH, Nicolas b: 12 Dec 1872 in Herborn, Lux

8 BLITSCH, Martin b: 23 Jul 1874

8 BLITSCH, Sophia-Maria b: 07 May 1876

8 BLITSCH, William-Joseph b: 06 Feb 1878

8 BLITSCH, Edward b: Abt. 1880 v: Waterloo, IA

7 WITRY, Dominic b: 19 Oct 1841 in Herborn, Lux d: 23 Oct 1912 in Waterloo, IA h: Kuhnen v: Waterloo, IA v: Herborn, Lux i: Emigrated to the U.S. o: Grocer r: bdx c: 3

+ seq: 288 POTT, Margaretha b: 10 Oct 1844 d: 14 Aug 1924 in Waterloo, IA w: 16 Feb 1869 v: Waterloo, IA c: 3

8 WITRY, Louis W. t: Vice President of John Deere b: 03 Mar 1870 in Waterloo, IA d: 14 Apr 1939 in Waterloo, IA v: Waterloo, IA o: Engineer

8 [1] WITRY, Peter (Perry) J. b: 13 Apr 1873 in Waterloo, IA d: 16 Jan 1940 in Waterloo, IA v: Waterloo, IA o: Machinist c: 5

+ seq: 289 M. M. b: Abt. 1875 w: Abt. 1896 v: Waterloo, IA c: 1

* 2nd Wife of [1] WITRY, Peter (Perry) J.:

+ seq: 290 WALCH, Philomena (Winnie) b: 1878 d: 1962 in Waterloo, IA w: 22 Apr 1898 in Waterloo, IA v: Waterloo, IA c: 4

8 WITRY, Mary (Mayme) A. b: 1883 in Waterloo, IA d: 16 Dec 1916 in Waterlo, IA v: Waterloo, IA c: 1

+ seq: 291.01 CONRY, Elmer b: Abt. 1870 in Waterloo, IA d: in Waterloo, IA w: Abt. 1910 v: Waterloo, IA c: 1

8 [1] WITRY, Peter (Perry) J. b: 13 Apr 1873 in Waterloo, IA d: 16 Jan 1940 in Waterloo, IA v: Waterloo, IA o: Machinist c: 5

+ seq: 289 M. M. b: Abt. 1875 w: Abt. 1896 v: Waterloo, IA c: 1

9 WITRY, Louis P. b: 1898 in Waterloo, IA d: 1918 in Waterloo, IA

* 2nd Wife of [1] WITRY, Peter (Perry) J.:

+ seq: 290 WALCH, Philomena (Winnie) b: 1878 d: 1962 in Waterloo, IA w: 22 Apr 1898 in Waterloo, IA v: Waterloo, IA c: 4

9 WITRY, Kathryn b: Abt. 1905 in Waterloo, IA v: Longmont, CO c: 1

+ seq: 290.01 SMITH, David w: Abt. 1930 v: Longmont, CO c: 1

9 WITRY, Louis b: Abt. 1905

9 WITRY, Margaret b: Abt. 1905

+ seq: 290.02 DAVIS b: Abt. 1900 w: Abt. 1930 in Waterloo, IA

9 WITRY, Frank A. b: 10 Nov 1909 in Waterloo, IA d: 24 Sep

1983 in Waterloo, IA v: Waterloo, IA o: U. S. Tank Corps o: Manager of apartment buildings o: Plumbing and heating sales
+ seq: 291 SEIBLE, Dolores S. b: 01 Oct 1923 in Mason City, IA d: 10 Sep 1998 in Waterloo, IA Cause of death: Cancer w: 19 Apr 1958 in Rockford, IL v: Waterloo, IA f: Eno Duvall m: Eva Duvall

290.01

9 WITRY, Kathryn b: Abt. 1905 in Waterloo, IA v: Longmont, CO c: 1
+ seq: 290.01 SMITH, David w: Abt. 1930 v: Longmont, CO c: 1
10SMITH, Royce-David

291.01

8 WITRY, Mary (Mayme) A. b: 1883 in Waterloo, IA d: 16 Dec 1916 in Waterlo, IA v: Waterloo, IA c: 1
+ seq: 291.01 CONRY, Elmer b: Abt. 1870 in Waterloo, IA d: in Waterloo, IA w: Abt. 1910 v: Waterloo, IA c: 1
9 CONRY, Cecil F. b: 16 Dec 1916 in Waterloo, IA d: 13 Aug 1984 in Waterloo, IA v: Waterloo, IA o: Water Works
+ seq: 291.02 QUINETT, Esther M. b: Abt. 1920 w: May 1942 in Bethany, MO v: Waterloo, IA

292

6 WITRY, Johann b: 04 Mar 1797 in Beidweiler, Lux d: 09 Mar 1865 in Beidweiler, Lux h: Hames v: Beidweiler, Lux i: Discharge from militia o: Day laborer o: Farmer r: bd c: 5
+ seq: 292 MEYERS, Barbara b: 19 Apr 1800 in Dickweiler, Lux d: 24 Feb 1874 in Beidweiler, Lux w: 21 Apr 1830 in Rodenbourg, Lux v: Beidweiler, Lux o: Farmer r: d r: m f: Nicolas Meyers m: Catherine Poos c: 5
7 WITRY, Nicolas b: 21 Jun 1831 in Beidweiler, Lux d: 16 Dec 1868 in Beidweiler, Lux v: Beidweiler, Lux o: Farmer r: bd c: 5
+ seq: 024 MULLER, Elisabeth b: 06 Apr 1837 in Zittig, Lux w: 23 Feb 1859 in Rodenbourg, Lux v: Beidweiler, Lux i: Both are descendents of the family tree o: Innkeeper r: b r: m f: Theodor Muller m: Anna Witry c: 5
7 WITRY, Elisabeth b: 02 Feb 1834 in Beidweiler, Lux d: 10 May 1834 in Beidweiler, Lux h: Hames v: Beidweiler, Lux o:

No profession r: bd

7 WITRY, Peter b: 12 May 1835 in Beidweiler, Lux d: 11 Dec
1908 in Graulinster, Lux v: Graulinster, Lux o: Day laborer o:
Farmer o: Tavern keeper r: bd c: 3

+ seq: 293 KELSEN, Johanna (Marie) (Jeanne) b: 24 Aug 1843
in Contern, Lux d: 16 Sep 1898 in Graulinster, Lux w: 05 Jul
1876 in Luxembourg, Lux v: Graulinster, Lux i: Born on
Krintgeshof farm o: Day laborer o: Tavern keeper r: d r: m f:
Nicolas Kelsen m: Marie Eckoltres c: 3

7 WITRY, Catherine b: 11 Apr 1838 in Beidweiler, Lux d: 17
May 1843 in Beidweiler, Lux h: Hames v: Beidweiler, Lux o:
No profession r: bd

7 [1] WITRY, Franz b: 25 Jun 1844 in Beidweiler, Lux v: Nancy,
France o: Restaranteur o: Stable-hand r: b

+ seq: 298 FRANCOIS, Marie-Louise b: 25 Aug 1849 in
Baccarat, France d: 14 Mar 1886 in Nancy, France w: 24 Nov
1877 in Rodenbourg, Lux v: Nancy, France o: Cook r: m f:
Johann-Nicolas Francois m: Marie-Amalieasette Benaud

* 2nd Wife of [1] WITRY, Franz:

+ seq: 299 TOUSSAINT, Marie-Pelagie b: 16 Apr 1849 in Rupt-
en-Meuse, France w: 19 Jul 1884 in Nancy, France v: Nancy,
France o: Cook r: m f: Joseph Toussaint m: Barbe Barniere

293

7 WITRY, Peter b: 12 May 1835 in Beidweiler, Lux d: 11 Dec
1908 in Graulinster, Lux v: Graulinster, Lux o: Day laborer o:
Farmer o: Tavern keeper r: bd c: 3

+ seq: 293 KELSEN, Johanna (Marie) (Jeanne) b: 24 Aug 1843
in Contern, Lux d: 16 Sep 1898 in Graulinster, Lux w: 05 Jul
1876 in Luxembourg, Lux v: Graulinster, Lux i: Born on
Krintgeshof farm o: Day laborer o: Tavern keeper r: d r: m f:
Nicolas Kelsen m: Marie Eckoltres c: 3

8 WITRY, Anna b: 08 Apr 1877 in Graulinster, Lux r: b

8 WITRY, Marie b: 11 Jan 1880 in Graulinster, Lux v:
Graulinster, Lux o: No profession r: b c: 4

+ seq: 293.01 KESSELER, Peter b: 30 Aug 1877 in Graulinster,
Lux w: 19 Feb 1902 in Junglinster, Lux v: Graulinster, Lux o:
Merchant o: Day laborer r: m f: Johann Kesseler m: Susanna
Schons c: 4

8 WITRY, Pierre b: 01 Mar 1883 in Graulinster, Lux d: 25 Mar
1956 in Paris, France v: Paris, France o: Cabinet maker r: b c:

3

+ seq: 294 HILTGEN, Angele b: 16 Apr 1887 in Berdorf, Lux d: 09 Dec 1961 in Paris, France w: 23 Feb 1906 in Berdorf, Lux v: Paris, France c: 3

293.01

8 WITRY, Marie b: 11 Jan 1880 in Graulinster, Lux v: Graulinster, Lux o: No profession r: b c: 4

+ seq: 293.01 KESSELER, Peter b: 30 Aug 1877 in Graulinster, Lux w: 19 Feb 1902 in Junglinster, Lux v: Graulinster, Lux o: Merchant o: Day laborer r: m f: Johann Kesseler m: Susanna Schons c: 4

9 KESSELER, Catherine b: 30 Jun 1903 in Graulinster, Lux r: b c: 1

+ seq: 293.02 PHILIPP, Mathias w: Abt. 1935 c: 1

9 KESSELER, Peter b: 18 Apr 1906 in Graulinster, Lux r: b

9 KESSELER, Johann-Peter b: 25 Apr 1909 in Graulinster, Lux r: b

9 KESSELER, Aloyse b: 18 Sep 1918 in Graulinster, Lux r: b

293.02

9 KESSELER, Catherine b: 30 Jun 1903 in Graulinster, Lux r: b c: 1

+ seq: 293.02 PHILIPP, Mathias w: Abt. 1935 c: 1

10PHILIPP, Marie-Paule c: 1

+ seq: 293.03 CIMENTI, Armando w: Abt. 1965 c: 1

293.03

10PHILIPP, Marie-Paule c: 1

+ seq: 293.03 CIMENTI, Armando w: Abt. 1965 c: 1

11CIMENTI, Claudia

294

8 WITRY, Pierre b: 01 Mar 1883 in Graulinster, Lux d: 25 Mar 1956 in Paris, France v: Paris, France o: Cabinet maker r: b c: 3

+ seq: 294 HILTGEN, Angele b: 16 Apr 1887 in Berdorf, Lux d: 09 Dec 1961 in Paris, France w: 23 Feb 1906 in Berdorf, Lux v: Paris, France c: 3

9 WITRY, Nicolas b: 30 Apr 1907 in Paris, France d: 17 Feb 1990 in Roullet St. Estephe, France v: Paris, France o: Cabinet

maker c: 2

+ seq: 295 CONTAMINES, Madeleine b: 12 Feb 1910 in St.
Barthelemy, France w: 26 Apr 1930 in Paris, France v: Paris,
France c: 2

9 WITRY, Alice b: 28 Jan 1909 in Paris, France d: 08 Mar 1909
in Paris, France

9 WITRY, Alice b: 01 Apr 1911 in Paris, France d: 29 Feb 1912
in Paris, France

295

9 WITRY, Nicolas b: 30 Apr 1907 in Paris, France d: 17 Feb
1990 in Roullet St. Estephe, France v: Paris, France o: Cabinet
maker c: 2

+ seq: 295 CONTAMINES, Madeleine b: 12 Feb 1910 in St.
Barthelemy, France w: 26 Apr 1930 in Paris, France v: Paris,
France c: 2

10 WITRY, Denise b: 31 Mar 1931 in Paris, France d: 19 Aug
1932

10 WITRY, Pierre b: 05 May 1932 in Paris, France v: Le Plessis
Trevise, France o: Industrial designer c: 2

+ seq: 296 CLAUSS, Anne-Marthe b: 29 Dec 1930 in Strasbourg,
France w: 06 Aug 1955 in Paris, France v: Le Plessis Trevise,
France f: Albert Clauss m: Marthe Hugel c: 2

296

10 WITRY, Pierre b: 05 May 1932 in Paris, France v: Le Plessis
Trevise, France o: Industrial designer c: 2

+ seq: 296 CLAUSS, Anne-Marthe b: 29 Dec 1930 in Strasbourg,
France w: 06 Aug 1955 in Paris, France v: Le Plessis Trevise,
France f: Albert Clauss m: Marthe Hugel c: 2

11 WITRY, Isabelle b: 18 Dec 1963 in Nogent-sur-Marne, France
v: Nogent-sur-Marne, France c: 2

+ seq: 296.01 GALLAIS, Lionel b: 09 Jul 1962 in Charenton,
France w: 06 Sep 1986 in Le Plessis Trevise, France o:
Professor of Business Management f: Pierre Gallais m: Denise
Alain c: 2

11 WITRY, Pascal b: 06 May 1966 in Nogent-sur-Marne, France
v: Le Plessis Trevise, France o: Commercial engineer c: 2

+ seq: 297 FALMOUTH, Sylvie b: 23 Jun 1966 in Champigny-
sur-Marne, France w: 25 Sep 1993 in Le Plessis Trevise,
France v: Le Plessis Trevise, France f: Jacques Falmouth m:

Alzira Lopes c: 2

296.01
11 WITRY, Isabelle b: 18 Dec 1963 in Nogent-sur-Marne, France
  v: Nogent-sur-Marne, France c: 2
+ seq: 296.01 GALLAIS, Lionel b: 09 Jul 1962 in Charenton,
  France w: 06 Sep 1986 in Le Plessis Trevise, France o:
  Professor of Business Management f: Pierre Gallais m: Denise
  Alain c: 2
12 GALLAIS, Melanie b: 27 Jan 1989 in Nogent-sur-Marne,
  France
12 GALLAIS, Marion b: 21 Jan 1992 in Nogent-sur-Marne, France

297
11 WITRY, Pascal b: 06 May 1966 in Nogent-sur-Marne, France
  v: Le Plessis Trevise, France o: Commercial engineer c: 2
+ seq: 297 FALMOUTH, Sylvie b: 23 Jun 1966 in Champigny-
  sur-Marne, France w: 25 Sep 1993 in Le Plessis Trevise,
  France v: Le Plessis Trevise, France f: Jacques Falmouth m:
  Alzira Lopes c: 2
12 WITRY, Romain b: 01 Nov 1994 in Nogent-sur-Marne, France
12 WITRY, Margot b: 08 Dec 1996 in Nogent-sur-Marne, France

300
6 WITRY, Peter b: 02 May 1802 in Beidweiler, Lux d: 03 Mar
  1847 in Osweiler, Lux v: Osweiler, Lux o: Laborer o: Farmer
  r: bd c: 3
+ seq: 300 NEU, Catherine b: 09 Nov 1810 in Osweiler, Lux w:
  22 Feb 1838 in Rosport, Lux v: Osweiler, Lux o: No profession
  r: b r: m f: Peter Neu m: Susanne Neu c: 3
7 WITRY, Nicolas b: 07 Jan 1841 in Osweiler, Lux d: 25 Nov
  1914 in Osweiler, Lux v: Osweiler, Lux o: Carpenter o:
  Furniture maker r: bd c: 6
+ seq: 301 ENDERS, Marie b: 03 Dec 1854 in Herborn, Lux d:
  07 Jan 1930 in Osweiler, Lux w: 23 Feb 1881 in Rosport, Lux
  v: Osweiler, Lux o: No profession r: m f: Johann Enders m:
  Catherine Klein c: 6
7 WITRY, Catherine b: 09 Sep 1843 in Osweiler, Lux d: 02 Jan
  1864 in Osweiler, Lux v: Osweiler, Lux o: No profession r: d
7 [1] WITRY, Marie b: 02 Jul 1846 in Osweiler, Lux d: 27 Oct
  1885 in Moesdorf, Lux v: Moesdorf, Lux v: Osweiler, Lux o:

No profession r: bd
+ seq: 308.01 KOHN, Heinrich b: Abt. 1852 w: Abt. 1875 v:
  Moesdorf, Lux o: Railroad worker
* 2nd Husband of [1] WITRY, Marie:
+ seq: 308.02 SCHWARTZ, Franz b: 15 Nov 1847 in Osweiler,
  Lux w: 22 Jan 1879 in Rosport, Lux v: Osweiler, Lux o:
  Mason r: b r: m f: Heinrich Schwartz m: Anna Hansen

301

7 WITRY, Nicolas b: 07 Jan 1841 in Osweiler, Lux d: 25 Nov
  1914 in Osweiler, Lux v: Osweiler, Lux o: Carpenter o:
  Furniture maker r: bd c: 6
+ seq: 301 ENDERS, Marie b: 03 Dec 1854 in Herborn, Lux d:
  07 Jan 1930 in Osweiler, Lux w: 23 Feb 1881 in Rosport, Lux
  v: Osweiler, Lux o: No profession r: m f: Johann Enders m:
  Catherine Klein c: 6
8 WITRY, Catherine b: 18 Jan 1882 in Osweiler, Lux d: 09 Nov
  1911 in Osweiler, Lux v: Osweiler, Lux o: No profession r: bd
  c: 2
+ seq: 301.01 [1] TOUSSING, Jacques b: 06 Sep 1873 in
  Consdorf, Lux d: 08 Feb 1933 w: 18 Nov 1907 in Rosport, Lux
  v: Osweiler, Lux i: Jacques married sisters (marriages seq. no.
  301.01 and 303.01) o: Farmer o: Laborer o: Smelter worker r:
  m f: Nicolas Toussing m: Maria Hansen c: 9
8 WITRY, Bernhard b: 01 Jun 1884 in Osweiler, Lux d: Abt.
  1960 in Chicago, IL v: Chicago, IL i: Emigrated to U.S. -
  Aurora, IL i: Arrived on the Kroonland from Antwerp o:
  Master carpenter r: b
+ seq: 302 DECKER, Margareta b: Abt. 1885 in Nommern, Lux
  w: Abt. 1910 v: Chicago, IL
8 WITTRY, Nicolas-Louis b: 28 Sep 1886 in Osweiler, Lux v:
  Chicago, IL i: Emigrated to the U.S. - Milwaukee, WI i:
  Arrived on the Zeeland from Antwerp r: b c: 2
+ seq: 303 BARTET, Elsie b: Abt. 1885 in Milwaukee, WI w:
  Abt. 1910 in Chicago, IL v: Chicago, IL c: 2
8 [2] WITRY, Angela b: 26 Oct 1889 in Osweiler, Lux v:
  Osweiler, Lux o: Farmer c: 7
+ seq: 303.01 [1] TOUSSING, Jacques b: 06 Sep 1873 in
  Consdorf, Lux d: 08 Feb 1933 w: 20 Nov 1912 in Rosport, Lux
  v: Osweiler, Lux i: Jacques married sisters (marriages seq. no.
  301.01 and 303.01) o: Farmer o: Laborer o: Smelter worker r:

m f: Nicolas Toussing m: Maria Hansen c: 9
* 2nd Husband of [2] WITRY, Angela:
+ seq: 303.02 KAUTH, Jean-Pierre b: Abt. 1885 in Osweiler, Lux
  w: 09 Nov 1935
8 WITRY, Anna b: 23 Aug 1893 in Osweiler, Lux d: 31 Oct 1911
  in Osweiler, Lux v: Osweiler, Lux o: No profession r: bd
8 WITRY, Pierre b: 02 Mar 1896 in Osweiler, Lux d: 1973 in
  Osweiler, Lux v: Osweiler, Lux o: Carpenter o: Furniture
  maker c: 4
+ seq: 304 KAUTH, Helena b: 14 Dec 1896 in Bastendorf, Lux d:
  26 Jun 1995 in Echternach, Lux w: 13 May 1921 in Rosport,
  Lux v: Osweiler, Lux o: No profession f: Johann Kauth m:
  Barbara Jungels c: 4

301.01

8 WITRY, Catherine b: 18 Jan 1882 in Osweiler, Lux d: 09 Nov
  1911 in Osweiler, Lux v: Osweiler, Lux o: No profession r: bd
  c: 2
+ seq: 301.01 TOUSSING, Jacques b: 06 Sep 1873 in Consdorf,
  Lux d: 08 Feb 1933 w: 18 Nov 1907 in Rosport, Lux v:
  Osweiler, Lux i: Jacques married sisters (marriages seq. no.
  301.01 and 303.01) o: Farmer o: Laborer o: Smelter worker r:
  m f: Nicolas Toussing m: Maria Hansen c: 9
9 TOUSSING, Anna b: 22 Aug 1908 in Osweiler, Lux o: Nun r:
  b
9 TOUSSING, Franz-Johann-Peter b: 30 Apr 1910 in Osweiler,
  Lux r: b
+ seq: 301.02 HOFFMANN, Maria b: Abt. 1910 in Reisdorf, Lux
  w: Abt. 1935

303

8 WITTRY, Nicolas-Louis b: 28 Sep 1886 in Osweiler, Lux v:
  Chicago, IL i: Emigrated to the U.S. - Milwaukee, WI i:
  Arrived on the Zeeland from Antwerp r: b c: 2
+ seq: 303 BARTET, Elsie b: Abt. 1885 in Milwaukee, WI w:
  Abt. 1910 in Chicago, IL v: Chicago, IL c: 2
9 WITTRY, Arthur b: 19 May 1913 in Aurora, IL d: 16 Aug
  1913 in Aurora, IL v: Aurora, IL
9 WITTRY, Louis b: 29 Apr 1914 in Frankville, WI d: 17 Dec
  1914 in Aurora, IL v: Aurora, IL

303.01

8 [1] WITRY, Angela b: 26 Oct 1889 in Osweiler, Lux v:
Osweiler, Lux o: Farmer c: 7

+ seq: 303.01 TOUSSING, Jacques b: 06 Sep 1873 in Consdorf,
Lux d: 08 Feb 1933 w: 20 Nov 1912 in Rosport, Lux v:
Osweiler, Lux i: Jacques married sisters (marriages seq. no.
301.01 and 303.01) o: Farmer o: Laborer o: Smelter worker r:
m f: Nicolas Toussing m: Maria Hansen c: 9

9 TOUSSING, Joseph b: 15 Mar 1913 in Osweiler, Lux r: b

9 TOUSSING, Johann b: 08 Feb 1915 in Osweiler, Lux d: 30 Oct
1953 r: b

9 TOUSSING, Peter-Andreas b: 02 Feb 1917 in Osweiler, Lux d:
07 Feb 1917 in Osweiler, Lux r: bd

9 TOUSSING, Eduard-Peter b: 07 Oct 1918 in Osweiler, Lux d:
27 Dec 1941 in Wahl, Lux r: b

9 TOUSSING, Emil b: 18 May 1921 in Osweiler, Lux d: 27 Dec
1921 in Osweiler, Lux r: bd

9 TOUSSING, Helena b: 18 Dec 1922 in Osweiler, Lux d: 09 Jun
1982 in Osweiler, Lux r: b

9 TOUSSING, Albert b: 22 Jul 1927 in Osweiler, Lux

* 2nd Husband of [1] WITRY, Angela:

+ seq: 303.02 KAUTH, Jean-Pierre b: Abt. 1885 in Osweiler, Lux
w: 09 Nov 1935

304

8 WITRY, Pierre b: 02 Mar 1896 in Osweiler, Lux d: 1973 in
Osweiler, Lux v: Osweiler, Lux o: Furniture maker c: 4

+ seq: 304 KAUTH, Helena b: 14 Dec 1896 in Bastendorf, Lux
d: 26 Jun 1995 in Echternach, Lux w: 14 May 1921 in Rosport,
Lux v: Osweiler, Lux c: 4

9 WITRY, Alfred b: 15 Dec 1922 in Osweiler, Lux d: 22 Mar
1973 in Ettelbruck, Lux v: Echternach, Lux o: Furniture maker
c: 2

+ seq: 305 MODERT, Maria b: 24 Apr 1930 in Uebersyren, Lux
w: 14 Jul 1952 in Rosport, Lux v: Osweiler, Lux c: 2

9 WITRY, Rene-Mathias b: 07 Jan 1925 in Osweiler, Lux d:
1945 in Russia

9 WITRY, Ernest-Nicolas b: 1927 in Osweiler, Lux d: 20 May
1932 in Osweiler, Lux v: Osweiler, Lux

9 WITRY, Francois b: 09 Oct 1933 in Osweiler, Lux d: 19 Oct
1933 in Osweiler, Lux v: Osweiler, Lux

9 WITRY, Johann-Alfred b: 15 Dec 1922 in Osweiler, Lux d: 22 Mar 1973 in Ettelbruck, Lux v: Echternach, Lux o: Furniture maker r: b c: 2

+ seq: 305 MODERT, Maria b: 24 Apr 1930 in Uebersyren, Lux w: 14 Jul 1952 in Rosport, Lux v: Osweiler, Lux c: 2

10 WITRY, Rene b: 25 Aug 1953 in Echternach, Lux v: Echternach, Lux o: Architect c: 3

+ seq: 306 WILLE, Ursula b: 29 Jan 1952 in Hildesheim-Bavevenstedt, Germany w: 11 Jul 1977 in Rosport, Lux v: Echternach, Lux o: Architect c: 3

10[1] WITRY, Marco b: 13 May 1955 in Echternach, Lux v: Osweiler, Lux o: Furniture maker c: 3

+ seq: 307 WOLF, Denise b: 30 Jun 1956 in Echternach, Lux w: 25 Jun 1982 in Rosport, Lux v: Osweiler, Lux c: 2

* 2nd Wife of [1] WITRY, Marco:

+ seq: 308 BATTEUX, Doris b: 03 Jan 1961 in Bitburg, Germany w: 25 Oct 1991 v: Luxembourg, Lux c: 1

10 WITRY, Rene b: 25 Aug 1953 in Echternach, Lux v: Echternach, Lux o: Architect c: 3

+ seq: 306 WILLE, Ursula b: 29 Jan 1952 in Hildesheim-Bavevenstedt, Germany w: 11 Jul 1977 in Rosport, Lux v: Echternach, Lux o: Architect c: 3

11 WITRY, Anabel b: 01 Dec 1977 in Kassel, Germany i: Studied in Munich

11 WITRY, Christopher b: 04 Oct 1980 in Osweiler, Lux

11 WITRY, Marie-Helene b: 18 Apr 1988 in Osweiler, Lux

10[1] WITRY, Marco b: 13 May 1955 in Echternach, Lux v: Osweiler, Lux o: Furniture maker c: 3

+ seq: 307 WOLF, Denise b: 30 Jun 1956 in Echternach, Lux w: 25 Jun 1982 in Rosport, Lux v: Osweiler, Lux c: 2

11 WITRY, Sam b: 20 Jan 1983 in Osweiler, Lux

11 WITRY, Lye b: 09 Apr 1984 in Osweiler, Lux

* 2nd Wife of [1] WITRY, Marco:

+ seq: 308 BATTEUX, Doris b: 03 Jan 1961 in Bitburg, Germany w: 25 Oct 1991 v: Luxembourg, Lux c: 1

11 WITRY, Alex b: 29 Sep 1993 in Osweiler, Lux

5 WITRY, Margaretha b: 14 Jul 1756 in Bergem, Lux h:
Scheurengs v: Mondercange, Lux o: Farmer r: b c: 10

+ seq: 308.03 DONDELINGER, Michel b: Abt. 1750 in
Mondercange, Lux d: 01 Jun 1839 in Bergem, Lux w: Abt.
1774 a: Scheurengs h: Scheurengs v: Mondercange, Lux o:
Farmer c: 10

6 DONDELINGER, Nicolas b: 20 Oct 1775 in Mondercange, Lux
r: b

6 DONDELINGER, Frederic b: 01 Feb 1779 in Mondercange,
Lux d: 07 Feb 1779 in Mondercange, Lux v: Mondercange, Lux
o: No profession r: bd

6 DONDELINGER, Nicolas b: 20 Oct 1780 in Mondercange, Lux
v: Mondercange, Lux r: b

+ seq: 308.04 ROESER, Magdalena b: Abt. 1788 in Fingig, Lux
w: 23 Jun 1813 in Mondercange, Lux v: Mondercange, Lux r:
m f: Michel Roeser

6 DONDELINGER, Ludwig b: 10 Nov 1782 in Mondercange,
Lux d: 23 Aug 1784 in Mondercange, Lux v: Mondercange,
Lux o: No profession r: bd

6 DONDELINGER, Margaretha b: 21 Apr 1785 in Mondercange,
Lux v: Mondercange, Lux r: b

+ seq: 308.05 BIVER, Nicolas b: Abt. 1777 in Mondercange, Lux
w: 03 Jan 1814 in Mondercange, Lux v: Mondercange, Lux r:
m f: Johann Biver m: Marie Goergen

6 DONDELINGER, Jacob b: 06 Jun 1787 in Mondercange, Lux
r: b

6 DONDELINGER, Johann b: 15 Jun 1789 in Mondercange, Lux
v: Bettembourg, Lux o: Farmer r: b

+ seq: 308.06 KNEIP, Agnese b: 09 May 1791 in Bettembourg,
Lux w: 26 Jan 1818 in Bettembourg, Lux v: Bettembourg, Lux
r: m f: Friederich Kneip m: Barbara Kirpach

6 DONDELINGER, Peter b: 18 Sep 1791 in Mondercange, Lux
d: 27 Jul 1793 in Mondercange, Lux v: Mondercange, Lux o:
No profession r: bd

6 DONDELINGER, Marie b: 09 Dec 1793 in Mondercange, Lux
r: b

6 DONDELINGER, Marie-Catherine b: 30 Nov 1797 in
Mondercange, Lux d: 07 Dec 1797 in Mondercange, Lux v:
Mondercange, Lux o: No profession r: bd

308.07

5 [1] WITRY, Magdalena b: 14 Oct 1758 in Bergem, Lux d: 21
  Apr 1823 in Strassem, Lux h: Schneider-Meyers v: Strassem,
  Lux r: bd c: 6
+ seq: 308.07 SCHMITT, Johann b: Abt. 1755 in Strassem, Lux
  d: 20 Nov 1802 in Strassem, Lux w: 26 Feb 1781 in Bertrange,
  Lux h: Schneider-Meyers v: Strassem, Lux o: Innkeeper o:
  Farmer r: d r: m f: Nicolas Schmitt m: Marie Dondelinger c:
  6
6 SCHMITT, Marie b: 10 Apr 1788 in Strassem, Lux r: b
6 SCHMITT, Marie-Catherine b: 09 Jul 1789 in Strassem, Lux r:
  b
6 SCHMITT, Margaretha b: 25 Aug 1791 in Strassem, Lux r: b
6 SCHMITT, Catherine b: 10 Jan 1793 in Strassem, Lux d: 13
  Apr 1793 in Strassem, Lux v: Strassem, Lux r: bd
6 SCHMITT, Peter b: 28 Feb 1794 in Strassem, Lux r: b
6 SCHMITT, Johann b: 24 Mar 1796 in Strassem, Lux r: b
* 2nd Husband of [1] WITRY, Magdalena:
+ seq: 308.08 SCHINTGEN, Nicolas b: Abt. 1780 in
  Mondercange, Lux w: 11 Jan 1804 in Bertrange, Lux v:
  Strassem, Lux o: Farmer r: m f: Johann Schintgen m: Marie
  Lantgen

310

5 WITRY, Nicolas b: Abt. 1766 in Schiffelange, Lux v:
  Dudelange, Lux o: Farmer c: 1
+ seq: 310 WEISGERBER, Margaretha b: Abt. 1765 w: Abt.
  1790 v: Dudelange, Lux c: 1
6 WITRY, Magdalena b: Abt. 1795 in Dudelange, Lux v:
  Bergem, Lux

311

3 WITRY, Peter b: 09 Apr 1654 in Schrondweiler, Lux d: 17 Feb
  1708 in Schrondweiler, Lux a: Weidert h: Weidert v:
  Schrondweiler, Lux o: Overseer o: Steward r: bd c: 7
+ seq: 311 GLASENER, Anna-Elisabeth b: Abt. 1660 in
  Schrondweiler, Lux w: 11 Nov 1685 in Nommern, Lux a:
  Weidert h: Weidert v: Schrondweiler, Lux r: m c: 7
4 WITRY, Johanna b: 30 Mar 1688 in Schrondweiler, Lux a:
  Weidert h: Weidert v: Schrondweiler, Lux r: b c: 8
+ seq: 311.01 RECKINGER, Bernard w: 14 Jan 1705 in

Nommern, Lux a: Holdschun a: Weidert h: Weidert v:
Schrondweiler, Lux o: Steward r: m c: 8

4 WITRY, Anna b: 07 Dec 1690 in Schrondweiler, Lux a:
Weidert h: Weidert r: b

4 WITRY, Johann b: 19 Sep 1693 in Schrondweiler, Lux a:
Weidert r: b

4 WITRY, Nicolas b: 10 Aug 1696 in Schrondweiler, Lux d: 20
Jun 1762 in Oberfeulen, Lux a: Weidert a: Welter v:
Oberfeulen, Lux i: 4th degree of consanguinity r: bd c: 6

+ seq: 311.06 WELTER, Susanne b: 24 Nov 1700 in Oberfeulen,
Lux d: 12 Dec 1770 in Oberfeulen, Lux w: 15 Oct 1734 in
Feulen, Lux v: Oberfeulen, Lux i: 4th degree of consanguinity
r: bd r: mx f: Johann Welter m: Marie Duhr c: 6

4 WITTRY, Catherine b: 04 Dec 1698 in Schrondweiler, Lux a:
Weidert r: b

4 WITTRY, Margaretha b: 13 Mar 1701 in Schrondweiler, Lux a:
Weidert r: b

4 WITRY, Peter b: 27 Apr 1703 in Schrondweiler, Lux a:
Weidert r: b

311.01

4 WITRY, Johanna b: 30 Mar 1688 in Schrondweiler, Lux a:
Weidert h: Weidert v: Schrondweiler, Lux r: b c: 8

+ seq: 311.01 RECKINGER, Bernard w: 14 Jan 1705 in
Nommern, Lux a: Holdschun a: Weidert h: Weidert v:
Schrondweiler, Lux o: Steward r: m c: 8

5 RECKINGER, Marie b: 29 Dec 1707 in Schrondweiler, Lux r:
b

5 RECKINGER, Michel b: 30 Sep 1709 in Schrondweiler, Lux r:
b

5 [1] RECKINGER, Johann-Michel b: 23 Mar 1712 in
Schrondweiler, Lux d: 11 May 1779 in Schrondweiler, Lux a:
Weidert h: Weidert v: Schrondweiler, Lux i: 3rd degree of
consanguinity o: Official o: Steward r: bd

+ seq: 311.02 KREMER, Magdalena b: Abt. 1715 in
Schrondweiler, Lux d: 06 Jan 1752 in Schrondweiler, Lux w:
Abt. 1739 a: Weidert h: Weidert v: Schrondweiler, Lux o:
Steward r: d

* 2nd Wife of [1] RECKINGER, Johann-Michel:

+ seq: 311.03 ATTEN, Anna-Catherine b: Abt. 1713 in Bissen,
Lux d: 15 Aug 1777 in Schrondweiler, Lux w: Feb 1753 in

Nommern, Lux h: Weidert v: Schrondweiler, Lux i: Buried by her brother, J. B. Atten, cure r: d

* 3rd Wife of [1] RECKINGER, Johann-Michel:

+ seq: 311.04 DELFELD, Marie-Catherine b: Abt. 1755 in Fels, Lux w: 13 May 1778 in Nommern, Lux h: Weidert v: Schrondweiler, Lux i: 3rd degree of consanguinity r: m

5 RECKINGER, Johann b: 29 Nov 1714 in Schrondweiler, Lux r: b

5 RECKINGER, Mathias b: 06 Jul 1717 in Schrondweiler, Lux a: Holdschun r: b

5 RECKINGER, Anna b: 06 Dec 1718 in Schrondweiler, Lux a: Holdschun r: b

5 RECKINGER, Anna-Margaretha b: 02 Jan 1728 in Schrondweiler, Lux r: b

5 RECKINGER, Marie-Margaretha b: 29 Oct 1735 in Schrondweiler, Lux v: Schrondweiler, Lux r: b

+ seq: 311.05 MEDERNACH, Johann b: Abt. 1730 in Rupe, Lux w: 04 Feb 1755 in Nommern, Lux v: Schrondweiler, Lux r: m f: Valentin Medernach

311.06

4 WITRY, Nicolas b: 10 Aug 1696 in Schrondweiler, Lux d: 20 Jun 1762 in Oberfeulen, Lux a: Weidert a: Welter v: Oberfeulen, Lux i: 4th degree of consanguinity r: bd c: 6

+ seq: 311.06 WELTER, Susanne b: 24 Nov 1700 in Oberfeulen, Lux d: 12 Dec 1770 in Oberfeulen, Lux w: 15 Oct 1734 in Feulen, Lux v: Oberfeulen, Lux i: 4th degree of consanguinity r: bd r: mx f: Johann Welter m: Marie Duhr c: 6

5 WITRY, Franzisca-Mauevia b: 12 Oct 1735 in Oberfeulen, Lux a: Weidert r: b

5 WITRY, Anna-Margaretha b: 04 Jul 1737 in Oberfeulen, Lux a: Weidert r: b

5 WITRY, Heinrich b: 02 Feb 1738 in Oberfeulen, Lux a: Weidert r: b

5 WITRY, Johann b: 28 Mar 1740 in Oberfeulen, Lux a: Weidert r: bx

5 WITRY, Anna-Maria b: 23 Jan 1743 in Oberfeulen, Lux d: 22 Aug 1777 in Niederfeulen, Lux a: Weidert v: Niederfeulen, Lux i: 4th degree of consanguinity r: bd c: 7

+ seq: 311.07 WILTGEN, Nicolas b: 21 Dec 1726 in Niederfeulen, Lux d: 26 Jun 1779 in Niederfeulen, Lux w: 08

Mar 1763 in Feulen, Lux a: Wiltges v: Niederfeulen, Lux i:
4th degree of consanguinity o: Farmer r: m f: Mathias Wiltgen
m: Catherine Junckers c: 7

5 WITRY, Franz b: 07 Sep 1745 in Oberfeulen, Lux d: 12 Aug
1746 in Oberfeulen, Lux a: Weidert r: bd

311.07

5 WITRY, Anna-Maria b: 23 Jan 1743 in Oberfeulen, Lux d: 22
Aug 1777 in Niederfeulen, Lux a: Weidert v: Niederfeulen, Lux
i: 4th degree of consanguinity r: bd c: 7

+ seq: 311.07 WILTGEN, Nicolas b: 21 Dec 1726 in
Niederfeulen, Lux d: 26 Jun 1779 in Niederfeulen, Lux w: 08
Mar 1763 in Feulen, Lux a: Wiltges v: Niederfeulen, Lux i:
4th degree of consanguinity o: Farmer r: m f: Mathias Wiltgen
m: Catherine Junckers c: 7

6 WILTGEN, Martin b: 06 Sep 1764 in Niederfeulen, Lux d: 21
Jul 1766 in Niederfeulen, Lux r: bd

6 WILTGEN, Marguerite b: 20 Oct 1766 in Niederfeulen, Lux r:
b

6 WILTGEN, Jean-Pierre b: 25 Mar 1769 in Niederfeulen, Lux r:
b

6 WILTGEN, Barbe b: 17 Nov 1770 in Niederfeulen, Lux d: 13
Jan 1772 in Niederfeulen, Lux r: bd

6 WILTGEN, Dominique b: 16 Oct 1772 in Niederfeulen, Lux d:
17 Apr 1830 in Oberglabach, Lux r: b c: 8

+ seq: 311.08 JACOBY, Susanne b: 03 Mar 1775 in
Oberglabach, Lux d: 19 Mar 1837 in Oberglabach, Lux w: 04
Nov 1793 in Nommern, Lux f: Johann Jacoby c: 8

6 [1] WILTGEN, Jean b: 16 Jun 1775 in Niederfeulen, Lux r: b
c: 9

+ seq: 311.22.50 WEYLAND, Marie b: 1777 w: 17 Mar 1799 in
Nommern, Lux c: 8

* 2nd Wife of [1] WILTGEN, Jean:

+ seq: 311.23 WAGNER, Catherine b: Abt. 1780 w: Abt. 1813
in Mersch, Lux c: 1

6 WILTGEN, Marguerite b: 21 Aug 1777 in Niederfeulen, Lux d:
16 May 1778 in Niederfeulen, Lux r: bd

311.08

6 WILTGEN, Dominique b: 16 Oct 1772 in Niederfeulen, Lux d:
17 Apr 1830 in Oberglabach, Lux r: b c: 8

+   seq: 311.08 JACOBY, Susanne b: 03 Mar 1775 in
Oberglabach, Lux d: 19 Mar 1837 in Oberglabach, Lux w: 04
Nov 1793 in Nommern, Lux f: Johann Jacoby c: 8
7 WILTGEN, Marie-Jeanne b: 28 Dec 1794 in Oberglabach, Lux
d: 02 Nov 1869 in Nommern, Lux c: 5
+   seq: 311.09 MONS, Heinrich b: Abt. 1789 in Essen, Germany
d: 11 Mar 1868 in Nommern, Lux w: 10 Feb 1819 in
Nommern, Lux f: Nikolas Mons m: Marie Strauss c: 5
7 WILTGEN, Marie-Franziska b: 10 Jul 1797 in Oberglabach,
Lux d: 17 Jan 1872 in Oberglabach, Lux c: 10
+   seq: 311.12 KAYSER, Nikolas b: Abt. 1795 in Jeanhartshof,
Lux w: 17 Nov 1819 in Nommern, Lux f: Henri Kayser m:
Marie Bertrang c: 10
7 WILTGEN, Nicolas b: 17 Dec 1799 in Oberglabach, Lux c: 1
+   seq: 311.20 RIES, Margaretha b: Abt. 1805 in Eichelbour, Lux
w: 18 Feb 1833 in Nommern, Lux f: Jacques Ries m: Marie
Matgen c: 1
7 WILTGEN, Nicolas b: 28 Jun 1802 in Oberglabach, Lux d: 12
Nov 1826 in Oberglabach, Lux
7 WILTGEN, Susanne b: 26 Dec 1804 in Oberglabach, Lux d: 27
Dec 1804 in Oberglabach, Lux
7 WILTGEN, Jean-Nicolas b: 21 Apr 1807 in Oberglabach, Lux
d: 12 Feb 1817 in Oberglabach, Lux
7 WILTGEN, Jean b: 18 Oct 1809 in Oberglabach, Lux
+   seq: 311.21 BILTGEN, Catherine b: Abt. 1810 w: 12 Feb 1837
in Nommern, Lux
7 WILTGEN, Barbara b: 08 May 1815 in Oberglabach, Lux
+   seq: 311.22 WAGNER, Peter b: Abt. 1815 in Petange, Lux w:
24 Jan 1838 in Mersch, Lux

311.09
7 WILTGEN, Marie-Jeanne b: 28 Dec 1794 in Oberglabach, Lux
d: 02 Nov 1869 in Nommern, Lux c: 5
+   seq: 311.09 MONS, Heinrich b: Abt. 1789 in Essen, Germany
d: 11 Mar 1868 in Nommern, Lux w: 10 Feb 1819 in
Nommern, Lux f: Nikolas Mons m: Marie Strauss c: 5
8 MONS, Catherine b: 28 Apr 1820 in Nommern, Lux d: 16 Feb
1880 in Nommern, Lux
+   seq: 311.10 GLOD, Pierre b: Abt. 1814 in Reckange, Lux d:
01 Apr 1893 in Nommern, Lux w: 02 Jan 1849 in Nommern,
Lux

8 MONS, Nikolaus b: 04 Jul 1822 in Nommern, Lux i: Emigrated
   to the U.S.A. with the children
+ seq: 311.11 HILBERT, Susanne b: Abt. 1827 in Nommern,
   Lux d: 04 Nov 1870 in Nommern, Lux w: Abt. 1848
8 MONS, Susanne b: 18 Sep 1831 in Nommern, Lux d: 17 Jun
   1905 in Nommern, Lux
8 MONS, Barbara b: 23 Aug 1833 in Nommern, Lux d: 22 May
   1875 in Nommern, Lux
8 MONS, Theodor b: 08 Mar 1835 in Nommern, Lux d: 22 Mar
   1835 in Nommern, Lux v: Nommern, Lux

311.12
7 WILTGEN, Marie-Franziska b: 10 Jul 1797 in Oberglabach,
   Lux d: 17 Jan 1872 in Oberglabach, Lux c: 10
+ seq: 311.12 KAYSER, Nikolas b: Abt. 1795 in Jeanhartshof,
   Lux w: 17 Nov 1819 in Nommern, Lux f: Henri Kayser m:
   Marie Bertrang c: 10
8 KAYSER, Marie b: 28 Sep 1820 in Nommern, Lux d: 07 Jan
   1821 in Nommern, Lux
8 KAYSER, Margaretha b: 01 Jan 1822 in Nommern, Lux
+ seq: 311.13 STRASSER, Michel b: Abt. 1818 in Flaxweiler,
   Lux w: 03 Apr 1848 in Nommern, Lux
8 KAYSER, Susanne b: 21 Dec 1823 in Nommern, Lux d: 22
   Dec 1823 in Nommern, Lux
8 KAYSER, Jeanne b: 19 Jan 1826 in Nommern, Lux d: 20 Jan
   1826 in Nommern, Lux
8 KAYSER, Jean b: 14 Jan 1830 in Nommern, Lux
+ seq: 311.14 SEIL, Anna b: Abt. 1835 in Bourglinster, Lux w:
   26 Mar 1857 in Nommern, Lux
8 KAYSER, Catherine b: 01 Sep 1832 in Nommern, Lux
+ seq: 311.15 LOMERTZ, Dominique b: Abt. 1817 in
   Erpeldange, Lux w: 24 Mar 1859 in Nommern, Lux
8 KAYSER, Wilhelm b: 02 Jan 1835 in Nommern, Lux d: 21
   Nov 1865 in Nommern, Lux
+ seq: 311.16 HOFFMANN, Catherine b: Abt. 1839 in Dillingen,
   Lux w: 11 Feb 1864 in Nommern, Lux
8 KAYSER, Nikolas b: 15 Mar 1837 in Nommern, Lux d: 03 Dec
   1895 in Nommern, Lux
+ seq: 311.17 GOERENS, Anna b: Abt. 1842 in Nommern, Lux
   d: 21 Dec 1892 in Nommern, Lux w: 09 Feb 1860 in
   Nommern, Lux

8 KAYSER, Marie-Catherine b: 23 Mar 1839 in Nommern, Lux
+ seq: 311.18 FRIEDRICH, Nikolas b: 23 Mar 1839 in
   Bettendorf, Lux w: 11 Feb 1863 in Nommern, Lux
8 KAYSER, Catherine b: 03 Apr 1841 in Nommern, Lux
+ seq: 311.19 WEYNANDT, Peter b: Abt. 1836 in Hosingen,
   Lux w: Abt. 1867

311.20

7 WILTGEN, Nicolas b: 17 Dec 1799 in Oberglabach, Lux c: 1
+ seq: 311.20 RIES, Margaretha b: Abt. 1805 in Eichelbour, Lux
   w: 18 Feb 1833 in Nommern, Lux f: Jacques Ries m: Marie
   Matgen c: 1
8 WILTGEN, Marie b: 04 May 1834

311.22.50

6 [1] WILTGEN, Jean b: 16 Jun 1775 in Niederfeulen, Lux r: b
   c: 9
+ seq: 311.22.50 WEYLAND, Marie b: 1777 w: 17 Mar 1799 in
   Nommern, Lux c: 8
7 WILTGEN, Pierre b: 08 Oct 1801 in Glabach, Lux o: Cobbler
   c: 1
+ seq: 311.22.55 STOPFEL, Elisabeth b: 1806 w: 28 Feb 1831
   in Nommern, Lux c: 1
7 WILTGEN, Apolonia b: 02 Dec 1803 in Glabach, Lux
7 WILTGEN, Susanne b: 28 Jul 1805 in Glabach, Lux
+ seq: 311.22.60 PHILIPPY, Jean b: 1803 w: 17 Apr 1828 in
   Larochette, Lux
7 WILTGEN, Anne-Marie b: 1807 in Glabach, Lux d: 20 Jan
   1877 in Bour, Lux c: 1
+ seq: 311.22.65 KLOPP, Nicolas b: Abt. 1804 d: 04 Jan 1868 in
   Bour, Lux w: Bef. 1840 c: 1
7 WILTGEN, Nicolas b: 15 Jul 1810 in Oberglabach, Lux d: 21
   Apr 1846 in Bissen, Lux c: 2
+ seq: 311.22.67 KREMER, Barbe b: 19 Jan 1812 in Bissen, Lux
   d: 30 May 1866 in Bissen, Lux w: Bef. 1841 f: Pierre Kremer
   m: Marguerite Kirsch c: 2
7 WILTGEN, Barbie b: 02 Jun 1813 in Glabach, Lux
+ seq: 311.22.70 FONCK, Michel b: Abt. 1816 w: 1837
7 WILTGEN, Rodolphe b: 27 Apr 1816 in Glabach, Lux
7 WILTGEN, Jeanne b: Abt. 1818 in Glabach, Lux d: 12 Dec
   1879 in Glabach, Lux c: 3

+ seq: 311.22.80 DICHTER, Mathias b: Abt. 1815 w: Aft. 1840
  c: 3
* 2nd Wife of [1] WILTGEN, Jean:
+ seq: 311.23 WAGNER, Catherine b: Abt. 1780 w: Abt. 1813
  in Mersch, Lux c: 1
7 WILTGEN, Jean b: 27 Oct 1815 in Niederfeulen, Lux

311.22.55
7 WILTGEN, Pierre b: 08 Oct 1801 in Glabach, Lux o: Cobbler
  c: 1
+ seq: 311.22.55 STOPFEL, Elisabeth b: 1806 w: 28 Feb 1831
  in Nommern, Lux c: 1
8 WILTGEN, Nicolas b: 08 Oct 1831 in Nommern, Lux

311.22.65
7 WILTGEN, Anne-Marie b: 1807 in Glabach, Lux d: 20 Jan
  1877 in Bour, Lux c: 1
+ seq: 311.22.65 KLOPP, Nicolas b: Abt. 1804 d: 04 Jan 1868 in
  Bour, Lux w: Bef. 1840 c: 1
8 KLOPP, Margaretha b: 1840

311.22.67
7 WILTGEN, Nicolas b: 15 Jul 1810 in Oberglabach, Lux d: 21
  Apr 1846 in Bissen, Lux c: 2
+ seq: 311.22.67 KREMER, Barbe b: 19 Jan 1812 in Bissen, Lux
  d: 30 May 1866 in Bissen, Lux w: Bef. 1841 f: Pierre Kremer
  m: Marguerite Kirsch c: 2
8 WILTGEN, Anne b: 22 Dec 1841 in Bissen, Lux
8 [1] WILTGEN, Marguerite b: 10 May 1846 in Bissen, Lux d:
  04 Jun 1904 in Vichten, Lux c: 3
+ seq: 311.22.68 GRAFF, Pierre b: 03 Feb 1845 in Kaundorf,
  Lux d: 22 Sep 1883 in Bissen, Lux w: Bef. 1869 f: Michel
  Graff m: Elisabeth Cleer c: 2
* 2nd Husband of [1] WILTGEN, Marguerite:
+ seq: 311.22.69 DELTGEN, Pierre b: 24 Oct 1841 in Vichten,
  Lux d: 12 Jul 1907 in Groseldange, Lux w: 05 May 1887 in
  Vichten, Lux o: Broom maker f: Michel Deltgen m: Catherine
  Maas c: 1

311.22.68
8 [1] WILTGEN, Marguerite b: 10 May 1846 in Bissen, Lux d:

04 Jun 1904 in Vichten, Lux c: 3
+ seq: 311.22.68 GRAFF, Pierre b: 03 Feb 1845 in Kaundorf,
   Lux d: 22 Sep 1883 in Bissen, Lux w: Bef. 1869 f: Michel
   Graff m: Elisabeth Cleer c: 2
9 GRAFF, Anne-Catherine b: 28 Oct 1869 in Bissen, Lux d: 09
   Jan 1955 in Vichten, Lux
9 GRAFF, Jean-Pierre b: 05 Dec 1873 in Bissen, Lux d: 17 Apr
   1945 in Vichten, Lux
* 2nd Husband of [1] WILTGEN, Marguerite:
+ seq: 311.22.69 DELTGEN, Pierre b: 24 Oct 1841 in Vichten,
   Lux d: 12 Jul 1907 in Groseldange, Lux w: 05 May 1887 in
   Vichten, Lux o: Broom maker f: Michel Deltgen m: Catherine
   Maas c: 1
9 DELTGEN, Jean b: 22 Jan 1890 in Vichten, Lux d: 17 Jun
   1891 in Vichten, Lux

311.22.80
7 WILTGEN, Jeanne b: Abt. 1818 in Glabach, Lux d: 12 Dec
   1879 in Glabach, Lux c: 3
+ seq: 311.22.80 DICHTER, Mathias b: Abt. 1815 w: Aft. 1840
   c: 3
8 DICHTER, Guillaume b: Aft. 1840
8 DICHTER, Pierre b: Aft. 1840
8 DICHTER, Marguerite b: Aft. 1840

321.08
3 WITRY, Franzisca b: 02 Jan 1656 in Schrondweiler, Lux a:
   Thies v: Schrondweiler, Lux r: b c: 6
+ seq: 321.08 GOEDERT, Mathias b: Abt. 1655 in
   Schrondweiler, Lux w: 02 Feb 1681 in Nommern, Lux v:
   Schrondweiler, Lux r: m c: 6
4 GOEDERT, Johann b: 10 Mar 1682 in Schrondweiler, Lux v:
   Schrondweiler, Lux r: b c: 6
+ seq: 321.09 GRALINGER, Marie-Barbara b: Abt. 1685 in
   Gralingen, Lux d: 02 Dec 1753 in Schrondweiler, Lux w: 12
   Nov 1708 in Nommern, Lux v: Schrondweiler, Lux r: d r: m
   c: 6
4 GOEDERT, Margaretha b: 03 May 1684 in Schrondweiler, Lux
   d: 27 Feb 1766 in Schrondweiler, Lux v: Schrondweiler, Lux r:
   bd c: 5
+ seq: 321.12 NEUENS, Nicolas b: Abt. 1685 in Schrondweiler,

Lux d: 01 Apr 1763 in Schrondweiler, Lux w: 17 Nov 1710 in
Nommern, Lux v: Schrondweiler, Lux o: Farmer r: d r: m c:
5
4 GOEDERT, Anna-Marie (Elisabeth) b: 25 Oct 1687 in
Schrondweiler, Lux a: Hitz v: Niederfeulen, Lux i: 4th degree
of consanguinity r: b c: 9
+ seq: 321.16 HITZ, Martin b: 14 Jul 1694 in Niederfeulen, Lux
d: 07 Jan 1772 in Niederfeulen, Lux w: 18 Feb 1715 in
Nommern, Lux a: Heintzen a: Hitzen v: Niederfeulen, Lux i:
4th degree of consanguinity o: Farmer r: bd r: m f: Peter Hitz
m: Elisabeth c: 9
4 GOEDERT, Marie b: 01 May 1690 in Schrondweiler, Lux r: b
4 GOEDERT, Nicolas b: 08 Mar 1693 in Schrondweiler, Lux d:
01 Oct 1722 in Schrondweiler, Lux v: Schrondweiler, Lux r: bd
4 GOEDERT, Catherine b: 12 Oct 1696 in Schrondweiler, Lux r:
b

321.09
4 GOEDERT, Johann b: 10 Mar 1682 in Schrondweiler, Lux v:
Schrondweiler, Lux r: b c: 6
+ seq: 321.09 GRALINGER, Marie-Barbara b: Abt. 1685 in
Gralingen, Lux d: 02 Dec 1753 in Schrondweiler, Lux w: 12
Nov 1708 in Nommern, Lux v: Schrondweiler, Lux r: d r: m
c: 6
5 GOEDERT, Marie b: Abt. 1713 in Schrondweiler, Lux d: 23
Apr 1778 in Schrondweiler, Lux h: Goedert v: Schrondweiler,
Lux o: Farmer r: d
+ seq: 321.10 THIEL, Dominic b: Abt. 1711 d: 01 Jun 1760 in
Schrondweiler, Lux w: Abt. 1735 a: Goedert h: Goedert v:
Schrondweiler, Lux o: Farmer r: d
5 GOEDERT, Catherine b: 10 Jul 1716 in Schrondweiler, Lux v:
Beaufort, Lux r: b
5 GOEDERT, Elisabeth b: 24 Aug 1718 in Schrondweiler, Lux v:
Petange, Lux r: b
+ seq: 321.11 ASSEL, Mathias b: Abt. 1715 in Beringen, Lux w:
23 Oct 1741 in Nommern, Lux v: Petange, Lux
5 GOEDERT, Mathias b: 10 Mar 1721 in Schrondweiler, Lux r: b
5 GOEDERT, Nicolas b: 24 Mar 1723 in Schrondweiler, Lux r: b
5 GOEDERT, Hubert b: 04 Nov 1725 in Schrondweiler, Lux r: b

321.12

4 GOEDERT, Margaretha b: 03 May 1684 in Schrondweiler, Lux
d: 27 Feb 1766 in Schrondweiler, Lux v: Schrondweiler, Lux r:
bd c: 5

+ seq: 321.12 NEUENS, Nicolas b: Abt. 1685 in Schrondweiler,
Lux d: 01 Apr 1763 in Schrondweiler, Lux w: 17 Nov 1710 in
Nommern, Lux v: Schrondweiler, Lux o: Farmer r: d r: m c:
5

5 [1] NEUENS, Nicolas b: 20 Oct 1711 in Schrondweiler, Lux d:
17 Jul 1796 in Schrondweiler, Lux v: Schrondweiler, Lux o:
Farmer r: bd

+ seq: 321.13 MEDERNACH, Margaretha b: Abt. 1715 w: Abt.
1740 v: Schrondweiler, Lux

* 2nd Wife of [1] NEUENS, Nicolas:

+ seq: 321.14 THINNES, Marie b: Abt. 1728 in Medernach, Lux
d: 08 Apr 1779 in Schrondweiler, Lux w: 02 Nov 1760 in
Nommern, Lux v: Schrondweiler, Lux o: Farmer r: d r: m

* 3rd Wife of [1] NEUENS, Nicolas:

+ seq: 321.15 MAJERUS, Margaretha b: Abt. 1722 in Rollingen,
Lux d: 14 Feb 1787 in Schrondweiler, Lux w: 01 Jul 1779 in
Nommern, Lux v: Schrondweiler, Lux o: Servant r: d r: m

5 NEUENS, Catherine b: Abt. 1714 in Schrondweiler, Lux v:
Bastendorf, Lux c: 10

+ seq: 321.15.01 CONZEMIUS, Joannis-Petrus b: 28 Jan 1702 in
Bastendorf, Lux d: 29 Mar 1766 in Bastendorf, Lux w: Abt.
1735 v: Bastendorf, Lux f: Petri Conzemius m: Jeanne
Eschette c: 10

5 NEUENS, Johann b: 02 Jan 1722 in Schrondweiler, Lux r: b

5 NEUENS, Elisabeth b: 27 Jan 1724 in Schrondweiler, Lux r: b

5 NEUENS, Peter b: 05 Dec 1729 in Schrondweiler, Lux r: b

321.15.01

5 NEUENS, Catherine b: Abt. 1714 in Schrondweiler, Lux v:
Bastendorf, Lux c: 10

+ seq: 321.15.01 CONZEMIUS, Joannis-Petrus b: 28 Jan 1702 in
Bastendorf, Lux d: 29 Mar 1766 in Bastendorf, Lux w: Abt.
1735 v: Bastendorf, Lux f: Petri Conzemius m: Jeanne
Eschette c: 10

6 CONZEMIUS, Marie-Marguerite b: 10 Apr 1736 in Bastendorf,
Lux

6 CONZEMIUS, Nikolas b: 08 Jul 1739 in Bastendorf, Lux

6 CONZEMIUS, Joes-Mathias b: 21 Jan 1742 in Bastendorf, Lux
  d: 03 May 1760 in Bastendorf, Lux
6 CONZEMIUS, Pierre b: 13 Aug 1744 in Bastendorf, Lux d: 22
  Jan 1776 in Bastendorf, Lux
+ seq: 321.15.02 PETERS, Susanne b: Abt. 1742 w: 10 Feb 1767
  in Diekirch, Lux
6 CONZEMIUS, Franciscus-Anselmus b: 03 Sep 1747 in
  Bastendorf, Lux
+ seq: 321.15.03 BIRCKELS, Barbe b: Abt. 1750 in Bastendorf,
  Lux w: 1769 in Diekirch, Lux
6 CONZEMIUS, Joannes-Nicolaus b: 04 May 1750 in Bastendorf,
  Lux d: 28 Feb 1771 in Bastendorf, Lux
6 CONZEMIUS, Claudius b: 25 Jun 1753 in Diekirch, Lux d: 12
  Feb 1792 in Bastendorf, Lux
+ seq: 321.15.04 MAJERUS, Anne-Marguerithe b: Abt. 1760 w:
  29 Nov 1780 in Diekirch, Lux
6 CONZEMIUS, Marie-Anna b: 27 Oct 1756 in Bastendorf, Lux
  d: 11 Jun 1829 in Colmar, Lux v: Colmar, Lux c: 6
+ seq: 321.15.05 OLSEM, Nicolas b: 16 Jan 1756 in Colmar, Lux
  d: 04 May 1824 in Colmar, Lux w: 11 Feb 1782 in Berg-
  Bissen, Lux v: Colmar, Lux f: Martinus Olsem m: Margaretha
  May c: 6
6 CONZEMIUS, Damien b: 16 Feb 1759 in Bastendorf, Lux
6 CONZEMIUS, Catherine b: Abt. 1760
+ seq: 321.15.29 LINCKELS, Jacques w: Abt. 1785

321.15.05
6 CONZEMIUS, Marie-Anna b: 27 Oct 1756 in Bastendorf, Lux
  d: 11 Jun 1829 in Colmar, Lux v: Colmar, Lux c: 6
+ seq: 321.15.05 OLSEM, Nicolas b: 16 Jan 1756 in Colmar, Lux
  d: 04 May 1824 in Colmar, Lux w: 11 Feb 1782 in Berg-
  Bissen, Lux v: Colmar, Lux f: Martinus Olsem m: Margaretha
  May c: 6
7 OLSEM, Francois b: 27 Aug 1785 in Colmar, Lux d: 29 Jul
  1860 in Colmar, Lux
7 OLSEM, Anne-Marguerite b: 16 Apr 1788 in Colmar, Lux d:
  02 Aug 1860 in Colmar, Lux
+ seq: 321.15.06 HEFFENISCH, Nikolas b: 24 Feb 1791 in
  Reckange, Lux d: 28 Sep 1848 in Colmar, Lux w: Bef. 1821
7 OLSEM, Nicolas b: 31 Oct 1790 in Colmar, Lux v: Goesdorf,
  Lux c: 4

+ seq: 321.15.07 MAJERUS, Anna-Maria b: 20 Jun 1806 in Goesdorf, Lux d: 25 Sep 1849 in Goesdorf, Lux w: 05 Apr 1826 in Goesdorf, Lux f: Gaspar Maiers m: Susanna Lanners c: 4

7 OLSEM, Marie b: 16 Jun 1793 in Colmar, Lux

7 OLSEM, Nicolas b: 16 May 1796 in Colmar, Lux d: 11 Mar 1848 in Schockville, ?

7 OLSEM, Catherine b: 14 Feb 1799 in Colmar, Lux

321.15.07

7 OLSEM, Nicolas b: 31 Oct 1790 in Colmar, Lux v: Goesdorf, Lux c: 4

+ seq: 321.15.07 MAJERUS, Anna-Maria b: 20 Jun 1806 in Goesdorf, Lux d: 25 Sep 1849 in Goesdorf, Lux w: 05 Apr 1826 in Goesdorf, Lux f: Gaspar Maiers m: Susanna Lanners c: 4

8 OLSEM, Anna-Marguerite b: 18 Nov 1830 in Goesdorf, Lux d: 28 Oct 1899 in Kaundorf, Lux v: Kaundorf, Lux c: 7

+ seq: 321.15.08 MACK, Nicolas b: 25 Feb 1832 in Dellen, Lux d: 09 Dec 1899 in Kaundorf, Lux w: 31 Jul 1858 in Heiderscheid, Lux v: Kaundorf, Lux f: Nicolas Mack m: Elisabeth Feck c: 7

8 [1] OLSEM, Maria b: 21 Jun 1834 in Goesdorf, Lux

+ seq: 321.15.25 SCHAULS, Peter b: 05 Nov 1840 in Kaundorf, Lux w: 28 Apr 1867 in Goesdorf, Lux f: Johann Schauls m: Elisabeth Reding

* 2nd Husband of [1] OLSEM, Maria:

+ seq: 321.15.26 BAULESCH, Nikolas b: 23 Jun 1844 in Goesdorf, Lux w: 15 Sep 1869 in Goesdorf, Lux f: Mathias Baulesch m: Katharina Kersch

8 OLSEM, Katharina b: 05 May 1837 in Goesdorf, Lux

+ seq: 321.15.27 FAUTSCH, Nikolas b: 17 May 1834 in Goesdorf, Lux w: 05 May 1861 in Goesdorf, Lux f: Peter Fautsch m: Anna-Maria Blaise

8 OLSEM, Nikolas b: 07 Apr 1841 in Goesdorf, Lux

+ seq: 321.15.28 KOETZ, Maria b: 30 May 1835 in Goesdorf, Lux w: 18 Apr 1866 in Goesdorf, Lux f: Wilhelm Koets m: Magdalena Zoller

321.15.08

8 OLSEM, Anna-Marguerite b: 18 Nov 1830 in Goesdorf, Lux d:

28 Oct 1899 in Kaundorf, Lux v: Kaundorf, Lux c: 7

+ seq: 321.15.08 MACK, Nicolas b: 25 Feb 1832 in Dellen, Lux
  d: 09 Dec 1899 in Kaundorf, Lux w: 31 Jul 1858 in
  Heiderscheid, Lux v: Kaundorf, Lux f: Nicolas Mack m:
  Elisabeth Feck c: 7

9 MACK, Marie b: 12 May 1859

9 MACK, Elisabetha b: 26 May 1863 in Heiderscheid, Lux

+ seq: 321.15.09 SCHWAB, Emile b: 13 Nov 1863 in
  Luxembourg, Lux w: 15 Apr 1885 in Mecher, Lux f: Frederick
  Schwab m: Magdalena Bolsen

9 MACK, Marie-Catherine b: 29 Jan 1866 in Heiderscheid, Lux

+ seq: 321.15.10 BLESER, Jean b: Abt. 1872 w: 29 Jan 1907 in
  Eschdorf, Lux

9 MACK, Anne b: 15 Feb 1867 in Heiderscheid, Lus

+ seq: 321.15.11 FAUTSCH, Jean-Francois b: 17 May 1865 in
  Kaundorf, Lux w: 24 Feb 1900 in Mecher, Lux f: Dominique
  Fautsch m: Elisabeth Wanderscheid

9 MACK, Andre b: 13 May 1868 in Heiderscheid, Lux d: Abt.
  1921 in Wiltz, Lux v: Wiltz, Lux c: 7

+ seq: 321.15.12 NOESEN, Katharina b: 01 Feb 1862 in Wiltz,
  Lux d: Abt. 1921 in Kautenbach, Lux w: 30 Dec 1890 in
  Wiltz, Lux v: Wiltz, Lux f: Johann Noesen m: Anna-Maria
  Theodory c: 7

9 MACK, Marie b: 31 Mar 1871 in Kaundorf, Lux d: 21 Jan 1872
  in Kaundorf, Lux

9 MACK, Mathias b: 31 Mar 1871 in Kaundorf, Lux d: 22 Feb
  1872 in Kaundorf, Lux

321.15.12

9 MACK, Andre b: 13 May 1868 in Heiderscheid, Lux d: Abt.
  1921 in Wiltz, Lux v: Wiltz, Lux c: 7

+ seq: 321.15.12 NOESEN, Katharina b: 01 Feb 1862 in Wiltz,
  Lux d: Abt. 1921 in Kautenbach, Lux w: 30 Dec 1890 in Wiltz,
  Lux v: Wiltz, Lux f: Johann Noesen m: Anna-Maria Theodory
  c: 7

10MACK, Joseph-Emile b: 14 Dec 1891 in Wiltz, Lux

10MACK, Nicolas-Andre b: 01 May 1893 in Wiltz, Lux d: 18
  May 1929 in Wiltz, Lux c: 2

+ seq: 321.15.13 MANDER, Claire-Eugenie-Anne b: 29 Apr 1894
  in Wiltz, Lux d: 07 Feb 1978 in Wiltz, Lux w: 28 Oct 1921 in
  Wiltz, Lux f: Frederic Mander m: Marie Kauth c: 2

10MACK, Jean-Pierre b: 25 Dec 1894 in Wiltz, Lux d: 10 Sep
  1958 in Wiltz, Lux
+ seq: 321.15.22 FOX, Margaretha b: 03 Jul 1895 in Niederwiltz,
  Lux w: 28 Feb 1919 in Wiltz, Lux f: Wilhelm Fox m: Eugenie
  Wietor
10MACK, Marie-Marguerite b: 04 Jan 1897 in Wiltz, Lux d: 04
  Mar 1959 in Wiltz, Lux
10MACK, Marie-Anna-Josephine b: 27 Oct 1898 in Wiltz, Lux d:
  31 Mar 1978 in St. Cloud, France
10MACK, Anna b: Abt. 1901 in Wiltz, Lux
+ seq: 321.15.23 WEHRLEN, Achille b: in Urschenheim.
  Germany w: Abt. 1925
10MACK, Joseph-Emile b: 09 Jan 1903 in Wiltz, Lux d: 30 Jun
  1953 in Clervaux, Lux
+ seq: 321.15.24 ROOB, Rose-Anna-Maria b: 26 Mar 1922 in
  Echternach, Lux d: 25 Feb 1999 in Wiltz, Lux w: 28 Apr 1944
  in Wiltz, Lux f: Johann Roob m: Maria Heitsch

321.15.13
10MACK, Nicolas-Andre b: 01 May 1893 in Wiltz, Lux d: 18
  May 1929 in Wiltz, Lux c: 2
+ seq: 321.15.13 MANDER, Claire-Eugenie-Anne b: 29 Apr
  1894 in Wiltz, Lux d: 07 Feb 1978 in Wiltz, Lux w: 28 Oct
  1921 in Wiltz, Lux f: Frederic Mander m: Marie Kauth c: 2
11MACK, Anne-Marie b: in Wiltz, Lux v: Wiltz, Lux c: 5
+ seq: 321.15.14 DELTGEN, Jacques-Jean-Pierre b: 05 Sep 1923
  in Wilwerwiltz, Lux d: 01 Apr 1999 in Wiltz, Lux w: Abt.
  1950 in Differdange, Lux v: Wiltz, Lux f: Jean-Pierre Deltgen
  m: Madeleine Theisen c: 5
11MACK, Joseph-Photographe b: 16 Aug 1922 in Wiltz, Lux d:
  19 Feb 1994 in Braine-l'Alleud, Belgium
+ seq: 321.15.21 DUPIRE, Paule (Paulette) b: 14 Feb 1918 in
  Braine-l'Alleud, Belgium d: 24 May 2002 in Braine-l'Alleud,
  Belgium w: 27 Jun 1964 in Braine-l'Alleud, Belgium

321.15.14
11MACK, Anne-Marie b: in Wiltz, Lux v: Wiltz, Lux c: 5
+ seq: 321.15.14 DELTGEN, Jacques-Jean-Pierre b: 05 Sep 1923
  in Wilwerwiltz, Lux d: 01 Apr 1999 in Wiltz, Lux w: Abt.
  1950 in Differdange, Lux v: Wiltz, Lux f: Jean-Pierre Deltgen
  m: Madeleine Theisen c: 5

12[1] DELTGEN, Jean-Pierre b: in Wiltz, Lux
+ seq: 321.15.15 BOONRUEN, Kitsuda b: in Thailand w: Abt.
   1920 in Luxembourg, Lux
* 2nd Wife of [1] DELTGEN, Jean-Pierre:
+ seq: 321.15.16 CARMES, Isabelle b: in Ettelbruck, Lux w:
   Abt. 1925
* 3rd Wife of [1] DELTGEN, Jean-Pierre:
+ seq: 321.15.17 LAU, Roxy b: in China w: Abt. 1930
12 DELTGEN, Robert-Joseph (Rob) b: 11 Jan 1950 in Wiltz, Lux
   v: Diekirch, Lux o: Photographer o: Genealogist c: 2
+ seq: 321.15.18 STEIWER, Marie-Josee b: in Ettelbruck, Lux
   w: 09 Jul 1971 in Wiltz, Lux v: Diekirch, Lux f: Joseph-Pierre
   Steiwer m: Regine-Anne Peters c: 2
12 DELTGEN, Antoine b: 19 Jan 1951 in Wiltz, Lux d: 05 Sep
   1988 in Luxembourg, Lux
+ seq: 321.15.19 VAN BENEDEN, Emilie-Anne-Germaine b: in
   Anderlecht, Belgium w: Abt. 1975 in Wiltz, Lux f: Emile-
   Juliaan Van Beneden m: Marie Heirens
12 DELTGEN, Albert-Joseph b: in Wiltz, Lux
+ seq: 321.15.20 URHAUSEN, Germaine w: Abt. 1980
12 DELTGEN, Viviane-Claire b: in Wiltz, Lux

321.15.18
12 DELTGEN, Robert-Joseph (Rob) b: 11 Jan 1950 in Wiltz, Lux
   v: Diekirch, Lux o: Photographer o: Genealogist c: 2
+ seq: 321.15.18 STEIWER, Marie-Josee b: in Ettelbruck, Lux
   w: 09 Jul 1971 in Wiltz, Lux v: Diekirch, Lux f: Joseph-Pierre
   Steiwer m: Regine-Anne Peters c: 2
13 DELTGEN, Giny b: 18 Sep 1973 in Ettelbruck, Lux c: 1
+ seq: 321.15.18.30 BAUS, Marco-Erny b: 16 Jul 1960 in
   Diekirch, Lux w: 20 May 2005 in Diekirch, Lux f: Fernand
   Baus m: Jeannette Grevig c: 1
13 DELTGEN, Marlene-Josee-Paule b: 15 Aug 1980 in Ettelbruck,
   Lux o: Teacher c: 1
+ seq: 321.15.18.60 NICOLAS, Tom b: 07 Apr 1977 w: Abt.
   2005 c: 1

321.15.18.30
13 DELTGEN, Giny b: 18 Sep 1973 in Ettelbruck, Lux c: 1
+ seq: 321.15.18.30 BAUS, Marco-Erny b: 16 Jul 1960 in
   Diekirch, Lux w: 20 May 2005 in Diekirch, Lux f: Fernand

Baus m: Jeannette Grevig c: 1

14 BAUS, Louis b: 23 Sep 2005 in Ettelbruck, Lux

321.15.18.60

13 DELTGEN, Marlene-Josee-Paule b: 15 Aug 1980 in Ettelbruck, Lux o: Teacher c: 1

+ seq: 321.15.18.60 NICOLAS, Tom b: 07 Apr 1977 w: Abt. 2005 c: 1

14 NICOLAS, Max b: 23 Jan 2007 in Ettelbruck, Lux

321.16

4 GOEDERT, Anna-Marie (Elisabeth) b: 25 Oct 1687 in Schrondweiler, Lux a: Hitz v: Niederfeulen, Lux i: 4th degree of consanguinity r: b c: 9

+ seq: 321.16 HITZ, Martin b: 14 Jul 1694 in Niederfeulen, Lux d: 07 Jan 1772 in Niederfeulen, Lux w: 18 Feb 1715 in Nommern, Lux a: Heintzen a: Hitzen v: Niederfeulen, Lux i: 4th degree of consanguinity o: Farmer r: bd r: m f: Peter Hitz m: Elisabeth c: 9

5 HITZ, Marie-Magdalena b: 09 Sep 1718 in Niederfeulen, Lux r: b

5 HITZ, Johann-Rudolph b: 02 Aug 1719 in Niederfeulen, Lux r: b

5 HITZ, Johann b: 17 Aug 1720 in Niederfeulen, Lux r: b

5 HITZ, Nicolas b: 11 Sep 1721 in Niederfeulen, Lux d: 11 Jan 1729 in Niederfeulen, Lux v: Niederfeulen, Lux r: bd

5 HITZ, Anna-Marie b: 07 Mar 1723 in Niederfeulen, Lux d: 10 May 1729 in Niederfeulen, Lux v: Niederfeulen, Lux r: bd

5 HITZ, Margaretha b: 16 Mar 1724 in Niederfeulen, Lux r: b

5 HITZ, Martin b: 02 Jun 1726 in Niederfeulen, Lux r: b

5 HITZ, Catherine b: 26 Jan 1727 in Niederfeulen, Lux r: b

5 HITZ, Johann-Wilhelm b: 22 May 1729 in Niederfeulen, Lux r: b

322

3 [1] ROB, Firmin b: Abt. 1660 in Budange, France d: 22 Jun 1756 in Useldange, Lux a: Thies a: Machus a: Witry a: Kob(?) a: Koob(?) a: Maclus a: Mockels h: Machus v: Useldange, Lux r: d c: 11

+ seq: 322 MATHIEU, Catherine b: Abt. 1675 in Useldange, Lux d: 14 Aug 1712 in Useldange, Lux w: 14 Nov 1700 in

Nommern, Lux a: Machus h: Machlus v: Useldange, Lux r: d
r: m f: Nicolas Mathieu c: 5

4 ROB, Nicolas b: 04 Mar 1703 in Useldange, Lux d: 02 Jul 1740
in Useldange, Lux a: Machus h: Machus v: Useldange, Lux r:
b c: 2

+ seq: 322.01 Catherine b: Abt. 1705 w: 1737 v: Useldange,
Lux c: 2

4 ROB, Marie-Catherine b: 16 Aug 1704 in Useldange, Lux d: 29
Mar 1744 in Niedermertzig, Lux a: Machus a: Moekles a:
Wiltges v: Niedermertzig, Lux r: bd c: 1

+ seq: 322.02 LEYDERS, Johann b: Abt. 1705 in Niedermertzig,
Lux d: 18 Feb 1756 in Niedermertzig, Lux w: 25 Sep 1732 in
Feulen, Lux a: Wiltges v: Niedermertzig, Lux r: d r: m c: 1

4 ROB, Marie-Agnes b: 07 Oct 1706 in Useldange, Lux a:
Machus r: b

4 ROB, Johann b: 31 Jul 1708 in Useldange, Lux a: Machus v:
Fischbach, Lux r: b

4 ROB, Johann-Jacob b: 15 Nov 1710 in Useldange, Lux a:
Machus r: b

* 2nd Wife of [1] ROB, Firmin:

+ seq: 323 MACHUS, Marie b: Abt. 1690 d: 02 Aug 1742 in
Useldange, Lux w: Abt. 1712 a: Mockels a: Macklus v:
Useldange, Lux c: 6

4 ROB, Anna-Marie b: 21 May 1713 in Useldange, Lux r: b

4 ROB, Susanne b: 28 Aug 1714 in Useldange, Lux r: b

4 ROB, Heinrich b: 28 Jul 1716 in Useldange, Lux d: 02 Jun
1754 in Useldange, Lux a: Machus v: Useldange, Lux r: bd

4 ROB, Anton b: 19 Mar 1718 in Useldange, Lux r: b

4 ROB, Clara b: 19 Mar 1718 in Useldange, Lux r: b

4 ROB, Conrad b: 07 Jul 1720 in Wahl, Lux r: b c: 1

+ seq: 323.00.01 RODENBOUR, Catherine b: Abt. 1725 w: Abt.
1745 c: 1

322.01

4 ROB, Nicolas b: 04 Mar 1703 in Useldange, Lux d: 02 Jul 1740
in Useldange, Lux a: Machus h: Machus v: Useldange, Lux r:
b c: 2

+ seq: 322.01 Catherine b: Abt. 1705 w: 1737 v: Useldange,
Lux c: 2

5 ROB, Marie-Salome b: 22 Jan 1738 in Useldange, Lux r: b

5 ROB, Heinrich b: 08 Jan 1739 in Useldange, Lux

322.02

4 ROB, Marie-Catherine b: 16 Aug 1704 in Useldange, Lux d: 29
Mar 1744 in Niedermertzig, Lux a: Machus a: Moekles a:
Wiltges v: Niedermertzig, Lux r: bd c: 1
+ seq: 322.02 LEYDERS, Johann b: Abt. 1705 in Niedermertzig,
Lux d: 18 Feb 1756 in Niedermertzig, Lux w: 25 Sep 1732 in
Feulen, Lux a: Wiltges v: Niedermertzig, Lux r: d r: m c: 1
5 LEYDERS, Firmin b: 19 Feb 1738 in Niedermertzig, Lux d: 07
May 1744 in Niedermertzig, Lux v: Niedermertzig, Lux r: bd

323.00.01

4 ROB, Conrad b: 07 Jul 1720 in Wahl, Lux r: b c: 1
+ seq: 323.00.01 RODENBOUR, Catherine b: Abt. 1725 w: Abt.
1745 c: 1
5 ROB, Maria-Catharina b: Abt. 1749 c: 4
+ seq: 323.00.02 MERSCH, Pierre b: 04 Aug 1749 in Grosbous,
Lux w: Abt. 1768 c: 4

323.00.02

5 ROB, Maria-Catharina b: Abt. 1749 c: 4
+ seq: 323.00.02 MERSCH, Pierre b: 04 Aug 1749 in Grosbous,
Lux w: Abt. 1768 c: 4
6 MERSCH, Marie-Catherine b: 09 Jun 1770 in Grosbous, Lux
+ seq: 323.00.03 GLAESENER, Charles b: Abt. 1770 in
Heiderscheid, Lux w: Abt. 1795
6 MERSCH, Gertrud b: 31 Dec 1771 in Grosbous, Lux
6 MERSCH, Marguerite b: 03 Jul 1774 in Grosbous, Lux
6 MERSCH, Margaretha b: 03 Jun 1779 in Grosbous, Lux
+ seq: 323.00.04 MILLANG, Anthonius b: 10 Apr 1779 in
Weidingen, Lux w: Abt. 1805

323.01

3 [1] WITRY, Johanna b: Abt. 1664 in Schrondweiler, Lux d: 02
Feb 1734 in Marnach, Lux a: Thies a: Schmitt v: Marnach, Lux
r: d c: 9
+ seq: 323.01 SCHMITT, Theodor t: Parish elder b: Abt. 1664 in
Marnach, Lux d: 1704 in Marnach, Lux w: 19 Feb 1691 in
Nommern, Lux v: Marnach, Lux r: d r: m c: 7
4 SCHMITT, Elisabeth b: Abt. 1693 in Marnach, Lux
+ seq: 323.02 FABER, Johann b: Abt. 1690 in Marbourg, Lux w:
Abt. 1715 v: Marnach, Lux r: m

4 SCHMITT, Anna-Catherine b: Abt. 1695 in Marnach, Lux h: Schmitt v: Marnach, Lux c: 7

+ seq: 323.03 THIVIS, Johann-Jacob b: Abt. 1690 in Weicherdange, Lux d: 13 May 1746 in Marnach, Lux w: 21 Dec 1717 in Munschausen, Lux a: Thies a: Schmitt h: Schmitt v: Marnach, Lux r: d r: m c: 7

4 SCHMITT, Catherine b: 11 Feb 1697 in Marnach, Lux d: 24 Jul 1722 in Marnach, Lux v: Marnach, Lux r: bd

4 SCHMITT, Jacob-Wilhelm b: Abt. 1698 in Marnach, Lux d: 28 Aug 1726 in Marnach, Lux v: Marnach, Lux r: d

4 SCHMITT, Nicolas b: 26 Oct 1699 in Marnach, Lux d: 06 Jan 1713 in Marnach, Lux v: Marnach, Lux r: bd

4 SCHMITT, Johann b: 18 Apr 1702 in Marnach, Lux v: Nommern, Lux r: b

4 SCHMITT, Anna-Marie b: 04 Oct 1704 in Marnach, Lux v: Marnach, Lux r: b

* 2nd Husband of [1] WITRY, Johanna:

+ seq: 323.04 SCHMITT, Johann-Wilhelm b: Abt. 1677 in Oberwampach, Lux d: 14 Dec 1754 in Marnach, Lux w: 07 Jan 1705 in Munschausen, Lux v: Marnach, Lux r: d r: m c: 2

4 SCHMITT, Peter b: 20 Feb 1707 in Marnach, Lux r: b

4 SCHMITT, Anton b: 21 Jul 1711 in Marnach, Lux r: b

323.03

4 SCHMITT, Anna-Catherine b: Abt. 1695 in Marnach, Lux h: Schmitt v: Marnach, Lux c: 7

+ seq: 323.03 THIVIS, Johann-Jacob b: Abt. 1690 in Weicherdange, Lux d: 13 May 1746 in Marnach, Lux w: 21 Dec 1717 in Munschausen, Lux a: Thies a: Schmitt h: Schmitt v: Marnach, Lux r: d r: m c: 7

5 THIVIS, Wilhelm b: 11 Oct 1718 in Marnach, Lux r: b

5 THIVIS, Susanne b: Abt. 1719 in Marnach, Lux d: 07 Sep 1726 in Marnach, Lux v: Marnach, Lux

5 THIVIS, Anna-Marie b: 21 Oct 1721 in Marnach, Lux d: 07 Aug 1725 in Marnach, Lux v: Marnach, Lux r: bd

5 THIVIS, Theodor b: 24 Jan 1724 in Marnach, Lux r: b

5 THIVIS, Susanne b: 29 Aug 1726 in Marnach, Lux d: 30 Aug 1726 in Marnach, Lux v: Marnach, Lux r: bd

5 THIVIS, Peter b: 05 Oct 1727 in Marnach, Lux r: b

5 THIVIS, Elisabeth b: 27 May 1731 in Marnach, Lux r: b

2 MARCHAL, Nicolas b: Abt. 1610 in Budange, France d: 06
Jan 1671 in Budange, France v: Budange, France r: d c: 4

+ seq: 324 PAULUS, Elisabeth b: Abt. 1610 d: 27 Jun 1688 in
Budange, France w: Abt. 1640 in Budange, France v:
Budange, France r: d c: 4

3 MARCHAL, Anna b: Abt. 1642 in Budange, France a: Robert
h: Robert v: Budange, France c: 5

+ seq: 324.01 VOLIBI, Peter b: Abt. 1640 w: Abt. 1668 a:
Robert h: Robert v: Budange, France o: Tailor c: 5

3 MARCHAL, Nicolas b: Abt. 1645 in Budange, France h:
Volibi v: Aix, France v: Edange, Lux o: Laborer o: Linen
draper c: 10

+ seq: 324.02 BEMER, Magdalena b: Abt. 1650 d: 16 Oct 1701
in Bruck, France w: Abt. 1670 a: Huen v: Aix, France v:
Edange, France o: Linen draper r: d f: Johann Bemer c: 10

3 MARCHAL, Susanne b: Abt. 1645 in Budange, France h:
Marchal v: Budange, France c: 8

+ seq: 324.08 FRANCOIS, Nicolas t: Mayor b: Abt. 1640 in
Budange, France d: 17 Dec 1689 in Budange, France w: Abt.
1669 a: Marchal h: Marchal v: Budange, France o: Tailor r: d
c: 8

3 MARCHAL, Margaretha b: Abt. 1650 in Budange, France v:
Budange, France c: 9

+ seq: 324.09 COLLET, Anton b: Abt. 1645 in Budange, France
d: 20 Jun 1709 in Budange, France w: 26 Nov 1672 in Fameck,
France v: Budange, France o: Cloth maker r: d r: m f: Johann
Collet m: Barbara Aubertin c: 9

324.01

3 MARCHAL, Anna b: Abt. 1642 in Budange, France a: Robert
h: Robert v: Budange, France c: 5

+ seq: 324.01 VOLIBI, Peter b: Abt. 1640 w: Abt. 1668 a:
Robert h: Robert v: Budange, France o: Tailor c: 5

4 VOLIBI, Margaretha b: 10 Jan 1671 in Budange, France r: b

4 VOLIBI, Anna b: 07 Feb 1672 in Budange, France r: b

4 VOLIBI, Franz b: 12 Nov 1679 in Budange, France r: b

4 VOLIBI, Catherine b: 08 Jun 1684 in Budange, France r: b

4 VOLIBI, Peter b: 31 Jul 1689 in Budange, France a: Robert r:
b

324.02

3 MARCHAL, Nicolas b: Abt. 1645 in Budange, France h:
Volibi v: Aix, France v: Edange, Lux o: Laborer o: Linen
draper c: 10

+ seq: 324.02 BEMER, Magdalena b: Abt. 1650 d: 16 Oct 1701
in Bruck, France w: Abt. 1670 a: Huen v: Aix, France v:
Edange, France o: Linen draper r: d f: Johann Bemer c: 10

4 [1] MARCHAL, Nicolas b: 18 Dec 1671 in Edange, France v:
Uckange, France i: Related in 4th degree r: b c: 1

+ seq: 324.03 BECKER, Anna b: Abt. 1680 in Monte, France w:
19 Aug 1703 in Uckange, France a: Beck v: Uckange, France
i: Related in 4th degree r: m

* 2nd Wife of [1] MARCHAL, Nicolas:

+ seq: 324.04 BONJEAN, Magdalena b: Abt. 1695 in Uckange,
France w: 26 Nov 1716 in Uckange, France v: Uckange,
France r: m f: Jacob Bonjean m: Magdalena De-la-Cour c: 1

4 MARCHAL, Mathias b: 26 Feb 1673 in Edange, France r: b

4 MARCHAL, Stephan b: 14 Oct 1674 in Edange, France r: b

4 MARCHAL, Johann b: 15 Sep 1676 in Edange, France r: b

4 MARCHAL, Peter b: 17 Mar 1680 in Uckange, France r: b

4 MARCHAL, Dominic b: 10 Oct 1683 in Uckange, France r: b

4 MARCHAL, Anna b: 05 Mar 1685 in Uckange, France v:
Uckange, France r: b

+ seq: 324.05 HOCH, Bernard b: Abt. 1680 in Weiningen, France
w: 27 Nov 1706 in Uckange, France v: Uckange, France r: m

4 MARCHAL, Margaretha b: 02 Mar 1687 in Uckange, France v:
Uckange, France r: b c: 6

+ seq: 324.06 COLLET, Johann b: Abt. 1685 w: 20 Jan 1711 in
Uckange, France v: Uckange, France r: m c: 6

4 MARCHAL, Johann b: 01 Nov 1688 in Uckange, France r: b

4 MARCHAL, Magdalena b: 14 Nov 1692 in Uckange, France d:
02 Dec 1720 in Uckange, France v: Uckange, France r: bd

+ seq: 324.07 DIDION, Johann b: Abt. 1690 in Uckange, France
w: 31 Jan 1719 in Uckange, France v: Uckange, France r: m f:
Johann Dideon m: Susanne Largan

324.03

4 [1] MARCHAL, Nicolas b: 18 Dec 1671 in Edange, France v:
Uckange, France i: Related in 4th degree r: b c: 1

+ seq: 324.03 BECKER, Anna b: Abt. 1680 in Monte, France w:
19 Aug 1703 in Uckange, France a: Beck v: Uckange, France

i: Related in 4th degree r: m
* 2nd Wife of [1] MARCHAL, Nicolas:
+ seq: 324.04 BONJEAN, Magdalena b: Abt. 1695 in Uckange,
France w: 26 Nov 1716 in Uckange, France v: Uckange,
France r: m f: Jacob Bonjean m: Magdalena De-la-Cour c: 1
5 MARCHAL, Nicolas b: 24 Oct 1732 in Uckange, France r: b

324.06

4 MARCHAL, Margaretha b: 02 Mar 1687 in Uckange, France v:
Uckange, France r: b c: 6
+ seq: 324.06 COLLET, Johann b: Abt. 1685 w: 20 Jan 1711 in
Uckange, France v: Uckange, France r: m c: 6
5 COLLET, Marie b: 11 Dec 1711 in Uckange, France r: b
5 COLLET, Claude b: 16 Jan 1714 in Uckange, France r: b
5 COLLET, Johann b: 04 Jun 1715 in Uckange, France r: b
5 COLLET, Margaretha b: Abt. 1721 in Uckange, France
5 COLLET, Mathias b: 12 May 1726 in Uckange, France r: b
5 COLLET, Margaretha b: 12 May 1726 in Uckange, France r: b

324.08

3 MARCHAL, Susanne b: Abt. 1645 in Budange, France h:
Marchal v: Budange, France c: 8
+ seq: 324.08 FRANCOIS, Nicolas t: Mayor b: Abt. 1640 in
Budange, France d: 17 Dec 1689 in Budange, France w: Abt.
1669 a: Marchal h: Marchal v: Budange, France o: Tailor r: d
c: 8
4 FRANCOIS, Nicolas b: 18 Jan 1671 in Budange, France a:
Marchal r: b
4 FRANCOIS, Catherine b: 12 May 1673 in Budange, France a:
Marchal r: b
4 FRANCOIS, Mathias b: 22 Dec 1675 in Budange, France a:
Marchal r: b
4 FRANCOIS, Peter b: 22 May 1677 in Budange, France a:
Marchal r: b
4 FRANCOIS, Margaretha b: Jul 1682 in Budange, France a:
Marchal r: b
4 FRANCOIS, Jeanne b: 11 Jun 1684 in Budange, France a:
Marchal r: b
4 FRANCOIS, Elisabeth b: 30 May 1686 in Budange, France a:
Marchal r: b
4 FRANCOIS, Agatha-Magdalena b: 05 Jul 1688 in Budange,

France a: Marchal r: b

324.09
3 MARCHAL, Margaretha b: Abt. 1650 in Budange, France v:
  Budange, France c: 9
+ seq: 324.09 COLLET, Anton b: Abt. 1645 in Budange, France
  d: 20 Jun 1709 in Budange, France w: 26 Nov 1672 in Fameck,
  France v: Budange, France Cloth maker r: d r: m f: Johann
  Collet m: Barbara Aubertin c: 9
4 COLLET, Johann b: Abt. 1673 in Budange, France d: 19 Aug
  1703 in Budange, France v: Budange, France r: d
4 COLLET, Claude b: 15 Jul 1675 in Budange, France d: 17 Jun
  1695 in Budange, France v: Budange, France r: bd
4 COLLET, Anna b: 24 Jan 1677 in Budange, France d: 04 Apr
  1696 in Budange, France v: Budange, France r: bd
4 COLLET, Johann b: 1679 in Budange, France v: Uckange,
  France
+ seq: 324.10 BONENFANT, Margaretha b: Abt. 1685 in
  Budange, France w: 29 Jan 1709 v: Uckange, France r: m f:
  Johann Bonenfant m: Magdalena Kaisse
4 COLLET, Barbara b: 06 Dec 1681 in Budange, France r: b
+ seq: 324.11 MASSON, Bernard b: Abt. 1680 w: 13 Sep 1707
  in Fameck, France r: m
4 COLLET, Peter b: 29 Feb 1684 in Budange, France r: b
4 COLLET, Mathias b: 09 Jul 1689 in Budange, France r: b
4 COLLET, Franz b: 11 Jun 1692 in Budange, France r: b
4 COLLET, Marie b: 14 Dec 1697 in Budange, France r: b

APPENDIX B

Marriage Index

Names of the married couple	Year	Marriage Seq. No.	Parents Seq. No.
<Unnamed> & Altmann, Rene	1960	095.11	095.10
<Unnamed> & Brotherhood, Tina	1990	015.41	015.40
<Unnamed> & Bryant, Kristen	2000	231.33.50	231.33
<Unnamed> & Elvsveen, Kristin	1990	103.00.50	103
<Unnamed> & Erpelding, Mathias	1925	095.07	095.06
<Unnamed> & Erpelding, Nicolas	1950	095.08	095.07
<Unnamed> & Erpelding, Pierre	1930	095.09	095.06
<Unnamed> & Heber, Robert-Wayne	1980	015.13	015.12
<Unnamed> & Kremer, Leonie	1930	119.01.50	119.00.50
<Unnamed> & Kremer, Nadine	1990	128.00.40	128.00.35
<Unnamed> & Kuntziger, Andre	1840	021.09	021.03
<Unnamed> & Kuntziger, Jacques	1835	021.08	021.03
<Unnamed> & Lenger, Francois	1910	141.05	141.04
<Unnamed> & Moos, Marie	1880	229.38.01	229.01
<Unnamed> & Muller, Juan-Mauricio	1920	031.00.10	031.00.05
<Unnamed> & Nieland, Jeanette	2000	248.02.02	248.02
<Unnamed> & Nieland, Jennifer	1993	248.05.00	248.05
<Unnamed> & Olinger, Johann	1850	009.05	009.04
<Unnamed> & Ondarcuhu, Luis	1945	128.03	128.02
<Unnamed> & Ondarcuhu, Pedro	1945	128.04	128.02

<Unnamed> & Schroeder, Paul J.	1930	015.59.30	015.06
<Unnamed> & Schroeder, Paula	1965	015.59.45	015.59.30
<Unnamed> & Theile, Dorian-Lee	1995	182.32	182.30
<Unnamed> & Theile, Lynn-Marie	2000	182.33	182.30
<Unnamed> & Thurston, Amanda	1997	231.25.50	231.25
<Unnamed> & Wagner, Debra	1995	015.24	015.19.50
<Unnamed> & Weiten, Kari	1995	204.18.02	204.18
<Unnamed> & Widdel, Erica	1998	229.25.10	229.25
<Unnamed> & Witry, Elizabeth	1980	128.09	128.08
<Unnamed> & Witry, Emilio-Carlos	1950	128.08	128.07
<Unnamed> & Witry, Francis	1980	095.15	095.14
<Unnamed> & Witry, Jean	1952	074.00.70	074.00.80
<Unnamed> & Witry, Johann-Nicolas	1805	008	007
<Unnamed> & Witry, Jorge-Nicolas	1980	128.11	128.08
<Unnamed> & Witry, Madeleine	1950	074.00.80	074.00.50
<Unnamed> & Witry, Maria	1920	166.02.02	166.02.01
<Unnamed> & Witry, Marie	1885	215.70	214
<Unnamed> & Witry, Marie-Elisabeth	1830	047	038
<Unnamed> & Witry, Peter	1600	001	
<Unnamed> & Witry, Pierre	1998	141.10.70	141.10.60
<Unnamed> & Witry, Unknown	1980	128.10	128.08
<Unnamed> & Zimmer, Johann	1830	021.04	021.03
Adam, Daniel & Nail, Lea	1991	204.13	204.12
Adam, David & Huss, Mona	1962	204.12	204.01
Adam, Heather & Ruffalo, Ken	1994	204.13.02	204.12
Adam, Timothy & Ravindran, Kay	1990	204.13.01	204.12
Adams, Anne & Reines, Raymond	1970	172.58	172.53
Adamy, Anne & Broos, Martin	1823	017.03.15	017.03.01
Adamy, Marguerite & Jung, Mathias	1857	017.03.05	017.03.04
Adamy, Marie & Laiches, Mathias	1818	017.03.03	017.03.01
Adamy, Mathias & Scholer, Anne	1787	017.03.01	017.03
Adamy, Nicolas & Majerus, Anne	1836	017.03.14	017.03.01
Adamy, Peter & Witry, Anna	1746	017.03	003
Adamy, Pierre & Keyser, Anne	1830	017.03.04	017.03.01
Adamy, Susanne & Michels, Mathias	1810	017.03.02	017.03.01
Adamy, Susanne & Schaaff, Henri	1865	017.03.13	017.03.04
Adkins, Theresa & Konen, Gilbert	1970	182.13	182.10
Albrecht, Michael & Spang, Mary C.	1981	171.20	171.16

Albright, Jean & Tannenbaum, James	1970	171.46	171.40
Alden, William & Graap, Frances	1967	231.50	231.49
Alderman, George & Wittry, Jeanne	1983	178.01	176
Alexander, Denise & Witry, David	1987	115	114
Allen, Clara & Wittry, Paul	1920	274	272
Allen, Guelda & Schmidt, Gordon	1984	240.31	240.23
Allen, Kathie & Tierney, Daniel	2002	204.17.02	204.17
Allen, Michele & Witry, John	2000	067.01	067
Alonso, Maria & Muller, Felix	1924	031.00.60	031.00.05
Altmann & Erpelding, Virginie	1930	095.10	095.06
Altmann, Rene & <Unnamed>	1960	095.11	095.10
Altura, Nina & Goblirsch, Mark	2002	261.30.03	261.29
Amaitis, Laurie & Carbery, John	1980	071.02	071.01
Anderson, Carl & Spang, Mary	1935	171.23	171.01
Anderson, Cynthia & Carlson, Geoffrey	1979	172.35	172.33
Anderson, Dean & Oberman, Cecelia	1970	171.50	171.47
Anderson, Kevin & Wittry, Margaret	1988	252.01	249
Anderson, Linda & Wyatt, Michael	1971	172.34	172.33
Anderson, Melanie & Nieland, Chad	1998	248.04.01	248.04
Anderson, Phyllis & Meyer, Jerry	1959	171.24	171.23
Anderson, William & Frieders, Anastasia	1946	172.33	172.24
Andring, Marie & Witry, Jean-Pierre	1955	223	221
Andring, Rene & Witry, Yvette	1983	222.01	222
Ange, Michael & Wagner, Dianne	1995	015.23	015.19.50
Anita & Theile, Michael-Paul	1990	182.31	182.30
Anna & Witry, Mathias	1720	005	003
Anso, Blanca & Muller, Felix-Raul	1945	031.00.65	031.00.60
Appel, Bryan & Spang, Diane	1990	171.22	171.16
Appel, Carl & Marmann, Elizabeth	1909	230.03	230.01
Arabuarena, Etelvina & Witry, Hector	1930	128.23	128.01
Arbogast, Grace & Tannenbaum, Raymond	1955	171.41	171.40
Arend, Jean & Witry, Appoline	1964	021.17	021.16
Arends, Ronald & Witry, Karen	1986	100.02	098
Armstrong, Larry & Salmen, Lisa	1993	270.02.50	270.02.30
Armstrong, Robert & Loser, Cinthia	1965	015.19.50	015.08
Armstrong, Sharon & Witry, Joseph	1970	072	071

Arndt, Michelle & Thooft, Dean	1990	261.26	261.21
Arterburn, Dale & Wittry, Elizabeth	1982	207.06	207
Assel, Mathias & Goedert, Elisabeth	1741	321.11	321.09
Atten, Anna & Reckinger, Johann	1753	311.03	311.01
Atten, Margaretha & Peffer, Peter	1764	119.08	119.05
Augustine, Todd & Reines, Therese	1987	172.57	172.54
Aultman, Bettideane & Nieland, Allen	1970	248.02	248.01
Avelar, Margareth & Muller, Guillermo	1990	031.00.85	031.00.80
Backes, Margareta & Witry, Mathias	1894	166.02.01	165
Bade & Witry, Theresa W.	1892	027.03	027
Baden, Anna-Maria & Reisch, Johann	1867	091.30	091.01
Baden, Corneil & Witry, Jeanette	1837	091.01	051
Baden, Theresia & Schwartz, Johann	1864	091.50	091.01
Bailey, John & Johannessen, Barbara	1980	172.62	172.59
Bailey, Luke & Witry, Laura	1983	069.01	069
Baker, Mary-Carolyn & Wittry, Paul	1942	274.03	272
Balk, Kathy & Wittry, Robert	1970	268	265
Baller, Michael & Salmen, Lisa	1997	270.02.55	270.02.30
Bamberg, Catherine & Wittry, Jacob	1898	264	262
Banwart, Scott & Nieland, LeAnn	1996	248.05.01	248.05
Barbiere, Lawrence & Johnsen, Jane	1980	208.13	208.09.01
Barbieri, Carlos & Zingoni, Maria	1985	128.15	128.13
Barile, Carla & Prado, Mariano	1998	031.00.72	031.00.60
Barker, Christine & Koehne, Mark	1995	231.47.01	231.45
Barnett, Dean & Venner, Susan	1974	236.05	236.02
Barnett, Lois & Koehne, Gerald	1971	231.03	231.02
Barnich, Catherine & Witry, Johann	1835	021.26.40	021.26
Barrera, Maria & Witry, Alfredo	1935	128.12	128.01
Barron, Daniel & McDaniel, Dawn	1998	201.03	201
Bartells, Robin & Conrad, Gregory	1986	229.37	229.35
Bartet, Elsie & Wittry, Nicolas	1910	303	301
Barth, Donald & Steimel, Julia-Ann	1973	096.07	096.06
Barth, Laura-Ann & Hoodjer, Jason	2000	096.07.50	096.06
Bartkowski, Mark & Cosgrove, Jill	1990	070.08	068
Bassani, Romain & Witry, Manon	1981	081.01	081
Bast, Cindy & Moss, David	1985	015.56	015.44
Bast, James & Wilde, Pamela	1984	015.57	015.44
Bast, Seno & Schroeder, Gloria	1961	015.55	015.44

Bastian, Lotty & Kosch, Carlo	1973	079.03	079.01
Batteux, Doris & Witry, Marco	1991	308	305
Batty, Brent & Carlson, Joanna	1989	182.27	182.25
Bauer, Fernande & Klosen, Joseph	1960	227.02	227.01
Bauer, James & Wittry, Judith	1975	268.02	265
Baulesch, Nikolas & Olsem, Maria	1869	321.15.26	321.15.07
Baum, Catherine & Schaaff, Jean	1902	017.03.13.30	017.03.13
Baum, Jean & Fixmer, Catherine	1880	164.20	164.01
Baumhover, Catherine & Wittry, Dale	1954	249	248
Baumhover, Laurie & Wiederin, Douglas	1986	261.09	261.08
Baumunk, Geri & Tapparo, John	1977	231.12	231.07
Bauske, Bonnie & Witry, Joseph	1985	066	063
Bayliss, Terry & Wiederin, Jodi	1990	261.10	261.08
Bearbower, Patricia & Conrad, James	1961	229.35	229.07
Beckel, Richard & Cavanaugh, Sarah	1971	096.05	096.02
Becker, Anna & Marchal, Nicolas	1703	324.03	324.02
Becker, Jean & Bettendorf, Susanne	1913	192.01.70	192.01
Beckers, Joseph & Lenger, Odette	1940	141.06	141.05
Behen, Edward & Walters, Katerine	1970	075.05.40	075.05
Behen, Francis & Winbech, Matilda	1950	075.05.30	075.05
Behen, Francis & Witry, Mary	1930	075.05	075
Behen, Mary & Holt, Raymond-Agner	1945	075.05.10	075.05
Beideler, Peter & Witry, Catherine	1858	021.26.70	021.26.50
Beller, Linda & Watgen, Thomas	1975	171.10	171.09
Bellion, Germaine & Witry, Ernest	1945	218.03	218.02
Bemer, Magdalena & Marchal, Nicolas	1670	324.02	324
Bemtgen, Adolf & Kirch, Margot	1959	215.65.40	215.65
Bemtgen, Adolf & Koch, Philomene	1948	215.65.20	215.65
Bemtgen, Alice & Geimer, Jacques	1945	215.65.70	215.65
Bemtgen, Johann & Fries, Helena	1915	215.60	215.50
Bemtgen, Johann & Fries, Helena	1915	215.60	215.50
Bemtgen, Johann & Fries, Helena	1917	215.65	215.50
Bemtgen, Johann & Fries, Helena	1917	215.65	215.50
Bemtgen, Johann & Witry, Anna	1916	216.50	216
Bemtgen, Magdalena & Wenmacher, Jos	1935	215.62	215.60

Bemtgen, Nico & Jost, Marie-France	1960	215.65.80	215.65
Bemtgen, Paul & Gaby	1960	215.65.90	215.65
Bemtgen, Peter & Weyer, Catherine	1948	215.65.60	215.65
Bennett, Cindy & Nieland, Daniel	1969	248.04	248.01
Benney, Jodi & Handzik, Thomas	1980	086.12	086.10
Benson, David & Hankins, Mary	1978	182.40	182.25
Benton, Michael & Bock, Lisa	1989	260.06	260.01
Berens, Anne & Schuster, Adam	1871	148.02	148.01
Berens, Jeanette & Witry, Jean	1836	126	124
Berens, Johann & Witry, Magdalena	1836	148.01	148
Berens, Marie & Witry, Jean	1855	127	126
Berens, Marie-Josefine & Witry, Jean	1885	128	127
Berenyi, Richard & Watgen, Katherine	1980	171.12	171.09
Bergerhaus, Carol J. & Dishong, John	1967	028.03	028.02
Bergerhaus, Leo & Wittry, Eleanor	1915	028.01	028
Bergerhaus, Maurice & Young, Merna	1943	028.02	028.01
Berna & Witry, Evelyne	1995	128.00.15	128.00.10
Bernardy, Angela & Luckhardt, Brian	2003	261.37	261.35
Bernardy, Catherine & Thooft, Ernest	1958	261.12	261.11
Bernardy, James & Coulter, Cindy	1987	261.34	261.11
Bernardy, Jean & Thooft, Raymond	1958	261.21	261.11
Bernardy, Linda & Chapman, Thomas	1970	261.33	261.11
Bernardy, Marlene & Heiling, Gerald	1965	261.31	261.11
Bernardy, Mary & Pohlen, Francis	1967	261.32	261.11
Bernardy, Mathew & Wittry, Mary	1935	261.11	231
Bernardy, Patricia & Goblirsch, Gerald	1962	261.29	261.11
Bernardy, Robert & Trexler, Linda	1975	261.28	261.11
Bernardy, Ronald & Strand, Lynette	1973	261.35	261.11
Bernardy, Staci & Halbersma, Justin	2002	261.36	261.35
Bernardy, Vicky & Main, Thomas	2001	261.28.01	261.28
Bernbrock, Mary & Weber, Carl	1938	208.02	208.01
Bertram, David & Handzik, Leslie	1978	086.13	086.10
Bertrang, Anna & Schwartz, Joseph	1890	009.20	009.16
Bertrang, Hubert & Pettinger, Marianna	1890	009.17	009.16
Bertrang, Marco & Rasquin, Mirielle	1990	014.77	014.75
Bertrang, Mathias & Wiltgen, Marie	1890	009.19	009.16
Bertrang, Nicolas & Muller, Leonie	1890	009.18	009.16
Bertrang, Peter & Stronck, Marie	1860	009.16	009.15

Besenius, Jeff & Kerger, Malou	2001	014.65.85	014.65.80
Betcher, Rose & Witry, Edward	1927	068	054
Bettendorf, Elisabeth & Frieden, Peter	1910	092.01.50	092.01
Bettendorf, Heinrich & Witry, Catherine	1878	092.01	092
Bettendorf, Margaretha & Schneider, Nicolas	1914	092.01.30	092.01
Bettendorf, Peter & Thies, Gertrud	1710	018.04	018
Bettendorf, Susanne & Poecker, Jean	1913	092.01.70	092.01
Bettendorf. Susanne & Becker, Jean	1913	192.01.70	192.01
Bieri, Margrit & Schroeder, Marcel	1955	015.88	015.87
Biever, Margaretha & Witry, Johann	1863	053	052
Biltgen, Catherine & Wiltgen, Jean	1837	311.21	311.08
Birckels, Barbe & Conzemius, Franciscus	1769	321.15.03	321.15.01
Bissener, Christina & Fabricius, Johann	1855	015.97.50	015.97
Bissener, Michel & Witry, Marie	1815	015.97	012
Biver, Nicolas & Dondelinger, Margaretha	1814	308.05	308.03
Biver, Yvonne & Witry, Egide	1960	227.00.01	227
Blair, Thomas & Conrad, Jamie	2001	229.12.01	229.12
Blanchette, Beatrice & Pape, Laverdos	1945	240.37	240.22
Bledsoe, Karen & Koehne, Gerald	2005	231.03.50	231.02
Bleser, Jean & Mack, Marie-Catherine	1907	321.15.10	321.15.08
Bley, Angelika & Witry, Johann	1892	218.01	214
Bley, Anna & Witry, Jean	1898	046.20	046
Bley, Peter & Witry, Elise	1913	046.70	046
Blitsch, Jacob & Witry, Catherine	1868	287.01	229
Blitsch, Lizzie & Witry, Peter	1893	096	094
Blommel, David & Glass, Jean-Marie	1973	233.06	233.01
Bob & Schroeder, Mary-Dell	1970	015.80	015.78
Bock, Christopher & Renholen, Wendy	2003	260.07	260.01
Bock, Howard & Wittry, Ruth	1953	260.01	260
Bock, Lisa & Benton, Michael	1989	260.06	260.01
Bock, Lori & Schaffer, Dennis	1980	260.04	260.01
Bock, Sharon & Bond, Patrick	1976	260.02	260.01
Bock, Sharon & Miller, Frederick	1982	260.03	260.01

Bock, Susan & Tollefson, Steven	1983	260.05	260.01
Bockman, Pam & Huss, Thomas	1975	204.15	204.01
Bockman, Patrick & Gary, Gwen	1975	204.05	204.02
Bofferding, Nicolas & Witry, Anna	1890	031.01.60	031
Bofferding, Nicolas & Witry, Elisabeth	1900	031.01.70	031
Bohanek, Therese & Wittry, David	1988	281.01	280
Bollig, Sanny & Witry, Jean	1930	227	219
Bond, Patrick & Bock, Sharon	1976	260.02	260.01
Bonenfant, Margaretha & Collet, Johann	1709	324.10	324.09
Bonifas, Barbara & Witry, Viktor	1886	145	143
Bonjean, Magdalena & Marchal, Nicolas	1716	324.04	324.02
Boomgaarden, Lynn & Witry, Scott	1989	119	118
Boonruen, Kitsuda & Deltgen, Jean	1920	321.15.17	321.15.14
Borland, Kevin & Johnsen, Mary-Sue	1975	208.10	208.09.01
Bosseler, Marguerite & Witry, Albert	1893	141.25	141.19
Bourgeois, Marie & Witry, Johann	1906	021.26.34	021.26.32
Bourgmeyer, Josette & Witry, Victor	1965	132	130
Bourtz, Marie & Radermacher, Heinrich	1735	020.02	020.01
Bous, Marco & Deltgen, Giny	2005	321.15.18.30	321.15.18
Brake, Debra & Brockberg, Jeffrey	1980	267.03	267.01
Brake, Donald & Wittry, Doris	1952	267.01	265
Brake, Douglas & Yackel, Marie	1975	267.02	267.01
Brake, Jeffrey & Brandt, Marlene	1980	267.04	267.01
Brake, Jerry & Thier, Julie	1985	267.06	267.01
Brake, Steven & Drealan, Mary	1980	267.05	267.01
Brakonier & Faber, Rene	1955	220.02	220.01
Brancho, Ann & Carlson, Joseph	2001	182.27.20	182.28
Brandt, Marlene & Brake, Jeffrey	1980	267.04	267.01
Brau, Leroy & Schmidt, Rosemary	1969	240.32	240.23
Braun, Alex & Witry, Sanny	1992	095.18	095.16
Braun, Nicolas & Kirsch, Margaretha	1810	009.43	009.40
Breckenridge, Douglas & Wittry, Debra	1979	257.02	256
Breckenridge, Tiffany & Rickbiel, Eric	2002	257.10	257.02

Brede, Nadia & Wittry, Steven	1980	281	280
Brennan, Celestine & Wittry, Edmund	1955	185	183
Brennan, Geraldine & Reines, Raymond	1952	172.54	172.53
Brenner, Craig & Johannessen, Karen	1985	172.61	172.59
Brenner, Mary & Wittry, David	1982	254	253
Breuer, Jaci & Wittry, Mark	1996	261.02.02	261
Brever, Marie & Witry, Emile	1945	155	152
Breyden, Angela & Radermacher, Peter	1736	020.03	020.01
Breyer, Elisabeth & Witry, Peter	1914	095.12	095
Bringen & Wittry, Mary-Clara	1945	274.01	273
Brinley, Kenneth & Nieland, Andrea	1998	248.02.01	248.02
Brinson, Cathleen & Tegels, Robert	1980	236.15	236.11
Britt, Brenda & Tannenbaum, Robert	1985	171.43	171.42
Brochmann, Louise & Witry, Jean	1925	074.00.90	074
Brockberg, Jeffrey & Brake, Debra	1980	267.03	267.01
Broos, Marie & Medernach, Balthasar	1880	017.03.18	017.03.17
Broos, Marie-Anne & Neu, Mathias	1886	017.03.19	017.03.17
Broos, Martin & Adamy, Anne	1823	017.03.15	017.03.01
Broos, Mathias & Konsbruck, Anne	1863	017.03.16	017.03.15
Broos, Theodor & Girst, Anne-Marie	1849	017.03.17	017.03.15
Brosius, Barbara & Witry, Jean	1773	021.02	021.01
Brotherhood, Roy & Schroeder, Sandra	1968	015.40	015.07
Brotherhood, Tina & <Unnamed>	1990	015.41	015.40
Brown, Clarice & Conrad, Robert	1952	229.10	229.07
Brown, Heather & Luhman, Edward	1999	229.14.01	229.14
Brown, Kimberly & Sharp, Ronald	2002	229.14.02	229.14
Brown, Lansing & Sachs, Suzanne	1973	229.14	229.13
Brown, Lynne & Wittry, Edmund	1985	187	185
Brown, Max & Plain, Margaret E.	1970	172.41	172.39
Brown, Sally & Russell, Michael	1976	229.23	229.21
Brownback, Bill & Wittry, Betty-Jo	1951	030.11	029
Brownback, Cynthia & Johnson, Jerry	1970	030.12	030.11
Bruck, Maria & Welter, Johann-Peter	1918	107.01.30	107.01
Brugeon, Pat & Wittrock, LeRoy	1960	270.06	270.04
Bruin, James & Witry, Anna	1925	075.03	075
Bruin, Nancy & Richter	1955	075.04	075.03

Bryan, Kathy & Loser, Steven-Mark	1974	015.27	015.08
Bryant, John & Koehne, Josephine	1984	231.33	231.29
Bryant, Kristen & <Unnamed>	2000	231.33.50	231.33
Brzycki, Alice & Schroeder, James	1935	015.44	015.06
Buchanan, Margaret & Cavanaugh, Erwin	1944	096.02	096.01
Buchet, Oscar & Witry, Octavie	1930	141.10	141.09
Buchmeier & Wenckus, Jennifer	1995	207.05	207.03
Buckley, Janet & Wittry, Robert	1985	189	188
Buelt, Carrie & Muell, Richard	2002	240.07.01	240.07
Buelt, Kathleen & Davis, Don	1979	240.02	240.01
Buelt, Leo & Flynn, Merrie	1978	240.07	240.01
Buelt, Leo & Wittry, Leona	1944	240.01	240
Buelt, Mary-Joan & Haller, Robert	1968	240.03	240.01
Buelt, Robert & Drey, Joan	1980	240.08	240.01
Buelt, Rose & Wiederin, Andrew	1970	240.05	240.01
Bulder, Regina & Wittry, Steven	1990	243	242
Bullerman, Susan & Hannasch, Thomas	1986	240.15	240.09
Bunkelman, Susan & Wittry, James	1980	199	198
Burditt, Valerie & Hannasch, Michael	1980	240.13	240.09
Burgholzer, Kim & Spang, Kim	1980	171.05	171.03
Burgin, John & Sitter, Katherine	1935	271.03	271.02
Burke, Catherine & Witry, Joseph	1932	071	054
Burke, John & Groble, Maryann	1980	060.02	060.01
Burke, Joseph & Dalton, Mary	1988	060.05	060.01
Burke, Kathleen & Wittry, Stephen	1976	194	193
Burke, Phillip & Witry, Jean	1950	060.01	060
Burke, Robert & Dettloff, Susan	1985	060.04	060.01
Burke, Thomas & Klein, Karen	1980	060.03	060.01
Burkel, John B. & Wittry, May A.	1936	181.02	173
Burns-Rakowski, Darlene & Witry, Richard	1972	117	109
Burritt, Jo-Anne & Wittry, Richard H.	1977	029.01	029
Burson, Douglas & Piron, Patricia	1970	172.30	172.29
Buss, Jan & Wittry, Edwin	1957	266	265
Butcher, Tammy & Thurston, Joseph	1989	231.27	231.21
Buzon, Alejandra & Zingoni, Martin	1991	128.14	128.13
Byers, Eva & Spang, Henry	1940	171.39	171.01

Callahan, Marcella & Wittry, Anthony	1922	278	272
Calvin, Cyrise & Sanders, Marc	1990	070.04	070.02
Calzolari & Mares, Maria-Clara	1950	128.06	128.05
Campbell, Cynthia & Wittry, Lyle	1996	247	241
Canueto, Blanca & Lance, Alfredo	1945	031.00.45	031.00.40
Canueto, Hilda & Duca, Esteban	1945	031.00.55	031.00.40
Canueto, Manuel & Muller, Maria	1915	031.00.40	031.00.05
Canueto, Mita & Vassolo, Ricardo	1945	031.00.50	031.00.40
Capus, Julie & Witry, Victor	1929	141.21	141.20
Caramelle, Anne & Witry, Eric	1990	090	089
Carbery, James & Mezmalis, Parsla	1985	071.03	071.01
Carbery, John & Witry, Patricia-Ann	1956	071.01	071
Carbery, John-W. & Amaitis, Laurie	1980	071.02	071.01
Carbery, Mary & Moderhack, Lawrence	1985	071.04	071.01
Carbery, Thomas & Padock, Marcia	1990	071.05	071.01
Carlson, Clarence & Konen, Verdell	1945	182.25	182.09
Carlson, Geoffrey & Anderson, Cynthia	1979	172.35	172.33
Carlson, James & Casey, Antoinette	1982	182.37	182.25
Carlson, James-Alan & Kohler, Kathy	1970	182.36	182.25
Carlson, Joanna & Batty, Brent	1989	182.27	182.28
Carlson, John & Evans, Jayme	1990	204.23	204.22
Carlson, Joseph & Brancho, Ann	2001	182.27.20	182.28
Carlson, Joseph & Szakacs, Amanda	2000	182.27.10	182.28
Carlson, Kira & Gross, Jason	1991	182.28	182.28
Carlson, Kira & McIntyre, Chip-Dio	1997	182.28.10	182.28
Carlson, Michael & Strickland, Kitina	1970	182.26	182.25
Carlson, Michael & Underhill, June	1975	182.29	182.25
Carlson, Peggy-Ann & Thiele, John	1966	182.30	182.25
Carlson, Peggy-Ann & Wilder, John	1989	182.34	182.25
Carlson, Raymond & Holmes, Patricia	1981	182.35	182.25
Carlson, Robert & Lemarand, Cinthia	1977	015.77	015.71
Carlson, Sally & Frye, Roger-Neal	1969	182.38	182.25
Carmes, Isabelle & Deltgen, Jean	1925	321.15.16	321.15.14
Carpenter, Rebecca & Wittry, Richard	1983	251	249
Carr, Kathleen & Handzik, Joseph	1985	086.15	086.10
Carson, Christine & Koehne, Terry	1993	231.54	231.49
Cartwright, Eli & Clemes, Lena	1935	086.02	086.01

Cartwright, Elizabeth & Soderholm	1965	086.03	086.02
Cartwright, Girl & Clancy	1965	086.04	086.02
Case, Patrick & Wittry, Rosemarie	1981	242.02	242
Casey, Antoinette & Carlson, James	1982	182.37	182.25
Castor, Eric & Schroeder, Robin	1974	015.62	015.59.30
Catherine & Rob, Nicolas	1737	322.01	322
Catherine & Schroeder, Clinton	1970	015.79	015.78
Cavanaugh, Charles & Witry, Clara	1920	096.01	096
Cavanaugh, Erwin & Buchanan, Margaret	1944	096.02	096.01
Cavanaugh, Michael & Huffman, Gloria	1984	096.04	096.02
Cavanaugh, Michael & Steege, Kathie	1965	096.03	096.02
Cavanaugh, Norma & Steimel, William	1949	096.06	096.01
Cavanaugh, Sarah & Beckel, Richard	1971	096.05	096.02
Caylor, Jeffrey & Wittry, Sandra	1982	249.02	249
Cernohaus, Sharon & Hannasch, Mark	1984	240.16	240.09
Cesarini, Gloria & Schroeder, Robert	1945	015.29	015.07
Chally, Gerald & Schramer, Kathleen	1980	172.10	172.09
Chan, Sonya & Wittry, Anthony	2004	259.01.50	259
Chang, Shu-mei & Wittry, David	1996	181.01.01	181
Chapman, Jennifer & Mack, Andrew	2003	261.33.50	261.33
Chapman, Thomas & Bernardy, Linda	1970	261.33	261.11
Charlier, Michel & Guerlet, Francine	1980	088.03	088.01
Chefner, Rose & Evans, Ronald	1970	204.25	204.21
Chris & Wittry, Edmund B.	2006	187.00.50	185
Christian, Sara & Tapparo, Troy	1993	231.09	231.08
Christian, Terri & Kraus, Gerald	1998	240.11	240.09
Christian, Terri & Kraus, Justin	1998	240.10.00	240.10
Christnach, Antoine & Witry, Marie	1810	021.11	021.02
Christopherson, Phyllis & Wittry, Jack	1980	277	276
Christy, Kent & Wittry, Kathryn	1973	177.01	176
Churrupit & Witry, Elvia	1965	128.21	128.20
Cimenti, Armando & Philipp, Marie	1965	293.03	293.02
Clancy & Cartwright, Girl	1965	086.04	086.02
Clark, David & Weddige, Carol	1988	173.08	173.02
Clark, Stephen & Koehne, Diane	1983	231.04	231.02
Clark, Steven & George, Ami-Sue	1999	182.22.01	182.22

Claudon, Susanne & Witry, Johann	1734	011	003
Clauson, Rose & Wittry, John	1920	275	272
Clauss, Anne & Witry, Pierre	1955	296	295
Clees, Susanna & Spanier, Nicolas	1840	015.94	015.03
Clementen, Johann & Radermacher, Catherine	1745	020.07	020.01
Clements, Melody & Tapparo, Michael	1981	231.13	231.07
Clemes, Annabelle & Stolarski, Leonard	1950	086.06	086.05
Clemes, Gail & Mengel	1965	086.22	086.21
Clemes, Genevieve & Handzik, Thomas	1952	086.10	086.05
Clemes, Jacqueline & Mulligan, Michael	1978	086.18	086.16
Clemes, Janis & DeVuono, Sam	1990	086.19	086.16
Clemes, John & Neffle, Winifred	1955	086.16	086.05
Clemes, John & Wierschem, Marie	1926	086.05	086.01
Clemes, John-Peter & Witry, Marie	1902	086.01	053
Clemes, Kimberly & Hamba, James	1985	086.20	086.16
Clemes, Lena & Cartwright, Eli	1935	086.02	086.01
Clemes, Patricia-Ann & Cook, James	1980	086.17	086.16
Clemes, William & Morrosco, Antoinette	1935	086.21	086.01
Cleo & Huss, Richard	1980	204.11.01	204.01
Cline, Frances & Schroeder, Paul	1935	015.59.60	015.06
Cloos, Mathias & Witry, Elisabeth	1903	044.01	040
Coggins, Christopher & Crenshaw, Brenda	1992	231.42	231.38
Cohen, Ellen & Wittry, Glen	1981	200	198
Cole, Andrea & Troutner, Jeff	2000	240.11.50	240.10
Cole, Doris & Schroeder, John	1946	015.83	015.06
Cole, Matthew & Strand, Susannah	1999	240.11.01	240.10
Cole, Sherry & Hight, William	1968	171.54	171.51
Collart, Mathias & Witry, Anne-Marie	1784	021.23	021.01
Colle, Michele & Kaell, Emile	1972	014.65.60	014.65
Collet, Anton & Marchal, Margaretha	1672	324.09	324
Collet, Barbara & Masson, Bernard	1707	324.11	324.09

Collet, Johann & Bonenfant, Margaretha	1709	324.10	324.09
Collet, Johann & Marchal, Margaretha	1711	324.06	324.02
Collins, Marget & Goblirsch, Eric	1988	261.30.01	261.29
Colllins, Teri & Stull, Michael-John	1992	182.24	182.14
Concha Contreras, Victoria & Witry, Horacio	1940	128.24	128.01
Connors, Michael & Frieders, Mary	1973	172.27	172.25
Conrad, Andrew & Runyan, Angela	1997	229.37.01	229.35
Conrad, Anita & Russell, Milo	1949	229.21	229.07
Conrad, Anthony & DeHeck, Kelly	1977	229.29	229.28
Conrad, Bernard & Moos, Margaretha	1884	229.06	229.01
Conrad, Christine & Harms, Barton	1985	229.36	229.35
Conrad, Craig & Pederson, Justine	1988	229.33	229.28
Conrad, David & McGrew, Mary	1999	229.12.02	229.10
Conrad, David & Riggle, Carla	1980	229.12	229.10
Conrad, Debra & Hill, Chad	1999	229.34	229.28
Conrad, Denise & Glenny, William	1979	229.30	229.28
Conrad, Diane & Elliott, Michael	1990	229.32	229.28
Conrad, Frances & Hollar, Donald	1944	229.08	229.07
Conrad, Gregory & Bartells, Robin	1986	229.37	229.35
Conrad, Holly & Goldsmith, Cory	2006	229.29.50	229.29
Conrad, James & Bearbower, Patricia	1961	229.35	229.07
Conrad, James & Follan, Marva	2003	229.37.02	229.07
Conrad, Jamie & Blair, Thomas	2001	229.12.01	229.12
Conrad, Joseph & Weber, Kristine	1994	229.20	229.18
Conrad, Louis & Hemmer, Teresa	1960	229.18	229.07
Conrad, Marie-Ann & Sachs, Merle	1953	229.13	229.07
Conrad, Nicole & Guenther, Timothy	2002	229.29.01	229.29
Conrad, Robert & Brown, Clarice	1952	229.10	229.07
Conrad, Robert & Nathem, Frances	1921	229.07	229.06
Conrad, Robert & Schares, Betty	1978	229.11	229.10
Conrad, Robert & Wittry, Mary	1925	229.09	229.06 231
Conrad, Roxane & Harms, Daniel	1987	229.19	229.18
Conrad, William & Smith, Carole	1957	229.28	229.07
Conry, Cecil & Quinett, Esther	1942	291.02	291.01
Conry, Elmer & Witry, Mary	1910	291.01	288
Conry, Lucille & Witry, Harold	1935	102	096

Consbruck, Susanne & Witry, Michel	1858	027	026
Contamines, Madeleine & Witry, Nicolas	1930	295	294
Conter, Dominique & Moos, Marie	1891	229.38	229.01
Contreras, Karen & Wittry, Stephen	1982	177	176
Conzemius, Catherine & Linckels, Jacques	1785	321.15.29	321.15.01
Conzemius, Claudius & Majerus, Anne	1780	321.15.04	321.15.01
Conzemius, Franciscus & Birckels, Barbe	1769	321.15.03	321.15.01
Conzemius, Joannis & Neuens, Catherine	1735	321.15.01	321.12
Conzemius, Marie & Olsem, Nicolas	1782	321.15.05	321.15.01
Conzemius, Pierre & Peters, Susanne	1767	321.15.02	321.15.01
Cook, James & Clemes, Patricia-Ann	1980	086.17	086.16
Cools, Karolien & Wittry, Bryon	2000	242.03	242
Cooper, Kim & Schroeder, Curtis	1983	015.33	015.29
Cooper, Mary & Witry, Nicolas	1873	285	229
Copons, Barbara & Witry, Johann	1806	032	022
Corken, Matthew & Witry, Alene	1985	061.03	061
Corkery, Lawrence & Sachs, Lori-Jean	1986	229.17	229.13
Corno, James & Pape, Tammy	1980	240.40	240.37
Corring, Antoine & Schroeder, Pia	1988	015.90	015.88
Corriveau, Dennis & Schroeder, Kathleen	1969	015.43	015.07
Cory, Jeffrey & Witry, Sharon-Ines	1980	100.01	098
Cory, Shawna-Lynn & Walton, Todd	2005	100.01.50	100.01
Cosgrove, Frank & Witry, Loretta	1960	070.05	068
Cosgrove, Jill & Bartkowski, Mark	1990	070.08	070.05
Cosgrove, Steven & Crilly, Joan	1990	070.06	
Cosgrove, Timothy & Winter, Pamela	1990	070.07	070.05
Coulter, Cindy & Bernardy, James	1987	261.34	261.11
Courtiol, Jeanne & Witry, Johann	1873	050	049
Couser, Scott & Crenshaw, Sara	1987	231.43	231.38
Crabbe, Kerry & Schramer, Gwen M.	1980	172.05	172.02
Craig & Davis, Shannon	1990	015.47	015.46
Crawford, Susan & Watgen, Donald	1980	171.14	171.09
Crenshaw, Billy & Koehne, Catherine	1955	231.38	231.01

Crenshaw, Brenda & Coggins, Christopher	1992	231.42	231.38
Crenshaw, Joan & Jones, Thorro	1980	231.39	231.38
Crenshaw, Mary & Phelps, Larry	1991	231.41	231.38
Crenshaw, Richard & Parella, Lisa	1986	231.40	231.38
Crenshaw, Sara & Couser, Scott	1987	231.43	231.38
Crenshaw, Sara & Villalpando, Jose	1992	231.44	231.38
Crilly, Joan & Cosgrove, Steven	1990	070.06	070.05
Crocker, Gary & Hankes, Kristen	1997	204.16.02	204.16
Cronister, Terri & Wittry, Thomas	1992	030.02	030
Cruts, Cathy & Salmen, David	2004	270.02.58	270.02.30
Culbertson, J. M. & Witry, Katherine	1885	027.05	027
Cumley, Earl R. & Dishong, Bridgette	1991	028.04	028.03
Czerkas, Jan & Wittry, Elissa	1975	280.01	280
Daetwyler, Peggy & Florence, John E.	1946	182.07	182.01
Dahling, Lori & Hannasch, Roch	1985	240.20	240.09
Dahm, Matilda & Schroeder, Johann	1902	015.06	015.05
Dalton, Mary & Burke, Joseph	1988	060.05	060.01
Danner, Lori & Derner, Tony	1999	261.07.01	261.03
Davidson, James & Wittry, Margaret	1930	169.01	169
Davidson, Marlene & Sanders, Jeffrey	1985	070.03	070.02
Davis & Witry, Margaret	1930	290.02	289
Davis, Don & Buelt, Kathleen	1979	240.02	240.01
Davis, Larry & Rasmussen, Patricia	1970	015.46	015.45
Davis, Shannon & Craig	1990	015.47	015.46
De Cosmo, Maria & Weddige, David	1986	173.14	173.13
De Jarlis, Helena & Wittry, Jacob	1935	269	264
De King, Brad & Huss, Bernadine	1980	204.19	204.01
De Phillips, Monica & Wittry, Dean	1982	250	249
De Vous, Margaret & Evans, Donald	1970	204.24	204.21
De Waha, Maria & Kaell, Jean	1854	014.50	014.01
De Waha, Nicolas & Witry, Margaretha	1836	014.01	013
Debbie & Wilde, Donald	1985	015.59	015.45
Decker, Catherine & Witry, Heinrich	1825	125	124
Decker, Margareta & Witry, Bernhard	1910	302	301
DeHeck, Kelly & Conrad, Anthony	1977	229.29	229.28
Delfeld, Marie & Reckinger, Johann	1778	311.04	311.01

Deltgen, Albert & Urhausen, Germaine	1980	321.15.20	321.15.14
Deltgen, Antoine & Van Beneden, Emilie	1975	321.15.19	321.15.14
Deltgen, Giny & Bous, Marco	2005	321.15.18.30	321.15.18
Deltgen, Jacques & Mack, Anne	1950	321.15.14	321.15.13
Deltgen, Jean & Boonruen, Kitsuda	1920	321.15.17	321.15.14
Deltgen, Jean & Carmes, Isabelle	1925	321.15.16	321.15.14
Deltgen, Jean & Lau, Roxy	1930	321.15.15	321.15.14
Deltgen, Marlene & Nicolas, Tom	2005	321.15.18.60	321.15.18
Deltgen, Pierre & Wiltgen, Marguerite	1887	311.22.69	311.22.67
Deltgen, Robert & Steiwer, Marie	1980	321.15.18	321.15.14
Demuth, Eduard & Witry, Jeanne	1959	132.01	130
Dennemeyer, Nicolas & Witry, Marie	1830	132.05	124
Dennis, Connie & Wittry, Lyle	1994	246	241
DePaolo, David & Wittry, Anne	1999	202.02	201
Derner, Carol & Tigges, Mark	1983	261.06	261.03
Derner, Dale & Grettenberg, Jeanean	1983	261.04	261.03
Derner, Eugene & Wittry, Vera	1959	261.03	260
Derner, Janet & Schulte, Dean	1987	261.05	261.03
Derner, Mary & Mikkelsen, Steve	1988	261.07	261.03
Derner, Pat & Tigges, Jennifer	1997	261.07.02	261.03
Derner, Tony & Danner, Lori	1999	261.07.01	261.03
Desmond, Judith & Gary, James	1980	204.06	204.02
Dettloff, Susan & Burke, Robert	1985	060.04	060.01
Deutsch, Michael & Kohley, Sandra	1980	171.34	171.30
DeVuono, Sam & Clemes, Janis	1990	086.19	086.16
Di Marco, Gustavo & Muller, Isabel	1985	031.00.25	031.00.15
Dichter, Mathias & Wiltgen, Jeanne	1840	311.22.80	311.22.50
Dickes, Margaretha & Witry, Willebrord	1791	123	121
Didier, Barbe & Schoedgen, Peter	1908	141.01.50	141.01
Didion, Johann & Marchal, Magdalena	1719	324.07	324.02
Diederich, Georges & Hoett, Yvonne	1955	227.07	227.06
Diefenbaugh, Mabel & Witry, Walter	1958	101	096
Diehl, Katherine & Kohley, Donald	1953	171.30	171.29
Dietrich, Dennis & Wittry, Janet	1981	250.01	249

Dilbeck, William & Thurston, Janice	1973	231.23	231.21
Dineen, Susan & Mertes, James	1987	173.11	173.09
Dinwiddie, Diane & Wittry, Donald J.	1950	184	183
Dion, George & Schramer, Dianne	1991	172.14	172.09
Dishong, Bridgette & Cumley, Earl R.	1991	028.04	028.03
Dishong, John & Bergerhaus, Carol J.	1967	028.03	028.02
Dockendorf, Lena & Wittry, Nick	1885	203	167
Dodson, Donna & Wittry, John-Paul	1986	179	176
Dohnalik, Wayne & Hipps, Margaret	1989	174.09	174.05
Donato, Ramona & Witry, John	1965	067	063
Donavan, Pete & Schmidt, Janice	1974	240.26	240.23
Donckel, Pierre & Putz, Marian	1960	132.04.00	132.04
Dondelinger, Catherine & Witry, Peter	1798	122	121
Dondelinger, Johann & Kneip, Agnese	1818	308.06	308.03
Dondelinger, Magdalena & Witry, Johann	1715	021	020
Dondelinger, Margaretha & Biver, Nicolas	1814	308.05	308.03
Dondelinger, Michel & Witry, Margaretha	1774	308.03	120
Dondelinger, Nicolas & Roeser, Magdalena	1813	308.04	308.03
Donka, Joy & Gary, Donald	1987	204.10	204.02
Donlinger, Theodor & Witry, Marie	1743	021.30	021
Donnelly, Raymond & Hannasch, Mary	1996	240.19	240.09
Donnersberger, Catherine & Witry, Bernard	1985	057	056
Dorothy & Plain, Clarence-Peter	1955	172.52	172.47
Dostert, Marie & Reiland, Nicolas	1870	009.29	009.26
Douglas, Patricia & Wittry, Delmar	1949	198	197
Doyle, Keith & Glass, Mary-Ellen	1974	233.05	233.01
Dozier, Joan & Witry, Gerald	1955	069	068
Drailly, Lambert & Witry, Margaretha	1737	017.02	003
Drauden, Martin & Witry, Susanne	1786	012.01	012
Draudt, Mary & Wittry, Henry	1908	172	168
Drealan, Mary & Brake, Steven	1980	267.05	267.01
Drey, Joan & Buelt, Robert	1980	240.08	240.01
Drum, Melissa & Wittry, Randal	1982	186	185

Drurnleller, Frank & Hoffman, Katherine	1910	015.92	015.91
Dubois, Mildred & Wittry, David	1955	282	279
Duca, Esteban & Canueto, Hilda	1945	031.00.55	031.00.40
Ducrocq, Arlette & Hebert, Georges	1967	095.04	095.02
Dugan, Leann & Schmidt, Gordon	1968	240.30	240.23
Duhr & Reiland, Marguerite	2000	009.31	009.29
Dunn, James & Joy, Sharon	1977	231.19	231.15
Dunn, Olivia & Hendrickson, Daren	2000	231.19.01	231.19
Dupire, Paule & Mack, Joseph	1964	321.15.21	321.15.13
Duryee, Donald & Thurston, Patricia	2002	231.24	231.21
Dusching, Nicolas & Groos, Elisabeth	1845	023.01.70	023.01
Dutton, Kirk & Wittry, Betty-Jo	1971	030.13	029
Dykstra, Andres & Wittry, Melanie	2004	259.10	259
Easterday, Geoffrey & Grattafiori, Cynthia	1980	173.04	173.03
Eastman, Robb & Wittry, Kristy	1989	255.01	253
Edwards, Judy & Thurston, John	1976	231.22	231.21
Edwards, Neil & Otte, Julie	1996	270.02.10	270.02.05
Efsic, Edward & Wilson, Barbara	1990	182.17.50	182.15
Efsic, Edward J. & Stull, Dianne M.	1962	182.15	182.14
Efsic, Ellen-Rose & Legg, Scott-Eric	1991	182.16	182.15
Efsic, Joni & Patterson, Doug	2000	182.17.60	182.50
Efsic, Maria & Van Boekel, Lambertus	2000	182.17.01	182.15
Efsic, Maria-Elena & Spoerri, Stefan	1986	182.17	182.15
Ehrke, Robert & Kohley, Nancy	1995	171.37	171.36
Eichhorn, Emilie & Jacques, Germaine	1933	141.17	141.14
Eiffes, Anna & Lick, Mathias	1879	161.04	161.03
Eiffes, Jean & Witry, Catherine	1913	050.00.60	050.00.50
Eiffes, Mathias & Witry, Anna	1848	161.03	157
Eischen, Catherine & Streff, Peter	1864	157.07	157.03
Eisen, Joseph & Kaell, Pauline	1955	014.65.90	014.55
Ekness, Michael & Wiederin, Lisa	1996	240.06	240.05
Elliott, Michael & Conrad, Diane	1990	229.32	229.28
Elsen, Helene & Witry, Henri	1950	095.13	095.12
Eltz, Johann & Muller, Catherine	1868	023.70	023.02
Elvsveen, Kristin & <Unnamed>	1990	103.00.50	103
Elvsveen, Robert & Tone	1990	103.01	103

Enders, Marie & Witry, Nicolas	1881	301	300
Engelbrecht, Mary & Witry, Nicolas	1913	287	229
Engh, Eli & Witry, William-Peter	1962	103	102
Ensch, Anna & Witry, Peter	1842	143	142
Ensweiler, Susanna & Witry, Peter	1881	139.03	134
Eppe, Anne & Witry, Victor	1925	128.00.05	128
Erath, Harry & Spang, Margaret	1943	171.57	171.01
Erath, Thomas & Wilson, Rose-Mary	1967	171.58	171.57
Erickson, Billye-Jo & Glass, Steven	1980	233.09	233.01
Ernst, Theresa & Wittry, John-Peter	1951	176	175
Erpelding, Jean & Witry, Susanne	1902	095.06	095
Erpelding, Mathias & <Unnamed>	1925	095.07	095.06
Erpelding, Nicolas & <Unnamed>	1950	095.08	095.07
Erpelding, Pierre & <Unnamed>	1930	095.09	095.06
Erpelding, Virginie & Altmann	1930	095.10	095.06
Esch, Hannelore & Zender, Edgar	1975	230.07	230.06
Esch, Willi & Jardin, Katharina	1950	230.06	230.05
Eskew, Dorothy & Witry, John	1943	043	042
Estrup, Jennifer & Wenckus, Neal	1998	207.04	207.03
Ettner, Thomas & Loser, Katherine	1976	015.17	015.08
Eubanks, Kenneth & Piron, Carol	1966	172.31	172.29
Eubanks, Laura & Wagenknecht, Gary	1993	172.32	172.31
Evans, Angiene & Van Fleet	2000	204.23.10	204.22
Evans, Donald & De Vous, Margaret	1970	204.24	204.21
Evans, James & Meyer, Susan	1965	204.22	204.21
Evans, Jayme & Carlson, John	1990	204.23	204.22
Evans, Kristin-Marie & Techmanski	2000	204.24.10	204.21
Evans, Robert & Wittry, Alice	1941	204.21	204
Evans, Ronald & Chefner, Rose	1970	204.25	204.21
Evans, Ronald & Sue	1977	204.26	204.21
Even, Marie & Streff, Reinhard	1851	157.05	157.03
Ewert, Nicolas & Witry, Marie	1840	147.03	142
Eyners, Anna & Witry, Johann	1735	004	003
Faber, Bernard & Witry, Maria	1912	220.01	219
Faber, Cecile & Heinerscheid	1955	220.03	220.01
Faber, Charles & Jung, Susanne	1888	017.03.11	017.03.05
Faber, Joelle & Witry, Patrick	1997	224.01	223
Faber, Johann & Schmitt, Elisabeth	1715	323.02	323.01

Faber, Maisy & Ney	1960	220.04	220.01
Faber, Rene & Brakonier	1955	220.02	220.01
Fabricius, Johann & Bissener, Christina	1855	015.97.50	015.97
Falmouth, Sylvie & Witry, Pascal	1993	297	296
Farley, Kris & Kohley, Laura	2000	171.37.01	171.36
Farrall, Edward & Wagner, Barbara	1984	015.21	015.19.50
Fautsch, Jean-Francois & Mack, Anne	1900	321.15.11	321.15.08
Fautsch, Nikolas & Olsem, Katharina	1861	321.15.27	321.15.07
Federspiel, Elisabeth & Witry, Johann	1885	050.00.50	049
Federspiel, Maria & Witry, Mathias	1882	160	158
Fehrentz, Elise & Schaaf, Jean	1943	017.03.13.50	017.03.13.30
Feliciano, Judith & Koehne, John	1959	231.45	231.01
Fell & Reiland, Marie	1860	009.33	009.26
Fell, Mathias & Klein, M.	1890	009.34	009.33
Feller, Christiane & Witry, Florent	1970	128.00.70	128.00.05
Feller, Francoise & Witry, Alphonse	1970	128.00.20	128.00.05
Feller, Joseph & Witry, Leonie	1915	143.70	143.50
Feller, Marie & Witry, Jean	1965	128.00.60	128.00.05
Felton, Jill-Ann & Witry, Gregory	1979	111	110
Fendrichs, Ella & Wittry, Nicholas	1924	234	231
Fernandez Salas, Elvia & Witry, Alberto	1933	128.20	128.01
Fetzer, Barbara & Tannenbaum, Kris	1978	171.44	171.42
Feuerborn, Joan F. & Spang, Thomas	1955	171.18	171.02
Feyereisen, Marthe & Witry, Claude	1989	138	137
Ficker, John & Weiten, Ericka	2001	204.18.01	204.18
Filbey, Edna & Wittry, Herman	1925	279	272
Finsterwald, Nicolas & Witry, Marie	1836	032.01	023
Fischer, Margaretha & Witry, Heinrich	1761	021.24	021
Fisher, Louise & Wittry, Michael	1920	190	182
Fitzloff, Lisa & Pohlen, Michael	2001	261.32.01	261.32
Fixmer, Catherine & Baum, Jean	1880	164.20	164.01
Fixmer, Elisabeth & Thill, Pierre	1880	164.10	164.01
Fixmer, Wilhelm & Witry, Catherine	1848	164.01	157
Flammang, Catherine & Schmidt, Johann	1903	166.02.00	166.02
Flammang, Josette & Witry, Nicolas	1970	218	217

Flammang, Marguerite & Jung, Pierre	1888	017.03.06	017.03.05
Flammang, Peter & Witry, Elisabeth	1879	166.02	165
Flannigan, Alice & Wittry, Elmer	1930	210	208
Florence, Barbara L. & Theis, John W.	1959	182.02	182.01
Florence, Edward & Wittry, Lena	1913	182.01	182
Florence, Emily H. & Sabo, Julius A.	1939	182.03	182.01
Florence, Joanne & Howard, Ronald	2002	182.08.01	182.07
Florence, John E. & Daetwyler, Peggy	1946	182.07	182.01
Florence, Marcia & Hazelwood, Richard	1980	182.08	182.07
Flores, Adrienne & Jacobsen, Eric	1980	231.36	231.29
Flynn, Merrie & Buelt, Leo	1978	240.07	240.01
Foehr, Mathias & Steyer, Magdalena	1903	024.20	024.01
Fogg & Witry, Maria-Josefa	1966	128.17	128.12
Fogg, Veronica & Imbrosciano	1995	128.18	128.17
Fogolin & Mores, Anna	1945	225.04	225.03
Follan, Marva & Conrad, James	2003	229.37.02	229.07
Fonck, Michel & Wiltgen, Barbie	1837	311.22.70	311.22.50
Forewood, Brant & Witry, Susan	2003	104.00.60	104
Forthman, Jill & Thooft, Brian	2000	261.27.01	261.21
Foster, Barbara & Wittry, Roy	1952	207	206
Foster, Jayce & Schramer, Margaret L.	1981	172.16	172.15
Fostervold, Kari & Witry, James	1989	113	110
Fourman, Therese & Jacques, Fortnnat	1905	141.14	141.13
Fourmond, Fanny & Hebert, Mathias	2000	095.04.50	095.04
Fowler, Anne & Spang, Kim	1985	171.06	171.03
Fox, Margaretha & Mack, Jean	1919	321.15.22	321.15.12
Fraley, Diane & Joy, Randall	1973	231.17	231.15
Frampton, Steven & Sachs, Kathleen	1981	229.16	229.13
Franck, Johann & Weis, Catherine	1811	037.02	037.01
Franck, Nicolas & Witry, Barbara	1781	037.01	037
Francois, Marie & Witry, Franz	1877	298	292
Francois, Nicolas & Marchal, Susanne	1669	324.08	324
Frank, Dorothy & Wittry, Alan	1977	030.01	030
Fransen, Leona & Pape, Laverdos	1980	240.42	240.37
Frantzen, Joseph & Kugener, Susanna	1921	024.00.97	024.00.95
Franz, Heinrich & Witry, Elisabeth	1826	035.02	033
Frazier, Jeffrey & Venner, Joan	1989	236.09	236.02
Frederes, Susanne & Witry, Heinrich	1877	041	039

Frederick, Roy & Wittry, Lena	1920	204.27	203
Frederickson, Judy & Huss, Richard	1963	204.11	204.01
Frederiks, Margaret & Koehne, Juvent	1950	231.05	231.01
Freie, Julie & Nieland, Allen	1982	248.03	248.01
Freiling, Peter & Witry, Maria-Theresa	1793	021.28	021.01
Freitag, Frieda & Witry, John-Peter	1920	055	054
French, Merle & Schroeder, Paul J.	1950	015.60	015.06
Friday, Carol & Witry, Thomas	1971	106	102
Frideres, Elise & Melsen, Leon	1940	074.02	074.01
Frieden, Peter & Bettendorf, Elisabeth	1910	092.01.50	092.01
Frieders, Anastasia & Anderson, William	1946	172.33	172.24
Frieders, Herman & Meyer, Ruth	1943	172.25	172.24
Frieders, John & Krantz, Susan	1933	172.33.50	168
Frieders, John & Swords, Suzanne	1987	172.28	172.25
Frieders, John & Wittry, Mary	1915	172.24	168
Frieders, Lawrence & Williams, Patricia	1971	172.26	172.25
Frieders, Leona & Piron, Ervin	1944	172.29	172.24
Frieders, Lydia-Jean & Lesniak, David	2000	172.26.01	172.26
Frieders, Mary & Connors, Michael	1973	172.27	172.25
Friedrich, Nikolas & Kayser, Marie	1863	311.18	311.12
Fries, Helena & Bemtgen, Johann	1915	215.60	215.50
Fries, Helena & Bemtgen, Johann	1917	215.65	215.50
Fries, Johann & Hoffmann, Catharina	1904	215.55	215.50
Fries, Pierre & Witry, Madeleine	1881	215.50	214
Friob, Anna & Witry, Pierre-Frederis	1920	042	040
Frisch, Susanne & Witry, Johann-Peter	1894	074	053
Frye, Roger & Carlson, Sally-Ann	1969	182.38	182.25
Fryer, Kelly & Schaffer, Brent	2003	260.04.01	260.04
Gaby & Bemtgen, Paul	1960	215.65.90	215.65
Galen, Janelle & Witry, Timothy	2006	066.01.50	064
Gallais, Lionel & Witry, Isabelle	1986	296.01	296
Gallup, Cynthia & Wittry, Mark	1992	252	249
Gamon, Mitzilyn & Hawking, Brian	2005	208.08.50	208.07
Gangler, Lucien & Witry, Julienne	1925	021.21	021.15
Garcia, Melinda & Koehne, Robert	1986	231.46	231.45
Garfield, Elaine & Witry, William	1960	077	076
Garrison, Robert & Wittry, Delores	1965	283.02	283

Gary, Arthur & Potts, Brenda	1989	204.03	204.02
Gary, Dean & Reckmeyer, Pamela	1976	204.04	204.02
Gary, Donald & Donka, Joy	1987	204.10	204.02
Gary, Eugene & Huss, Donna	1954	204.02	204.01
Gary, Gwen & Bockman, Patrick	1975	204.05	204.02
Gary, James & Desmond, Judith	1980	204.06	204.02
Gary, Marianne & McCormick, Daniel	1981	204.07	204.02
Gary, Phillip & Northrup, Sherri	1985	204.08	204.02
Gary, Vincent & Spears, Cindy	1987	204.09	204.02
Garza, Emma & Hankins, Robert	1978	182.39	182.25
Gaspar, Donna & Spang, Gerald	1950	171.03	171.02
Gehling, Marceal & Wittry, John	1956	253	248
Geimer, Jacques & Bemtgen, Alice	1945	215.65.70	215.65
Geistfeld, Janna & Goblirsch, Mark	1995	261.30.02	261.29
Gengler, Catherine & Witry, Johann	1880	144	143
Gengler, Marie & Witry, Nicolas	1873	141.08	141
George, Ami-Sue & Clark, Steven	1999	182.22.01	182.22
George, Cory & Yarbrough, Kelly	2002	236.06.00	236.05
George, Johann & Witry, Anna-Marie	1801	119.02	037
George, Margaretha & Kiefer, Franz	1826	119.04	119.02
George, Margaretha & Wagner, Mathias	1825	119.03	119.02
George, Robert & Stull, Margaret	1967	182.22	182.14
Gevelinger, Agnese & Goedert, Nicolas	1953	229.05	229.03
Geyton, Donald & Wittry, Charmian	1985	184.01	184
Giamprini, Diana & Kosch, Marco	1989	079.04	079.02
Giliano, Michael & Witry, Mary	1990	066.02	064
Gilles, Barbara & Witry, Peter	1845	165	157
Gillessen, Pierre & Jung, Catherine	1919	017.03.07	017.03.06
Girst, Anne-Marie & Broos, Theodor	1849	017.03.17	017.03.15
Givenes, Albertine & Witry, Johann	1914	050.00.70	050.00.50
Gjerde, Kenneth & Schmidt, Genevieve	1957	240.24	240.24
Gjerde, Kenneth & Wendy	1985	240.25	240.23
Glaesener, Charles & Mersch, Marie	1795	323.00.03	323.00.02
Glange, Anna & Witry, Matthias	1935	226	219
Glange, Marguerite & Witry, Jean	1920	220	219
Glasener, Anna & Witry, Peter	1685	311	002

Glaser, Neil & Witry, Theresa	1993	105.01	105
Glass, Jean-Marie & Blommel, David	1973	233.06	233.01
Glass, Jean-Marie & Zumburge, Fred	1982	233.07	233.01
Glass, Jon & Palmer, Marian	1978	233.08	233.01
Glass, Louis & Green, Kelly	1981	233.11	233.01
Glass, Mary-Ellen & Doyle, Keith	1974	233.05	233.01
Glass, Robert & Wittry, Marie	1947	233.01	232
Glass, Steven & Erickson, Billye-Jo	1980	233.09	233.01
Glass, Steven & Justice, Leneatha	1990	233.10	233.01
Glass, William & McCarthy, Wanda	1982	233.03	233.01
Glass, William & Stark, Tara	1990	233.04	233.01
Glass, William & Trent, Beverly	1968	233.02	233.01
Glenny, William & Conrad, Denise	1979	229.30	229.28
Glod, Pierre & Mons, Catherine	1849	311.10	311.09
Glodt, Marie & Kugener, Lambert	1862	161.02	161.01
Glomski, Tom & Schmidt, Marlene	1967	240.27	240.23
Goblirsch, Eric & Collins, Marget	1988	261.30.01	261.29
Goblirsch, Eric & Johnston, Wendy	1986	261.30	261.29
Goblirsch, Gerald & Bernardy, Patricia	1962	261.29	261.11
Goblirsch, Heidi & Winter, Jeremy	2002	261.30.04	261.29
Goblirsch, Mark & Altura, Nina	2002	261.30.03	261.29
Goblirsch, Mark & Geistfeld, Janna	1995	261.30.02	261.29
Goblish, Stephen & Thooft, Carol	1983	261.22	261.21
Godefroy, Marie & Witry, Jean	1810	021.10	021.02
Goedert, Anna & Hitz, Martin	1715	321.16	321.08
Goedert, Elisabeth & Assel, Mathias	1741	321.11	321.09
Goedert, Johann & Gralinger, Marie	1708	321.09	321.08
Goedert, Margaretha & Neuens, Nicolas	1710	321.12	321.08
Goedert, Marie & Thiel, Dominic	1735	321.10	321.09
Goedert, Marie-Paule & Zappone, Marco	2002	229.05.01	229.05
Goedert, Mathias & Witry, Franzisca	1681	321.08	002
Goedert, Michel & Moos, Catherine	1887	229.02	229.01
Goedert, Nicolas & Gevelinger, Agnese	1953	229.05	229.03
Goedert, Peter & Kaiser, Barbara	1914	229.03	229.02
Goeller, Susanne & Witry, Michel	1831	158	157
Goerens, Anna & Kayser, Nikolas	1860	311.17	311.12

Goerens, Susanne & Witry, Jean	1880	021.26.32	021.26.20
Goerke, Victoria & Wittry, Robert	1976	270.01	270
Goicochea, Gladis & Muller, Carlos	1955	031.00.15	031.00.10
Goldsmith, Cory & Conrad, Holly	2006	229.29.50	229.29
Golladay, David & Witry, Anne	1973	043.01	043
Gomez, Alicia & Witry, Emilio-Carlos	1920	128.07	128.01
Gomez, Dolores & Koehne, Scott	1987	231.47	231.45
Gonzalez, Hector & Hankes, Amy	1997	204.16.01	204.16
Goolsby & Witry, Anna	1880	092.02	092
Gordinaire, Nicole & Hankes, Aaron	2001	204.16.04	204.16
Gorham, John P. & Witry, Suzanne	1970	077.03	076
Gormley, Thomas & Wittry, Anna	1935	174.01	173
Gorner, Denis & Witry, Joan-Marie	1968	071.06	071
Gosset, Kyle & Hankins, Eugene	1977	182.43	182.25
Graap, Frances & Alden, William	1967	231.50	231.49
Graap, Frances & Jones, David	1973	231.51	231.49
Graap, Frances & O'Steen, Chester	1977	231.52	231.49
Graap, Nancy & Lee, Mick	1970	231.53	231.49
Graff, Pierre & Wiltgen, Marguerite	1845	311.22.68	311.22.67
Gralinger, Marie & Goedert, Johann	1708	321.09	321.08
Grattafiori, Alan & Weddige, Carol	1958	173.03	173.02
Grattafiori, Cynthia & Easterday, Geoffrey	1980	173.04	173.03
Grattafiori, Cynthia & Strohmenger, Brian	1983	173.05	173.03
Grattafiori, Michael & Kreul, Diane	1985	173.06	173.03
Graziano, Teresa & Przybyl, Steven	1994	015.36	015.35
Green, Kelly & Glass, Louis	1981	233.11	233.01
Greisch, Theodore & Jung, Catherine	1930	017.03.10	017.03.06
Greischer, Michel & Witry, Susanne	1913	160.20	160
Greiveldinger, Nicolas & Witry, Marie	1872	143.01	143
Grelon, Christian & Hebert, Christiane	1964	095.03	095.02
Grelon, Jean & Lilaz-Polletaz, Nadege	2000	095.03.50	095.03
Grettenberg, Jeanean & Derner, Dale	1983	261.04	261.03
Groble, Maryann & Burke, John	1980	060.02	060.01
Groff, Susanna & Witry, Michel	1888	143.50	143
Groos, Anne & Huss, Heinrich	1840	023.01.75	023.01
Groos, Anne & Philips, Jean	1850	023.01.80	023.01
Groos, Barbara & Philipps, Jean-Pierre	1839	023.01.01	023.01

Groos, Catharina & Ludwig, Nicolas	1851	023.01.85	023.01
Groos, Elisabeth & Dusching, Nicolas	1845	023.01.70	023.01
Groos, Maria & Huss, Heinrich	1843	023.01.50	023.01
Groos, Nicolas & Witry, Marie	1815	023.01	023
Gross, Jason & Carlson, Kira	1991	182.28	182.28
Groth, Eunice & Witry, Joseph	1955	110	109
Groud, Henriette & Witry, Pierre	1915	091	087
Gruber, Francoise & Witry, Theodor	1889	164	162
Gudendorf, Simone & Klosen, Georges	1990	227.04	227.02
Guenther, Timothy & Conrad, Nicole	2002	229.29.01	229.29
Guerlet, Francine & Charlier, Michel	1980	088.03	088.01
Guerlet, Gilbert & Witry, Elisabeth	1953	088.01	088
Guerlet, Marie & Parmentier, Thierry	1985	088.02	088.01
Guerlet, Sylvette & Ramires de la Rosa, Hector	1978	088.04	088.01
Guess, Robert & Wittry, Myrna	1965	283.01	283
Guest, Guy & King, Shawna H.	1990	172.51	172.50
Guillaume, Maria & Witry, Henri	1788	021.25	021.01
Haas, Fernand & Witry, Marie-Paule	1983	225.01	225
Haas, Rene & Witry, Marie	1925	021.22	021.15
Hackett, Pamela & Kraus, Gerald	1971	240.10	240.09
Hager & Witry, Mary	1880	027.04	027
Hagerty, Kathleen & Wittry, John	1950	276	275
Halbersma, Justin & Bernardy, Staci	2002	261.36	261.35
Hall, Mary & Witry, Bernard	1966	105	102
Hall, Nadine & Wittry, James	1997	282.00.01	282
Haller, Jennifer & Wilkens, Gary	1991	240.04	240.03
Haller, Laura & Stapleton, Timothy	2000	240.04.01	240.03
Haller, Robert- & Buelt, Mary-Joan	1968	240.03	240.01
Halling, David & Meyer, Lianne-Kay	1979	171.25	171.24
Halsdorf, Jos & Witry, Annick	2002	086.00.01	086
Hamba, James & Clemes, Kimberly	1985	086.20	086.16
Hames, Apollonia & Peffer, Nicolas	1754	119.07	119.05
Hames, Corneille & Witry, Marie	1754	119.10	020
Hames, Monique & Sales, Jean-Louis	1990	166.02.05	166.02.04
Handzik, Joseph & Carr, Kathleen	1985	086.15	086.10
Handzik, Joyce & Nahorski, Jan	1975	086.11	086.10
Handzik, Karla & Kraemer, Garry	1980	086.14	086.10

Handzik, Leslie & Bertram, David	1978	086.13	086.10
Handzik, Thomas & Benney, Jodi	1980	086.12	086.10
Handzik, Thomas & Clemes, Genevieve	1952	086.10	086.05
Hankenne, Marguerite & Witry, Georges	1930	141.10.50	141.09
Hankes, Aaron & Gordinaire, Nicole	2001	204.16.04	204.16
Hankes, Amy & Gonzalez, Hector	1997	204.16.01	204.16
Hankes, Eva & Wittry, Henry	1925	206	203
Hankes, John & Huss, Anna-Jean	1969	204.16	204.01
Hankes, Kristen & Crocker, Gary	1997	204.16.02	204.16
Hankes, Nicholas & Whitecotton, Kristie	1997	204.16.03	204.16
Hankes, Suzon & Hawking, John	1963	208.07	208.06
Hankins, Carol & McDaniel, Philip	1977	182.42	182.25
Hankins, Clare & Ritli, Charles	1978	182.45	182.25
Hankins, Eugene & Gosset, Kyle	1977	182.43	182.25
Hankins, Eugene & Roselli, Debra	1981	182.44	182.25
Hankins, Mary & Benson, David	1978	182.40	182.25
Hankins, Mary & Swartout, Seldon	1991	182.41	182.25
Hankins, Robert & Garza, Emma	1978	182.39	182.25
Hankins, Robert & Konen, Verdell	1954	182.38.50	182.09
Hanna, Mari & Piscitelli, Michael	1990	075.02.02	075.02.01
Hanna, Thomas & Witry, Marilyn	1960	075.02.01	075.02
Hannasch, James & Peterson, Linda	1991	240.21	240.09
Hannasch, Jane & Walter, Gary	1978	240.14	240.09
Hannasch, Jerome & Wittry, Joan	1954	240.12	240
Hannasch, Mark & Cernohaus, Sharon	1984	240.16	240.09
Hannasch, Mary & Donnelly, Raymond	1996	240.19	240.09
Hannasch, Mary & McCann, Daniel	1984	240.18	240.09
Hannasch, Michael & Burditt, Valerie	1980	240.13	240.09
Hannasch, Richard & Lampe, Kay	1987	240.17	240.09
Hannasch, Roch & Dahling, Lori	1985	240.20	240.09
Hannasch, Thomas & Bullerman, Susan	1986	240.15	240.09
Hansen & Simon, Angela	1860	009.02	009.01
Hansen, Angela & Witry, Johann-Peter	1731	006	003
Hansen, Anna & Witry, Willebrord	1754	022	021

Hansen, Jennifer & Wittry, Christopher	2001	270.01.01	270.01
Hansen, Laurent & Witry, Catherine	2003	128.00.25	128.00.20
Hansen, Nicolas & Streff, Elisabeth	1854	157.04	157.03
Hansen, Peter & Witry, Anna	1862	086.23	052
Harken, Sheree & Witry, Craig	1993	100	098
Harms, Barton & Conrad, Christine	1985	229.36	229.35
Harms, Daniel & Conrad, Roxane	1987	229.19	229.18
Harrell, Sue & Warnell, Jeffrey-Glen	1995	104.02	104.01
Harvey, Michael & Wittry, Laurie	1986	236.01	235
Harwood, Faye & Witry, Craig-Joseph	1979	099	098
Hass, Megan-Marie & Konen, Michael	2003	182.12.05	182.11
Haufle, Helen-Jane & Wittry, Frank J.	1965	181	180
Haugen, Karen & Hoflock, Ronald	1977	240.46	240.43
Hauser, Mark & Reines, Mary	1975	172.55	172.54
Hawking, Brian & Gamon, Mitzilyn	2005	208.08.50	208.07
Hawking, J. Wilfrid & Weber, Marian	1939	208.06	208.01
Hawking, John & Hankes, Suzon	1963	208.07	208.06
Hawking, Karen & Lawson, Robert	1988	208.08	208.07
Hawking, Michael & Repass, Robin	2000	208.09	208.07
Haynes, Kenny & Jillan	1995	015.51	015.50
Haynes, Kenny & Rasmussen, Terry	1975	015.50	015.45
Hazelwood, Richard & Florence, Marcia	1980	182.08	182.07
Healey, Joan-Rita & Witry, Richard	1953	114	109
Heaton, Eileen & Huss, Joseph	1979	204.20	204.01
Hebeler, Nicolas & Witry, Marie	1837	032.02	023
Heber, David & Winiarski, Wendy	1995	015.15	015.12
Heber, Paul & Loser, Katherine-Marie	1965	015.12	015.08
Heber, Robert-Wayne & <Unnamed>	1980	015.13	015.12
Heber, Robert-Wayne & Laurie	1990	015.14	015.12
Hebert, Christiane & Grelon, Christian	1964	095.03	095.02
Hebert, Georges & Ducrocq, Arlette	1967	095.04	095.02
Hebert, Georges & Witry, Suzanne	1931	095.02	095.01
Hebert, Keith & Warnell, Jami-Marie	1980	104.03	104.01
Hebert, Mathias & Fourmond, Fanny	2000	095.04.50	095.04
Hecht, Susanne & Ries, Valentin	1778	020.05.02	020.05
Heck, Jacques & Witry, Magdalena	1901	215.10	215
Heffenisch, Nikolas & Olsem, Anne	1821	321.15.06	321.15.05

Heiling, Ann-Marie & Smith-Tosomeen, Craig	1991	261.31.01	261.31
Heiling, Gerald & Bernardy, Marlene	1965	261.31	261.11
Hein, Nadia & Kerger, Claude	1977	014.65.88	014.65.80
Heinerscheid & Faber, Cecile	1955	220.03	220.01
Heinrichs, Sara & Wittry, Thomas	1983	257	256
Heisten, Jean & Schanen, Marcelle	1955	132.02.02	132.02
Hellers & Olinger, Barbara	1860	009.09	009.04
Hellers & Olinger, Margareta	1880	009.08	009.05
Hellers, Catherine & Wilmes	1890	009.10	009.09
Hellers, Jacob & Steid	1890	009.13	009.09
Hellers, Jean & Kurth	1890	009.11	009.09
Hellers, Mathias & Schiltz	1890	009.12	009.09
Hemmer, Teresa & Conrad, Louis	1960	229.18	229.07
Henderson, Russell & Loser, Stacy	1997	015.11	015.09
Hendrickson, Daren & Dunn, Olivia	2000	231.19.01	231.19
Hennes, Susanne & Witry, Heinrich	1867	040	039
Henrickson, Christine & Weddige, Paul	1936	173.02	173.01
Herges, Johann & Witry, Barbara	1841	147.04	142
Hess, Claude & Witry, Claudine	1988	225.02	225
Hettinger, George & Schramer, Sharon	1975	172.12	172.09
Heuardt, Petronille & Witry, Heinrich	1839	036	033
Heuschling, Anna & Witry, Jacob	1895	219	214
High, Thomas & Hold, Diane	1980	075.05.27	075.05.01
Hight, Charles & Spang, Theresa	1940	171.51	171.01
Hight, Charles-Peter & Jean	1975	171.55	171.51
Hight, Cynthia & Rudigier, Bruce	1980	171.56	171.51
Hight, Kathleen & Lonsway, John	1965	171.52	171.51
Hight, William & Cole, Sherry	1968	171.54	171.51
Hilbert, Johann & Nepper, Anna	1861	031.50	031.02
Hilbert, Nicolas & Witry, Marie	1823	031.02	023
Hilbert, Susanne & Mons, Nikolaus	1848	311.11	311.09
Hildman, Paul & Wittry, Lois	1974	235.01	235
Hilger, Jean & Witry, Eugenie	1910	134.02	134.01
Hill, Chad & Conrad, Debra	1999	229.34	229.28
Hill, Gary-Dee & Wittry, Sandra-Lynn	1969	198.01	198
Hill, Matthew & Simmons, Tanya	2001	198.02	198.01
Hill, Pamela-Dee & Kaarg, Jason P.	2001	198.03	198.01

Hillard, Carolyn & Warnell, Chris	1990	104.05	104.01
Hiltgen, Angele & Witry, Pierre	1906	294	293
Hinterlang, Leny & Witry, Rudi	1955	217.01	217
Hipp, Margaret & Schroeder, Michel	1905	015.86	015.85
Hipps, Elizabeth & Russie, Daniel	1978	174.06	174.05
Hipps, Harold & Pobstman, Dorothy	1955	174.05	174.02
Hipps, Margaret & Dohnalik, Wayne	1989	174.09	174.05
Hipps, Margaret & Nordman, Alan	1985	174.08	174.05
Hipps, Rebecca & Powell, Kenneth	1983	174.07	174.05
Hirschler, Alice & Kosch, Roger	1949	079.02	079.01
Hirschler, Mathias & Witry, Josephine	1925	079.01	079
Hirtz, Anna-Marie & Witry, Jean	1848	094	051
Hirtzig, Marie & Witry, Johann	1848	045	038
Hitz, Martin & Goedert, Anna	1715	321.16	321.08
Hoch, Bernard & Marchal, Anna	1706	324.05	324.02
Hockstein, Linda & Weber, William	1980	208.04	208.02
Hodge, Richard & Witry, Lucy	1890	030.14	027
Hodges, Edna Mae & Witry, George	1958	064	063
Hoett, Pierre & Witry, Eugenie	1929	227.06	219
Hoett, Raymond & Ney, Tilly	1955	227.06.01	227.06
Hoett, Yvonne & Diederich, Georges	1955	227.07	227.06
Hoffman, Katherine & Drurnleller, Frank	1910	015.92	015.91
Hoffman, Mark & Wittry, Barbara	1979	253.01	253
Hoffman, Peter & Schroeder, Josephine	1871	015.91	015.04
Hoffmann, Catherine & Fries, Peter	1904	215.55	215.50
Hoffmann, Catherine & Kayser, Wilhelm	1864	311.16	311.12
Hoffmann, Gerard & Witry, Anna-Margaretha	1806	009.39	007
Hoffmann, Johann & Witry, Margaretha	1849	147.06	142
Hoffmann, Maria & Toussing, Jean	1935	301.02	301.01
Hoffmann, Marie-Anna & Witry, Peter	1835	052	051
Hoflock, Gary & Labat, Mary-Kay	1973	240.45	240.43
Hoflock, Kevin & Van Moer, Nancy	1978	240.47	240.43
Hoflock, Larry & Kuehl, Cheryl	1977	240.44	240.43
Hoflock, Raymond & Pape, Betty	1952	240.43	240.22

Hoflock, Ronald & Haugen, Karen	1977	240.46	240.43
Hoflock, Todd & Schmitt, Melissa	1984	240.48	240.43
Hoflock, Wesley & Statler, Tamara	1986	240.49	240.43
Hollar, Donald & Conrad, Frances	1944	229.08	229.07
Holly & Stolarski, Paul-Edward	1995	086.09	086.06
Holmberg, Arvid & Wittry, Clara	1937	270.03	264
Holmberg, Darlene & Krafka, Arnold	2003	270.03.10	270.03
Holmberg, Darlene & Pelc, Gordon	1990	270.03.05	270.03
Holmberg, Michelle & Tutender	2000	270.03.20	270.03.15
Holmberg, Patrick & Lange, Marian	1973	270.03.15	270.03
Holmes, Jennifer & Vanderheiden, Trenton	1994	236.13	236.12
Holmes, Patricia & Carlson, Raymond	1981	182.35	182.25
Holt, Diane & High, Thomas	1980	075.05.27	075.05.10
Holt, Diane & Raber, Conrad	1970	075.05.25	075.05.10
Holt, Raymond-Agner & Behen, Mary	1945	075.05.10	075.05
Holzmacher, Catherine & Witry, Heinrich	1859	107	051
Homolar, Darlene & Witry, Robert	1959	104	102
Hoodjer, Jason & Barth, Laura-Ann	2000	096.07.50	096.07
Hora, Jill & Spang, David	1982	171.21	171.16
Hoss, Anna & Witry, Emile	1940	154	152
Hotchkiss, Todd & Wittry, Karman	1990	259.01	259
Houle, Ray & Lemarand, Connie	1972	015.76	015.71
Howard, Ronald & Florence, Joanne	2002	182.08.01	182.07
Howard, Tamara & Theis, James E.	1983	172.23	172.22
Huberty, Camille & Lies, Eugenie	1964	014.80	014.70
Huberty, Pascale &Kaiser, Frank	1995	014.85	014.80
Huberty, Patrick & Straus, Annik	1995	014.90	014.80
Huettenmueller, Karen & Wittry, Carl	1986	030.05	030
Huffman, Gloria & Cavanaugh, Michael	1984	096.04	096.02
Humphrey, Kimberly & Witry, Gregory	1987	112	110
Hunter, Christopher & Wittry, Karen	1987	207.12	207
Hunter, Jason & Weddige, Carol	1970	173.07	173.02
Huss, Anna-Jean & Hankes, John	1969	204.16	204.01
Huss, Bernadine & De King, Brad	1980	204.19	204.01
Huss, Donna & Gary, Eugene	1954	204.02	204.01

Huss, Edwin & Pilch, Judith	1969	204.14	204.01
Huss, Elisabeth & Witry, Nicolas	1786	228	120
Huss, Heinrich & Groos, Anne	1840	023.01.75	023.01
Huss, Heinrich & Groos, Maria	1843	023.01.50	023.01
Huss, Henry & Wittry, Julia	1933	204.01	204
Huss, Jacob & Lida	1998	204.14.01	204.14
Huss, Joseph & Heaton, Eileen	1979	204.20	204.01
Huss, Kathy-Jo & Tierney, Michael	1969	204.17	204.01
Huss, Margaret & Weiten, Ronald	1972	204.18	204.01
Huss, Mary & Wittry, Adam	1889	208	167
Huss, Michel & Mathieu, Susanne	1759	018.02	018.01
Huss, Mona & Adam, David	1962	204.12	204.01
Huss, Richard & Cleo	1980	204.11.01	204.01
Huss, Richard & Frederickson, Judy	1963	204.11	204.01
Huss, Richard & Priscilla	1990	204.11.02	204.01
Huss, Thomas & Bockman, Pam	1975	204.15	204.01
Huss, Virginie & Witry, Mathias	1904	095.01	095
Hutchinson, Sally & Weddige, David	1960	173.13	173.02
Hutton, Timothy & Koehne, Ethel	1993	231.34	231.29
Huveler, Barbara & Witry, Michel	1849	159	157
Hylaczek, Estelle & Witry, Henry	1940	075.07	075
Hymbert, Marie & Witry, Nicolas	1765	309	020
Imbrosciano & Fogg, Veronica	1995	128.18	128.17
Ingerski, Vic & Witry, Louis-John	1925	060	054
Ingram, Kristin & Wittry, Evan	2006	195.50	194
Ionica, Dumitrel & Rasquin, Carmen	1980	014.78	014.75
Irwin, Mary & Wittry, John B.	1915	183	182
Jacobs, Peter & Witry, Marie	1835	133.01	124
Jacobsen, De-Anne & Morgan, Art	1981	231.37	231.29
Jacobsen, Eric & Flores, Adrienne	1980	231.36	231.29
Jacobsen, Noelle & Thompson, John	1990	231.37.01	231.29
Jacoby, Adam & Witry, Catherine	1891	151.01	151
Jacoby, Catherine & Kaell, Charles	1900	014.55	014.50
Jacoby, Susanne & Wiltgen, Dominique	1793	311.08	311.07
Jacque, Albertine & Witry, Leon	1925	146	145
Jacque, Nicolas & Witry, Anna	1880	139.04	134
Jacquemin, Julie & Stronck, Michel	1870	009.23	009.15
Jacques, Amant & Sinner, Aline	1918	141.18	141.13

Jacques, Emile & Jungels, Josephine	1936	141.16	141.14
Jacques, Ferdnand & Van Verweck, Joanne	1934	141.15	141.14
Jacques, Fortnnat & Fourman, Therese	1905	141.14	141.13
Jacques, Germaine & Eichhorn, Emilie	1933	141.17	141.14
Jacques, Joseph & Witry, Eudalie	1865	141.13	141
Jacques, Victor & Witry, Sylvie	1930	141.11	141.09
Jado, Catherine C. & Sitter, Joseph	1910	271.02	271.01
Jado, Michael & Wittry, Marie	1885	271.01	271
Jansz, Mary & Wittry, John	1884	272	271
Jantz, Jessica & Witry, Timothy-Conry	2005	104.00.30	104
Jardin, Josef & Marmann, Susanna	1915	230.05	230.01
Jardin, Katharina & Esch, Willi	1950	230.06	230.05
Jarka, Tim & Meyer, Dawn-Corrine	1987	171.28	171.24
Jean & Hight, Charles-Peter	1975	171.55	171.51
Jenkins, Johnny & Russell, Stacy	1999	229.22.01	229.22
Jenkins, Thomas & Witry, Cynthia	1978	043.02	043
Jensen, John & Koehne, Stephanie	1989	231.48	231.45
Jenson, Darlene & Witry, Charles	1956	118	109
Jillan & Haynes, Kenny	1995	015.51	015.50
Johannessen, Barbara & Bailey, John	1980	172.62	172.59
Johannessen, Howard & Reines, Virginia	1952	172.59	172.53
Johannessen, Karen & Brenner, Craig	1985	172.61	172.59
Johannessen, Karen & Kieres, Michael	1974	172.60	172.59
Johnsen, Debra & Swaidan, George	1980	208.12	208.09.01
Johnsen, Donald & Weber, Dorothy	1950	208.09.01	208.01
Johnsen, Jane & Barbiere, Lawrence	1980	208.13	208.09.01
Johnsen, Joyce & North, John	1980	208.14	208.09.01
Johnsen, Mary & Silver, Robert	1982	208.11	208.09.01
Johnsen, Mary-Sue & Borland, Kevin	1975	208.10	208.09.01
Johnson, Craig & Nieland, Sharon	1983	248.08	248.01
Johnson, Craig & Wilson, Darlene	1950	015.71	015.70
Johnson, Ione & Wittry, Alois	1960	171	169
Johnson, Jerry & Brownback, Cynthia	1970	030.12	030.11
Johnson, Rick & Laura	1980	015.73	015.71
Johnson, Rick & Redeford, Carmen	1975	015.72	015.71
Johnson, Ronald & Mertes, Jean	1982	173.12	173.09
Johnson, Shirley & Thooft, Richard	1985	261.13	261.12

Johnston, Todd & Salmen, Lisa	1988	270.02.45	270.02.30
Johnston, Wendy & Goblirsch, Eric	1986	261.30	261.29
Jones, Betty-Ann & Konen, Donald M.	1963	182.11	182.10
Jones, David & Graap, Frances	1973	231.51	231.49
Jones, Thomas A. & Plain, Gail-Marie	1975	172.45	172.44
Jones, Thorro & Crenshaw, Joan	1980	231.39	231.38
Jordan, Elisabeth & Peffer, Heinrich	1773	119.06	119.05
Jost, Marie-France & Bemtgen, Nico	1960	215.65.80	215.65
Joy, Peter-Douglas & Spang, Tracy	1985	171.08	171.03
Joy, Randall & Fraley, Diane	1973	231.17	231.15
Joy, Randall & Kinman, Kathleen	1969	231.16	231.15
Joy, Randall & Thomas, Linda	1990	231.18	231.15
Joy, Robert & Koehne, Magdalen	1946	231.15	231.01
Joy, Sharon & Dunn, James	1977	231.19	231.15
Joy, Sharon & Lemay, Richard	1992	231.20	231.15
Julia & Schroeder, John-Paul	1985	015.63	015.59.30
June & Witry, Albert	1930	075.05.50	075
Jung, Anne & Jung, Mathias	1895	017.03.12	017.03.05
Jung, Catherine & Gillessen, Pierre	1919	017.03.07	017.03.06
Jung, Catherine & Greisch, Theodore	1930	017.03.10	017.03.06
Jung, Charles & Karels, Marie	1922	017.03.08	017.03.06
Jung, Jean & Prim, Berthie	1952	017.03.09	017.03.08
Jung, Mathias & Adamy, Marguerite	1857	017.03.05	017.03.04
Jung, Mathias & Jung, Anne	1895	017.03.12	017.03.05
Jung, Pierre & Flammang, Marguerite	1888	017.03.06	017.03.05
Jung, Susanne & Faber, Charles	1888	017.03.11	017.03.05
Jungels, Josephine & Jacques, Emile	1936	141.16	141.14
Jungers, Elisabeth & Witry, Jean	1895	132.04.01	127
Jungers, Marie-Anne & Witry, Michel	1830	021.13	021.02
Jungers, Sonja & Leyers, Carol	2001	166.40	166.20
Jungles, Nicolas & Witry, Theresa W.	1876	027.01	027
Jungles, Norma & Mutscheler, C. E.	1915	027.02	027.01
Juppin, Germaine & Witry, Henri	1930	088	087
Justice, Leneatha & Glass, Steven	1990	233.10	233.01
Kaarg, Jason P. & Hill, Pamela-Dee	2001	198.03	198.01
Kaell, Charles & Jacoby, Catherine	1900	014.55	014.50
Kaell, Charles & Stroesser, Anne	1908	014.60	014.50
Kaell, Emile & Colle, Michele	1972	014.65.60	014.65

Kaell, Francois & Siebenaler, Marguerite	1945	014.65	014.55
Kaell, Francois & Van Grysperre, Isabel	2000	014.65.40	014.65
Kaell, Jean & De Waha, Maria	1854	014.50	014.01
Kaell, Joseph & Oduber, Marlene	1971	014.65.20	014.65
Kaell, Marguerite & Lies, Alphonse	1940	014.70	014.55
Kaell, Marianne & Kerger, Paul	1974	014.65.80	014.65
Kaell, Pauline & Eisen, Joseph	1955	014.65.90	014.55
Kaepppeli, Paul & Schaaf, Elaine	1986	017.03.13.70	017.03.13.50
Kaiser, Barbara & Goedert, Peter	1914	229.03	229.02
Kaiser, Frank & Huberty, Pascale	1995	014.85	014.80
Kalsow, Thomas & Kohley, Donna	1977	171.32	171.30
Kammes, Josephine & Wittry, Jacob	1912	204	203
Kane, Candace & Whitfield, Robert	1975	171.17	171.16
Kane, Randy & Sachs, Mary-Kay	1979	229.15	229.13
Kane, Ted & Spang, Joan	1950	171.16	171.02
Kanne, Jayne & Welch, Randy	1990	243.03	243.01
Kanne, Michael & McBride, Joy	1996	243.04	243.01
Kanne, Ralph & Wittry, Janice	1958	243.01	241
Kanne, Roxanne & Roush, Kent	1988	243.02	243.01
Kaplun, Luis & Muller, Maria-Ines	1993	031.00.95	031.00.90
Kardong, Matthew & Witry, Margaretha	1921	108.01	108
Karels, Marie & Jung, Charles	1922	017.03.08	017.03.06
Kariger, Anne & Witry, Mathias	1910	095.05	095
Karpes, Lucia & Witry, Michel	1860	262	229
Kathleen M. & Witry, John	1930	075.01	075
Kathy & Schroeder, Randy-John	1980	015.84	015.83
Katzer, Jo-Ann & Wittry, Christopher	1985	030.04	030
Kauffmann, Nicolas & Witry, Regina	1817	015.02	012
Kauth, Helena & Witry, Pierre	1921	304	301
Kauth, Jean & Witry, Angele	1935	303.02	301
Kayser, Catherine & Lomertz, Dominique	1859	311.15	311.12
Kayser, Catherine & Weynandt, Peter	1867	311.19	311.12
Kayser, Jean & Seil, Anna	1857	311.14	311.12
Kayser, Margaretha & Strasser, Michel	1848	311.13	311.12

Kayser, Marie & Friedrich, Nikolas	1863	311.18	311.12
Kayser, Marie & Kugener, Johann	1922	074.00.99	074.00.95
Kayser, Nikolas & Goerens, Anna	1860	311.17	311.12
Kayser, Nikolas & Wiltgen, Marie	1819	311.12	311.08
Kayser, Wilhelm & Hoffmann, Catherine	1864	311.16	311.12
Keenan, Karen & Schramer, Robert	1965	172.08	172.01
Kelley, Charles A. & Wittry, Helen	1942	030.08	029
Kelley, Richard & McKay, Margie	1955	277.03	277.01
Kelley, Sharlys & Viergever, James	1970	030.09	030.08
Kelley, William & Maryann	1955	277.02	277.01
Kelley, William & Wittry, Elizabeth	1920	277.01	272
Kelly, Geraldine & Spang, Brian J.	1980	171.07	171.03
Kelsen, Johanna & Witry, Peter	1876	293	292
Kennedy, Mary & Witry, Bernard	1950	056	055
Kerger, Claude & Hein, Nadia	1977	014.65.88	014.65.80
Kerger, Malou & Besenius, Jeff	2001	014.65.85	014.65.80
Kerger, Paul & Kaell, Marianne	1974	014.65.80	014.65
Kerschen, Leon & Origer, Sylvie	1910	141.24	141.22
Kerzmann, John & Witry, Johanna	1892	107.02	107
Kesseler, Claude & Thill, Nathalie	2004	153.02.01	153.02
Kessler, Catherine & Philipp, Mathias	1935	293.02	293.01
Kessler, Peter & Witry, Marie	1902	293.01	293
Keyser, Anne & Adamy, Pierre	1830	017.03.04	017.03.01
Kiefer, Franz & George, Margaretha	1826	119.04	119.02
Kiefer, Patricia & Wittry, Delbert	1949	201	197
Kieres, Michael & Johannessen, Karen	1974	172.60	172.59
King, Jimmy & Martin, Helen M.	1970	172.50	172.48
King, Leslie & Thurston, Joseph	1979	231.26	231.21
King, Shawna H. & Guest, Guy	1990	172.51	172.50
Kinman, Kathleen & Joy, Randall	1969	231.16	231.15
Kipgen, Catherine & Ries, Mathias	1788	020.05.03	020.05
Kipgen, Jacob & Witry, Catherine	1770	015.98	011
Kirsch, Anna & Weidert, Peter	1794	009.41	009.40
Kirsch, Barbara & Stiren, Nicolas	1796	009.42	009.40
Kirsch, Jean-Pierre & Witry, Anna	1840	125.01	125
Kirsch, Margaretha & Braun, Nicolas	1810	009.43	009.40
Kirsch, Margot & Bemtgen, Adolf	1959	215.65.40	215.65
Kirsch, Marie-Anna & Witry, Heinrich	1867	151	148

Kirsch, Nicolas & Witry, Marie	1749	036.03	021
Kirsch, Valentin & Witry, Anna	1770	009.40	006
Kirsh, Robert & Thooft, Suzanne	1989	261.19	261.12
Kleber, Marie-Louise & Witry, Alfred	1923	136	135
Klees, Valerie & Witry, Marcel	1955	217.03	217
Klein, H. & Spanier, Susanne	1850	015.96	015.03
Klein, Karen & Burke, Thomas	1980	060.03	060.01
Klein, M. & Fell, Mathias	1890	009.34	009.33
Klein, Marie & Marx, Jean Baptiste	1853	035.01.50	035.01
Klein, Nicolas & Witry, Marie	1821	035.01	033
Klein, Peter & Witry, Anna	1785	010.01	006
Kleinfeldt, Janet & Stolarski, Leonard	1978	086.08	086.06
Klensch & Mom	1970	074.00.85	074.00.80
Kleppe, Joan & Wittry, Warren	1950	280	279
Klopp, Nicolas & Wiltgen, Anne	1840	311.22.65	311.22.50
Klosen, Franz & Witry, Suzanne	1933	227.01	219
Klosen, Georges & Gudendorf, Simone	1990	227.04	227.02
Klosen, Joseph & Bauer, Fernande	1960	227.02	227.01
Klosen, Michel & Weirich, Viviane	1995	227.05	227.02
Klosen, Paul & Terao, Eriko	1990	227.03	227.02
Kneip, Agnese & Dondelinger, Johann	1818	308.06	308.03
Kneip, Anna & Witry, Jean-Mathias	1766	012	011
Kneipper, Margaret & Wittry, Albert	1925	192	182
Knips, Earl & Wittry, Arlene	1955	267.07	265
Knips, Kristi & Reker, Gary	1980	267.08	267.07
Knisley, Edward & Wittry, Theresa	1945	274.02	273
Knobbe, Julie & Venner, Thomas	1986	236.07	236.02
Koch, Philomene & Bemtgen, Adolf	1959	215.65.20	215.65
Koehne, Adelaide & Thurston, John	1948	231.21	231.01
Koehne, Catherine & Crenshaw, Billy	1955	231.38	231.01
Koehne, Debra & Rossi, Ralph	1973	231.30	231.29
Koehne, Diane & Clark, Stephen	1983	231.04	231.02
Koehne, Ethel & Hutton, Timothy	1993	231.34	231.29
Koehne, Gerald & Barnett, Lois	1971	231.03	231.02
Koehne, Gerald & Bledsoe, Karen	2005	231.03.50	231.02
Koehne, Harold & Ramos, Isabel	1947	231.02	231.01
Koehne, John & Feliciano, Judith	1959	231.45	231.01
Koehne, Joseph & Martin, Dorotha	1951	231.29	231.01

Koehne, Joseph & Roth, Auldene	1986	231.35	231.01
Koehne, Josephine & Bryant, John	1984	231.33	231.29
Koehne, Juvent & Frederiks, Margaret	1950	231.05	231.01
Koehne, Juvent & Wall, Sallie	1975	231.06	231.01
Koehne, Magdalen & Joy, Robert	1946	231.15	231.01
Koehne, Margaret & Reading, Joseph	1993	231.32	231.29
Koehne, Marianne & Tapparo, John	1945	231.07	231.01
Koehne, Mark & Barker, Christine	1995	231.47.01	231.45
Koehne, Paul & Ramirez, Dolores	1961	231.14	231.01
Koehne, Robert & Garcia, Melinda	1986	231.46	231.45
Koehne, Scott & Gomez, Dolores	1987	231.47	231.45
Koehne, Stephanie & Jensen, John	1989	231.48	231.45
Koehne, Terry & Carson, Christine	1993	231.54	231.49
Koehne, Thomas & Pimental, Lori	1976	231.31	231.29
Koehne, William & Martin, Frances	1962	231.49	231.01
Koehne, William & Wittry, Sophia	1916	231.01	231
Koemptgen, Susanna & Stronck, Nicolas	1860	009.21	009.15
Koentge, Catherine & Witry, Peter	1885	087	052
Koerner, Adam & Witry, Barbara	1867	166.01	165
Koetz, Catherine & Witry, Michel	1894	050.01	049
Koetz, Maria & Olsem, Nikolas	1866	321.15.28	321.15.07
Kohl, Barbara & Witry, Michel	1867	263	229
Kohler, Kathy & Carlson, James-Alan	1970	182.36	182.25
Kohley, Donald & Diehl, Katherine	1953	171.30	171.29
Kohley, Donna & Kalsow, Thomas	1977	171.32	171.30
Kohley, Karen & Ostrander, Mark	1975	171.31	171.30
Kohley, Kenneth & Messmer, Susan	1966	171.38	171.29
Kohley, Laura & Farley, Kris	2000	171.37.01	171.36
Kohley, Louise & Ziman, John G.	1955	171.35	171.29
Kohley, Nancy & Ehrke, Robert	1995	171.37	171.36
Kohley, Ralph & Spang, Agnes	1929	171.29	171.01
Kohley, Richard J. & Mielke, Karen	1965	171.36	171.29
Kohley, Sandra & Deutsch, Michael	1980	171.34	171.30
Kohley, Thomas & Kunde, Becky	1991	171.33	171.30
Kohn, Heinrich & Witry, Marie	1875	308.01	300
Kolbach, Silvie & Witry, Andre	1984	218.05	218.04
Kolp, Sharon & Schroeder, Thomas	1965	015.37	015.07
Konen, Donald M. & Jones, Betty-Ann	1963	182.11	182.10

Konen, Dorothy M. & Stull, Emil W.	1937	182.14	182.09
Konen, Gilbert & Adkins, Theresa	1970	182.13	182.10
Konen, John M. & Mezan, Frances	1937	182.10	182.09
Konen, John-Irvin & Pellegrino, Diane	1989	182.12	182.11
Konen, Michael & Hass, Megan-Marie	2003	182.12.05	182.11
Konen, Michael & Wittry, Laura-Lena	1913	182.09	182
Konen, Verdell & Carlson, Clarence	1945	182.25	182.09
Konen, Verdell & Hankins, Robert	1954	182.38.50	182.09
Konsbruck, Anne & Broos, Mathias	1863	017.03.16	017.03.15
Konsbruck, Pierre & Steyer, Maria	1902	024.50	024.01
Korier, Nicolas & Witry, Anna	1866	086.50	052
Kosch, Carlo & Bastian, Lotty	1973	079.03	079.02
Kosch, Marco & Giamprini, Diana	1989	079.04	079.02
Kosch, Roby & Thornton, Josette	1994	079.05	079.02
Kosch, Roger & Hirschler, Alice	1949	079.02	079.01
Koteles, Gary & O'Leary, Maureen	1980	278.02	278.01
Kraemer, Garry & Handzik, Karla	1980	086.14	086.10
Kraemer, John & Thooft, Karen	1989	261.17	261.12
Krafka, Arnold & Holmberg, Darlene	2003	270.03.10	270.03
Krant, David & Schramer, Kathleen	1982	172.11	172.09
Krantz, Eugene & Lanham, Rita	1945	209.02	209.01
Krantz, Maretta & Schmidt, Donald	1970	209.03	209.02
Krantz, Susan & Frieders, John	1933	172.33.50	168
Kraus, Clarence & Wittry, Joan	1949	240.09	240
Kraus, Gerald & Christian, Terri	1998	240.11	240.09
Kraus, Gerald & Hackett, Pamela	1971	240.10	240.09
Kraus, Justin & Christian, Terri	1998	240.10.00	240.10
Kraus, Mary & Thooft, Dennis	1989	261.24	261.21
Kraus, Theresa & Witry, Johann-Peter	1899	108	107
Kremer, Barbe & Wiltgen, Nicolas	1841	311.22.67	311.22.50
Kremer, Isabelle & Rasquin, Jean	1964	128.00.50	128.00.35
Kremer, Joseph & Witry, Marie	1965	128.00.35	128.00.05
Kremer, Leonie & <Unnamed>	1930	119.01.50	119.00.50
Kremer, Magdalena & Reckinger, Johann	1739	311.02	311.01
Kremer, Nadine & <Unnamed>	1990	128.00.40	128.00.35
Kremer, Peter & Witry, Catherine	1898	119.01	107
Kreul, Diane & Grattafiori, Michael	1985	173.06	173.03
Krier, Margaretha & Witry, Theodor	1836	039	038

Krippeler, Marco & Witry, Victorine	2000	128.00.22	128.00.20
Krippes, Catherine & Ries, Heinrich	1760	020.05.01	020.05
Kubacki, Stanley & Sitter, Bernadine	1935	271.04	271.02
Kuehl, Cheryl & Hoflock, Larry	1977	240.44	240.43
Kugener, Anton, & Witry, Anna	1895	074.00.95	053
Kugener, Johann & Kayser, Marie	1922	074.00.99	074.00.95
Kugener, Lambert & Glodt, Marie	1862	161.02	161.01
Kugener, Mathias & Witry, Margaretha	1835	161.01	157
Kugener, Susanna & Frantzen, Joseph	1921	024.00.97	024.00.95
Kuhnen, Catherine & Witry, Nicolas	1818	229	156
Kuhnen, Johann & Witry, Elisabeth	1835	157.02	157
Kuhnen, Marie & Witry, Nicolas	1774	156	120
Kuhnen, Marie-Magdalena & Witry, Adam	1685	003	002
Kultgen, Catherine & Witry, Francois	1870	021.14	021.13
Kunde, Becky & Kohley, Thomas	1991	171.33	171.30
Kuntziger, Andre & <Unnamed>	1840	021.09	021.03
Kuntziger, Barbe & Waver, Joseph	1840	021.06	021.03
Kuntziger, Francoise & Moeris, Michel	1840	021.07	021.03
Kuntziger, Jacques & <Unnamed>	1835	021.08	021.03
Kuntziger, Jacques & Witry, Marie	1808	021.05	021.02
Kurt, Tom & Venner, Elizabeth	1994	236.06.01	236.02
Kurth & Hellers, Jean	1890	009.11	009.09
Kyhn, Steven & Otte, Coleen	1991	270.02.20	270.02.05
Labat, Mary-Kay & Hoflock, Gary	1973	240.45	240.43
Lacare, Catheine & Witry, Philippe	1919	046.65	046
Laiches, Mathias & Adamy, Marie	1818	017.03.03	017.03.01
Lamote, Brenda & Thooft, Douglas	1984	261.14	261.12
Lampe, Kay & Hannasch, Richard	1987	240.17	240.09
Lance, Alfredo & Canueto, Blanca	1945	031.00.45	031.00.40
Lange, Marian & Holmberg, Patrick	1973	270.03.15	270.03
Lanham, Paul & McCulloh, Lori	1991	209.05	209.04
Lanham, Rita & Krantz, Eugene	1945	209.02	209.01
Lanham, Robert & McWain, Jacquelyn	1955	209.04	209.01
Lanham, Robert & Wittry, Dorothy	1925	209.01	208
Lanhers, Margit & Schroeder, Francois	1930	015.87	015.86

Lanteigne, Michele & Thurston, James	1977	231.25	231.21
Larsen, Marie & Schroeder, Paul J.	1934	015.59.40	015.06
Larson, Dorothy & Schroeder, Edward	1939	015.78	015.06
Larson, Kimberly & Venner, Dale	1988	236.08	236.02
Larson, Lloyd & Verdeck, Bonnie	1966	240.35	240.34
Laschette, Anna & Witry, Mathias	1850	214	157
Lau, Roxy & Deltgen, Jean	1930	321.15.15	321.15.14
Laura & Johnson, Rick	1980	015.73	015.71
Laurie & Heber, Robert-Wayne	1990	015.14	015.12
Laux, Marie-Catherine & Witry, Jean	1765	121	120
Lavallaye, Nicolas & Witry, Catherine	1880	036.01	036
LaVoy, Gary & Thooft, Joan	1994	261.25	261.21
Lawson, Robert & Hawking, Karen	1988	208.08	208.07
Layman, Richard & Wittry, Christine	1981	207.10	207
Leclerc, Theodore & Quiring, Marianne	1960	139.02.01	139.02
Leclerc, Victor & Witry, Marie	1923	139.02	135
Lee, Mick & Graap, Nancy	1970	231.53	231.49
Lefebvre, Marie & Witry, Auguste	1880	141.25.50	141.19
Legg, Scott-Eric & Efsic, Ellen-Rose	1991	182.16	182.15
Lego, Thomas & Witry, Nancy-Jean	1990	062.01	061
Lehnen, Marie & Marmann, Peter	1921	230.02	230.01
Leider, Josephine & Wittry, George H.	1932	180	173
Leisen, Nicole & Witry, Charles	1970	086	085
Leitgen, Philippe & Philippart, Anna	1905	144.50	144.01
Leiting, Marc & Wittry, Peggy	1975	257.01	256
Lemarand, Cinthia & Carlson, Robert	1977	015.77	015.71
Lemarand, Connie & Houle, Ray	1972	015.76	015.71
Lemarand, Robert & Wilson, Darlene	1952	015.75	015.70
Lemay, Richard & Joy, Sharon	1992	231.20	231.15
Lemus, Nestor & Muller, Monica	1985	031.00.20	031.00.15
Lenger, Anatol & Parisse, Marie	1880	141.04	141.03
Lenger, Anne-Marie & Witry, Nicolas	1849	141.19	140
Lenger, Francois & <Unnamed>	1910	141.05	141.04
Lenger, Francois & Witry, Catherine	1855	141.03	141
Lenger, Marie & Stoffel, Jean-Nicolas	1910	141.07	141.04
Lenger, Odette & Beckers, Joseph	1940	141.06	141.05
Leonard, Margaretha & Witry, Nicolas	1875	046	045
Leonard, Marie & Witry, Arthur	1887	141.20	141.19

Lepley, Helene & Reider, William	1955	208.16	208.15
Lesniak, David & Frieders, Lydia-Jean	2000	172.26.01	172.26
Lester, John-Jay & Witry, Mary-Ellen	1974	056.01	056
Letellier, Gustav & Witry, Josefine	1889	035.00.50	035
Lethal, Anne-Marie & Witry, Johann	1899	132.04.02	127
Lewis, Patricia & Witry, Richard-James	1980	073	071
Leyders, Johann & Rob, Marie	1732	322.02	322
Leyers, Albertine & Streng, Romain	1996	166.30	166.20
Leyers, Camille & Putz, Nicole-Barbe	1965	166.20	166.05
Leyers, Carol & Jungers, Sonja	2001	166.40	166.20
Lhotelain, Monique & Witry, Michel	1958	089	088
Lichter, Susanna & Witry, Johann	1850	230	229
Lick, Mathias & Eiffes, Anna	1879	161.04	161.03
Lida & Huss, Jacob	1998	204.14.01	204.14
Lies, Alphonse & Kaell, Marguerite	1940	014.70	014.55
Lies, Anne-Marie & Rasquin, Jeff	1964	014.75	014.70
Lies, Eugenie & Huberty, Camille	1964	014.80	014.70
Lies, Peter-Paul & Wittry, Theresa	1918	172.36	168
Lilaz-Polletaz, Nadege & Grelon, Jean	2000	095.03.50	095.03
Limpach, Monique & Witry, Leon	1961	021.18	021.16
Linckels, Jacques & Conzemius, Catherine	1785	321.15.29	321.15.01
Link, Nancy-Ann & Wittry, Eugene	1954	193	192
Linster, Robert & Witry, Maria	1930	132.03	129
Litsch, Frances & Wittry, Arthur O.	1919	029	028
Lodraga, Judy & Tapparo, Ronald	1975	231.11	231.07
Logelin, Leonie & Witry, Nicolas	1925	166.04	166.03
Lomertz, Dominique & Kayser, Catherine	1859	311.15	311.12
Lonsway, John & Hight, Kathleen	1965	171.52	171.51
Lonsway, Patrick & MacKenzie, Karen	1990	171.53	171.52
Lopez, Crystal & Smith, Steven	1999	207.09	207.08
Lopez, Phillip & Wittry, Marianne	1980	207.08	207
Lordong, Jean-Pierre & Witry, Josiane	1980	227.00.02	227.00.01
Loretta & Schroeder, Paul J.	1935	015.59.50	015.06
Losch, John & Witry, Margaretha	1920	050.01.50	050.01
Loser, Brandy & Lund, Mike	1995	015.28	015.27

Loser, Cinthia & Armstrong, Robert	1965	015.19.50	015.08
Loser, Cinthia & Thomfohrda, Woody	1991	015.26	015.08
Loser, Cinthia-Ann & Wagner, Rick	1965	015.20	015.08
Loser, George & Schroeder, Barbara	1942	015.08	015.07
Loser, George & Steadman, Loraine	1965	015.09	015.08
Loser, Katherine & Ettner, Thomas	1976	015.17	015.08
Loser, Katherine & McKenna, Kenneth	1972	015.16	015.08
Loser, Katherine & Offling, Frank	1980	015.18	015.08
Loser, Katherine-Marie & Heber, Paul	1965	015.12	015.08
Loser, Katherine-Marie & Smell, Jack	1986	015.19	015.08
Loser, Michelle & Tueber, Christopher	1987	015.10	015.09
Loser, Stacy & Henderson, Russell	1997	015.11	015.09
Loser, Steven-Mark & Bryan, Kathy	1974	015.27	015.08
Louwagie, Debbie & Thooft, Scott	1992	261.20	261.12
Lucas, Christina & Witry, Michael	1828	021.26.50	021.26
Lucius, Sisy & Witry, Emile	1955	222	221
Lucius, Susanne & Witry, Jacques	1958	225	221
Luckhardt, Brian & Bernardy, Angela	2003	261.37	261.35
Ludwig, Nicolas & Groos, Catharina	1851	023.01.85	023.01
Ludwigs, Catherine & Witry, Georg	1876	215	214
Lugo, Sonya & Wittry, Kristopher	1989	282.01	282
Luhman, Edward & Brown, Heather	1999	229.14.01	229.14
Lun, Christine & Witry, Michel	1835	141	140
Lund, Mike & Loser, Brandy	1995	015.28	015.27
Lutgen, Margaretha & Witry, Heinrich	1874	095	094
Lutgen, Susanne & Witry, Gregoire	1932	166.02.03	166.02.01
M. M. & Witry, Peter	1896	289	288
Machus, Marie & Rob, Firmin	1712	323	002
Mack, Andre & Noesen, Katharina	1890	321.15.12	321.15.08
Mack, Andrew & Chapman, Jennifer	2003	261.33.50	261.33
Mack, Anna & Wehrlen, Achille	1925	321.15.23	321.15.12
Mack, Anne & Deltgen, Jacques	1950	321.15.14	321.15.13
Mack, Anne & Fautsch, Jean-Francois	1900	321.15.11	321.15.08
Mack, Charles & Stolarski, Judith-Ann	1975	086.07	086.06
Mack, Elisabetha & Schwab, Emile	1885	321.15.09	321.15.08
Mack, Jean & Fox, Margaretha	1919	321.15.22	321.15.12
Mack, Joseph & Dupire, Paule	1964	321.15.21	321.15.13
Mack, Joseph & Roob, Rose	1944	321.15.24	321.15.12

Mack, Marie-Catherine & Bleser, Jean	1907	321.15.10	321.15.08
Mack, Nicolas & Mander, Claire	1921	321.15.13	321.15.12
Mack, Nicolas & Olsem, Anna	1858	321.15.08	321.15.07
MacKenzie, Karen & Lonsway, Patrick	1990	171.53	171.52
Main, Thomas & Bernardy, Vicky	2001	261.28.01	261.28
Majerus, Anna & Olsem, Nicolas	1826	321.15.07	321.15.05
Majerus, Anne & Adamy, Nicolas	1836	017.03.14	017.03.01
Majerus, Anne & Conzemius, Claudius	1780	321.15.04	321.15.01
Majerus, Margaretha & Neuens, Nicolas	1779	321.15	321.12
Malding, Johann & Witry, Anna	1799	009.38	007
Malhaiuk, Julie & Wittry, Thomas	1983	239	238
Mallory & Schroeder, Penny	1969	015.61	015.59.30
Malone, Timothy & Wittry, Shanna	2000	194.01	194
Mander, Claire & Mack, Nicolas	1921	321.15.13	321.15.12
Mangerich, Marguerite & Witry, Roger	1954	218.04	218.02
Marchal, Anna & Hoch, Bernard	1706	324.05	324.02
Marchal, Anna & Volibi, Peter	1668	324.01	324
Marchal, Jean & Witry, Jacqueline	1980	218.04.50	218.04
Marchal, Magdalena & Didion, Johann	1719	324.07	324.02
Marchal, Margaretha & Collet, Anton	1672	324.09	324
Marchal, Margaretha & Collet, Johann	1711	324.06	324.02
Marchal, Nicolas & Becker, Anna	1703	324.03	324.02
Marchal, Nicolas & Bemer, Magdalena	1670	324.02	324
Marchal, Nicolas & Bonjean, Magdalena	1716	324.04	324.02
Marchal, Nicolas & Paulus, Elisabeth	1640	324	001
Marchal, Susanne & Francois, Nicolas	1669	324.08	324
Mares, Aristobulo & Witry, Clara	1920	128.05	128.01
Mares, Maria-Clara & Calzolari	1950	128.06	128.05
Margaret T. & Witry, Nicholas	1899	075	053
Margaretha & Thies, Johann	1675	018	002
Marie & Reuter, Nicolas	1717	017.08	017.05
Marie & Wittry, Paul	1915	273	272
Marmann, Elizabeth & Appel, Carl	1909	230.03	230.01

Marmann, Katharina & Stubert, Christophe	1914	230.04	230.01
Marmann, Mathias & Witry, Katharina	1880	230.01	230
Marmann, Peter & Lehnen, Marie	1921	230.02	230.01
Marmann, Susanna & Jardin, Josef	1915	230.05	230.01
Marsch, Susan & Schroeder, Kenneth	1973	015.30	015.29
Martin, Albert & Plain, Ruth-Helen	1945	172.49	172.47
Martin, Dorotha & Koehne, Joseph	1951	231.29	231.01
Martin, Frances & Koehne, William	1962	231.49	231.01
Martin, Helen M. & King, Jimmy	1970	172.50	172.48
Martin, Marie & Witry, William	1940	076	075
Martinez, Cindy & Wittry, Christopher	1995	259.02	259
Martinez, Enrique & Thurston, Patricia	1998	231.25.01	231.25
Marx, Jean Baptiste & Klein, Marie	1853	035.01.50	035.01
Maryann & Kelley, William	1955	277.02	277.01
Marzuki, Henry, Jr. & Stull, Laura-Li	1960	182.18	182.14
Mason, James & Wittry, Mary-Jo	1976	249.01	249
Masselter, Clara & Spanier, Nicolas	1860	015.95	015.03
Masson, Bernard & Collet, Barbara	1707	324.11	324.09
Mathey, Barbara & Witry, Johann	1849	134	124
Mathey, Catherine & Witry, Michel	1802	140	121
Mathieu, Catherine & Rob, Firmin	1700	322	002
Mathieu, Catherine & Weber, Conrad	1758	018.03	018.01
Mathieu, Johann & Thies, Marie	1716	018.01	018
Mathieu, Susanne & Huss, Michel	1759	018.02	018.01
Mathis, Jeanne & Plain, John M.	1970	172.42	172.39
Mattioli, Diane & Seil, Guy	2000	084.50	084.02
Matyas, Marsha & Stull, Nicholas	1966	182.19	182.14
McBride, Joy & Kanne, Michael	1996	243.04	243.01
McCann, Daniel & Hannasch, Mary	1984	240.18	240.09
McCarthy, Wanda & Glass, William	1982	233.03	233.01
McCormick, Daniel & Gary, Marianne	1981	204.07	204.02
McCulloh, Lori & Lanham, Paul	1991	209.05	209.04
McDaniel, Dawn & Barron, Daniel	1998	201.03	201.02
McDaniel, James & Wittry, Debra	1970	201.02	201
McDaniel, Philip & Hankins, Carol	1977	182.42	182.25
McGrath, Alice & Witry, George	1930	063	054
McGrew, Mary & Conrad, David	1999	229.12.02	229.10
McGuffin, Craig & Orizondo, Amy	2003	182.06.01	182.06

McIntyre, Chip-Dio & Carlson, Kira	1997	182.28.10	182.28
McIntyre, Dan & Wittry, Barbara	1967	270.02	270
McKay, Margie & Kelley, Richard	1955	277.03	277.01
McKenna, Kenneth & Loser, Katherine	1972	015.16	015.08
McKnight, Forrest & Wittry, Helen	1956	030.10	029
McMahan, Robert & Wittry, Catherine	1975	201.01	201
McQueen, Angelica & Schopp, Troy	1994	207.02	207.01
McQueen, Joseph & Wittry, Theresa	1973	207.01	207
McWain, Jacquelyn & Lanham, Robert	1955	209.04	209.01
Mears, Elizabeth & Wittry, Nickolas	1903	169	168
Medernach, Balthasar & Broos, Marie	1880	017.03.18	017.03.17
Medernach, Johann & Reckinger, Marie	1755	311.05	311.01
Medernach, Margaretha & Neuens, Nicolas	1740	321.13	321.12
Mehlen & Reiland, Catherine	1860	009.32	009.26
Melsen, Anna & Sher, Mathias	1940	074.03	074.01
Melsen, Anna & Witry, John	1890	054	053
Melsen, J. & Witry, Helene	1900	074.01	053
Melsen, Leon & Frideres, Elise	1940	074.02	074.01
Menage, Pierre & Witry, Margaretha	1810	021.12	021.02
Mengel & Clemes, Gail	1965	086.22	086.21
Menne, Anne & Witry, Johann	1935	217	216
Meny, Peter & Streff, Margaretha	1863	157.06	157.03
Mercer, John & Wittry, Debra	1973	201.04	201
Mergen, Catherine & Witry, Mathias	1925	046.30	046.20
Merkle, James & Witry, Julie	1990	070.01	069
Mersch, Margaretha & Millang, Anthonius	1805	323.00.04	323.00.02
Mersch, Marie & Glaesener, Charles	1795	323.00.03	323.00.02
Mersch, Pierre & Rob, Maria	1768	323.00.02	323.00.01
Mertes, Edward & Weddige, Pauline	1958	173.09	173.02
Mertes, James & Dineen, Susan	1987	173.11	173.09
Mertes, Jean & Johnson, Ronald	1982	173.12	173.09
Mertes, Susan & Nitschke, Robert	1981	173.10	173.09
Messmer, Susan & Kohley, Kenneth	1966	171.38	171.29
Messmore, Gregory & Wittry, Linda	1984	261.01	261

Metz, Evrard & Muller, Catherine	1861	023.50	023.02
Meunier, Martine & Witry, Michel	1990	021.20	021.18
Meyer, Dawn-Corrine & Jarka, Tim	1987	171.28	171.24
Meyer, Esther & Schroeder, Ernest	1924	015.07	015.06
Meyer, Gregory & Weistroffer, Jane	1986	171.27	171.24
Meyer, Jerry & Anderson, Phyllis	1959	171.24	171.23
Meyer, Lianne-Kay & Halling, David	1979	171.25	171.24
Meyer, Lianne-Kay & Spencer, John	1985	171.26	171.24
Meyer, Ruth & Frieders, Herman	1943	172.25	172.24
Meyer, Susan & Evans, James	1965	204.22	204.21
Meyers, Barbara & Witry, Johann	1830	292	156
Meyers, Catherine & Witry, Valentin	1796	157	156
Meyers, Marie & Reuter, Johann	1715	017.06	017.05
Mezan, Frances & Konen, John M.	1937	182.10	182.09
Mezmalis, Parsla & Carbery, James	1985	071.03	071.01
Michaelis, Marie & Witry, Theodor	1870	163	162
Michaelis, Mich & Witry, Marie-Paule	1985	225.01.50	225
Michaely, Geraldine & Witry, Romain	1995	217.05	217.04
Michaux, Marguerite & Witry, Joseph	1942	083	079
Michels, Mathias & Adamy, Susanne	1810	017.03.02	017.03.01
Michels, William & Weddige, Diana	1986	173.15	173.13
Mielke, Karen & Kohley, Richard J.	1965	171.36	171.29
Mikel, Steve & Pape, Brenda	1984	240.41	240.37
Mikkelsen, Steve & Derner, Mary	1988	261.07	261.03
Millang, Anthonius & Mersch, Margaretha	1805	323.00.04	323.00.02
Miller, Frederick & Bock, Sharon	1982	260.03	260.01
Miller, Pearl & Witry, Joseph	1928	109	108
Mitchell, Donald & Schramer, Gayle	1975	172.04	172.02
Mitchell, Mary & Witry, Paul	1990	059	056
Modaff, Janet & Stull, Gary-Michael	1977	182.23	182.14
Moderhack, Lawrence & Carbery, Mary	1985	071.04	071.01
Modert, Maria & Witry, Alfred	1952	305	304
Moeris, Michel & Kuntziger, Francoise	1840	021.07	021.03
Moiss, Anna-Marie & Witry, Johann	1847	049	038
Molitor, Margaret & Wittry, Henry	1882	173	167
Mom & Klensch	1970	074.00.85	074.00.80

Monique & Sher, Leon	1970	074.04	074.03
Mons, Catherine & Glod, Pierre	1849	311.10	311.09
Mons, Heinrich & Wiltgen, Marie	1819	311.09	311.08
Mons, Karl & Witry, Marie-Catherine	1796	015.01	012
Mons, Nikolaus & Hilbert, Susanne	1848	311.11	311.09
Moore, Kelly-Jo & Wittry, Philip-John	1991	196	193
Moore, Kristi & Weddige, Michael	2004	173.16	173.13
Moore, Nicole & Wittry, James	1996	245	244
Moore, Sheila & Thurston, Steven	1984	231.28	231.21
Moos, Catherine & Goedert, Michel	1887	229.02	229.01
Moos, Jacob & Witry, Elisabeth	1846	229.01	229
Moos, Margaretha & Conrad, Bernard	1884	229.06	229.01
Moos, Marie & <Unnamed>	1880	229.38.01	229.01
Moos, Marie & Conter, Dominique	1891	229.38	229.01
Morang, Joseph & Witry, Maria	1935	153.04	152
Mores, Anna & Fogolin	1945	225.04	225.03
Mores, Nicolas & Witry, Virginie	1920	225.03	219
Mores, Simone & Schueren	1960	225.05	225.03
Morette, Madeleine & Witry, Pierre	1925	221	219
Morgan, Art & Jacobsen, De-Anne	1981	231.37	231.29
Morgan, Phillip & Skoglie, Tammy	1995	015.49	015.48
Morgan, Randy & Weber, Caryl	1980	208.05	208.02
Morganstein, Sanford & Sabo, Monica	1970	182.05	182.03
Morge, Marion & Witry, Peter J.	1930	075.02	075
Moriame, Anne & Witry, Heinrich	1745	021.01	021
Moris, Charles & Witry, Marie	1775	015.99.01	011
Morrosco, Antoinette & Clemes, William	1935	086.21	086.01
Moss, David & Bast, Cindy	1985	015.56	015.45
Mouchant, Anna & Witry, Johann	1767	007	006
Muell, Richard & Buelt, Carrie	2002	240.07.01	240.07
Muller, Alberto-Raul & Re, Andrea	1980	031.00.75	031.00.60
Muller, Alfredo & Zubiri, Ana-Maria	1964	031.00.90	031.00.60
Muller, Ana & Olsen, Pablo	1992	031.01.30	031.00.90
Muller, Blanca & Prado, Ruben	1975	031.00.70	031.00.65
Muller, Carlos & Goicochea, Gladis	1955	031.00.15	031.00.10
Muller, Catharina & Welter, Johann	1920	107.01.60	107.01
Muller, Catherine & Eltz, Johann	1868	023.70	023.02
Muller, Catherine & Metz, Evrard	1861	023.50	023.02

Muller, Elisabeth & Witry, Johann	1862	031	026
Muller, Elisabeth & Witry, Nicolas	1859	024	023.02 292
Muller, Felix & Alonso, Maria	1924	031.00.60	031.00.05
Muller, Felix-Raul & Anso, Blanca	1945	031.00.65	031.00.60
Muller, Guillermo & Avelar, Margareth	1990	031.00.85	031.00.80
Muller, Hugo & Zapetini, Lydia	1955	031.00.80	031.00.60
Muller, Isabel & Di Marco, Gustavo	1985	031.00.25	031.00.15
Muller, Johann & Witry, Anna	1900	284.50	284
Muller, Juan-Mauricio & <Unnamed>	1920	031.00.10	031.00.05
Muller, Leonie & Bertrang, Nicolas	1890	009.18	009.16
Muller, Ludwig & Witry, Marie	1886	031.00.05	031
Muller, Margaretha & Witry, Heinrich	1848	149	148
Muller, Margaretha & Witry, Peter	1856	150	148
Muller, Maria & Canueto, Manuel	1915	031.00.40	031.00.05
Muller, Maria-Ines & Kaplun, Luis	1993	031.00.95	031.00.90
Muller, Marie & Witry, Michel	1841	014	013
Muller, Monica & Lemus, Nestor	1985	031.00.20	031.00.15
Muller, Paola & Sepulveda, Alejandro	1985	031.00.30	031.00.15
Muller, Theodor & Witry, Anna	1818	023.02	023
Muller, Vilma & Zubillaga	1960	031.00.35	031.00.10
Mulligan, Michael & Clemes, Jacqueline	1978	086.18	086.16
Munnerlyn, Lou-Dean & Plain, Jacob	1945	172.44	172.38
Murphy, Lois & Sitter, Gerald	1945	271.05	271.02
Murphy, Shannon & Wittry, Raymond	1953	188	183
Murray, Bruce & Wittry, Mary-Ellen	1964	238.02	238
Murtagh, Catalina & Witry, Nicolas	1892	128.01	127
Muschang, Barbe & Wouters, Emile	1876	140.12	140.06
Mutscheler, C. E. & Jungles, Norma	1915	027.02	027.01
Nagl, Lucille & Wittry, Lawrence	1950	235	232
Nahorski, Jan & Handzik, Joyce	1975	086.11	086.10
Nail, Lea & Adam, Daniel	1991	204.13	204.12
Nallinger, Mary & Wittry, Paul	1941	209	208
Napruszewski, Alyce & Schroeder, Ernest	1942	015.34	015.06
Nathem, Frances & Conrad, Robert	1921	229.07	229.06
Neffle, Winifred & Clemes, John	1955	086.16	086.05

Nelson, Curtis & Rasmussen, Theresa	1976	015.52	015.45
Nelson, Jane & Wittry, Kenneth	1964	259	248
Nelson, Pamela & Russell, Steven	1973	229.22	229.21
Nepper, Anna & Hilbert, Johann	1861	031.50	031.02
Nepper, Marie & Witry, Heinrich	1817	026	023
Nepper, Marie & Witry, Henri	1897	129	127
Nepper, Susanne & Witry, Johann	1806	142	121
Neu, Catherine & Witry, Peter	1838	300	156
Neu, Mathias & Broos, Marie-Anne	1886	017.03.19	017.03.17
Neuens, Catherine & Conzemius, Joannis	1735	321.15.01	321.12
Neuens, Nicolas & Goedert, Margaretha	1710	321.12	321.08
Neuens, Nicolas & Majerus, Margaretha	1779	321.15	321.12
Neuens, Nicolas & Medernach, Margaretha	1740	321.13	321.12
Neuens, Nicolas & Neuens, Nicolas	1760	321.14	321.12
Ney & Faber, Maisy	1960	220.04	220.01
Ney, Tilly & Hoett, Raymond	1955	227.06.01	227.06
Nichols, Roy & Wittry, Gladys	1947	030.07	029
Nicolas, Tom & Deltgen, Marlene	2005	321.15.18.60	321.15.18
Nieland, Allen & Aultman, Bettideane	1970	248.02	248.01
Nieland, Allen & Freie, Julie	1982	248.03	248.01
Nieland, Andrea & Brinley, Kenneth	1998	248.02.01	248.02
Nieland, Anna & Wittry, Jacob	1921	240	231
Nieland, Chad & Anderson, Melanie	1998	248.04.01	248.04
Nieland, Craig & Pelz, Nikki	1971	248.05	248.01
Nieland, Daniel & Bennett, Cindy	1969	248.04	248.04
Nieland, Douglas & Tjebbens, Mary	1976	248.06	248.01
Nieland, Douglas & Weldon, Mindy	1986	248.07	248.01
Nieland, Jeanette & <Unnamed>	2000	248.02.02	248.02
Nieland, Jennifer & <Unnamed>	1993	248.05.00	248.05
Nieland, Kimberly & Smith, Justin	2003	248.05.50	248.05
Nieland, LeAnn & Banwart, Scott	1996	248.05.01	248.05
Nieland, Lindsay & Underberg, Gabriel	2006	248.04.50	248.04
Nieland, Marie & Wittry, Carl	1942	233	232

Nieland, Patricia & Wetzel, Robert	1992	248.09	248.01
Nieland, Patrick & Wittry, Della	1948	248.01	248
Nieland, Sharon & Johnson, Craig	1983	248.08	248.01
Niesen, Sylvie & Seil, Rene	1970	084.02	084.01
Nilles, Jean & Reuland, Anne-Marie	1897	044.50	044.02
Nilles, Marie & Witry, Johann	1788	023	022
Nilles, Peter & Witry, Catherine	1877	159.01	158
Nitschke, Robert & Mertes, Susan	1981	173.10	173.09
Noesen, Katharina & Mack, Andre	1890	321.15.12	321.15.08
Nordman, Alan & Hipps, Margaret	1985	174.08	174.05
North, John & Johnsen, Joyce	1980	208.14	208.09.01
Northey, Jill & Otte, Mark	1996	270.02.15	270.02.05
Northrup, Sherri & Gary, Phillip	1985	204.08	204.02
Northstrum, Mary & Witry, Robert	1980	078	076
Nowicki, Michael & Schramer, Gina	1984	172.07	172.02
Nuetzman, Steven & Wittry, Susan	1980	250.02	249
Oberman, Cecelia & Anderson, Dean	1970	171.50	171.47
Oberman, Diane & Orland, Clinton	1963	171.48	171.47
Oberman, John P. & Spang, Ursula	1940	171.47	171.01
Oberman, Sharon & Sickles, Ronald	1968	171.49	171.47
O'Connor, Charlotte & Witry, Harlan	1953	098	097
O'Connor, Kathryn & Wittry, Elmer	1945	211	208
Oduber, Marlene & Kaell, Joseph	1971	014.65.20	014.65
Offling, Frank & Loser, Katherine	1980	015.18	015.08
O'Leary, Aileen & Seckman, Michael	1975	278.03	278.01
O'Leary, Donald & Wittry, Mary-Lou	1948	278.01	278
O'Leary, Maureen & Koteles, Gary	1980	278.02	278.01
Olinger, Anna & Witry, Jean	1795	124	121
Olinger, Barbara & Hellers	1860	009.09	009.04
Olinger, Johann & <Unnamed>	1850	009.05	009.04
Olinger, Johann & Pirry	1880	009.06	009.05
Olinger, Johann & Witry, Margaretha	1830	009.04	009
Olinger, Margareta & Hellers	1880	009.08	009.05
Olinger, Marie & Weiss	1870	009.14	009.04
Olinger, Marie-Anna & Witry, Peter	1892	216	214
Olinger, Mathias & Swoboda, Olga	1880	009.07	009.05
Olsem, Anna & Mack, Nicolas	1858	321.15.08	321.15.07
Olsem, Anne & Heffenisch, Nikolas	1821	321.15.06	321.15.05

Olsem, Katharina & Fautsch, Nikolas	1861	321.15.27	321.15.07
Olsem, Maria & Baulesch, Nikolas	1869	321.15.26	321.15.07
Olsem, Maria & Schauls, Peter	1867	321.15.25	321.15.07
Olsem, Nicolas & Conzemius, Marie	1782	321.15.05	321.15.01
Olsem, Nicolas & Majerus, Anna	1826	321.15.07	321.15.05
Olsem, Nikolas & Koetz, Maria	1866	321.15.28	321.15.07
Olsen, Pablo & Muller, Ana	1992	031.01.30	031.00.90
Olson, Kathryn & Tegels, Kenneth	1984	236.17	236.11
Ondarcuhu, Jose & Witry, Maria	1915	128.02	128.01
Ondarcuhu, Luis & <Unnamed>	1945	128.03	128.02
Ondarcuhu, Pedro & <Unnamed>	1945	128.04	128.02
O'Neill, Mellissa & Witry, Thomas	1986	116	114
Origer, Anne & Witry, Albert	1900	141.09	141.22
			141.08
Origer, Arthur & Sinner, Eugenie	1919	141.23	141.22
Origer, Francois & Witry, Marie	1878	141.22	141.19
Origer, Sylvie & Kerschen, Leon	1910	141.24	141.22
Orizondo, Amy & McGuffin, Craig	2003	182.06.01	182.06
Orizondo, Frank & Sabo, Sarah-Jo	1977	182.06	182.03
Orland, Clinton & Oberman, Diane	1963	171.48	171.47
O'Steen, Chester & Graap, Frances	1977	231.52	231.49
Osterholt, Angela & Wittry, Marvin	1956	242	241
Ostrander, Mark & Kohley, Karen	1975	171.31	171.30
Oswald, Elizabeth & Wittry, Gustave	1890	028	027
Otte, Bowdie & Pick, Heather	1994	270.02.25	270.02.05
Otte, Coleen & Kyhn, Steven	1991	270.02.20	270.02.05
Otte, Gerald & Wittry, Marilyn	1964	270.02.05	270
Otte, Julie & Edwards, Neil	1996	270.02.10	270.02.05
Otte, Mark & Northey, Jill	1996	270.02.15	270.02.05
Otten, Carol & Wittry, Steven	2000	181.01.03	181
Padilla, Brenda & Thurston, Joseph	2005	231.27.50	231.21
Padock, Marcia & Carbery, Thomas	1990	071.05	071.01
Palasz, Patricia & Schroeder, Thomas	1956	015.36.50	015.07
Palmer, Marian & Glass, Jon	1978	233.08	233.01
Palmer, Paul & Schroeder, Romayne	1965	015.59.55	015.59.30
Pape, Annabella & Schmidt, Kenneth	1937	240.23	240.22
Pape, Annabella & Turbos, Ray	1968	240.33	240.23
Pape, Betty & Hoflock, Raymond	1952	240.43	240.22
Pape, Brenda & Mikel, Steve	1984	240.41	240.37

Pape, John & Wittry, Clara	1917	240.22	231
Pape, Judith & Taylor, Arthur	1983	240.39	240.37
Pape, Judith & Wills, Robert	1968	240.38	240.37
Pape, Laverdos & Blanchette, Beatrice	1945	240.37	240.22
Pape, Laverdos & Fransen, Leona	1980	240.42	240.37
Pape, Margorie & Verdeck, Francis	1940	240.34	240.22
Pape, Mayme & Wittry, John	1917	237	231
Pape, Tammy & Corno, James	1980	240.40	240.37
Parella, Lisa & Crenshaw, Richard	1986	231.40	231.38
Parisse, Marie & Lenger, Anatol	1880	141.04	141.03
Parker, Jeffery & Wagner, Barbara	1987	015.22	015.19.50
Parmentier, Thierry & Guerlet, Marie	1985	088.02	088.01
Partaka, Barbara & Salmen, Richard	1983	270.02.35	270.02.30
Patrick, Michael & Witry, Mary-Alice	1985	066.01	064
Patterson, Doug & Efsic, Joni	2000	182.17.60	182.50
Paulus, Caroline & Witry, Peter	1887	166.03	165
Paulus, Elisabeth & Marchal, Nicolas	1640	324	001
Pearson, Gail & Wittry, Kevin	1987	255	253
Pearson, William & Schroeder, Edna	1935	015.81	015.06
Peckham, Richard & Wittry, Diane	1999	282.02	282
Pederson, Ingrid & Weber, Elwyn	1968	208.03	208.02
Pederson, Justine & Conrad, Craig	1988	229.33	229.28
Peffer, Adam & Witry, Marie	1720	119.05	020
Peffer, Dominic & Sintgen, Margaretha	1775	119.09	119.05
Peffer, Heinrich & Jordan, Elisabeth	1773	119.06	119.05
Peffer, Nicolas & Hames, Apollonia	1754	119.07	119.05
Peffer, Peter & Atten, Margaretha	1764	119.08	119.05
Peiffer, Patricia & Schramer, David	1956	172.15	172.01
Pelc, Gordon & Holmberg, Darlene	1990	270.03.05	270.03
Pellegrino, Diane & Konen, John-Irvin	1989	182.12	182.11
Pelz, Nikki & Nieland, Craig	1971	248.05	248.01
Perez, Maximo & Wittry, Patricia	1983	030.03	030
Perquin, Eugenie & Witry, Peter	1889	025	024
Peters, Susanne & Conzemius, Pierre	1767	321.15.02	321.15.01
Peterson, Linda & Hannasch, James	1991	240.21	240.09
Peterson, Mike & Verdeck, Beverly	1966	240.36	240.34
Petry, Anna-Marie & Witry, Theodor	1759	037	021
Pettinger, Daniele & Rugo, Robert	1992	085.02	085.01

Name	Year	Col1	Col2
Pettinger, Marianna & Bertrang, Hubert	1890	009.17	009.16
Pettinger, Nic & Witry, Lucianne	1963	085.01	085
Pfaff, Bruce & Tierney, Joelle	1999	204.17.01	204.17
Pfister, Lillian & Wittry, Alfred	1935	283	272
Phelps, Larry & Crenshaw, Mary	1991	231.41	231.38
Philipp, Marie & Cimenti, Armando	1965	293.03	293.02
Philipp, Mathias & Kessler, Catherine	1935	293.02	293.01
Philippart, Anna & Leitgen, Philippe	1905	144.50	144.01
Philippart, Frederic & Witry, Susanne	1876	144.01	143
Philipps, Jean-Pierre & Groos, Barbara	1839	023.01.01	023.01
Philippy, Jean & Wiltgen, Susanne	1828	311.22.60	311.22.50
Philips, Jean & Groos, Anne	1850	023.01.80	023.01
Phillipart, Leonie, & Weber, Mathias	1918	144.70	144.01
Pick, Heather & Otte, Bowdie	1994	270.02.25	270.02.05
Piere, Anna & Witry, Nicolas	1744	120	020
Pierre, Johann & Witry, Anne-Marie	1839	009.35	009
Pilch, Judith & Huss, Edwin	1969	204.14	204.01
Pilier, Pierre & Witry, Marie	1820	021.26.10	021.26
Pillatsch, Herman & Wittry, Dorothy	1940	172.19	172
Pillatsch, Mary & Ruppert, Edwin	1975	172.20	172.19
Pimental, Lori & Koehne, Thomas	1976	231.31	231.29
Pink, Susanne & Witry, Peter	1800	010	006
Piron, Carol & Eubanks, Kenneth	1966	172.31	172.29
Piron, Ervin & Frieders, Leona	1944	172.29	172.24
Piron, Patricia & Burson, Douglas	1970	172.30	172.29
Pirry & Olinger, Johann	1880	009.06	009.05
Piscitelli, Michael & Hanna, Mari	1990	075.02.02	075.01
Pixius, Jacques & Schroeder, Margot	1981	015.89	015.88
Plain, Barbara & Reines, Frank H.	1911	172.53	172.37
Plain, Clarence-Peter & Dorothy	1955	172.52	172.47
Plain, Gail-Marie & Jones, Thomas A.	1975	172.45	172.44
Plain, Gilbert & Swan, Felice-Bancroft	1940	172.39	172.38
Plain, Jacob & Munnerlyn, Lou-Dean	1945	172.44	172.38
Plain, Janet B. & Stanley, Gregory	1980	172.43	172.39
Plain, John M. & Mathis, Jeanne	1970	172.42	172.39
Plain, John W. & Wittry, Anna	1878	172.37	167
Plain, Karen E. & Switzer, Robert	1970	172.40	172.39
Plain, Margaret E. & Brown, Max	1970	172.41	172.39

Plain, Michael D. & Viebig, Gail	1984	172.46	172.44
Plain, Michael W. & Pung, Anna	1907	172.38	172.37
Plain, Peter J. & Schuster, Helen	1914	172.47	172.37
Plain, Ruth & Schassow, Wayburn	1940	172.48	172.47
Plain, Ruth-Helen & Martin, Albert	1945	172.49	172.47
Platt, Jason & Wittry, Nicole	2000	268.00.50	268
Pletschet, Peter & Witry, Anne-Marie	1839	009.36	009
Pobstman, Dorothy & Hipps, Harold	1955	174.05	174.02
Pobstman, James & Wittry, Margaret	1924	174.02	173
Pobstman, Lorraine & White, Francis	1946	174.03	174.02
Pobstman, Mary & Wittry, Adam	1922	174	173
Poecker, Anny & Witry, Francis	1955	095.16	095.12
Poecker, Jean & Bettendorf, Susanne	1913	092.01.70	092.01
Poerters, Susanne & Reiland, Michel	2000	009.30	009.29
Pohlen, Francis & Bernardy, Mary	1967	261.32	261.11
Pohlen, Michael & Fitzloff, Lisa	2001	261.32.01	261.32
Pott, Margaretha & Witry, Dominic	1869	288	229
Potter, Beatrice & Tapparo, William	1969	231.08	231.07
Potts, Brenda & Gary, Arthur	1989	204.03	204.02
Powell, Kenneth & Hipps, Rebecca	1983	174.07	174.05
Powers, Elisabeth & Smith, Steve	2001	236.03.01	236.03
Prado, Mariano & Barile, Carla	1998	031.00.72	031.00.70
Prado, Ruben & Muller, Blanca	1975	031.00.70	031.00.65
Prim, Berthie & Jung, Jean	1952	017.03.09	017.03.08
Printz, Heinrich & Reuter, Margaretha	1720	017.07	017.05
Priscilla & Huss, Richard	1990	204.11.02	204.01
Probst, Margaretha & Witry, Johann	1848	015	013
Protsman, Ron & Russell, Julia	1997	229.26	229.21
Pruisner, Robin & Venner, Mark	1995	236.10	236.02
Przybyl, Philip & Schroeder, Judy	1966	015.35	015.07
Przybyl, Steven & Graziano, Teresa	1994	015.36	015.35
Pudenz, Joan & Wittry, Eugene	1954	256	248
Pung, Anna & Plain, Michael W.	1907	172.38	172.37
Putz, Edouard & Witry, Carola	1945	166.05	166.04
Putz, Marian & Donckel, Pierre	1960	132.04.00	132.04
Putz, Nicolas & Witry, Hortense	1930	132.04	129
Putz, Nicole-Barbe & Leyers, Camille	1965	166.20	166.05
Quarberg, Mark & Witry, Patricia	1976	114.01	114

Quinett, Esther & Conry, Cecil	1942	291.02	291.01
Quintus, Josefine & Witry, Jacques	1918	218.02	218.01
Quiring, Marianne & Leclerc, Theodore	1960	139.02.01	139.02
Raber, Conrad & Holt, Diane	1970	075.05.25	075.05.10
Radermacher, Anna & Weiland, Johann	1742	020.06	020.01
Radermacher, Anton & Witry, Marie	1705	020.01	020
Radermacher, Catherine & Clementen, Johann	1745	020.07	020.01
Radermacher, Heinrich & Bourtz, Marie	1735	020.02	020.01
Radermacher, Johann & Schons, Susanne	1738	020.04	020.01
Radermacher, Marie & Ries, Johann	1735	020.05	020.01
Radermacher, Peter & Breyden, Angela	1736	020.03	020.01
Radford, Carol & Wittry, Warren	1965	281.50	279
Ramires de la Rosa, Hector & Guerlet, Sylvette	1978	088.04	088.01
Ramirez, Dolores & Koehne, Paul	1961	231.14	231.01
Ramos, Isabel & Koehne, Harold	1947	231.02	231.01
Rashid, Jeffrey & Wittry, Susan-Anne	2000	196.01	193
Raska, Kathryn & Russell, Michael	1995	229.24	229.21
Rasmussen, Dawn & Watts, Steve	1985	015.54	015.45
Rasmussen, Debbra & Slade, William	1977	015.53	015.45
Rasmussen, Douglas & Thooft, Janine	1982	261.15	261.12
Rasmussen, Pamela & Skoglie, Lawrence	1971	015.48	015.45
Rasmussen, Patricia & Davis, Larry	1970	015.46	015.45
Rasmussen, Robert & Schroeder, Gloria	1952	015.45	015.44
Rasmussen, Terry & Haynes, Kenny	1975	015.50	015.45
Rasmussen, Theresa & Nelson, Curtis	1976	015.52	015.45
Rasque, Jean & Kremer, Isabelle	1989	128.00.50	128.00.35
Rasque, Jeff & Lies, Anne-Marie	1970	014.75	014.70
Rasquin, Carmen & Ionica, Dumitrel	1980	014.78	014.75
Rasquin, Mirielle & Bertrang, Marco	1990	014.77	014.75
Rausch, Claude & Strotz, Nadine	1993	083.02	083.01

Rausch, Peter & Witry, Catharina	1896	284.20	284
Ravindran, Kay & Adam, Timothy	1990	204.13.01	204.12
Re, Andrea & Muller, Alberto-Raul	1980	031.00.75	031.00.60
Reading, Joseph & Koehne, Margaret	1993	231.32	231.29
Reckinger, Bernard & Witry, Johanna	1705	311.01	311
Reckinger, Johann & Atten, Anna	1753	311.03	311.01
Reckinger, Johann & Delfeld, Marie	1778	311.04	311.01
Reckinger, Johann & Kremer, Magdalena	1739	311.02	311.01
Reckinger, Marie & Medernach, Johann	1755	311.05	311.01
Reckinger, Nicolas & Witry, Marie	1844	026.02	026
Reckmeyer, Pamela & Gary, Dean	1976	204.04	204.02
Redeford, Carmen & Johnson, Rick	1975	015.72	015.71
Reding, Catherine & Stronck, Johann	1870	009.24	009.15
Reding, Johannr & Witry, Suzanne	1930	074.00.60	074.00.50
Reding, Nicolas & Witry, Susanne	1782	022.02	022
Reedy, Nancy & Schroeder, Duane	1981	015.31	015.29
Regenwetter, Anna & Witry, Reinhard	1833	161	157
Reichenberger, John & Witry, Helen	1935	075.06	075
Reichling & Simon, Jean	1860	009.03	009.01
Reid, Stacy & Wiederin, Tom	2002	261.10.01	261.08
Reider, William & Lepley, Helene	1955	208.16	208.15
Reider, William & Wittry, Rose	1920	208.15	208
Reiland, Catherine & Mehlen	1860	009.32	009.26
Reiland, Marguerite & Duhr	2000	009.31	009.29
Reiland, Marie & Fell	1860	009.33	009.26
Reiland, Michel & Poerters, Susanne	2000	009.30	009.29
Reiland, Nicolas & Dostert, Marie	1870	009.29	009.26
Reiland, Nicolas & Witry, Susanne	1835	009.26	009
Reiland, Susanne & Terrens	1880	009.27	009.26
Reinert, Anne & Witry, Peter	1793	021.26	021.01
Reines, Frank H. & Plain, Barbara	1911	172.53	172.37
Reines, Mary & Hauser, Mark	1975	172.55	172.54
Reines, Raymond & Adams, Anne	1970	172.58	172.53
Reines, Raymond & Brennan, Geraldine	1952	172.54	172.53
Reines, Regina F. & Theis, William J.	1949	172.63	172.53
Reines, Robert & Winthers, Linda	1991	172.56	172.54

Reines, Therese & Augustine, Todd	1987	172.57	172.54
Reines, Virginia & Johannessen, Howard	1952	172.59	172.53
Reisch, Johann & Baden, Anna-Maria	1867	091.30	091.01
Reiser, Marie & Wittry, Christian	1935	270	264
Reitz, August & Wittry, Lena	1892	213.01	167
Reker, Gary & Knips, Kristi	1980	267.08	267.07
Renholen, Wendy & Bock, Christopher	2003	260.07	260.01
Repass, Robin & Hawking, Michael	2000	208.09	208.07
Repele, Marie & Witry, Henri-Lucien	1910	139	135
Rettenmaier, Anna & Wittry, Nicholas	1916	232	231
Retterer, Wendy & Watgen, William	1985	171.15	171.09
Reuland, Anne-Marie & Nilles, Jean	1897	044.50	044.02
Reuland, Johann & Witry, Anna	1866	044.02	039
Reuland, Susanne & Thies, Johann	1675	019	002
Reuter, Elisabeth & Witry, Nicolas	1688	020	002
Reuter, Jean & Weis, Denise	1980	146.02	146.01
Reuter, Johann & Meyers, Marie	1715	017.06	017.05
Reuter, Louis & Thies, Margaretha	1688	017.05	002
Reuter, Margaretha & Printz, Heinrich	1720	017.07	017.05
Reuter, Marie-Barbe & Witry, Nicolas	1920	046.60	046
Reuter, Melissa & Wittry, Brett	1985	267	266
Reuter, Nicolas & Marie	1717	017.08	017.05
Reynolds, Alan & Wilson, Darlene	1950	015.74	015.70
Rhea, Bruce & Witry, Cynthia	1984	118.01	118
Rice, Helen-Ann & Schroeder, Bruce	1974	015.32	015.29
Riche, Todd & Witry, Catherine	2007	072.50	072
Richter & Bruin, Nancy	1955	075.04	075.03
Rickbiel, Eric & Breckenridge, Tiffany	2002	257.10	257.02
Ries, Heinrich & Krippes, Catherine	1760	020.05.01	020.05
Ries, Johann & Radermacher, Marie	1735	020.05	020.01
Ries, Johann & Witry, Josefine	1838	026.01	026
Ries, Margaretha & Wiltgen, Nicolas	1833	311.20	311.08
Ries, Mathias & Kipgen, Catherine	1788	020.05.03	020.05
Ries, Valentin & Hecht, Susanne	1778	020.05.02	020.05
Riggle, Carla & Conrad, David	1980	229.12	229.12
Ritli, Charles & Hankins, Clare	1978	182.45	182.25
Rivoire, Charles & Witry, Victorine	1930	153.03	152

Rob, Conrad & Rodenbour, Catherine	1745	323.00.01	322
Rob, Firmin & Machus, Marie	1712	323	002
Rob, Firmin & Mathieu, Catherine	1700	322	002
Rob, Maria & Mersch, Pierre	1768	323.00.02	323.00.01
Rob, Marie & Leyders, Johann	1732	322.02	322
Rob, Nicolas & Catherine	1737	322.01	322
Robert, Claudine & Witry, Alain	1988	082	081
Robertson, Christopher & Wittry, Jennifer	2006	195	194
Robles, Susan & Wittry, Michael	1991	207.07	207
Rodenbour, Catherine & Rob, Conrad	1745	323.00.01	322
Roemeling, Lawrence & Wittry, Lezlee	1980	266.01	266
Roeser, Magdalena & Dondelinger, Nicolas	1813	308.04	308.03
Roisin, Francois & Witry, Astrid	1989	021.19	021.18
Rollin, Jean-Francois & Witry, Anna	1840	133.03	124
Roob, Rose & Mack, Joseph	1944	321.15.24	321.15.12
Roos, Catherine & Witry, Nicolas	1934	080	079
Roosa, Jack & Wittry, Nannon K.	1986	187.01	185
Roselli, Debra & Hankins, Eugene	1981	182.44	182.25
Ross, Johann-Peter & Witry, Irma	1916	145.01	145
Ross, Margot & Schmitt, Pierre	1940	145.02	145.50
Rossi, Ralph & Koehne, Debra	1973	231.30	231.29
Roth, Auldene & Koehne, Joseph	1986	231.35	231.01
Rouillon, Ivonne & Witry, Manuel	1970	128.19	128.12
Roush, Kent & Kanne, Roxanne	1988	243.02	243.01
Rousseau, Zoe & Witry, Johann	1860	128.26	127
Rudigier, Bruce & Hight, Cynthia	1980	171.56	171.51
Ruffalo, Ken & Adam, Heather	1994	204.13.02	204.12
Rugo, Robert & Pettinger, Daniele	1992	085.02	085.01
Runyan, Angela & Conrad, Andrew	1997	229.37.01	229.35
Ruppert, Edwin & Pillatsch, Mary	1975	172.20	172.19
Russell, Julia & Protsman, Ron	1997	229.26	229.21
Russell, Julia & Widdel, John	1977	229.25	229.21
Russell, Michael & Brown, Sally	1976	229.23	229.21
Russell, Michael & Raska, Kathryn	1995	229.24	229.21
Russell, Milo & Conrad, Anita	1949	229.21	229.07
Russell, Stacy & Jenkins, Johnny	1999	229.22.01	229.22

Russell, Steven & Nelson, Pamela	1973	229.22	229.21
Russell, Timothy & Woolsey, Jamie	1989	229.27	229.21
Russie, Daniel & Hipps, Elizabeth	1978	174.06	174.05
Ruth, Marie & Witry, Nicolas	1838	162	157
Sabo, Julius A. & Florence, Emily H.	1939	182.03	182.01
Sabo, Mary-Ellen & Wittman, Thomas	1976	182.04	182.03
Sabo, Monica & Morganstein, Sanford	1970	182.05	182.03
Sabo, Sarah-Jo & Orizondo, Frank	1977	182.06	182.03
Sachs, Kathleen & Frampton, Steven	1981	229.16	229.13
Sachs, Lori-Jean & Corkery, Lawrence	1986	229.17	229.13
Sachs, Mary-Kay & Kane, Randy	1979	229.15	229.13
Sachs, Merle & Conrad, Marie-Ann	1953	229.13	229.07
Sachs, Suzanne & Brown, Lansing	1973	229.14	229.13
Sales, Jean-Louis & Hames, Monique	1990	166.02.05	166.02.04
Sales, Pierre & Witry, Jeanne	1959	166.02.04	166.02.03
Salmen, Amy & Smith	1990	270.02.60	270.02.30
Salmen, Amy & Thomas, Rodney	2002	270.02.65	270.02.30
Salmen, David & Cruts, Cathy	2004	270.02.58	270.02.30
Salmen, Lisa & Armstrong, Larry	1993	270.02.50	270.02.30
Salmen, Lisa & Baller, Michael	1997	270.02.55	270.02.30
Salmen, Lisa & Johnston, Todd	1988	270.02.45	270.02.30
Salmen, Richard & Partaka, Barbara	1983	270.02.35	270.02.30
Salmen, Richard & Sheldon, Lisa	1987	270.02.40	270.02.30
Salmen, Richard & Wittry, Catherine	1962	270.02.30	270
Salmen, Sophia & Witry, Nicolas	1876	286	285
Samuelson, Robert & Schramer, Sharon	1985	172.13	172.09
Sand, Amelie & Witry, Mathias	1923	166.03.50	166.03
Sand, Anna & Witry, Johann	1889	093	092
Sanders, Jeffrey & Davidson, Marlene	1985	070.03	070.02
Sanders, Marc & Calvin, Cyrise	1990	070.04	070.02
Sanders, Norbert & Witry, Dorinne	1957	070.02	068
Sandy & Tannenbaum, Robert	1968	171.45	171.40
Santo, Susan & Thooft, Edward	1986	261.16	261.12
Sauber, Lucie & Witry, Charles	1902	084	053
Schaaf, Elaine & Kaeppeli, Paul	1986	017.03.13.70	017.03.13.50
Schaaf, Jean & Baum, Catherine	1902	017.03.13.30	017.03.13

Schaaf, Jean & Fehrentz, Elise	1943	017.03.13.50	017.03.13.30
Schaaff, Henri & Adamy, Susanne	1865	017.03.13	017.03.04
Schaal, Bobbette & Witry, George	1984	065	064
Schaedle, Allen & Witry, Eugenia	1913	093.01	093
Schaffer, Brent & Fryer, Kelly	2003	260.04.01	260.04
Schaffer, Dennis & Bock, Lori	1980	260.04	260.01
Schalbar, Nelly & Witry, Francois	1959	081	080
Schanen, Fernand & Schweitzer, Nicole	1955	132.02.01	132.02
Schanen, Joseph & Witry, Marie	1929	132.02	129
Schanen, Marcelle & Heisten, Jean	1955	132.02.02	132.02
Schares, Betty & Conrad, Robert	1978	229.11	229.10
Schartz, Jean& Witry, Fernande	1991	131.00.01	131
Schassow, Wayburn & Plain, Ruth	1940	172.48	172.47
Schaub, Gladys & Wittry, Nickolaus J.	1920	191	182
Schauls, Peter & Olsem, Maria	1867	321.15.25	321.15.07
Scheur, Nicolas & Witry, Susanne	1766	015.99	011
Schiltz & Hellers, Mathias	1890	009.12	009.09
Schindlbeck, Joyce & Watgen, Dennis	1975	171.11	171.09
Schintgen, Jeanette & Witry, Pierre	1809	148	121
Schintgen, Nicolas & Witry, Magdalena	1804	308.08	120
Schirdelly, Erma & Tannenbaum, Robert	1952	171.42	171.40
Schleich, Denis & Witry, Catherine	1830	036.02	033
Schlesser, Marguerite & Witry, Jacques	1928	153	152
Schlick, Pamela & Tapparo, Brian	1991	231.10	231.08
Schmidt, Allen & Zwach, Carol	1963	240.28	240.23
Schmidt, Donald & Krantz, Maretta	1970	209.03	209.02
Schmidt, Genevieve & Gjerde, Kenneth	1957	240.24	240.23
Schmidt, Gordon & Allen, Guelda	1984	240.31	240.23
Schmidt, Gordon & Dugan, Leann	1968	240.30	240.23
Schmidt, Janice & Donavan, Pete	1974	240.26	240.23
Schmidt, JoAnn & Stattelman, Tom	1963	240.29	240.23
Schmidt, Johann & Flammang, Catherine	1903	166.02.00	166.02

Name	Year	Col1	Col2
Schmidt, Kenneth & Pape, Annabella	1937	240.23	240.22
Schmidt, Marlene & Glomski, Tom	1967	240.27	240.23
Schmidt, Rosemary & Brau, Leroy	1969	240.32	240.23
Schmit, Catharina & Witry, Emil	1907	144.00	144
Schmit, Marie & Witry, Johann	1901	147	143
Schmit, Nathalie & Witry, Alain	2000	128.00.17	128.00.10
Schmit, Nicolas & Witry, Magdalena	1860	150.01	148
Schmitt, Anna & Thivis, Johann	1717	323.03	323.01
Schmitt, Elisabeth & Faber, Johann	1715	323.02	323.01
Schmitt, Girl & Wirion	1970	145.03	145.02
Schmitt, Johann & Witry, Johanna	1705	323.04	002
Schmitt, Johann & Witry, Magdalena	1781	308.07	120
Schmitt, Marie & Witry, Pierre	1885	134.01	134
Schmitt, Melissa & Hoflock, Todd	1984	240.48	240.43
Schmitt, Pierre & Ross, Margot	1940	145.02	145.50
Schmitt, Theodor & Witry, Johanna	1691	323.01	002
Schneider, Johann & Witry, Angela	1792	009.37	007
Schneider, Michel & Witry, Josee	1996	131.01	131
Schneider, Nicolas & Bettendorf, Margaretha	1914	092.01.30	192.01
Schoedgen, Peter & Didier, Barbe	1906	141.01.50	141.01
Schoedgen, Peter & Witry, Marie	1865	141.01	141
Scholer, Anne & Adamy, Mathias	1787	017.03.01	017.03
ScHollar, Claudine & Witry, Luc	1996	082.02	081
Scholtus, Lucie & Witry, Marcel	1964	128.00.10	128.00.05
Schons, Magdalena & Wittry, Jacob	1851	167	157
Schons, Susanne & Radermacher, Johann	1738	020.04	020.01
Schoomars, N. & Terrens, Susanne	1910	009.28	009.27
Schopp, Troy & McQueen, Angelica	1994	207.02	207.01
Schoug, Johann & Witry, Anna	1875	049.01	049
Schramer, Carolyn & Trosine, Kevin	1988	172.17	172.15
Schramer, Daniel & Walker, Charlotte	1955	172.09	172.01
Schramer, David & Peiffer, Patricia	1956	172.15	172.01
Schramer, Dianne & Dion, George	1991	172.14	172.09
Schramer, Gayle & Mitchell, Donald	1975	172.04	172.02
Schramer, Gayle & Severson, Steven	1975	172.03	172.02
Schramer, Gill & Viereckl, Rudolph	1985	172.06	172.02
Schramer, Gina & Nowicki, Michael	1984	172.07	172.02

Schramer, Gwen M. & Crabbe, Kerry	1980	172.05	172.02
Schramer, James & Wittry, Rose-Mary	1969	179.01	175
Schramer, Kathleen & Chally, Gerald	1980	172.10	172.09
Schramer, Kathleen & Krant, David	1982	172.11	172.09
Schramer, Margaret L. & Foster, Jayce	1981	172.16	172.15
Schramer, Merri-Kay & Sullivan, John	1984	172.18	172.15
Schramer, Ralph & Wittry, Margaret	1928	172.01	172
Schramer, Robert & Keenan, Karen	1965	172.08	172.01
Schramer, Robert & Stanek, Rose	1952	172.02	172.01
Schramer, Sharon & Hettinger, George	1975	172.12	172.09
Schramer, Sharon & Samuelson, Robert	1985	172.13	172.09
Schrobiltgen, Appoline & Witry, Andre	1893	021.15	021.13
Schroeder, Anna-Marie & Witry, Jean	1798	051	037
Schroeder, Barbara & Loser, George	1942	015.08	015.07
Schroeder, Bruce & Rice, Helen-Ann	1974	015.32	015.29
Schroeder, Clinton & Catherine	1970	015.79	015.78
Schroeder, Curtis & Cooper, Kim	1983	015.33	015.29
Schroeder, Duane & Reedy, Nancy	1981	015.31	015.29
Schroeder, Edna & Pearson, William	1935	015.81	015.06
Schroeder, Edward & Larson, Dorothy	1939	015.78	015.06
Schroeder, Ernest & Meyer, Esther	1924	015.07	015.06
Schroeder, Ernest & Napruszewski, Alyce	1942	015.34	015.06
Schroeder, Francois & Lanhers, Margit	1930	015.87	015.86
Schroeder, Franz & Staudt, Catherine	1873	015.85	015.04
Schroeder, Gloria & Bast, Seno	1961	015.55	015.44
Schroeder, Gloria & Rasmussen, Robert	1952	015.45	015.44
Schroeder, Gloria & Wilde, Donald	1965	015.58	015.44
Schroeder, James & Brzycki, Alice	1935	015.44	015.06
Schroeder, Johann & Dahm, Matilda	1902	015.06	015.05
Schroeder, Johann & Thies, Catherine	1716	018.05	018
Schroeder, John & Cole, Doris	1946	015.83	015.06
Schroeder, John & Spanier, Marie	1838	015.04	015.03
Schroeder, John & Virginia	1950	015.84.50	015.06
Schroeder, John-Paul & Julia	1985	015.63	015.59.30

Schroeder, Josephine & Hoffman, Peter	1871	015.91	015.04
Schroeder, Josephine & Wilson, Hjalmer	1933	015.70	015.06
Schroeder, Judy & Przybyl, Philip	1966	015.35	015.07
Schroeder, Kathleen & Corriveau, Dennis	1969	015.43	015.07
Schroeder, Kenneth & Marsch, Susan	1973	015.30	015.29
Schroeder, Leslie & Zeimet, Michael	1999	015.38	015.36.50
Schroeder, Marcel & Bieri, Margrit	1955	015.88	015.87
Schroeder, Margot & Pixius, Jacques	1981	015.89	015.88
Schroeder, Mary-Dell & Bob	1970	015.80	015.78
Schroeder, Michel & Hipp, Margaret	1905	015.86	015.85
Schroeder, Michel & Wagener, Josephine	1868	015.05	015.04
Schroeder, Paul & Cline, Frances	1935	015.59.60	015.06
Schroeder, Paul J. & <Unnamed>	1930	015.59.30	015.06
Schroeder, Paul J. & French, Merle	1950	015.60	015.06
Schroeder, Paul J. & Larsen, Marie	1934	015.59.40	015.06
Schroeder, Paul J. & Loretta	1935	015.59.50	015.06
Schroeder, Paula & <Unnamed>	1965	015.59.45	015.59.30
Schroeder, Penny & Mallory	1969	015.61	015.59.30
Schroeder, Pia & Corring, Antoine	1988	015.90	015.88
Schroeder, Randy-John & Kathy	1980	015.84	015.83
Schroeder, Robert & Cesarini, Gloria	1945	015.29	015.07
Schroeder, Robin & Castor, Eric	1974	015.62	015.59.30
Schroeder, Romayne & Palmer, Paul	1965	015.59.55	015.59.30
Schroeder, Sandra & Brotherhood, Roy	1968	015.40	015.07
Schroeder, Sandra & Stelmaszewski, Robert	1990	015.42	015.07
Schroeder, Thomas & Kolp, Sharon	1965	015.37	015.07
Schroeder, Thomas & Palasz, Patricia	1956	015.36.50	015.07
Schueren & Mores, Simone	1960	225.05	225.03
Schuh, Elisabeth & Thomas, Heinrich	1886	021.26.65	021.26.60
Schulte, Dean & Derner, Janet	1987	261.05	261.03
Schultz, Karen & Witry, David-Allen	1985	062	061
Schumacher, Greg & Wittry, Karen	1987	261.02.01	261
Schuster, Adam & Berens, Anne	1871	148.02	148.01

Schuster, Helen & Plain, Peter J.	1914	172.47	172.37
Schuster, Magdalena & Witry, Peter	1895	079	053
Schwab, Emile & Mack, Elisabetha	1885	321.15.09	321.15.08
Schwachtgen, Gertrude & Witry, Marcel	1954	137	136
Schwartz, Catherine & Witry, Nicolas	1853	092	051
Schwartz, Franz & Witry, Marie	1879	308.02	300
Schwartz, Johann & Baden, Theresia	1864	091.50	091.01
Schwartz, Joseph & Bertrang, Anna	1890	009.20	009.16
Schwartz, Mary & Wittrock, Marvin	1965	270.05	270.04
Schweitzer, Nicole & Schanen, Fernand	1955	132.02.01	132.02
Seckman, Michael & O'Leary, Aileen	1975	278.03	278.01
Seible, Dolores & Witry, Frank	1958	291	288
Seil, Andre & Witry, Anna	1948	084.01	084
Seil, Anna & Kayser, Jean	1857	311.14	311.12
Seil, Guy & Mattioli, Diane	2000	084.50	084.02
Seil, Rene & Niesen, Sylvie	1970	084.02	084.01
Sekelsky, Mark & Witry, Barbara	1987	112.01	110
Sendens, Tom & Wittry, Shirley	1963	238.01	238
Sepulveda, Alejandro & Muller, Paola	1985	031.00.30	031.00.15
Seth, Karen & Wittry, Jonathan	1981	202	201
Setter, Ruth & Wittry, Gustave	1955	030	029
Severson, Connie & Thooft, David	1991	261.23	261.21
Severson, Steven & Schramer, Gayle	1975	172.03	172.02
Shaeffer, Joan & Wittry, Lyle	1964	244	241
Sharp, Ronald & Brown, Kimberly	2002	229.14.02	229.14
Sheahan, Michael & Witry, Kathleen	1985	058.01	056
Sheldon, Lisa & Salmen, Richard	1987	270.02.40	270.02.30
Sher, Leon & Monique	1970	074.04	074.03
Sher, Mathias & Melsen, Anna	1940	074.03	074.01
Sherwood, Edwin & White, Mary	1989	174.04	174.03
Sickles, Ronald & Oberman, Sharon	1968	171.49	171.47
Siebenaler, Marguerite & Kaell, Francois	1945	014.65	014.55
Silver, Robert & Johnsen, Mary	1982	208.11	208.09.01
Simmons, Tanya & Hill, Matthew	2001	198.02	198.01
Simon, Andre & Witry, Anna	1797	021.29	021.01
Simon, Angela & Hansen	1860	009.02	009.01

Simon, Jean & Reichling	1860	009.03	009.01
Simon, Johann & Witry, Johanna	1828	009.01	009
Simons, Grace & Witry, Walter-John	1929	097	096
Sinner, Aline & Jacques, Amant	1918	141.18	141.13
Sinner, Eugenie & Origer, Arthur	1919	141.23	141.22
Sintgen, Margaretha & Peffer, Dominic	1775	119.09	119.05
Sitter, Bernadine & Kubacki, Stanley	1935	271.04	271.02
Sitter, Gerald & Murphy, Lois	1945	271.05	271.02
Sitter, Joseph & Jado, Catherine	1910	271.02	271.01
Sitter, Katherine & Burgin, John	1935	271.03	271.02
Skoglie, Lawrence & Rasmussen, Pamela	1971	015.48	015.45
Skoglie, Tammy & Morgan, Phillip	1995	015.49	015.48
Slade, William & Rasmussen, Debbra	1977	015.53	015.45
Slocum, Debra & Spang, John T.	1981	171.19	171.16
Smaldt, Alan & Warnell, Jami-Marie	1990	104.04	104.01
Smell, Jack & Loser, Katherine-Marie	1986	015.19	015.08
Smith & Salmen, Amy	1990	270.02.60	270.02.30
Smith, Carole & Conrad, William	1957	229.28	229.07
Smith, David & Witry, Kathryn	1930	290.01	289
Smith, Frank & Venner, Christy	1973	236.03	236.02
Smith, Justin & Nieland, Kimberly	2003	248.05.50	248.05
Smith, Olive L. & Wittry, Peter H.	1928	175	173
Smith, Steve & Powers, Elisabeth	2001	236.03.01	236.03
Smith, Steven & Lopez, Crystal	1999	207.09	207.08
Smith-Tosomeen, Craig & Heiling, Ann-Marie	1991	261.31.01	261.31
Snyder, Magdalene & Wittry, Bernard	1928	248	231
Soanny, George & Spanier, Marie	1840	015.93	015.03
Soderholm & Cartwright, Elizabeth	1965	086.03	086.02
Solecki, Michael & Watgen, Deborah	1976	171.13	171.09
Souvignier, Catherine & Witry, Michel	1836	141.02	140
Souvignier, Jean & Witry, Helene	1840	141.26	140
Spang, Agnes & Kohley, Ralph	1929	171.29	171.01
Spang, Ann & Tannenbaum, George	1931	171.40	171.01
Spang, Brian J. & Kelly, Geraldine	1980	171.07	171.03
Spang, Choral & Watgen, Robert	1951	171.09	171.02
Spang, David & Hora, Jill	1982	171.21	171.16

Spang, Diane & Appel, Bryan	1990	171.22	171.16
Spang, Gerald & Gaspar, Donna	1950	171.03	171.02
Spang, Henry & Byers, Eva	1940	171.39	171.01
Spang, Joan & Kane, Ted	1950	171.16	171.02
Spang, John & Stull, Hildegarde	1926	171.02	171.01
Spang, John T. & Slocum, Debra	1981	171.19	171.18
Spang, Kim & Burgholzer, Kim	1980	171.05	171.03
Spang, Kim & Fowler, Anne	1985	171.06	171.03
Spang, Margaret & Erath, Harry	1943	171.57	171.01
Spang, Mark & Tillis, Cheryl	1980	171.04	171.03
Spang, Mary & Anderson, Carl	1935	171.23	171.01
Spang, Mary C. & Albrecht, Michael	1981	171.20	171.16
Spang, Peter J. & Wittry, Elizabeth	1903	171.01	168
Spang, Theresa & Hight, Charles	1940	171.51	171.01
Spang, Thomas & Feuerborn, Joan F.	1955	171.18	171.02
Spang, Tracy & Joy, Peter-Douglas	1985	171.08	171.03
Spang, Ursula & Oberman, John P.	1940	171.47	171.01
Spanier, Dominique & Witry, Marie	1811	015.03	012
Spanier, Marie & Schroeder, John	1838	015.04	015.03
Spanier, Marie & Soanny, George	1840	015.93	015.03
Spanier, Nicolas & Clees, Susanna	1840	015.94	015.03
Spanier, Nicolas & Masselter, Clara	1860	015.95	015.03
Spanier, Susanne & Klein, H.	1850	015.96	015.03
Sparrow, Robert & Witry, Beth-Ann	1983	061.01	061
Spears, Cindy & Gary, Vincent	1987	204.09	204.02
Spencer, John & Meyer, Lianne-Kay	1985	171.26	171.24
Speyer, Peter & Witry, Margaretha	1835	133.02	124
Spoerri, Stefan & Efsic, Maria-Elena	1986	182.17	182.15
Spoetler, Johann & Witry, Anna	1791	037.03	037
Stanek, Rose & Schramer, Robert	1952	172.02	172.01
Stanfield, Jim & Thurston, Cindy	1999	231.28.01	231.21
Stanley, Gregory & Plain, Janet B.	1980	172.43	172.39
Stapleton, Timothy & Haller, Laura	2000	240.04.01	240.03
Stark, Tara & Glass, William	1990	233.04	233.01
Statler, Tamara & Hoflock, Wesley	1986	240.49	240.43
Stattelman, Tom & Schmidt, JoAnn	1963	240.29	240.23
Staudt, Catherine & Schroeder, Franz	1873	015.85	015.04
Steadman, Loraine & Loser, George	1965	015.09	015.08

Steege, Kathie & Cavanaugh, Michael	1965	096.03	096.02
Steichen, Paul & Witry, Maria	1905	144.00.50	144
Steichen, Peter & Witry, Barbara	1830	140.01	140
Steid & Hellers, Jacob	1890	009.13	009.09
Steimel, Julia-Ann & Barth, Donald	1973	096.07	096.06
Steimel, Mary-Ellen & Yusko, Mark	1980	096.08	096.06
Steimel, William & Cavanaugh, Norma	1949	096.06	096.01
Steiwer, Marie & Deltgen, Robert-	1980	321.15.18	321.15.14
Stelmaszewski, Robert & Schroeder, Sandra	1990	015.42	015.07
Stepenske, Marilyn & Wittry, Elmer	1970	212	210
Stevens, Scott & Weber, Jennifer	2000	208.03.05	208.03
Stevens, Vicki & Stull, Nicholas	1994	182.20	182.19
Steyer, Heinrich & Witry, Anna	1879	024.01	024
Steyer, Magdalena & Foehr, Mathias	1903	024.20	024.01
Steyer, Maria & Konsbruck, Pierre	1902	024.50	024.01
Stimac, Frank & Wittry, Kathleen	1952	205.01	205
Stiren, Margaretha & Witry, Peter	1847	165	157
Stiren, Nicolas & Kirsch, Barbara	1796	009.42	009.40
Stirn, Anna & Witry, Nicolas	1910	046.5	046
Stocklausen, Marie & Witry, Stephan	1905	152	151
Stoffel, Jean-Nicolas & Lenger, Marie	1910	141.07	141.04
Stolarski, Judith-Ann & Mack, Charles	1975	086.07	086.06
Stolarski, Leonard & Clemes, Annabelle	1950	086.06	086.05
Stolarski, Leonard & Kleinfeldt, Janet	1978	086.08	086.06
Stolarski, Paul-Edward & Holly	1995	086.09	086.06
Stoltz, Valentin & Witry, Therese	1857	031.01.80	026
Stoos, Louise & Witry, Jean-Pierre	1940	085	084
Stopfel, Elisabeth & Wiltgen, Pierre	1831	311.22.55	311.22.50
Stracke, Marie & Wittry, Louis	1959	261	260
Straight, Phillip & Wittry, Judith	1970	268.01	265
Strand, Lynette & Bernardy, Ronald	1973	261.35	261.11
Strand, Susannah & Cole, Matthew	1999	240.11.01	240.10
Strasser, Michel & Kayser, Margaretha	1848	311.13	311.12
Straus, Annik & Huberty, Patrick	1995	014.90	014.80
Streff, Elisabeth & Hansen, Nicolas	1854	157.04	157.03
Streff, Johann & Witry, Elisabeth	1824	157.03	157

Streff, Margaretha & Meny, Peter	1863	157.06	157.03
Streff, Peter & Eischen, Catherine	1864	157.07	157.03
Streff, Reinhard & Even, Marie	1851	157.05	157.03
Streng, Romain & Leyers, Albertine	1996	166.30	166.20
Strickland, Kitina & Carlson, Michael	1970	182.26	182.25
Stroesser, Anne & Kaell, Charles	1908	014.60	014.50
Strohmenger, Brian & Grattafiori, Cynthia	1983	173.05	173.03
Stronck, Johann & Reding, Catherine	1870	009.24	009.15
Stronck, Johann & Witry, Catherine	1829	009.15	009
Stronck, Johanna & Wolter, Nicolas	1900	009.25	009.24
Stronck, Marie & Bertrang, Peter	1860	009.16	009.15
Stronck, Michel & Jacquemin, Julie	1870	009.23	009.15
Stronck, Nicolas & Koemptgen, Susanna	1860	009.21	009.15
Stronck, Peter & Weiss, Helena	1890	009.22	009.21
Strotz, Fernand & Witry, Monique	1967	083.01	083
Strotz, Nadine & Rausch, Claude	1993	083.02	083.01
Stubert, Christophe & Marmann, Katharina	1914	230.04	230.01
Stuhr, Jodi & Wittry, James	1990	258	256
Stull, Dianne M. & Efsic, Edward J.	1962	182.15	182.14
Stull, Dorothy-Ann & Sucik, John M.	1970	182.21	182.14
Stull, Emil W. & Konen, Dorothy M.	1937	182.14	182.09
Stull, Gary-Michael & Modaff, Janet	1977	182.23	182.14
Stull, Hildegarde & Spang, John	1926	171.02	171.01
Stull, Laura-Li & Marzuki, Henry, Jr.	1960	182.18	182.14
Stull, Margaret & George, Robert	1967	182.22	182.14
Stull, Michael-John & Colllins, Teri	1992	182.24	182.14
Stull, Nicholas & Matyas, Marsha	1966	182.19	182.14
Stull, Nicholas & Stevens, Vicki	1994	182.20	182.19
Suarez & Witry, Cristina	1965	128.22	128.20
Sucik, John M. & Stull, Dorothy-Ann	1970	182.21	182.14
Sue & Evans, Ronald	1977	204.26	204.21
Sullivan, John & Schramer, Merri-Kay	1984	172.18	172.15
Swaidan, George & Johnsen, Debra	1980	208.12	208.09.01
Swan, Felice-Bancroft & Plain, Gilbert	1940	172.39	172.38
Swartout, Seldon & Hankins, Mary	1991	182.41	182.25
Sweeney, Catherine & Witry, Louis	1955	061	060

Switzer, Robert & Plain, Karen E.	1970	172.40	172.39
Swoboda, Olga & Olinger, Mathias	1880	009.07	009.05
Swords, Suzanne & Frieders, John	1987	172.28	172.25
Szakacs, Amanda & Carlson, Joseph	2000	182.27.10	182.28
Tank, Becky & Venner, James	1975	236.04	236.02
Tannenbaum, George & Spang, Ann	1931	171.40	171.01
Tannenbaum, James & Albright, Jean	1970	171.46	171.40
Tannenbaum, Kris & Fetzer, Barbara	1978	171.44	171.42
Tannenbaum, Raymond & Arbogast, Grace	1955	171.41	171.40
Tannenbaum, Robert & Britt, Brenda	1985	171.43	171.42
Tannenbaum, Robert & Sandy	1968	171.45	171.40
Tannenbaum, Robert & Schirdelly, Erma	1952	171.42	171.40
Tapparo, Brian & Schlick, Pamela	1991	231.10	231.08
Tapparo, John & Baumunk, Geri	1977	231.12	231.07
Tapparo, John & Koehne, Marianne	1945	231.07	231.01
Tapparo, Michael & Clements, Melody	1981	231.13	231.07
Tapparo, Ronald & Lodraga, Judy	1975	231.11	231.07
Tapparo, Troy & Christian, Sara	1993	231.09	231.08
Tapparo, William & Potter, Beatrice	1969	231.08	231.07
Taylor, Arthur & Pape, Judith	1983	240.39	240.37
Techmanski & Evans, Kristin-Marie	2000	204.24.10	204.24
Tegels, Gerald & Weise, Shelley	1985	236.18	236.11
Tegels, Joseph & Wittry, Anita	1953	236.11	232
Tegels, Karen & Wood, Robert	1977	236.16	236.11
Tegels, Kenneth & Olson, Kathryn	1984	236.17	236.11
Tegels, LuAnn & Vanderheiden, Randall	1972	236.12	236.11
Tegels, Robert & Brinson, Cathleen	1980	236.15	236.11
Tegels, Timothy & Tiefenthaler, Jill	1991	236.19	236.11
Tellison, Dorothy & Wittry, Alois	1940	170	169
Terao, Eriko & Klosen, Paul	1990	227.03	227.02
Terrens & Reiland, Susanne	1880	009.27	009.26
Terrens, Susanne & Schoomars, N.	1910	009.28	009.27
Terzer, Aloyse & Witry, Leonie-Anna	1950	153.01	153
Terzer, Josiane & Thill, Eloi	1976	153.02	153.01
Tescher, Paul & Witry, Sanny	1980	095.17	095.16

Theile, Dorian-Lee & <Unnamed>	1995	182.32	182.30
Theile, Lynn-Marie & <Unnamed>	2000	182.33	182.30
Theile, Michael-Paul & Anita	1990	182.31	182.30
Theis, James E. & Howard, Tamara	1983	172.23	172.22
Theis, Johann & Witry, Babette	1834	147.01	142
Theis, John J. & Zmuda, Lucille	1951	172.22	172.21
Theis, John W. & Florence, Barbara L.	1959	182.02	182.01
Theis, Nicholas A. & Wittry, Anna	1910	172.21	168
Theis, William J. & Reines, Regina F.	1949	172.63	172.53
Theophillus, Morgan & Witry, Ardith	1970	104.06	102
Therens, Catherine & Witry, Peter	1798	038	037
Thiel, Dominic & Goedert, Marie	1735	321.10	321.09
Thiel, Marie & Witry, Johann-Michel	1794	016	011
Thiele, John & Carlson, Peggy-Ann	1966	182.30	182.25
Thier, Julie & Brake, Jerry	1985	267.06	267.01
Thies, Anna & Witry, Peter	1635	002	001
Thies, Catherine & Schroeder, Johann	1716	018.05	018
Thies, Gertrud & Bettendorf, Peter	1710	018.04	018
Thies, Johann & Margaretha	1675	018	002
Thies, Johann & Reuland, Susanne	1675	019	002
Thies, Margaretha & Reuter, Louis	1688	017.05	002
Thies, Marie & Mathieu, Johann	1716	018.01	018
Thill, Eloi & Terzer, Josiane	1976	153.02	153.01
Thill, Josy & Witry, Monique	2002	128.00.30	128.00.20
Thill, Nathalie & Kesseler, Claude	2004	153.02.01	153.02
Thill, Pierre & Fixmer, Elisabeth	1880	164.10	164.01
Thines, Marie & Neuens, Nicolas	1760	321.14	321.12
Thinnes, Pierre & Witry, Barbara	1864	283.03	229
Thiry, Barbara & Witry, Michel	1830	034	033
Thivis, Johann & Schmitt, Anna	1717	323.03	323.01
Tholen, Susan & Thooft, Thomas	1990	261.18	261.12
Tholl, Gaston & Witry, Caroline	1952	224.02	221
Thomas, Heinrich & Schuh, Elisabeth	1886	021.26.65	021.26.60
Thomas, Jeanne & Witry, Jean	1857	021.26.30	021.26.20
Thomas, Josephine & Witry, Andre	1923	021.16	021.15
Thomas, Linda & Joy, Randall	1990	231.18	231.15
Thomas, Rodney & Salmen, Amy	2002	270.02.65	270.02.30
Thomas, Wilhelm & Witry, Susanne	1852	021.26.60	021.26.50

Thomfohrda, Woody & Loser, Cinthia	1991	015.26	015.08
Thompson, John & Jacobsen, Noelle	1990	231.37.01	231.29
Thooft, Brian & Forthman, Jill	2000	261.27.01	261.21
Thooft, Carol & Goblish, Stephen	1983	261.22	261.21
Thooft, David & Severson, Connie	1991	261.23	261.21
Thooft, Dean & Arndt, Michelle	1990	261.26	261.21
Thooft, Dennis & Kraus, Mary	1989	261.24	261.21
Thooft, Douglas & Lamote, Brenda	1984	261.14	261.12
Thooft, Edward & Santo, Susan	1986	261.16	261.12
Thooft, Ernest & Bernardy, Catherine	1958	261.12	261.11
Thooft, Janine & Rasmussen, Douglas	1982	261.15	261.12
Thooft, Joan & LaVoy, Gary	1994	261.25	261.21
Thooft, Karen & Kraemer, John	1989	261.17	261.12
Thooft, Kevin & Youngerberg, Kristin	1993	261.27	261.21
Thooft, Raymond & Bernardy, Jean	1958	261.21	261.11
Thooft, Richard & Johnson, Shirley	1985	261.13	261.12
Thooft, Scott & Louwagie, Debbie	1992	261.20	261.12
Thooft, Suzanne & Kirsh, Robert	1989	261.19	261.12
Thooft, Thomas & Tholen, Susan	1990	261.18	261.12
Thornton, Josette & Kosch, Roby	1994	079.05	079.02
Thurston, Amanda & <Unnamed>	1997	231.25.50	231.25
Thurston, Cindy & Stanfield, Jim	1999	231.28.01	231.21
Thurston, James & Lanteigne, Michele	1977	231.25	231.21
Thurston, Janice & Dilbeck, William	1973	231.23	231.21
Thurston, John & Edwards, Judy	1976	231.22	231.21
Thurston, John & Koehne, Adelaide	1948	231.21	231.01
Thurston, Joseph & Butcher, Tammy	1989	231.27	231.21
Thurston, Joseph & King, Leslie	1979	231.26	231.21
Thurston, Joseph & Padilla, Brenda	2005	231.27.50	231.21
Thurston, Patricia & Duryee, Donald	2002	231.24	231.21
Thurston, Patricia & Martinez, Enrique	1998	231.25.01	231.25
Thurston, Steven & Moore, Sheila	1984	231.28	231.21
Tiefenthaler, Jill & Tegels, Timothy	1991	236.19	236.11
Tierney, Daniel & Allen, Kathie	2002	204.17.02	204.17
Tierney, Joelle & Pfaff, Bruce	1999	204.17.01	204.17
Tierney, Michael & Huss, Kathy-Jo	1969	204.17	204.01
Tigges, Jennifer & Derner, Pat	1997	261.07.02	261.03
Tigges, Mark & Derner, Carol	1983	261.06	261.03

Tillis, Cheryl & Spang, Mark	1980	171.04	171.03
Tix, Nicolas & Witry, Marie	1899	151.02	151
Tjarks, Michael & Wittry, Nancy	1986	261.02	261
Tjebbens, Mary & Nieland, Douglas	1976	248.06	248.01
Toledo, Tannia & Wittry, Daniel	2000	181.01.02	181
Tollefson, Steven & Bock, Susan	1983	260.05	260.01
Tomaszek, Margaret & Witry, Lawrence	1981	058	056
Tone & Elvsveen, Robert	1990	103.01	103
Tourner, Nicolas & Witry, Elisabeth	1823	157.01	157
Toussaint, Marie & Witry, Franz	1884	299	292
Toussaint, Michel & Witry, Margaretha	1835	147.02	142
Toussing, Jacques & Witry, Angele	1912	303.01	301
Toussing, Jacques & Witry, Catherine	1907	301.01	301
Toussing, Jean & Hoffmann, Maria	1935	301.02	301.01
Tracey, Deborah & Wittry, Dennis	1975	213	210
Trausch, Janine & Witry, Theodor	1905	164.00.50	162
Trent, Beverly & Glass, William	1968	233.02	233.01
Trexler, Linda & Bernardy, Robert	1975	261.28	261.11
Trosine, Kevin & Schramer, Carolyn	1988	172.17	172.15
Troutner, Jeff & Cole, Andrea	2000	240.11.50	240.10
Tueber, Christopher & Loser, Michelle	1987	015.10	015.09
Turbos, Ray & Pape, Annabella	1968	240.33	240.23
Tutender & Holmberg, Michelle	2000	270.03.20	270.03.15
Ulen, Charles & Wittry, Karen	1981	242.01	242
Unden, Heinrich & Witry, Marie	1779	017.01	011
Underberg, Gabriel & Nieland, Lindsay	2006	248.04.50	248.04
Underhill, June & Carlson, Michael	1975	182.29	182.25
Urban, Robert & Witry, Patricia	1990	061.02	061
Urhausen, Germaine & Deltgen, Albert	1980	321.15.20	321.15.14
Uscheldinger, Wilhelm & Witry, Johanna	1906	166.01.50	166.01
Uselding, Anton & Witry, Anna	1794	032.03	022
Van Beneden, Emilie & Deltgen, Antoine	1975	321.15.19	321.15.14

Van Boekel, Lambertus & Efsic, Maria	2000	182.17.01	182.15
Van Fleet & Evans, Angiene	2000	204.23.10	204.22
Van Grysperre, Isabel & Kaell, Francois	2000	014.65.40	014.65
Van Moer, Nancy & Hoflock, Kevin	1978	240.47	240.43
Van Verweck, Joanne & Jacques, Ferdnand	1934	141.15	141.14
Vanderheiden, Carin & Wallace, Thomas	1997	236.14	236.12
Vanderheiden, Randall & Tegels, LuAnn	1972	236.12	236.11
Vanderheiden, Trenton & Holmes, Jennifer	1994	236.13	236.12
VanDyck, Victor & Witry, Marie	1924	139.01	135
Vassolo, Ricardo & Canueto, Mita	1945	031.00.50	031.00.40
Venner, Christy & Smith, Frank	1973	236.03	236.02
Venner, Dale & Larson, Kimberly	1988	236.08	236.02
Venner, Elizabeth & Kurt, Tom	1994	236.06.01	236.02
Venner, James & Tank, Becky	1975	236.04	236.02
Venner, Joan & Frazier, Jeffrey	1989	236.09	236.02
Venner, Mark & Pruisner, Robin	1995	236.10	236.02
Venner, Paul & Wittry, Rita	1951	236.02	232
Venner, Susan & Barnett, Dean	1974	236.05	236.02
Venner, Susan & Yarbrough, Joe	1983	236.06	236.02
Venner, Thomas & Knobbe, Julie	1986	236.07	236.02
Verdeck, Beverly & Peterson, Mike	1966	240.36	240.34
Verdeck, Bonnie & Larson, Lloyd	1966	240.35	240.34
Verdeck, Francis & Pape, Margorie	1940	240.34	240.22
Veyder, Elise & Witry, Johann	1923	218.00.50	216
Viaene, Margaret & Wittry, Leonard	1944	238	237
Viebig, Gail & Plain, Michael D.	1984	172.46	172.44
Viereckl, Rudolph & Schramer, Gill	1985	172.06	172.02
Viergever, James & Kelley, Sharlys	1970	030.09	030.08
Villalpando, Jose & Crenshaw, Sara	1992	231.44	231.38
Virginia & Schroeder, John	1950	015.84.50	015.06
Volibi, Peter & Marchal, Anna	1668	324.01	324
Wade, Tristan & Zingoni, Maria-Ines	1990	128.16	128.13

Wagener, Josephine & Schroeder, Michel	1868	015.05	015.04
Wagenknecht, Gary & Eubanks, Laura	1993	172.32	172.31
Wagner & Wittry, Karen	1985	207.11	207
Wagner, Barbara & Farrall, Edward	1984	015.21	015.19.50
Wagner, Barbara & Parker, Jeffery	1987	015.22	015.19.50
Wagner, Catherine & Wiltgen, Jean	1813	311.23	311.07
Wagner, Christina & Witry, Dominic	1809	013	012
Wagner, Debra & <Unnamed>	1995	015.24	015.19.50
Wagner, Dianne & Ange, Michael	1995	015.23	015.19.50
Wagner, Heinrich & Witry, Anna	1788	022.03	022
Wagner, Mathias & George, Margaretha	1825	119.03	119.02
Wagner, Paul & Wittry, Judith	1991	252.02	249
Wagner, Peter & Wiltgen, Barbara	1838	311.22	311.08
Wagner, Rick & Loser, Cinthia-Ann	1965	015.20	015.08
Wagner, Romain & Witry, Viviane	1980	217.02	217.01
Wagner, Susanna & Witry, Johann	1923	160.50	160
Wagner, Susanne & Witry, Johann	1829	017	016
Wagner, Susanne & Witry, Peter	1855	048	047
Waind, Patrick & Wittry, Anne	1990	202.01	201
Walch, Philomena & Witry, Peter	1898	290	288
Waldbillig, Germaine & Witry, Jean	1950	095.14	095.12
Walker, Charlotte & Schramer, Daniel	1955	172.09	172.01
Walker, Kim & Wittry, Susan	1986	177.02	176
Wall, Sallie & Koehne, Juvent	1975	231.06	231.01
Wallace, Thomas & Vanderheiden, Carin	1997	236.14	236.12
Walter, Gary & Hannasch, Jane	1978	240.14	240.09
Walters, Katerine & Behen, Edward	1970	075.05.40	075.05
Walton, Todd & Shawna-Lynn Cory	2005	100.01.50	100.01
Wambach, Barbara & Witry, Pierre	1918	074.00.50	074
Warlies, Alexa & Witry, Joseph	1985	224	223
Warnell, Chris & Hillard, Carolyn	1990	104.05	104.01
Warnell, Gary & Witry, Ardith-Elaine	1959	104.01	102
Warnell, Jami-Marie & Hebert, Keith	1980	104.03	104.01
Warnell, Jami-Marie & Smaldt, Alan	1990	104.04	104.01
Warnell, Jeffrey-Glen & Harrell, Sue	1995	104.02	104.01
Watgen, Deborah & Solecki, Michael	1976	171.13	171.09

Watgen, Dennis & Schindlbeck, Joyce	1975	171.11	171.09
Watgen, Donald & Crawford, Susan	1980	171.14	171.09
Watgen, Katherine & Berenyi, Richard	1980	171.12	171.09
Watgen, Robert & Spang, Choral	1951	171.09	171.02
Watgen, Thomas & Beller, Linda	1975	171.10	171.09
Watgen, William & Retterer, Wendy	1985	171.15	171.09
Watts, Steve & Rasmussen, Dawn	1985	015.54	015.45
Waver, Joseph & Kuntziger, Barbe	1840	021.06	021.03
Weber, Carl & Bernbrock, Mary	1938	208.02	208.01
Weber, Caryl & Morgan, Randy	1980	208.05	208.02
Weber, Conrad & Mathieu, Catherine	1758	018.03	018.01
Weber, Dorothy & Johnsen, Donald	1950	208.09.01	208.01
Weber, Elwyn & Pederson, Ingrid	1968	208.03	208.02
Weber, Ferdinand & Wittry, Emma	1913	208.01	208
Weber, Jacob & Witry, Marie	1790	050.02	037
Weber, Jennifer & Stevens, Scott	2000	208.03.05	208.03
Weber, Johann & Witry, Catherine	1896	119.00.50	107
Weber, Kristine & Conrad, Joseph	1994	229.20	229.18
Weber, Marian & Hawking, J. Wilfrid	1939	208.06	208.01
Weber, Marie & Wittry, Paul	1858	271	229
Weber, Mathias & Phillipart, Leonie	1918	144.70	144.01
Weber, William & Hockstein, Linda	1980	208.04	208.02
Weddige, Carol & Clark, David	1988	173.08	173.02
Weddige, Carol & Grattafiori, Alan	1958	173.03	173.02
Weddige, Carol & Hunter, Jason	1970	173.07	173.02
Weddige, David & De Cosmo, Maria	1986	173.14	173.13
Weddige, David & Hutchinson, Sally	1960	173.13	173.02
Weddige, Diana & Michels, William	1986	173.15	173.13
Weddige, Frederick & Wittry, Barbara	1908	173.01	173
Weddige, Michael & Moore, Kristi	2004	173.16	173.13
Weddige, Paul & Henrickson, Christine	1936	173.02	173.01
Weddige, Pauline & Mertes, Edward	1958	173.09	173.02
Wegman, Carol & Wittry, Lawrence	1990	236	235
Wehden, Lillian & Wittry, Ferdinand	1925	197	182
Wehrlen, Achille & Mack, Anna	1925	321.15.23	321.15.12
Weidert, Peter & Kirsch, Anna	1794	009.41	009.40
Weiland, Johann & Radermacher, Anna	1742	020.06	020.01

Weiland, Margritha & Witry, Nicolas	1823	021.26.20	021.26
Weirich, Viviane & Klosen, Michel	1995	227.05	227.02
Weis, Angela & Witry, Nicolas	1797	033	022
Weis, Camille & Witry, Irene-Eugenie	1950	146.01	146
Weis, Catherine & Franck, Johann	1811	037.02	037.01
Weis, Denise & Reuter, Jean	1980	146.02	146.01
Weise, Shelley & Tegels, Gerald	1985	236.18	236.11
Weisgerber, Anna & Witry, Peter	1867	284	229
Weisgerber, Margaretha & Witry, Nicolas	1790	310	120
Weiss & Olinger, Marie	1870	009.14	009.04
Weiss, Helena & Stronck, Peter	1890	009.22	009.21
Weistroffer, Jane & Meyer, Gregory	1986	171.27	171.24
Weiten, Ericka & Ficker, John	2001	204.18.01	204.18
Weiten, Kari & <Unnamed>	1995	204.18.02	204.018
Weiten, Ronald & Huss, Margaret	1972	204.18	204.01
Welch, Randy & Kanne, Jayne	1990	243.03	243.01
Weldon, Mindy & Nieland, Douglas	1986	248.07	248.01
Welsch, Elisabetha & Zahn, Philippe	1922	146.03.70	146.03
Welter, Agnes & Wittry, Michel	1877	168	167
Welter, Johann & Muller Catharina	1920	107.01.60	107.01
Welter, Johann-Peter & Bruck, Maria	1918	107.01.30	107.01
Welter, Nicolas & Witry, Margaretha	1889	107.01	107
Welter, Susanne & Witry, Nicolas	1734	311.06	311
Wenckus & Wittry, Elizabeth	1970	207.03	207
Wenckus, Jennifer & Buchmeier	1995	207.05	207.03
Wenckus, Neal & Estrup, Jennifer	1998	207.04	207.03
Wendy & Gjerde, Kenneth	1985	240.25	240.24
Wenmacher, Jos & Bemtgen, Magdalena	1935	215.62	215.60
Weskott, Denny & Wittry, Carol	1975	238.03	238
Wester, Catherine & Witry, Jean	1809	133	121
Wester, Susanne & Witry, Johann	1799	009	007
Wetzel, Robert & Nieland, Patricia	1992	248.09	248.01
Weyer, Catherine & Bemtgen, Peter	1948	215.65.60	215.65
Weyland, Clotilde & Witry, Joseph	1909	141.12	141.08
Weyland, Elisabeth & Witry, Jacob	1792	022.01	022
Weyland, Marie & Wiltgen, Jean	1799	311.22.50	311.07
Weynandt, Peter & Kayser, Catherine	1867	311.19	311.12

White, Francis & Pobstman, Lorraine	1946	174.03	174.02
White, Mary & Sherwood, Edwin	1989	174.04	174.03
Whitecotton, Kristie & Hankes, Nicholas	1997	204.16.03	204.16
Whitfield, Robert & Kane, Candace	1975	171.17	171.16
Widdel, Erica & <Unnamed>	1998	229.25.10	229.25
Widdel, John & Russell, Julia	1977	229.25	229.21
Wiebe, Thomas & Wittry, Darlene	1979	238.04	238
Wiederin, Andrew & Buelt, Rose	1970	240.05	240.01
Wiederin, Douglas & Baumhover, Laurie	1986	261.09	261.08
Wiederin, Eugene & Wittry, Marcia	1962	261.08	260
Wiederin, Jodi & Bayliss, Terry	1990	261.10	261.08
Wiederin, Lisa & Ekness, Michael	1996	240.06	240.05
Wiederin, Tom & Reid, Stacy	2002	261.10.01	261.08
Wierschem, Marie & Clemes, John	1926	086.05	086.01
Wilberding, Frances & Wittry, Nicholas	1931	265	264
Wilberding, Rose & Wittry, Joseph	1933	241	231
Wilde, Donald & Debbie	1985	015.59	015.45
Wilde, Donald & Schroeder, Gloria	1965	015.58	015.44
Wilde, Pamela & Bast, James	1984	015.57	015.45
Wilder, John & Carlson, Peggy-Ann	1989	182.34	182.25
Wilhelm, Henriette & Witry, Heinrich	1966	131	130
Wilkens, Gary & Haller, Jennifer	1991	240.04	240.03
Wille, Ursula & Witry, Rene	1977	306	305
Williams, Beatrice & Wittry, Michael	1980	178	176
Williams, Patricia & Frieders, Lawrence	1971	172.26	172.25
Wills, Robert & Pape, Judith	1968	240.38	240.37
Wilmes & Hellers, Catherine	1890	009.10	009.09
Wilson, Barbara & Efsic, Edward	1990	182.17.50	182.15
Wilson, Darlene & Johnson, Craig	1950	015.71	015.70
Wilson, Darlene & Lemarand, Robert	1952	015.75	015.70
Wilson, Darlene & Reynolds, Alan	1950	015.74	015.70
Wilson, Hjalmer & Schroeder, Josephine	1933	015.70	015.06
Wilson, Rose-Mary & Erath, Thomas	1967	171.58	171.57
Wiltgen, Anne & Klopp, Nicolas	1840	311.22.65	311.22.50

Name	Year	Code 1	Code 2
Wiltgen, Barbara & Wagner, Peter	1838	311.22	311.08
Wiltgen, Barbie & Fonck, Michel	1837	311.22.70	311.22.50
Wiltgen, Dominique & Jacoby, Susanne	1793	311.08	311.07
Wiltgen, Jean & Biltgen, Catherine	1837	311.21	311.08
Wiltgen, Jean & Wagner, Catherine	1813	311.23	311.07
Wiltgen, Jean & Weyland, Marie	1799	311.22.50	311.07
Wiltgen, Jeanne & Dichter, Mathias	1840	311.22.80	311.22.50
Wiltgen, Marguerite & Deltgen, Pierre	1887	311.22.69	311.22.67
Wiltgen, Marguerite & Graff, Pierre	1845	311.22.68	311.22.67
Wiltgen, Marie & Bertrang, Mathias	1890	009.19	009.16
Wiltgen, Marie & Kayser, Nikolas	1819	311.12	311.08
Wiltgen, Marie & Mons, Heinrich	1819	311.09	311.08
Wiltgen, Nicolas & Kremer, Barbe	1841	311.22.67	311.22.50
Wiltgen, Nicolas & Ries, Margaretha	1833	311.20	311.08
Wiltgen, Nicolas & Witry, Anna	1763	311.07	311.06
Wiltgen, Pierre & Stopfel, Elisabeth	1831	311.22.55	311.22.50
Wiltgen, Susanne & Philippy, Jean	1828	311.22.60	311.22.50
Wilwertz, Christophe & Witry, Anna	1790	021.27	021.01
Winbech, Matilda & Behen, Francis	1950	075.05.30	075.05
Winiarski, Wendy & Heber, David	1995	015.15	015.12
Winter, Jeremy & Goblirsch, Heidi	2002	261.30.04	261.29
Winter, Pamela & Cosgrove, Timothy	1990	070.07	070.05
Winter, Robert & Witry, Lisa	1990	077.02	077
Winthers, Linda & Reines, Robert	1991	172.56	172.54
Wirion & Schmitt, Girl	1970	145.03	145.02
Wirtz, Anna & Witry, Jacob	1888	231	230
Witry, Adam & Kuhnen, Marie-Magdalena	1685	003	002
Witry, Alain & Robert, Claudine	1988	082	081
Witry, Alain & Schmit, Nathalie	2000	128.00.17	128.00.10
Witry, Albert & Bosseler, Marguerite	1893	141.25	141.19
Witry, Albert & June	1930	075.05.50	075
Witry, Albert & Origer, Anne	1900	141.09	141.08 141.22
Witry, Alberto & Fernandez Salas, Elvia	1933	128.20	128.01
Witry, Alene & Corken, Matthew	1985	061.03	061
Witry, Alfred & Kleber, Marie-Louise	1923	136	135

Witry, Alfred & Modert, Maria	1952	305	304
Witry, Alfredo & Barrera, Maria	1935	128.12	128.01
Witry, Alphonse & Feller, Francoise	1970	128.00.20	128.00.05
Witry, Andre & Kolbach, Sylvie	1984	218.05	218.04
Witry, Andre & Schrobiltgen, Appoline	1893	021.15	021.13
Witry, Andre & Thomas, Josephine	1923	021.16	021.15
Witry, Angela & Schneider, Johann	1792	009.37	007
Witry, Angele & Kauth, Jean	1935	303.02	301
Witry, Angele & Toussing, Jacques	1912	303.01	301
Witry, Anna & Adamy, Peter	1746	017.03	003
Witry, Anna & Bemtgen, Johann	1916	216.50	216
Witry, Anna & Bofferding, Nicolas	1890	031.01.60	031
Witry, Anna & Bruin, James	1925	075.03	075
Witry, Anna & Eiffes, Mathias	1848	161.03	157
Witry, Anna & Goolsby	1880	092.02	092
Witry, Anna & Hansen, Peter	1862	086.23	052
Witry, Anna & Jacque, Nicolas	1880	139.04	134
Witry, Anna & Kirsch, Jean-Pierre	1840	125.01	125
Witry, Anna & Kirsch, Valentin	1770	009.40	006
Witry, Anna & Klein, Peter	1785	010.01	006
Witry, Anna & Korier, Nicolas	1866	086.50	052
Witry, Anna & Kugener, Anton	1895	074.00.95	053
Witry, Anna & Malding, Johann	1799	009.38	007
Witry, Anna & Muller, Johann	1900	284.50	284
Witry, Anna & Muller, Theodor	1818	023.02	023
Witry, Anna & Reuland, Johann	1866	044.02	039
Witry, Anna & Rollin, Jean-Francois	1840	133.03	124
Witry, Anna & Schoug, Johann	1875	049.01	049
Witry, Anna & Seil, Andre	1948	084.01	084
Witry, Anna & Simon, Andre	1797	021.29	021.01
Witry, Anna & Spoetler, Johann	1791	037.03	037
Witry, Anna & Steyer, Heinrich	1879	024.01	024
Witry, Anna & Uselding, Anton	1794	032.03	022
Witry, Anna & Wagner, Heinrich	1788	022.03	022
Witry, Anna & Wiltgen, Nicolas	1763	311.07	311.06
Witry, Anna & Wilwertz, Christophe	1790	021.27	021.01
Witry, Anna-Margaretha & Hoffmann, Gerard	1806	009.39	007

Witry, Anna-Marie & George, Johann	1801	119.02	037
Witry, Anne & Golladay, David	1973	043.01	043
Witry, Anne-Marie & Collart, Mathias	1784	021.23	021.01
Witry, Anne-Marie & Pierre, Johann	1839	009.35	009
Witry, Anne-Marie & Pletschet, Peter	1839	009.36	009
Witry, Annick & Halsdorf, Jos	2002	086.00.01	086
Witry, Appoline & Arend, Jean	1964	021.17	021.16
Witry, Ardith & Theophillus, Morgan	1970	104.06	102
Witry, Ardith-Elaine & Warnell, Gary	1959	104.01	102
Witry, Arthur & Leonard, Marie	1887	141.20	141.19
Witry, Astrid & Roisin, Francois	1989	021.19	021.18
Witry, Auguste & Lefebvre, Marie	1880	141.25.50	141.19
Witry, Babette & Theis, Johann	1834	147.01	142
Witry, Barbara & Franck, Nicolas	1781	037.01	037
Witry, Barbara & Herges, Johann	1841	147.04	142
Witry, Barbara & Koerner, Adam	1867	166.01	165
Witry, Barbara & Sekelsky, Mark	1987	112.01	110
Witry, Barbara & Steichen, Peter	1830	140.01	140
Witry, Barbara & Thinnes, Pierre	1864	283.03	229
Witry, Barbara & Zahn, Dominic	1880	146.03	143 147.04
Witry, Barbara & Zahn, Dominic	1846	147.05	142
Witry, Bernard & Donnersberger, Catherine	1985	057	055
Witry, Bernard & Hall, Mary	1966	105	102
Witry, Bernard & Kennedy, Mary	1950	056	055
Witry, Bernhard & Decker, Margareta	1910	302	301
Witry, Beth-Ann & Sparrow, Robert	1983	061.01	060
Witry, Carola & Putz, Edouard	1945	166.05	166.04
Witry, Caroline & Tholl, Gaston	1952	224.02	221
Witry, Catharina & Rausch, Peter	1896	284.20	284
Witry, Catherine & Beideler, Peter	1858	021.26.70	021.26.50
Witry, Catherine & Bettendorf, Heinrich	1878	092.01	092
Witry, Catherine & Blitsch, Jacob	1868	287.01	229
Witry, Catherine & Eiffes, Jean	1913	050.00.60	050.00.50
Witry, Catherine & Fixmer, Wilhelm	1848	164.01	157
Witry, Catherine & Hansen, Laurent	2003	128.00.25	128.00.05
Witry, Catherine & Jacoby, Adam	1891	151.01	151

Witry, Catherine & Kipgen, Jacob	1770	015.98	011
Witry, Catherine & Kremer, Peter	1898	119.01	107
Witry, Catherine & Lavallaye, Nicolas	1880	036.01	036
Witry, Catherine & Lenger, Francois	1855	141.03	141
Witry, Catherine & Nilles, Peter	1877	159.01	158
Witry, Catherine & Riche, Todd	2007	072.50	072
Witry, Catherine & Schleich, Denis	1830	036.02	033
Witry, Catherine & Stronck, Johann	1829	009.15	009
Witry, Catherine & Toussing, Jacques	1907	301.01	301
Witry, Catherine & Weber, Johann	1896	119.00.50	107
Witry, Catherine & Witry, Emil	1867	035	036 034
Witry, Charles & Jenson, Darlene	1956	118	109
Witry, Charles & Leisen, Nicole	1970	086	085
Witry, Charles & Sauber, Lucie	1902	084	053
Witry, Christopher & Young, Kim	1990	077.01	077
Witry, Clara & Cavanaugh, Charles	1920	096.01	096
Witry, Clara & Mares, Aristobulo	1920	128.05	128.01
Witry, Claude & Feyereisen, Marthe	1989	138	137
Witry, Claudine & Hess, Claude	1988	225.02	225
Witry, Craig & Harken, Sheree	1993	100	098
Witry, Craig-Joseph & Harwood, Faye	1979	099	098
Witry, Cristina & Suarez	1965	128.22	128.20
Witry, Cynthia & Jenkins, Thomas	1978	043.02	043
Witry, Cynthia & Rhea, Bruce	1984	118.01	118
Witry, David & Alexander, Denise	1987	115	114
Witry, David-Allen & Schultz, Karen	1985	062	061
Witry, Dominic & Pott, Margaretha	1869	288	229
Witry, Dominic & Wagner, Christina	1809	013	012
Witry, Dorinne & Sanders, Norbert	1957	070.02	068
Witry, Edward & Betcher, Rose	1927	068	054
Witry, Egide & Biver, Yvonne	1960	227.00.01	227
Witry, Elisabeth & Bofferding, Nicolas	1900	031.01.70	031
Witry, Elisabeth & Cloos, Mathias	1903	044.01	040
Witry, Elisabeth & Flammang, Peter	1879	166.02	165
Witry, Elisabeth & Franz, Heinrich	1826	035.02	033
Witry, Elisabeth & Guerlet, Gilbert	1953	088.01	088

Witry, Elisabeth & Kuhnen, Johann	1835	157.02	157
Witry, Elisabeth & Moos, Jacob	1846	229.01	229
Witry, Elisabeth & Streff, Johann	1824	157.03	157
Witry, Elisabeth & Tourner, Nicolas	1823	157.01	157
Witry, Elisabeth & Wouters, Pierre	1835	140.06	140
Witry, Elise & Bley, Peter	1913	046.70	046
Witry, Elizabeth & <Unnamed>	1980	128.09	128.08
Witry, Elvia & Churrupit	1965	128.21	128.20
Witry, Emil & Schmit, Catharina	1907	144.00	144
Witry, Emil & Witry, Catherine	1867	035	034 036
Witry, Emile & Brever, Marie	1945	155	152
Witry, Emile & Hoss, Anna	1940	154	152
Witry, Emile & Lucius, Sisy	1955	222	221
Witry, Emilio-Carlos & <Unnamed>	1950	128.08	128.07
Witry, Emilio-Carlos & Gomez, Alicia	1920	128.07	128.01
Witry, Eric & Caramelle, Anne	1990	090	089
Witry, Ernest & Bellion, Germaine	1945	218.03	218.02
Witry, Eudalie & Jacques, Joseph	1865	141.13	141
Witry, Eugenia & Schaedle, Allen	1913	093.01	093
Witry, Eugenie & Hilger, Jean	1910	134.02	134.01
Witry, Eugenie & Hoett, Pierre	1929	227.06	219
Witry, Evelyne & Berna	1995	128.00.15	128.00.10
Witry, Fernande & Schartz, Jean	1991	131.00.01	131
Witry, Florent & Feller, Christiane	1970	128.00.70	128.00.05
Witry, Francis & <Unnamed>	1980	095.15	095.14
Witry, Francis & Poecker, Anny	1955	095.16	095.12
Witry, Francois & Kultgen, Catherine	1870	021.14	021.13
Witry, Francois & Schalbar, Nelly	1959	081	080
Witry, Frank & Seible, Dolores	1958	291	288
Witry, Franz & Francois, Marie	1877	298	292
Witry, Franz & Toussaint, Marie	1884	299	292
Witry, Franzisca & Goedert, Mathias	1681	321.08	002
Witry, Georg & Ludwigs, Catherine	1876	215	214
Witry, George & Hodges, Edna-Mae	1958	064	063
Witry, George & McGrath, Alice	1930	063	054
Witry, George & Schaal, Bobbette	1984	065	064

Witry, Georges & Hankenne, Marguerite	1930	141.10.50	141.09
Witry, Georges & Wohl, Aloysia	1960	217.04	217
Witry, Gerald & Dozier, Joan	1955	069	068
Witry, Gregoire & Lutgen, Susanne	1932	166.02.03	166.02.01
Witry, Gregory & Felton, Jill-Ann	1979	111	110
Witry, Gregory & Humphrey, Kimberly	1987	112	110
Witry, Harlan& O'Connor, Charlotte	1953	098	097
Witry, Harold & Conry, Lucille	1935	102	096
Witry, Hector & Arabuarena, Etelvina	1930	128.23	128.01
Witry, Heinrich & Decker, Catherine	1825	125	124
Witry, Heinrich & Fischer, Margaretha	1761	021.24	021
Witry, Heinrich & Frederes, Susanne	1877	041	039
Witry, Heinrich & Hennes, Susanne	1867	040	039
Witry, Heinrich & Heuardt, Petronille	1839	036	033
Witry, Heinrich & Holzmacher, Catherine	1859	107	051
Witry, Heinrich & Kirsch, Marie-Anna	1867	151	148
Witry, Heinrich & Lutgen, Margaretha	1874	095	094
Witry, Heinrich & Moriame, Anne	1745	021.01	021
Witry, Heinrich & Muller, Margaretha	1848	149	148
Witry, Heinrich & Nepper, Marie	1817	026	023
Witry, Heinrich & Wilhelm, Henriette	1966	131	130
Witry, Helen & Reichenberger, John	1935	075.06	075
Witry, Helene & Melsen, J.	1900	074.01	053
Witry, Helene & Souvignier, Jean	1840	141.26	140
Witry, Henri & Elsen, Helene	1950	095.13	095.12
Witry, Henri & Guillaume, Maria	1788	021.25	021.01
Witry, Henri & Juppin, Germaine	1930	088	087
Witry, Henri & Nepper, Marie	1897	129	127
Witry, Henri-Lucien & Repele, Marie	1910	139	135
Witry, Henry & Hylaczek, Estelle	1940	075.07	075
Witry, Horacio & Concha Contreras, Victoria	1940	128.24	128.01
Witry, Hortense & Putz, Nicolas	1930	132.04	129
Witry, Irene-Eugenie & Weis, Camille	1950	146.01	146
Witry, Irma & Ross, Johann-Peter	1916	145.01	145
Witry, Isabelle & Gallais, Lionel	1986	296.01	296

Witry, Jacob & Heuschling, Anna	1895	219	214
Witry, Jacob & Weyland, Elisabeth	1792	022.01	022
Witry, Jacob & Wirtz, Anna	1888	231	230
Witry, Jacqueline & Marchal, Jean	1980	218.04.50	218.04
Witry, Jacqueline & Zimmer, Georges	1995	227.00.03	227.00.01
Witry, Jacques & Lucius, Susanne	1958	225	221
Witry, Jacques & Quintus, Josefine	1918	218.02	218.01
Witry, Jacques & Schlesser, Marguerite	1928	153	152
Witry, James & Fostervold, Kari	1989	113	110
Witry, Jean & <Unnamed>	1952	074.00.70	074.00.50
Witry, Jean & Berens, Jeanette	1836	126	124
Witry, Jean & Berens, Marie	1855	127	126
Witry, Jean & Berens, Marie-Josefine	1885	128	127
Witry, Jean & Bley, Anna	1898	046.20	046
Witry, Jean & Bollig, Sanny	1930	227	219
Witry, Jean & Brochmann, Louise	1925	074.00.90	074
Witry, Jean & Brosius, Barbara	1773	021.02	021.01
Witry, Jean & Burke, Phillip	1950	060.01	060
Witry, Jean & Feller, Marie	1965	128.00.60	128.00.05
Witry, Jean & Glange, Marguerite	1920	220	219
Witry, Jean & Godefroy, Marie	1810	021.10	021.02
Witry, Jean & Goerens, Susanne	1880	021.26.32	021.26.20
Witry, Jean & Hirtz, Anna-Marie	1848	094	051
Witry, Jean & Laux, Marie-Catherine	1765	121	120
Witry, Jean & Olinger, Anna	1795	124	121
Witry, Jean & Schroeder, Anna-Marie	1798	051	037
Witry, Jean & Thomas, Jeanne	1857	021.26.30	021.26.20
Witry, Jean & Waldbillig, Germaine	1950	095.14	095.12
Witry, Jean & Wester, Catherine	1809	133	121
Witry, Jeanette & Baden, Corneil	1837	091.01	051
Witry, Jean-Mathias & Kneip, Anna	1766	012	011
Witry, Jeanne & Demuth, Eduard	1959	132.01	130
Witry, Jeanne & Sales, Pierre	1959	166.02.04	166.02.03
Witry, Jean-Pierre & Andring, Marie	1955	223	221
Witry, Jean-Pierre & Stoos, Louise	1940	085	084
Witry, Joan-Marie & Gorner, Denis	1968	071.06	071
Witry, Johann & Barnich, Catherine	1835	021.26.40	021.26
Witry, Johann & Biever, Margaretha	1863	053	052

Witry, Johann & Bley, Angelika	1892	218.01	214
Witry, Johann & Bourgeois, Marie	1906	021.26.34	021.26.32
Witry, Johann & Claudon, Susanne	1734	011	003
Witry, Johann & Copons, Barbara	1806	032	022
Witry, Johann & Courtiol, Jeanne	1873	050	049
Witry, Johann & Dondelinger, Magdalena	1715	021	020
Witry, Johann & Eyners, Anna	1735	004	003
Witry, Johann & Federspiel, Elisabeth	1885	050.00.50	049
Witry, Johann & Gengler, Catherine	1880	144	143
Witry, Johann & Givenes, Albertine	1914	050.00.70	050.00.50
Witry, Johann & Hirtzig, Marie	1848	045	038
Witry, Johann & Lethal, Anne-Marie	1899	132.04.02	127
Witry, Johann & Lichter, Susanna	1850	230	229
Witry, Johann & Mathey, Barbara	1849	134	124
Witry, Johann & Menne, Anne	1935	217	216
Witry, Johann & Meyers, Barbara	1830	292	156
Witry, Johann & Moiss, Anna-Marie	1847	049	038
Witry, Johann & Mouchant, Anna	1767	007	006
Witry, Johann & Muller, Elisabeth	1862	031	026
Witry, Johann & Nepper, Susanne	1806	142	121
Witry, Johann & Nilles, Marie	1788	023	022
Witry, Johann & Probst, Margaretha	1848	015	013
Witry, Johann & Rousseau, Zoe	1860	128.26	127
Witry, Johann & Sand, Anna	1889	093	092
Witry, Johann & Schmit, Marie	1901	147	143
Witry, Johann & Veyder, Elise	1923	218.00.50	216
Witry, Johann & Wagner, Susanna	1923	160.50	160
Witry, Johann & Wagner, Susanne	1829	017	016
Witry, Johann & Wester, Susanne	1799	009	007
Witry, Johanna & Kerzmann, John	1892	107.02	107
Witry, Johanna & Reckinger, Bernard	1705	311.01	311
Witry, Johanna & Schmitt, Johann	1705	323.04	002
Witry, Johanna & Schmitt, Theodor	1691	323.01	002
Witry, Johanna & Simon, Johann	1828	009.01	009
Witry, Johanna & Uscheldinger, Wilhelm	1906	166.01.50	166.01
Witry, Johann-Michel & Thiel, Marie	1794	016	011
Witry, Johann-Nicolas & <Unnamed>	1805	008	007

Witry, Johann-Peter & Frisch, Susanne	1894	074	053
Witry, Johann-Peter & Hansen, Angela	1731	006	003
Witry, Johann-Peter & Kraus, Theresa	1899	108	107
Witry, John & Allen, Michele	2000	067.01	067
Witry, John & Donato, Ramona	1965	067	063
Witry, John & Eskew, Dorothy	1943	043	042
Witry, John & Kathleen M.	1930	075.01	075
Witry, John & Melsen, Anna	1890	054	053
Witry, John & Woodson, Sue	1980	044	043
Witry, John-Peter & Freitag, Frieda	1920	055	054
Witry, Jorge-Nicolas & <Unnamed>	1980	128.11	128.08
Witry, Josee & Schneider, Michel	1996	131.01	131
Witry, Josefine & Letellier, Gustav	1889	035.00.50	035
Witry, Josefine & Ries, Johann	1838	026.01	026
Witry, Joseph & Armstrong, Sharon	1970	072	071
Witry, Joseph & Bauske, Bonnie	1985	066	064
Witry, Joseph & Burke, Catherine	1932	071	054
Witry, Joseph & Groth, Eunice	1955	110	109
Witry, Joseph & Michaux, Marguerite	1942	083	079
Witry, Joseph & Miller, Pearl	1928	109	108
Witry, Joseph & Warlies, Alexa	1985	224	223
Witry, Joseph & Weyland, Clotilde	1909	141.12	141.08
Witry, Josephine & Hirschler, Mathias	1925	079.01	079
Witry, Josiane & Lordong, Jean-Pierre	1980	227.00.02	227.00.01
Witry, Jules & Witry, Marie-Therese	1927	130	145 129
Witry, Julie & Merkle, James	1990	070.01	069
Witry, Julienne & Gangler, Lucien	1925	021.21	021.15
Witry, Karen & Arends, Ronald	1986	100.02	098
Witry, Katharina & Marmann, Mathias	1880	230.01	230
Witry, Katherine & Culbertson, J. M.	1885	027.05	027
Witry, Kathleen & Sheahan, Michael	1985	058.01	05
Witry, Kathryn & Smith, David	1930	290.01	289
Witry, Laura & Bailey, Luke	1983	069.01	069
Witry, Lawrence & Tomaszek, Margaret	1981	058	056
Witry, Leon & Jacque, Albertine	1925	146	145
Witry, Leon & Limpach, Monique	1961	021.18	021.16
Witry, Leonie & Feller, Joseph	1915	143.70	143.50

Witry, Leonie-Anna & Terzer, Aloyse	1950	153.01	153
Witry, Lisa & Winter, Robert	1990	077.02	077
Witry, Loretta & Cosgrove, Frank	1960	070.05	068
Witry, Louis & Sweeney, Catherine	1955	061	060
Witry, Louis-John & Ingerski, Vic	1925	060	054
Witry, Luc & ScHollar, Claudine	1996	082.02	081
Witry, Lucianne & Pettinger, Nic	1963	085.01	085
Witry, Lucy & Hodge, Richard	1890	030.14	027
Witry, Madeleine & <Unnamed>	1950	074.00.80	074.00.50
Witry, Madeleine & Fries, Pierre	1881	215.50	214
Witry, Magdalena & Berens, Johann	1836	148.01	148
Witry, Magdalena & Heck, Jacques	1901	215.10	215
Witry, Magdalena & Schintgen, Nicolas	1804	308.08	120
Witry, Magdalena & Schmit, Nicolas	1860	150.01	148
Witry, Magdalena & Schmitt, Johann	1781	308.07	120
Witry, Manon & Bassani, Romain	1981	081.01	081
Witry, Manuel & Rouillon, Ivonne	1970	128.19	128.12
Witry, Marc & Witry, Nicole	1965	141.10.60	141.21 141.10.50
Witry, Marcel & Klees, Valerie	1955	217.03	217
Witry, Marcel & Scholtus, Lucie	1964	128.00.10	128.00.05
Witry, Marcel & Schwachtgen, Gertrude	1954	137	136
Witry, Marco & Batteux, Doris	1991	308	305
Witry, Marco & Wolf, Denise	1982	307	305
Witry, Margaret & Davis	1930	290.02	289
Witry, Margaretha & De Waha, Nicolas	1836	014.01	013
Witry, Margaretha & Dondelinger, Michel	1774	308.03	120
Witry, Margaretha & Drailly, Lambert	1737	017.02	003
Witry, Margaretha & Hoffmann, Johann	1849	147.06	142
Witry, Margaretha & Kardong, Matthew	1921	108.01	108
Witry, Margaretha & Kugener, Mathias	1835	161.01	157
Witry, Margaretha & Losch, John	1920	050.01.50	050.01

Witry, Margaretha & Menage, Pierre	1810	021.12	021.02
Witry, Margaretha & Olinger, Johann	1830	009.04	009
Witry, Margaretha & Speyer, Peter	1835	133.02	124
Witry, Margaretha & Toussaint, Michel	1835	147.02	142
Witry, Margaretha & Welter, Nicolas	1889	107.01	107
Witry, Maria & <Unnamed>	1920	166.02.02	166.02.01
Witry, Maria & Faber, Bernard	1912	220.01	219
Witry, Maria & Linster, Robert	1930	132.03	129
Witry, Maria & Morang, Joseph	1935	153.04	152
Witry, Maria & Ondarcuhu, Jose	1915	128.02	128.01
Witry, Maria & Steichen, Paul	1905	144.00.50	144
Witry, Maria del Carmen & Zingoni, Horacio	1959	128.13	128.12
Witry, Maria-Josefa & Fogg	1966	128.17	128.12
Witry, Maria-Theresa & Freiling, Peter	1793	021.28	021.01
Witry, Marie & <Unnamed>	1885	215.70	214
Witry, Marie & Bissener, Michel	1815	015.97	012
Witry, Marie & Christnach, Antoine	1810	021.11	021.02
Witry, Marie & Clemes, John-Peter	1902	086.01	053
Witry, Marie & Dennemeyer, Nicolas	1830	132.05	124
Witry, Marie & Donlinger, Theodor	1743	021.30	021
Witry, Marie & Ewert, Nicolas	1840	147.03	142
Witry, Marie & Finsterwald, Nicolas	1836	032.01	023
Witry, Marie & Greiveldinger, Nicolas	1872	143.01	143
Witry, Marie & Groos, Nicolas	1815	023.01	023
Witry, Marie & Haas, Rene	1925	021.22	021.15
Witry, Marie & Hames, Corneille	1754	119.10	020
Witry, Marie & Hebeler, Nicolas	1837	032.02	023
Witry, Marie & Hilbert, Nicolas	1823	031.02	023
Witry, Marie & Jacobs, Peter	1835	133.01	124
Witry, Marie & Kessler, Peter	1902	293.01	293
Witry, Marie & Kirsch, Nicolas	1749	036.03	021
Witry, Marie & Klein, Nicolas	1821	035.01	033
Witry, Marie & Kohn, Heinrich	1875	308.01	300
Witry, Marie & Kremer, Joseph	1965	128.00.35	128.00.05
Witry, Marie & Kuntziger, Jacques	1808	021.05	021.02
Witry, Marie & Leclerc, Victor	1923	139.02	135
Witry, Marie & Moris, Charles	1775	015.99.01	011

Witry, Marie & Muller, Ludwig	1886	031.00.05	031
Witry, Marie & Origer, Francois	1878	141.22	141.19
Witry, Marie & Peffer, Adam	1720	119.05	020
Witry, Marie & Pilier, Pierre	1820	021.26.10	021.26
Witry, Marie & Radermacher, Anton	1705	020.01	020
Witry, Marie & Reckinger, Nicolas	1844	026.02	026
Witry, Marie & Schanen, Joseph	1929	132.02	129
Witry, Marie & Schoedgen, Peter	1865	141.01	141
Witry, Marie & Schwartz, Franz	1879	308.02	300
Witry, Marie & Spanier, Dominique	1811	015.03	012
Witry, Marie & Tix, Nicolas	1899	151.02	151
Witry, Marie & Unden, Heinrich	1779	017.01	011
Witry, Marie & VanDyck, Victor	1924	139.01	135
Witry, Marie & Weber, Jacob	1790	050.02	037
Witry, Marie & Witry, Michel	1879	135	150 134
Witry, Marie & Zimmer, Johann	1800	021.03	021.02
Witry, Marie-Catherine & Mons, Karl	1796	015.01	012
Witry, Marie-Elisabeth & <Unnamed>	1830	047	038
Witry, Marie-Paule & Haas, Fernand	1983	225.01	225
Witry, Marie-Paule & Michaelis, Mich	1985	225.01.50	225
Witry, Marie-Therese & Witry, Jules	1927	130	129 145
Witry, Marilyn & Hanna, Thomas	1960	075.02.01	075.02
Witry, Mary & Conry, Elmer	1910	291.01	288
Witry, Mary & Giliano, Michael	1990	066.02	064
Witry, Mary & Hager	1880	027.04	027
Witry, Mary-Agnes & Behen, Francis	1930	075.05	075
Witry, Mary-Alice & Patrick, Michael	1985	066.01	064
Witry, Mary-Ellen & Lester, John-Jay	1974	056.01	056
Witry, Mathias & Anna	1720	005	003
Witry, Mathias & Backes, Margareta	1894	166.02.01	165
Witry, Mathias & Federspiel, Maria	1882	160	158
Witry, Mathias & Huss, Virginie	1904	095.01	095
Witry, Mathias & Kariger, Anne	1910	095.05	095
Witry, Mathias & Laschette, Anna	1850	214	157
Witry, Mathias & Mergen, Catherine	1925	046.30	046.20
Witry, Mathias & Sand, Amelie	1923	166.03.50	166.03
Witry, Matthew & Wolff, Mary-Pat	1987	070	069

Witry, Matthias & Glange, Anna	1935	226	219
Witry, Michael & Lucas, Christina	1828	021.26.50	021.26
Witry, Michel & Consbruck, Susanne	1858	027	026
Witry, Michel & Goeller, Susanne	1831	158	157
Witry, Michel & Groff, Susanna	1888	143.50	143
Witry, Michel & Huveler, Barbara	1849	159	157
Witry, Michel & Jungers, Marie-Anne	1830	021.13	021.02
Witry, Michel & Karpes, Lucia	1860	262	229
Witry, Michel & Koetz, Catherine	1894	050.01	049
Witry, Michel & Kohl, Barbara	1867	263	229
Witry, Michel & Lhotelain, Monique	1958	089	088
Witry, Michel & Lun, Christine	1835	141	140
Witry, Michel & Mathey, Catherine	1802	140	121
Witry, Michel & Meunier, Martine	1990	021.20	021.18
Witry, Michel & Muller, Marie	1841	014	013
Witry, Michel & Souvignier, Catherine	1836	141.02	140
Witry, Michel & Thiry, Barbara	1830	034	033
Witry, Michel & Witry, Marie	1879	135	134 150
Witry, Monique & Strotz, Fernand	1967	083.01	083
Witry, Monique & Thill, Josy	2002	128.00.30	128.00.20
Witry, Nancy-Jean & Lego, Thomas	1990	062.01	061
Witry, Nicholas & Margaret T.	1899	075	053
Witry, Nicolas & Contamines, Madeleine	1930	295	294
Witry, Nicolas & Cooper, Mary	1873	285	229
Witry, Nicolas & Enders, Marie	1881	301	300
Witry, Nicolas & Engelbrecht, Mary	1913	287	229
Witry, Nicolas & Flammang, Josette	1970	218	217
Witry, Nicolas & Gengler, Marie	1873	141.08	141
Witry, Nicolas & Huss, Elisabeth	1786	228	120
Witry, Nicolas & Hymbert, Marie	1765	309	020
Witry, Nicolas & Kuhnen, Catherine	1818	229	156
Witry, Nicolas & Kuhnen, Marie	1774	156	120
Witry, Nicolas & Lenger, Anne-Marie	1849	141.19	140
Witry, Nicolas & Leonard, Margaretha	1875	046	045
Witry, Nicolas & Logelin, Leonie	1925	166.04	166.03
Witry, Nicolas & Muller, Elisabeth	1859	024	292 023.02

Witry, Nicolas & Murtagh, Catalina	1892	128.01	127
Witry, Nicolas & Piere, Anna	1744	120	020
Witry, Nicolas & Reuter, Elisabeth	1688	020	002
Witry, Nicolas & Reuter, Marie-Barbe	1920	046.60	046
Witry, Nicolas & Roos, Catherine	1934	080	079
Witry, Nicolas & Ruth, Marie	1838	162	157
Witry, Nicolas & Salmen, Sophia	1876	286	285
Witry, Nicolas & Schwartz, Catherine	1853	092	051
Witry, Nicolas & Stirn, Anna	1910	046.5	046
Witry, Nicolas & Weiland, Margritha	1823	021.26.20	021.26
Witry, Nicolas & Weis, Angela	1797	033	022
Witry, Nicolas & Weisgerber, Margaretha	1790	310	120
Witry, Nicolas & Welter, Susanne	1734	311.06	311
Witry, Nicole & Witry, Marc	1965	141.10.60	141.10.50 141.21
Witry, Octavie & Buchet, Oscar	1930	141.10	141.09
Witry, Pascal & Falmouth, Sylvie	1993	297	296
Witry, Pascal, & Wyrwik, Claudia	1995	218.05.50	218.04
Witry, Patricia & Quarberg, Mark	1976	114.01	114
Witry, Patricia & Urban, Robert	1990	061.02	061
Witry, Patricia-Ann & Carbery, John	1956	071.01	071
Witry, Patrick & Faber, Joelle	1997	224.01	223
Witry, Paul & Mitchell, Mary	1990	059	056
Witry, Peter & <Unnamed>	1600	001	
Witry, Peter & Blitsch, Lizzie	1893	096	094
Witry, Peter & Breyer, Elisabeth	1914	095.12	095
Witry, Peter & Dondelinger, Catherine	1798	122	121
Witry, Peter & Ensch, Anna	1842	143	142
Witry, Peter & Ensweiler, Susanna	1881	139.03	134
Witry, Peter & Gilles, Barbara	1845	165	157
Witry, Peter & Glasener, Anna	1685	311	002
Witry, Peter & Hoffmann, Marie-Anna	1835	052	051
Witry, Peter & Kelsen, Johanna	1876	293	292
Witry, Peter & Koentge, Catherine	1885	087	052
Witry, Peter & M. M.	1896	289	288
Witry, Peter & Muller, Margaretha	1856	150	148
Witry, Peter & Neu, Catherine	1838	300	156
Witry, Peter & Olinger, Marie-Anna	1892	216	214

Witry, Peter & Paulus, Caroline	1887	166.03	166
Witry, Peter & Perquin, Eugenie	1889	025	024
Witry, Peter & Pink, Susanne	1800	010	006
Witry, Peter & Reinert, Anne	1793	021.26	021.01
Witry, Peter & Schuster, Magdalena	1895	079	053
Witry, Peter & Stiren, Margaretha	1847	165	157
Witry, Peter & Therens, Catherine	1798	038	037
Witry, Peter & Thies, Anna	1635	002	001
Witry, Peter & Wagner, Susanne	1855	048	047
Witry, Peter & Walch, Philomena	1898	290	288
Witry, Peter & Weisgerber, Anna	1867	284	229
Witry, Peter J. & Morge, Marion	1930	075.02	075
Witry, Philippe & Lacare, Catherine	1919	046.65	046
Witry, Pierre & <Unnamed>	1998	141.10.70	141.10.60
Witry, Pierre & Clauss, Anne	1955	296	295
Witry, Pierre & Groud, Henriette	1915	091	087
Witry, Pierre & Hiltgen, Angele	1906	294	293
Witry, Pierre & Kauth, Helena	1921	304	301
Witry, Pierre & Morette, Madeleine	1925	221	219
Witry, Pierre & Schintgen, Jeanette	1809	148	121
Witry, Pierre & Schmitt, Marie	1885	134.01	134
Witry, Pierre & Wambach, Barbara	1918	074.00.50	074
Witry, Pierre-Frederis & Friob, Anna	1920	042	040
Witry, Regina & Kauffmann, Nicolas	1817	015.02	012
Witry, Reinhard & Regenwetter, Anna	1833	161	157
Witry, Rene & Wille, Ursula	1977	306	305
Witry, Richard & Burns-Rakowski, Darlene	1972	117	109
Witry, Richard & Healey, Joan-Rita	1953	114	109
Witry, Richard-James & Lewis, Patricia	1980	073	071
Witry, Robert & Homolar, Darlene	1959	104	102
Witry, Robert & Northstrum, Mary	1980	078	076
Witry, Roger & Mangerich, Marguerite	1954	218.04	218.02
Witry, Romain & Michaely, Geraldine	1995	217.05	217.04
Witry, Rudi & Hinterlang, Leny	1955	217.01	217
Witry, Sanny & Braun, Alex	1992	095.18	095.16
Witry, Sanny & Tescher, Paul	1980	095.17	095.16

Witry, Scott & Boomgaarden, Lynn	1989	119	118
Witry, Sharon-Ines & Cory, Jeffrey	1980	100.01	098
Witry, Stephan & Stocklausen, Marie	1905	152	151
Witry, Susan & Forewood, Brant	2003	104.00.60	104
Witry, Susanne & Drauden, Martin	1786	012.01	012
Witry, Susanne & Erpelding, Jean	1902	095.06	095
Witry, Susanne & Greischer, Michel	1913	160.20	160
Witry, Susanne & Philippart, Frederic	1876	144.01	143
Witry, Susanne & Reding, Nicolas	1782	022.02	022
Witry, Susanne & Reiland, Nicolas	1835	009.26	009
Witry, Susanne & Scheur, Nicolas	1766	015.99	011
Witry, Susanne & Thomas, Wilhelm	1852	021.26.60	021.26.50
Witry, Suzanne & Gorham, John P.	1970	077.03	076
Witry, Suzanne & Hebert, Georges	1931	095.02	095.01
Witry, Suzanne & Klosen, Franz	1933	227.01	219
Witry, Suzanne & Reding, Johann	1930	074.00.60	074.00.50
Witry, Sylvie & Jacques, Victor	1930	141.11	141.09
Witry, Theodor & Gruber, Francoise	1889	164	162
Witry, Theodor & Krier, Margaretha	1836	039	038
Witry, Theodor & Michaelis, Marie	1870	163	162
Witry, Theodor & Petry, Anna-Marie	1759	037	021
Witry, Theodor & Trausch, Janine	1905	164.00.50	162
Witry, Theresa & Glaser, Neil	1993	105.01	105
Witry, Theresa W. & Bade	1892	027.03	027
Witry, Theresa W. & Jungles, Nicolas	1876	027.01	027
Witry, Therese & Stoltz, Valentin	1857	031.01.80	026
Witry, Thomas & Friday, Carol	1971	106	102
Witry, Thomas & O'Neill, Mellissa	1986	116	114
Witry, Timothy & Galen, Janelle	2006	066.01.50	064
Witry, Timothy-Conry & Jantz, Jessica	2005	104.00.30	104
Witry, Unknown & <Unnamed>	1980	128.10	128.08
Witry, Valentin & Meyers, Catherine	1796	157	156
Witry, Victor & Bourgmeyer, Josette	1965	132	130
Witry, Victor & Capus, Julie	1929	141.21	141.20
Witry, Victor & Eppe, Anne	1925	128.00.05	128
Witry, Victorine & Krippeler, Marco	2000	128.00.22	128.00.20
Witry, Victorine & Rivoire, Charles	1930	153.03	152
Witry, Viktor & Bonifas, Barbara	1886	145	143

Witry, Virginie & Mores, Nicolas	1920	225.03	219
Witry, Viviane & Wagner, Romain	1980	217.02	217.01
Witry, Walter & Diefenbaugh, Mabel	1958	101	096
Witry, Walter-John & Simons, Grace	1929	097	096
Witry, Willebrord & Dickes, Margaretha	1791	123	121
Witry, Willebrord & Hansen, Anna	1754	022	021
Witry, William & Garfield, Elaine	1960	077	076
Witry, William & Martin, Marie	1940	076	075
Witry, William-Peter & Engh, Eli	1962	103	102
Witry, Yvette & Andring, Rene	1983	222.01	222
Witry,Jean & Jungers, Elisabeth	1895	132.04.01	127
Wittman, Thomas & Sabo, Mary-Ellen	1976	182.04	182.03
Wittrock, Anton & Wittry, Elizabeth	1934	270.04	264
Wittrock, LeRoy & Brugeon, Pat	1960	270.06	270.04
Wittrock, Marvin & Schwartz, Mary	1965	270.05	270.04
Wittry, Adam & Huss, Mary	1889	208	167
Wittry, Adam & Pobstman, Mary	1922	174	173
Wittry, Alan & Frank, Dorothy	1977	030.01	030
Wittry, Albert & Kneipper, Margaret	1925	192	182
Wittry, Alfred & Pfister, Lillian	1935	283	272
Wittry, Alice & Evans, Robert	1941	204.21	204
Wittry, Alois & Johnson, Ione	1960	171	169
Wittry, Alois & Tellison, Dorothy	1940	170	169
Wittry, Andrew & Wolterman, Leola	1933	260	231
Wittry, Anita & Tegels, Joseph	1953	236.11	232
Wittry, Anna & Gormley, Thomas	1935	174.01	173
Wittry, Anna & Plain, John W.	1878	172.37	167
Wittry, Anna & Theis, Nicholas A.	1910	172.21	168
Wittry, Anne & DePaolo, David	1999	202.02	201
Wittry, Anne & Waind, Patrick	1990	202.01	201
Wittry, Anthony & Callahan, Marcella	1922	278	272
Wittry, Anthony & Chan, Sonya	2004	259.01.50	259
Wittry, Arlene & Knips, Earl	1955	267.07	265
Wittry, Arthur O. & Litsch, Frances	1919	029	028
Wittry, Barbara & Hoffman, Mark	1979	253.01	253
Wittry, Barbara & McIntyre, Dan	1967	270.02	270
Wittry, Barbara & Weddige, Frederick	1908	173.01	173

Wittry, Barbara & Wittry, John	1886	182	271 167
Wittry, Bernard & Snyder, Magdalene	1928	248	231
Wittry, Betty-Jo & Brownback, Bill	1951	030.11	029
Wittry, Betty-Jo & Dutton, Kirk	1971	030.13	029
Wittry, Brett & Reuter, Melissa	1985	267	266
Wittry, Bryon & Cools, Karolien	2000	242.03	242
Wittry, Carl & Huettenmueller, Karen	1986	030.05	030
Wittry, Carl & Nieland, Marie	1942	233	232
Wittry, Carol & Weskott, Denny	1975	238.03	238
Wittry, Catherine & McMahan, Robert	1975	201.01	201
Wittry, Catherine & Salmen, Richard	1962	270.02.30	270
Wittry, Charmian & Geyton, Donald	1985	184.01	184
Wittry, Christian& Reiser, Marie	1935	270	264
Wittry, Christine & Layman, Richard	1981	207.10	207
Wittry, Christopher & Hansen, Jennifer	2001	270.01.01	270.01
Wittry, Christopher & Katzer, Jo-Ann	1985	030.04	030
Wittry, Christopher & Martinez, Cindy	1995	259.02	259
Wittry, Clara & Holmberg, Arvid	1937	270.03	264
Wittry, Clara & Pape, John	1917	240.22	231
Wittry, Dale & Baumhover, Catherine	1954	249	248
Wittry, Daniel & Toledo, Tannia	2000	181.01.02	181
Wittry, Darlene & Wiebe, Thomas	1979	238.04	238
Wittry, David & Bohanek, Therese	1990	281.01	280
Wittry, David & Brenner, Mary	1982	254	253
Wittry, David & Chang, Shu-mei	1996	181.01.01	181
Wittry, David & Dubois, Mildred	1955	282	279
Wittry, Dean & De Phillips, Monica	1982	250	249
Wittry, Debra & Breckenridge, Douglas	1979	257.02	256
Wittry, Debra & McDaniel, James	1970	201.02	201
Wittry, Debra & Mercer, John	1973	201.04	201
Wittry, Delbert & Kiefer, Patricia	1949	201	197
Wittry, Della & Nieland, Patrick	1948	248.01	248
Wittry, Delmar & Douglas, Patricia	1949	198	197
Wittry, Delores & Garrison, Robert	1965	283.02	283
Wittry, Dennis & Tracey, Deborah	1975	213	210
Wittry, Diane & Peckham, Richard	1999	282.02	282

Wittry, Donald J. & Dinwiddie, Diane	1950	184	183
Wittry, Doris & Brake, Donald	1952	267.01	265
Wittry, Dorothy & Lanham, Robert	1925	209.01	208
Wittry, Dorothy & Pillatsch, Herman	1940	172.19	172
Wittry, Edmun & Brennan, Celestine	1955	185	183
Wittry, Edmund & Brown, Lynne	1985	187	185
Wittry, Edmund B. & Chris	2006	187.00.50	185
Wittry, Edwin & Buss, Jan	1957	266	265
Wittry, Eleanor & Bergerhaus, Leo	1915	028.01	028
Wittry, Elissa & Czerkas, Jan	1975	280.01	280
Wittry, Elizabeth & Arterburn, Dale	1982	207.06	207
Wittry, Elizabeth & Kelley, William	1920	277.01	272
Wittry, Elizabeth & Spang, Peter J.	1903	171.01	168
Wittry, Elizabeth & Wenckus	1994	207.03	207
Wittry, Elizabeth & Wittrock, Anton	1934	270.04	264
Wittry, Elmer & Flannigan, Alice	1930	210	208
Wittry, Elmer & O'Connor, Kathryn	1945	211	208
Wittry, Elmer & Stepenske, Marilyn	1970	212	210
Wittry, Emma & Weber, Ferdinand	1913	208.01	208
Wittry, Eugene & Link, Nancy-Ann	1954	193	192
Wittry, Eugene & Pudenz, Joan	1954	256	248
Wittry, Evan & Ingram, Kristin	2006	195.50	194
Wittry, Ferdinand & Wehden, Lillian	1925	197	182
Wittry, Frank J. & Haufle, Helen-Jane	1965	181	180
Wittry, George H. & Leider, Josephine	1932	180	173
Wittry, Gladys & Nichols, Roy	1947	030.07	029
Wittry, Glen & Cohen, Ellen	1981	200	198
Wittry, Gustave & Oswald, Elizabeth	1890	028	027
Wittry, Gustave & Setter, Ruth	1955	030	029
Wittry, Helen & Kelley, Charles A.	1942	030.08	029
Wittry, Helen & McKnight, Forrest	1956	030.10	029
Wittry, Henry & Draudt, Mary	1908	172	168
Wittry, Henry & Hankes, Eva	1925	206	203
Wittry, Henry & Molitor, Margaret	1882	173	167
Wittry, Herman & Filbey, Edna	1925	279	272
Wittry, Jack & Christopherson, Phyllis	1980	277	276
Wittry, Jacob & Bamberg, Catherine	1898	264	263
Wittry, Jacob & De Jarlis, Helena	1935	269	264

Wittry, Jacob & Kammes, Josephine	1912	204	203
Wittry, Jacob & Nieland, Anna	1921	240	231
Wittry, Jacob & Schons, Magdalena	1851	167	157
Wittry, James & Bunkelman, Susan	1980	199	198
Wittry, James & Hall, Nadine	1997	282.00.01	282
Wittry, James & Moore, Nicole	1996	245	244
Wittry, James & Stuhr, Jodi	1990	258	256
Wittry, Janet & Dietrich, Dennis	1981	250.01	249
Wittry, Janet-Susan & Wright, James	1990	030.06	030
Wittry, Janice & Kanne, Ralph	1958	243.01	241
Wittry, Jeanne & Alderman, George	1983	178.01	176
Wittry, Jennifer & Robertson, Christopher	2006	195	194
Wittry, Joan & Hannasch, Jerome	1954	240.12	240
Wittry, Joan & Kraus, Clarence	1949	240.09	240
Wittry, John & Clauson, Rose	1920	275	272
Wittry, John & Gehling, Marceal	1956	253	248
Wittry, John & Hagerty, Kathleen	1950	276	275
Wittry, John & Jansz, Mary	1884	272	271
Wittry, John & Pape, Mayme	1917	237	231
Wittry, John & Wittry, Barbara	1886	182	167 271
Wittry, John B. & Irwin, Mary	1915	183	182
Wittry, John-Paul & Dodson, Donna	1986	179	176
Wittry, John-Peter & Ernst, Theresa	1951	176	175
Wittry, Jonathan & Seth, Karen	1981	202	201
Wittry, Joseph & Wilberding, Rose	1933	241	231
Wittry, Judith & Bauer, James	1975	268.02	265
Wittry, Judith & Straight, Phillip	1970	268.01	265
Wittry, Judith & Wagner, Paul	1991	252.02	249
Wittry, Julia & Huss, Henry	1933	204.01	204
Wittry, Karen & Hunter, Christopher	1987	207.12	207
Wittry, Karen & Schumacher, Greg	1987	261.02.01	261
Wittry, Karen & Ulen, Charles	1981	242.01	242
Wittry, Karen & Wagner	1985	207.11	207
Wittry, Karman & Hotchkiss, Todd	1990	259.01	259
Wittry, Kathleen & Stimac, Frank	1952	205.01	205
Wittry, Kathryn & Christy, Kent	1973	177.01	176
Wittry, Kenneth & Nelson, Jane	1964	259	248

Wittry, Kevin & Pearson, Gail	1987	255	253
Wittry, Kristopher & Lugo, Sonya	1989	282.01	282
Wittry, Kristy & Eastman, Robb	1989	255.01	253
Wittry, Laura-Lena & Konen, Michael	1913	182.09	182
Wittry, Laurie & Harvey, Michael	1986	236.01	235
Wittry, Lawrence & Nagl, Lucille	1950	235	232
Wittry, Lawrence & Wegman, Carol	1990	236	235
Wittry, Lena & Florence, Edward	1913	182.01	182
Wittry, Lena & Frederick, Roy	1920	204.27	203
Wittry, Lena & Reitz, August	1892	213.01	167
Wittry, Leona & Buelt, Leo	1944	240.01	240
Wittry, Leonard & Viaene, Margaret	1944	238	237
Wittry, Lezlee & Roemeling, Lawrence	1980	266.01	266
Wittry, Linda & Messmore, Gregory	1984	261.01	261
Wittry, Lois & Hildman, Paul	1974	235.01	235
Wittry, Louis & Stracke, Marie	1959	261	260
Wittry, Lyle & Campbell, Cynthia	1996	247	241
Wittry, Lyle & Dennis, Connie	1994	246	241
Wittry, Lyle & Shaeffer, Joan	1964	244	241
Wittry, Marcia & Wiederin, Eugene	1962	261.08	260
Wittry, Margaret & Anderson, Kevin	1988	252.01	249
Wittry, Margaret & Davidson, James	1930	169.01	169
Wittry, Margaret & Pobstman, James	1924	174.02	173
Wittry, Margaret & Schramer, Ralph	1928	172.01	172
Wittry, Marianne & Lopez, Phillip	1980	207.08	207
Wittry, Marie & Glass, Robert	1947	233.01	232
Wittry, Marie & Jado, Michael	1885	271.01	271
Wittry, Marilyn & Otte, Gerald	1964	270.02.05	270
Wittry, Mark & Breuer, Jaci	1996	261.02.02	261
Wittry, Mark & Gallup, Cynthia	1992	252	249
Wittry, Marvin & Osterholt, Angela	1956	242	241
Wittry, Mary & Bernardy, Mathew	1935	261.11	231
Wittry, Mary & Conrad, Robert-Louis	1925	229.09	231 229.06
Wittry, Mary & Frieders, John	1915	172.24	168
Wittry, Mary-Clara & Bringen	1945	274.01	273
Wittry, Mary-Ellen & Murray, Bruce	1964	238.02	238
Wittry, Mary-Jo & Mason, James	1976	249.01	249

Wittry, Mary-Lou & O'Leary, Donald	1948	278.01	278
Wittry, May A. & Burkel, John B.	1936	181.02	173
Wittry, Melanie & Dykstra, Andres	2004	259.10	259
Wittry, Michae & Fisher, Louise	1920	190	182
Wittry, Michael & Robles, Susan	1991	207.07	207
Wittry, Michael & Williams, Beatrice	1980	178	176
Wittry, Michel & Welter, Agnes	1877	168	167
Wittry, Mike & Zebel, Vita	1925	205	203
Wittry, Myrna & Guess, Robert	1965	283.01	283
Wittry, Nancy & Tjarks, Michael	1986	261.02	261
Wittry, Nannon K. & Roosa, Jack	1986	187.01	185
Wittry, Nicholas & Fendrichs, Ella	1924	234	231
Wittry, Nicholas & Rettenmaier, Anna	1916	232	231
Wittry, Nicholas & Wilberding, Frances	1931	265	264
Wittry, Nick & Dockendorf, Lena	1885	203	167
Wittry, Nickolas & Mears, Elizabeth	1903	169	168
Wittry, Nickolaus J. & Schaub, Gladys	1920	191	182
Wittry, Nicolas & Bartet, Elsie	1910	303	301
Wittry, Nicole & Platt, Jason	2000	268.00.50	268
Wittry, Patricia & Perez, Maximo	1983	030.03	030
Wittry, Paul & Allen, Clara-Mary	1920	274	272
Wittry, Paul & Baker, Mary-Carolyn	1942	274.03	272
Wittry, Paul & Marie	1915	273	272
Wittry, Paul & Nallinger, Mary	1941	209	208
Wittry, Paul & Weber, Marie	1858	271	229
Wittry, Peggy & Leiting, Marc	1975	257.01	256
Wittry, Peter H. & Smith, Olive L.	1928	175	173
Wittry, Philip-John & Moore, Kelly-Jo	1991	196	193
Wittry, Randal & Drum, Melissa	1982	186	185
Wittry, Raymond & Murphy, Shannon	1953	188	183
Wittry, Richard & Carpenter, Rebecca	1983	251	249
Wittry, Richard H. & Burritt, Jo-Anne	1977	029.01	029
Wittry, Rita & Venner, Paul	1951	236.02	232
Wittry, Robert & Balk, Kathy	1970	268	265
Wittry, Robert & Buckley, Janet	1985	189	188
Wittry, Robert & Goerke, Victoria	1976	270.01	270
Wittry, Rose & Reider, William	1920	208.15	208
Wittry, Rosemarie & Case, Patrick	1981	242.02	242

Wittry, Rose-Mary & Schramer, James	1969	179.01	175
Wittry, Roy & Foster, Barbara	1952	207	206
Wittry, Ruth & Bock, Howard	1953	260.01	260
Wittry, Sandra & Caylor, Jeffrey	1982	249.02	249
Wittry, Sandra-Lynn & Hill, Gary-Dee	1969	198.01	198
Wittry, Shanna & Malone, Timothy	2000	194.01	194
Wittry, Shirley & Sendens, Tom	1963	238.01	238
Wittry, Sophia & Koehne, William	1916	231.01	231
Wittry, Sophia & Wretstrom, Joseph	1987	270.03.25	264
Wittry, Stephen & Burke, Kathleen	1976	194	193
Wittry, Stephen & Contreras, Karen	1982	177	176
Wittry, Steven & Brede, Nadia	1980	281	280
Wittry, Steven & Bulder, Regina	1990	243	242
Wittry, Steven & Otten, Carol	2000	181.01.03	181
Wittry, Susan & Nuetzman, Steven	1980	250.02	249
Wittry, Susan & Walker, Kim	1986	177.02	176
Wittry, Susan-Anne & Rashid, Jeffrey	2000	196.01	193
Wittry, Theresa & Knisley, Edward	1945	274.02	273
Wittry, Theresa & Lies, Peter-Paul	1918	172.36	168
Wittry, Theresa & McQueen, Joseph	1973	207.01	207
Wittry, Thomas & Cronister, Terri	1992	030.02	030
Wittry, Thomas & Heinrichs, Sara	1983	257	256
Wittry, Thomas & Malhaiuk, Julie	1983	239	238
Wittry, Vera- & Derner, Eugene	1959	261.03	260
Wittry, Warren & Kleppe, Joan	1950	280	279
Wittry, Warren & Radford, Carol	1965	281.50	279
Wohl, Aloysia & Witry, Georges	1960	217.04	217
Wolf, Denise & Witry, Marco	1982	307	305
Wolff, Mary-Pat & Witry, Matthew	1987	070	069
Wolff, Susanna & Zahn, Philippe	1908	146.03.50	146.03
Wolter, Nicolas & Stronck, Johanna	1900	009.25	009.24
Wolterman, Leola & Wittry, Andrew	1933	260	231
Wood, Robert & Tegels, Karen	1977	236.16	236.11
Woodson, Sue & Witry, John	1980	044	043
Woolsey, Jamie & Russell, Timothy	1989	229.27	229.21
Wouters, Emile & Muschang, Barbe	1876	140.12	140.06
Wouters, Pierre & Witry, Elisabeth	1835	140.06	140
Wretstrom, Joseph & Wittry, Sophia	1987	270.03.25	264

Name	Year	Value 1	Value 2
Wright, James & Wittry, Janet-Susan	1990	030.06	030
Wyatt, Michael & Anderson, Linda	1971	172.34	172.33
Wyrwik, Claudia & Witry, Pascal	1995	218.05.50	218.04
Yackel, Marie & Brake, Douglas	1975	267.02	267.01
Yarbrough, Joe & Venner, Susan	1983	236.06	236.02
Yarbrough, Kelly & George, Cory	2002	236.06.00	236.05
Young, Kim & Witry, Christopher	1990	077.01	077
Young, Merna & Bergerhaus, Maurice	1943	028.02	028.01
Youngerberg, Kristin & Thooft, Kevin	1993	261.27	261.21
Yusko, Mark & Steimel, Mary-Ellen	1980	096.08	096.06
Zahn, Dominic & Witry, Barbara	1880	146.03	147.04 143
Zahn, Dominic & Witry, Barbara	1846	147.05	142
Zahn, Philippe & Welsch, Elisabetha	1922	146.03.70	146.03
Zahn, Philippe & Wolff, Susanna	1908	146.03.50	146.03
Zapetini, Lydia & Muller, Hugo	1955	031.00.80	031.00.60
Zappone, Marco & Goedert, Marie-Paule	2002	229.05.01	229.05
Zebel, Vita & Wittry, Mike	1925	205	203
Zeimet, Michael & Schroeder, Leslie	1999	015.38	015.36.50
Zender, Edgar & Esch, Hannelore	1975	230.07	230.06
Ziman, John G. & Kohley, Louise	1955	171.35	171.29
Zimmer, Georges & Witry, Jacqueline	1995	227.00.03	227.00.01
Zimmer, Johann & <Unnamed>	1830	021.04	021.03
Zimmer, Johann & Witry, Marie	1800	021.03	021.02
Zingoni, Horacio & Witry, Maria del Carmen	1959	128.13	128.12
Zingoni, Maria & Barbieri, Carlos	1985	128.15	128.13
Zingoni, Maria-Ines & Wade, Tristan	1990	128.16	128.13
Zingoni, Martin & Buzon, Alejandra	1991	128.14	128.13
Zmuda, Lucille & Theis, John J.	1951	172.22	172.21
Zubillaga & Muller, Vilma	1960	031.00.35	031.00.10
Zubiri, Ana-Maria & Muller, Alfredo	1964	031.00.90	031.00.60
Zumburge, Fred & Glass, Jean-Marie	1982	233.07	233.01
Zwach, Carol & Schmidt, Allen	1963	240.28	240.23

ABOUT THE AUTHOR

The author, EUGENE J. WITTRY, began to search for the roots of the family in 1990. He found the origin of the family name, and the oldest existing documents that report significant events in the history of the family. His language competency in German, French and Latin enabled him to translate the contents of about 4,000 original historical documents about members of the family between the years 1638 and 1923. In 1996 he wrote a history of the family that is still in print at Heritage Books. He has published a quarterly family newsletter since 1997, motivating family members to share information with him about their branches of the family. He has attended numerous reunions of the family, including four that he organized in Luxembourg. He is generally recognized as the family genealogist.